Prague
& the Czech Republic

"All you've got to do is decide to go
and the hardest part is over.

So go!"

Contents

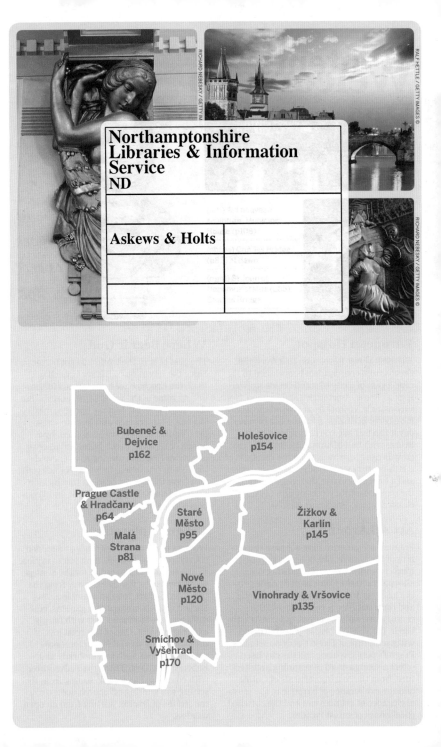

Welcome to Prague & the Czech Republic

Prague is the equal of Paris in terms of beauty. Its history goes back a millennium. And the beer? The best in Europe.

European Hotspot

The 1989 Velvet Revolution that freed the Czechs from communism bequeathed to Europe a gem of a city to stand beside stalwarts such as Rome, Amsterdam and London. Not surprisingly, visitors from around the world have come in droves, and on a hot summer's day it can feel like you're sharing Charles Bridge with half of humanity. But even the crowds can't take away from the spectacle of a 14th-century stone bridge, a hilltop castle and a lovely, lazy river that inspired one of the most beautiful pieces of 19th-century classical music, Smetana's *Moldau*.

Art All Around

Prague's art galleries may not have the allure of the Louvre, but Bohemian art offers much to admire, from the glowing Gothic altarpieces in the Convent of St Agnes, to the luscious art nouveau of Alfons Mucha, and the magnificent collection of 20th-century surrealists, cubists and constructivists in the Veletržní Palác. The weird and witty sculpture of David Černý punctuates Prague's public spaces, and the city itself offers a smorgasbord of stunning architecture, from the soaring verticals of Gothic and the exuberance of baroque to the sensual elegance of art nouveau and the chiselled cheekbones of cubist facades.

Where Beer is God

The best beer in the world just got better. Since the invention of Pilsner Urquell in 1842, the Czechs have been famous for producing some of the world's finest brews. But the internationally famous brand names – Urquell, Staropramen and Budvar – have been equalled, and even surpassed, by a bunch of regional Czech beers and microbreweries that are catering to a renewed interest in traditional brewing. Names you'll now have to get your head around include Kout na Šumavě, Svijanský Rytíř and Velkopopovický Kozel.

Urban Explorations

Prague's maze of cobbled lanes and hidden courtyards, always beckoning you to explore a little further, is a paradise for the aimless wanderer. Just a few blocks away from the Old Town Square you can stumble across ancient chapels, unexpected gardens, cute cafes and old-fashioned bars with hardly a tourist in sight. One of the great joys of the city is its potential for exploration – neighbourhoods such as Vinohrady and Bubeneč can reward the urban adventurer with countless memorable scenes, from the setting sun glinting off church domes, to the strains of Dvořák wafting from an open window.

Why I Love Prague

By Neil Wilson

How can you not love a city that has a pub with cushions above the gents' urinal, so you can rest your head while you 'go'? Where you can order a beer without speaking, simply by placing a beer mat on the table? And where the beer is probably the best in the world? But it's not just exquisite ale and a wonderfully relaxed drinking culture that keep bringing me back to Prague – there's wit and weirdness in equal measure: a public fountain where two figures pee in a puddle, spelling out literary quotations; a 1950s nuclear bunker hidden beneath a city-centre hotel; and a cubist lamp post. Quirky doesn't even begin to describe it.

For more about our authors, see p352.

Lobkowicz Palace (p72), Prague Castle

Prague &
the Czech Republic's
Top 10

Charles Bridge (p83)

1 Whether you visit alone in the early morning mist or shoulder your way through the afternoon crowds, crossing Charles Bridge is the quintessential Prague experience. Built in 1357, its 16 elegant arches withstood wheeled traffic for 500-odd years – thanks, legend claims, to eggs mixed into the mortar – until it was made pedestrian-only after WWII. By day, the famous baroque statues stare down with stony indifference on a fascinating parade of buskers, jazz bands and postcard sellers; at dawn, they regain something of the mystery and magic their creators sought to capture.

⊙ *Malá Strana*

Prague Castle (p66)

2 A thousand years of history is cradled within the walls of Prague's hilltop castle, a complex of churches, towers, halls and palaces that is almost a village in its own right. This is the cultural and historical heart of the Czech Republic, comprising not only collections of physical treasures such as the golden reliquaries of St Vitus Treasury and the Bohemian crown jewels, but also the sites of great historic events such as the murder of St Wenceslas and the Second Defenestration of Prague.

⊙ *Prague Castle & Hradčany*

MIROSLAV PETRASKO / GETTY IMAGES ©

SIGFRID LOPE / GETTY IMAGES ©

Prague, Queen of Music *(p43)*

3 The city that nurtured Smetana, Dvořák and Janáček, and saw performances by Wolfgang Amadeus Mozart in his prime, has a place in musical history alongside that of Vienna. Two major festivals of classical music – Prague Spring and Strings of Autumn – grace the calendar, but the city is famous for more than just the classics. Prague has been a hotbed of European jazz since the late 1940s, and there's now a thriving live music scene that spans genres from hard rock to electronica.

TOP LEFT: THE CZECH PHILHARMONIC ORCHESTRA PERFORMS AT THE RUDOLFINUM (P106)

☆ *Entertainment*

Old Town Square *(p103)*

4 Despite the swarms of tourists, crowded pavement cafes and over-the-top commercialism, it's impossible not to enjoy the spectacle of Prague's premier public space: tour leaders, with umbrellas borne aloft like battle standards, thrusting through the crowds gathered to watch the Old Town Hall's amazing Astronomical Clock; students dressed as frogs and chickens handing out flyers for a drama production; middle-aged couples in matching rain jackets and sensible shoes walking past pink-haired, leather-clad punks with too many piercings; and a bored-looking guy with a placard advertising a museum of torture instruments. Verily, all of human life is here.

⊙ *Staré Město*

St Vitus Cathedral *(p73)*

5 Occupying the site of a 10th-century Romanesque rotunda built by the Good King Wenceslas of Christmas-carol fame, St Vitus is the heart of Czech Catholicism, and its spires and bell tower are the focus of Prague's skyline. Commenced in 1344 but not completed until 1929, the cathedral's soaring Gothic nave is lit by gorgeous stained glass, and is home to the cultural jewels of Chapel of St Wenceslas, the priceless medieval mosaics of the Golden Gate and the magnificent silver tomb of St John of Nepomuk.

ABOVE: CHAPEL OF ST WENCESLAS

⊙ *Prague Castle & Hradčany*

Amazing Architecture (p50)

6 One of Prague's prime attractions is its physical appearance. Prague Castle and the city centre are a textbook display of around 900 years of architectural evolution – bluff Romanesque, sublime Gothic, elegant Renaissance and dazzling baroque, plus 19th-century revivals of all of these styles – all amazingly undisturbed by the modern world and folded into a compact network of lanes and passages. And that's before you get started on the 20th century's sleek and sensual art nouveau, and Prague's uniquely Czech cubist and rondocubist buildings.

BELOW: KLEMENTINUM (P108)

⊙ *Architecture*

Czech Beer (p39)

7 'Where beer is brewed, life is good', according to an old Czech proverb. This means that life in the Czech Republic must be very good indeed, as the country is awash in breweries both large and small. Czech beer has been famous for its quality and flavour since the invention of Pilsner Urquell in 1842, but in recent years there has been a renaissance of microbreweries and craft beers, and you can now enjoy everything from classic *ležák* (pale lager) to *kvasnicové* (yeast beer) and *kávové pivo* (coffee-flavoured beer).

🍷 *Drinking & Nightlife*

Prague Jewish Museum (p97)

8 The slice of Staré Město bounded by Kaprova, Dlouhá and Kozí streets is home to the remains of the once-thriving mini-town of Josefov, Prague's former Jewish ghetto. The museum encompasses half a dozen ancient synagogues, a ceremonial hall and former mortuary, and the powerful melancholy of the Old Jewish Cemetery. These exhibits tell the often tragic and moving story of Prague's Jewish community, from the 16th-century creator of the Golem, Rabbi Loew, to the horrors of Nazi persecution. LEFT: KLAUS SYNAGOGUE (P99), PRAGUE JEWISH MUSEUM

◉ **Staré Město**

Veletržní Palác *(p156)*

9 In 1996 the huge, grimly functionalist Veletržní Palác, built in 1928 to house international trade fairs, became the new home of the National Gallery's museum of 19th-, 20th- and 21st-century art. This vast, ocean-liner-like building can now lay claim to being one of Prague's best (and biggest) galleries, displaying works by Van Gogh, Picasso, Klimt and Mucha, as well as impressionist works and masterpieces by Czech expressionist, cubist and surrealist artists.

⊙ *Holešovice*

Český Krumlov *(p208)*

10 The sleepy, southern Bohemian town of Český Krumlov is arguably the Czech Republic's only other world-class, must-see sight outside of Prague. None other than *National Geographic* has dubbed this former medieval stronghold one of the 'world's greatest places', and once you catch a glimpse of the rocky, rambling Renaissance castle (the second-biggest in the country after Prague Castle), with its mesmerising multicoloured tower, you'll feel the appeal. Yes, this really is the fairytale town the tourist brochures promised.

⊙ *Best of Bohemia*

What's New

The Riverfront

Praguers have finally woken up to the leisure potential of the Vltava riverfront, notably at Náplavka in Nové Město. Formerly the site of a timber quay (that's what the name means), this stretch of embankment now hosts a popular weekly farmers market, and on summer evenings comes alive with cocktail boats, live-music stages, and crowds of promenading locals. It's also the starting point for a riverside bike trail much used by cyclists, walkers and inline skaters. (p134)

Karel Zeman Museum

A new museum packed with fascinating exhibits, dedicated to the work of Czech film director, animator and special-effects pioneer Karel Zeman. (p87)

Hotel Jalta Nuclear Bunker

A communist-era hotel on Wenceslas Square has opened up the secret nuclear bunker and surveillance control room hidden beneath the building. (p125)

Room

With actor Tommy Lee Jones' personal chef as a consultant, this new tapas restaurant has ready-made PR appeal; and the food is every bit as good as the hype. (p131)

Vršovice

Who would've thought it? The venerable neighbourhood of Vršovice has found itself at the epicentre of Prague hipsterdom. It's no Brooklyn, but if this is your scene, in Prague at least, this is your place. (p135)

Bisos

A sure sign of the gentrification of the Žižkov district was the opening in December 2013 of this superb Sardinian eatery, sister to Malá Strana's Ichnusa. (p151)

Dish

This Vinohrady restaurant is the reigning king of Prague's burger boom. We love the classic 'Dish' bacon and cheese. Vegetarians can savour a beetroot burger with red lentils, caper mayonnaise and courgette (zucchini) chips. (p137)

EU 'Cultural Capital'

The western Bohemian metropolis of Plzeň (p220) is no longer all about the beer. The European Union's 'Cultural Capital' for 2015 has rolled out an ambitious programme of concerts, shows and exhibitions.

Český Krumlov Synagogue

To Český Krumlov's innumerable charms has just been added another: a beautifully and sensitively renovated former synagogue with an instructive and moving exhibition on Jewish history in southern Bohemia. (p210)

Techmania

Plzeň's spiffy interactive science and technology centre opened in 2014 amid squeals of delight from adolescent techno geeks around the country. Well-designed exhibits prove museums can be both educational and a blast. (p222)

For more recommendations and reviews, see **lonelyplanet. com/czech-republic**

Need to Know

For more information, see Survival Guide (p295)

Currency
Czech crown (Koruna česká; Kč)

Language
Czech

Visas
Generally not needed for stays of up to 90 days. Some nationalities require a Schengen visa.

Money
ATMs widely available. Credit cards accepted in most hotels and restaurants. Non-European credit cards are sometimes rejected.

Mobile Phones
GSM 900/1800 system is used. Czech SIM cards can be used in European and Australian mobile phones. Standard North American GSM 1900 phones will not work, though dual-band GSM 1900/900 phones will.

Time
Central European Time (GMT/ UTC plus one hour)

Tourist Information
Prague City Tourism (Prague Welcome; Map p332; ☑221 714 444; www.prague.eu; Old Town Hall, Staroměstské náměstí 5; ⊙9am-7pm; ⓂStaroměstská) Good free maps, detailed brochures, and information on guided tours; also sells public transport tickets.

Daily Budget

Budget:
less than €80

➡ Dorm bed: €15

➡ Self-catering and lunch specials: €15

➡ Admission to major tourist attractions: €10

Midrange:
€80–200

➡ Double room: €120–160

➡ Three-course dinner in casual restaurant: €30

➡ Concert ticket: €10–30

Top End:
more than €200

➡ Double room in luxury hotel: €260

➡ Seven-course tasting menu in top restaurant: €90

➡ Private guided tour of Prague with driver: €200

Advance Planning

Three months before Book accommodation if visiting in high season. Check Prague Spring or Strings of Autumn programs and book tickets.

One month before Reserve tables at top-end restaurants, and buy tickets online for a weekend visit to Karlštejn Castle.

One week before Make Friday- or Saturday-night reservations for any restaurants you don't want to miss. Check website programs for art galleries, jazz clubs and music venues.

Useful Websites

Living Prague (www. livingprague.com) Insider guide to the city by a British expat.

Lonely Planet (www.lonely-planet.com/prague) Destination information, hotel bookings, traveller forum and more.

Prague Events Calendar (www. pragueeventscalendar.com) Covers music, entertainment, culture, sport etc.

Prague City Tourism (www. prague.eu) Official tourist information website.

CzechTourism (www.czechtour-ism.com) Official tourist information for the Czech Republic.

IDOS (jizdnirady.idnes.cz) Train and bus timetables, and fares for the Czech Republic.

WHEN TO GO

May and June are peak season, with fine weather and major festivals. April and October have decent weather and smaller crowds.

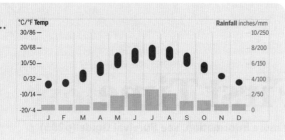

Arriving in the Czech Republic

Prague Airport Buses to Dejvice (service No 119) and Zličín (No 100) metro stations depart every 10 minutes from 4am to midnight, from stops just outside the arrivals terminal (32Kč). A taxi to the city centre costs 560Kč.

Prague's main train station (Praha hlavní nádraží) In the centre of Prague, a short walk from Wenceslas Square; all international rail connections arrive here. The station is on metro line C, one stop from Florenc bus station, and on tram lines 5, 9 and 26.

Florenc bus station International buses arrive here, just east of Prague centre, with metro and tram links to the rest of the city. Some domestic bus services leave from Florenc; others depart from Holešovice in the north (eg to Mělník) and Smíchov in the southwest.

Car The Czech Republic is surrounded by EU Schengen countries; there are no passport checks on the border. Prague lies at the nexus of several European highways and is an easy drive from many major cities, including Munich (four hours) and Vienna (four hours).

 For much more on **arrival** see p296

Getting Around

Within the Czech Republic, buses are often faster, cheaper and more convenient than trains. Outside Prague, the easiest way to get around is by car. Prague has an integrated metro, tram and bus network – tickets are valid on all types of transport, and for transfers between them. A basic ticket (32Kč) is valid for 90 minutes – validate tickets once in yellow machines on trams and buses, and at the entrance to metro stations.

➡ **Walking** Central Prague is fairly compact, and individual neighbourhoods are easily explored on foot.

➡ **Tram** Extensive network; best way to get around shorter distances between neighbourhoods.

➡ **Metro** Fast and frequent, good for visiting outlying areas or covering longer distances.

➡ **Bus** Not much use in city centre, except for airport and part of Žižkov; operates in areas not covered by tram or metro.

➡ **Taxi** Relatively expensive, and prone to rip-off drivers.

For much more on **getting around** see p298

Sleeping

Gone are the days when Prague was a cheap destination. The Czech capital now ranks alongside most western European cities when it comes to the quality, range and price of hotels. Book as far in advance as possible (especially during festival season in spring and autumn, at weekends, and at Easter and Christmas/New Year). Many central hotels are set in charming historic buildings, and there is a new generation of funky design hotels and hostels. There are also dozens of backpacker hostels, most of them geared towards youthful party animals.

Useful Websites

➡ **AVE Travel** (www.praguehotellocator.com) Offers a huge range of hotels and apartments.

➡ **Mary's Travel & Tourist Services** (www.marys.cz) Offers private rooms, hostels, pensions, apartments and hotels in all price ranges.

➡ **Hostel.cz** (www.hostel.cz) Database of hostels and budget hotels, with online booking.

For much more on **sleeping** see p190

First Time

For more information, see Survival Guide (p295)

Checklist

➡ Make sure your passport is valid for at least six months after your arrival date.

➡ Inform your debit-/credit-card company of your intended travel dates and destination.

➡ Arrange for appropriate travel insurance.

➡ Contact your cell-phone provider to inquire about roaming charges or getting an international plan.

What to Pack

➡ European two-pin electrical adapter. When there, consider buying an extension cord with multiple sockets – lots of tourist accommodation is sadly lacking in electrical outlets.

➡ Comfortable walking shoes – Prague is best appreciated on foot.

➡ Umbrella and/or packable waterproof jacket.

➡ A small day-pack (the smaller the better to avoid having to check it when visiting museums).

Top Tips for Your Trip

➡ Plan your time – although Prague's public transport system is top-notch, criss-crossing the city will eat into your time. Choose just one or two neighbourhoods to explore in a single day.

➡ Buy a map! It's easy to get lost in Prague's medieval maze of backstreets. Most bookshops sell excellent large-scale maps of the city centre (look for the Kartografie Praha brand) which include tram and bus info.

➡ Sightsee by foot. Walking is one of the best ways to get around within each neighbourhood – it's quick, cheap and provides the opportunity to explore hidden lanes and shops you might otherwise miss.

What to Wear

Most Praguers are pretty style-conscious and take pleasure in looking good. Folk here still dress up for dinner, and as for going to the opera in anything but your best, well, you must be a tourist.

Pack layers of clothing – Prague's weather can be fickle, with thunderstorms and cool spells even in summer. In spring and autumn, a light trench jacket and a small umbrella will mean you're prepared for the odd shower. In winter, bring a warm coat, hat and gloves to ward off the sub-zero temperatures, and footwear that can cope with snow and ice.

Be Forewarned

➡ Prague is as safe as any European capital, but pickpockets can be a problem. There's no need to be paranoid, but keep valuables well out of reach, and be alert in crowds and on public transport.

➡ Prime pickpocket spots are Prague Castle (especially at the changing of the guard), Charles Bridge, Old Town Square (in the crowd watching the Astronomical Clock), the entrance to the Old Jewish Cemetery and Wenceslas Square.

➡ Carry shoulder bags or backpacks in front of you on crowded trams (especially Nos 9 and 22), metro carriages and escalators.

Money

ATMS are everywhere, and will generally accept Visa, MasterCard, Cirrus or Maestro cards. There is nearly always a cash withdrawal fee (around 2%) for foreign cards. Many Prague ATMs dispense 2000Kč notes, which are hard to change in shops or pubs.

Most hotels accept credit cards, but a fair number of restaurants, shops and other businesses do not. Some businesses levy a 5% surcharge (or more) on credit-card purchases. Always check first.

To change cash, use a bank. Avoid private exchange booths (*směnárna*).

National Theatre (p126)

Taxes & Refunds

Value-added tax (VAT, or DPH in Czech) is applied at 10% on food (including restaurant meals), books and periodicals, and 20% on the sale of most goods and services. This tax is included in the marked price.

It's sometimes possible for visitors to claim a refund of VAT paid on goods (see p306).

Tipping

➡ **Hotels** Porters expect 20Kč to 50Kč per bag in top-end hotels; not typical for cleaning staff.

➡ **Restaurants** Normal practice is to add around 10% if service has been good.

➡ **Pubs and bars** For table service, round up to the next 10Kč (or 20Kč for bills over 200Kč).

➡ **Taxis** A 5% tip is expected, rising to 10% if they haul your bags.

Etiquette

➡ **Greetings** It's customary to say *dobrý den* (good day) to all and sundry when entering a shop, cafe or pub, and to say *na shledanou* (goodbye) when you leave. When meeting people for the first time a firm handshake, for both men and women, is the norm.

➡ **Visiting** If you're invited to someone's home, bring flowers or some other small gift for your host, and remove your shoes when you enter the house.

➡ **Manners** On tram and metro, it's good manners to give up a seat for an elderly or infirm passenger.

➡ **Beer** Never, ever, pour the dregs of your previous glass of beer into a newly served one. This is considered to be the behaviour of barbarians!

Language

English is widely spoken in the tourist areas of Prague, especially among the younger generation, and most important signage (eg on public transport) is bilingual. It's possible to enjoy a visit without knowing a word of Czech, but learning a few basic phrases, if only hello, goodbye, please and thank you, will ensure a warmer reception in restaurants and pubs. See Language (p309) for more information.

Getting Around

For more information, see Transport (p296)

Tickets

Prague has an integrated metro, tram and bus network – tickets are valid on all types of transport, and for transfers between them.

Tram

Extensive network of routes, best way for getting around shorter distances between neighbourhoods. Full service from 5am to 12.30am; limited service through the night.

Metro

Fast and frequent, good for visiting outlying areas or covering longer distances. Runs 5am to midnight.

Bus

Not much use in city centre, except for airport and parts of Žižkov; operates in areas not covered by tram or metro. Runs 4.30am to 12.30am, plus limited night service.

Taxi

Relatively expensive, and prone to rip-off drivers in tourist areas, especially late at night.

Walking

Central Prague is fairly compact; individual neighbourhoods are easily explored on foot.

Key Phrases

Přestupní stanice Transfer/interchange station

Kolej Platform

Výstup Exit

Přistí zastávka/stanice... Next tram stop/metro station is...

Mimo Provoz Out of service

How to Hail a Taxi

➡ Look for a cab with its yellow roof lamp lit, and raise your hand. Establish your destination and a likely fare before getting in, and make sure the meter is switched on.

➡ Only hail official, registered cabs – these are yellow, have a permanently installed roof lamp with the word TAXI on it, and have the driver's name and licence number printed on both front doors.

Key Routes

Tram No 22 The classic tram line that climbs to Prague Castle from Malá Strana, though you can board it in Vinohrady, at Národní třída, or Národní Divadlo (National Theatre) too.

Tram No 9 One of Prague's busiest cross-city tram routes, linking Žižkov, the main train station, Wenceslas Square, the National Theatre and Smíchov. Transfer to line No 22 at Národní třída, Národní Divadlo or Újezd.

Metro Line A (Shown on transport maps in green.) Links airport bus to Malá Strana, Old Town Square, Wenceslas Square and Vinohrady

Metro Line B (Yellow) Cross-river route from Smíchov in southwest to Náměstí Republiky and Florenc bus station.

Metro Line C (Red) Links main train station to Florenc bus station, Wenceslas Square and Vyšehrad.

TOP TIPS

➡ Children under 10 years of age travel free, but be sure to carry proof of age.

➡ If you plan to make four or more tram/metro trips per day, then a 24-hour or three-day pass will be cheaper than buying individual tickets.

➡ Be aware that you need a 16Kč half-fare ticket for large items of luggage (more than 25cm x 45cm x 70cm). A 24-hour or three-day pass includes one such item of luggage.

➡ If you're going to be in Prague for a week or more, a 30-day transferable pass (670Kč) is worth thinking about.

When to Travel

➡ Public transport is usually very crowded during weekday rush hours, between 7.30am and 9.30am, and from 4.30pm to 6.30pm. However, services are more frequent, with metro trains every two or three minutes, rather than the four to 10-minute gaps during off-peak periods.

➡ Although the normal tram and metro network closes down between midnight and 5am, a night tram service continues to operate with trams every half hour or so. Only full-fare (32Kč) tickets and multi-day passes are valid on night trams.

Travel Etiquette

➡ On metro escalators it's important to stand on the right-hand side or use the left if you want to walk down. Failure to observe this can cause consternation among other users, especially during rush hour.

➡ The large seatless area at the tail end of older trams is generally reserved for pushchairs – be sure to make room here if someone boards with a pram.

➡ Except in the oldest trams, you have to press a green button (marked *dveře*) to make the doors open; if you're at the front of the queue, press it smartly if you don't want to incur the wrath of those behind!

Tickets & Passes

➡ A basic ticket (32Kč) is valid for 90 minutes. Validate tickets once only, on first boarding, in the yellow machines found on trams and buses, and at the entrance to metro stations. A short-term ticket (24Kč) is valid for only 30 minutes.

➡ You can buy tickets in metro stations, from Prague Public Transport Authority (DPP) information offices, from ticket machines at tram and bus stops, and from grocery shops, newsagents and kiosks (look for a sign saying '*jizdenky*'). You can not buy tickets from a tram or bus driver.

➡ You can buy a 24-hour pass from ticket machines, but for three-day passes or longer you need to go to a metro station ticket office. For 30-day non-transferable passes you have to go to the ticket office in the Line B station at Můstek.

For much more on **getting around** see p298

USING TICKET MACHINES

Press the button for the ticket you need – probably the 32Kč PLNOCENNÁ (full fare) at top left – once for one ticket, twice for two etc. You will see the price clocking up in the display. Put your coins in the slot – as soon as the correct fare (or more) has been inserted, your tickets will be printed, and change given if necessary. If you make a mistake, press the STORNO (cancel) button and start again.

Top Itineraries

Day One

Prague Castle & Hradčany (p64)

☀️ Wander through **Prague Castle's** courtyards before the main sights open, then spend the morning visiting **St Vitus Cathedral**, the **Old Royal Palace** and the **Lobkowicz Palace**; try and time things to catch the **changing of the guard** at noon.

🍴 **Lunch** Lobkowicz Palace Café (p80) serves good food with a view.

Malá Strana (p81)

☀️ Descend from the castle to Malá Strana along **Nerudova** street, and stop to admire the baroque beauty of **St Nicholas Church**. From here, head to the **Wallenstein Garden** for some peace and quiet, then exit on the far side and follow the backstreets south to **Kampa**. If it's sunny, hang out in the park, and grab a drink at **Mlýnská Kavárna**, or pay a visit to the **Kampa Museum**. As day fades, stroll across **Charles Bridge** in the evening light.

🍴 **Dinner** Elegantes (p93) is a sophisticated place for a special dinner.

Malá Strana (p81)

🌙 Malá Strana is full of buzzy bars – **U Malého Glena** is a classic Prague bar and jazz club, with live music every night.

Day Two

Staré Město (p95)

☀️ Start the day in the **Old Town Square**; after watching the **Astronomical Clock** do its thing, climb to the top of the **Old Town Hall Tower** for a great view of the square. Head along Celetná to the **Municipal House** and have a coffee while you admire the art nouveau decor. Buy a ticket for a concert; if you have time before lunch, take a guided tour.

🍴 **Lunch** Try Lokál (p111) for an authentically Czech lunch, and great beer.

Staré Město (p95)

☀️ Dedicate the afternoon to visiting the half-dozen monuments that comprise the **Prague Jewish Museum**; if you don't have the time or energy for all of them, concentrate on the **Old-New Synagogue**, the **Old Jewish Cemetery** and the **Spanish Synagogue**.

🍴 **Dinner** Kalina (p113) is good for French food and wine.

Staré Město (p95)

🌙 Attend a concert in the Municipal House's **Smetana Hall** or the Klementinum's **Chapel of Mirrors**, or spend a night at the opera at the **Estates Theatre**. Afterwards, explore Old Town cocktail joints such as **Hemingway Bar** and **Čili Bar**.

Day Three

Nové Město (p120)

☀ Explore the passages and arcades around **Wenceslas Square**, and (if time and inclination allow) take in the historical and artistic treasures of the **National Museum**, the **Prague City Museum** and the **Mucha Museum**.

> ✗ **Lunch** Le Patio (p131) is a favourite local lunch spot.

Smíchov & Vyšehrad (p170)

☼ In the afternoon, take a metro ride out to Vyšehrad and explore Prague's other castle, the **Vyšehrad Citadel**, with its gorgeous views along the Vltava. Don't miss the impressive tombs of composers Dvořák and Smetana and other famous Czechs in the **Vyšehrad Cemetery**. Walk back to the city centre along the embankment.

> ✗ **Dinner** Head to Sansho (p131) for a memorable meal (book in advance).

Nové Město (p120)

☾ The New Town is home to the city's most prestigious classical-music venues – try to catch a performance at the **National Theatre** (ballet), the **Prague State Opera** or the **Dvořák Museum** (concerts of Dvořák's music).

Day Four

Holešovice (p154)

☀ Time to escape the city for a while: take a boat trip to the rural suburb of Troja (or hire a bike and ride there) and visit **Prague Zoo**. Walk back into the city centre through Stromovka park.

> ✗ **Lunch** Enjoy a picnic lunch in leafy Stromovka park (p164).

Holešovice (p154)

☼ You could spend an entire afternoon admiring modern art in the **Veletržní Palác**, but if the outdoor bug has bitten keep walking (or take a tram) to Letná Gardens for some afternoon drinking at **Letná Beer Garden**, the city's premier open-air chill-out spot.

> ✗ **Dinner** Sasazu (p157) captures the vibe of this up-and-coming area.

Žižkov & Karlín (p145)

☾ Take the metro across town to Jiřího z Poděbrad station, and go up the **TV Tower** (open until midnight) for a night-time city panorama. From here, the legendary bars of Žižkov await – **Bukowski's** cocktail dive is just two blocks downhill.

If You Like...

Art & Literature

Veletržní Palác This magnificent functionalist building harbours four floors of 20th-century and contemporary art. (p156)

Franz Kafka Museum Offers a comprehensive exploration of the claustrophobic and paranoid world of Kafka's novels, and their relation to Prague. (p88)

David Černý The witty and provocative works of Prague's most famous living artist pop up all over the city. (p288)

U Kalicha A place of pilgrimage for fans of Jaroslav Hašek's novel *The Good Soldier Švejk* – this pub is where the novel's opening scene is set. (p129)

Convent of St Agnes This branch of the National Gallery houses a precious collection of glowing Gothic altarpieces and religious sculpture. (p106)

Beer

Prague Beer Museum Not a museum but a hugely popular pub, with 30 varieties of beer on tap. (p114)

Pivovarský Dům One of the city's best microbreweries, offering classic lagers and fruit-flavoured beers produced on the premises. (p131)

U Zlatého Tygra The classic Prague drinking den, where Václav Havel took Bill Clinton in 1994 to show him a real Czech pub. (p115)

Pivní Galerie If the idea of shopping leaves you cold, how about shopping for beer? This booze boutique stocks nearly 150

David Černý's *Miminka* (Mummy) statues (p149) outside the TV Tower

varieties from around the world. (p161)

Pivovarský Klub Six guest beers on tap and more than 200 international brands in bottles make this welcoming pub a great place to drink your way around the world. (p152)

Budvar Brewery Fountainhead of the original Budweiser beer, and still wrangling over the name. (p203)

Parks & Gardens

Wallenstein Garden Hidden away behind high walls, this gorgeous 17th-century Italianate garden is a haven of peace and tranquillity. (p88)

Letná Gardens Huge open space, once used for military pa-rades, now home to skateboard-ers, inline skaters, and glorious city panoramas. (p157)

Riegrovy sady A 19th-century park with a grandstand view of Prague Castle, and home to one of the city's most popular beer gardens. (p137)

Vrtbov Garden Perhaps Prague's least-known garden: an 18th-century retreat peopled by stone figures from Roman mythology. (p89)

Kampa This leafy Malá Strana island, bounded by the Devil's Stream, is one of the city's most popular chill-out spots. (p88)

Music

Prague Spring The Czech Re-public's biggest annual cultural event, and one of Europe's most important festivals of classical music. (p25)

Palác Akropolis A Prague institution that hosts live music performances of all kinds, from

ethnic folk to heavy metal to string quartets. (p153)

Rudolfinum Home to the Czech Philharmonic Orchestra, this complex of concert halls is decorated with statues of famous composers. (p106)

Jazz Dock Most of Prague's jazz clubs are hidden away in Old Town cellars, but this floating venue offers music with a view over the Vltava. (p179)

Municipal House Prague's most beautiful art nouveau building houses Smetana Hall, the city's largest concert venue. (p108)

Prague State Opera The State Opera is a glorious neo-rococo setting for a late-summer pro-gramme devoted to the works of Verdi. (p133)

Original Music Theatre of Prague This ensemble performs the works of Antonín Dvořák in the baroque setting of the 18th-century Vila Amerika. (p133)

History

Prague Castle A thousand years of Bohemian history clustered on a hilltop. (p66)

Prague Jewish Museum An ancient cemetery and exhibits spread across half-a-dozen synagogues, telling the story of Prague's Jewish community. (p97)

National Monument A brutalist building and monumental statue, bearing witness to the turbulent 20th-century history of Czechoslovakia. (p147)

National Memorial to the Heroes of the Heydrich Terror A moving memorial to those who died in one of the key events of WWII. (p128)

Prague City Museum Recounts the story of the Czech capital

For more top Prague spots, see the following:
➡ Eating (p35)
➡ Drinking & Nightlife (p39)
➡ Entertainment (p43)
➡ Shopping (p47)

from prehistoric times to the 20th century. (p124)

Terezin Former WWII concentra-tion camp, and a sobering memorial to the horrors of the Holocaust. (p188)

Offbeat Attractions

TV Tower Prague's futuristic three-legged TV Tower looks unconventional enough from a distance, but when you get up close and see the giant crawling babies… (p149)

KGB Museum The enthusiastic Russian owner of this quirky lit-tle museum will talk you through his collection of spy cameras, torture kits and gruesome garrottes. (p89)

Hotel Jalta Nuclear Bunker A 1950s nuclear shelter hidden beneath a communist-era hotel right on Wenceslas Square. (p125)

Miniature Museum If the preserved whale penises in the Strahov Library aren't weird enough for you, how about a flea wearing microscopic golden horseshoes? (p76)

Cubist Lamp Post How many cities can boast a humble lamp post designed in the cubist style? (p130)

Konopiště Chateau A fascinat-ing testament to the eccentric obsessions of Archduke Franz Ferdinand. (p183)

Month by Month

January

Days are short – the sun sets around 4.30pm in mid-January – but post– New Year accommodation prices are the cheapest you'll find, ideal for that romantic getaway in a cosy hotel with an open fireplace.

✷ Three Kings' Day (Svátek Tří králů)

On 6 January, Three Kings' Day (also known as Twelfth Night) marks the formal end of the Christmas season. The Czechs celebrate with carol-singing, bell-ringing and gifts to the poor.

✷ Anniversary of Jan Palach's Death

A gathering in Wenceslas Square on 19 January commemorates the Charles University student Jan Palach (www.janpalach.cz) who burned himself to death in 1969 in protest against the Soviet occupation.

February

Prague's frost can be cruel in February, with temperatures plunging below -10°C, so wrap up well. But Prague certainly looks mighty pretty in the snow.

✷ Masopust

Once banned by the communists, the Czech version of carnival (www.carnevale.cz) is marked by street parties, fireworks, concerts and revelry. Celebrations start on the Friday before Shrove Tuesday (aka Mardi Gras), and end with a masked parade.

March

The first buds of spring begin to green Prague's parks and gardens, and the Easter holidays bring Easter markets, hand-painted Easter eggs, and the first tourist influx of the year.

☆ St Matthew Fair (Matějská pouť')

From the Feast of St Matthew (24 February) up to and including Easter weekend, Výstaviště (exhibition grounds) fills with roller coasters, shooting galleries and stalls selling traditional heart-shaped cookies. Open 2pm to 10pm Tuesday to Friday; 10am to 10pm Saturday and Sunday.

✷ Easter Monday (Pondělí velikonoční)

Mirthful spring! Czech boys chase girls and swat them on the legs with willow switches decked with ribbons; the girls respond with gifts of hand-painted eggs, then everyone parties. It's the culmination of several days of spring-cleaning, cooking and visiting family and friends.

☆ One World (Jeden Svět)

This week-long film festival (www.oneworld.cz) is dedicated to documentaries on the subject of human rights. Screenings are held at some of the smaller cinemas around Prague, including Kino Světozor (p133).

☆ Febiofest

This festival (www.febiofest.cz) of film, TV and video features new works by international film-makers. It continues throughout the Czech Republic after the Prague festival.

April

The weather transforms from shivers to sunshine. By the end of the month the sidewalks and squares are covered with outdoor cafe tables, and peak tourist season begins.

🎭 Burning of the Witches (Pálení čarodějnic)

This Czech pre-Christian (pagan) festival for warding off evil features the burning of brooms at Výstaviště and all-night, end-of-winter bonfire parties on Kampa island and in suburban backyards. It's held on 30 April.

May

May is Prague's busiest and most beautiful month, with trees and gardens in full blossom, and a string of major festivals. Book accommodation well in advance, and expect to pay top dollar.

🎭 Labour Day (Svátek práce)

Once sacred to the communists, the 1 May holiday is now mostly a picnic opportunity. To celebrate the arrival of spring, couples lay flowers at the statue of the 19th-century Romantic poet Karel Hynek Mácha, author of *Máj* (May), a poem about unrequited love.

☆ Prague Spring (Pražské jaro)

Running from 12 May to 3 June, this international music festival (p45) is Prague's most prestigious event, with classical music concerts held in theatres, churches and historic buildings.

🍴 Prague Food Festival

A Friday-to-Sunday festival (www.praguefoodfestival.com) spread throughout the gardens on the south side of Prague Castle. Celebrates the best of Czech and international cuisine, with cooking demonstrations, food stalls, beer- and wine-tastings and children's events.

🍺 Czech Beer Festival (Český pivní festival)

During the second half of May, part of Letná park is consumed by the country's largest beer tent. The festival (www.ceskypivnifestival.cz) celebrates the nation's most famous product. Hog roasts, live music and 70 brands of beer.

🎭 Khamoro

This festival (www.khamoro.cz) of Roma culture – with performances of traditional music and dance, exhibitions of art and photography, and a parade through Staré Město – is usually held in late May.

June

Something of a shoulder season, June promises great weather for beer gardens and river cruises without the May festival crowds or the hordes of

students who descend on the city in July and August.

🎭 Prague Fringe Festival

This nine-day binge of international theatre, dance, comedy and music (www.praguefringe.com), inspired by the innovative Edinburgh Fringe, takes place in late May/early June. Hugely popular with visitors and now pulling in more and more locals.

🎭 Prague Writers' Festival

A meeting of writers from around the world (www.pwf.cz), with public readings, lectures, discussions and bookshop events.

☆ Dance Prague (Tanec Praha)

International festival of modern dance (www.tanecpraha.cz) held at theatres around Prague throughout June.

September

The hot and humid August weather is mellowing as autumn approaches, and the hordes of visiting backpackers, students and school groups have thinned out, making this a great month to visit.

☆ Dvořák Festival

Two weeks in September are given over to the Dvořák Festival, a celebration of the works of the Czech Republic's most famous classical composer, with a programme of performances by the world's top orchestras, chamber ensembles and soloists.

(Top) Masked ball during Masopust
(Bottom) Easter-egg decorating, Old Town Square

October

Autumn is one of the most pleasant times of year in Prague – the tourist crowds start to diminish, it's still pleasantly warm, and the Strings of Autumn festival is less frenetic than the Prague Spring.

☆ Strings of Autumn (Struny podzimu)

Strings (www.struny-podzimu.cz) is an eclectic program of musical performances, from classical and baroque to avant-garde jazz, Sardinian vocal polyphony and contemporary Swiss yodelling. It runs for eight weeks from mid-September to mid-November.

December

Cold and dark the weather may be, but a warming glass of *svařák* (mulled wine) will set you up to enjoy the city's Christmas markets and New Year celebrations. Expect peak season hotel prices.

✲ Christmas & New Year (Vánoce & Nový Rok)

From 24 December to 1 January, tourists engulf Prague and many Czechs take an extended holiday. From early December a Christmas market takes over the Old Town Square, around a huge Christmas tree: also here on New Year's Eve, massive crowds gather here for a huge midnight fireworks display.

MARK READ / LONELY PLANET ©

RICHARD NEBESKY/ROBERT HARDING / GETTY IMAGES ©

With Kids

Czechs are very family-oriented, and there are plenty of activities around the city for children. An increasing number of Prague restaurants cater specifically for children, with play areas and so on, and many offer a children's menu (dětský jídelníček).

RICHARD NEBESKY / GETTY IMAGES ©

Sculpture at the National Gallery, Schwarzenberg Palace (p78)

Outdoor Fun

Petřín

The classic outdoor play area in central Prague, Petřín (p90) has a whole range of diversions, from the Lookout Tower and observatory to the Mirror Maze.

Prague Zoo

As it's located on the northern outskirts of the city, just getting to the zoo can be part of the adventure. Take a boat trip along the river with Prague Passenger Shipping (p32), enjoy a walk through lovely Stromovka (p164), or rent bikes and cycle through the park. Once there, as well as the animals, you'll find a children's zoo (petting allowed), a miniature cable car and a huge kids' play area.

Children's Island

At the southern end of Malá Strana, traffic-free Children's Island (p90) is equipped with playground equipment, rope swings, a mini football pitch, a skateboarding area and a cafe-bar where parents can sip a coffee or beer.

Skateboarding & Skating

The area around the metronome monument in Letná (p157), the huge park to the east of the castle, is a favourite with local skateboarders, while the park's paths provide a perfect surface for inline skating.

If you're visiting in winter, an outdoor ice rink (10am to 9.30pm December to February) gets set up at Ovocný Trh (behind the Estates Theatre) in Staré Město. Skate hire is available.

Parks & Playgrounds

There are safe, well-designed playgrounds all over the city, with convenient city-centre ones at the north end of Kampa (p88) island (at the Malá Strana end of Charles Bridge) and on **Slav Island** (Slovanský ostrov; Map p338; Masarykovo nábřeží; 🚋17, 21). There's an extensive list of play areas at www.livingprague.com/kids.htm.

Messing about on the River

In summer (generally April to October) you can hire rowing boats and pedalos from several jetties dotted around Slav Island, and splash around on the Vltava. If that sounds too energetic, there are lots of organised boat trips on offer.

Child-Friendly Restaurants

Hergetova Cihelna

Long famed among Prague parents for its family-friendly Sunday brunch, riverside Hergetova Cihelna (p93) now actively encourages you to bring the kids any day of the week. The upper lounge is equipped with high chairs, a nappy-changing station, a breastfeeding area and a play area with lots of toys.

Kogo

An upmarket but relaxed Italian restaurant with outdoor tables in summer, Kogo (p131) welcomes families and provides high chairs and a separate children's menu.

Sakura

Sakura (p167) is an unpretentious Japanese sushi restaurant that has a children's play area.

Vozovna Stromovka

Vozovna (p167) is a garden restaurant in the middle of leafy Stromovka park, next door to a playground – parents can eat and drink while the kids can run around in safety.

Rainy-Day Fun

Puppets & Plays

Children's theatre is a long-standing Czech tradition, and there are several places in Prague that stage regular children's entertainment. The Spejbl & Hurvínek Theatre (p169) puts on puppet shows, while Minor Theatre (p134) stages live children's theatre.

Zoo Mořský Svět

Shark tanks and touch pools are among the attractions at Zoo Mořský Svět (p164), Prague's only aquarium.

NEED TO KNOW

➡ Admission costs The maximum age for child discounts on admission fees varies from 12 to 18; children under six often get in for free.

➡ Kids in Prague (www.kidsinprague.com) Has loads of useful information on places to go and things to do.

➡ Babysitting Most top-end hotels provide a babysitting service. **Prague Family** (☑737 749 019; www.prague-family.cz) is an agency that provides English-speaking babysitters.

TV Tower

Prague's space-age TV Tower (p149) offers a trip in a high-speed elevator to the 93m-high observation decks – if the view proves 'boring', there are suspended chairs and free wi-fi for WhatsApping and SnapChatting.

Prague Planetarium

Regular tours of the heavens (in Czech, but a summary text in English is available) are on offer at the Prague Planetarium (p164).

Child-Friendly Museums & Galleries

Art Gallery for Children

The clue is in the name: at the Art Gallery for Children (p104) the kids not only get to look at art, but make it, add to it and alter it. There are paints and materials to play with, and even workshops for five- to 12-year-olds (only in Czech at present, though staff speak English).

Lego Museum

The Lego Museum (p111) is Europe's largest private collection of Lego models, with a play area at the end where kids can build stuff from Lego themselves.

National Technical Museum

Sadly, all those vintage trains, planes, cars and buses are off-limits at the National Technical Museum (p157), but there are interactive exhibits in the photography and printing-industry sections.

Like a Local

Central Prague can often feel like it's populated entirely by tourists. Where are all the locals? If it's the weekend, they're probably either picking wild mushrooms or at a football or ice-hockey match.

RICHARD NEBESKY / GETTY IMAGES ©

omovka (p164)

Eat Like a Local

Lunchtime Bargains

Praguers enjoy eating out, and weekday lunchtime is when office workers, shoppers and parents with toddlers go looking for a bargain. You'll see lots of restaurants and pubs with signs advertising *polední menu* (lunch menu) or *denní nabídka* (today's offer), usually offering a set menu of one or two courses and a drink for a set price, often as little as 100Kč or 150Kč. There's even a website (www.lunchtime.cz) dedicated to publicising these deals (English version available).

Foraging for Fun

It has been estimated that Czechs pick more than 20 million kilograms of wild mushrooms each year. From May to October, foraging for fungi and wild berries is one of the nation's most popular pastimes, when Prague's Divoká Šárka (p166) and Michelský Les woodlands (southeast of the city centre) are thronged with locals clutching wicker baskets. Czechs learn young how to identify edible fungi, so unless you've mastered the art of mushroom identification you'd better tag along with a local expert; otherwise you can sample the fruits of the forest at a farmers market, or at restaurants advertising *hřiby* (mushrooms) or *lesní houby* (forest mushrooms).

Relaxation

Picnic in the Park

Get a taste for local produce by browsing the weekend farmers markets at Vinohrady (p144) or Náplavka (p134) and putting together the makings of a picnic. Then join the crowds at Riegrovy sady in Vinohrady for an alfresco lunch (there's a beer garden here, too), or head down to Havlíčkovy sady, where you can sample Czech wine at Viniční Altán. From Náplavka, climb up to Vyšehrad – a favourite spot for weekend strolls – for a picnic with a view.

Head to the Embankment

From late April to September, as evening approaches, the river embankment at Náplavka in Nové Město swells with crowds of walkers and gawkers, cyclists and strollers who throng here to take in various live-music events, evening drinks on quayside boats, and the breathtaking views towards floodlit Prague Castle.

Celebration Days

Easter

Come Easter, the country celebrates with a mirthful rite of spring: Czech boys swat their favourite girls on the legs with braided willow switches (you'll see them on sale in street markets) or splash them with water, and the girls respond with gifts of hand-painted eggs. Afterwards the whole family parties – the culmination of several days of serious spring-cleaning, cooking and visiting relatives and friends.

May Day

The May Day holiday *(Svátek práce)* on May 1 – once the communist 'holy' day, marked by huge parades – is now just a chance for a picnic or a day in the country. To celebrate the arrival of spring, many couples lay flowers at the statue of the 19th-century poet Karel Hynek Mácha (author of *Máj,* a poem about unrequited love) on Petřín.

Majáles

Prague students celebrate the first weekend of May with Majáles, a festival dating back to at least the early 19th century, which was banned under communism but revived in 1997. It starts with a midday parade – with bands, students in fancy dress, and a float bearing the Kral Majáles (King of Majáles) and Miss Majáles – from Wenceslas Square to Stromovka park, and there is an open-air party including live bands, student theatre and non-stop sausages and beer. For dates and details, check www.majales.cz (Czech only).

Sporting Obsessions

Ice Hockey

It's a toss-up whether football or ice hockey inspires more passion in the hearts of Prague sports fans, but hockey probably wins. Games are fast and furious, and the atmosphere can be electrifying – it's well worth making the effort to see a game, and take part in a genuinely Czech experience.

Prague's two big hockey teams are HC Sparta Praha (www.hcsparta.cz) and HC Slavia Praha (www.hc-slavia.cz), both of which compete in the 14-team national league (known as the Extraliga). Gifted young players are often lured away by the promise of big money in North America's National Hockey League, and there is a sizeable Czech contingent in the National Hockey League (NHL).

Sparta plays at the huge, slightly run-down Tipsport Aréna (p161) at the Výstaviště exhibition grounds in Holešovice, and Slavia Praha at **O2 Arena** (☑266 212 111; www.o2arena.cz; Českomoravská 17, Vysočany; underground rail Českomoravská). The season runs from September to early April. Buy tickets online at www.sazkaticket.cz or www.ticketportal.cz, or at the stadium box office before matches.

Football

Prague's two big football (soccer) clubs, SK Slavia Praha (www.slavia.cz) and AC Sparta Praha (www.sparta.cz), are both leading contenders in the national *fotbal* (football) league, with fiercely partisan supporters all over the country. Two other Prague-based teams – FC Bohemians (www.bohemians1905.cz) and FK Viktoria Žižkov (www.fkvz.cz) – attract fervent local support.

The season runs from August to December and February to June, and matches are mostly played on Wednesday, Saturday and Sunday afternoons. You can buy tickets (100Kč to 400Kč) at stadium box offices on match days.

The Czech national team performs well in international competitions, having won the European Championship in 1976 (as Czechoslovakia), and reached the final in 1996 and the semifinal in 2004. Home international matches are played at Slavia Praha's 21,000-seat Eden stadium (also known as the Synot Tip Aréna in eastern Prague).

Prague for Free

Once a famously inexpensive destination, Prague is no longer cheap; there's not much on offer without a price attached. Parks and gardens, some museums and galleries, and gazing at the glorious architecture are all free, as is the street entertainment on Charles Bridge.

Prague Without a Ticket

Without having to buy a ticket, you can wander through the courtyards and gardens of Prague Castle (p66), watch the changing of the guard ceremony and visit the western end of the nave of St Vitus Cathedral (p73). Charles Bridge (p83), with its array of jazz bands, buskers, caricature artists and postcard sellers, is a smorgasbord of free entertainment.

Over in the Old Town Square, the hourly performance by the Astronomical Clock (p100) is a classic sight without a ticket, as is the baroque glory of the nearby Church of St Nicholas (p105). Although you'll have to pay for a guided tour of the Municipal House (p108), you can wander through the glorious art nouveau cafe, the lobby and to the downstairs American Bar without a ticket.

Visits to most churches in Prague (except St Nicholas Church in Malá Strana)

are free, as is the beautiful Wallenstein Garden (p88) and imposing Vyšehrad Citadel (p173).

Public Art

Prague has a fine collection of public art on show, all viewable for free, including the provocative and often humorous modern works of David Černý and the magnificent art nouveau monuments to **Jan Hus** (Map p332; ⓂStaroměstská) in the Old Town Square, and Josef Palácký on Paláckého náměstí.

Free Museums & Galleries

Museums, art galleries and other attractions with free admission include the following:

➡ Museum of the Infant Jesus of Prague (p89)
➡ Dvorak Sec Contemporary (p104)
➡ Wallenstein Palace (p88)
➡ Mánes Gallery (p127)
➡ Futura Gallery (p175)
➡ Meet Factory (p175)
➡ Karlín Studios (p149)
➡ Army Museum (p149)

On the first Thursday of every month, entrance to the Prague City Museum (p124) is free for students, and is reduced to 10Kč (from 120Kč) for everyone else.

Free Tours

A number of outfits, including the recommended **Prague Extravaganza** (www.extravaganzafreetour.com), offer guided walking tours 'for free' (ie on a no-fee, tips-only basis). The guides are local volunteers, and tours depart twice daily from outside the Cartier store on the corner of the Old Town Square and Pařížská. See also Royal Walk Free Tour (p32).

Prague Tours

Prague offers so much intriguing history and culture that it's easy to feel overwhelmed. A guided tour can ease you into an aspect of the city that reflects your interests. The Prague City Tourism office in the Old Town Hall (p100) provides details of tours.

Boat tour along the Vltava River

OLIVIERO OLIVIERI/ROBERT HARDING / GETTY IMAGES ©

Walking Tours

The corner of the Old Town Square outside the Old Town Hall is usually clogged with dozens of people touting for business as walking guides; the quality varies, but some of the better ones are listed here. Most operators don't have an office – you can join a walk by just turning up at the starting point and paying your money.

➜ **Context Tours** (☑246 019 648; www. contexttravel.com; per person 1050Kč) US-based outfit that employs specialist guides to lead three-hour walking tours (maximum six persons) exploring various aspects of Prague – architecture, art, history, Jewish Prague and communism. Online booking.

➜ **Amazing Walks of Prague** (☑777 069 685; sites.google.com/site/ amazingtoursofprague; group tours per person 300-600Kč, private tours from 900Kč) Guide Roman Bílý is especially strong on WWII, the communist era and the Jewish Quarter.

➜ **Royal Walk Free Tour** (www.discover-prague.com) FREE One of Prague's most popular and highly rated walking tours, operated on a tips-only basis, provides an entertaining introduction to the city's history. No booking needed, just turn up at the Astronomical Clock.

➜ **World War II in Prague** (☑605 918 596; www.ww2inprague.com; per person 600Kč) Highly recommended for anyone interested in military history, with a chance to visit the underground HQ of the Prague resistance, and compare archive photos of WWII Prague with their present-day locations.

➜ **Prague Special Tours** (☑777 172 177; www.prague-special-tours.com; per person 600Kč) The communism tour visits a genuine 1950s underground nuclear bunker, beneath Parukářka hill in Žlžkov.

Boat Tours

➜ **Prague Boats** (Evropská Vodní Doprava; ☑224 810 030; www.prague-boats.cz; Čechův most; 🚊17) Offers a one-hour cruise departing hourly from 10am to 6pm (adult/child 220/110Kč); and a two-hour cruise to Vyšehrad (350/270Kč), departing at 3.30pm.

➜ **Prague Passenger Shipping** (Pražská Paroplavební Společnost, PPS; Map p338; ☑224 930 017; www.paroplavba.cz; Rašínovo nábřeží 2; ☺Apr-Oct; Ⓜ Karlovo Náměstí) Runs a photogenic one-hour cruise taking in the National Theatre, Střelecký island and Vyšehrad, departing at 11am, 2pm, 4pm, 5pm and 6pm April to September (adult/child 240/120Kč). Also offers a 1¼-hour boat trip to Troja (near the zoo; one-way 180/100Kč, return 290/150Kč) departing four times daily from May to August, and three times daily at weekends only in April and September.

➡ **Prague Venice** (🕿 776 776 779; www. prague-venice.cz; Platnéřská 4; per person 280Kč; ☺10.30am-10pm Jul & Aug, to 8pm Apr-Jun & Sep, to 6pm Oct-Mar; 🚈17) Runs entertaining 45-minute cruises in small boats under the hidden arches of Charles Bridge and along the Čertovka millstream in Kampa.

Bike Tours

➡ Biko Adventures (p301) Excellent guided tours, on either road or mountain bikes, ranging from a half-day urban tour of Prague's communist-era tower blocks (1150Kč) to a full-day trip to Karlštejn (returning by train; 1250Kč). Also offers proper off-road mountain-biking, trail running, and (in winter) cross-country skiing.

➡ **Praha Bike** (🕿 732 388 880; www. prahabike.cz; Dlouhá 24, Staré Město; rental per day 550Kč, tours per person from 540Kč; ☺9am-8pm; Ⓜ Náměstí Republiky) Offers a 2½-hour guided cycling tour through the city or an easy evening pedal through the parks. Tours depart at 11.30am mid-March to October and also at 2.30pm May to September. Trips outside the city can also be arranged, including a full day's tour to Karlštejn Castle (returning by train; 1140Kč).

➡ **AVE Bicycle Tours** (Map p342; 🕿 251 551 011; www.bicycle-tours.cz; Pod Barvirkou 6, Smíchov; guided tour 1190Kč, self-guided tour 600Kč; ☺Apr-Oct) Operates a full-day guided bicycle tour from Prague to Karlštejn Castle (one-way), including hotel pick-up, bike hire, lunch at Karlštejn and a train ticket back to the city. It also offers bike trips to Konopiště and one-week tours through the Czech countryside.

Segway Tours

A Segway (an electrically powered, two-wheeled 'personal transportation system')

allows you to cover more ground in less time than on foot.

➡ **Prague Segway Tours** (Map p328; 🕿 724 280 838; www.prague-segway-tours. com; Maltézské náměstí 7; per person 1250-1990Kč; 🚈12, 20, 22) Offers three-hour guided tours of the Old Town and Malá Strana, which depart daily at 10am and 2pm.

➡ **Prague on Segway** (Map p328; 🕿 775 588 588; www.pragueonsegway.com; Vlašská 2; per person 1250-1990Kč; 🚈12, 20, 22) Offers three-hour private, customised guided tours by Segway for one or two people.

Tram Tours

➡ **Nostalgic Tram No 91** (🕿 233 343 349; www.dpp.cz; Public Transport Museum, Patočkova 4, Střešovice; adult/child 35/20Kč; ☺departs hourly noon-5.30pm Sat, Sun & holidays Mar–mid-Nov) Vintage tram cars dating from 1908 to 1924 trundle along a special route, starting at the Public Transport Museum and travelling via stops at Prague Castle, Malostranské náměstí, the National Theatre, Wenceslas Square, náměstí Republiky and Štefánikův most to finish at Výstaviště. You can get on and off at any stop, and buy tickets on board (ordinary public transport tickets and passes are not valid).

Jewish-Interest Tours

➡ **Wittmann Tours** (Map p332; 🕿 222 252 472; www.wittmann-tours.com; Novotného lávka 5; 🚈17, 18) The experts on Jewish Prague offer a three-hour walking tour of Josefov (per person 880Kč; ☺tours 10.30am & 2pm Sun-Fri mid-Mar–Dec), as well as seven-hour day trips to Terezín (1250Kč per person), daily May to October, four times a week April, November and December.

➡ **Precious Legacy Tours** (Map p332; 🕿 222 321 954; www.legacytours.net; Kaprova 13; per person 880Kč; ☺tours 10.30am & 2pm Sun-Fri; Ⓜ Staroměstská) Offers a three-hour walking tour of Prague's Josefov district (the fee includes admission to four synagogues; Staronová Synagogue is 200Kč extra). There's also a daily six-hour excursion to Terezín (1160Kč per person; departs 10am).

Czech Republic by Bike

Prague has a long way to go before it's a cycling town comparable with big cities in Germany. Nevertheless, there's a group of hard-core cyclists promoting commuter cycling, extending bike paths and raising driver awareness. Their efforts are starting to bear fruit.

Recommended Routes

Prague has a relatively complete, if disjointed, network of bike paths, signposted in yellow, that criss-cross the city centre and fan out in all directions. Recreational cyclists will probably be content just to tootle around on one of the tours offered by the bike-rental companies, but more serious cyclists should consider buying a good map, hiring a bike and hitting the outlying trails for a day or two.

Arguably the best cycling trails lead off to the north following the Vltava River in the direction of Germany. Someday, the Prague–Dresden run will be the stuff of cycling legend, but for now there are still significant gaps in the route. That said, the path northward along the river is nearly complete as far as the town of Kralupy nad Vltavou (20km from Prague; it's possible to return by rail), from where you can continue on back roads to Mělník. There are plenty of bridges and ferries to take you back and forth across the river, and some really great trails leading inland along

the way. From the centre of Prague, start off at Čechův most (the bridge over the Vltava by the InterContinental Hotel), ride across the bridge and up the hill to Letná. From there, follow the signs to Stromovka and on to Prague Zoo. The riverside trail (waymarked A2) continues northward from here.

There's also a cycle track that heads south along the east bank of the Vltava as far as Zbraslav, where you can cross the river and continue on a mix of minor roads and cycle tracks to Karlštejn Castle.

Remember to pack water and sunscreen and always watch out for cars. Many Czech drivers, inexplicably, are rabidly anti-cyclist.

Maps

Most large bookstores stock cycling maps (*cycloturisticka mapa*). One of the best maps to look out for is the latest Freytag & Berndt *Praha a Okoli* (Prague & Surroundings; 1:75,000), which costs about 150Kč. Another good choice for the northwestern section of the city is *Z prahy na kole, Severozapad* (Around Prague by Bike, Northwest; 1:65,000) for about 75Kč.

Websites

➡ **Open Cycle Map** (www.opencyclemap.org) Open-source, community-maintained map of cycle routes worldwide; useful for checking out the fine detail of any city's cycle trail network.

➡ **Prague by Bike** (http://prahounakole.cz) Czech-only for now, but click on 'Mapa' for a cycle route map (dark purple for traffic-free paths, pale purple for quiet streets). You can use Google Translate to make sense of most of the site content.

➡ **Grant's Prague Bike Blog** (http://praguebikeblog.blogspot.com) An American expat's cycling exploits, with great ride ideas, maps and photos.

➡ **Greenways** (www.pragueviennagreenways.org) Details of a 402km cycle trail linking Prague and Vienna.

➡ **Biko Adventures** (www.bikoadventures.com) Hires out quality road and mountain bikes, and provides great advice on routes, including off-road and local MTB singletrack.

Traditional Czech fare

Eating

Traditional Czech cuisine is a cardiologist's nightmare, a cholesterol-laden menu of meat accompanied by high-calorie dumplings washed down with copious quantities of beer. When it comes to food, the ultimate Czech put-down is to describe it as neslaný or nemaslý ('not salty' or 'not fatty'). But if you put aside your notions of healthy eating for a few days, you'll find traditional Czech food to be very tasty.

When to Eat

➡ **Breakfast** Served from 7am to 9am, a typical Czech breakfast *(snídaně)* is a light affair consisting of *chléb* (bread) or *rohlík* (bread roll) with butter, cheese, jam or yoghurt, washed down with tea or coffee. A hotel breakfast buffet will normally also include cereals, eggs, ham or sausage. Many cafes serve British- and American-style breakfasts. You can also go to a *pekárna* or *pekařství* (bakery), or to one of the French or Viennese bakeries, for *loupáčky* (like croissants

but smaller and heavier). Czech bread, especially rye, is excellent and varied.

➡ **Lunch** *Oběd* (lunch) is traditionally the main meal of the day and, except for Sundays, it's often a hurried affair. Czechs are usually early risers, and so they may sit down to lunch as early as 11.30am, though many restaurants continue to serve lunch as late as 3pm.

➡ **Dinner** Having stuffed themselves at lunchtime, for many Czechs *večeře* (dinner) is a light meal, perhaps only a platter of cold meats, cheese and pickles with bread. However, tourist restaurants

NEED TO KNOW

Price Ranges

We use the following price ranges to indicate the cost of a main course at dinner:

€ less than 200Kč

€€ 200Kč to 450Kč

€€€ more than 450Kč

Opening Hours

Lunch is generally from noon to 3pm, and dinner from 6pm to 9pm. Most Prague restaurants, however, are open all day, from 11am or noon to 10pm or 11pm.

Reservations

It's a good idea to reserve a table at upmarket restaurants, especially during the high season; almost always the phone will be answered by someone who speaks English.

Tipping

In most tourist-area places the helpful message 'Tips Not Included', in English (hint, hint), is printed on the bill. The usual rate is 10% of the total. Usual practice in pubs, cafes and midrange restaurants is to round up the bill to the next 10Kč (or the next 20Kč if it's over 200Kč).

Smoking

In 2010, pubs and restaurants in the Czech Republic had to choose one of the following three labels to be displayed at the entrance to the premises: smoking allowed, smoking prohibited, or mixed. The latter is used for places that have separate (ie physically isolated) spaces for smokers and nonsmokers.

gear up for a three-course dinner from 6pm to 10pm.

Local Specialities

➡ **Dumplings** The traditional source of carbs in Czech meals. There are two main kinds – *houskové knedlíky* (bread dumplings) are made from flour, yeast, egg yolk and milk, and are left to rise like bread before being cooked in boiling water and then sliced. Alternatively, you may be served *bramborové knedlíky* (potato dumplings); if you thought bread dumplings were filling, just wait until you try these stodge-bombs. The best *knedlíky* are homemade, but the ones in most pubs and restaurants are factory-produced. The classic Czech dessert is *ovocné knedlíky* (fruit dumplings). Large, round dumplings made with sweetened, flour-based dough are stuffed with berries, plums or apricots, and served drizzled with melted butter and a sprinkle of sugar.

➡ **Roast pork** What roast beef and Yorkshire pudding is to the English, *vepřová pečeně s knedlíky a kyselé zelí* (roast pork with dumplings and sauerkraut) is to the Czechs; it's a dish so ubiquitous that it is often abbreviated to *vepřo-knedlo-zelo*. The pork is rubbed with salt and caraway seeds, and roasted long and slow – good roast pork should fall apart, meltingly tender, at the first touch of a fork or finger.

➡ **Svíčková** Another staple of Czech restaurant menus is *svíčková na smetaně* – slices of marinated roast beef served with a sour-cream sauce garnished with lemon and cranberries.

➡ **Poultry & Game** Poultry is a popular main course, either roasted or served as *kuře na paprice* (chicken in spicy paprika-cream sauce). *Kachna* (duck), *husa* (goose) and *krůta* (turkey) usually come roasted, with gravy, dumplings and sauerkraut. A few restaurants specialise in game; the most common are *jelení* (venison), *bažant* (pheasant), *zajíc* (hare) and *kanec* (boar) – fried or roasted and served in a wild mushroom sauce or as *guláš*.

Celebrating with Food

Christmas is the most important celebration on the Czech domestic calendar, and food and drink play an important part. Christmas Eve (*Štědrý den,* or 'generous day') is a day of abstinence from meat, with people saving their appetite for the evening meal, which is traditionally *smažený kapr* (crispy, fried carp) served with *bramborový salát* (potato salad). The carp are farmed in medieval *rybníky* (fish ponds) in the countryside, mostly in South Bohemia, and in December they are brought to city markets where they are sold, live, from water-filled barrels. In many homes, the Christmas carp then gets to swim around in the bathtub until it's time for the frying pan.

There is no national tradition as to what is served on Christmas Day *(Vánoce),* but meat is definitely back on the menu; *pečená kachna* (roast duck), served with gravy and dumplings, is a widespread favourite. There are also *vánoční cukroví* (Christmas cookies), baked according to traditional family recipes, and *vánočka,*

FUNNY, I DON'T REMEMBER ORDERING THAT!

Keep in mind that nothing comes for free in Prague restaurants – if the waiter offers you fries with that, and you accept, you'll be charged for them. Bread, mayonnaise, mustard, vegetables... almost everything has a price tag. If the menu has no prices, ask for them. Don't be intimidated by the language barrier; know exactly what you're ordering. If something is not available and the waiter suggests an alternative, ask for the price. Immediately return anything you didn't order and don't want, such as bread, butter or side dishes; don't just leave it to one side or chances are they'll appear on your bill. Most importantly, though, don't let paranoia ruin your meal. The majority of overcharging happens at tourist-oriented restaurants in the city centre. If you're not eating in the Old Town Square or Wenceslas Square, or if you're at a new place run by young Czechs, you're unlikely to have any problems.

Bohemia's answer to Christmas cake, made with bread dough, sweetened with sugar, flavoured with lemon, nutmeg, raisins and almonds, and plaited; it is usually served after the Christmas Eve dinner.

New Year's Eve *(Silvestr)* is also a big celebration. Few people still prepare the traditional New Year's Eve dinner of *vepřový ovar (*boiled pig's head) served with grated horseradish and apple, but the day is still a big party day, with plates of *chlebíčky* (small, open sandwiches), *brambůrky* (potato pancakes) and other snacks, and bottles of *šampaňské* or other sparkling wine on hand to toast the bells at midnight.

Etiquette

Although the vast majority of Prague's tourist-oriented restaurants have long since adopted international manners, a dinner in a Czech home or a traditional eatery still demands traditional local etiquette.

To the Czech way of thinking, only barbarians would begin a meal without first saying *dobrou chuť* (the Czech equivalent of *bon appetit* – the correct response is to repeat the phrase); even the waiters in tourist restaurants will murmur *dobrou chuť* as they place the plates on your table. The first drink of the evening is accompanied by a toast – usually *na zdraví* (nahz-drahvee; 'to health') – as you clink first the tops and then the bottoms of your glasses, then touch the glass to the table.

It's considered bad manners to talk while eating, and especially to distract a guest while they are enjoying their food, so conversation is usually kept to a minimum while food is being consumed; the time for talk is between courses and after the meal.

Best Food & Drink Blogs

➡ **Czech Please** (czechoutchannel.blogspot.co.uk)

➡ **Bohemian Bites** (bohemianbites.wordpress.com)

➡ **Prague Post** (www.praguepost.com/food-and-drink)

➡ **Pivní Filosof** (www.pivni-filosof.com)

➡ **Taste of Prague** (www.tasteofprague.com/pragueblog)

Eating in Prague by Neighbourhood

➡ **Prague Castle & Hradčany** Surprisingly few places to eat, with one or two hidden gems.

➡ **Malá Strana** Lots of quality restaurants, and more touristy spots with great riverside settings.

➡ **Staré Město** Tourist central around the Old Town Square, but plenty of good Czech eateries to be found in backstreets.

➡ **Nové Město** Lots of fast food and street kiosks, but also many good restaurants.

➡ **Vinohrady & Vršovice** Upmarket area that is home to some of the city's best restaurants.

➡ **Žižkov & Karlín** Rough and ready – mostly pub grub and pizza, plus some good Indian and Pakistani restaurants.

➡ **Holešovice** By general acclaim, a culinary wasteland with a few notable (and excellent) exceptions.

➡ **Bubeneč & Dejvice** Affluent residential area with some very good destination restaurants, spread thinly apart.

➡ **Smíchov & Vyšehrad** Not much choice in Vyšehrad, but Smíchov has a decent range of restaurants.

Lonely Planet's Top Choices

Sansho (p131) Local produce with Asian flavours and shared, informal dining.

Bisos (p151) Fresh and flavourful Sardinian cuisine.

Kofein (p140) Hopping tapas joint in Vinohrady; must pre-book but worth the effort.

Mozaika (p140) Vinohrady locals can't get enough of this French-inspired bistro.

Kalina (p113) A little touch of Gallic sophistication in Staré Město.

Sasazu (p157) The best Asian cuisine north of the river, with a great nightclub attached.

Best by Budget

$

Café Lounge (p91) Art deco atmosphere, superb coffee, exquisite pastries, extensive wine list.

Cukrkávalimonáda (p91) Cute little cafe with Renaissance-era painted roof beams.

Las Adelitas (p139) The closest thing to authentic Tex-Mex you're likely to find in Prague.

Mistral Café (p111) Possibly the coolest bistro in the Old Town.

Lokál (p111) Classic Czech dishes and great beer in a bright, modern beer hall.

$$

Ichnusa Botega Bistro (p91) Family bistro serving superb Sardinian cuisine.

Room (p131) Authentic Spanish tapas from accomplished Argentinian chef.

Kofein (p140) Spanish-style tapas at one of the hottest restaurants in town.

Sansho (p131) Ground-breaking menu, created from locally sourced produce, changes daily.

Argument (p167) Great food in Bubeneč at half the price you would pay in the centre.

$$$

Aromi (p141) Has a well-deserved reputation for authentic, excellent Italian cuisine.

V zátiší (p114) From high-end Indian cuisine to gourmet versions of traditional Czech dishes.

Kalina (p113) Takes the best of fresh Czech produce and gives it the French gourmet treatment.

Chagall's (p114) Understated style, French flair and a warm welcome.

Elegantes (p93) Classy, sophisticated hotel restaurant with an international menu.

Best by Cuisine

Czech

Lokál (p111) Daily-changing menu of traditional Bohemian dishes and great beer.

Kolkovna (p113) A stylish, modern take on the traditional Prague pub.

Zelená Zahrada (p141) This secluded, upscale restaurant draws a star-studded crowd.

Restaurace U Veverky (p164) Classic Czech pub with home-made cooking fit for a gourmet.

Zlatý klas (p177) Very popular pub-restaurant offering well-prepared Czech grub such as roast pork and goulash.

Italian

Vino di Vino (p113) Intimate restaurant and attached deli stuffed with Italian goodies.

Al Forno (p131) Honest and authentic Italian dishes, from pizza to lasagne.

Bisos (p151) Cool little restaurant serving up flavourful Sardinian fare.

Osteria da Clara (p140) A tiny Tuscan-style trattoria offering some of the city's most authentic Italian cuisine.

Asian

Sakura (p167) One of Prague's best sushi restaurants, set in a smart 1930s functionalist building.

Hanil (p151) Hosts a mixed crowd of businesspeople, locals and expats enjoying the authentic Japanese and Korean cuisine.

Sasazu (p157) Perhaps the best high-end Asian cooking in Prague.

Pho Viet (p129) Basic, canteen-like place serving fresh Vietnamese food laced with fiery chillis.

Best for Vegetarians

Country Life (p113) Prague's first-ever health-food shop is an all-vegan cafeteria and sandwich bar.

Lehká Hlava (p113) Features an exotically decorated dining room with emphasis on freshly prepared vegetarian and vegan dishes.

Maitrea (p111) Quality vegetarian and vegan cuisine amid unexpected designer decor.

Loving Hut (p139) Part of a citywide chain of nonsmoking, no-alcohol, vegan/vegetarian restaurants.

Plevel (p137) The best hummus in the city, and many great vegetarian choices.

Wheat beer, Pivovarský Dům brewery (p131)

Drinking & Nightlife

Bars in Prague go in and out of fashion with alarming speed, and trend spotters are forever flocking to the latest 'in' place only to desert it as soon as it becomes mainstream. The best areas to go looking for good drinking dens include Vinohrady, Žižkov, Holešovice, the area south of Národní třída in Nové Město and the lanes around the Old Town Square in Staré Město.

Drinking
BEER

Even in these times of encroaching coffee culture, *pivo* (beer) remains the lifeblood of Prague. Many people drink at least one glass of beer every day – local nicknames for beer include *tekutý chleb* (liquid bread) and *živá voda* (life-giving water) – and it's still possible to see people stopping off for a small glass of beer on their way to work in the morning. And come the evening, beer reigns supreme. There's nothing Praguers enjoy more than

getting together in a local bar and swapping stories over a *pivo* or two. Or three...

There are two main varieties of beer: *světlé* (light) and *tmavy* or *černé* (dark). The *světlé* is a pale amber or golden lager-style beer with a crisp, refreshing, hoppy flavour. Dark beers are sweeter and more full-bodied, with a rich, malty or fruity flavour.

Czechs like their beer served at cellar temperature (around 6°C to 10°C) with a tall, creamy head (known as *pěna,* meaning 'foam'). Americans and Australians may find it a bit warm, but this improves the flavour.

NEED TO KNOW

Opening Hours

Most bars are open from 11am until midnight, though many stay open until 1am or later, especially on Friday and Saturday nights.

How Much?

The price of a half-litre of draught beer varies enormously, from around 25Kč to 40Kč in pubs catering mainly to local drinkers, to 90Kč and up at outdoor tables in the tourist-thronged Old Town Square. Most tourist-oriented bars in the city centre charge 40Kč to 80Kč.

Cocktails in the city centre range from 150Kč to 300Kč, depending on the quality of the ingredients and the fanciness of the surroundings, while good-quality Czech wine in a specialist wine bar will cost from 300Kč to 500Kč a bottle.

Tipping

Normal practice is to round up the bill to the next 10Kč (or the next 20Kč if it's over 200Kč). Change is usually counted out starting with the big notes, then on down to the smallest coins. If you say *děkuji* (thank you) during this process, the bartender will stop and assume that the rest is a tip.

Most draught beer is sold in *půl-litr* (0.5L) glasses; if you prefer a small beer, ask for a *malé pivo* (0.3L). Some bars confuse the issue by using 0.4L glasses, while others offer a German-style 1L mug known as a *tuplák*.

A recent trend has seen the emergence of the 'fourth pipe' (*čtvrtá pípa*) pub. Prague pubs traditionally offered just three beers on tap, all from one large brewery such as Pilsner Urquell; some pioneering bar owners added a 'fourth pipe' to allow them to offer a rotating range of guest beers from various independent regional breweries. Many now have five, six or even more pipes.

PUB ETIQUETTE

There's an etiquette to be observed if you want to sample the atmosphere in a traditional *hospoda* (pub) without drawing disapproving stares from the regulars. First off, don't barge in and start rearranging chairs – if you want to share a table or take a spare seat, first ask *'je tu volno?'* (is

this free?). It's normal practice in crowded Czech pubs to share tables with strangers.

Take a beer mat from the rack and place it in front of you, and wait for the bar staff to come to you; waving for service is guaranteed to get you ignored. When the waiter approaches, just raise your thumb for one beer, thumb and index finger for two, etc – it's automatically assumed that you're here for the beer. Even just a nod will do. The waiter will keep track of your order by marking a slip of paper that stays on your table; whatever you do, don't write on it or lose it (you'll have to pay a fine if you do).

As soon as the level of beer in your glass falls to within an inch of the bottom, the eagle-eyed waiter will be on his/her way with another. But never, as people often do in Britain, pour the dregs of the old glass into the new – this is considered to be deeply uncivilised behaviour.

If you don't want any more beer brought to your table, place a beer mat on top of your glass. When you want to pay up and go, get the waiter's attention and say *'za-platím'* (I'll pay). He or she will total up the marks on your slip of paper, and you pay there, at the table.

WINE

Grapes have been grown in the Czech lands since the 14th century, when Charles IV imported vines from Burgundy; their descendants are still thriving on the slopes beneath Mělník Chateau.

The standard of Czech wine has soared since the fall of communism, as small producers have concentrated on the quality end of the market. Although Czech red wines – such as the South Moravian speciality Svatovavřinecké (St Lawrence) – are mostly pretty average, Czech whites can be very good indeed. The varieties to look out for are Veltínské zelené (Grüner Veltlin), Rýnský ryzlink (riesling) and Müller-Thurgau. Tanzberg and Sonberk are both excellent winemakers.

For about three weeks each year, from the end of September to mid-October, you will see shops and street stalls selling *burčak*. This is 'young wine', freshly extracted grape juice in the early stages of fermentation. It is cloudy yellow in appearance and innocently sweet in flavour, more like a soft drink than a wine. But beware – it contains 5% to 8% alcohol.

Later in the year, as winter sets in, you'll notice the *svařák* stalls appearing in the

TANKOVÉ PIVO

One recent innovation that you will
come across in many Prague pubs is the
phenomenon of *tankové pivo* (tanked
beer). Ordinarily beer goes stale through
contact with oxygen in the air. Tanked
beer is delivered in sterile plastic bags
that are stored in chilled stainless steel
tanks (often in plain view in the pub).
Compressed air forced between the tank
and the bag forces the beer through the
tap without it having to come into contact with oxygen, a system that allows
pubs to serve fresh, unpasteurised beer
(vastly superior in flavour to the more
common, heat-treated keg beer).

streets. Short for *svařené víno* (mulled
wine), *svařák* is red wine heated and flavoured with sugar and spices.

SPIRITS

Probably the most distinctive of Czech
lihoviny (spirits) is Becherovka. Produced
in the West Bohemian spa town of Karlovy
Vary, famous for its 12 sulphurous, thermal
springs, the bitter, herbal liqueur is often
served as an aperitif, and is increasingly
used as an ingredient in cocktails.

The fiery and potent *slivovice* (plum
brandy) is said to have originated in
Moravia, where the best brands still come
from. The best commercially produced
slivovice is R Jelínek from Vizovice. Other
regional spirits include *meruňkovice*
(apricot brandy) and juniper-flavoured
borovička.

The deadliest locally produced spirit
is absinthe. While it's banned in many
countries, in part because of its high alcohol content, absinthe is legal in the Czech
Republic. Unfortunately, connoisseurs of
absinthe consider Hill's absinthe –
the biggest-selling brand of Czech-made
absinthe – little better than highly alcoholic
mouthwash. However, it does form the
basis of an evil cocktail that was popular
among clubbers a few years ago – the H-
Bomb (Hill's mixed with Semtex, a Czech
brand of energy drink).

Clubbing

Prague's club scene is nothing to rave about.
With few exceptions, the city's dance clubs
cater to crowds of partying teenagers and
tourists weaned on MTV Europe – if you
want to dance to anything other than '80s
hits or happy house, you'll have to look long
and hard. Prague's main strengths are its
alternative music clubs, DJ bars, and 'experimental' venues such as Palác Akropolis
(p153) and the Roxy (p116).

Refreshingly, dress codes don't seem to
have reached Prague yet, and it's unlikely
you'll be knocked back anywhere unless
you're stark naked. And there are even a
few places that would probably be OK with
that...

Check out www.prague.tv, www.techno.
cz/party or www.hip-hop.cz for up-to-date
club listings (the latter two are in Czech,
but you can work out what's going on).

Drinking & Nightlife in Prague by Neighbourhood

➡ **Prague Castle & Hradčany** The area has a
couple of interesting cafes and pubs, but goes
very quiet in the evenings.

➡ **Malá Strana** A lively drinking scene with
smart, modern bars and plenty of live music.

➡ **Staré Město** Classic outdoor tables around
the Old Town Square, and snug atmospheric
bars and jazz joints in the backstreets.

➡ **Nové Město** A hotbed of sports bars, Irish
pubs and girlie bars much frequented by visiting
stag parties.

➡ **Vinohrady & Vršovice** Trendy
neighbourhoods where you can seek out the
latest cocktail bars and cool cafes.

➡ **Žižkov & Karlín** The best areas for down-to-
earth pubs packed with locals downing glasses
of the city's cheapest beer.

➡ **Holešovice** Working-class neighbourhood
that's big on pubs and some surprisingly classy
cafes.

➡ **Bubeneč & Dejvice** Aside from a few pockets
of life, residents here tend to turn in early.

➡ **Smíchov & Vyšehrad** Smíchov has the
rowdiest pubs per square metre in Prague; in
Vyšehrad, you can hear a pin drop at night.

Lonely Planet's Top Choices

Pivovarský Klub (p152) A dream come true for fans of real ale.

U Vystřeleného oka (p152) The quintessential Žižkov neighbourhood pub.

Sasazu (p160) Prague's classiest and most popular dance club.

Fraktal (p168) Expat hangout on the far side of the river.

Zlatý klas (p177) Awesome unfiltered Pilsner-Urquell in an authentic, always boisterous pub atmosphere.

Best Grand Cafes

Kavárna Obecní dům (p116) Extravaganza of art nouveau excess.

Café Imperial (p132) Famous for its ornate ceramic-tile decor.

Café Savoy (p91) Elegant waitstaff in black waistcoats and white aprons.

Grand Cafe Orient (p116) The world's only cubist cafe?

Kavárna Slavia (p126) Art deco literary cafe.

Kavárna Lucerna (p132) Hidden gem in heart of art nouveau arcade.

Best Traditional Pubs

U Zlatého Tygra (p115) Novelist Bohumil Hrabal's favourite hostelry.

U Slovanské Lípy (p152) Friendly, traditional pub in heart of Žižkov.

Pivnice U Černého Vola (p80) Classic old beer hall close to the castle.

Hospůdka Obyčejný Svět (p142) Good range of hard-to-find artisan beers.

Klášterní Pivnice (p160) Perfectly preserved, old-fashioned Prague pub.

Best Cocktail Bars

Hemingway Bar (p114) Snug and sophisticated hideaway.

Hoffa (p132) Popular new bar, completely smoke-free.

Bukowski's (p152) Dark and smoky expat cocktail dive.

Čili Bar (p115) Cute and compact, serves rum with chopped chillis.

Bar & Books Mánesova (p142) Upmarket New York–style cocktail and cigar bar.

Best for Regional Beers

Prague Beer Museum (p114) Thirty beers on tap – 'nuff said. Now has Vinohrady branch.

Klášterní Pivnice (p160) Serves excellent, hard-to-find Klášter beers.

Jáma (p132) Rotating selection of regional beers and microbrews.

Pivovarský Klub (p152) Six guest beers on tap and hundreds of bottled varieties.

U Slovanské Lípy (p152) Cherished for its Kout na Šumavě beers.

Best Alternative Clubs

Palác Akropolis (p153) Established venue for all things alternative.

Roxy (p116) Legendary independent club venue.

Fatal Music Club (p152) Classic, old-skool Žižkov rock club.

Radost FX (p144) Chilled-out, bohemian atmosphere.

Best Microbreweries

Pivovarský Dům (p131) Known for its fruit-flavoured beers.

Klášterní pivovar Strahov (p80) Makes full-bodied, hoppy St Norbert amber ale.

U Medvídků (p115) Famous for strong (11.8%) X-Beer.

Pivovar U Bulovky (p152) Hospitable neighbourhood brewpub, well off beaten track.

U Tří růží (p114) Re-creation of Old Town brewery, with six home-brewed beers on tap.

Best Wine Bars

Bokovka (p132) Extensive menu of top-notch Moravian wines.

Vinograf (p132) Popular and appealingly modern wine bar.

Monarch Vinný Sklep (p115) One of the best places to get to know Czech wines.

Viniční Altán (p141) Prague's most pleasant open-air wine garden

Best Beer Gardens

Letná Beer Garden (p158) In summer there's no better place from which to admire Prague's golden spires.

Riegrovy Sady Beer Garden (p141) Popular spot with sports events screened on open-air TVs.

Hospoda Parukářka (p153) Friendly community pub and garden, set in a public park.

Buskers on Charles Bridge (p83)

☆ Entertainment

Across the spectrum, from ballet to blues, jazz to rock and theatre to film, there's a bewildering range of entertainment on offer in this eclectic city. Prague is now as much a European centre for jazz, rock and hip hop as it is for classical music. The biggest draw, however, is still the Prague Spring festival of classical music and opera.

Music
CLASSICAL MUSIC

There are half a dozen concerts of one kind or another in Prague almost every day during the summer, making a fine soundtrack to accompany the city's visual delights. Many of these are chamber concerts performed by aspiring musicians in the city's churches – gorgeous but chilly (take an extra layer, even on a summer day), and not always with the finest of acoustics. However, a good number of concerts, especially those promoted by

people handing out flyers in the street, are second-rate, despite the premium prices that foreigners pay. If you want to be sure of quality, go for a performance by one of the city's professional orchestras.

Box offices are open from 30 minutes to one hour before the start of a performance. For classical music, opera and ballet listings, check out www.heartofeurope.cz and www.czechopera.cz.

In summer, the spa towns of Karlovy Vary and Mariánské Lázně stage daily concerts of classical music among their pavilions and

NEED TO KNOW

Listings

For reviews, day-by-day listings and a directory of venues, consult the 'Night & Day' section of the weekly *Prague Post* (www.praguepost.com). Monthly listings booklets include *Culture in Prague* and the Czech-language *Přehled*, available from Prague Information Service tourist offices.

For web-based entertainment listings, check out:

➡ www.praguewelcome.cz/en/events

➡ www.pragueeventscalendar.com

Buying Tickets

The 'wholesalers' with the largest agency networks are Bohemia Ticket International (BTI), FOK and Ticketpro; the others probably get their tickets from them.

➡ **Bohemia Ticket** (☑224 227 832; www.ticketsbti.cz; Malé náměstí 13; ⊙9am-5pm Mon-Fri) Provides tickets for all kinds of events. There's another **branch** (☑224 215 031; Na příkopě 16; ⊙10am-7pm Mon-Fri, to 5pm Sat, to 3pm Sun) near the Municipal House.

➡ **FOK Box Office** (☑222 002 336; www.fok.cz; U Obecního Domu 2; ⊙10am-6pm Mon-Fri) Prague Symphony Orchestra box office, for classical concert tickets; also open for one hour before performances begin.

➡ **Ticketpro** (www.ticketpro.cz; Pasáž Lucerna, Vodičkova 36; ⊙noon-4pm & 4.30-8.30pm Mon-Fri) Tickets are available here for all kinds of events. There are Ticketpro branches in Prague City Tourism offices and many other places.

➡ **Ticketstream** (www.ticketstream.cz) Internet-based booking agency that covers events in Prague and all over the Czech Republic.

colonnades, while Český Krumlov hosts an international music festival.

LIVE MUSIC

Prague has a high-energy live-music scene, with rock, metal, punk, electro, industrial, hip hop and newer sounds at a score of DJ and live-music venues; most have a cover charge of around 50Kč to 200Kč. Most clubs stay open until at least 2am or 3am, and some keep going until 6am. Clubs such as Palác Akropolis (p153) and Roxy (p116) also host live rock bands. Keep an eye open for flyers that are posted around town.

JAZZ

Prague has lots of good jazz clubs, many of which have been around for decades. Most have a cover charge of 100Kč to 300Kč.

Film

Prague has more than 30 cinemas, some showing first-run Western films, some showing Czech films, and several excellent art-house cinemas. For cinema listings check the 'Night & Day' section of the *Prague Post* or www.prague.tv.

Most films are screened in their original language with Czech subtitles (*české titulky*), but Hollywood blockbusters are often dubbed into Czech (*dabing*); look for the labels 'tit' or 'dab' on cinema listings. Czech-language films with English subtitles are listed as having *anglický titulky*.

Movies are normally screened twice in the evening, at around 7pm and 9pm, though multiplexes show films all day. Most cinemas screen matinees on weekends.

Theatre

Most Czech drama is, not surprisingly, performed in Czech. However, there are some English-language productions, as well as many predominantly visual shows at which language is not a barrier. There's also the Prague Fringe Festival (www.praguefringe.com), which takes place in early June and offers plenty of English-language theatre.

Prague is famous for its black-light theatre – occasionally called just 'black theatre' – a hybrid of mime, drama, dance and special effects in which actors wearing fluorescent costumes do their thing in front of a black backdrop lit only by ultraviolet light (it's a growth industry in Prague, with at least half a dozen venues). An even older Czech tradition is puppetry, and the city has several marionette shows on offer.

Entertainment in Prague by Neighbourhood

➡ **Prague Castle & Hradčany** Very little happens in this neighbourhood after dark – best head elsewhere!

PRAGUE SPRING

First held in 1946, the Prague Spring (Pražské jaro) international music festival is the Czech Republic's best-known annual cultural event. It begins on 12 May, the anniversary of composer Bedřich Smetana's death, with a procession from his grave at Vyšehrad to the Municipal House (p108), and a performance there of his patriotic song cycle *Má vlast* (*My Homeland*). The festival runs until 3 June, and the beautiful concert venues are as big a drawcard as the music.

Tickets can be obtained through the official **Prague Spring Box Office** (Map p332; ☏227 059 234; www.festival.cz; náměstí Jana Palacha; ☉10am-6pm Mon-Fri; 🚊17, 18) in the Rudolfinum, or from any branch of Ticketpro.

If you want a guaranteed seat at a Prague Spring concert, book it by mid-March at the latest, though a few seats may still be available as late as the end of May.

➡ **Malá Strana** Good selection of small, intimate live-music venues.

➡ **Staré Město** Home to many classical-music venues and old-school jazz clubs.

➡ **Nové Město** Prague State Opera and the National Theatre rub shoulders with sports bars and stag parties.

➡ **Vinohrady & Vršovice** The heart of Prague's gay scene also has lots of trendy clubs and bars.

➡ **Žižkov & Karlín** The place for classic, sticky-floored, down-and-dirty rock joints.

➡ **Holešovice** Home to up-and-coming nightclubs and experimental venues.

➡ **Bubeneč & Dejvice** Few entertainment options here, but catching a Sparta Praha football match is usually pretty entertaining.

➡ **Smíchov & Vyšehrad** Some good experimental venues in Smíchov; open-air classical concerts in Vyšehrad.

Lonely Planet's Top Choices

Cross Club (p160) The ultimate in Prague's 'industrial' nightclubs, packed with mechanical gadgets.

Palác Akropolis (p153) A long-standing Prague institution, host to all kinds of live music.

Roxy (p116) The queen of the city's experimental scene, mixing art, music and live performance.

Smetana Hall (p117) An art-nouveau setting to match the splendour of Smetana's music.

JazzDock (p179) Evening jazz gigs with a view over the Vltava River.

Best Jazz & Blues

Jazz Republic (p133) Stages all kinds of live music, including rock, blues, reggae and fusion, as well as jazz.

AghaRTA Jazz Centrum (p116) As well as hosting local musicians, occasionally stages gigs by leading international artists.

Blues Sklep (p116) Typical Old Town basement provides atmospheric setting for nightly jazz sessions.

Jazz Club U Staré Paní (p116) Varied program of modern jazz, soul, blues and Latin rhythms.

U Malého Glena (p94) Lively bar where hard-swinging local jazz or blues bands play every night.

Best Live Music

Malostranská beseda (p93) Fabled music club with a lively roster of cabaret acts, jazz bands and old Czech rockers.

Lucerna Music Bar (p133) Atmospheric old theatre hosts '90s video parties and eclectic program of live bands.

Rock Café (p133) Mostly local bands ranging from nu-metal to folk rock to Doors tribute acts.

Fatal Music Club (p152) Scruffy, laid-back Žižkov club with bands ranging from heavy metal to acoustic singer-songwriters.

Vagon (p116) Live music pretty much every night, from local blues artists to classic Czech rock bands.

Divadelní Klub Ántré (p213) Great place to hear up-and-coming Czech bands in Český Krumlov.

Best Clubbing

Cross Club (p160) An industrial club in every sense of the word with DJs and live acts.

Sasazu (p160) One of the most fashionable and popular dance clubs in the city.

Roxy (p116) The place to see the Czech Republic's top DJs.

Radost FX (p144) Chilled-out, bohemian atmosphere, with themed dance parties each night of the week.

Best Classical & Opera

National Theatre (p133) Spectacular venue providing a stage for traditional opera, drama and ballet.

Prague State Opera (p133) An impressive neo-rococo building makes a glorious setting for performances of opera and ballet.

Estates Theatre (p116) The oldest theatre in Prague, famed as the place where Mozart conducted the premiere of *Don Giovanni* in 1787.

Dvořák Hall (p116) Home to the world-renowned Czech Philharmonic Orchestra.

Chapel of Mirrors (p109) Baroque chapel glittering with decorative mirrors; venue for daily concerts of classical music.

Janáček Theatre (p248) Provincial theatre in Brno that stages top-quality opera and ballet.

Shopping

In the past decade or so the Czech Republic's shopping scene has changed beyond recognition. An influx of global brand names and glitzy new malls has left the city's main shopping streets looking very much like those of any other European capital. Imported goods often carry Western European prices, but Czech products remain affordable for Czechs and cheap for Westerners.

Specialities

GLASS & CRYSTAL

One of the Czech Republic's best buys is Bohemian crystal (*sklo*) – anything from simple glassware to stupendous works of art, sold at some three-dozen upmarket places in Prague's shopping zone. Prices aren't radically different from shop to shop, though they are highest in the city centre.

Karlovy Vary is the spiritual home of Bohemian crystal – the famous Moser glass-making company opened its first shop there in 1857, and still operates a glass-making factory in the town.

HANDICRAFTS

In the tourist areas of Prague, many shops – notably Manufaktura (p118) – stock quality craft items made of wood, ceramic, straw, textiles and other materials, handmade in traditional styles. Things to look for include painted Easter eggs, wooden utensils, ceramics with traditional designs, linen with traditional stitching, and Bohemian lacework. Notably popular are figures of Krtek (Little Mole), a Czech cartoon character dating from the 1950s.

Traditional wooden marionettes (and more delicate and lifelike ones made of plaster) are also available in many shops.

JEWELLERY

Amber (*jantar*) from the Baltic and gemstones mined in the Czech Republic are good value, and popular as souvenirs or gifts. Amber is better value here than over the border in Germany. This fossilised tree resin is usually honey-yellow in colour, although it can be white, orange, red or brown. Czech garnets (*český granát*) – sometimes called 'Czech rubies' – are usually red but can be many other colours, or even colourless.

MUSIC

Good buys include CDs and sheet music of the works of famous Czech composers (such as Smetana, Dvořák, Janáček and Martinů) as well as Bohemian folk music – even *dechovka* (brass-band 'polka' music). There are almost as many music shops in Prague as there are bookshops.

Shopping Areas

WENCESLAS SQUARE

The city centre's single biggest – and most exhausting – retail zone is around Wenceslas Square (Václavské náměstí), its pavements jammed with browsing visitors and locals making beelines for their favourite stores. You can find pretty much everything here, from high fashion and music megastores to run-of-the-mill department stores and gigantic book emporia. Many of the more interesting shops are hidden away in arcades and passages, such as the Lucerna Palace (p124).

The other main shopping drag intersects with the lower end of Wenceslas Square, comprising Na Příkopě, 28.října and Národní třída. Most of the big stores and malls are concentrated on Na Příkopě, with the biggest of them all – the **Palladium Praha Shopping Centre** (Map p336; náměstí Republiky; Ⓜ Náměstí

NEED TO KNOW

Opening Hours

Prague shops usually open anywhere between 8am and 10am, and close between 5pm and 7pm Monday to Friday. They open from 8.30am to noon or 1pm on Saturday. Major shops, department stores and tourist businesses also open on weekends (usually from 9am to 6pm), but local shops may be closed on Saturday afternoon and Sunday.

Consumer Taxes

Value-added tax (VAT, or DPH in Czech) is applied at 10% on food (including restaurant meals), books and periodicals, and 20% on the sale of most goods and services. This tax is included in the marked price and not added at the cash register.

It is possible to claim VAT refunds of up to 14% of the purchase price for purchases totalling more than 2000Kč that are made in shops displaying the 'Tax Free Shopping' sticker. They will give you a Tax Free Shopping voucher, which you then need to present to customs for validation when you leave the country (which must be within three months of the date of purchase). You can then claim your refund either at a duty-free shop in the airport (after passing through passport control) or from a cash-refund office back home (within six weeks of the purchase date). For more information, see www.global-refund.com.

Republiky) – at its northeast end, opposite Municipal House.

STARÉ MĚSTO

In Staré Město the elegant avenue of Pařížská is lined with international designer houses including Dior, Boss, Armani and Louis Vuitton. In contrast, the winding lanes between the Old Town Square and Charles Bridge are full of tacky souvenir shops flaunting puppets, Russian dolls and 'Czech This Out' T-shirts. However, other parts of Staré Město – notably Dlouhá, Dušní and Karoliny Světlé – are becoming known for their concentration of designer fashion boutiques, art galleries and quirky independent shops.

VINOHRADY

As Prague's ritziest residential district, it's not surprising that Vinohrady is also home to the greatest number of furniture and home-decor shops in the city. If you are a fan of design or decoration, you should definitely hike the miracle mile along Vinohradská between the Muzeum and Jiřího z Poděbrad metro stations to see the latest in couches, kitchens and carpets.

Shopping by Neighbourhood

➡ **Prague Castle & Hradčany** There's not much in the way of shopping here.

➡ **Malá Strana** Mostly tourist-oriented shopping, with a few designer boutiques and bookshops tucked away in back alleys.

➡ **Staré Město** The best area in the city for Czech designer fashion.

➡ **Nové Město** This is the main shopping area, with all the big European high-street names from Marks & Spencer to Mothercare.

➡ **Vinohrady & Vršovice** Upmarket neighbourhoods with chic arty-crafty shops and designer furniture.

➡ **Žižkov & Karlín** As yet, there's not much of interest here for the dedicated shopper.

➡ **Holešovice** Home to the city's biggest open-air market, but more interesting for people-watching than actually buying.

➡ **Bubeneč & Dejvice** Some interesting specialist shops, plus the city's oldest farmers market.

➡ **Smíchov & Vyšehrad** Home to Nový Smíchov, one of Prague's biggest and busiest shopping malls.

Lonely Planet's Top Choices

Art Deco Galerie (p117) Antique and reproduction items from the 1920s and '30s.

Modernista (p117) Beautiful reproduction furniture in classic styles from art deco and cubist to functionalist and Bauhaus.

Globe Bookstore & Café (p134) A great selection of new and secondhand books in English, and a cafe to read them in.

Klara Nademlýnská (p118) High fashion from one of the Czech Republic's best-known and most respected designers.

Obchod s Uměním (p144) Original paintings, prints and sculpture from 1900 to 1940, when Czech artists were at the forefront of the European avant-garde.

Pivní Galerie (p161) A beer-drinker's heaven, with 150 varieties from all over the Czech Republic.

Best for Fashion

Dušní 3 (p117) Ready-to-wear fashion and accessories from a range of international designers.

Bohème (p118) Collections of knitwear, leather and suede clothes by designer Hana Stocklassa.

Leeda (p117) Colourful, hip and stylish clothes, from T-shirts to designer dresses.

Pavla & Olga (p94) A unique collection of quirky and cute hats, clothes and accessories.

TEG (p118) Boutique showcasing two of Prague's most respected fashion designers.

Best for Food & Drink

Dejvice Farmers Market (p168) The first, and still the best, of Prague's farmers markets.

Náplavka Farmers Market (p134) Weekly foodie market with lovely riverside setting.

Pivní Galerie (p161) Sample and purchase a huge range of Bohemian and Moravian beers.

Wine Food Market (p179) Italian food store where you can eat in or pack a picnic lunch fit for a king.

Best for Arts & Crafts

Manufaktura (p118) Traditional Czech crafts including wooden toys and hand-painted Easter eggs.

Kubista (p118) Limited-edition reproductions of distinctive cubist furniture and ceramics.

Artěl (p94) Traditional Bohemian glass-making meets modern design.

Best for Antiques

Antikvita (p169) Vintage toys, dolls, coins, medals, jewellery, watches, militaria, postcards and much more.

Bric A Brac (p119) A wonderfully cluttered cave of old household items and glassware and, well... bric-a-brac.

Antique Music Instruments (p80) A real treasure-trove of vintage stringed instruments.

Starožitnosti Robert Pavlů (p169) Fans of art deco and art nouveau will enjoy poking around the several rooms of this noted antique dealer.

Vetešnictvi (p94) An Aladdin's cave of secondhand goods, bric-a-brac and junk.

Best for Glass, Crystal & Ceramics

Moser (p134) One of the most exclusive and respected of Bohemian glassmakers.

St.Vol (p118) A showroom for the colourful glassware of top Czech designers.

Dům Porcelánu (p144) Factory outlet for the best Czech porcelain makers.

Le Patio Lifestyle (p118) Lots of high-quality household accessories, including chunky crystal wine glasses.

Best for Music

Bazar (p134) Vast selection of secondhand CDs, LPs and videos.

Maximum Underground (p119) Crammed with CDs and LPs of indie, punk, hip hop, techno and other genres.

Talacko (p119) The place to go for sheet music scores of the great composers.

Architecture

Prague's stunning architecture, stretching back more than 1000 years to the present day, is a major drawcard. The backstreets of Staré Město and Malá Strana, in particular, are living textbooks of the steady march of European styles over the centuries. Thankfully, the city's historic core escaped significant damage in WWII.

Romanesque

Romanesque architecture, characterised by rounded facades, arched doorways and massive walls, was all the rage in Europe from the 10th to the 12th centuries, and was the reigning style during the rise of the early Bohemian kings. The oldest buildings in Prague date from this period, but regrettably not many original structures survived intact. Prague's finest Romanesque building is the **Basilica of St George** (p71) at Prague Castle, but the style is perhaps best preserved in the handful of rotundas (circular churches) that are, amazingly, still standing. The finest examples include the **Rotunda of St Longinus** (early 12th century) in Nové Město and the late-11th century **Rotunda of St Martin** (p173) in Vyšehrad.

Gothic

Romanesque evolved into Gothic architecture in the 13th and 14th centuries. This is Prague's signature style and is characterised by tall, pointed arches, ribbed vaults, external flying buttresses, and tall, narrow windows with intricate tracery supporting massive stained glass. Gothic architecture flourished in the 14th century during the rule of Charles IV, especially in the hands of architect Peter Parler (Petr Parléř), who was best known for the eastern part of St Vitus Cathedral at Prague Castle. Parler was also responsible for the Gothic design of Charles Bridge and the **Old Town Bridge Tower** (p83). Another master builder was Benedikt Rejt, whose finest legacy is the petal-shaped vaulting of **Vladislav Hall** (p69; 1493–1500) in the **Old Royal Palace** (p69) at Prague Castle. The **Old Town Hall** (p100), with its Astronomical Clock, dates from this period as well. Curiously, the golden spires that crown the many Gothic steeples around town were not part of the original design, but were added in the 19th century, when the craze of neo-Gothic swept the city.

Renaissance

When the Habsburgs assumed the Bohemian throne in the early 16th century, they invited Italian architects to Prague to help create a royal city worthy of their status. The Italians brought a new enthusiasm for classical forms, an obsession with symmetry and a taste for exuberant decoration.

BEST HISTORICAL ARCHITECTURE

→ **Basilica of St George** (p71)
→ **St Vitus Cathedral** (p73)
→ **Charles Bridge** (p83)
→ **St Nicholas Church** (p86)
→ **Municipal House** (p108)

1. Vladislav Hall (p69) **2.** Basilica of St George (p71)

The mix of local and Italian styles gave rise to a distinctive 'Bohemian Renaissance', featuring the technique of sgraffito – from the Italian word 'to scrape' – literally creating design patterns by scraping through an outer layer of pale plaster to reveal a darker surface underneath. The **Summer Palace** (p67; 1538–60), or Belvedere, found in the gardens north of Prague Castle, was built for Queen Anna, the consort of Prague's first Habsburg ruler Ferdinand I. It is almost pure Italian Renaissance. The **Schwarzenberg Palace** (p78; 1546–67) in Hradčany and the House at the Minute (1546–1610) in Staré Město, just to the left of the **Astronomical Clock** (p100), are good examples of sgraffito.

Baroque

In the aftermath of the Thirty Years' War (1618–48), the Habsburg Empire embarked on a campaign to rebuild and re-Catholicise the Czech lands. The ornate baroque style, with its marble columns,

florid sculpture, frescoed ceilings and rich ornamentation, was used by the church as an instrument of persuasion. The most impressive example of baroque style is **St Nicholas Church** (p86; 1704–55) in Malá Strana, the work of Bavarian father and son Kristof and Kilian Ignatz Dientzenhofer. Its massive green dome dominates Malá Strana in a fitting symbol of the Catholic Church's dominance over 18th-century Prague. The final flourish of late baroque was rococo, featuring even more-elaborate decoration. The **Kinský Palace** (p103; 1755–65), overlooking Old Town Square, has a gleaming rococo facade.

Neoclassical

After the exuberance of the 17th and 18th centuries, the architecture of the 19th century was comparatively dull. There was a feeling among architects that baroque and rococo had taken pure decoration as far as it could go and there was a need to simplify styles. They looked to classical Greece and

1. St Nicholas Church (p86) 2. Estates Theatre (p108)

Rome for inspiration. Neoclassical and other 'historicist' styles (in other words styles that consciously imitate earlier forms such as Gothic and Renaissance; usually given the prefix 'neo') are closely associated with the 19th-century Czech National Revival. The **Estates Theatre** (p108; 1783) is a good example of neoclassical theatre design. The **National Theatre** (p126; 1888) and **National Museum** (p123; 1891) were built in neo-Renaissance style. The buildings are noteworthy not so much for the architecture but for what they represented: the chance for Czechs to show they were the equals of their Viennese overlords. The flamboyant **Spanish Synagogue** (p99; 1868) in Josefov is another good example of neoclassicism, though here the style imitated is Moorish, recalling Jewish roots in Spain.

Art Nouveau

As the 19th century drew to a close, Czech architects began to tire of linear neoclassical facades and the pompous style of imperial Vienna. They were looking for something new and found inspiration in Paris with art nouveau and its flowing lines and emphasis on natural

MODERN TRENDS

While it's true that modern architecture (styles from the 1920s to the present) doesn't have the pedigree of the older styles, there are several interesting buildings here and there. Czech modernism got off to a promising start in the 1920s and '30s with functionalism, which was heavily influenced by the German Bauhaus movement. Many of the functionalists' best ideas, including building to purpose and eschewing unnecessary design clutter, were co-opted – badly – by the communists from the 1950s to the 1980s. The post-'89 period has been relatively disappointing, by contrast, and no single style has dominated.

beauty. The city's finest expression of art nouveau is the magnificent **Municipal House** (p108; 1906–12). Every aspect of the building's decoration was designed by leading Czech artists of the time, most famously Alfons Mucha, who decorated the Lord Mayor's Hall. Art nouveau was also frequently applied to upmarket hotels, including the **Hotel Central** (1899–1901) on Hybernská in Nové Město, and the **Grand Hotel Evropa** (p122; 1906) on Wenceslas Square.

Cubist

In just one decade (1910–20), barely half a dozen architects bequeathed to Prague a unique legacy of buildings that were influenced by the cubist art movement. The cubist style spurned the regular lines of traditional architecture and the sinuous forms of art nouveau in favour of triangular and pyramidal forms, emphasising diagonals rather than horizontals and verticals, and achieving a jagged, almost crystalline effect. Many have likened the style to a Picasso painting in 3D, and in many ways that was the idea. Some of Prague's finest **cubist houses** can be seen in the neighbourhood below the Vyšehrad fortress. Another appealing example is the **House of the Black Madonna** (1912) at Celetná 34 in Staré Město. Prague also boasts a **Cubist lamp post** (p130; 1915).

Functionalist

The early-modern mantra that 'form follows function' found a receptive audience among architects who came of age in the 1920s and '30s. Functionalism – similar to Germany's Bauhaus school – appealed to architects for its conscious rejection of superfluous ornamentation. Instead, functionalist architects tended to prefer clean lines and high-quality materials. Notable functionalist works in Prague include the **Baťa** (p134; 1929) shoe store on Wenceslas Square, **Veletržní palác** (p156; 1928) in Holešovice, and Adolf Loos's **Villa Müller** (1930) in the suburb of Střešovice.

Communist

The communists, in power from 1948 to 1989, are usually derided for building ugly, nondescript buildings from cookie-cutter designs and using the cheapest materials available, but some critics are starting to soften their views. It's not that the buildings are good, but at least they're bad in an interesting way. In the 1950s, architects were forced to design in the bombastic Stalinist, socialist-realist style, as seen in the former Hotel International (now the **Hotel Crowne**

BEST MODERN ARCHITECTURE IN PRAGUE
....
➡ Villa Müller
➡ Veletržní palác (p156)
➡ Hotel Crowne Plaza (p164)
➡ TV Tower (p149)
➡ Dancing Building (p127)

1. Stained-glass window, Municipal House (p108)
2. House of the Black Madonna (p107) **3.** Veletržní Palác (p156)

Plaza, p164; 1954) in Dejvice. The **TV Tower** (p149; 1987) in Žižkov dates from the end of the communist period. Its sheer scale dwarfs everything around.

Post-1989

Arguably the most interesting structure of the post-Velvet Revolution period is the so-called **Dancing Building** (p127; 1992-96) in Nové Město, designed by Czech-based Croatian architect Vlado Milunić and American Frank Gehry. The building's resemblance to a pair of dancers spurred the nickname 'Fred and Ginger', after the legendary dancing duo of Astaire and Rogers. Some of the best new architecture is going up in former industrial districts, such as Smíchov, Karlín and Holešovice, including the refurbishment of a former factory to create a space for the **DOX Centre for Contemporary Art** (p157; 2008).

....

1. Dancing Building (p127) **2.** TV Tower with David Černý's *Miminka* (Mummy) sculptures (p149)

JOHN ELK / GETTY IMAGES ©

1. Sedlec Ossuary (p184) 2. Colonnade (p234), Mariánské Lázně
3. Hluboká Chateau (p207) 4. Český Krumlov State Castle (p210)

JOHN ELK / GETTY IMAGES ©

Architectural Highlights of the Czech Republic

Many of the architectural movements that swept through Prague were felt in the countryside as well. From the Gothic splendours of Karlštejn to the breathtaking Renaissance castle at Český Krumlov and the wacky bone church in Kutná Hora, the country's architectural treasures are not limited to the capital.

Spa Architecture

The spa craze that swept Europe in the 19th and early 20th centuries gave the Czech Republic some of the continent's most stunningly beautiful spas, including the main **Colonnade** (p234) in Mariánské Lázně.

The Bone Church

The eerie **ossuary** (p184) at the Sedlec monastery near Kutná Hora, dating from the 19th century, defies easy architectural description, or any other type of description for that matter.

Český Krumlov State Castle

This soaring **Renaissance tower** (p210), remodelled in the 16th century, dominates the charming riverside town below and is visible for miles around. Český Krumlov itself is a nearly perfectly preserved example of Renaissance town planning.

Karlštejn Castle

Emperor Charles IV had this **Gothic castle** (p181) built in the mid-14th century to house the crown jewels. Now it's the most popular destination for day-trippers outside of Prague; book your tour in advance and get an early start.

Hluboká Chateau

The 19th century was all about imitation in architecture. This **delightful folly** (p207), in neo-Gothic style, was created by the noble Schwarzenberg family, who consciously modelled their home after Windsor Castle in the UK.

Explore Prague

PRAGUE'S
TOP SIGHTS

Neighbourhoods at a Glance

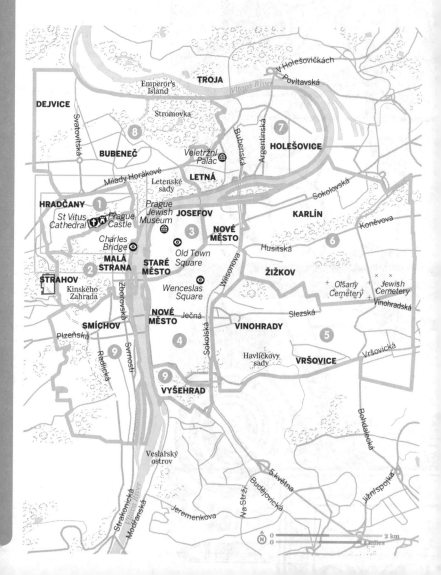

TROJA

V Holešovičkách

Povltavská

Vltava River

Emperor's Island

DEJVICE

Stromovka

Svatovítská

8

BUBENEČ

Veletržní Palác

Bubenská

Argentinská

7

HOLEŠOVICE

Milady Horákové

LETNÁ

Letenské sady

Sokolovská

HRADČANY

1

Prague Jewish Museum

JOSEFOV

KARLÍN

St Vitus Cathedral

Prague Castle

Koněvova

Charles Bridge

3

NOVÉ MĚSTO

6

MALÁ STRANA

2

STARÉ MĚSTO

Old Town Square

Husitská

Wilsonova

ŽIŽKOV

STRAHOV

Zborovská

Wenceslas Square

Olšany Cemetery

Jewish Cemetery

Kinského Zahrada

Vinohradská

Slezská

NOVÉ MĚSTO

Ječná

SMÍCHOV

Plzeňská

4

Sokolská

VINOHRADY

5

Radlická

Svornosti

Havlíčkovy sady

VRŠOVICE

Vršovická

9

9

VYŠEHRAD

Veslařský ostrov

Bohdalecká

Vltava River

Strakonická

Modřanská

5.května

Budějovická

Na Strži

Jeremenkova

Jižní spojka

N

0

0

2 km

miles

① Prague Castle & Hradčany p64

The tourist hotspot of Prague Castle is perched on a hilltop above the Vltava River, with the attractive and peaceful residential area of Hradčany stretching westward to the Loreta and Strahov Monastery. Hradčany became a borough of Prague in 1598, after which the Habsburg nobility built many palaces here in the hope of cementing their influence with the rulers in the castle.

② Malá Strana p81

Malá Strana (the 'Little Quarter') is a charming district of Renaissance palaces and gardens, with an idyllic riverside setting. It is home to the beautiful baroque Church of St Nicholas, the elegant Wallenstein Garden and museums of music and modern art, as well as many excellent restaurants and bars. Prague's scenic centrepiece, Charles Bridge, links Malá Strana to Staré Město on the far side of the river.

③ Staré Město p95

Staré Město – meaning 'Old Town' – is the historic heart of medieval Prague, centred on one of Europe's most spectacular town squares (Old Town Square, or Staroměstské náměstí). It is home to some of the city's most iconic sights, including the Old Town Hall Tower, the Astronomical Clock, the Municipal House and the Prague Jewish Museum. The maze of cobbled streets and narrow alleys leading away from Old Town Square is perfect for exploring.

④ Nové Město p120

The 'New Town' – new in the 14th century, that is – wraps around the Old Town, and finds a focus in the broad, historic boulevard of Wenceslas Square. Its sprawl of mostly 19th- and early 20th-century buildings encompasses important museums and galleries, impressive architecture and the city centre's main shopping streets.

⑤ Vinohrady & Vršovice p135

Vinohrady (literally 'vineyards') is one of the city's most desirable residential neighbourhoods, known for its excellent restaurants and fashionable bars and cafes. Adjacent Vršovice is not quite as sophisticated, though parts are slowly gentrifying.

⑥ Žižkov & Karlín p145

Žižkov is one of the city's liveliest districts, with more bars per capita than any other part of Prague, and home to two prominent, communist-vintage hilltop landmarks: the TV Tower and the National Monument. Karlín, to the north of Žižkov, is undergoing massive redevelopment, but along Křižíkova is an up-and-coming area with lovely art nouveau buildings.

⑦ Holešovice p154

A working-class area north of the centre, Holešovice is short on sights and good restaurants, but has some emerging art galleries and trendy clubs. Letná park is on the extreme western end.

⑧ Bubeneč & Dejvice p162

Bubeneč and Dejvice are adjoining residential neighbourhoods north of the Old Town. Considered the city's most prestigious address, Bubeneč has nice hotels and a few good restaurants scattered about. Within its boundaries is the city's largest park, Stromovka.

⑨ Smíchov & Vyšehrad p170

Smíchov, south of Malá Strana, is a former industrial area that has seen a recent boom in office and luxury hotel construction. The area has few sights but lots of pubs. Vyšehrad, south of Nové Město, is a leafy residential area, dominated by an ancient castle said to be where Prague was founded.

Prague Castle & Hradčany

Neighbourhood Top Five

1 Explore the historic palaces, churches and glorious gardens of **Prague Castle** (p66).

2 Soak up the stunning view from the summit of the **Great South Tower of St Vitus Cathedral** (p74).

3 Absorb the atmosphere of ancient wisdom at the **Strahov Library** (p75).

4 Admire the baroque beauty of the **Loreta** (p77).

5 Wander through the peaceful medieval backstreets of the **Nový Svět** (p78) district.

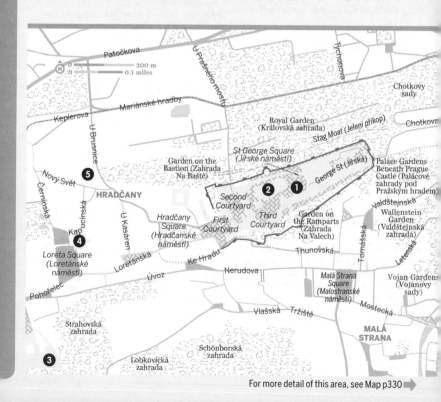

For more detail of this area, see Map p330 ➡

Explore: Prague Castle & Hradčany

Weirdly, this can be both the most crowded and the least crowded neighbourhood in the city. While Prague Castle is thronging with tourists, just a few blocks away you can find yourself alone in the cobbled backstreets of Nový Svět.

The castle is the big attraction, of course, but crowds can spoil the experience. To avoid the worst of the crowds, try to visit the castle early or late – before 10.30am or after 3.30pm – and on a weekday if possible. Your ticket is valid for two consecutive days – better two quiet mornings than cramming it all into one crowded day.

Start with the castle's main entrance at the western end, then move through the various courtyards and sights before exiting at the eastern end. You'll need at least two hours to see the main sights, and a full day if you want to visit everything.

Note that you can wander through the castle grounds and gardens without a ticket – this can be a magical experience on a summer evening, when the courtyards are almost deserted – but you'll need a ticket for all of the main historic buildings.

Local Life

➡ **Hangouts** This may be the most tourist-heavy district in Prague, but there are still some hangouts that are favoured by locals, notably the cool cafe-bar U Zavěšeného Kafe (p80), and the traditional beer hall called Pivnice U Černého Vola (p80).

➡ **Walking the dog** Hradčany residents out for a stroll avoid the crowds by taking to the Stag Moat on the north side of the castle – you can walk in peace from the Powder Bridge east to Pod Bruskou, near Malostranská metro station (April to October only).

Getting There & Away

➡ **Metro** The nearest metro station is Malostranská, but from there it's a stiff climb up the Old Castle Steps to the eastern end of the castle. Hradčanská station is about 10 minutes' walk north of the castle, but it's an easy, level walk to Hradčany and the castle.

➡ **Tram** Take line 22 from Národní třída on the southern edge of Staré Město, Malostranské náměstí in Malá Strana, or Malostranská metro station to the Pražský hrad stop. If you want to explore Hradčany first, stay on the tram until Pohořelec, the second stop after this one.

Lonely Planet's Top Tip

Prague Castle is perched on a steep hill – a sweaty climb in warm weather. To explore the neighbourhood without having to walk uphill, begin at the Pohořelec tram stop (p65) and wander via Strahov Monastery and the Loreta to the castle – all downhill. From the castle it's downhill again through Malá Strana to Charles Bridge.

⚔ Best Places to Eat

➡ Host (p78)
➡ Lobkowicz Palace Café (p80)
➡ Villa Richter (p80)

 For reviews, see p78.➡

🍷 Best Places to Drink

➡ U Zavěšeného Kafe (p80)
➡ Pivnice U Černého Vola (p80)
➡ Klášterní pivovar Strahov (p80)

For reviews, see p80.➡

◉ Best Museums

➡ Strahov Library (p75)
➡ Story of Prague Castle (p70)
➡ St Vitus Treasury (p67)

TOP SIGHT
PRAGUE CASTLE

Prague Castle – Pražský hrad, or just *hrad* to Czechs – is Prague's most popular attraction. Looming above the Vltava's left bank, its serried ranks of spires, towers and palaces dominate the city centre like a fairy-tale fortress. Within its walls lies a varied and fascinating collection of historic buildings, museums and galleries that are home to some of the Czech Republic's greatest artistic and cultural treasures.

The castle has always been the seat of Czech monarchs as well as the official residence of the head of state. Its history begins in the 9th century, when Prince Bořivoj founded a fortified settlement here. It grew haphazardly as rulers made their own additions – there have been four major reconstructions, from that of Prince Soběslav in the 12th century to a classical facelift under Empress Maria Theresa (r 1740–80) – creating an eclectic mixture of architectural styles.

First Courtyard

The First Courtyard lies within the castle's **main gate** (Map p330) on Hradčany Square (Hradčanské náměstí), flanked by huge, baroque statues of battling Titans (1767–70) that dwarf the castle guards standing beneath them. After the fall of communism in 1989, then-president Václav Havel hired his old pal Theodor Pistek, the costume designer on the film *Amadeus* (1984), to replace their communist-era khaki uniforms with the stylish pale blue kit they now wear, which harks back to the army of the first Czechoslovak Republic of 1918 to 38.

DON'T MISS...

➡ Story of Prague Castle
➡ Lobkowicz Palace
➡ St Vitus Treasury
➡ Basilica of St George
➡ Golden Lane

PRACTICALITIES

➡ Pražský hrad
➡ Map p330
➡ ☏224 372 423
➡ www.hrad.cz
➡ Hradčanské náměstí
➡ grounds free
➡ ⊙ gardens 10am-6pm Apr & Oct, to 7pm May & Sep, to 9pm Jun-Aug, closed Nov-Mar, historic buildings 9am-5pm Apr-Oct, to 4pm Nov-Mar
➡ 🚋22, Ⓜ Malostranská

The **changing of the guard** takes place every hour on the hour, but the longest and most impressive display is at noon, when banners are exchanged while a brass band plays a fanfare from the windows of the **Plečnik Hall** (Plečnikova síň; Map p330), which overlooks the First Courtyard.

Second Courtyard

You pass through the Matthias Gate into the Second Courtyard, centred on a baroque fountain and a 17th-century well with lovely Renaissance latticework. On the right is the **Chapel of the Holy Cross** (1763).

St Vitus Treasury

The 18th-century Chapel of the Holy Cross houses the **St Vitus Treasury** (Svatovítský poklad; Map p330; ☑224 373 442; www.kulturanahrade.cz; II. nádvoří, Pražský hrad; adult/concession/family 300/150/600Kč; ☺10am-6pm Apr-Oct, to 5pm Nov-Mar), a spectacular collection of ecclesiastical bling that was founded by Charles IV in the 14th century. Gold and silver reliquaries crusted in diamonds, emeralds and rubies contain saintly relics ranging from fragments of the True Cross to the withered hand of a Holy Innocent. The oldest items include a reliquary arm of St Vitus dating from the early 10th century, while the most impressive treasures range from a gold coronation cross of Charles IV (1370) to a diamond-studded baroque monstrance of 1708.

Royal Garden

A gate on the northern side of the Second Courtyard leads to the 1540 **Powder Bridge** (Prašný most), which spans the Stag Moat and leads to the **Royal Garden** (Královská zahrada; ☺10am-dusk Apr-Oct) FREE, which started life as a Renaissance garden built by Ferdinand I in 1534. It is graced by several gorgeous Renaissance structures.

The most beautiful of the garden's buildings is the 1569 **Ball-Game House** (Míčovna; Map p330), a masterpiece of Renaissance sgraffito where the Habsburgs once played a primitive version of badminton. To the east is the **Summer Palace** (Letohrádek, Belvedere; Map p330), built betwen 1538 and 1860, and the most authentic Italian Renaissance building outside Italy; to the west is the 1695 former **Riding School** (Jízdárna; Map p330). All three are used as venues for temporary exhibitions of modern art.

Prague Castle Picture Gallery

The Swedish army that looted the famous bronzes in the Wallenstein Garden (p88) in 1648 also nicked Rudolf II's art treasures. This **gallery** (Map p330; www.kulturanahrade.cz; adult/child 150/80Kč; ☺9am-6pm

PRAGUE CASTLE & HRADČANY PRAGUE CASTLE PRAGUE CASTLE

THE STAG MOAT

A footpath on the west side of the Powder Bridge leads down to the Stag Moat (Jelení příkop; open April to October), and doubles back through a modern (and rather Freudian) red-brick tunnel beneath the bridge. If you follow the path east along the moat you'll end up at a busy road that leads down to Malostranská metro station. A gate on the outer wall of the castle, overlooking the moat, leads to a nuclear shelter started by the communists in the 1950s but never completed; its tunnels run beneath most of the castle.

In the 1920s President Masaryk hired a Slovene architect, Jože Plečnik, to renovate the castle; his changes created some of its most memorable features and made the complex more tourist friendly.

A WORLD RECORD

According to *Guinness World Records*, Prague Castle is the largest ancient castle in the world – 570m long, an average of 128m wide and occupying 7.28 hectares.

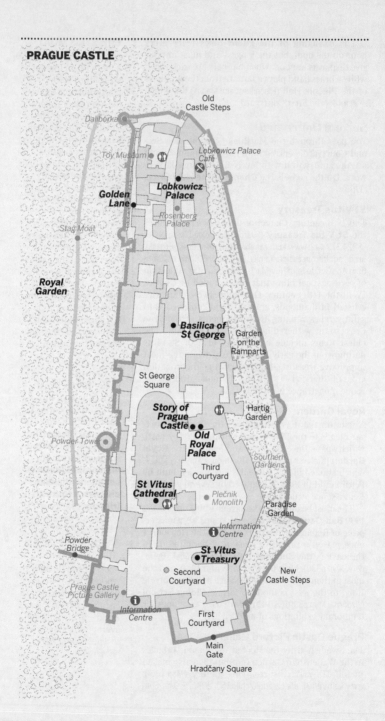

PRAGUE CASTLE

Old Castle Steps

Daliborka

Toy Museum

Lobkowicz Palace Café

Golden Lane

Lobkowicz Palace

Rosenberg Palace

Stag Moat

Royal Garden

Basilica of St George

Garden on the Ramparts

St George Square

Story of Prague Castle

Old Royal Palace

Hartig Garden

Powder Tower

Southern Gardens

Third Courtyard

St Vitus Cathedral

Plečnik Monolith

Paradise Garden

Information Centre

Powder Bridge

St Vitus Treasury

Second Courtyard

New Castle Steps

Prague Castle Picture Gallery

Information Centre

First Courtyard

Main Gate

Hradčany Square

Changing of the guard

Apr-Oct, to 4pm Nov-Mar) in the castle's beautiful Renaissance stables houses an exhibition of 16th- to 18th-century European art, based on the Habsburg collection that was begun in 1650 to replace the lost paintings; it includes works by Cranach, Holbein, Rubens, Tintoretto and Titian.

Third Courtyard

As you pass through the passage on the eastern side of the Second Courtyard, the huge western facade of St Vitus Cathedral soars directly above you; to its south (to the right as you enter) lies the Third Courtyard. At its entrance you'll see a 16m-tall **granite monolith** dedicated to the victims of WWI, designed by Jože Plečnik in 1928, and a copy of a 14th-century bronze figure of **St George** slaying the dragon; the original is on display in the Story of Prague Castle exhibition.

The courtyard is dominated by the southern facade of St Vitus Cathedral, with its grand centrepiece the Golden Gate.

Old Royal Palace

The **Old Royal Palace** (Starý královský palác; Map p330; admission with Prague Castle tour ticket) at the courtyard's eastern end is one of the oldest parts of the castle, dating from 1135. It was originally used only by Czech princesses, but from the 13th to the 16th centuries it was the king's own palace.

The **Vladislav Hall** (Vladislavský sál) is famous for its beautiful, late-Gothic vaulted ceiling

St George may be most familiar as the patron saint of England, but he was also an important royal saint in Bohemia. George's legendary slaying of the dragon came to represent the triumph of Christianity over paganism, a symbol eagerly adopted by devout monarchs, including Vratislav I, the founder of the Basilica of St George.

(1493–1500) designed by Benedikt Rejt. Though more than 500 years old, the flowing, interwoven lines of the vaults have an almost art nouveau feel, in contrast to the rectilinear form of the Renaissance windows. The vast hall was used for banquets, councils and coronations, and for indoor jousting tournaments – hence the **Riders' Staircase** (Jezdecké schody) on the northern side, designed to admit a knight on horseback. All the presidents of the republic have been sworn in here.

A door in the hall's southwestern corner leads to the former offices of the **Bohemian Chancellery** (České kanceláře). On 23 May 1618, in the second room, Protestant nobles rebelling against the Bohemian Estates and the Habsburg emperor threw two of his councillors and their secretary out of the window. They survived, as their fall was broken by the dung-filled moat, but this Second Defenestration of Prague sparked off the Thirty Years' War.

At the eastern end of the Vladislav Hall, steps lead up to a balcony that overlooks **All Saints' Chapel** (kaple Všech svatých; Map p330); a door to the right leads to a terrace with great views of the city. To the right of the Riders' Staircase you'll spot an unusual Renaissance doorway framed by twisted columns, which leads to the **Diet** (Sněmovna), or Assembly Hall, which displays another beautifully vaulted ceiling and a case containing replicas of the **Bohemian crown jewels**.

Story of Prague Castle

Housed in the Gothic vaults beneath the Old Royal Palace, this huge and impressive **museum** (www.kulturnahrade.cz; adult/child 140/70Kč, incl with Prague Castle tour ticket) ranks alongside the Lobkowicz Palace as one of the most interesting collections of artefacts in the castle. It traces 1000 years of the castle's history, from the building of the first wooden palisade to the present day, illustrated by models of the site at various stages in its development.

The exhibits include the grave of a 9th-century warrior discovered in the castle grounds, the helmet and chain mail worn by St Wenceslas, and a replica of the gold crown of St Wenceslas, which was made for Charles IV in 1346. Anyone with a serious interest in Prague Castle should visit here first.

St George Square

St George Square (Jiřské náměstí), the plaza to the east of St Vitus Cathedral, lies at the heart of the castle complex.

PRAGUE CASTLE TICKETS

There are two kinds of tickets for Prague Castle (each valid for two days), which allow entry to different combinations of sights:

➡ **Long Tour** (adult/child/family 350/175/700Kč) Includes St Vitus Cathedral, Old Royal Palace, Story of Prague Castle, Basilica of St George, Powder Tower, Golden Lane and Daliborka, Prague Castle Picture Gallery, Powder Tower and Rosenberg Palace.

➡ **Short Tour** (adult/child/family 250/125/500Kč) Includes St Vitus Cathedral, Old Royal Palace, Basilica of St George, Golden Lane and Daliborka.

You can buy tickets at the two information centres in the **Second** (Map p330; ☑224 372 423; ⊗9am-5pm Apr-Oct, to 4pm Nov-Mar) and **Third Courtyards** (Map p330; ☑224 372 434; ⊗9am-5pm Apr-Oct, to 4pm Nov-Mar), or from ticket offices at the entrances to all the main sights.

Basilica of St George

The striking, brick red, early baroque facade that dominates the square conceals the Czech Republic's best-preserved Romanesque **basilica** (Bazilika Sv Jiří; Map p330; Jiřské náměstí; admission with Prague Castle tour ticket; ☺9am-6pm Apr-Oct, to 4pm Nov-Mar), established in the 10th century by Vratislav I (the father of St Wenceslas). What you see today is mostly the result of restorations made between 1887 and 1908.

The austerity of the Romanesque nave is relieved by a baroque double staircase leading to the apse, where fragments of 12th-century frescoes survive. In front of the stairs lie the tombs of Prince Boleslav II (d 997; on the left) and Prince Vratislav I (d 921). The arch beneath the stairs allows a glimpse of the **12th-century crypt**; Přemysl kings are buried here and in the nave.

On the right side of the crypt is a gruesome statue of a decomposing corpse, complete with a snake coiled in its abdominal cavity. Dating from the 16th century, it is an allegory of Vanity although it is known as **Brigita** after a Prague legend. An Italian sculptor murdered his girlfriend, a local girl named Brigita, but when her buried body was discovered he was driven by remorse to create this sculpture of her decaying corpse.

Powder Tower

A passage to the north of St Vitus Cathedral leads to the **Powder Tower** (Prašná Věž; Map p330; adult/concession 70/40Kč, incl with Prague Castle long-tour ticket; ☺9am-6pm Apr-Oct, to 4pm Nov-Mar), also called Mihulka, which was built in the 15th century as part of the castle's defences. Later it became the workshop of cannon- and bell-maker Tomáš Jaroš, who cast the bells for St Vitus Cathedral. Today it houses an exhibition on the history of the Castle Guard.

George Street & Around

George St (Jiřská) runs from the Basilica of St George to the castle's eastern gate.

Golden Lane

The picturesque alley known as **Golden Lane** (Zlatá ulička; admission with Prague Castle tour ticket) runs along the northern wall of the castle. Its tiny, colourful cottages were built in the 16th century for the sharpshooters of the castle guard, but were later used by goldsmiths. In the 19th and early 20th centuries they were occupied by artists, including the writer Franz Kafka (who frequently visited his sister's house at No 22 from 1916 to 1917).

The cottages have been restored to show a variety of former uses. One is a goldsmith's workshop,

GARDEN ON THE RAMPARTS

At the castle's eastern gate, you can either descend the Old Castle Steps to Malostranská metro station or take a sharp right and wander back to Hradčany Square through the **Garden on the Ramparts** (Zahrada na valech; admission free; ☺10am-6pm Apr & Oct, to 7pm May & Sep, to 9pm Jun & Jul, to 8pm Aug, closed Nov-Mar). The terrace garden offers superb views across the rooftops of Malá Strana and permits a peek into the back garden of the British embassy. Alternatively, you can descend to Malá Strana through the terraced Palace Gardens Beneath Prague Castle (p87).

Performances of classical music are staged at 1pm each day in the late-17th-century baroque concert hall in the Lobkowicz Palace. The program includes works by Beethoven, Chopin, Dvořák, Haydn, Vivaldi and Smetana, among others; tickets (340Kč to 440Kč) can be bought online at www.lobkowicz.cz or at the palace ticket office.

another a tavern, and one the home of celebrated Prague fortune-teller Matylda Průšová, who died at the hands of the Gestapo during WWII; Kafka's sister's cottage is now a bookshop. The most evocative is No 12 at the far eastern end, the cosy former home of an amateur film historian who seems to have just popped out for lunch – archive footage of the castle is projected on the living-room wall.

Daliborka

This **tower** (Zlatá ulička; admission with Prague Castle tour ticket; ⊙9am-6pm Apr-Oct, to 4pm Nov-Mar) is named after the knight Dalibor of Kozojedy, imprisoned here in 1498 for supporting a peasant rebellion, and later executed. According to legend, he played a violin that could be heard throughout the castle; composer Bedřich Smetana based his 1868 opera *Dalibor* on the tale. You can peer into the bottle dungeon, and see a small display of torture instruments.

Lobkowicz Palace

This 16th-century **palace** (Lobkovický palác; ☑233 312 925; www.lobkowicz.cz; Jiřská 3; adult/concession/family 275/200/690Kč; ⊙10am-6pm) houses a private museum known as the **Princely Collections**, which includes priceless paintings, furniture and musical memorabilia. Your tour includes an audio guide dictated by owner William Lobkowicz and his family – this personal connection really brings the displays to life, and makes the palace one of the castle's most interesting attractions.

Built in the 16th century, the palace has been home to the aristocratic Lobkowicz family for around 400 years. Confiscated by the Nazis in WWII, and again by the communists in 1948, the palace was finally returned in 2002 to William Lobkowicz, an American property developer and grandson of Maximilian, the 10th Prince Lobkowicz, who fled to the USA in 1939.

Highlights of the museum include paintings by Cranach, Breughel the Elder, Canaletto and Piranesi, original musical scores annotated by Mozart, Beethoven and Haydn (the 7th prince was a great patron of music – Beethoven dedicated three symphonies to him), and an impressive collection of musical instruments. But it's the personal touches that make an impression, such as the 16th-century portrait of a Lobkowicz ancestor wearing a ring that William's mother still wears today, and an old photo album with a picture of a favourite family dog smoking a pipe.

The palace has an excellent cafe (p80).

Rosenberg Palace

This Renaissance **palace** (Rožmberský palác; Jiřská 1; admission included with Prague Castle long-tour ticket) once served as the 'Institute of Noblewomen' – effectively a home for aristocratic ladies fallen on hard times, founded by Empress Maria Theresa in 1755. The palace chapel soars three storeys high, decorated with trompe l'œil paintings and frescoes, and there's a re-creation of a lady's bed-chamber, complete with commode and elaborate period mousetrap!

Toy Museum

The second-largest **toy museum** (Muzeum Hraček; ☑224 372 294; Jiřská 6; adult/concession/family 70/30/120Kč; ⊙9.30am-5.30pm) in the world houses an amazing collection, with some artefacts dating back to ancient Greece, but it can be a bit frustrating for the kids as most displays are hands-off. Toys range from model trains and teddy bears to Victorian dolls, Action Men and the definitive Barbie collection.

TOP SIGHT
ST VITUS CATHEDRAL

Built over a time span of almost 600 years, St Vitus is one of the most richly endowed cathedrals in central Europe. It is pivotal to the religious and cultural life of the Czech Republic, housing treasures that range from the 14th-century Bohemian crown jewels to glowing art nouveau stained glass, and the tombs of Bohemian saints and rulers from St Wenceslas to Charles IV.

The Nave

The foundation stone of the cathedral was laid in 1344 by Emperor Charles IV, on the site of a 10th-century Romanesque rotunda dedicated to St Wenceslas. The architect, Matthias of Arras, began work on the choir in the French Gothic style, but died eight years later. His German successor, Peter Parler – a veteran of Cologne's cathedral – built most of the eastern part, but it remained unfinished. It was only in 1861 that a concerted effort was made to complete the project – everything between the western door and the crossing was built during the late 19th and early 20th centuries, and it was finally consecrated in 1929.

Inside, the nave is flooded with colour from **stained-glass windows** created by eminent Czech artists of the early 20th century – note the one by **Alfons Mucha** in the third chapel on the northern side, which depicts the lives of Sts Cyril and Methodius (1909). Nearby is a **wooden sculpture of the crucifixion** (1899) by František Bílek.

Walk up to the crossing, where the nave and transept meet, which is dominated by the huge and colourful **south window** (1938) by Max Švabinský, depicting the Last Judgment – note the fires of Hell burning brightly in the lower

DON'T MISS...

➡ Stained-glass window by Alfons Mucha
➡ South window
➡ Tomb of St John of Nepomuk
➡ Chapel of St Wenceslas
➡ Golden Gate

PRACTICALITIES

➡ Katedrála Sv Víta
➡ Map p330
➡ ☏ 257 531 622
➡ www.katedralasvate hovita.cz
➡ Third Courtyard, Prague Castle
➡ admission incl in Prague Castle tour ticket
➡ ⏰ 9am-5pm Mon-Sat, noon-5pm Sun Apr-Oct, to 4pm Nov-Mar
➡ 🚊 22

THE GOLDEN GATE

The cathedral's south entrance is known as the Golden Gate (Zlatá brána), an elegant, triple-arched Gothic porch designed by Peter Parler. Above it is a mosaic of the Last Judgment (1370–71): on the left, the godly are raised into heaven by angels; on the right, sinners are cast down into hell by demons; and in the centre, Christ reigns in glory with Saints Procopius, Sigismund, Vitus, Wenceslas, Ludmila and Adalbert below. Beneath them Charles IV and his wife kneel in prayer.

The cathedral crypt (no longer open to the public) contains sarcophagi with the remains of Czech rulers including Charles IV, Wenceslas IV, George of Poděbrady and Rudolf II. You can see it in the Virtual Tour on the cathedral's website.

CROWN JEWELS

On the southern side of the Chapel of St Wenceslas, a small door, sealed with seven locks, hides a staircase leading up to the Crown Chamber, where the Bohemian crown jewels are kept. You can see replicas in the Old Royal Palace (p69).

right-hand corner. In the north transept, beneath the baroque organ, are three carved wooden doors decorated with **reliefs of Bohemian saints**, with smaller panels beneath each saint depicting their martyrdom – look on the left-hand door for St Vitus being tortured in a cauldron of boiling oil. Next to him is the martyrdom of St Wenceslas; he is down on one knee, clinging to a lion's-head door handle, while his treacherous brother Boleslav drives a spear into his back. You can see that very door handle on the other side of the church, on the door to the Chapel of St Wenceslas.

The Ambulatory

The eastern end of the cathedral is capped with graceful late-Gothic vaulting dating from the 14th century. In the centre lies the ornate **Royal Mausoleum** (1571–89) with its cold marble effigies of Ferdinand I, his wife Anna Jagellonská and their son Maximilián II.

As you round the far end of the ambulatory you pass the **tomb of St Vitus** – as well as being a patron saint of Bohemia, Vitus is a patron of actors, entertainers and dancers. Further round is the spectacular, baroque silver **tomb of St John of Nepomuk**, its draped canopy supported by a squadron of silver angels (the tomb contains two tons of silver in all).

The nearby **Chapel of St Mary Magdalene** contains the grave slabs of cathedral architects Matthias of Arras and Peter Parler. Beyond is the ornate, late-Gothic **Royal Oratory**, a fancy balcony with ribbed vaulting carved to look like tree branches. The biggest and most beautiful of the cathedral's numerous side chapels is Parler's **Chapel of St Wenceslas**. Its walls are adorned with gilded panels containing polished slabs of semiprecious stones. Wall paintings from the early 16th century depict scenes from the life of the Czechs' patron saint, while even older frescos show scenes from the life of Christ.

Great South Tower

The cathedral's **bell tower** (admission 150Kč; ☉10am-6pm Apr-Oct, to 5pm Nov-Mar) was left unfinished in the 15th century; its soaring Gothic lines are capped by a Renaissance gallery added in the late 16th century, and a bulging spire that dates from the 1770s. You can climb the 297 steps to the top for excellent views; the entrance is in Prague Castle's Third Courtyard (admission not included in castle tour ticket). You also get a close look at the clockworks, dating from 1597. The tower's **Sigismund Bell**, cast in 1549, is the largest bell in the Czech Republic.

TOP SIGHT
STRAHOV MONASTERY

In 1140 Vladislav II founded Strahov Monastery for the Premonstratensian order. The present monastery buildings, completed in the 17th and 18th centuries, functioned until the communist government closed them down and imprisoned most of the monks; they returned in 1990.

Inside the main gate is the **Church of St Roch** (Kostel sv Rocha), which was built in 1612 and is now an art gallery, and the **Church of the Assumption of Our Lady** (Kostel Nanebevzetí Panny Marie; Map p330), built in 1143 and heavily decorated in the 18th century in the baroque style; Mozart is said to have played the organ here.

Strahov Library

This **library** (Strahovská knihovna; Map p330; ☑233 107 716; www.strahovskyklaster.cz; Strahovské nádvoří 1; adult/concession 80/50Kč; ☉9am-noon & 1-5pm; 🚌22) is the largest monastic library in the country, with two magnificent baroque halls dating from the 17th and 18th centuries. You can peek through the doors but, sadly, you can't go into the halls themselves – it was found that fluctuations in humidity caused by visitors' breath was endangering the frescos. There's also a display of historical curiosities.

The stunning interior of the two-storey-high **Philosophy Hall** (Filozofický sál; 1780–97) was built to fit around the carved and gilded floor-to-ceiling walnut shelving that was rescued from another monastery in South Bohemia (access to the upper gallery is via spiral staircases concealed in the corners). The feeling of height here is accentuated by a grandiose ceiling fresco, *Mankind's Quest for True Wisdom* – the figure of Divine Providence is enthroned in the centre amid a burst of golden light, while around the edges are figures ranging from Adam and Eve to the Greek philosophers.

The lobby outside the hall contains an 18th-century **Cabinet of Curiosities**, displaying the grotesquely shrivelled remains of sharks, skates, turtles and other sea creatures;

DON'T MISS...

➡ Strahov Library
➡ Miniature Museum

PRACTICALITIES

➡ Strahovský klášter
➡ Map p330
➡ ☑233 107 711
➡ www.strahovs-kyklaster.cz
➡ Strahovské nádvoří 1
➡ 🚌22

EXIT TO PETŘÍN

The doorway at the eastern end of Strahov Monastery's main courtyard leads into the terraced orchards and parkland of Petřín, which enjoys some of the finest panoramas in Prague. A pleasant stroll leads southeast to the Petřín Lookout Tower (p90), with grand views over Malá Strana and the Vltava River to the spires of the Old Town, the TV Tower and the National Monument on Vítkov Hill.

Lying on a table in the corridor connecting Strahov Library's two baroque halls, beside the model ship and narwhal tusk, are two long, brown, leathery things. The prudish attendant will tell you they're elephants' trunks, but they're actually preserved whales' penises.

TIME FOR A PINT...

The monks of Strahov were known not only for their academic prowess, but also for their ale – a brewery was built here in 1628. It closed in 1907 but was reopened in 2000, and now the Klášterní pivovar Strahov (p80) serves up some of Prague's best beers.

these flayed and splayed corpses were prepared by sailors, who passed them off to credulous landlubbers as 'sea monsters'. Another case (beside the door to the corridor) contains historical items, including a miniature coffee service made for the Habsburg empress Marie Louise in 1813, which fits into four false books.

The corridor leads to the older and even more beautiful **Theology Hall** (Teologiský sál; 1679). The low, curved ceiling is thickly encrusted in ornate baroque stuccowork, and decorated with painted cartouches depicting the theme of 'True Wisdom', which was acquired, of course, through piety; one of the mottoes that adorns the ceiling is 'initio sapientiae timor domini' ('the beginning of wisdom is the fear of God').

On a stand outside the hall door is a facsimile of the library's most prized possession, the **Strahov Evangeliary**, a 9th-century codex in a gem-studded, 12th-century binding. A nearby bookcase houses the **Xyloteka** (1825), a set of booklike boxes, each one bound in the wood and bark of the tree it describes, with samples of leaves, roots, flowers and fruits inside.

Strahov Picture Gallery

In Strahov Monastery's second courtyard is the **Strahov Picture Gallery** (Strahovská Obrazárna; Map p330; 220 517 278; www.strahovskyklaster.cz; Strahovské nádvoří II; adult/child 80/40Kč; 9am-noon & 12.30-5pm; 22), with a valuable collection of Gothic, baroque, rococo and romantic art on the 1st floor, and temporary exhibits on the ground floor. Some of the medieval works are extraordinary – don't miss the very modern-looking 14th-century Jihlava Crucifix. You can also wander around the monastery's cloister, refectory and chapter house.

Miniature Museum

Siberian technician Anatoly Konyenko used to manufacture tools for microsurgery, but these days he prefers to spend 7½ years crafting a pair of golden horseshoes for a flea. This **museum** (Muzeum Miniatur; Map p330; 233 352 371; Strahovské nádvoří II; adult/child 100/50Kč; 9am-5pm; 22) displays his handiwork, which includes the Lord's Prayer inscribed on a single human hair, a grasshopper clutching a violin, and a camel caravan silhouetted in the eye of a needle. Weird but fascinating.

TIBOR BOGNAR / GETTY IMAGES ©

TOP SIGHT
LORETA

The Loreta is a baroque place of pilgrimage founded by Benigna Kateřina Lobkowicz in 1626, and designed as a replica of the supposed Santa Casa (Sacred House; the home of the Virgin Mary) in the Holy Land.

Santa Casa

Loreta's duplicate Santa Casa is in the centre of a courtyard complex, surrounded by cloistered arcades, churches and chapels. The interior is adorned with 17th-century frescos and reliefs depicting the life of the Virgin Mary, and an ornate silver altar with a wooden effigy of Our Lady of Loreto. Above the entrance to the courtyard 27 bells play 'We Greet Thee a Thousand Times' on the hour.

Churches

Behind the Santa Casa is the **Church of the Nativity of Our Lord** (Kostel Narození Páně), built in 1737 to a design by Kristof Dientzenhofer. The claustrophobic interior includes skeletons of the Spanish saints Felicissima and Marcia.

At the corner of the courtyard is the **Chapel of Our Lady of Sorrows** (Kaple Panny Marie Bolestné). She was St Starosta, pious daughter of a Portuguese king who promised her to the king of Sicily against her wishes. After a night of tearful prayers she awoke with a beard, the wedding was called off, and her father had her crucified. She was later made patron saint of the needy and the godforsaken.

Treasury

The church's treasury has been ransacked several times over the centuries, but it remains a bastion of over-the-top religious bling centred on the 90cm-tall Prague Sun (Pražské slunce), made of solid silver and gold and studded with 6222 diamonds.

DON'T MISS...

➡ Santa Casa
➡ Treasury

PRACTICALITIES

➡ Map p330
➡ ☎ 220 516 740
➡ www.loreta.cz
➡ Loretánské náměstí 7
➡ adult/concession/family 130/100/270Kč
➡ ⊘9am-12.15pm & 1-5pm Apr-Oct, 9.30am-12.15pm & 1-4pm Nov-Mar
➡ 🚊22

SIGHTS

PRAGUE CASTLE CASTLE
See p66.

ST VITUS CATHEDRAL CHURCH
See p73.

STRAHOV MONASTERY MONASTERY
See p75.

LORETA CHURCH
See p77.

BÍLEK VILLA GALLERY
Map p330 (Bílkova Vila; ☎233 323 631; www.citygalleryprague.cz; Mickiewiczova 1; adult/child 120/60Kč; ⊙10am-6pm Tue-Sun; ☒18, 22) This striking art nouveau villa, designed by sculptor František Bílek in 1911, now houses a museum of his unconventional works. Bílek's distinctive sculptures, mostly in wood, take inspiration from his religious beliefs. Dramatic compositions such as *The Fall* show Adam and Eve cowering in fear of God's wrath, while *Wonderment* expresses the feeling of awe at God's presence.

NOVÝ SVĚT QUARTER NEIGHBOURHOOD
Map p330 (☒22) In the 16th century, houses were built for castle staff in an enclave of curving cobblestone streets down the slope north of the Loreta. Today, these diminutive cottages have been restored and painted in pastel shades, making the 'New World' quarter a perfect alternative to the castle's crowded Golden Lane. Danish astronomer Tycho Brahe once lived at Nový Svět 1.

ŠTERNBERG PALACE GALLERY
Map p330 (Šternberský palác; ☎233 090 570; www.ngprague.cz; Hradčanské náměstí 15; incl admission to Schwarzenberg Palace adult/child 150/80Kč; ⊙10am-6pm Tue-Sun; ☒22) The baroque Šternberg Palace is home to the National Gallery's collection of 14th- to 18th-century European art, including works by Goya and Rembrandt. Fans of medieval altarpieces will be in heaven; there are also several Rubens, some Rembrandts and Breughels, and a large collection of Bohemian miniatures.

SCHWARZENBERG PALACE GALLERY
Map p330 (Schwarzenberský palác; ☎224 810 758; www.ngprague.cz; Hradčanské náměstí 2; incl admission to Šternberg Palace adult/child 150/80Kč; ⊙10am-6pm Tue-Sun; ☒22) Sporting a beautifully preserved facade of black-and-white Renaissance sgraffito, the Schwarzenberg Palace houses the National Gallery's collection of baroque art. A lot of the paintings are poorly lit and suffer from reflections from nearby windows – a shame, as the inside of the palace itself is less impressive than the outside, and the collection is really only of interest to aficionados.

SALM PALACE GALLERY
(Salmovský Palác; ☎233 081 713; www.ngprague.cz; Hradčanské náměstí 1; adult/child 100/50Kč, incl admission to Schwarzenberg & Šternberg Palaces 200/100Kč; ⊙10am-6pm Tue-Sun; ☒22) Overlooking the entrance to Prague Castle, the austerely neoclassical Salm Palace – built in 1810 as a luxury aristocratic residence – provides hanging space for the National Gallery's temporary exhibitions (see website for latest program), and is slated to house the NG's collection of medieval art. Tickets can be bought in the new, glass-fronted information office between the Salm and Schwarzenberg Palaces.

EATING

Most of the restaurants in the castle district are aimed squarely at the tourist crowds, and the whole area becomes pretty quiet in the evenings after the castle closes. The following places, which are a cut above the usual tourist eateries regarding character and cuisine, are worth seeking out.

MALÝ BUDDHA ASIAN €
Map p330 (☎220 513 894; www.malybuddha.cz; Úvoz 46; mains 140-250Kč; ⊙noon-10.30pm Tue-Sun; ☒; ☒22) Candlelight, incense and a Buddhist shrine characterise this intimate, vaulted restaurant that tries to capture the atmosphere of an oriental tearoom. The menu is a mix of Asian influences, with authentic Thai, Chinese and Vietnamese dishes, many of them vegetarian, and a drinks list that includes ginseng wine, Chinese rose liqueur and all kinds of tea. Credit cards are not accepted.

HOST MEDITERRANEAN, ASIAN €€
Map p330 (☎728 695 793; www.hostrestaurant.cz; Loretánská 15; mains 300-400Kč; ⊖☎; ☒22) Hidden away down a narrow staircase between streets, Host impresses with its sleekly modern dining room, decorated with old monochrome photos, and the

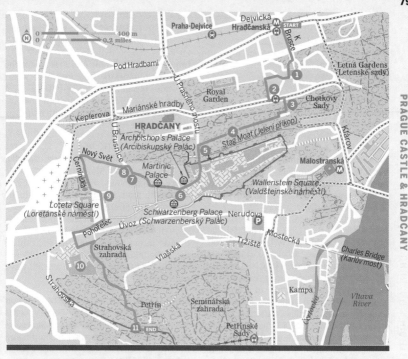

🏃 Neighbourhood Walk
Hradčany

START HRADČANSKÁ METRO STATION
END PETŘÍN
LENGTH 2.5KM; ONE HOUR

From the metro station follow K Brusce towards the stone portal of the **①Písek Gate**. This baroque gateway, decorated with carved military emblems, was built in 1721 as part of Prague's new fortifications; the streets on either side still follow the outlines of the bastions.

Turn right on U Písecké Brány, and then left onto Tychonova. Here you will pass two **②Cubist houses** designed by Josef Gočár. Cross Mariánské hradby and enter the Royal Garden (open April to October only) beside the beautiful, Renaissance **③Summer Palace**.

Turn right, continue past the stunning **④Ball-Game House**, and follow the upper rim of the Stag Moat to the western end of the gardens. Go through the gate and turn left to enter the Second Courtyard of Prague Castle via the **⑤Powder Bridge**.

Leave the courtyard via the first gate on the right, which leads into **⑥Hradčany Square**, once the heart of the aristocratic quarter. At the far end bear right on Kanovnická, past the **⑦Church of St John Nepomuk**, built in 1729 by the king of Prague baroque, Kilian Dientzenhofer.

Turn left into Nový Svět, a picturesque cluster of cottages once inhabited by court artisans. **⑧No 1 Nový Svět** was once the home of astronomer Tycho Brahe and, after 1600, his successor Johannes Kepler. Turn left on Černínská to the pretty square in front of the extravagantly baroque **⑨Loreta** (p77); opposite is the imposing facade of the Černín Palace, dating from 1692.

Turn right into Pohořelec – a little alley at No 9 leads into the courtyard of **⑩Strahov Monastery** (p75), where you can visit the library before going through the gate at the eastern end of the courtyard into the gardens above Malá Strana. Turn right on the footpath (signposted 'Rozhledna & Bludiště') and finish with a stroll along to the **⑪Petřín Lookout Tower** (p90).

stunning view from its outdoor terrace. Friendly staff will guide you through a competent menu that ranges from steaks and burgers to traditional Czech dishes to Asian favourites such as spring rolls and Thai-style prawn stir-fry.

LOBKOWICZ PALACE CAFÉ CAFE €€

Map p330 (☎233 312 925; Jiřská 3; mains 200-300Kč; ⏰10am-6pm; 📶👪; 🚋22) This cafe, housed in the 16th-century Lobkowicz Palace, is the best eatery in the castle complex by an imperial mile. Try to grab one of the tables on the balconies at the back – the view over Malá Strana is superb, as is the goulash. The coffee is good, too, and service is fast and friendly.

VILLA RICHTER CZECH, FRENCH €€

Map p330 (☎257 219 079; www.villarichter.cz; Staré zamecké schody 6; mains 150-300Kč, 3-course dinner 945Kč; ⏰11am-11pm; Ⓜ Malostranská) Housed in a restored 18th-century villa in the middle of a replanted medieval vineyard, this place is aimed squarely at the hordes of tourists thronging up and down the Old Castle Steps. But the setting is special – outdoor tables on terraces with one of the finest views in the city – and the menu of classic Czech dishes doesn't disappoint.

If you want something fancier, the Piano Nobile restaurant within the villa itself offers a French-influenced fine-dining menu.

U ZLATÉ HRUŠKY CZECH €€€

Map p330 (☎220 941 244; www.restaurantuzlatehrusky.cz; Nový Svět 3; mains 450-700Kč; ⏰11am-1am; 🚋22) 'At the Golden Pear' is a cosy, wood-panelled gourmets' corner, serving Bohemian fish, fowl and game dishes (tripe fricassee is a speciality) and frequented by locals and visiting dignitaries as well as tourists (the Czech foreign ministry is just up the road, and Margaret Thatcher once dined here). In summer get a table in its leafy *zahradní restaurace* (garden restaurant) across the street.

DRINKING & NIGHTLIFE

This is a fairly quiet district, with drinking venues limited to laid-back cafes and a couple of traditional pubs.

U ZAVĚŠENÝHO KAFE BAR

Map p330 (☎605 294 595; www.uzavesenyhokafe.cz; Úvoz 6; ⏰11am-midnight; 📶; 🚋12, 20, 22) A superb drinking den barely five minutes' walk from the castle. Head for the back room, quirkily decorated with weird art and mechanical curiosities by local artist Kuba Krejci, and an ancient jukebox. Foaming Pilsner Urquell is 38Kč a half-litre, and the coffee is damn fine too.

PIVNICE U ČERNÉHO VOLA PUB

Map p330 (☎220 513 481; Loretánské náměstí 1; ⏰10am-10pm; 🚋22) Many religious people make a pilgrimage to the Loreta, but just across the road, the 'Black Ox' is a shrine that pulls in pilgrims of a different kind. This surprisingly inexpensive beer hall is visited by real-ale aficionados for its authentic atmosphere and lip-smackingly delicious draught beer, Velkopopovický Kozel (30Kč for 0.5L), brewed in a small town southeast of Prague.

KLÁŠTERNÍ PIVOVAR STRAHOV BREWERY

Map p330 (Strahov Monastery Brewery; ☎233 353 155; www.klasterni-pivovar.cz; Strahovské nádvoří 301; ⏰10am-10pm; 🚋22) Dominated by two polished copper brewing kettles, this convivial little pub serves up two varieties of its St Norbert beer – *tmavý* (dark), a rich, tarry brew with a creamy head, and *polotmavý* (amber), a full-bodied, hoppy lager; both are 59Kč per 0.4L. There's also a strong (6.3% abv) IPA-style beer.

SHOPPING

ANTIQUE MUSIC INSTRUMENTS ANTIQUES

Map p330 (☎220 514 287; Pohořelec 9; ⏰9am-6pm; 🚋22) It may not get the prize for most inventive shop name, but this place is a real treasure trove of vintage stringed instruments. You'll find an interesting stock of antique violins, violas and cellos dating from the 18th century to the mid-20th century, as well as bows, cases and other musical accessories.

In the same premises you'll find **Icons Gallery** (Map p330; ☎233 353 777; Pohořelec 9; ⏰9am-6pm; 🚋22), a luminous collection of Russian and Eastern European religious icons, as well as lots of other decorative objets d'art, watches, porcelain and art nouveau glassware.

Malá Strana

PRAGUE CASTLE TO CHARLES BRIDGE | NORTHERN MALÁ STRANA | SOUTHERN MALÁ STRANA | PETŘÍN

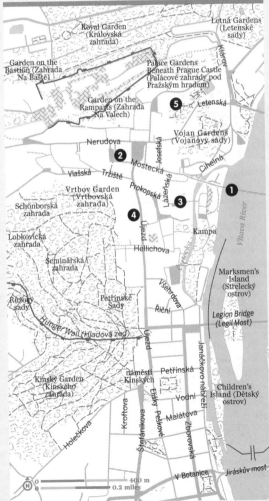

Neighbourhood Top Five

❶ Experience the bustle and throng of **Charles Bridge** (p83), a crowded half-kilometre of baroque statues, busking musicians, postcard sellers, caricature artists, snapshotting tourists and stunning views. Better still, experience the bridge at its most romantic, at dawn.

❷ Gaze at the florid frescoes and *trompe l'œil* trickery that adorn the soaring vaults and domes of **St Nicholas Church** (p86).

❸ Remember the repression of communist-era Prague with a visit to the **John Lennon Wall** (p87), where youths once gathered in a spirit of rebellion.

❹ Admire the faith and passion that has gone into creating the countless costumes worn by the **Infant Jesus of Prague** (p89).

❺ Escape from the crowds with a stroll among the aristocratic fripperies of the impressive – and unexpected – **Wallenstein Garden** (p88).

For more detail of this area, see Map p328 ➡

Lonely Planet's Top Tip

Charles Bridge is a victim of its own popularity – too often your visit to Prague's most beautiful location will be spent squeezing through the crowds, trying to catch a glimpse of the view. If you want to experience the bridge at its most atmospheric, set your alarm clock for an early start. Try to arrive around dawn (check http://timeanddate.com for sunrise times), and enjoy a leisurely stroll across the bridge in perfect peace before returning to your hotel for breakfast.

✗ Best Places to Eat

➡ Elegantes (p93)

➡ Café Lounge (p91)

➡ Ichnusa Botega Bistro (p91)

➡ U Malé Velryby (p91)

➡ Café de Paris (p91)

For reviews, see p91. ➡

🍷 Best Places to Drink

➡ Mlýnská Kavárna (p93)

➡ Klub Újezd (p93)

➡ Malostranská beseda (p93)

➡ U Malého Glena (p94)

For reviews, see p93. ➡

◉ Best Viewpoints

➡ Petřín Lookout Tower (p90)

➡ Malá Strana Bridge Tower (p84)

➡ St Nicholas Church Bell Tower (p86)

For reviews, see p86. ➡

Explore: Malá Strana

Almost too picturesque for its own good, the baroque district of Malá Strana (Little Quarter) tumbles down the hillside between Prague Castle and the river. The focal point of the neighbourhood is Nerudova street, which links the castle to Malostranské náměstí, Malá Strana's main square, dominated by the soaring green dome of St Nicholas Church. To its north is a maze of palaces and gardens, home to government offices and foreign embassies; to the south are more parks and gardens straggling along the banks of the Vltava before merging into the more commercialised streets of Smíchov.

Once you get away from the crowded pavements of Nerudova and Mostecká – the main tourist route between the castle and Charles Bridge – there are cobbled backstreets to explore, with hidden historic gardens, quaint and colourful house signs perched above doorways, and countless little bars and cafes where you can while away an afternoon.

Local Life

➡ **Popular Parks** Though it may be picturesque, Malá Strana is also a place of work for many Praguers, filled as it is with government offices, embassies and consulates. Favourite parks where locals relax during lunch break include **Vojan Gardens** and **Kampa Park** (p88).

➡ **Hangouts** Kafíčko (p94) and Mlýnská Kavárna (p93) are popular venues for after-work drinks among local artists, journalists and politicians.

➡ **Petřín** Summer or winter, Petřín (p90) is every bit as popular with local families as it is with tourists. On the weekend, the hill's lookout tower and mirror maze are thronging with excited kids.

Getting There & Away

➡ **Metro** Malostranská metro station is in northern Malá Strana, about five minutes' walk from Malostranské náměstí.

➡ **Tram** Lines 12, 20 and 22 run along Újezd with stops at Hellichová and Malostranské náměstí.

➡ **Funicular** A funicular railway links Malá Strana with the summit of Petřín Hill.

TOP SIGHT
CHARLES BRIDGE

Strolling across Charles Bridge is everybody's favourite Prague activity. However, by 9am it can be a 500m-long fairground, with an army of tourists squeezing through a gauntlet of hawkers and buskers beneath the impassive gaze of the baroque statues that line the parapets – try to visit early or late. In the crush, don't forget to look at the bridge itself (the bridge towers have great views) and the grand vistas up and down the river.

History

In 1357 Charles IV commissioned Peter Parler (the architect of St Vitus Cathedral) to replace the 12th-century Judith Bridge, which had been washed away by floods in 1342. (You can see the only surviving arch of the Judith Bridge by taking a boat trip with Prague Venice, p33).

The new bridge was completed in 1390, and took Charles' name only in the 19th century – before that it was known simply as Kamenný most (Stone Bridge). Despite occasional flood damage, it withstood wheeled traffic for 500-odd years – thanks, legend says, to eggs mixed into the mortar (though recent investigations have disproved this myth) – until it was made pedestrian-only after WWII.

The Bridge Towers

Perched at the eastern end of Charles Bridge in Staré Město, the elegant late-14th-century **Old Town Bridge Tower** (Staroměstská mostecká věž; Map p332; ☎ 224 220 569; en.muzeumprahy. cz/prague-towers; Charles Bridge; adult/child 90/65Kč; ⏰ 10am-10pm Apr-Sep, to 8pm Mar & Oct, to 6pm Nov-Feb; 🚊 17, 18) was built not only as a fortification but also as a triumphal arch marking the entrance to the Old Town. Here, at the end of the Thirty Years' War, an invading

DON'T MISS

→ The view from the Old Town Bridge Tower
→ St John of Nepomuk Statue
→ Busking jazz musicians

PRACTICALITIES

→ Karlův most
→ Map p328
→ admission free
→ ⏰24hr
→ 🚊17, 18 to Karlovy lázně, 12, 20, 22 to Malostranské náměstí

BRADÁČ

At the Staré Město end of the bridge, look over the downstream parapet at the retaining wall on the right and you'll see a carved stone head known as Bradáč (Bearded Man). When the river level rose above this medieval marker, Praguers knew it was time to head for the hills. A blue line on the modern flood gauge nearby shows the level of the 2002 flood, no less than 2m above Bradáč!

Pickpocket gangs work the bridge day and night, so keep your purse or wallet safe.

Swedish army was finally repulsed by a band of students and Jewish ghetto residents. Like the bridge itself, the tower was designed by Peter Parler and incorporates many symbolic elements.

On the 1st floor there's a small exhibition and a video explaining the astronomical and astrological symbolism of Charles Bridge and the bridge tower, while the 2nd floor has a rather dull exhibit about Charles IV. The main justification for paying the admission fee, however, is the amazing view from the top of the tower.

There are actually two towers at the Malá Strana end of Charles Bridge. The lower one was originally part of the long-gone 12th-century Judith Bridge, while the taller one was built in the mid-15th century in imitation of the Staré Město tower. The taller **Malá Strana Bridge Tower** (Map p328; en.muzeumprahy.cz; Mostecká; adult/child 90/65Kč; ☉10am-10pm Apr-Sep, to 8pm Mar & Oct, to 6pm Nov-Feb; ⛟ 12, 20, 22) is open to the public and houses an exhibit on alchemists during the reign of Rudolf II, though like its Staré Město counterpart, the main attraction is the view from the top.

The Statues

The first monument erected on the bridge was the crucifix near the eastern end, in 1657. The first statue – the Jesuits' 1683 tribute to St John of Nepomuk – inspired other Catholic orders, and over the next 30 years a score more went up, like ecclesiastical billboards. New ones were added in the mid-19th century, and one (plus replacements for some lost to floods) in the 20th. As most of the statues were carved from soft sandstone, several weathered originals have been replaced with copies. Some originals are housed in the Casements at Vyšehrad (p174); others are in the Lapidárium (p164) in Holešovice.

The most famous figure is the monument to **St John of Nepomuk**. According to the legend on the base of the statue, Wenceslas IV had him trussed up in armour and thrown off the bridge in 1393 for refusing to divulge the queen's confessions (he was her priest), though the real reason had to do with the bitter conflict between church and state; the stars in his halo allegedly followed his corpse down the river. Tradition says that if you rub the bronze plaque, you will one day return to Prague. A bronze cross set in the parapet between statues 17 and 19 marks the point where he was thrown off.

Starting from the western (Malá Strana) end, with odd numbers on your left and even ones on your right, the statues that line the bridge are as follows:

→ **1 Sts Cosmas & Damian** (1709) Third-century physician brothers.

→ **2 St Wenceslas** (sv Václav; 1858) Patron saint of Bohemia.

→ **3 St Vitus** (sv Víta; 1714) Patron saint of Prague (and of dogs, dancers, actors and comedians).

→ **4 Sts John of Matha & Félix de Valois** (1714) The 12th-century French founders of the Trinitarian order, whose mission was the ransom of enslaved Christians (represented by a Tatar standing guard over a group of slaves).

→ **5 St Philip Benizi** (sv Benicius; 1714) Miracle worker and healer.

→ **6 St Adalbert** (sv Vojtěch; 1709; replica) Prague's first Czech bishop, canonised in the 10th century.

→ **7 St Cajetan** (1709) Italian founder of the Theatine order in the 15th century.

→ **8 The Vision of St Luitgard** (1710) Arguably the finest piece on the bridge, in which Christ appears to the blind saint and allows her to kiss his wounds.

→ **9 St Augustine** (1708; replica) Reformed hedonist, famous for his *Confessions*, theological fountainhead of the Reformation. Patron saint of brewers.

→ **10 St Nicholas of Tolentino** (1706; replica) Patron of Holy Souls.

→ **11 St Jude Thaddaeus** (1708) Apostle and patron saint of hopeless causes. Further on the right, beyond the railing, is a column with a statue of the eponymous hero of the 11th-century epic poem *Song of Roland* (Bruncvík).

→ **12 St Vincent Ferrer** (1712) A 14th-century Spanish priest, shown with St Procopius, Hussite warrior-priest.

→ **13 St Anthony of Padua** (1707) The 13th-century disciple of St Francis of Assisi.

→ **14 St Francis Seraphinus** (1855) Patron of the poor and abandoned.

→ **15 St John of Nepomuk** (1683) Bronze. Patron saint of Czechs.

→ **16 St Wenceslas as a boy** (c 1730) With his grandmother and guardian St Ludmilla, patroness of Bohemia.

→ **17 St Wenceslas** (1853) With St Sigismund, son of Charles IV, and St Norbert, 12th-century German founder of the Premonstratensian order.

→ **18 St Francis Borgia** (1710) A 16th-century Spanish priest.

→ **19 St John the Baptist** (1857) By Josef Max.

→ **20 St Christopher** (1857) Patron saint of travellers.

→ **21 Sts Cyril & Methodius** (1938) The newest statue. These two introduced Christianity and a written script (Cyrillic) to the Slavs in the 9th century.

→ **22 St Francis Xavier** (1711; replica) A 16th-century Spanish missionary celebrated for his work in the Orient.

→ **23 St Anne with Madonna & Child** (1707) The mother of the Virgin Mary.

→ **24 St Joseph** (1854) Husband of the Virgin Mary.

→ **25 Crucifix** (1657) Gilded bronze. Has an invocation in Hebrew saying 'holy, holy, holy Lord'; the stone figures date from 1861.

→ **26 Pietá** (1859) Mary holding the body of Christ following the crucifixion.

→ **27 Madonna with St Dominic** (1709; replica) Spanish founder of the Dominicans, with St Thomas Aquinas.

→ **28 Sts Barbara, Margaret & Elizabeth** (1707) St Barbara, 2nd-century patron saint of miners; St Margaret, 3rd- or 4th-century patron saint of expectant mothers; and St Elizabeth, a 13th-century Slovak princess who renounced the good life to serve the poor.

→ **29 Madonna with St Bernard** (1709; replica) Founder of the Cistercian order in the 12th century.

→ **30 St Ivo of Kermartin** (1711; replica) A 13th-century Breton, patron saint of lawyers and orphans.

SIGHTS

MALÁ STRANA SIGHTS

Prague Castle to Charles Bridge

CHARLES BRIDGE   BRIDGE
See p83.

NERUDOVA   STREET
Map p328 (🚋 12, 20, 22) Following the tourist crowds downhill from the castle via Ke Hradu, you will arrive at Nerudova, architecturally the most important street in Malá Strana. Most of its old Renaissance facades were 'baroquefied' in the 18th century. It's named after the Czech poet Jan Neruda (famous for his short stories, *Tales of Malá Strana*), who lived at the **House of the Two Suns** (dům U dvou slunců; Map p328; Nerudova 47) from 1845 to 1857.

The **House of the Golden Horseshoe** (dům U zlaté podkovy; Map p328; Nerudova 34) is named after the relief of St Wenceslas above the doorway – his horse was said to be shod with gold. From 1765 Josef of Bretfeld made his **Bretfeld Palace** (Map p328; Nerudova 33) a social hot spot, entertaining Mozart and Casanova. The baroque **Church of Our Lady of Unceasing Succour** (Kostel Panny Marie ustavičné pomoci; Map p328; Nerudova 24; 🚋 12, 20, 22) was a theatre from 1834 to 1837, and staged Czech plays during the Czech National Revival.

Most of the buildings bear house signs. Built in 1566, **St John of Nepomuk House** (Map p328; Nerudova 18) is adorned with the image of one of Bohemia's patron saints, while the **House at the Three Fiddles** (dům U tří housliček; Map p328; Nerudova 12), a Gothic building rebuilt in Renaissance style during the 17th century, once belonged to a family of violin makers.

MUSEUM MONTANELLI   GALLERY
Map p328 (📞257 531 220; www.muzeummontanelli.com; Nerudova 13; adult/child 80/40Kč; ⊗2-6pm Tue-Fri; 🚋12, 20, 22) Tourists, drawn in by an attractive cafe and bookshop, rub shoulders with connoisseurs of the Czech art world in this private gallery. Having rapidly become a focus for contemporary art in Prague, it provides a showcase for up-and-coming artists from Central and Eastern Europe, as well as staging exhibitions by more established international names.

TOP SIGHT
ST NICHOLAS CHURCH

Malá Strana is dominated by the huge green cupola of St Nicholas Church, one of Central Europe's finest baroque buildings. Begun by famed architects Kristof and Kilian Dientzenhofer, Anselmo Lurago finished it in 1755.

On the ceiling, Johann Kracker's 1770 *Apotheosis of St Nicholas* is Europe's largest fresco. In the first chapel on the left is a mural by Karel Škréta, which includes the church official who kept track of the artist as he worked; he is looking out through a window in the upper corner.

Mozart himself tickled the ivories on the 2500-pipe organ in 1787, and was honoured with a requiem Mass here (14 December, 1791). Take the stairs up to the **gallery** to see Škréta's gloomy 17th-century Passion Cycle paintings and the scratchings of bored 1820s tourists.

You can climb the church's **bell tower** (Map p328; http://en.muzeumprahy.cz/prague-towers; Malostranské náměstí; adult/child 90/65Kč; ⊗ 10am-10pm Apr-Sep, to 8pm Mar & Oct, to 6pm Nov-Feb; 🚋 12, 20, 22) via a separate entrance on the corner of Malostranské náměstí and Mostecká. During the communist era, the tower was used to spy on the nearby American embassy – on the way up you can still see a small, white, cast-iron urinal that was installed for the use of the watchers.

DON'T MISS
➡ Ceiling frescoes
➡ 2500-pipe organ
➡ Gallery
➡ Bell tower

PRACTICALITIES
➡ Kostel sv Mikuláše
➡ Map p328
➡ 📞257 534 215
➡ www.stnicholas.cz
➡ Malostranské náměstí 38
➡ adult/child 70/50Kč
➡ ⊗9am-5pm Mar-Oct, to 4pm Nov-Feb
➡ 🚋12, 20, 22

TOP SIGHT
JOHN LENNON WALL

After his murder on 8 December 1980, John Lennon became a pacifist hero for many young Czechs. An image of Lennon was painted on a wall in a secluded square opposite the French Embassy (there is a niche on the wall that looks like a tombstone), along with political graffiti and Beatles lyrics. Despite repeated coats of whitewash, the secret police never managed to keep it clean for long, and the Lennon Wall became a political focus for Prague youth (most Western pop music was banned by the communists, and some Czech musicians were even jailed for playing it).

Post-1989 weathering and lightweight graffiti ate away at the political messages and images, until little remained of Lennon but his eyes, but visiting tourists began making their own contributions. The wall is the property of the Knights of Malta, and they have repainted it several times, but it soon gets covered with more Lennon images, peace messages and inconsequential tourist graffiti. In recent years the Knights have bowed to the inevitable and now don't bother to whitewash it any more.

DON'T MISS

➡ Trying to spot the image of Lennon among the myriad graffiti

PRACTICALITIES

➡ Map p328
➡ Velkopřevorské náměstí
➡ 🚋12, 20, 22

MALOSTRANSKÉ NÁMĚSTÍ SQUARE

Map p328 (🚋12, 20, 22) Malostranské náměstí, Malá Strana's main square, is divided into an upper and lower part by St Nicholas Church (p86), the district's most distinctive landmark. The square has been the hub of Malá Strana since the 10th century, though it lost some of its character when Karmelitská street was widened early in the 20th century, and a little more when Prague's first Starbucks opened here in 2008.

Today, it's a mixture of official buildings and touristy restaurants, with a tram line through the middle of the lower square. The nightclub and bar at No 21, Malostranská beseda (p93), was once the old town hall. It was here in 1575 that non-Catholic nobles wrote the so-called České Konfese (Czech Confession), a demand for religious tolerance addressed to the Habsburg emperor that was eventually passed into Czech law in 1609. On 22 May 1618, Czech nobles gathered at the **Smiřický Palace** (Map p328; Malostranské náměstí 18; 🚋12, 20, 22) to plot a rebellion against the Habsburg rulers – the next day they flung two Habsburg councillors out of a window in Prague Castle.

KAREL ZEMAN MUSEUM MUSEUM

Map p328 (Museum of Film Special Effects; ☎724 341 091; www.muzeumkarlazemana.cz; Saský dvůr, Saská 3; adult/child 200/140Kč; ◷10am-7pm, last admission 6pm; 🚋12, 20, 22) Bohemia-born director Karel Zeman (1910–89) was a pioneer of movie special effects whose work is little known outside the Czech Republic. This fascinating museum reveals the tricks and techniques he perfected, and allows visitors a bit of hands-on interaction – you can film yourself on your smartphone against painted backgrounds and 3D models.

◉ Northern Malá Strana

PALACE GARDENS BENEATH PRAGUE CASTLE GARDENS

Map p328 (Palácové zahrady pod Pražským hradem; ☎257 010 401; www.palacove-zahrady.cz; Valdštejnská 12-14; adult/child 80/50Kč; ◷10am-9pm Jun & Jul, to 8pm Aug, to 7pm May & Sep, to 6pm Apr & Oct; MMalostranská, 🚋12, 20, 22) The beautiful, terraced gardens on the steep southern slopes below the castle date from the 17th and 18th centuries, when they were created for the owners of the adjoining palaces. They were restored in the 1990s and contain a Renaissance loggia with frescoes of Pompeii and a baroque portal with sundial that cleverly catches the sunlight reflected off the water in a Triton fountain.

There are two entrances: one on Valdštejnská next to the Palffy Palace Restaurant, and one at the top of the hill in the Garden on the Ramparts (p71) at Prague Castle.

WALLENSTEIN GARDEN
GARDENS

Map p328 (Valdštejnská zahrada; Letenská 10; ⊙7.30am-6pm Mon-Fri, 10am-6pm Sat & Sun Mar-Oct, to 7pm daily Jun-Sep; MMalostranská, ⊞12, 20, 22) FREE This huge, baroque garden is an oasis of peace amid the bustle of Malá Strana's streets. Created for Duke Albrecht of Wallenstein in the 17th century, its finest feature is the huge loggia decorated with scenes from the Trojan War, flanked to one side by an enormous fake stalactite grotto – see how many hidden animals and grotesque faces you can spot.

The bronze statues of Greek gods lining the avenue opposite the loggia are copies – the originals were carted away by marauding Swedes in 1648 and now stand outside the royal palace of Drottningholm near Stockholm. At the eastern end of the garden is an ornamental pond, home to some seriously large carp, and the **Wallenstein Riding School** (Valdštejnská jízdárna; Map p328; ⊉257 073 136; www.ngprague.cz; Valdštejnská 3; adult/child 150/80Kč; ⊙10am-6pm Tue-Sun; MMalostranská), which hosts changing exhibitions of modern art. Enter the garden on Letenská (beside Malostranská metro station) or via the Wallenstein Palace.

WALLENSTEIN PALACE
PALACE

Map p328 (Valdštejnský palác; ⊉257 075 707; Valdštejnské náměstí 4; ⊙10am-4pm first Sat & Sun of the month; MMalostranská, ⊞12, 20, 22) FREE Valdštejnské náměstí, a small square northeast of Malostranské náměstí, is dominated by the monumental 1630 palace of Albrecht of Wallenstein, general of the Habsburg armies, who financed its construction with properties confiscated from Protestant nobles he defeated at the Battle of Bílá Hora in 1620. It now houses the Senate of the Czech Republic, with limited public access.

Enter via the Senate Information Centre in the first courtyard – the self-guided tour takes in the more spectacularly decorated parts of the palace. The ceiling fresco in the Baroque Hall shows Wallenstein as a warrior at the reins of a chariot, while the unusual oval Audience Hall has a fresco of Vulcan at work in his forge.

FRANZ KAFKA MUSEUM
MUSEUM

Map p328 (Muzeum Franzy Kafky; ⊉257 535 373; www.kafkamuseum.cz; Cihelná 2b; adult/child 200/120Kč; ⊙10am-6pm; MMalostranská, ⊞12, 20, 22) This much-hyped exhibition on the life and work of Prague's most famous literary son, entitled 'City of K', explores the intimate relationship between the writer and the city that shaped him, through the use of original letters, photographs, quotations, period newspapers and publications, and video and sound installations.

PROUDY (DAVID ČERNÝ SCULPTURE)
MONUMENT

Map p328 (Streams; Hergetova Cihelná; MMalostranská) Sounds of laughter and clicking cameras greet *Proudy* (Streams; 2004) by David Černý, a saucy animatronic sculpture of two guys pissing in a puddle shaped like the Czech Republic. The microchip-controlled sculptures are writing out famous quotations from Czech literature with their 'pee'.

⊙ Southern Malá Strana

KAMPA
PARK

Map p328 (⊞ 12, 20, 22) Kampa – an 'island' bounded by the Vltava and Čertovka (the Devil's Stream) – is the most peaceful and picturesque part of Malá Strana. It was once farmland (the name Kampa comes from *campus*, Latin for 'field'), but in the 13th century Prague's first mill, the **Sovovský mlýn** (now Kampa Museum), was built here, and other mills followed.

The north part of the island was settled in the 16th century after being raised above flood level. (In 1939 the river was so low that it was again joined to the mainland, and coins and jewellery were found in the dry channel.) The houses are clustered around a picturesque little square called **Na Kampě**; at its northern end, at about waist height on the wall to the left of the little gallery under the stairs leading up to Charles Bridge, is a small **memorial plaque** that reads *Výska vody 4.září 1890* (height of waters, 4 September 1890), marking the level reached by the floodwaters of 1890. Directly over it – above head height – is another marking the height of the 2002 floods.

The area where the Čertovka passes under Charles Bridge is sometimes called **Prague's Venice** – the channel is often crowded with dinky tour boats.

KAMPA MUSEUM
GALLERY

Map p328 (Muzeum Kampa; ☑257 286 147; www.museumkampa.cz; U Sovových mlýnů 2; adult/concession 220/110Kč; ☺10am-6pm; ☐12, 20, 22) Housed in a renovated mill building, this gallery is devoted to 20th-century and contemporary art from Central Europe. The highlights of the permanent exhibition are extensive collections of bronzes by Cubist sculptor Otto Gutfreund and paintings by František Kupka, a pioneer of abstract art.

MALTESE SQUARE
SQUARE

Map p328 (Maltézské náměstí; ☐12, 20, 22) References to the Knights of Malta around Malá Strana hark back to 1169, when that military order established a monastery in the Church of Our Lady Beneath the Chain on this square. Disbanded by the communists, the Knights have regained much property under post-1989 restitution laws, including the John Lennon Wall.

CZECH MUSEUM OF MUSIC
MUSEUM

Map p328 (České muzeum hudby; ☑257 257 777; www.nm.cz; Karmelitská 2/4; adult/concession 120/60Kč; ☺10am-6pm Wed-Mon; ☐12, 20, 22) A 17th-century baroque monastery building with an impressive central atrium makes a beautiful setting for Prague's Museum of Music. The museum's permanent exhibition, entitled 'Man-Instrument-Music', explores the relationship between human beings and musical instruments through the ages, and showcases an incredible collection of violins, guitars, lutes, trumpets, flutes and harmonicas.

VRTBOV GARDEN
GARDENS

Map p328 (Vrtbovská zahrada; ☑257 531 480; www.vrtbovska.cz; Karmelitská 25; adult/concession 62/52Kč; ☺10am-6pm Apr-Oct; ☐12, 20, 22) This 'secret garden', hidden along an alley at the corner of Tržiště and Karmelitská, was built in 1720 for the Earl of Vrtba, the senior chancellor of Prague Castle. It's a formal baroque garden, climbing steeply up the hillside to a terrace graced with baroque statues of Roman mythological figures by Matthias Braun – see if you can spot Vulcan, Diana and Mars.

KGB MUSEUM
MUSEUM

Map p328 (☑272 048 047; kgbmuzeum.com; Vlašská 13; admission 300Kč; ☺9am-6pm; ☐12, 20, 22) The enthusiastic Russian collector of KGB memorabilia who established this small

MALÁ STRANA SIGHTS

TOP SIGHT
MUSEUM OF THE INFANT JESUS

The **Church of Our Lady Victorious** (kostel Panny Marie Vítězné), built in 1613, has on its central altar a 47cm-tall waxwork figure of the baby Jesus, brought from Spain in 1628. Known as the Infant Jesus of Prague (Pražské Jezulátko), it is said to have protected Prague from the plague and from the destruction of the Thirty Years' War. An 18th-century German prior, ES Stephano, wrote about the miracles, kicking off what became a worldwide cult; today the statue is visited by a steady stream of pilgrims, especially from Italy, Spain and Latin America. It was traditional to dress the figure in beautiful robes, and over the years various benefactors donated richly embroidered dresses. Today the Infant's wardrobe consists of more than 70 costumes; these are changed regularly in accordance with a religious calendar.

At the back of the church is the **museum**, displaying a selection of the frocks used to dress the Infant; shops in the street nearby sell copies of the wax figure. Looking at all this, you can't help thinking about the Second Commandment ('Thou shalt not make unto thee any graven image...') and the objectives of the Reformation. Jan Hus must be spinning in his grave.

DON'T MISS
➡ Wax figure of the Infant Jesus of Prague
➡ Clothing worn by the Infant Jesus
➡ Nearby souvenir shops

PRACTICALITIES
➡ Muzeum Pražského Jezulátka
➡ Map p328
➡ ☑257 533 646
➡ www.pragjesu.info
➡ Karmelitská 9
➡ ☺museum 9.30am-5.30pm Mon-Sat & 1-6pm Sun
➡ ☐12, 20, 22

museum will insist on showing you around his treasure trove of spy cameras, concealed pistols, weapons (including an original garotte, known as 'Stalin's scarf') and sinister electrical 'interrogation equipment'. There are also rare photographs of Prague taken in 1968 by a KGB officer, with ordinary citizens strangely absent from the street scenes.

QUO VADIS (DAVID ČERNÝ SCULPTURE)   MONUMENT

Map p328 (Where Are You Going; Vlašská 19; 🚊12, 20, 22) This golden Trabant car on four legs is a David Černý tribute to 4000 East Germans who occupied the garden of the then–West German embassy in 1989, before being granted political asylum and leaving their Trabants behind. You can see the sculpture through the fence behind the German embassy. Head uphill along Vlašská, turn left into a park, and left again to find it.

CHILDREN'S ISLAND   PARK

(Dětský ostrov; access from Nábřežní; ⊘24hr; Ⓜ Anděl) FREE Prague's smallest island offers a respite from the hustle and bustle of the city, with a selection of swings, slides, climbing frames and sandpits to keep the kids busy, as well as a rope swing, skate ramp, mini football pitch, netball court, and lots of open space for older siblings to run wild.

◉ Petřín

This 318m-high hill is one of Prague's largest green spaces. It's great for quiet walks and fine views over the 'City of a Hundred Spires'. There were once vineyards here, and a quarry that provided the stone for most of Prague's Romanesque and Gothic buildings.

Petřín (Map p328) is easily accessible on foot from Strahov Monastery, or you can ride the funicular railway from Újezd up to the top. You can also get off two-thirds of the way up at Nebozízek.

In the peaceful **Kinský Garden** (Kinského zahrada), on the southern side of Petřín, is the 18th-century wooden **Church of St Michael** (Kostel sv Michala), transferred here, log by log, from the village of Medveďov in Ukraine. Such structures are rare in Bohemia, though still common in Ukraine and northeastern Slovakia.

PETŘÍN FUNICULAR RAILWAY   RAILWAY

Map p328 (Lanová draha na Petřín; 🖉800 191 817; www.dpp.cz; Újezd; adult/child 24/12Kč; ⊘9am-11.30pm Apr-Oct, 9am-11.20pm Nov-Mar; 🚊6, 9, 12, 20, 22 to Újezd) First opened in 1891, Prague's funicular railway now uses modern coaches that trundle back and forth on 510m of track, saving visitors a climb up Petřín. It runs every 10 minutes (every 15 minutes November to March) from Újezd to the **Petřín Lookout Tower** (Petřínská Rozhledna; Map p328; 🖉257 320 112; www.petrinska-Rozhledna.cz; Petřínské sady; adult/child 120/65Kč; ⊘10am-10pm Apr-Sep, to 8pm Mar & Oct, to 6pm Nov-Feb; 🚠Funicular), with a stop at Nebozízek. A full-price ticket or day-pass is required to ride.

MIRROR MAZE   HISTORIC BUILDING

Map p328 (Zrcadlové bludiště; www.petrinska-rozhledna.cz; Petřínské sady; adult/child 75/55Kč; ⊘10am-10pm Apr-Sep, 10am-8pm Mar & Oct, 10am-6pm Nov-Feb; 🚠Funicular) Below the Petřín Lookout Tower is the Mirror Maze, built for the 1891 Prague Exposition. As well as the maze of distorting mirrors, which was based on the Prater in Vienna, there's a diorama of the 1648 battle between Praguers and Swedes on Charles Bridge.

Opposite is the **Church of St Lawrence** (Kostel sv Vavřince), which contains a fresco depicting the founding of the church in 991.

MUSAION   MUSEUM

Map p328 (Ethnographical Museum; 🖉257 214 806; Kinského zahrada 98; adult/child 70/40Kč; ⊘10am-6pm Tue-Sun; 🚊6, 9, 12, 20) This renovated summer palace houses the National Museum's ethnographic collection, with exhibits covering traditional Czech folk culture and art, including music, costume, farming methods and handicrafts. There are regular folk concerts and workshops demonstrating traditional crafts such as blacksmithing and woodcarving; in the summer months there's a garden cafe.

MEMORIAL TO THE VICTIMS OF COMMUNISM   MONUMENT

Map p328 (Památník obětem komunismu; cnr Újezd & Vítězná; 🚊6, 9, 12, 20, 22) This striking sculptural group consists of several ragged human figures (controversially, all are male) in progressive stages of disintegration, descending a staggered slope. A bronze strip inlaid into the ground in front of them records the terrible human toll of the communist era – 205,486 arrested; 170,938 driven into exile; 248 executed; 4500 died in prison; and 327 shot while trying to escape across the border.

✕ EATING

You'll be spoilt for choice looking for somewhere to eat in Malá Strana. Many of the best restaurants take advantage of a riverside location, or are perched on a hillside with a view over the city.

CAFÉ LOUNGE
CAFE €

Map p328 (☑257 404 020; www.cafe-lounge.cz; Plaská 8; mains 120-390Kč; ⊘7.30am-10pm Mon-Fri, 9am-10pm Sat, 9am-5pm Sun; ⊖🐾; ⊞6, 9, 12, 20, 22) Cosy and welcoming, Café Lounge sports an art deco atmosphere, superb coffee, exquisite pastries and an extensive wine list. The all-day cafe menu offers freshly made salads and corn-bread sandwiches, while lunch and dinner extends to dishes such as beef cheeks braised in red wine, or roast pike-perch with caraway seeds. Great breakfasts too (served until 11am weekdays, noon on weekends).

CUKRKÁVALIMONÁDA
EUROPEAN €

Map p328 (☑257 225 396; www.cukrkavalimona-da.com; Lázeňská 7; mains 100-200Kč; ⊘9am-7pm; ⊞12, 20, 22) A cute little cafe-cum-restaurant that combines minimalist modern styling with Renaissance-era painted timber roof-beams, CKL offers fresh, home-made pastas, frittatas, ciabattas, salads and pancakes (sweet and savoury) by day and a slightly more sophisticated bistro menu in the early evening. There's also a good breakfast menu offering ham and eggs, croissants and yoghurt, and the hot chocolate is to die for.

Since you ask, the name means 'sugar, coffee, lemonade' – the phrase is the Czech equivalent of 'eeny-meeny-miny-moe'.

★ICHNUSA BOTEGA BISTRO
ITALIAN €€

Map p328 (☑605 375 012; www.ichnusaboteg-abistro.cz; Plaská 5; mains 250-400Kč; ⊘11am-midnight Mon-Fri, 4pm-midnight Sat; ⊖🐾; ⊞6, 9, 12, 20, 22) The 'Ichnusa' refers to the ancient name for Sardinia, which is where owner Antonella Pranteddu sources all of the meats, cheeses and wines he serves in this inviting, family-run bistro. Let the server run through the day's starters and mains. The grilled tuna is Prague's best. Reservations essential.

U MALÉ VELRYBY
SEAFOOD, MEDITERRANEAN €€

Map p328 (☑ 257 214 703; www.umalevelryby.cz; Maltézské náměstí 15; mains 360-410Kč; ⊘10am-10pm; ⊖; ⊞12, 20, 22) 'The Little Whale' is a tiny place – only eight tables – run by chef-proprietor Jason from Cork, Ireland, who gets fresh seafood flown in daily from French markets. The seafood chowder is tasty and filling, the braised pork ribs with cauliflower and sesame purée are tender, and the tapas exceedingly moreish. Make sure Jason himself is in the kitchen to be sure of a top-quality dinner.

CAFÉ DE PARIS
FRENCH €€

Map p328 (☑603 160 718; www.cafedeparis.cz; Maltézské náměstí 4; mains 245-425Kč; ⊘noon-midnight; ⊞12, 20, 22) A little corner of France tucked away on a quiet square, the Café de Paris is straightforward and unpretentious. So is the menu – onion soup or foie gras terrine to start, followed by entrecôte steak with chips, salad and a choice of sauces (they're very proud of the Café de Paris sauce, made to a 75-year-old recipe). There are also one or two daily specials, including a vegetarian alternative.

BAR BAR
CZECH, EUROPEAN €€

Map p328 (☑ 257 312 246; www.bar-bar.cz; Všehrdova 17; mains 170-320Kč; ⊘noon-midnight Mon-Sat, noon-6pm Sun; ☑; ⊞6, 9, 12, 20, 22) This friendly cellar bar is frequented more by locals than tourists, but the healthy-eating menu is chalked on a blackboard in both Czech and English. It ranges from chicken breast with honey, lemon and chilli to grilled salmon with creamed spinach, with a couple of good veggie alternatives. The weekday lunch menu offers soup and a main course for 120Kč.

CAFÉ SAVOY
EUROPEAN €€

Map p328 (☑ 257 311 562; cafesavoy.ambi.cz; Vítězná 5; mains 125-500Kč; ⊘8am-10.30pm Mon-Fri, 9am-10.30pm Sat & Sun; 🐾; ⊞6, 9, 12, 20, 22) The Savoy is a beautifully restored belle époque cafe, with haughty black-and-white-suited waiting staff and a Viennese-style menu of hearty soups, salads, roast meats and schnitzels. There's also a good breakfast menu with plenty of healthy choices, including a 'Full English', an American breakfast, and eggs cooked half-a-dozen ways.

NOI
THAI €€

Map p328 (☑257 311 411; www.noirestaurant. cz; Újezd 19; mains 180-290Kč; ⊘11am-1am; 🐾; ⊞12, 20, 22) A restaurant that feels a bit like a club, Noi is super stylish but with a chilled-out atmosphere and oriental design. The decor is based around lotus blossoms,

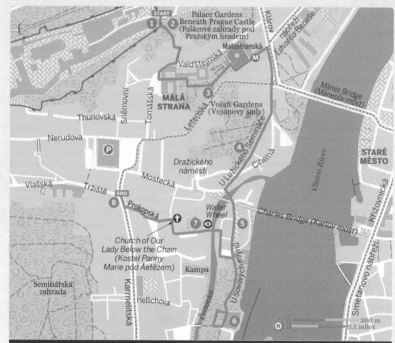

Neighbourhood Walk
Malá Strana Gardens

START PRAGUE CASTLE
END PETŘÍN
LENGTH 2.5KM; 1½ HOURS

Except for Vojan, the gardens are open April to October; in winter the walk is still worth doing, beginning from Malostranská metro.

From the ① **lookout** at the eastern entrance to Prague Castle, go into the Garden on the Ramparts and find the entrance to the ② **Palace Gardens beneath Prague Castle** (p87). Exit the Palace Gardens on Valdštejnská and turn right, then left into the Wallenstein Palace and through the courtyard to the ③ **Wallenstein Garden** (p88). Head for the northeastern corner and leave through the gate beside Malostranská metro station. Turn right on Klárov and continue along U Lužického Semináře. A gate on the right leads to the ④ **Vojan Gardens**, a peaceful corner where local folk sit in the sun on the park benches.

Continue along U Lužického Semináře and bear left across the little bridge over the Čertovka. Pass under Charles Bridge and through the picturesque square of ⑤ **Na Kampě** into the leafy riverside park known as Kampa, one of the city's favourite chill-out zones and home to the modern art collections of the ⑥ **Kampa Museum** (p89).

Retrace your steps and bear left along Hroznová, which leads to a bridge over the Čertovka beside a water wheel. The bridge is covered in padlocks placed there by couples as a sign of enduring love.

The bridge leads to a tiny cobbled square with the ⑦ **John Lennon Wall** (p87) on one side and the baroque palace that houses the French embassy on the other. The far end of the square curves right, past the severe Gothic towers of the Church of Our Lady Below the Chain. Turn left opposite the church and bear right along Prokopská; cross busy Karmelitská and turn right.

Just past the bar called U Malého Glena is an alley on your left that leads to the ⑧ **Vrtbov Garden** (p89), one of Malá Strana's least visited, but most beautiful, gardens.

lanterns and soft lighting, and the menu follows the Asian theme with competent Thai dishes such as chicken in red curry, and pad thai noodles, which – unusually for a Prague restaurant – have a hefty chilli kick.

★ELEGANTES CZECH, EUROPEAN €€€

Map p328 (☑266 112 280; www.elegantes.cz; Letenská 12; mains 490-990Kč; ☺noon-10.30pm; ☑; ☑12, 20, 22) Hidden away in the historic Augustine Hotel (check out the ceiling fresco in the bar), this sophisticated yet relaxed restaurant is well worth seeking out. The menu ranges from down-to-earth but delicious dishes such as veal shank braised in the hotel's own St Thomas beer, to inventive dishes built around Czech game, such as wild boar ragout with chestnut pappardelle.

TERASA U ZLATÉ STUDNĚ EUROPEAN, ASIAN €€€

Map p328 (☑ 257 533 322; www.terasauzlatestudne.cz; U Zlaté Studně 4; mains 750-1150Kč; ☺noon-11pm; Ⓜ Malostranská) Perched atop a Renaissance mansion within a champagne cork's pop of the castle, 'At the Golden Well' combines some of Prague's finest dining with one of the finest settings in the city. Weather will dictate whether you sit in the plush dining room or on the outdoor terrace – both command a stunning panorama across the red-tiled rooftops of Malá Strana.

The kitchen, which has French, Mediterranean and Asian influences, conjures up dishes such as fennel and saffron velouté with mixed fish and shellfish, to the signature dish of Argentinian steak with foie gras and truffles.

U MODRÉ KACHNIČKY CZECH €€€

Map p328 (☑257 320 308; www.umodrekachnicky.cz; Nebovidská 6; mains 450-600Kč; ☺noon-4pm & 6.30pm-midnight; ☑; ☑12, 20, 22) A plush and chintzy 1930s-style hunting lodge hidden away on a quiet side street, 'At the Blue Duckling' is a pleasantly old-fashioned place with quiet, candlelit nooks perfect for a romantic dinner. The menu is heavy on traditional Bohemian duck and game dishes, such as roast duck with *slivovice* (plum brandy), plum sauce and potato pancakes.

HERGETOVA CIHELNA MEDITERRANEAN, ASIAN €€€

Map p328 (☑296 826 103; www.kampagroup.com; Cihelná 2b; mains 300-600Kč; ☺11.30am-1am; ☑☑; Ⓜ Malostranská) Housed in a converted 18th-century *cihelná* (brickworks), this place enjoys one of Prague's hottest locations, with a riverside terrace offering sweeping views of Charles Bridge and the Old Town waterfront. The menu is as sweeping as the view, ranging from seafood and upmarket burgers to Asian dishes such as Thai beef salad and chicken stir fry. There's also a decent kids' menu and play area.

🍷 DRINKING & NIGHTLIFE

Malá Strana is the place to go for pavement table people-watching, with lots of cafes and bars spilling out onto the streets. Places here range from cute teahouses and cafes to traditional cellar-pubs and funky bars.

MLÝNSKÁ KAVÁRNA BAR

Map p328 (☑257 313 222; Všehrdova 14; ☺noon-midnight; ☑; ☑6, 9, 12, 20, 22) This cafe-bar in Kampa Park has existed in various guises since the communist era, and you might still hear it called Tato Kejkej, its previous incarnation, or just Mlýn (the mill). A wooden footbridge leads from Kampa to the smoky, dimly lit interior which is peopled with local artists, writers and politicians.

KLUB ÚJEZD BAR

Map p328 (☑251 510 873; www.klubujezd.cz; Újezd 18; ☺2pm-4am; ☑6, 9, 12, 20, 22) Klub Újezd is one of Prague's many 'alternative' bars, spread over three floors (DJs in the cellar, and a cafe upstairs) and filled with a fascinating collection of original art and weird wrought-iron sculptures. Clamber onto a two-tonne bar stool in the agreeably grungy street-level bar, and sip on a beer beneath a scaly, fire-breathing sea-monster.

MALOSTRANSKÁ BESEDA BAR, CLUB

Map p328 (☑257 409 123; www.malostranska-beseda.cz; Malostranské náměstí 21; shows 120-250Kč; ☺bar 4pm-1am, box office 5-9pm Mon-Sat, to 8pm Sun; ☑12, 20, 22) Malá Strana's four-storey pleasure palace reopened in 2010 after a five-year reconstruction. The fabled music club on the 2nd floor is better than ever, with a lively roster of cabaret acts, jazz and old Czech rockers. There's also an art gallery on the top floor and a big beer hall in the basement, with a bar and restaurant on the ground floor.

MALÁ STRANA DRINKING & NIGHTLIFE

MALÁ STRANA SHOPPING

U MALÉHO GLENA
BAR, JAZZ

Map p328 (☑257 531 717; www.malyglen.cz; Karmelitská 23; ⊙10am-2am, to 3am Fri & Sat, music from 8.30pm; ☎; 🚋12, 20, 22) 'Little Glen's' is a lively American-owned bar and restaurant where hard-swinging local jazz or blues bands play every night in the cramped and steamy stone-vaulted cellar. There are Sunday-night jam sessions where amateurs are welcome (as long as you're good!). It's a small venue, so get here early if you want to see as well as hear the band.

KAFÍČKO
CAFE

Map p328 (☑724 151 795; Míšeňská 10; ⊙10am-10pm; 🚼; 🚋12, 20, 22) This little cafe is an unexpected setting for some of Prague's best tea and coffee. Choose from a wide range of roasted beans from all over the world, and have them freshly ground into espresso, cappuccino or latte (40Kč to 55Kč).

U ZELENÉHO ČAJE
CAFE

Map p328 (☑257 530 027; www.uzelenehocaje.cz; Nerudova 19; ⊙11am-8pm; 🚋12, 20, 22) 'At the Green Tea' is a charming little olde-worlde teahouse on the way up to the castle. The menu offers a wide range of teas (70Kč to 95Kč a pot) from all over the world, ranging from classic green and black teas from China and India to fruit-flavoured teas and herbal infusions, as well as tempting cakes and tasty sandwiches.

BLUE LIGHT
COCKTAIL BAR

Map p328 (☑257 533 126; www.bluelightbar.cz; Josefská 1; ⊙6pm-3am; 🚋12, 20, 22) The Blue Light is a dark and atmospheric hangout, as popular with locals as with tourists, where you can sip a caipirinha or cranberry colada as you cast an eye over the vintage jazz posters, records, old photographs and decades-worth of scratched graffiti that adorn the walls. The background jazz is recorded rather than live, and never overpowers your conversation. Often heaving on weekend nights.

HOSTINEC U KOCOURA
PUB

Map p328 (☑257 530 107; Nerudova 2; 🚋12, 20, 22) 'The Tomcat' is a long-established traditional pub, still enjoying its reputation as a former favourite of the late president Havel, and still managing to pull in a mostly Czech crowd despite being in the heart of touristville (maybe it's the ever-present pall of cigarette smoke). It has relatively inexpensive beer for this part of town – 35Kč for 0.5L of draught Pilsner Urquell.

🔒 SHOPPING

SHAKESPEARE & SONS
BOOKS

Map p328 (☑257 531 894; www.shakes.cz; U Lužického semináře 10; ⊙11am-9pm; 🚋12, 20, 22) Though its shelves groan with a formidable range of literature in English, French and German, this is more than just a bookshop (with Prague's best range of titles on east European history) – it's a congenial literary hangout with knowledgeable staff, occasional author events, and a cool downstairs space for sitting and reading.

MARIONETY TRUHLÁŘ
CRAFT

Map p328 (☑606 924 392; www.marionety.com; U Lužického semináře 5; ⊙10am-7pm; 🚋12, 20, 22) On a back street beneath the western end of Charles Bridge, this palace of puppetry stocks traditional marionettes from more than 40 workshops around the Czech Republic, as well as offering DIY puppet kits, courses on puppet-making, and the chance to order a custom-made marionette in your own (or anyone else's) likeness.

ARTĚL
GLASS, INTERIOR DESIGN

Map p328 (www.artelglass.com; U Lužickeho semináře 7; ⊙10am-7pm; 🚋12, 20, 22) Traditional Bohemian glass-making meets modern design in this shop founded by US designer Karen Feldman. In addition to hand-blown designer crystal, you'll find a range of vintage and modern items of Czech design.

VETEŠNICTVI
ANTIQUES

Map p328 (☑257 530 624; Vítězná 16; ⊙10am-5pm Mon-Fri, to noon Sat; 🚋6, 9, 12, 20, 22) This is an Aladdin's cave of secondhand goods, bric-a-brac and junk with, in all likelihood, some genuine antiques for those who know what they're looking for. There's affordable stuff for all, from communist-era lapel pins, medals, postcards, old beer mugs and toys to crystal, shot glasses, porcelain, china, pipes and spa cups.

PAVLA & OLGA
FASHION

Map p328 (☑728 939 872; Tržiště 3; ⊙2-6pm Mon-Fri; 🚋12, 20, 22) Sisters Pavla and Olga Michalková originally worked in the film and TV industry before setting up their own fashion label, creating a unique collection of quirky and cute hats, clothes and accessories. Past customers have included Czech supermodel Tereza Maxová, Britpop band Blur and photographer Helmut Newton.

Staré Město

OLD TOWN SQUARE & AROUND | JOSEFOV | ALONG THE ROYAL WAY | SOUTHWESTERN STARÉ MĚSTO

Neighbourhood Top Five

1 Tour the half-dozen monuments that comprise the **Prague Jewish Museum** (p97), a moving memorial to the Czech capital's once-thriving Jewish community.

2 Check out Prague's **Municipal House** (p108) – a tour de force of art nouveau extravagance.

3 Join the crowds in the Old Town Square to witness the **Astronomical Clock** (p100) do its thing.

4 Admire the skill of master craftspeople at the **Museum of Decorative Arts** (p102).

5 **Shop** (p117) for art, antiques and designer fashion in the atmospheric Staré Město backstreets.

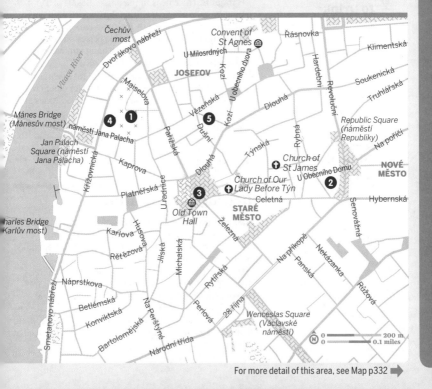

For more detail of this area, see Map p332 ➡

Lonely Planet's Top Tip

Get away from the Old Town Square and Karlova! Huge crowds throng the square and the narrow street that links it to Charles Bridge, but just a few blocks away – try wandering along Anenská – you can find yourself exploring back-streets almost on your own.

✖ Best Places to Eat

➡ Mistral Café (p111)

➡ Lokál (p111)

➡ Kalina (p113)

➡ Indian Jewel (p113)

➡ Chagall's (p114)

For reviews, see p111. ➡

🍷 Best Places to Drink

➡ Prague Beer Museum (p114)

➡ Hemingway Bar (p114)

➡ Krásný ztráty (p114)

➡ U Tří růží (p114)

➡ Čili Bar (p115)

For reviews, see p114. ➡

◉ Best Museums

➡ Prague Jewish Museum (p97)

➡ Museum of Decorative Arts (p102)

➡ Charles Bridge Museum (p109)

➡ Gastronomy Museum (p107)

For reviews, see p103. ➡

Explore: Staré Město

If the labyrinth of narrow streets around the Old Town Square can be said to have a 'main drag', it's the so-called Royal Way, the ancient coronation route to Prague Castle, running from the Powder Gate along Celetná to the Old Town Square and Little Square (Malé náměstí), then along Karlova and across Charles Bridge.

To the north of the Old Town Square, half-a-dozen historic synagogues, a town hall and the Old Jewish Cemetery are all that survive of the once-thriving Jewish quarter of Josefov – the slice of Staré Město bounded by Kaprova, Dlouhá and Kozí. Most of the district's buildings were demolished around the turn of the 20th century, when massive redevelopment saw the old slums replaced with expensive new apartments.

To the south, the meandering lanes and passageways between Karlova and Národní třída are Prague's best territory for aimless wandering. When the crowds thin out late in the day, this area can cast such a spell that it's quite a surprise to emerge from its peaceful backstreets into the bustle of the 21st century.

Local Life

➡**Hangouts** The clue is in the name: Lokál (p111), a modern take on the traditional *pivnice* (small beer hall), has proved a hit with Praguers looking for good Czech food and beer at reasonable prices. Meanwhile, students from Charles University hang out over coffee and magazines at Krásný ztráty (p114).

➡**Clubs** Students flock to Vagon (p116) for live music from up-and-coming local bands, while an older crowd prefers the laid-back atmosphere and chilled tunes at Duende (p115).

➡**Shopping** Staré Město is where Prague's fashionistas come to track down the hottest threads among the dozens of designer boutiques that proliferate in the streets around Dlouhá, Dušní and Karolíny Světlé.

Getting There & Away

➡**Metro** Staroměstská station is a few minutes' walk northwest of the Old Town Square, Můstek station is five minutes' walk to the south, and Náměstí Republiky is five minutes to the east.

➡**Tram** No trams run close to the Old Town Square. Trams 17 and 18 run along the western edge of Staré Město near the river, while lines 5, 8 and 24 stop at Republic Square (náměstí Republiky), across the street from the Municipal House (Obecní dům). Trams 6, 9, 18, 21 and 22 run along Národní třída on the southern edge of Staré Město.

PRAGUE JEWISH MUSEUM

In one of the most grotesquely ironic acts of WWII, the Nazis took over the management of Prague's Jewish Museum – established in 1906 to preserve artefacts from synagogues demolished during slum clearances in Josefov – with the intention of creating a 'museum of an extinct race'. They shipped in materials and objects from destroyed Jewish communities throughout Bohemia and Moravia, helping to amass what is probably the world's biggest collection of sacred Jewish artefacts, and a moving memorial to seven centuries of oppression.

Old-New Synagogue

Completed around 1270, the **Old-New Synagogue** (Staro-nová synagóga; Map p332; www.jewishmuseum.cz; Červená 2; adult/child 200/140Kč; ⛟17) is Europe's oldest working synagogue and one of Prague's earliest Gothic buildings. You step down into it because it predates the raising of Staré Město's street level in medieval times to guard against floods. Men must cover their heads (a hat or bandanna will do; paper yarmulkes are handed out at the entrance). Note that entry is not included with a Prague Jewish Museum ordinary ticket.

Around the central chamber are an entry hall, a winter prayer hall and the room from which women watch the men-only services. The interior, with a pulpit surrounded by a 15th-century wrought-iron grill, looks much as it would have 500 years ago. The 17th-century scriptures on the walls were recovered from beneath a later 'restoration'. On the eastern wall is the Holy Ark that holds the Torah

DON'T MISS...

➡ Old-New Synagogue

➡ Old Jewish Cemetery

➡ Spanish Synagogue

PRACTICALITIES

➡ Židovské muzeum Praha

➡ Map p332

➡ ☑222 317 191

➡ www.jewishmuseum.cz

➡ Reservation Centre, U starého hřbitova 3a

➡ ordinary ticket adult/child 300/200Kč, combined ticket incl entry to Old-New Synagogue 480/320Kč

➡ ⊙9am-6pm Sun-Fri Apr-Oct, to 4.30pm Nov-Mar

➡ ⛟17, Ⓜ Staroměstská

BUYING TICKETS

Buy tickets at the Reservation Centre, the Pinkas Synagogue, the Spanish Synagogue and the shop opposite the Old-New Synagogue. Queues are shortest at the Spanish Synagogue.

One of the oldest gravestones in the Old Jewish Cemetery is that of Rabbi Judah Loew ben Bezalel, chief rabbi of Prague in the late 16th century. Rabbi Loew is famously associated with the legend of the Golem, a supernatural being created from the mud of the Vltava. Loew breathed life into the creature using secret incantations, and bid it to protect the Jews of Prague from harm.

MORDECHAI MAISEL

Mordechai Maisel (1528–1601), a contemporary of Rabbi Loew, was one of Prague's wealthiest men. He was known for his philanthropy, paying for the paving of the ghetto streets, providing for Jewish widows and orphans, and building and bequeathing the beautiful Maisel Synagogue.

scrolls. In a glass case at the rear, little light bulbs beside the names of the prominent deceased are lit on their death days.

With its steep roof and Gothic gables, this looks like a place with secrets, and at least one version of the Golem legend ends here. Left alone on the Sabbath, the creature runs amok; Rabbi Loew rushes out in the middle of a service, removes its magic talisman and carries the lifeless body into the synagogue's attic, where some insist it still lies.

Across the narrow street is the elegant 16th-century **High Synagogue** (Vysoká synagóga; Map p332; Červená 2), so-called because its prayer hall (closed to the public) is upstairs. Around the corner is the **Jewish Town Hall** (Židovská radnice; Map p332; Maiselova 18; ⊘ closed to the public), built by Mordechai Maisel in 1586 and given its rococo facade in the 18th century. It has a clock tower with one Hebrew face where the hands, like the Hebrew script, run 'backwards'.

Pinkas Synagogue

Handsome **Pinkas Synagogue** (Pinkasova synagóga; Map p332) was built in 1535 and used for worship until 1941. After WWII it was converted into a memorial, with wall after wall inscribed with the names, birth dates, and dates of disappearance of the 77,297 Czech victims of the Nazis. It also has a collection of paintings and drawings by children held in the Terezín concentration camp during WWII.

Old Jewish Cemetery

The Pinkas Synagogue contains the entrance to the **Old Jewish Cemetery** (Starý židovský hřbitov; Map p332; Pinkas Synagogue, Široká 3), Europe's oldest surviving Jewish graveyard. Founded in the early 15th century, it has a palpable atmosphere of mourning even after two centuries of disuse (it was closed in 1787); however, this is one of Prague's most popular sights, so if you're hoping to have a moment of quiet contemplation you'll probably be disappointed. Around 12,000 crumbling stones (some brought from other, long-gone cemeteries) are heaped together, but beneath them are perhaps 100,000 graves, piled in layers because of the lack of space.

The most prominent graves, marked by pairs of marble tablets with a 'roof' between them, are near the main gate; they include those of Mordechai Maisel and Rabbi Loew. The oldest stone (now replaced by a replica) is that of Avigdor Karo, a chief rabbi and court poet to Wenceslas IV, who died in 1439. Most stones bear the name of the deceased and his or her father, the date of death (and sometimes of burial), and poetic texts. Elaborate markers from

MENDELSSOHN IS ON THE ROOF

The roof of the Rudolfinum (p106), on the western edge of Josefov, is decorated with statues of famous composers. It housed the German administration during WWII, when the Nazi authorities ordered that the statue of Felix Mendelssohn – who was Jewish – must be removed.

In *Mendelssohn is on the Roof,* a darkly comic novella about life in wartime Prague, the Jewish writer Jiří Weil weaves a wryly amusing story around this true-life event. The two Czech labourers given the task of removing the statue can't tell which of the two dozen or so figures is Mendelssohn – they all look the same, as far as they can tell. Their Czech boss, remembering his lectures in 'racial science', tells them that Jews have big noses. 'Whichever one has the biggest conk, that's the Jew.'

So the workmen single out the statue with the biggest nose – 'Look! That one over there with the beret. None of the others has a nose like his' – then sling a noose around its neck and start to haul it over. As their boss walks across to check on their progress, he gapes in horror as they start to topple the figure of the only composer on the roof that he does recognise – Richard Wagner.

the 17th and 18th centuries are carved with symbols representing the deceased's name or occupation, eg hands (giving a blessing) for a Cohen (Cohens are descended from temple priests), a violin for a musician.

Since the cemetery was closed, Jewish burials have taken place at the Jewish Cemetery in Žižkov. There are remnants of another old Jewish burial ground at the foot of the TV Tower in Žižkov.

Exit through a gate between the Klaus Synagogue and the Ceremonial Hall.

Ceremonial Hall & Klaus Synagogue

Built in 1912, the **Ceremonial Hall** (Obřadní síň; Map p332) was formerly the mortuary for the Old Jewish Cemetery, and is the site of an interesting exhibition on Jewish traditions relating to illness and death. The neighbouring baroque **Klaus Synagogue** (Klauzová synagóga; Map p332; U starého hřbitova 1) houses a good exhibit on Jewish ceremonies of birth and death, worship and special holy days.

Maisel Synagogue

A block to the southeast of the Ceremonial Hall and Klaus Synagogue lies the neo-Gothic **Maisel Synagogue** (Maiselova synagóga; Map p332; Maiselova 10; ⊘9am-6pm Sun-Fri Apr-Oct, to 4.30pm Nov-Mar; Ⓜ Staroměstská), which replaced a Renaissance original built by Mordechai Maisel, mayor of the Jewish community, in 1592. It houses an exhibit on the history of the Jews in Bohemia and Moravia from the 10th to the 18th centuries, with displays of ceremonial silver, textiles, prints and books.

Spanish Synagogue

About two blocks east of the Maisel Synagogue is the **Spanish Synagogue** (Španělská synagóga; Map p332; Vězeňská 1). Named after its striking Moorish interior and dating from 1868, its exhibit continues the story of the Jews in the Czech Republic from emancipation to the present day.

TRAVELLIBUG / GETTY IMAGES ©

OLD TOWN HALL & ASTRONOMICAL CLOCK

Prague's Old Town Hall, founded in 1338, is a hotchpotch of medieval buildings presided over by a tall Gothic tower with a splendid Astronomical Clock. The town hall has several historic attractions, and hosts art exhibitions on the ground floor and the 2nd floor.

Astronomical Clock

Every hour, on the hour, crowds gather beneath the Old Town Hall Tower to watch the **Astronomical Clock** (Map p332; ⊙chimes on the hour 9am-9pm) in action. Despite a slightly underwhelming performance that takes only 45 seconds, the clock is one of Europe's best-known tourist attractions, and a 'must-see' for visitors to Prague. After all, it's historic, photogenic and – if you take time to study it – rich in intriguing symbolism.

Four figures beside the clock represent the deepest civic anxieties of 15th-century Praguers: **Vanity** (with a mirror), **Greed** (with his money bag; originally a Jewish money-lender, but cosmetically altered after WWII), **Death** (the skeleton) and **Pagan Invasion** (represented by a Turk). The four figures below these are the Chronicler, Angel, Astronomer and Philosopher.

On the hour, Death rings a bell and inverts his hourglass, and the **12 Apostles** parade past the windows above the clock, nodding to the crowd. On the left side are Paul (with a sword and a book), Thomas (lance), Jude (book), Simon (saw), Bartholomew (book) and Barnabas (parchment); on the right side are Peter (with a key), Matthew

DON'T MISS...

➡ The parade of Apostles during the hourly chiming of the Astronomical Clock

➡ The view from the top of the tower

➡ The guided tour, where you can see the inner workings of the 12 Apostles

PRACTICALITIES

➡ Staroměstská radnice

➡ Map p332

➡ 🖊236 002 629

➡ www.staromestskaradnicepraha.cz

➡ Staroměstské náměstí 1

➡ guided tour adult/child 100/50Kč, incl tower 160Kč

➡ ⊙11am-6pm Mon, 9am-6pm Tue-Sun

➡ Ⓜ Staroměstská

(axe), John (snake), Andrew (cross), Philip (cross) and James (mallet). At the end, a cock crows and the hour is rung.

Exterior

The town hall's best feature is the view from the 60m-tall **tower** (Věž radnice; Map p332; adult/child 100/50Kč, incl Old Town Hall 160Kč; ☉11am-10pm Mon, 9am-10pm Tue-Sun), which is well worth the climb (there's also a lift).

A plaque on the building's eastern face lists the 27 Protestant nobles who were beheaded here in 1621 after the Battle of Bílá Hora; white crosses on the ground mark where the deed was done. If you look at the neo-Gothic eastern gable, you can see that its right-hand edge is ragged – the wing that once extended north from here was blown up by the Nazis in 1945, on the day before the Soviet army marched into the city.

Guided Tour

The guided tour of the town hall takes you through the council chamber and assembly room, with beautiful mosaics dating from the 1930s, before visiting the Gothic chapel and taking a look at the inner workings of the 12 Apostles who parade above the Astronomical Clock every hour. The tour is rounded off with a trip through the Romanesque and Gothic cellars beneath the building.

THE CLOCK FACE

On the upper face, the disk in the middle of the fixed part depicts the world known at the time – with Prague at the centre. The gold sun traces a circle through the blue zone of day, the brown zone of dusk in the west, the black disc of night, and dawn in the east. From this the hours of sunrise and sunset can be read.

The Old Town Hall's original clock of 1410 was improved in 1490 by Master Hanuš, producing the mechanical marvel you see today. Legend has it that Hanuš was blinded afterwards so he could not duplicate his work elsewhere.

THE CALENDAR WHEEL

The calendar wheel beneath the clock's astronomical wizardry, with 12 seasonal scenes celebrating rural Bohemian life, is a duplicate of one painted in 1866 by the Czech Revivalist Josef Mánes. You can have a close look at the beautiful original in the Prague City Museum (p124). Most of the dates around the calendar wheel are marked with the names of their associated saints; 6 July honours Jan Hus.

MUSEUM OF DECORATIVE ARTS

This museum opened in 1900 as part of a European movement to encourage a return to the aesthetic values sacrificed to the Industrial Revolution. Its four halls are a feast for the eyes, full of 16th- to 19th-century artefacts such as furniture, tapestries, porcelain and a fabulous collection of glasswork.

Exhibition

The neo-Renaissance building is itself a work of art, the facade decorated with reliefs representing the various decorative arts and the Bohemian towns famous for them. The staircase leading from the entrance hall to the main exhibition on the 2nd floor is beautifully decorated with colourful ceramics, stained-glass windows and frescos representing graphic arts, metalworking, ceramics, glassmaking and goldsmithing. It leads to the Votive Hall, which houses the **Karlštejn Treasure**, a hoard of 14th-century silver found in the walls of Karlštejn Castle in the 19th century.

To the right is a textiles exhibit and a fascinating collection of clocks, watches, sundials and astronomical devices, but the good stuff is to the left in the **glass and ceramics hall** – exquisite baroque glassware, a fine collection of Meissen porcelain and a range of Czech glass, ceramics and furniture in cubist, art nouveau and art deco styles, the best pieces being by Josef Gočár and Pavel Janák.

The **graphic arts section** has some fine art nouveau posters, and the **gold and jewellery exhibit** contains some real curiosities; amid the Bohemian garnet brooches, 14th-century chalices, diamond-studded monstrances and art nouveau silverware you will find a Chinese rhino-horn vase in a silver mount, a delicate nautilus shell engraved with battle scenes, and a silver watchcase in the shape of a skull.

DON'T MISS...

➡ Karlštejn Treasure
➡ Cubist ceramics
➡ Art nouveau posters

PRACTICALITIES

➡ Umělecko-průmyslové muzeum
➡ Map p332
➡ ☎251 093 111
➡ www.upm.cz
➡ 17.listopadu 2
➡ whole gallery adult/child 120/70Kč, temporary exhibition only 80/40Kč
➡ ☺10am-7pm Tue, to 6pm Wed-Sun
➡ ☷17

SIGHTS

◉ Old Town Square & Around

OLD TOWN HALL   HISTORIC BUILDING
See p100.

ASTRONOMICAL CLOCK   HISTORIC SITE
See p100.

OLD TOWN SQUARE   SQUARE
Map p332 (Staroměstské náměstí; MStaro-městská) One of Europe's biggest and most beautiful urban spaces, the Old Town Square (Staroměstské náměstí, or Staromák for short) has been Prague's principal public square since the 10th century, and was its main marketplace until the beginning of the 20th century.

There are busking jazz bands and alfresco concerts, political meetings and fashion shows, plus Christmas and Easter markets, all watched over by Ladislav Šaloun's brooding art nouveau **statue of Jan Hus**. It was unveiled on 6 July 1915, which was the 500th anniversary of Hus' death at the stake.

The brass strip on the ground to the south of the Hus statue is the so-called **Prague Meridian**. Until 1915 the square's main feature was a 17th-century plague column, the shadow of which used to cross the meridian at high noon.

KINSKÝ PALACE   GALLERY
Map p332 (Palác Kinských; ☎224 810 758; www.ngprague.cz; Staroměstské náměstí 12; adult/child 150/80Kč; ☺10am-6pm Tue-Sun; MStaroměstská) The late-baroque Kinský Palace sports Prague's finest rococo facade, completed in 1765 by the redoubtable Kilian Dientzenhofer. Today, the palace is home to a branch of the National Gallery, housing its collection of ancient and oriental art, ranging from ancient Egyptian tomb treasures and Greek Apulian pottery (4th century BC) to Chinese and Japanese decorative art and calligraphy.

Alfred Nobel, the Swedish inventor of dynamite, once stayed in the palace; his crush on pacifist Bertha von Suttner (née Kinský) may have influenced him to establish the Nobel Peace Prize (she was the first woman laureate in 1905). Many older Praguers have

STARÉ MĚSTO SIGHTS

◉ TOP SIGHT
CHURCH OF OUR LADY BEFORE TÝN

Its distinctive twin Gothic spires make the Church of Our Lady Before Týn (Kostel Panny Marie před Týnem) an unmistakable Old Town landmark. Like something out of a 15th-century – and probably slightly cruel – fairy tale, they loom over the Old Town Square, decorated with a golden image of the Virgin Mary made from the melted-down Hussite chalice that had adorned the church.

Though impressively Gothic on the outside, the church's interior is smothered in heavy baroque. Two of the most interesting features are the huge rococo **altar** on the northern wall and the **tomb of Tycho Brahe**, the Danish astronomer who was one of Rudolf II's most illustrious court scientists (he died in 1601 of a burst bladder following a royal piss-up – he was too polite to leave the table to relieve himself).

As for the exterior of the church, the north portal overlooking Týnská ulička is topped by a remarkable **14th-century tympanum** that shows the Crucifixion and was carved by the workshop of Charles IV's favourite architect, Peter Parler. Note that this is a copy; the original is in the Lapidárium (p164).

The church is an occasional concert venue and has a very grand-sounding pipe organ.

DON'T MISS...
→ View of the floodlit spires at night
→ Tympanum depicting the Crucifixion
→ Tomb of Tycho Brahe

PRACTICALITIES
→ Map p332
→ ☎222 318 186
→ www.tyn.cz
→ Staroměstské náměstí
→ suggested donation 25Kč
→ ☺10am-1pm & 3-5pm Tue-Sat, 10.30am-noon Sun Mar-Oct
→ MStaroměstská

a darker memory of the place, for it was from its balcony in February 1948 that Klement Gottwald proclaimed communist rule in Czechoslovakia. There are Kafka connections here, too – young Franz once attended a school around the back of the building, and his father ran a shop in the premises next to the House at the Stone Bell, now occupied by the Kafka Bookshop.

CLAM-GALLAS PALACE PALACE
Map p332 (Clam-Gallasův palác; ☎236 002 068; Husova 20; exhibition adult/child 80/40Kč; ◎10am-6pm Tue-Sun; MStaroměstská) Designed by Viennese court architect Johann Bernhard Fischer von Erlach in 1713, the Clam-Gallas Palace is one of the most extravagantly baroque buildings in Prague, decorated with sculptures and frescos depicting scenes of ancient mythology. The 1st floor houses exhibitions staged by the Prague City Archives, while the courtyard and Marble Hall (visited by Mozart and Beethoven) host performances by Opera Barocca.

COLLOREDO-MANSFELD PALACE PALACE
Map p332 (Colloredo-Mansfeldský palác; ☎222 232 053; www.ghmp.cz; Karlova 2; adult/child 60/30Kč; ◎10am-6pm Tue-Sun; ☐17, 18) Recently taken over by the City of Prague Gallery, the shabby halls of this decaying 18th-century aristocratic palace are being restored as an information centre and exhibition space. Meanwhile you can wander its baroque corridors and visit the grand ballroom – which appeared in Miloš Forman's 1984 film *Amadeus* – with ceiling frescoes untouched since the 1760s.

ART GALLERY FOR CHILDREN GALLERY
Map p332 (Galerie umění pro děti; ☎732 513 559; www.galeriegud.cz; náměstí Franze Kafky 3; adult/child aged 3-15/family 170/80/300Kč, child aged 2 & under free; ◎1-6pm Tue-Fri, 10am-6pm Sat & Sun; MStaroměstská) The clue is in the name: at the Art Gallery for Children the kids not only get to look at art, but make it, add to it and alter it. There are paints and materials to play with, and even workshops for five- to 12-year-olds (only in Czech at present, though staff speak English).

DVORAK SEC CONTEMPORARY GALLERY
Map p332 (☎607 262 617; www.dvoraksec.com; Dlouhá 5; ◎10am-6pm Mon-Fri, 11am-7pm Sat; MStaroměstská) **FREE** One of Prague's leading independent art galleries, the Dvorak

STARÉ MĚSTO SIGHTS

◉ TOP SIGHT
CHURCH OF ST JAMES

The great Gothic mass of the Church of St James began in the 14th century as a Minorite monastery church, and was given a beautiful baroque facelift in the early 18th century. But in the midst of the gilt and stucco is a grisly memento: on the inside of the western wall (look up to the right as you enter) hangs a **shrivelled human arm**. Legend claims that when a thief tried to steal the jewels from the statue of the Virgin around the year 1400, the Virgin grabbed his wrist in such an iron grip that his arm had to be lopped off. (The truth may not be far behind: the church was a favourite of the guild of butchers, who may have administered their own justice.)

Pride of place inside goes to the over-the-top **tomb**, found in the northern aisle, of Count Jan Vratislav of Mitrovice, an 18th-century lord chancellor of Bohemia. It's well worth a visit to enjoy St James' splendid **pipe organ** and famous acoustics. Recitals – free ones at 10.30am or 11am after Sunday Mass – and occasional concerts are not always advertised by ticket agencies, so check the noticeboard outside.

DON'T MISS...
➡ The thief's arm
➡ The tomb of Count Jan Vratislav of Mitrovice
➡ An organ recital

PRACTICALITIES
➡ Kostel sv Jakuba
➡ Map p332
➡ Malá Štupartská 6
➡ ◎9.30am-noon & 2-4pm Tue-Sat, 2-4pm Sun
➡ MNáměstí Republiky

Sec specialises in promoting modern art of international importance from the United States, Britain, Germany and the Czech Republic. Past exhibitions have included the likes of Julian Opie, Jiří David, Paul Brainard, Dana Bell, Peter Černý and Roman Týc.

VÁCLAV HAVEL LIBRARY GALLERY
Map p332 (Knihovna Václava Havla; ☎222 220 112; www.vaclavhavel-library.org; Galerie Montmartre, Řetězová 7; ☺noon-8pm Tue-Sun; ☒17, 18) This small gallery, supported by the foundation that protects the legacy of the Czech Republic's late playwright-president, houses a permanent exhibition on the life and work of Václav Havel, and a series of temporary exhibitions of art on related themes such as human rights, samizdat publishing, and the struggle for freedom and democracy.

HOUSE AT THE STONE BELL GALLERY
Map p332 (Dům U kamenného zvonu; ☎224 828 245; www.ghmp.cz; Staroměstské náměstí 13; adult/child 120/60Kč; ☺10am-8pm Tue-Sun; ⓂStaroměstská) During restoration in the 1980s a baroque stucco facade was stripped away from this elegant medieval building to reveal the original 14th-century Gothic stonework; the eponymous stone bell is on the building's corner. Inside, two restored Gothic chapels now serve as branches of the Prague City Gallery (with exhibits of modern art) and as chamber-concert venues.

CHURCH OF ST NICHOLAS CHURCH
Map p332 (Kostel sv Mikuláše; www.svmikulas. cz/en; Staroměstské náměstí; ☺10am-4pm; ⓂStaroměstská) FREE The baroque wedding cake in the northwestern corner of the Old Town Square is the Church of St Nicholas, built in the 1730s by Kilian Dientzenhofer (not to be confused with the Dientzenhofers' masterpiece in Malá Strana). Considerable grandeur has been worked into a tight space; originally the church was behind the Old Town Hall's north side (destroyed in 1945).

Chamber concerts are often held beneath its stucco decorations, a visually splendid (though acoustically mediocre) setting.

TÝN COURTYARD SQUARE
Map p332 (Týnský dvůr; entrances on Malá Štupartská & Týnská ulička; ☺24hr; ⓂNáměstí Republiky) This picturesque courtyard tucked behind the Church of Our Lady Before Týn (p103) was originally a sort of medieval caravanserai – a fortified hotel, trading centre and customs office for vis-

OLD TOWN ORIGINS

The origins of Staré Město (Old Town) date back to the 10th century, when a marketplace and settlement grew up on the east bank of the river. In the 12th century this was linked to the castle district by Judith Bridge, the forerunner of Charles Bridge, and in 1231 Wenceslas I honoured it with a town charter and the beginnings of a fortification.

The town walls are long gone, but their line can still be traced along the streets of Národní třída, Na příkopě (which means 'on the moat') and Revoluční, and the Old Town's main gate – the Powder Gate – still survives.

iting foreign merchants. Now attractively renovated, the courtyard houses shops, restaurants and hotels. The courtyard is still often referred to by its German name, Ungelt (meaning 'customs duty').

Established as long ago as the 11th century, it was busiest and most prosperous during the reign of Charles IV. In the northwest corner is the 16th-century **Granovsky Palace** (Map p332), with an elegant Renaissance loggia, and sgraffito and painted decoration depicting biblical and mythological scenes. Across the yard, to the right of the V Ungeltu shop, is the **House at the Black Bear** (dům U černého medvěda; Map p332), the baroque facade of which is adorned with a statue of St John of Nepomuk above the door and a bear in chains on the corner, a reminder of the kind of 'entertainment' that once took place here.

Josefov

PRAGUE JEWISH MUSEUM MUSEUM
See p97.

MUSEUM OF DECORATIVE ARTS MUSEUM
See p102.

PAŘÍŽSKÁ STREET
Map p332 (ⓂStaroměstská) When the Josefov ghetto was cleared at the turn of the 20th century, the broad boulevard of Pařížská třída (Paris Ave) was driven in a straight line through the heart of the old slums. This was a time of widespread infatuation

STARÉ MĚSTO SIGHTS

TOP SIGHT
CONVENT OF ST AGNES

In the northeastern corner of Staré Město is the former Convent of St Agnes, Prague's oldest surviving Gothic building. The 1st-floor rooms hold the National Gallery's permanent collection of medieval and early Renaissance art (1200–1550) from Bohemia and Central Europe, a treasure house of glowing **Gothic altar paintings** and polychrome religious sculptures.

In 1234 the Franciscan Order of the Poor Clares was founded by Přemysl king Wenceslas I, who made his sister Anežka (Agnes) the first abbess of the convent. Agnes was beatified in the 19th century; Pope John Paul II canonised her weeks before the events of November 1989.

In the 16th century the convent was handed over to the Dominicans, and after Joseph II dissolved the monasteries it became a squatters' paradise. It is only since the 1980s that the complex has been restored and renovated. In addition to the 13th-century cloister, you can visit the French Gothic **Church of the Holy Saviour** (Map p332), which contains the tombs of St Agnes and of Wenceslas I's Queen Cunegund. Alongside this is the smaller **Church of St Francis** (Map p332), where Wenceslas I is buried; part of its ruined nave serves as a chilly concert hall.

DON'T MISS...

➡ Gothic altarpieces painted by medieval masters

➡ Church of the Holy Saviour

PRACTICALITIES

➡ Klášter sv Anežky

➡ Map p332

➡ ☎224 810 628

➡ www.ngprague.cz

➡ U Milosrdných 17

➡ adult/child 150/80Kč

➡ ⊙10am-6pm Tue-Sun

➡ ⬛5, 8, 24

---

with the French art nouveau style, and the avenue is lined with elegant apartment buildings adorned with stained glass and sculptural flourishes.

In the last decade Pařížská has become a glitzy shopping strand, studded with expensive brand names such as Dior, Louis Vuitton and Fabergé.

FRANZ KAFKA MONUMENT MONUMENT
Map p332 (cnr Vězeňská & Dušní; ⓂStaroměstská) Commissioned by Prague's Franz Kafka Society in 2003, Jaroslav Róna's unusual sculpture of a mini-Kafka riding on the shoulders of a giant empty suit was based on the writer's story *Description of a Struggle,* in which the author explores a fantasy landscape from the shoulders of 'an acquaintance' (who may be another aspect of the author's personality).

JAN PALACH SQUARE SQUARE
Map p332 (náměstí Jana Palacha; ⬛17, 18) Jan Palach Square is named after the young Charles University student who in January 1969 set himself alight in Wenceslas Square in protest against the Soviet invasion. On the eastern side of the square, beside the

entrance to the philosophy faculty building where Palach was a student, is a bronze memorial plaque with a ghostly death mask.

RUDOLFINUM HISTORIC BUILDING
Map p332 (☎227 059 270; www.ceskafilharmonie.cz; Alšovo nábřeží 12; ⬛17, 18) Presiding over Jan Palach Square is the Rudolfinum, home to the Czech Philharmonic Orchestra. This and the National Theatre, both designed by architects Josef Schulz and Josef Zítek, are considered Prague's finest neo-Renaissance buildings. Completed in 1884, the Rudolfinum served as the seat of the Czechoslovak parliament between the wars, and as the administrative offices of the occupying Nazis during WWII.

The impressive **Dvořák Hall**, its stage dominated by a vast organ, is one of the main concert venues for the Prague Spring festival. The northern part of the complex houses the Galerie Rudolfinum. There's also a cafe with tables ranged amid the Corinthian pillars of the Column Hall.

GALERIE RUDOLFINUM GALLERY
Map p332 (☎227 059 205; www.galerierudolfinum.cz; Alšovo nábřeží 12; adult/child 140/90Kč;

⊙10am-6pm Tue, Wed & Fri-Sun, to 8pm Thu; 🖪17, 18) Housed in the Rudolfinum complex of concert halls, this gallery specialises in changing exhibitions of contemporary art. The entrance is on the riverfront (northern) side of the Rudolfinum building.

⊙ Along the Royal Way

GASTRONOMY MUSEUM   MUSEUM
Map p332 (Muzeum Gastronomie; 🗹602 108 017; www.muzeumgastronomie.cz; Jakubská 12; adult/child 180/65Kč; ⊙10am-7pm, closed Mon Oct-Mar; 🅼Náměstí Republiky) Dedicated to 'history through the kitchen window', this museum tells the story of food, drink and cooking from prehistoric times to the present day, focusing on Czech cuisine in particular. You can arrange special group tours that involve cookery demonstrations (eg how to make Czech dumplings) and drinks tastings (learn about *slivovice, hruškovice, meruňkovice* and other '-vices').

POWDER GATE   TOWER
Map p332 (Prašná brána; http://en.muzeumprahy. cz/prague-towers; Na příkopě; adult/child 90/65Kč; ⊙10am-10pm Apr-Sep, to 8pm Oct & Mar, to 6pm Nov-Feb; 🅼Náměstí Republiky) The 65m-tall Powder Gate was begun in 1475 on the site of one of Staré Město's original 13 gates. The tower above the arch houses exhibitions of medieval weapons and instruments, many of which were used in films shot in Prague, including *Van Helsing, Chronicles of Narnia* and *Blade II*, but the main attraction is the view from the top.

The gate was built during the reign of King Vladislav II Jagiello as a ceremonial

STARÉ MĚSTO SIGHTS

THE ROYAL WAY

The Royal Way (Královská cesta) was the ancient processional route followed by Czech kings on their way to St Vitus Cathedral for coronation. The route leads from the Powder Gate (Prašná brána) along Celetná, through the Old Town Square and Little Square (Malé náměstí), along Karlova (Charles St) and across **Charles Bridge** to Malá Strana Square (Malostranské náměstí), before climbing up Nerudova to the castle. The only procession that makes its way along these streets today is the daily crush of tourists shouldering their way past a gauntlet of gaudy souvenir shops and bored-looking leaflet touts.

Celetná, leading from the Powder Gate to the Old Town Square, is an open-air museum of pastel-painted baroque facades covering Gothic frames resting on Romanesque foundations, deliberately buried to raise Staré Město above the floods of the Vltava River. But the most interesting building – Josef Gočár's delightful **House of the Black Madonna** (dům U černé Matky Boží) – dates only from 1912.

Little Square, the southwestern extension of the Old Town Square, has a Renaissance fountain with a 16th-century wrought-iron grill. Here, several fine baroque and neo-Renaissance exteriors adorn some of Staré Město's oldest structures. The most colourful is the 1890 **VJ Rott Building** (Map p332), decorated with wall paintings by Mikuláš Aleš, which now houses the Prague incarnation of the Hard Rock Café.

A dog-leg from the southwestern corner of the square leads to narrow, cobbled Karlova, which continues as far as Charles Bridge – this section is often choked with tourist crowds. On the corner of Liliová is the house called **At the Golden Snake** (U zlatého hada; Map p332), the site of Prague's first coffee house, opened in 1708 by an Armenian named Deomatus Damajan.

Karlova sidles along the massive southern wall of the Klementinum before emerging at the riverside on Křížovnické náměstí. On the north side of the square is the 17th-century **Church of St Francis Seraphinus** (Kostel sv Františka Serafinského; Map p332; 🔊), its dome decorated with a fresco of the Last Judgment. It belongs to the Order of the Knights of the Cross with the Red Star, the only Bohemian order of Crusaders still in existence.

Just south of Charles Bridge, at the site of the former Old Town mill, is **Novotného lávka** (Map p332), a riverside terrace full of sunny, overpriced *vinárny* (wine bars) with great views of the bridge and castle, its far end dominated by a statue of composer Bedřich Smetana.

entrance to the city, but was left unfinished after the king moved from the neighbouring Royal Court to Prague Castle in 1483. The name comes from its use as a gunpowder magazine in the 18th century. Josef Mocker rebuilt and decorated it and put up a steeple between 1875 and 1886, giving it its neo-Gothic icing.

ESTATES THEATRE
HISTORIC BUILDING

Map p332 (Stavovské divadlo; ☎224 902 231; www.narodni-divadlo.cz; Ovocný trh 1; MMůstek) Prague's oldest theatre and finest neoclassical building, the Estates Theatre is where the premiere of Mozart's *Don Giovanni* was performed on 29 October 1787, with the maestro himself conducting. Opened in 1783 as the Nostitz Theatre (after its founder, Count Anton von Nostitz-Rieneck), it was patronised by upper-class German citizens and thus came to be called the Estates Theatre – the Estates being the traditional nobility.

After WWII it was renamed the Tyl Theatre (Tylovo divadlo) in honour of the 19th-century Czech playwright Josef Kajetán Tyl. One of his claims to fame is the Czech national anthem, 'Kde domov můj?' (Where is My Home?), which came from one of his plays. In the early 1990s the theatre's name

reverted to Estates Theatre. To see the interior you'll need to attend a performance – the program is on the website.

KLEMENTINUM
HISTORIC BUILDING

Map p332 (☎222 220 879; www.klementinum.cz; entrances on Křížovnická, Karlova & Mariánské náměstí; guided tour adult/child 220/140Kč; ☺10am-5pm Apr-Oct, to 4pm Nov, Dec & Mar; MStaroměstská) The Klementinum is a vast complex of beautiful baroque and rococo halls, now mostly occupied by the Czech National Library. Most of the buildings are closed to the public, but you can walk freely through the courtyards, or take a 50-minute **guided tour** of the baroque Library Hall, the Astronomical Tower and the Chapel of Mirrors.

When the Habsburg emperor Ferdinand I invited the Jesuits to Prague in 1556 to boost the power of the Roman Catholic Church in Bohemia, they selected one of the city's choicest pieces of real estate and in 1587 set to work on the **Church of the Holy Saviour** (Kostel Nejsvětějšího Spasitele; Map p332), Prague's flagship of the Counter-Reformation. Its western facade faces Charles Bridge, its sooty stone saints

◉ TOP SIGHT
MUNICIPAL HOUSE

Restored in the 1990s, Prague's most exuberantly art nouveau building is a labour of love, every detail of its design and decoration carefully considered. The restaurant and cafe (p116) are like walk-in museums of art nouveau design; upstairs are half-a-dozen sumptuously decorated halls that you can visit by guided tour.

The Municipal House stands on the site of the Royal Court, seat of Bohemia's kings from 1383 to 1483, which was demolished at the end of the 19th century. Between 1906 and 1912 this magnificent palace was built in its place – a lavish joint effort by around 30 leading artists of the day, creating a cultural centre that was the architectural climax of the Czech National Revival.

Highlights of the tour include **Smetana Hall**, Prague's biggest concert hall, with seating for 1200 beneath a glass dome, and the dramatic **Lord Mayor's Hall**, designed by Alfons Mucha, who also painted the superbly moody murals that adorn the walls and ceiling.

The Prague Spring music festival always opens on 12 May, the anniversary of Smetana's death, with a procession from Vyšehrad to the Municipal House followed by a gala performance of Smetana's symphonic cycle *Má vlast* (My Homeland) in Smetana Hall.

DON'T MISS

➡ Mosaics
➡ Smetana Hall
➡ Lord Mayor's Hall

PRACTICALITIES

➡ Obecní dům
➡ Map p332
➡ ☎222 002 101
➡ www.obecnidum.cz
➡ náměstí Republiky 5
➡ tour adult/child under 10/concession 290/free/240Kč
➡ ☺public areas 7.30am-11pm, information centre 10am-8pm
➡ MNáměstí Republiky

glaring down at the traffic jam of trams and tourists on Křížovnické náměstí.

After gradually buying up most of the adjacent neighbourhood, the Jesuits started building their college, the Klementinum, in 1653. By the time of its completion a century later, it was the largest building in the city after Prague Castle. When the Jesuits fell out with the pope in 1773, it became part of Charles University.

The baroque **Library Hall** (1727), magnificently decorated with ornate gilded carvings and a ceiling fresco depicting the Temple of Wisdom, houses thousands of theological volumes dating back to 1600. Also dating from the 1720s, the **Astronomical Tower** (Map p332) is capped with a huge bronze of Atlas and was used as an observatory until the 1930s; it houses a display of 18th-century astronomical instruments.

The **Chapel of Mirrors** (Zrcadlová kaple; Map p332; ☑222 220 879; www.klementinum. com; adult/child incl Astronomical Tower & Baroque Library 220/140Kč; ☻10am-7pm, tours hourly Mon-Thu, every 30min Fri-Sun; ☒17) also dates from the 1720s and is an ornate confection of gilded stucco, marbled columns, fancy frescos and ceiling mirrors – think baroque on steroids. Concerts of classical music are held here daily (tickets are available at most ticket agencies).

There are two other interesting churches in the Klementinum. The **Church of St Clement** (Kostel sv Klimenta; Map p332; ☻services 8.30am & 10am Sun), lavishly redecorated in the baroque style from 1711 to 1715 to plans by Kilian Dientzenhofer, is now a Greek Catholic chapel. Conservatively dressed visitors are welcome to attend the services. And then there's the elliptical **Chapel of the Assumption of the Virgin Mary** (Vlašská kaple Nanebevzetí Panny Marie; Map p332), built in 1600 for the Italian artisans who worked on the Klementinum (it's still technically the property of the Italian government).

CHARLES BRIDGE MUSEUM   MUSEUM
Map p332 (Muzeum Karlova Mostu; ☑776 776 779; www.charlesbridgemuseum.com; Křížovnické náměstí 3; adult/concession 150/70Kč; ☻10am-8pm May-Sep, to 6pm Oct-Apr; ☒17, 18) Founded in the 13th century, the Order of the Knights of the Cross with the Red Star were the guardians of Judith Bridge (and its successor Charles Bridge), with their 'mother house' at the Church of St Francis Seraphinus on Křížovnické náměstí. This museum, housed in the order's headquarters, covers the history of Prague's most famous landmark.

There are displays on ancient bridge-building techniques, masonry and carpentry, and models of both the Judith and Charles Bridges. In Room 16 you can descend into the foundations of the building to see some of the original stonework of Judith Bridge (dating from 1172), but perhaps the most impressive exhibits are the old photographs of flood damage to Charles Bridge in 1890, when three arches collapsed and were swept away.

SMETANA MUSEUM   MUSEUM
Map p332 (Muzeum Bedřicha Smetany; ☑222 220 082; www.nm.cz; Novotného lávka 1; adult/child 50/25Kč; ☻10am-noon & 12.30-5pm Wed-Mon; ☒17, 18) This small museum is devoted to Bedřich Smetana, Bohemia's favourite composer. It isn't that interesting unless you're a Smetana fan, and has only limited labelling in English, but there's a good exhibit on popular culture's feverish response to Smetana's opera *The Bartered Bride* – it seems Smetana was the Andrew Lloyd Webber of his day.

⊙ Southwestern Staré Město

BETHLEHEM CHAPEL   CHURCH
Map p332 (Betlémská kaple; ☑224 248 595; Betlémské náměstí 3; adult/child 60/30Kč; ☻10am-6.30pm Apr-Oct, to 5.30pm Nov-Mar; ☒6, 9, 18, 21, 22) The Bethlehem Chapel is a national cultural monument, being the birthplace of the Hussite cause. Jan Hus preached here from 1402 to 1412, marking the emergence of the Reform movement from the sanctuary of the Karolinum (where he was rector). Every year on the night of 5 July, the eve of Hus' burning at the stake in 1415, a memorial is held here with speeches and bell-ringing.

In 1391, Reformist Praguers won permission to build a church where services could be held in Czech instead of Latin, and proceeded to construct the biggest chapel Bohemia had ever seen, able to hold 3000 worshippers.

In the 18th century the chapel was torn down. Remnants were discovered around 1920, and from 1948 to 1954 – because Hussitism had official blessing as an ancient form of communism – the whole thing was

THE MISSING MONUMENTS

Prague witnessed several profound changes of political regime during the 20th century: from Habsburg empire to independent Czechoslovak Republic in 1918; to Nazi Protectorate from 1938 to 1945; to communist state in 1948; and back to democratic republic in 1989.

Each change was accompanied by widespread renaming of city streets and squares to reflect the heroes of the new regime. The square in front of the Rudolfinum, for example, has been known variously as Smetanovo náměstí (Smetana Square; 1919–42 and 1945–52); Mozartplatz (Mozart Square; 1942–45); náměstí Krasnoarmějců (Red Army Square; 1952–90); and náměstí Jana Palacha (Jan Palach Square; 1990–present).

This renaming was often followed by the removal of monuments erected by the previous regime. Here are three of Prague's most prominent 'missing monuments'.

The Missing Virgin

If you look at the ground in the Old Town Square (Staroměstské náměstí) about 50m south of the Jan Hus statue, you'll see a circular stone slab set among the cobblestones at the far end of the brass strip marking the Prague Meridian. This was the site of a **Marian column** (a pillar bearing a statue of the Virgin Mary), erected in 1650 in celebration of the Habsburg victory over the Swedes in 1648. It was surrounded by figures of angels crushing and beating down demons – a rather unsubtle symbol of a resurgent Catholic Church defeating the Protestant Reformation.

The column was toppled by a mob – who saw it as a symbol of Habsburg repression – on 3 November 1918, five days after the declaration of Czechoslovak independence. Its remains can be seen in the Lapidárium (p164).

The Missing Dictator

If you stand in the Old Town Square and look north along the arrow-straight avenue of Pařížská you will see, on a huge terrace at the far side of Čechův most, a giant metronome. If the monumental setting seems out of scale that's because the terrace was designed to accommodate the world's biggest statue of Stalin. Unveiled in 1955 – two years after Stalin's death – the 30m-high, 14,000-tonne colossus showed Uncle Joe at the head of two lines of communist heroes, Czech on one side, Soviet on the other. Cynical Praguers accustomed to constant food shortages quickly nicknamed it *fronta na maso* (the queue for meat).

The monument was dynamited in 1962, in deference to Khrushchev's attempt to airbrush Stalin out of history. The demolition crew was instructed, 'it must go quickly, there mustn't be much of a bang, and it should be seen by as few people as possible'. The Museum of Communism (p125) has a superb photo of the monument – and of its destruction.

The Missing Tank

Náměstí Kinských, at the southern edge of Malá Strana, was until 1989 known as náměstí Sovětských tankistů (Soviet Tank Crews Square), named in memory of the Soviet soldiers who 'liberated' Prague on 9 May 1945. For many years a Soviet T-34 tank – allegedly the first to enter the city (in fact it was a later Soviet 'gift') – squatted menacingly atop a pedestal here.

In 1991 artist David Černý decided that the tank was an inappropriate monument to the Soviet soldiers and painted it bright pink. The authorities had it painted green again, and charged Černý with a crime against the state. This infuriated many parliamentarians, 12 of whom repainted the tank pink. Their parliamentary immunity saved them from arrest and secured Černý's release.

After complaints from the Soviet Union the tank was removed. Its former setting is now occupied by a circular fountain surrounded by park benches; the vast granite slab in the centre is split by a jagged fracture, perhaps symbolic of a break with the past. The tank still exists, and is still pink – it's at the Military Museum in Lešany, near Týnec nad Sázavou, 30km south of Prague.

painstakingly reconstructed in its original form, based on old drawings, descriptions, and traces of the original work. Architecturally it was a radical departure, with a simple square hall focused on the pulpit rather than the altar.

An explanatory text in English is available at the chapel entrance. Only the southern wall of the chapel is brand new, and you can still see some original parts in the eastern wall: the pulpit door, several windows and the door to the preacher's quarters. These quarters, including the rooms used by Hus and others, are also original; they are now used for exhibits. The wall paintings are modern, and are based on old Hussite tracts. The indoor well pre-dates the chapel.

NÁPRSTEK MUSEUM   MUSEUM

Map p332 (Náprstkovo muzeum; ☎224 497 500; www.nm.cz; Betlémské náměstí 1; adult/child 80/50Kč; ☺10am-6pm Tue-Sun; ☒6, 9, 18, 21, 22) The small Náprstek Museum houses an ethnographic collection of Asian, African and American cultures, founded by Vojta Náprstek, a 19th-century industrialist with a passion for both anthropology and modern technology; his technology exhibits are now part of the National Technical Museum, p157, in Holešovice.

LEGO MUSEUM   MUSEUM

Map p332 (Muzeum Lega; ☎775 446 677; www. muzeumlega.cz; Národní 31; adult/child/family 200/50/470Kč; ☺10am-8pm; ☒6, 9, 18, 21, 22) The Lego Museum is Europe's largest private collection of Lego models, with a play area at the end where kids can build stuff from Lego themselves.

 EATING

The Old Town is littered with tourist traps, especially around the Old Town Square, but there are also plenty of excellent restaurants to discover. The maze of streets leading away from the Old Town Square contains many hidden gems, while the swanky strip of Pařížská boasts a more obvious string of stylish, upmarket eateries. The classic Staré Město dining room is in a brick-lined cellar – you'll soon become a connoisseur of subterranean decor.

MISTRAL CAFÉ   BISTRO €

Map p332 (☎222 317 737; www.mistralcafe.cz; Valentinská 11; mains 100-260Kč; ☺10am-11pm; ☎; Ⓜ Staroměstská) Is this the coolest bistro in the Old Town? Pale stone, bleached birchwood and potted shrubs make for a clean, crisp, modern look, and the clientele of local students and office workers clearly appreciate the competitively priced, well-prepared food. Fish and chips in crumpled brown paper with lemon and black-pepper mayo – yum!

LOKÁL   CZECH €

Map p332 (☎222 316 265; lokal-dlouha.ambi.cz; Dlouhá 33; mains 110-270Kč; ☺11am-1am Mon-Fri, noon-1am Sat, noon-10pm Sun; ☒5, 8, 24) Who'd have thought it possible? A classic Czech beer hall (albeit with slick modern styling); excellent *tankové pivo* (tanked Pilsner Urquell); a daily-changing menu of traditional Bohemian dishes; smiling, efficient, friendly service; and a no-smoking area! Top restaurant chain Ambiente has turned its hand to Czech cuisine, and the result has been so successful that the place is always busy, mostly with locals.

MAITREA   VEGETARIAN €

Map p332 (☎221 711 631; www.restaurace-maitrea.cz; Týnská ulička 6; mains 145-165Kč; weekday lunch 115Kč; ☺11.30am-11.30pm Mon-Fri, noon-11.30pm Sat & Sun; ☺☒; Ⓜ Staroměstská) Maitrea (a Buddhist term meaning 'the future Buddha') is a beautifully designed space full of flowing curves and organic shapes, from the sensuous polished-oak furniture and fittings to the blossomlike lampshades. The menu is inventive and wholly vegetarian, with dishes such as Tex-Mex quesadillas, spicy goulash with wholemeal dumplings, and pasta with smoked tofu, spinach and parmesan.

KAFKA SNOB FOOD   ITALIAN €

Map p332 (☎725 915 505; Široká 12; mains 150-280Kč; ☺8.30am-10pm; ☎☒; Ⓜ Staroměstská) A favourite hangout for fashion-conscious employees of the Old Town's many designer boutiques, this smoky bistro models a self-consciously hip look that combines turquoise-painted panelling and tan leather banquettes with brushed steel ducting and painted brick. The menu offers authentically Italian pasta and risotto dishes, plus great cakes and coffee. And no, we don't know what the name means either.

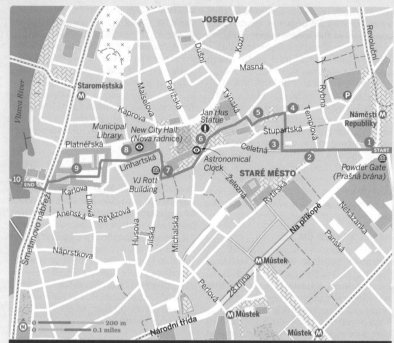

Neighbourhood Walk
Not Quite the Royal Way

START REPUBLIC SQUARE (NÁMĚSTÍ REPUBLIKY)
END CHARLES BRIDGE
LENGTH 1.5KM, 45 MINUTES

From ❶ **Republic Square** head towards the Powder Gate and set off along Celetná, which is lined with interesting buildings including the ❷ **House of the Black Madonna**, a fine example of cubist architecture.

Turn right into the passage at Celetná 17, which leads past the ❸ **Celetna Theatre**, and then go straight ahead along Malá Štupartská for a look at the baroque sculptures of the ❹ **Church of St James**. The cobbled passage leads to the ❺ **Týn Courtyard**, a lovely square with a Renaissance loggia. Exit at the far end and go along the alley to the right of the Church of Our Lady Before Týn.

You emerge into the ❻ **Old Town Square**, dominated by the brooding statue of Jan Hus and the Gothic tower of the Old Town Hall. Continue past the clock to reach ❼ **Little Square**; bear right and then left into Linhartská.

This leads to the quieter ❽ **Mariánské náměstí** (Virgin Mary Square) and New City Hall, seat of Prague's city council. Nip into the lobby of the Municipal Library (on the north side of the square) for a peek at the interesting book tower sculpture by Matej Kren.

Facing New City Hall is the main gate of the ❾ **Klementinum**. Go through the gate and turn left; on your right is the Chapel of Mirrors, where classical concerts are held daily. Continue through the triple arch, then turn right to pass through quiet courtyards (look up to your right to spot a modern sculpture of a child with a paper plane, perched on a ledge).

At the far end of the Klementinum you emerge into the bustling crowds of Křížovnické náměstí. End your walk by climbing up the ❿ **Old Town Bridge Tower** for a view over Charles Bridge.

LEHKÁ HLAVA
VEGETARIAN €

Map p332 (☑222 220 665; www.lehkahlava.cz; Boršov 2; mains 150-185Kč; ☺11.30am-11.30pm Mon-Fri, noon-11.30pm Sat & Sun; ⊜ ☑ ⛾; 🚇17, 18) Tucked away down a narrow cul-de-sac, Lehká Hlava (the name means 'clear head') exists in a little world of its own. There are two exotically decorated dining rooms, both with a vaguely psychedelic vibe – tables lit from within, studded with glowing glass spheres or with a radiant wood-grain effect. In the kitchen the emphasis is on healthy, freshly prepared vegetarian and vegan dishes.

COUNTRY LIFE
VEGETARIAN €

Map p332 (☑224 213 366; www.countrylife.cz; Melantrichova 15; mains 90-180Kč; ☺10.30am-7.30pm Mon-Thu, 10.30am-3.30pm Fri, noon-6pm Sun; 🕿☑; Ⓜ Můstek) Prague's first-ever health-food shop opened in 1991, and is an all-vegan cafeteria and sandwich bar offering inexpensive salads, sandwiches, pizzas, vegetarian goulash, sunflower-seed burgers and soy drinks (food is sold by weight, around 30Kč per 100g). There is plenty of seating in the rear courtyard but it can still get crowded at lunchtime, so go early or buy sandwiches to go.

BAKESHOP PRAHA
BAKERY, SANDWICHES €

Map p332 (☑222 316 823; www.bakeshop.cz; Kozí 1; sandwiches 75-200Kč; ☺7am-9pm; ⊜; Ⓜ Staroměstská) This fantastic bakery sells some of the best bread in the city, along with pastries, cakes and takeaway sandwiches, wraps, salads and quiche. Very busy at lunchtime.

INDIAN JEWEL
INDIAN €€

Map p332 (☑222 310 156; www.indianjewel. cz; Týn 6; mains 300-400Kč; ☺11am-11pm; 🕿; Ⓜ Staroměstská) A long, vaulted room in a medieval building makes an elegant setting for one of Prague's best Indian restaurants, with marble floors, chunky wooden chairs, copper tableware and restrained oriental decor; tables spill into the courtyard in summer. The food impresses, too, with light and flaky parathas, richly spiced sauces, and plenty of fire in the hotter curries.

VINO DI VINO
ITALIAN €€

Map p332 (☑222 311 791; www.vinodivinopraha. cz; Štupartská 18; mains 240-490Kč; ☺noon-10pm; 🕿; Ⓜ Náměstí Republiky) This Italian wine shop and delicatessen doubles as a restaurant, with a menu that makes the most of all those imported goodies – bresaola with smoked mozzarella, *spaghetti alla chitarra* (with squid and pecorino), and *saltimbocca alla Romana* (beef fillet with prosciutto and sage). Good list of Italian wines too, including excellent Montepulciano d'Abbruzzo from 610Kč a bottle.

FISH & CHIPS
FISH & CHIPS €€

Map p332 (☑606 881 414; fishandchipsprague. cz; Dlouhá 21; mains 200-270Kč; ☺11am-midnight Sun-Thu, to 1am Fri & Sat; 🚇5, 8, 24) Prague's first proper fish-and-chip shop goes a bit over the top with its 'British' theme, sporting white London Underground tiles, chandeliers, a red telephone box, and photos of the Beatles, Prince Charles and a Mini. But the eponymous signature dish is pretty good – crisp battered cod and chunky chips, with malt vinegar and Heinz ketchup. Takeaway available.

AMBIENTE PIZZA NUOVA
ITALIAN €€

Map p332 (☑221 803 308; pizzanuova.ambi. cz; Revoluční 1; mains 165-500Kč; ☺11.30am-11.30pm; ⊜🕿⛾; Ⓜ Náměstí Republiky) This cool 1st-floor space filled with big tables and banquettes with picture windows overlooking náměstí Republiky showcases a good idea from the Ambiente team: for a fixed price (298Kč per person before 6pm, 365Kč after) you get an all-you-can-eat pasta and pizza deal. (Without the deal, the salad and antipasti buffet and pizza-pasta combined costs 475/555Kč.) Wine by the glass is 75Kč to 120Kč.

KOLKOVNA
CZECH €€

Map p332 (☑224 819 701; www.kolkovna-restaurant.cz; V Kolkovně 8; mains 110-360Kč; ☺11am-midnight; 🕿; Ⓜ Staroměstská) Owned and operated by the Pilsner Urquell brewery, Kolkovna is a stylish, modern take on the traditional Prague pub, with decor by top Czech designers, and posh (but hearty) versions of classic Czech dishes such as goulash, roast duck and Moravian sparrow, as well as the Czech favourite, roast pork knuckle. All washed down with exquisite Urquell beer, of course.

★KALINA
FRENCH €€€

Map p332 (☑222 317 715; www.kalinarestaurant. cz; Dlouhá 12; mains 330-720Kč; ☺noon-3pm & 6-11.30pm Mon-Sat; ⊜🕿; 🚇5, 8, 24) Setting a trend for taking the best of fresh Czech produce and giving it the French gourmet treatment, this smart but unfailingly friendly little restaurant offers dishes such as duck pâté with rowan berries, smoked eel with beetroot and hazelnut, and roast wild boar with red wine and juniper. The set two-course lunch menu costs 330Kč.

CHAGALL'S
FRENCH €€€

Map p332 (☑739 002 347; www.chagalls.cz; Kozí 5; mains lunch 160-300Kč, dinner 460-510Kč; ⊙11am-midnight; ☺☎; ◰5, 8, 24) Stylishly understated decor in black, white and grey (with a hint of a Czech cubist vibe) is leavened with splashes of colour from old oil paintings and coloured fabrics in this sophisticated dining room. But it's the warmth of the welcome you notice first, followed by the quality of the menu – fresh seasonal produce prepared with Gallic care and flair.

V ZÁTIŠÍ
INTERNATIONAL, MODERN CZECH €€€

Map p332 (☑222 221 155; www.vzatisi.cz; Liliová 1; 2-/3-course meals 990/1090Kč; ⊙noon-3pm & 5.30-11pm; ☺☎; ◰17, 18) 'Still Life' is one of Prague's top restaurants, famed for the quality of its cuisine. The decor is bold and modern, with quirky glassware, boldly patterned wallpapers and cappuccino-coloured crushed-velvet chairs. The menu ranges from high-end Indian cuisine to gourmet versions of traditional Czech dishes – the South Bohemian duck with cabbage and herb dumplings is superb.

If the three-course dinner is not enough, you can lash out on the five-course *dégustation* menu (1390Kč; plus 790Kč extra for wines to match the dishes).

GEORGE PRIME STEAK
STEAKHOUSE €€€

Map p332 (☑226 202 599; http://georgeprimesteak.com; Platnéřská 19; mains 350-1000Kč; ⊙noon-2.30pm & 6-10.30pm; ☎; Ⓜ Staroměstská) One hundred per cent Black Angus Prime Beef imported from the American Midwest is the name of the game here, whether you order a charcoal-broiled T-bone steak in the elegant surroundings of the main restaurant, or opt for a house burger in the less formal bar. The presence on the menu of the 1000Kč 'Oligarch Burger' (with foie gras and gold leaf) gives a clue as to the target market.

🍷 DRINKING & NIGHTLIFE

The Old Town is tourist central, with crowded pubs and prices to match. But
all you have to do is explore the maze of narrow backstreets that radiate from the Old Town Square to find hidden gems such as Čili Bar, Duende and Literární Kavárna Řetězová.

PRAGUE BEER MUSEUM
PUB

Map p332 (☑732 330 912; www.praguebeer-museum.com; Dlouhá 46; ⊙noon-3am; ☎; ◰5, 8, 24) Although the name seems aimed at the tourist market, this lively and always heaving pub is very popular with Praguers. There are no fewer than 30 Czech-produced beers on tap (plus a beer menu with tasting notes to guide you). Try a sample board – a wooden platter with five 0.15L glasses containing five beers of your choice.

HEMINGWAY BAR
COCKTAIL BAR

Map p332 (☑773 974 764; www.hemingwaybar. eu; Karolíny Světlé 26; ⊙5pm-1am Mon-Thu, 5pm-2am Fri, 7pm-2am Sat, 7pm-1am Sun; ☎; ◰17, 21) The Hemingway is a snug and sophisticated hideaway with dark leather benches, a library-like back room, flickering candlelight, and polite and professional bartenders. There's a huge range of quality spirits (especially rum), first-class cocktails, champagne and cigars.

KRÁSNÝ ZTRÁTY
CAFE

Map p332 (☑775 755 143; www.krasnyztraty.cz; Náprstkova 10; ⊙9am-1am Mon-Fri, noon-1am Sat & Sun; ☎; ◰17, 18) This cool cafe – the name translates to something like 'beautiful destruction' – doubles as an art gallery and occasional music venue, and is hugely popular with students from nearby Charles University. There are Czech newspapers and books to leaf through and chilled tunes on the sound system, plus a menu of gourmet teas and coffees to choose from.

U TŘÍ RŮŽÍ
BREWERY

Map p332 (☑601 588 281; www.u3r.cz; Husova 10; ⊙11am-11pm Sun-Thu, to midnight Fri & Sat; ◰17, 18) In the 19th century there were more than 20 breweries in Prague's Old Town, but by 1989 there was only one left (U Medvídku). The Three Roses brewpub, on the site of one of those early breweries, helps revive the tradition, offering six beers on tap, including a tasty *světlý ležák* (pale lager), good food and convivial surroundings.

ČILI BAR
COCKTAIL BAR

Map p332 (⏱724 379 117; www.cilibar.cz; Kožná 8; ☺5pm-2am; 🚇; MMůstek) This tiny cocktail bar could not be further removed in atmosphere from your typical Old Town drinking place. Cramped and smoky – there are Cuban cigars for sale – with battered leather armchairs competing for space with a handful of tables, it's friendly, relaxed and lively. Try the speciality of the house – rum mixed with finely chopped red chillis.

U MEDVÍDKŮ
BEER HALL

Map p332 (At the Little Bear; ⏱224 211 916; www.umedvidku.cz; Na Perštýně 7; ☺beer hall 11.30am-11pm, museum noon-10pm; 🚇; 📳6, 9, MMůstek) The most micro of Prague's microbreweries, with a capacity of only 250L, U Medvídků started producing its own beer in 2005, though its trad-style beer hall has been around for many years. What it lacks in size, it makes up for in strength – the dark lager, marketed as X-Beer, is the strongest in the country, with an alcohol content of 11.8%.

Available in bottles (122Kč for 0.33L), it's a malty, bitter-sweet brew with a powerful punch; handle with caution! There's also Budvar on tap at 32Kč for 0.4L.

KOZIČKA
BAR

Map p332 (⏱224 818 308; www.kozicka.cz; Kozí 1; ☺4pm-4am Mon-Thu, 5pm-4am Fri, 6pm-4am Sat, 7pm-3am Sun; 🚇; MStaroměstská) The 'Little Goat' is a buzzing, red-brick basement bar decorated with cute steel goat sculptures, serving Krušovice on tap at 45Kč for 0.5L (though watch out – the bartenders will occasionally sling you a 1L *tuplák* if they think you're a tourist). It fills up later in the evening with a mostly Czech crowd, and makes a civilised setting for a late-night session.

DUENDE
BAR

Map p332 (⏱775 186 077; www.barduende.cz; Karolíny Světlé 30; ☺1pm-midnight Mon-Fri, 3pm-midnight Sat, 4pm-midnight Sun; 📳17, 18) Barely five minutes' walk from Charles Bridge but half a world away in atmosphere, this cute little bar is the opposite of touristy – a bohemian drinking den that pulls in an arty, mixed-age crowd of locals. Here you can enjoy a drink while casting an eye over the fascinating photos and quirky art that cover the walls, or listen to live guitar or violin.

JAMES JOYCE
PUB

Map p332 (⏱224 818 851; www.jamesjoyceprague.cz; U obecního dvora 4; ☺11am-12.30am Sun-Thu, to 2am Fri & Sat; 🚇; 📳5,8,24) You probably don't go to Prague to visit an Irish bar, but if you're here in winter this friendly pub offers something rarely seen in Prague bars: an open fire. Toast your toes while sipping a Guinness, or downing the all-day Irish breakfast fry-up, including Clonakilty black pudding.

LITERÁRNÍ KAVÁRNA ŘETĚZOVÁ
CAFE

Map p332 (⏱222 220 681; Řetězová 10; ☺noon-11pm Mon-Fri, 5-11pm Sat & Sun; 📳17, 21) This is the kind of place where you can imagine yourself tapping out the Great Prague Novel on your laptop with a half-finished coffee on the table beside you. It's a plain, vaulted room with battered wooden furniture, a scatter of rugs on the floor, old black-and-white photos on the wall, and a relaxed – if smoky – atmosphere.

U ZLATÉHO TYGRA
PUB

Map p332 (⏱222 221 111; www.uzlatehotygra.cz; Husova 17; ☺3-11pm; MStaroměstská) The 'Golden Tiger' is one of the few Old Town drinking holes that has hung on to its soul – and its reasonable prices (40Kč per 0.5L of Pilsner Urquell), considering its location. It was novelist Bohumil Hrabal's favourite hostelry – there are photos of him on the walls – and the place that Václav Havel took Bill Clinton in 1994 to show him a real Czech pub.

MONARCH VINNÝ SKLEP
WINE BAR

Map p332 (⏱224 239 602; www.monarch.cz; Na Perštýně 15; ☺3pm-midnight Mon-Fri, 5pm-midnight Sat & Sun; MNárodní Třída, 📳6, 9) The Monarch wine cellar is one of the best places in town to get to know Czech wines. Despite its knowledgable staff and vast selection of vintages, it manages to avoid any air of pretentiousness, and has a tempting menu of nibbles – cheeses, olives, prosciutto, salami and smoked duck – to accompany your wine.

FRIENDS
CLUB

Map p332 (⏱226 211 920; www.friendsclub.cz; Bartolomějská 11; ☺7pm-6am; 🚇; MNárodní Třída, 📳6, 9) Friends is a welcoming gay bar and club serving excellent coffee, cocktails and wine. It's a good spot to sit back with a drink and check out the crowd, or join in the party spirit on assorted theme nights, which range from Czech pop music and movies to beach parties and comedy nights (see website for listings).

STARÉ MĚSTO DRINKING & NIGHTLIFE

KAVÁRNA OBECNÍ DŮM
CAFE

Map p332 (☑222 002 763; www.kavarnaod. cz; náměstí Republiky 5; ☻7.30am-11pm; ☏; ⓂNáměstí Republiky) The spectacular café in Prague's opulent Municipal House (Obecní dům; p108) offers the opportunity to sip your cappuccino amid an orgy of art nouveau splendour. Also worth a look is the neat little American Bar in the basement of the building, all polished wood, stained glass and gleaming copper.

GRAND CAFE ORIENT
CAFE

Map p332 (☑224 224 240; www.grandcafeorient. cz; Ovocný trh 19; ☻9am-10pm Mon-Fri, 10am-10pm Sat & Sun; ⓂNáměstí Republiky) Prague's only cubist cafe, the Orient was designed by Josef Gočár in 1912 and flaunts its cubist styling down to the smallest detail, including the lampshades and coat hooks. It was restored and reopened in 2005, having been closed since 1920. Decent coffee and inexpensive cocktails, but occasionally surly service.

☆ ENTERTAINMENT

ROXY
CLUB, PERFORMING ARTS

Map p332 (☑224 826 296; www.roxy.cz; Dlouhá 33; cover Fri & Sat free-300Kč; ☻7pm-5am; ☒5, 8, 24) Set in the ramshackle shell of an art deco cinema, the legendary Roxy has nurtured the more independent and innovative end of Prague's club spectrum since 1987 – this is the place to see the Czech Republic's top DJs. On the 1st floor is NoD, an 'experimental space' that stages drama, dance, performance art, cinema and live music. Best nightspot in Staré Město.

JAZZ CLUB U STARÉ PANÍ
JAZZ

Map p332 (☑605 285 211; www.jazzstarapani.cz; Michalská 9; cover 100-250Kč; ☻7pm-1am Wed-Sun, music from 9pm; ⓂMůstek) Located in the basement of the Hotel U Staré Paní, this long-established but recently revamped jazz club caters to all levels of musical appreciation. There's a varied program of modern jazz, soul, blues and Latin rhythms, and a dinner menu if you want to make a full evening of it.

AGHARTA JAZZ CENTRUM
JAZZ

Map p332 (☑222 211 275; www.agharta.cz; Železná 16; cover 250Kč; ☻7pm-1am, music 9pm-midnight; ⓂMůstek) AghaRTA has been staging top-notch modern jazz, blues, funk and fusion since 1991, but moved into this central Old Town venue only in 2004. A typical jazz cellar with red-brick vaults, the centre also has a music shop (open 7pm to midnight) which sells CDs, T-shirts and coffee mugs. As well as hosting local musicians, AghaRTA occasionally stages gigs by leading international artists.

BLUES SKLEP
JAZZ

Map p332 (☑221 466 138; www.bluessklep.cz; Liliová 10; cover 100-150Kč; ☻bar 7pm-2.30am, music 9pm-midnight; ☒17, 18) One of the city's newer jazz clubs, the Blues Sklep (*sklep* means 'cellar') is a typical Old Town basement with dark, Gothic-vaulted rooms that provide an atmospheric setting for regular nightly jazz sessions. Bands play anything from trad New Orleans jazz to bebop, blues, funk and soul.

VAGON
LIVE MUSIC

Map p332 (☑733 737 301; www.vagon.cz; Palác Metro, Národní třída 25; gigs 100-200Kč, cover after midnight free; ☻7pm-5am Mon-Thu, to 6am Fri & Sat, to 1am Sun; ☏; ⓂNárodní Třída) Vagon is more like a student-union bar than a club as such, but it always has a friendly, chilled-out atmosphere. There's live music pretty much every night, from local blues artists, to Pink Floyd and Led Zep tribute bands, to classic Czech rock bands. From midnight into the small hours the dancing continues as a DJ-hosted 'rockothèque'.

DVOŘÁK HALL
CONCERT VENUE

Map p332 (Dvořákova síň; ☑227 059 227; www. ceskafilharmonie.cz; náměstí Jana Palacha 1; tickets 120-800Kč; ☻box office 10am-12.30pm & 1.30-6pm Mon-Fri; ⓂStaroměstská) The Dvořák Hall in the neo-Renaissance Rudolfinum (p106) is home to the world-renowned Czech Philharmonic Orchestra (Česká filharmonie). Sit back and be impressed by some of the best classical musicians in Prague.

ESTATES THEATRE
OPERA, BALLET

Map p332 (Stavovské divadlo; ☑224 902 322; www.narodni-divadlo.cz; Ovocný trh 1; tickets 50-1290Kč; ☻box office 10am-6pm; ⓂMůstek) The Estates is the oldest theatre in Prague, famed as the place where Mozart conducted the premiere of *Don Giovanni* on 29 October 1787. Mozartissimo – a medley of highlights from several of Mozart's operas, including *Don Giovanni* – is performed here from March to May (see www.bmart. cz); the rest of the year sees various opera, ballet and drama productions.

SMETANA HALL CLASSICAL MUSIC
Map p332 (Smetanova síň; ☑222 002 101; www. obecnidum.cz; náměstí Republiky 5; tickets 300-600Kč; ⊙box office 10am-6pm; ⓂNáměstí Republiky) The Smetana Hall, centrepiece of the stunning Municipal House (p108), is the city's largest concert hall, with seating for 1200. This is the home venue of the Prague Symphony Orchestra (Symfonický orchestr hlavního města Prahy), and it also stages performances of folk dance and music.

IMAGE THEATRE PERFORMING ARTS
Map p332 (Divadlo Image; ☑222 314 448; www. imagetheatre.cz; Pařížská 4; tickets 480Kč; ⊙box office 9am-8pm; ⓂStaroměstská) Founded in 1989 this company uses creative black-light theatre along with pantomime, modern dance and video – not to mention liberal doses of slapstick – to tell its stories. The staging can be very effective, but the atmosphere is often dictated by audience reaction.

NATIONAL MARIONETTE THEATRE PERFORMING ARTS
Map p332 (Národní divadlo marionet; ☑224 819 323; www.mozart.cz; Žatecká 1; adult/child 590/490Kč; ⊙box office 10am-8pm; ⓂStaroměstská) Touted as the longest-running marionette show in the city – performed almost continuously since 1991 (a fact, some say, that is reflected in the enthusiasm of the performances) – *Don Giovanni* is a life-sized puppet version of the Mozart opera, and has spawned imitations around town. Younger kids' attention might begin to wander fairly early on during this two-hour show.

TA FANTASTIKA PERFORMING ARTS
Map p332 (☑222 221 364; www.tafantastika. cz; Karlova 8; tickets 720Kč; ⊙box office 11am-9.30pm; ⓂStaroměstská) Established in New York in 1981 by Czech émigré Petr Kratochvil, Ta Fantastika moved to Prague in 1989. The company produces black-light theatre based on classic literature and legends such as *Excalibur, The Picture of Dorian Gray* and *Joan of Arc,* but the program is dominated by *Aspects of Alice,* based on *Alice in Wonderland.*

THEATRE ON THE BALUSTRADE THEATRE
Map p332 (Divadlo Na Zábradlí; ☑222 868 868; www.nazabradli.cz; Anenské náměstí 5; tickets

150-350Kč; ⊙box office 2-8pm Mon-Fri, 2hr before show starts Sat & Sun; 🚊17, 18) The theatre where Václav Havel honed his skills as a playwright four decades ago is now the city's main venue for serious Czech-language drama, including works by a range of foreign playwrights translated into Czech. There are occasional performances in English, and some with English subtitles.

🛍 SHOPPING

DUŠNÍ 3 FASHION
Map p332 (☑234 095 870; www.dusni3.cz; Dušní 3; ⊙10am-7pm Mon-Sat; ⓂStaroměstská) Established as an alternative to the superbrand stores on nearby Pařížská, this welcoming boutique offers a range of ready-to-wear fashion and accessories from a range of international designers, including clothes by Tara Jarmon, Ilaria Nistri and Vivienne Westwood, bags by Lulu Guinness, shoes by Mellow Yellow, sunglasses by Victoria Beckham and perfumes by Andrea Maack.

LEEDA FASHION
Map p332 (☑775 601 185; www.leeda.cz; Bartolomějská 1; ⊙11am-7pm Mon-Sat; 🚊6, 9, 18, 22) This original Czech label, created by two young Prague designers, Lucie Kutálková and Lucie Trnkov, has established a well-earned reputation for turning out colourful, hip and stylish clothes, from T-shirts to designer dresses – and all at very reasonable prices.

ART DECO GALERIE ANTIQUES
Map p332 (☑224 223 076; www.artdecogaleriemili.com; Michalská 21; ⊙2-7pm Mon-Fri; ⓂMůstek) Specialising in early-20th-century items, this shop has a wide range of 1920s and '30s stuff, including clothes, handbags, jewellery, glassware and ceramics, along with knick-knacks such as the kind of cigarette case you might imagine Dorothy Parker pulling from her purse.

MODERNISTA HOMEWARES
Map p332 (☑224 241 300; www.modernista.cz; Obecní dům, náměstí Republiky 5; ⊙11am-6pm; ⓂNáměstí Republiky) Modernista specialises in reproduction 20th-century furniture, ceramics, glassware and jewellery in classic styles ranging from art deco and cubist to functionalist and Bauhaus, including sensuously curved chairs that are a feature

of the Icon Hotel, and an unusual chaise lounge by Adolf Loos. The shop is in the information centre at the Municipal House (p108).

ART DÉCORATIF   ARTS & CRAFTS
Map p332 ([⌖]222 002 350; www.artdecoratif.cz; U Obecního Domu 2; ☺10am-8pm; [M]Náměstí Republiky) This beautiful shop deals in Czech-made reproductions of fine art nouveau and art deco glassware, jewellery and fabrics, including some stunning vases and bowls. It's also an outlet for the gorgeously delicate creations of Jarmila Plockova, granddaughter of Alfons Mucha, who uses elements of his paintings in her work.

KUBISTA   HOMEWARES
Map p332 ([⌖]224 236 378; www.kubista.cz; Ovocný trh 19; ☺10am-7pm Tue-Sat, noon-7pm Sun; [M]Náměstí Republiky) Appropriately located in Prague's finest cubist building, this shop specialises in limited-edition reproductions of distinctive cubist furniture and ceramics, and designs by masters of the form such as Josef Gočár and Pavel Janák. It also has a few original pieces for serious collectors with serious cash to spend.

ST.VOL   GLASS
Map p332 ([⌖]224 814 099; www.stvol.eu; Valentinská 11; ☺10am-6pm Mon-Fri, 11am-5pm Sun; [M]Staroměstská) This gallery-shop is showroom for the striking and colourful glassware of Czech designers, including Jiří Pačínek and Bořek Šípek. Their work may not be to everyone's taste, but their eccentric creations are certainly eye-catching.

KLARA NADEMLÝNSKÁ   FASHION
Map p332 ([⌖]224 818 769; www.klaranademlynska.cz; Dlouhá 3; ☺10am-7pm Mon-Fri, to 6pm Sat; [M]Staroměstská) Klara Nademlýnská is one of the Czech Republic's top fashion designers, having trained in Prague and worked for almost a decade in Paris. Her clothes are characterised by clean lines, simple styling and quality materials, making for a very wearable range that covers the spectrum from swimwear to evening wear via jeans, halter tops, colourful blouses and sharply styled suits.

TEG   FASHION
Map p332 ([⌖]222 327 358; www.timoure.cz; V Kolkovně 6; ☺10am-7pm Mon-Fri, 11am-5pm Sat; [M]Staroměstská) TEG (Timoure et Group) is the design team created by Alexandra Pavalová and Ivana Šafránková, two of Prague's most respected fashion designers. This boutique showcases their quarterly collections, which feature a sharp, imaginative look that adds zest and sophistication to everyday, wearable clothes. There's a second **branch** (Map p332; [⌖]224 240 737; www.timoure.cz; Martinská 4; ☺10am-7pm Mon-Fri, to 5pm Sat; [M]Národní Třída) near Národní třída.

BOHÈME   FASHION
Map p332 ([⌖]224 813 840; www.boheme.cz; Dušní 8; ☺11am-7pm Mon-Fri, to 5pm Sat; [M]Staroměstská) This boutique showcases the designs of Hana Stocklassa and her associates, with collections of knitwear, leather and suede clothes for women. Sweaters, turtlenecks, suede skirts, linen blouses, knit dresses and stretch denim suits seem to be the stock in trade, and there's a range of jewellery to choose from as well.

LE PATIO LIFESTYLE   HOMEWARES
Map p332 ([⌖]222 310 310; www.lepatiolifestyle.com; Dušní 8; ☺10am-7pm Mon-Sat, 11am-7pm Sun; [M]Staroměstská) There are lots of high-quality household accessories here, from wrought-iron chairs and lamps forged by Bohemian blacksmiths to scented wooden chests made by Indian carpenters. Plus you'll find funky earthenware plant pots, chunky crystal wine glasses in contemporary designs, and many more tempting items that you just *know* will fit into your already crammed suitcase...

DENIM HEADS   FASHION
Map p332 ([⌖]222 313 151; www.denimheads.cz; Rámová 3; ☺11am-7pm Mon-Sat; [🚊]5, 8, 24) Probably the city's best outlet for denim goods, this stylish boutique stocks more than two dozen brands from around the world, including Denim Demon and Indigofera from Sweden, and quality Japanese jeans from Momotaro and Japan Blue.

MANUFAKTURA   ARTS & CRAFTS
Map p332 ([⌖]257 533 678; www.manufaktura.cz; Melantrichova 17; ☺10am-8pm; [M]Můstek) There are several Manufaktura outlets across town, but this small branch near the Old Town Square seems to keep its inventory especially enticing. You'll find great Czech wooden toys, beautiful-looking (if extremely chewy) honey gingerbread made from elaborate medieval moulds, and seasonal gifts such as hand-painted Easter eggs.

FREY WILLE
JEWELLERY

Map p332 (📞272 142 228; www.frey-wille.com; Havířská 3; ⏱10am-7pm Mon-Sat, noon-6pm Sun; Ⓜ Můstek) An Austrian jewellery maker famed for enamel work, Frey Wille produces a distinctive range of highly decorative pieces. Its traditional paisley and Egyptian designs are complemented by a range of art nouveau designs based on the works of Alfons Mucha.

GRANÁT TURNOV
JEWELLERY

Map p332 (📞222 315 612; www.granat.eu; Dlouhá 28-30; ⏱10am-6pm Mon-Fri, to 1pm Sat; Ⓜ Náměstí Republiky) Part of the country's biggest jewellery chain, Granát Turnov specialises in Bohemian garnet, and has a huge range of gold and silver rings, brooches, cufflinks and necklaces featuring these small, dark blood red stones. There's also pearl and diamond jewellery, and less expensive pieces set with the dark green semiprecious stone known in Czech as *vltavín* (moldavite).

MAXIMUM UNDERGROUND
MUSIC

Map p332 (📞724 307 198; www.maximum.cz; Jílská 22; ⏱11am-7pm Mon-Sat; Ⓜ Můstek) On the 1st floor in an arcade just off Jílská, this place is stocked with CDs and LPs of indie, punk, hip hop, techno and other genres. It also has a selection of new and secondhand street and club wear for those seeking that Central European grunge look.

TALACKO
MUSIC

Map p332 (📞224 813 039; www.talacko.cz; Rybná 29; ⏱10am-6pm Mon-Fri, to 4pm Sat; Ⓜ Náměstí Republiky) Pick up the score for Mozart's *Don Giovanni* or Dvořák's *New World Symphony* at this eclectic sheet-music shop. Or you might enjoy some popular music favourites – how about '101 Beatles Songs for Buskers'?

BRIC A BRAC
ANTIQUES

Map p332 (📞222 326 484; Týnská 7; ⏱11am-6pm; Ⓜ Náměstí Republiky) This is a wonderfully cluttered cave of old household items, glassware, toys, apothecary jars, 1940s leather jackets, cigar boxes, typewriters and stringed instruments and... Despite the junky look of the place, the knick-knacks are surprisingly expensive, but the affable Serbian owner can give you a guided tour around every piece in his extensive collection.

HAVELSKÁ MARKET
MARKET

Map p332 (Havelská; ⏱7.30am-6pm Mon-Fri, 8.30am-6pm Sat & Sun; Ⓜ Můstek) Souvenirs have insinuated themselves among the fruit and veg of this formerly produce-only market. While the shops on either side of the street are selling entirely resistible tat, the market stalls are worth a quick browse for fresh honey or sweets, as well as colourfully painted eggs sold in the run-up to Easter.

STARÉ MĚSTO SHOPPING

Nové Město

NORTHERN NOVÉ MĚSTO | WENCESLAS SQUARE & AROUND | ALONG THE RIVER | CHARLES SQUARE & AROUND

Neighbourhood Top Five

1 Admire some of the city's finest 20th-century architecture in and around **Wenceslas Square** (p122), from the art nouveau extravagance of the Grand Hotel Evropa to the sleekly functionalist **Mánes Gallery** (p127) and the exuberant **Dancing Building** (p127).

2 Attend a performance of Dvořák's music by the **Original Music Theatre of Prague** (p133) in the Víla Amerika.

3 Learn about one of WWII's most dramatic assassinations in the **National Memorial to the Heroes of the Heydrich Terror** (p128).

4 Discover the beautiful art nouveau masterpieces of Prague's most famous artist at the **Mucha Museum** (p126).

5 Explore the magnificent arcades, such as those in **Lucerna Palace** (p124), and hidden gardens of Nové Město on foot.

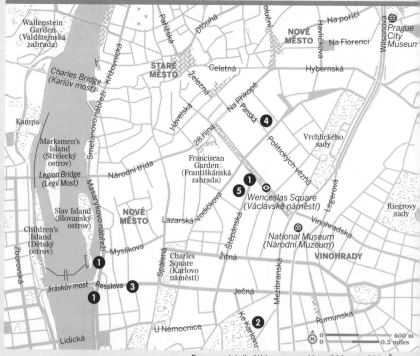

For more detail of this area, see Map p336 and p338 ➡

Explore: Nové Město

Nové Město means 'New Town', although this crescent-shaped district to the east and south of Staré Město was new only when it was founded by Charles IV in 1348. It extends eastwards from Revoluční and Na Příkopě to Wilsonova and the main railway line, and south from Národní třída to Vyšehrad.

Most of Nové Město's outer fortifications were demolished in 1875, though a section of wall still survives in the south, facing Vyšehrad. However, the original street plan has been essentially preserved, with three large market squares that once provided the district's commercial focus: Hay Market Square (Senovážné náměstí), Wenceslas Square (Václavské náměstí) and Charles Square (Karlovo náměstí).

Most of the surviving buildings are from the 19th and early 20th centuries, many of them among the city's finest examples of art nouveau, neo-Renaissance, Czech National Revival and functionalist architecture. Many blocks are honeycombed with pedestrian-only arcades – Prague's famous *pasáže* (passages) – lined with shops, cafes, cinemas and theatres.

Local Life

➡ **A Night at the Opera** Get dressed up to the nines and join the crowds of similarly spruced-up Praguers attending a performance at the Prague State Opera (p133) – only tourists dress down.

➡ **Hangouts** The Bokovka (p132) wine bar is owned by a couple of Czech film directors, and is a popular meeting place for local arty types. Kávovarna (p132) is another place where locals outnumber tourists by a long way, despite being a few steps from Wenceslas Square.

➡ **Markets** Crowds of locals throng the river embankment at Náplavka for the Saturday farmers market (p134); in summer, stalls are augmented by music, barbecues and cocktail boats moored alongside.

Getting There & Away

➡ **Metro** The city's three metro lines all intersect in Nové Město: at Muzeum and Můstek stations at the eastern and western ends (respectively) of Wenceslas Square, and at Florenc station in northern Nové Město, while Karlovo Náměstí station on line B serves southern Nové Město.

➡ **Tram** Cutting across the middle of Wenceslas Square, trams 3, 9, 14 and 24 run along Vodičkova and Jindřišská. Lines 14 and 17 run along the river embankment in the west.

Lonely Planet's Top Tip

If you want to get away from the crowds and constant traffic of Wenceslas Square, find your way to the **Franciscan Garden** (p127) – an oasis of peace just a short stroll away from the urban madness.

Best Places to Eat

➡ Sansho (p131)
➡ Room (p131)
➡ Al Forno (p131)
➡ Siam Orchid (p131)
➡ Kogo (p131)

For reviews, see p129.➡

Best Places to Drink

➡ Bokovka (p132)
➡ Pivovarský Dům (p131)
➡ Hoffa (p132)
➡ Red Room (p132)
➡ Vinograf (p132)

For reviews, see p131.➡

Best Art Galleries

➡ Mucha Museum (p126)
➡ Leica Gallery (p125)
➡ Mánes Gallery (p127)

For reviews, see p124.➡

NOVÉ MĚSTO

TOP SIGHT
WENCESLAS SQUARE

More a broad boulevard than a typical city square, Wenceslas Square has witnessed a great deal of Czech history – a giant Mass was held here during the revolutionary upheavals of 1848; in 1918 the creation of the new Czechoslovak Republic was celebrated here; and in 1989 the fall of communism was announced here. Originally a medieval horse market, Václavské náměstí was named after Bohemia's patron saint during the nationalist revival of the mid-19th century.

DON'T MISS

➡ St Wenceslas Statue
➡ Memorial to the Victims of Communism
➡ Grand Hotel Evropa
➡ Bat'a Shoe Store

PRACTICALITIES

➡ Václavské náměstí
➡ Map p338
➡ Ⓜ Můstek, Muzeum

Velvet Revolution

Following a police attack on a student demonstration on 17 November 1989, angry citizens gathered in Wenceslas Square by the thousands night after night. A week later, in a stunning mirror image of Klement Gottwald's 1948 proclamation of communist rule in Old Town Square, Alexander Dubček and Václav Havel stepped onto the balcony of the Melantrich Building to a thunderous and tearful ovation, and proclaimed the end of communism in Czechoslovakia.

St Wenceslas Statue

At the southern end of the square is Josef Myslbek's muscular equestrian statue of St Wenceslas (sv Václav), the 10th-century pacifist Duke of Bohemia and the 'Good King Wenceslas' of Christmas-carol fame. Flanked by other patron saints of Bohemia – Prokop, Adalbert, Agnes and Ludmila – he has been plastered with posters and bunting at every one of the square's historical moments.

Memorial to the Victims of Communism

Near the statue, a small memorial to the victims of communism bears photographs and handwritten epitaphs to Jan Palach and other anticommunist rebels. In contrast to the solemnity of this shrine, the square around it has become a monument to capitalism, a gaudy gallery of fast-food outlets and expensive shops.

Architecture

Grand Hotel Evropa (Map p338; No 25; 1906) Perhaps the most beautiful building on the square, art nouveau inside and out; currently closed for reconstruction.

Melantrich Building (Map p338; No 36; 1914) Now a Marks & Spencer; the balcony overlooking the Tramvaj Café is where Havel and Dubček appeared to announce the end of communist rule in November 1989.

Wiehl House (Wiehlův dům; Map p338; No 34; 1896) Has a gorgeous facade decorated with neo-Renaissance murals by top Czech artist Mikuláš Aleš and others; it's named after its designer, Antonín Wiehl.

Bat'a shoe store (Map p338; No 6; 1929) A functionalist masterpiece, designed by Ludvík Kysela for Tomáš Bat'a, art patron, industrialist and founder of the shoe empire.

Lindt Building (Map p338; No 4; 1927) Also designed by Ludvík Kysela, it's one of the republic's earliest functionalist buildings.

Koruna Palace (Palác Koruna; Map p338; No 1; 1914) An art nouveau design by Antonín Pfeiffer; has a tower topped with a crown of pearls. Note its tiny but charming facade around the corner on Na Příkopě.

NOVÉ MĚSTO

TOP SIGHT
NATIONAL MUSEUM

Looming above Wenceslas Square is the neo-Renaissance bulk of the National Museum, designed in the 1880s by Josef Schulz as an architectural symbol of the Czech National Revival. Its magnificent interior is a shrine to the cultural, intellectual and scientific history of the Czech Republic.

DON'T MISS...

➡ Main staircase
➡ Pantheon
➡ Jan Palach memorial

PRACTICALITIES

➡ Národní muzeum
➡ Map p338
➡ ☑224 497 111
➡ www.nm.cz
➡ Václavské náměstí 68
➡ Ⓜ Muzeum

History

Completed in 1891, the imposing facade of the National Museum dominates the southern end of Wenceslas Square, and has played a part in many of the historical events that happened here. The building was occupied by the Nazis during WWII, and was damaged by a bomb on 7 May 1945, allegedly dropped by the last enemy plane to fly over the city during the German withdrawal. In 1968, invading Warsaw Pact troops apparently mistook the museum for the former National Assembly or the radio station, and raked it with gunfire; the light-coloured areas on the facade are patched-up bullet holes. And in January 1969, student Jan Palach set himself on fire here in protest at the Warsaw Pact invasion – you'll find a cross-shaped **memorial** set into the pavement, to the left of the fountain in front of the museum, that marks the spot where he fell.

Main Building

The museum's main building was closed until 2015 for a major overhaul that extended exhibition spaces, and created covered courtyards and a museum shop and cafe. The marbled splendour of the interior has appeared in several Hollywood films including *Mission Impossible* with Tom Cruise, *From Hell* starring Johnny Depp, and *Casino Royale* with Daniel Craig. The opulent **main staircase** is an extravaganza of polished limestone and serpentine, lined with paintings of Bohemian castles and medallions of kings and emperors. The domed **pantheon**, with four huge lunette paintings of (strangely womanless) Czech legend and history by František Ženíšek and Václav Brožík, houses bronze busts and statues of the great and the good of Czech art and science.

New Building

In 2009 the museum expanded into the old Radio Free Europe/Radio Liberty building next door. The so-called **New Building** (Map p338; ☑224 497 111; www.nm.cz; Vinohradská 1; adult/child 110/75Kč; ⊙10am-6pm; Ⓜ Muzeum) now hosts changing exhibitions on various historical, scientific and technological themes. These range from subjects such as the gold treasure of Košice (a hoard of gold coins and jewellery discovered in Slovakia in 1935), famous Czech and Slovak inventors, and 100 years of the Olympic games, to an exhibition on Czechoslovakia under communist rule, which provided some grimly fascinating insights into this dark period of recent history. Between 1948 and 1989 at least 280 civilians died trying to cross the border to the west. During the same period 584 of the 19,000-strong border guard died, including 185 suicides, 39 shot, and 243 through injury and accident; only 11 were killed by escapees.

◉ SIGHTS

◉ Northern Nové Město

PRAGUE MAIN
TRAIN STATION ARCHITECTURE
Map p336 (Praha Hlavní Nádraží; Wilsonova; ◷3.15am-12.40am; Ⓜ Hlavní Nádraží) What? The railway station is a tourist attraction? Perhaps not all of it, but it's certainly worth heading to the top floor for a look at the newly renovated splendour of the original art nouveau entrance hall, designed by Josef Fanta and built between 1901 and 1909.

JINDŘIŠSKÁ TOWER TOWER
Map p336 (Jindřišská věž; ☏224 232 429; www.jindrisskavez.cz/en; Jindřišská 1; adult/child 90/40Kč; ◷10am-6pm; ☒3, 9, 14, 24) This bell tower, dating from the 15th century but rebuilt in Gothic style in the 1870s, dominates the end of Jindřišská, a busy street running northeast from Wenceslas Square. Having stood idle for decades, the tower was renovated and reopened in 2002 as a tourist attraction, complete with exhibition space, whisky bar, cafe and restaurant, and a lookout gallery on the 10th floor.

JUBILEE SYNAGOGUE SYNAGOGUE
Map p338 (Jubilejní synagóga; ☏222 319 002; www.synagogue.cz; Jeruzalémská 7; adult/child 80/50Kč; ◷11am-5pm Sun-Fri Apr-Oct, closed on Jewish hols; Ⓜ Hlavní Nádraží) The colourful Moorish facade of the Jubilee Synagogue, also called the Velká synagóga (Great Synagogue), dates from 1906; note the names of the donors on the stained-glass windows, and the grand organ above the entrance. It houses an exhibition of artefacts, photographs and films charting the post-WWII history of Prague's Jewish community.

◉ Wenceslas Square & Around

WENCESLAS SQUARE SQUARE
See p122.

NATIONAL MUSEUM MUSEUM
See p123.

LUCERNA PALACE ARCHITECTURE
Map p338 (Palác Lucerna; www.lucerna.cz; Vodičkova 36; ☒3, 9, 14, 24) The most elegant of Nové Město's many shopping arcades runs through the art nouveau Lucerna

◉ TOP SIGHT
PRAGUE CITY MUSEUM

This excellent museum, opened in 1898, is devoted to the history of Prague from prehistoric times to the 20th century. Among the many intriguing exhibits are the Astronomical Clock's (p100) original 1866 calendar wheel with Josef Mánes' beautiful painted panels representing the months – that's January at the top, toasting his toes by the fire, and August near the bottom, sickle in hand, harvesting the corn.

The medieval and Renaissance galleries display lots of fascinating household artefacts, including a reliquary made of carved bone, plus more valuable items such as a 16th-century bronze figure of Hercules which was perhaps created for the Wallenstein Palace (it was found in a private house in the Old Town in 1905).

But what everybody comes to see is Antonín Langweil's astonishing 1:480 scale model of Prague as it looked between 1826 and 1834. The display is most rewarding after you get to know Prague a bit, as you can spot the changes – look at St Vitus Cathedral, for example, still only half-finished. Labels are in English as well as Czech.

DON'T MISS...
➡ Antonín Langweil's model of Prague
➡ Manes' beautiful calendar wheel

PRACTICALITIES
➡ Muzeum hlavního města Prahy
➡ Map p336
➡ ☏224 816 773
➡ www.muzeumprahy.cz
➡ Na Poříčí 52, Karlín
➡ adult/child 120/50Kč
➡ ◷9am-6pm Tue-Sun
➡ Ⓜ Florenc

Palace (1920), between Štěpánská and Vodičkova streets. The complex was designed by Václav Havel (grandfather of the former president), and is still partially owned by the family. It includes theatres, a cinema, shops, a rock club and several cafes and restaurants.

In the marbled atrium hangs artist David Černý's sculpture *Kun* (Horse), a wryly amusing counterpart to the equestrian statue of St Wenceslas in Wenceslas Square. Here St Wenceslas sits astride a horse that is decidedly dead; Černý never comments on the meaning of his works, but it's safe to assume that this Wenceslas (Václav in Czech) is a reference to Václav Klaus, president of the Czech Republic from 2003 to 2013.

The neighbouring **Novák Arcade**, connected to the Lucerna and riddled by a maze of passages, has one of Prague's finest art nouveau facades (overlooking Vodičkova), complete with mosaics of country life.

MUSEUM OF COMMUNISM MUSEUM
Map p338 (Muzeum Komunismu; ☑224 212 966; www.muzeumkomunismu.cz; Na Příkopě 10; adult/concession/child under 10 years 190/150Kč/free; ⊗9am-9pm; ⓂMůstek) It's difficult to think of a more ironic site for a museum of communism – in an 18th-century aristocrat's palace, with a casino on one side and a McDonald's on the other. Put together by an American expat and his Czech partner, the museum tells the story of Czechoslovakia's years behind the Iron Curtain in photos, words and a fascinating and varied collection of...well, stuff.

HOTEL JALTA NUCLEAR BUNKER HISTORIC BUILDING
Map p338 (☑222 822 111; www.hoteljalta.com; Václavské náměstí 45; per person 75Kč; ⊗5-8pm Mon & Wed even weeks, Tue & Thu odd weeks; ⓂMuzeum) Hidden beneath the 1950s Hotel Jalta on Wenceslas Square lies a communist-era nuclear shelter that was opened to the public in 2013. The tour (in Czech, with an English text), led by a guide in period security police uniform, takes in a series of secret chambers; the highlight is the comms room, where wiretaps in the bedrooms of important guests were monitored.

LEICA GALLERY GALLERY
Map p338 (☑222 211 567; www.lgp.cz; Školská 28; adult/child 70/40Kč; ⊗9am-9pm Mon-Fri, noon-8pm Sat & Sun; ☎; ☷3, 9, 14, 24) The Leica Gallery stages exhibitions of 20th-century and contemporary photography by both Czech and international photographers; past exhibitions have featured the work of Helmut Newton, Leni Riefenstahl, and Magnum Photo Agency photographer Elliott Erwitt. There's also a comfortable cafe and bookshop.

NA PŘÍKOPĚ STREET
(ⓂMůstek) Na Příkopě (On the Moat), along with Revoluční (Revolution), 28.října (28 October 1918; Czechoslovak Independence Day) and Národní třída (National Ave), follows the line of the moat that once ran along the foot of Staré Město's city walls.

Na Příkopě meets Wenceslas Square at Na Můstku (On the Little Bridge). A small stone bridge once crossed the moat here – you can still see a remaining arch in the underground entrance to Můstek metro station, on the left just past the ticket machines.

In the 19th century this fashionable street was the haunt of Prague's German cafe society. Today it is (along with Wenceslas Square and Pařížská) the city's main upmarket shopping precinct, lined with banks, shopping malls and tourist cafes.

NÁRODNÍ TŘÍDA STREET
Map p338 (☷6, 9, 18, 22) Národní třída (National Ave) is central Prague's 'high street', a stately row of midrange shops and grand public buildings, notably the National Theatre at the Vltava River end.

Fronting Jungmannovo náměstí, at the eastern end, is an imitation Venetian palace known as the **Adria Palace** (Map p338; Národní třída 36). Its distinctive, chunky architectural style, dating from the 1920s, is known as 'rondocubism'. Note how the alternating angular and rounded window pediments echo similar features in neoclassical baroque buildings such as the Černín Palace.

Beneath it is the **Adria Theatre**, birthplace of Laterna Magika and meeting place of the Civic Forum in the heady days of the Velvet Revolution. From here, Dubček and Havel walked to the Lucerna Palace and their 24 November 1989 appearance on the balcony of the Melantrich Building. Wander through the arcade for a look at the lovely marble, glass and brass decoration; the main atrium has a 24-hour clock from the 1920s, flanked by sculptures depicting the signs of the zodiac. It was once the entrance

TOP SIGHT
MUCHA MUSEUM

This fascinating (and busy) museum features the sensuous art nouveau posters, paintings and decorative panels of Alfons Mucha (1860–1939), as well as many sketches, photographs and other memorabilia. The exhibits include countless artworks showing Mucha's trademark Slavic maidens with flowing hair and piercing blue eyes, bearing symbolic garlands and linden boughs.

There are also photos of the artist's Paris studio, one of which shows a trouserless Gaugin playing the harmonium; a powerful canvas entitled *Old Woman in Winter*; and the original of the 1894 poster of actress Sarah Bernhardt as Giselda, which shot Mucha to international fame. In 1910 he was invited to design the Lord Mayor's Hall in Prague's Municipal House and, following the creation of Czechoslovakia in 1918, he designed the new nation's banknotes and postage stamps. But his crowning achievement was the *Slav Epic*, a series of huge, historical paintings, now on display at the Veletržní Palác (p156).

The fascinating 30-minute video documentary about Mucha's life is well worth watching, and helps to put his achievements into perspective.

DON'T MISS...

➔ 1894 poster of Sarah Bernhardt

➔ The photograph of a trouserless Gaugin in Mucha's studio

➔ The video documentary about Mucha's life and work

PRACTICALITIES

➔ Muchovo muzeum

➔ Map p336

➔ ☑221 451 333

➔ www.mucha.cz

➔ Panská 7

➔ adult/child 240/140Kč

➔ ⊙10am-6pm

➔ Ⓜ Můstek

to the offices of the Adriatica insurance company (hence the building's name).

Along the street, inside the arcade near No 16, is the **1989 students' memorial** – a bronze plaque on the wall with a cluster of hands making the peace sign and the date '17.11.89', in memory of students beaten up by police on that date.

West of Voršilská, the lemon-yellow walls of the **Convent of St Ursula** (klášter sv Voršila; Map p338; Národní třída 10) frame a pink church, which has a lush baroque interior that includes a battalion of Apostle statues. Out front is the figure of St John of Nepomuk, and in the facade's lower-right niche is a statue of St Agatha holding her severed breasts – one of the more gruesome images in Catholic hagiography.

Across the road at No 7 is the art nouveau facade (by Osvald Polívka) of the **Viola Building** (Map p332; Národní třída 7), former home of the Prague Insurance Co, with the huge letters 'PRAHA' entwined around five circular windows, and mosaics spelling out *život, kapitál, důchod, věno* and *pojišťuje* (life, capital, income, dowry and insurance). The building next door, a former publishing house, is also a Polívka design.

On the southern side at No 4, looking like it has been built out of old TV screens, is the **Nová Scéna** (1983), the 'New National Theatre' building, now home of Laterna Magika (p134).

Finally, facing the Vltava near Smetanovo nábřeží is the magnificent National Theatre. Across from the theatre is the **Kavárna Slavia**, known for its art deco interior and river views, and once the place to be seen or to grab an after-theatre meal. Now renovated, it's once again the place to be seen – though mainly by other tourists.

NATIONAL THEATRE   ARCHITECTURE
Map p338 (Národní divadlo; www.narodni-divadlo.cz; Ostrovní 1, main entrance on Národní třída; ⬚6, 9, 18, 22) The National Theatre is the neo-Renaissance architectural flagship of the Czech National Revival, and one of Prague's most impressive buildings. Funded entirely by private donations and decorated inside and out by a roll-call of prominent Czech artists, architect Josef Zítek's masterpiece burned down within weeks of its 1881 opening but, incredibly, was funded again and restored in less than two years.

CHURCH OF OUR LADY
OF THE SNOWS
CHURCH

Map p338 (Kostel Panny Marie Sněžné; www.pms.
ofm.cz; Jungmannovo náměstí 18; MMůstek)
This Gothic church at the northern end of
Wenceslas Square was begun in the 14th
century by Charles IV, but only the chan-
cel was ever completed, which accounts
for the building's proportions – seemingly
taller than it is long. Charles had intended
it to be the grandest church in the whole of
Prague; the nave is higher than that of St
Vitus Cathedral, and the altar is the city's
tallest.

It was a Hussite stronghold, ringing
with the sermons of Jan Želivský, who led
the 1419 defenestration that touched off the
Hussite Wars. The church is approached
through an arch in the Austrian Cultural
Institute on Jungmannovo náměstí, but
you can get a good view of the exterior from
the neighbouring **Franciscan Garden** (Map
p338; entrances on Jungmannovo náměstí, pasáž
Vodičkova ulice & pasáž Václavské náměstí). Beside the church is the Chapel of the Pasov
Virgin, now a venue for temporary art
exhibitions.

⊙ Along the River

DANCING BUILDING
ARCHITECTURE

Map p338 (Tančící dům; www.tancici-dum.cz;
Rašínovo nábřeží 80; 14, 17) The Dancing
Building was built in 1996 by architects
Vlado Milunić and Frank Gehry. The
curved lines of the narrow-waisted glass
tower clutched against its more upright and
formal partner led to it being christened
the 'Fred & Ginger' building, after legendary dancing duo Fred Astaire and Ginger
Rogers. It's surprising how well it fits in
with its ageing neighbours.

MÁNES GALLERY
GALLERY

Map p338 (Výstavní síň Mánes; ✆224 932 938;
www.ncvu.cz/manes; Masarykovo nábřeží 1;
⏰10am-8pm Tue-Sun; 14, 17) **FREE** Spanning a branch of the river beneath a 15th-
century water tower is the Mánes Building
(1927–30), a masterpiece of functionalist architecture designed by Otakar Novotný. It
houses an art gallery founded in the 1920s
by a group of artists, headed by painter Josef Mánes, and is still one of Prague's best
venues for viewing contemporary art.

NOVÉ MĚSTO SIGHTS

RIVERFRONT ARCHITECTURE

The Nové Město riverfront, stretching south from the National Theatre to Vyšehrad, is
lined with some of Prague's grandest 19th- and early-20th-century architecture. It's a
great place for an evening stroll, when the sun gilds the facades with golden light.

Masarykovo nábřeží (Masaryk Embankment) sports a series of stunning art nouveau buildings. At No 32 is the duck-egg green **Goethe Institute** (Map p338; Masarykovo nábřeží 32), once the East German embassy. No 26 is a beautiful apartment building
with owls perched in the decorative foliage that twines around the door, dogs peeking
from the balconies on the 5th floor, and birds perched atop the balustrade.

No 16 is the **House of the Hlahol Choir** (Map p338; Masarykovo nábřeží 16), built in
1906 by Josef Fanta for a patriotic choral society associated with the Czech National
Revival. It's decorated with elaborate musical motifs and topped by a giant mosaic
depicting Music – the motto beneath translates as 'Let the song reach the heart; let
the heart reach the homeland'.

At the next bridge is **Jirásek Square** (Jiráskovo náměstí), dedicated to writer
Alois Jirásek (1851–1930), author of Old Czech Legends (studied by all Czech school-
children) and an influential figure in the drive towards Czechoslovak independence.
His statue is overlooked by the famous Dancing Building.

A little further along the riverbank is **Rašínovo nábřeží 78** (Map p338), an apartment building designed by the grandfather of the late president Václav Havel – this was
where Havel first chose to live (in preference to Prague Castle) after being elected as
president in December 1989, surely the world's least pompous presidential residence.

Two blocks south, sitting on Palackého náměstí, is Stanislav Sucharda's extraordinary art nouveau **František Palacký Memorial** (Map p338; Palackého náměstí);
a swarm of haunted bronze figures (allegories of the writer's imagination) swirling
around a stodgy statue of the 19th-century historian and giant of the Czech National
Revival.

TOP SIGHT
NATIONAL MEMORIAL TO THE HEROES OF THE HEYDRICH TERROR

The Church of Sts Cyril & Methodius houses a moving memorial to the seven Czech paratroopers who were involved in the assassination of Reichsprotektor Reinhard Heydrich in 1942, with an exhibit and video about Nazi persecution of the Czechs. The church appeared in the 1975 movie based on the assassination, *Operation Daybreak*.

The paratroopers hid in the church's crypt for three weeks after the killing, until their hiding place was betrayed by the Czech traitor Karel Čurda. The Germans besieged the church, first attempting to smoke the paratroopers out and then flooding the crypt with fire hoses. Three paratroopers were killed in the ensuing fight; the other four took their own lives rather than surrender to the Germans.

In the crypt itself you can still see the bullet marks and shrapnel scars on the walls, and signs of the paratroopers' last desperate efforts to dig an escape tunnel to the sewer under the street. On the Resslova side of the church, the narrow gap in the wall of the crypt where the Germans inserted their fire hoses is still pitted with bullet marks.

DON'T MISS...

➡ The bullet-scarred gap in the exterior wall of the church

➡ Crypt exhibit

PRACTICALITIES

➡ Národní památník hrdinů Heydrichiády

➡ Map p338

➡ ☎224 916 100

➡ www.pamatnik-heydrichiady.cz

➡ Resslova 9

➡ adult/concession 75/35Kč

➡ ☺9am-5pm Tue-Sun Mar-Oct, 9am-5pm Tue-Sat Nov-Feb

➡ Ⓜ Karlovo Náměstí

However, half of the building is now leased as a restaurant and office space, following financial problems that arose during a major renovation from 2012 to 2014.

◉ Charles Square & Around

CHARLES SQUARE   SQUARE
Map p338 (Karolovo náměstí; Ⓜ Karlovo Náměstí) With an area of more than seven hectares, Charles Square is the city's biggest square; it's more like a small park, really, and was originally the city's cattle market. Presiding over it is the **Church of St Ignatius** (Kostel sv Ignáce; Map p338; Ječná 2), a 1660s baroque tour de force designed for the Jesuits by Carlo Lurago.

The baroque palace at the southern end of the square belongs to Charles University. It's known as **Faust House** (Faustův dům; Map p338; Karlovo náměstí 40) because, according to a popular story, this house was where Mephisto took Dr Faust away to hell through a hole in the ceiling, and because

of associations with Rudolf II's English court alchemist, Edward Kelley, who toiled here in the 16th century trying to convert lead into gold.

NEW TOWN HALL   HISTORIC BUILDING
Map p338 (Novoměstská radnice; ☎224 948 229; www.nrpraha.cz; Karlovo náměstí 23; adult/child 50/30Kč; ☺10am-6pm Tue-Sun Apr-Sep; Ⓜ Karlovo Náměstí) The New Town Hall was built in the late 14th century, when the New Town was still new. From the window of the main hall (the tower was not built until 1456), two of Wenceslas IV's Catholic councillors were flung to their deaths in 1419 by followers of the Hussite preacher Jan Želivský, sparking the Hussite Wars.

DVOŘÁK MUSEUM   MUSEUM
Map p338 (Muzeum Antonína Dvořáka; ☎224 923 363; www.nm.cz; Ke Karlovu 20; adult/child 50/25Kč; ☺10am-1.30pm & 2-5pm Tue-Sun; Ⓜ IP Pavlova) The most striking building in the drab neighbourhood south of Ječná is the energetically baroque Vila Amerika, a 1720s, French-style summer house designed

by (you guessed it) Kilian Dientzenhofer. It's one of the city's finest baroque buildings and now houses a museum dedicated to the composer Antonín Dvořák. Special concerts (p133) of Dvořák's music are staged here from May to October.

CHARLES UNIVERSITY
BOTANICAL GARDEN
GARDEN

Map p338 (Botanická zahrada Univerzity Karlovy; ☑221 951 879; www.bz-uk.cz; Viničná 7, main entrance on Na Slupi; garden free, glasshouses adult/child 55/30Kč; ◷10am-7.30pm Apr-Aug, to 6pm Sep & Oct, to 5pm Feb & Mar, to 4pm Nov-Jan; ☐6, 18, 24) Just south of Karlovo náměstí is Charles University's botanical garden. Founded in 1775 and moved from Smíchov to its present site in 1898, it's the country's oldest botanical garden.

U KALICHA
HISTORIC BUILDING

Map p338 (At the Chalice; ☑224 912 557; www.ukalicha.cz; Na Bojišti 12; ◷11am-11pm; ⓜIP Pavlova) This is where the eponymous antihero was arrested at the beginning of Jaroslav Hašek's comic novel of WWI, *The Good Soldier Švejk*. The pub is milking the connection for all it's worth – it's an essential port of call for Švejk fans, but the rest of us can find cheaper beer and dumplings elsewhere.

 EATING

The New Town has an eclectic collection of eating places. The main eating areas are Wenceslas Square and Na Příkopě;

there are also lots of less obvious and more appealing eateries hidden in the backstreets between Wenceslas Square and the river.

PHO VIET
VIETNAMESE €

Map p332 (☑777 724 489; Národní třídá 25; mains 60-90Kč; ◷10am-11pm; ⓜNárodní třídá) Tucked away in the far corner of a shopping arcade, this unassuming little place serves up fresh *nem tuoi* (prawn rolls) and aromatic *pho* (beef and noodle soup with coriander) with searingly hot chillis. No prizes for decor – think workers' canteen – but the price/tastiness ratio can't be beat.

GLOBE BOOKSTORE & CAFÉ
CAFE €

Map p338 (☑224 934 203; www.globebookstore.cz; Pštrossova 6; mains 160-200Kč; ◷9.30am-midnight, to 1am Fri & Sat; ☜; ⓜKarlovo Náměstí) This appealing expat bookshop-cafe serves nachos, burgers, chicken wings and salads until 11pm nightly, and also offers an excellent brunch menu (from 9.30am to 4pm Saturday and Sunday) that includes the classic bacon, egg and hash browns, the full English, blueberry pancakes, and freshly squeezed juices. Lighter breakfasts are served from 9.30am to 11.30am weekdays.

KLUB CESTOVATELŮ
MIDDLE EASTERN €

Map p338 (☑734 322 729; www.klubcestovatelu.cz; Masarykovo nábřeží 22; mains 130-230Kč; ◷11am-11pm Mon-Thu, to midnight Fri, noon-midnight Sat, noon-10pm Sun; ☜☜☑; ☐14, 17) This restaurant and tearoom cultivates a ramshackle, relaxed and welcoming atmosphere, with its batik tablecloths, wicker chairs, oriental knick-knacks and library

NOVÉ MĚSTO EATING

THE HEYDRICH ASSASSINATION

In 1941, in response to a series of crippling strikes and sabotage operations by the Czech resistance movement, the German government appointed SS general Reinhard Heydrich, an antisubversion specialist, as Reichsprotektor of Bohemia and Moravia. Heydrich immediately cracked down on resistance activities with a vengeance.

In a move designed to support the resistance and boost Czech morale, Britain secretly trained a team of Czechoslovak paratroopers to assassinate Heydrich. The daring mission was code-named Operation Anthropoid and, against all odds, it succeeded. On 27 May 1942, two paratroopers, Jan Kubiš and Jozef Gabčík, attacked Heydrich as he rode in his official car through the city's Libeň district – he later died from the wounds. The assassins and five co-conspirators fled but were betrayed in their hiding place in the Church of Sts Cyril & Methodius (p128); all seven died in the ensuing siege.

The Nazis reacted with a frenzied wave of terror, which included the annihilation of two entire Czech villages, Ležáky and Lidice, and the shattering of the underground movement.

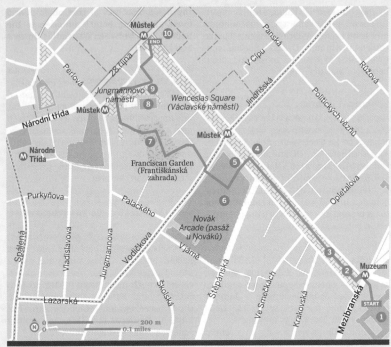

Neighbourhood Walk
Around Wenceslas Square

START NATIONAL MUSEUM
END NA MŮSTKU
LENGTH 1.5KM; 45 MINUTES

Begin at the **1** **National Museum** (p123), at the upper end of Wenceslas Square. At the foot of the steps is a pavement memorial to student Jan Palach.

Cross Mezibranská to the equestrian **2** **statue of St Wenceslas**, the 10th-century 'Good King Wenceslas' of Christmas-carol fame. A flower bed just downhill from the statue contains the **3** **Memorial to the Victims of Communism** (p122).

Wander down the middle of the square admiring the grand buildings such as the **4** **Grand Hotel Evropa** (p122) at No 25. Opposite at No 36 is the **5** **Melantrich Building** (p122), where the death of Czech communism was pronounced by Alexander Dubček and Václav Havel in 1989.

Turn left into Pasáž Rokoko, a mirror-lined art deco arcade. It leads to the central atrium of the **6** **Lucerna Palace** (p124) arcade, dominated by David Černý's *Kun* (Horse), an ironic twist on the St Wenceslas statue outside. Turn right and exit onto Vodičkova, and bear right across the street to enter the Světozor arcade, with a beautiful stained-glass window dating from the late 1940s.

At the far end of the arcade, turn left into the **7** **Franciscan Garden**, a hidden oasis of peace and greenery. Exit diagonally opposite into Jungmannovo náměstí, go past the arch leading to the **8** **Church of Our Lady of the Snows** (p127) and turn right.

Keep to the right of the Lancôme shop, and you will find what must be the only **9** **Cubist lamp post** in the world, dating from 1915. Turn left here and then right through the **10** **Lindt arcade** to emerge at the foot of Wenceslas Square.

of travel guidebooks. The menu is mostly Lebanese – baba ganoush, falafel, hummus and lamb kebabs – with a couple of Indian dishes thrown in, and there's a huge range of speciality teas to choose from.

★ SANSHO
ASIAN, FUSION €€
Map p336 (📱222 317 425; www.sansho.cz; Petrská 25; lunch mains 110-225Kč, 6-course dinner 850-950Kč; ⏱11.30am-3pm & 6-11pm Tue-Thu, to 11.30pm Fri, 6-11.30pm Sat, last orders 10pm; 🚇🍽; 🚊3, 8, 24) Friendly and informal best describes the atmosphere at this ground-breaking restaurant where British chef Paul Day champions Czech farmers by sourcing all his meat and vegetables locally. There's no menu – the waiter will explain what dishes are available, depending on market produce – typical dishes include curried rabbit, pork belly with watermelon salad, and 12-hour beef rendang.

★ ROOM
SPANISH €€
Map p338 (📱221 634 103; www.tapasroom.cz; Icon Hotel, V Jámě 6; tapas 50-320Kc, mains 230-400Kč; ⏱7am-1am; 🛜; 🚊3, 9, 14, 24) Cool, angular and precise in shades of grey, black and avocado green, Room provides the perfect setting for some of Prague's most carefully crafted flavours. With an accomplished kitchen team working from a menu created by actor Tommy Lee Jones's personal chef, it's no surprise that the food – *gambas pil pil* (garlic prawns), clams and chorizo in cider, oxtail with parsnip purée – is top-notch.

AL FORNO
ITALIAN €€
Map p336 (📱222 316 011; al-forno.cz; Petrské náměstí 4; mains 150-350Kč; ⏱11am-11pm; 🚇🛜; 🚊3, 8, 14) As the name suggests ('al forno' means 'cooked in the oven'), this rustic Italian place with warm yellow walls, old wooden furniture and checked tablecloths sports a wood-fired oven that turns out authentic pizza, focaccia, lasagne, cannelloni and a range of roast meat dishes. There's a wide choice of reasonably priced Italian wines, and desserts include tiramisu and *panna cotta*.

LA GARE/LE WINSTUB
FRENCH €€
Map p336 (📱222 313 712; www.lagare.cz; V Celnici 3; mains 150-300Kč; ⏱8am-midnight; 🛜🍽; 🚇Náměstí Republiky) It might not impress a Parisian, but La Gare is a passable imitation of a bustling French brasserie, offering classics such as fish soup, frog legs, coq au vin and bœuf bourguignon. Downstairs is Le Winstub, an Alsace-themed cellar serving *tartes flambées* (a traditional, wood-fired Alsatian dish that resembles a thin and crispy pizza). Family-friendly brunch is served from 10.30am to 3pm Sundays.

KOGO
ITALIAN €€
Map p336 (📱221 451 259; www.kogo.cz; Slovanský dům, Na Příkopě 22; mains 250-680Kč; ⏱11am-11pm; 🛜🍽; 🚇Náměstí Republiky) Chic and businesslike, but also relaxed and family-friendly (highchairs provided), Kogo is a stylish restaurant serving pizza, pasta, and Italian meat and seafood dishes – the rich, tomatoey *zuppa di pesce* (fish soup) is delicious, as is the *risotto alla pescatora* (risotto with squid, mussels, shrimp and octopus). On summer evenings, candlelit tables spill over into the leafy courtyard.

SIAM ORCHID
THAI €€
Map p336 (📱222 319 410; www.siamorchid.cz; Na poříčí 21; mains 160-240Kč; ⏱10am-10pm; 🛜🛜; 🚊3, 8, 24, 26) The setting – a scatter of plastic tables and chairs on a 1st-floor balcony – looks none too promising, but this restaurant, tucked away beside a Thai massage studio, offers some of the city's most authentic Thai cuisine.

LE PATIO
INTERNATIONAL €€
Map p338 (📱274 810 262; www.le-patio.cz; Národní třída 22; mains 225-565Kč; ⏱8am-11pm; 🛜; 🚇Můstek, Národní Třída) It's easy to walk past this place without noticing it, but it's well worth dropping in to sample its accomplished menu of Czech and international dishes in a relaxed atmosphere that hints of foreign travel – a ship's prow, lots of Asian-style lamps, paintings and textiles. There's a good breakfast menu too (served until 11am) with English, American and healthy options.

🍷 DRINKING & NIGHTLIFE

Nové Město, particularly the area around Wenceslas Square, is still a bit of a magnet for stag parties and groups of young lads on the piss. Check out the streets south of Národní třída near the river, where you'll find lots of student cafes, quirky wine bars and trendy new bars.

PIVOVARSKÝ DŮM
BREWERY
Map p338 (📱296 216 666; www.pivovarskydum.com; cnr Ječná & Lipová; ⏱11am-11.30pm; 🚊4,

10, 16, 22) While the tourists flock to U Fleků (p133), locals gather here to sample the classic Czech lager (44Kč per 0.5L) that is produced on the premises, as well as wheat beer and a range of flavoured beers (including coffee, banana and cherry, 44Kč per 0.3L). The pub itself is a pleasant place to linger, decked out with polished copper vats and brewing implements, and smelling faintly of malt and hops.

KÁVOVARNA   CAFE
Map p338 (☎296 236 233; Pasáž Lucerna, Štěpánská 61; ⊗8am-midnight; MMůstek) This retro-styled place has bentwood chairs and curved wooden benches in the smoky, dimly lit front room, with exhibitions of arty black-and-white photography on the walls. The coffee is good and reasonably priced, and the service is friendly and relaxed.

HOFFA   COCKTAIL BAR
Map p336 (☎601 359 659; www.hoffa.cz; Senovážné náměstí 22; ⊗11am-2am Mon-Fri, 6pm-2am Sat & Sun; 🖃; MI5, 9, 26) One of Prague's first entirely smoke-free bars, Hoffa matches clean air with clean design: a long (12m long!) bar fronts a room with sleek, functional decor and a wall of windows looking out onto Senovážné náměstí's fountain of dancing sprites. Friendly staff, accomplished cocktails, and good snacks; there's homemade lemonade and iced tea at lunchtime.

RED ROOM   BAR
Map p338 (☎222 520 084; www.redroom.cz; Myslíkova 28; ⊗6pm-1am Tue-Thu, 6pm-2am Fri, 7pm-2am Sat, 7pm-1am Sun; 🖃; MKarlovo Náměstí, 🚋14 to Myslíkova) The American-expat owners of this tiny bar, just off of Karlovo náměstí, are musicians, so most nights you can usually count on some impromptu guitar playing or an open-mic night. Other times it's quieter and a good spot to start or end your night over a beer and friendly conversation. Mainly students and backpackers.

VINOGRAF   WINE BAR
Map p336 (☎224 142 050; www.vinograf.cz; Senovážné náměstí 23; ⊗11.30am-midnight Mon-Sat; 🖃; 🚋5, 9, 26) With knowledgeable staff and a relaxed atmosphere, this modern wine bar is a great place to discover Moravian wines. There's good finger-food to accompany, mostly cheese and charcuterie, with menus (in Czech and English) on big blackboards behind the bar. Very busy at weekends, when it's worth booking a table.

JÁMA   BAR
Map p338 (☎222 967 081; www.jamapub.cz; V Jámě 7; ⊗11am-1am; 🖃; MMuzeum) Jáma is a popular American-expat bar plastered with old rock gig posters ranging from Led Zep and REM to Kiss and Shania Twain. There's a little beer garden out the back shaded by lime and walnut trees, smiling staff serving up a rotating selection of regional beers and microbrews, and a menu that includes good burgers, steaks, ribs and chicken wings.

BOKOVKA   WINE BAR
Map p338 (☎222 544 014; www.bokovka.com; Pštrossova 8; ⊗4pm-1am Mon-Sat; 🖃; MKarlovo Náměstí) Owned by a syndicate of oenophiles including film directors Jan Hřebejk and David Ondříček, this quaint little bar is named after the movie *Sideways* (*Bokovka* in Czech), which was set in the California vineyards. The main attraction (other than the chance of being served by a film director) is the extensive menu of top-notch Moravian wines.

CAFÉ IMPERIAL   CAFE
Map p336 (☎246 011 440; www.cafeimperial.cz; Na poříčí 15; ⊗7am-11pm; 🖃; MNáměstí Republiky) First opened in 1914, the Imperial is a tour de force of art nouveau tiling – the walls and ceiling are covered in original ceramic tiles, mosaics, sculptured panels and bas-reliefs, with period light fittings and bronzes scattered about. Good coffee, cocktails in the evening, and the menu has all-day English and American breakfasts.

FRIENDS COFFEE HOUSE   CAFE
Map p338 (☎272 049 665; www.milujikavu.cz; Palackého 7; ⊗9am-9pm Mon-Fri, noon-8pm Sat & Sun; 🖃; 🚋3, 9, 14, 24) It's easy to walk past this place, but it's worth seeking out – head through the back to find a couple of relaxing rooms, one fitted out as a library, with well-spaced tables and comfy chairs. Coffee is taken seriously here; only freshly roasted and ground coffee beans are used. Freshly prepared sandwiches also available.

KAVÁRNA LUCERNA   CAFE
Map p338 (☎224 215 495; www.restauracemonarchie.cz; Lucerna Pasáž, Štěpánská 61; ⊗10am-midnight; 🖃; MMůstek, 🚋3, 9, 14, 24) The least touristy of Prague's grand cafes, the Lucerna is part of an art nouveau shopping arcade designed by the grandfather of ex-president Václav Havel. Filled with faux marble, ornamental metalwork and glit-

tering crystal lanterns, this 1920s gem has arched windows overlooking David Černý's famous *Kun* (Horse) sculpture hanging beneath the glass-domed atrium.

U FLEKŮ
BREWERY

Map p338 (☑224 934 019; www.ufleku.cz; Křemencová 11; ◷10am-11pm; Ⓜ Karlovo Náměstí) A festive warren of drinking and dining rooms, U Fleků is a Prague institution, though it's usually clogged with tour groups high on oompah music and the tavern's home-brewed, 13° black beer (59Kč for 0.4L), known as Flek. Purists grumble but go along anyway, though tourist prices have nudged out many locals.

 **ENTERTAINMENT**

JAZZ REPUBLIC
LIVE MUSIC

Map p332 (☑224 282 235; www.jazzrepublic.cz; 28.října 1; admisson to gigs 100Kč; ◷5pm-late, music from 9pm) Despite the name, this relaxed club stages all kinds of live music, including rock, blues, reggae and fusion as well as jazz. Bands are mostly local, and the music is not overpowering – you can easily hold a conversation. Enter at the foot of the stairs leading down to Můstek metro station.

REDUTA JAZZ CLUB
JAZZ

Map p338 (☑224 933 487; www.redutajazzclub.cz; Národní třída 20; cover 330Kč; ◷9pm-3am; 🛜; Ⓜ Národní Třída) The Reduta is Prague's oldest jazz club, founded in 1958 during the communist era – it was here in 1994 that former US president Bill Clinton famously jammed on a new saxophone presented to him by Václav Havel. Smartly dressed patrons squeeze into tiered seats and lounges to soak up the big band, swing and Dixieland.

ROCK CAFÉ
LIVE MUSIC

Map p338 (☑224 933 947; www.rockcafe.cz; Národní třída 20; cover free-300Kč; ◷10am-3am Mon-Fri, 5pm-3am Sat, 5pm-1am Sun; Ⓜ Národní Třída) Not to be confused with the Hard Rock Café, this multifunction club is the offspring of the influential Nový Horizont art movement of the 1990s. It sports a stage for DJs and live rock bands, a funkily decorated 'rock cafe', a cinema, a theatre, an art gallery and a CD shop.

LUCERNA MUSIC BAR
LIVE MUSIC

Map p338 (☑224 217 108; www.musicbar.cz; Palác Lucerna, Vodičkova 36; cover 100-500Kč;

◷8pm-4am; Ⓜ Můstek) Nostalgia reigns supreme at this atmospheric old theatre, now looking a little dog-eared, which hosts a hugely popular 1980s and '90s video party every Friday and Saturday night, with crowds of young locals bopping along to Duran Duran and Gary Numan. There's an impressively eclectic program of live bands on midweek nights.

ORIGINAL MUSIC THEATRE OF PRAGUE
CLASSICAL MUSIC

Map p338 (Originální hudební divadlo Praha; ☑281 932 662; www.musictheatre.cz; Vila Amerika, Ke Karlovu 20; tickets 595Kč; ◷concerts 8pm Tue & Fri May-Oct; Ⓜ IP Pavlova) Vila Amerika was built in 1717 as an aristocrat's immodest summer retreat. These days it's home to the Dvořák Museum (p128) and stages performances of Dvořák's works by the Original Music Theatre of Prague, complete with period costume. Tickets are available through ClassicTic and PragueExperience.

NATIONAL THEATRE
OPERA, BALLET

Map p338 (Národní divadlo; ☑224 901 448; www.narodni-divadlo.cz; Národní třída 2; tickets 50-1100Kč; ◷box offices 10am-6pm; 🚊6, 9, 18, 22) The much-loved National Theatre provides a stage for traditional opera, drama and ballet by the likes of Smetana, Shakespeare and Tchaikovsky, sharing the program alongside more modern works by composers and playwrights such as Philip Glass and John Osborne. The box offices are in the Nový síň building next door, in the Kolowrat Palace (opposite the Estates Theatre) and at the State Opera.

PRAGUE STATE OPERA
OPERA, BALLET

Map p338 (Státní opera Praha; ☑224 901 448; www.narodni-divadlo.cz; Wilsonova 4; tickets 180-1190Kč; ◷box office 10am-6pm; Ⓜ Muzeum) The impressive home of the Prague State Opera provides a glorious setting for performances of opera and ballet. An annual Verdi festival takes place here in August and September, and less conventional shows, such as Leoncavallo's rarely staged version of *La Bohème,* are also performed here.

KINO SVĚTOZOR
CINEMA

Map p338 (☑224 946 824; www.kinosvetozor.cz; Vodičkova 41; tickets 60-120Kč; 🛜; Ⓜ Můstek) The Světozor is under the same management as Žižkov's famous Kino Aero (p153), but is more central. It has the same emphasis on classic cinema, documentary and art-house films screened in their original language plus critically acclaimed box-office hits.

LATERNA MAGIKA   PERFORMING ARTS

Map p338 (☑224 901 448; www.narodni-divadlo. cz; Nová Scéna, Národní třída 4; tickets 260-690Kč; ☺box office 9am-6pm Mon-Fri, 10am-6pm Sat & Sun; ☒6, 9, 18, 22) Laterna Magika has been wowing audiences since its first cutting-edge multimedia show in 1958. Its imaginative blend of dance, music and projected images continues to pull in the crowds. Nová Scena, the building next to the National Theatre, has been home to Laterna Magika since it moved here in the mid-1970s.

MINOR THEATRE   THEATRE

Map p338 (Divadlo Minor; ☑222 231 351; www. minor.cz; Vodičkova 6; adult/child 150/100Kč; ☺box office 10am-1.30pm & 2.30-8pm Mon-Fri, 11am-6pm Sat & Sun; Ⓜ Karlovo Náměstí) Divadlo Minor is a wheelchair-accessible children's theatre that offers a fun mix of puppets, clown shows and pantomime. There are performances (in Czech) at 3pm Saturday and Sunday, and at 6pm Thursday and Friday.

🛍 SHOPPING

NÁPLAVKA FARMERS MARKET   MARKET

(www.farmarsketrziste.cz; Rašínovo nábřeží; ☺8am-2pm Sat; ☒3, 7, 17) Stretching along the embankment from Trojická to Výton, this weekly market makes the most of its riverside setting with live music and outdoor tables scattered among stalls selling freshly baked bread, local vegetables, homemade cakes and pastries, wild mushrooms (in season), herbs, flowers, wild honey, hot food, and a range of arts and crafts.

GLOBE BOOKSTORE & CAFÉ   BOOKS

Map p338 (☑224 934 203; www.globebookstore. cz; Pštrossova 6; ☺9.30am-midnight Mon-Thu, 9.30am-1am Fri-Sun; ☎; Ⓜ Karlovo Náměstí) A popular hang out for book-loving expats, the Globe is a cosy English-language bookshop with an excellent cafe-bar (p129) in which to peruse your purchases. There's a good range of fiction and nonfiction, a big selection of secondhand books, and newspapers and magazines in English, French, Spanish, Italian, German and Russian.

PALÁC KNIH NEO LUXOR   BOOKS

Map p338 (☑296 110 368; www.neoluxor.cz; Václavské náměstí 41; ☺8am-8pm Mon-Fri, 9am-7pm Sat, 10am-7pm Sun; Ⓜ Muzeum) This is Prague's biggest bookshop – head for the basement to find a wide selection of fiction and nonfiction in English, German, French and Russian, including Czech authors in translation. Also has internet access, a cafe and international newspapers and magazines.

MOSER   GLASS

Map p336 (☑224 211 293; www.moser-glass.com; Na Příkopě 12; ☺10am-8pm; Ⓜ Můstek) One of the most exclusive and respected of Bohemian glassmakers, Moser was founded in Karlovy Vary in 1857 and is famous for its rich and flamboyant designs. The shop on Na Příkopě is worth a browse; it's in a magnificently decorated, Gothic building called the House of the Black Rose (dům U černé růže).

BELDA JEWELLERY   JEWELLERY

Map p338 (☑224 931 052; www.belda.cz; Mikulandská 10; ☺11am-6pm Mon-Fri; Ⓜ Národní Třída) Belda & Co is a long-established Czech firm dating from 1922. It creates gold and silver jewellery of a very high standard. Its range includes its own angular, contemporary designs, as well as reproductions based on art nouveau designs by Alfons Mucha.

BAZAR   MUSIC

Map p338 (☑602 313 730; www.cdkrakovska. cz; Krakovská 4; ☺11am-7pm Mon-Fri, 10am-4pm Sat; Ⓜ Muzeum) There's a vast selection of secondhand CDs, LPs and videos to browse through here. Czech and Western pop jostle with jazz, blues, heavy metal, country and world music, though with most LPs costing around 300Kč to 450Kč, this place is not exactly what you'd call a bargain basement.

JAN PAZDERA   PHOTOGRAPHY

Map p338 (☑224 216 197; www.fotopazdera.cz; Vodičkova 28; ☺10am-6pm Mon-Fri, to 1pm Sat; ☒3, 9, 14, 24) The knowledgeable staff members at this long-standing shop are happy to show you around their impressive stock of secondhand cameras, darkroom gear, lenses, binoculars and telescopes.

BAT'A   SHOES

Map p338 (☑221 088 478; www.bata.cz; Václavské náměstí 6; ☺9am-9pm Mon-Fri, 9am-8pm Sat, 10am-8pm Sun; Ⓜ Můstek) Established by Tomáš Bat'a in 1894, the Bat'a footwear empire is one of the Czech Republic's most successful companies. The flagship store on Wenceslas Square, built in the 1920s, is considered a masterpiece of modern architecture, and houses six floors of shoes, handbags, luggage and leather goods.

Vinohrady & Vršovice

Neighbourhood Top Five

1 Stroll lovely **Riegrovy sady** (p137), with photo-op vistas out over to Prague Castle in the distance and to the Old Town and the main train station below. Follow your walk with a visit to the park's cheery **beer garden** (p141).

2 Sip some wine in the open air at Vinohrady's **Viniční Altán** (p141).

3 Have a meal to remember at a great restaurant such as **Aromi** (p141).

4 Sneak a peek inside the modern masterpiece that is the **Church of the Most Sacred Heart of Our Lord** (p137).

5 Try out some of the new pubs around Peace Square – such as Vinohradský Parlament – on an impromptu **pub crawl** (p143).

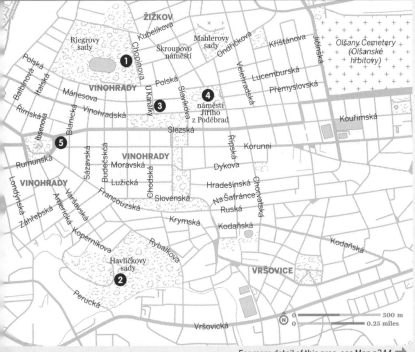

For more detail of this area, see Map p344 ➡

Lonely Planet's Top Tip

There aren't many traditional sights in Vinohrady, so the best way to enjoy this part of Prague is to put the map away and amble at will, admiring the fine townhouses and lovely quality of life in one of Prague's nicest residential areas.

Best Places to Eat

➡ Mozaika (p140)
➡ Kofein (p140)
➡ Aromi (p141)
➡ Osteria Da Clara (p140)
➡ Dish (p137)

For reviews, see p137. ➡

⬤ Best Places to Drink

➡ Riegrovy Sady Beer Garden (p141)
➡ Viniční Altán (p141)
➡ Café Kaaba (p142)
➡ Coffee Source (p142)
➡ Prague Beer Museum (p142)

For reviews, see p141. ➡

☆ Best Places to Party

➡ Techtle Mechtle (p144)
➡ Radost FX (p144)
➡ Termix (p144)
➡ Infinity (p144)
➡ Cafe V Lese (p142)

For reviews, see p144. ➡

Explore: Vinohrady & Vršovice

Vinohrady and Vršovice are largely residential, and mostly off the tourist trail. Upscale Vinohrady has a well-earned reputation as the stomping ground for well-to-do singles and young marrieds. Most of the best places are clustered within walking distance of the main metro stops: Náměstí Míru and Jiřího z Poděbrad. Vršovice is scruffier, but in some ways more interesting. There's a nascent hipster subcommunity evolving around Krymská street, which poses an interesting contrast to Vinohrady's finery.

Local Life

➡ **Hangouts** If you get a warm evening, head to the beer garden in Riegrovy sady (p141). Favourite neighbourhood cafes include Café Kaaba (p142), Coffee Source (p142) and Cafe Sladkovsky (p137), all of which offer great coffee and free wi-fi.

➡ **Markets** The grassy area above the Jiřího z Poděbrad metro station is home to a popular farmers market (p144) every Wednesday, Friday and Saturday. Come for home-grown food and lots of fun.

➡ **Shopping** Vinohrady's main street, Vinohradská, is the centre of home design in Prague, and even if you're not here to buy, it's fun to poke around the shops and see the latest in interior fashion. To see what we're talking about, stop by Vinohradský Pavilon (p144).

Getting There & Away

➡ **Metro** Vinohrady is easily reached from around the city by metro line A (green), which stops at Náměstí Míru, Jiřího z Poděbrad and Flora. Trams are better for getting to Vršovice.

➡ **Tram** Several tram lines service Vinohrady. Popular tram 22 runs all the way from Prague Castle to Peace Square (náměstí Míru) and continues into Vršovice. Tram 11 links Muzeum with several points in Vinohrady, including Jiřího z Poděbrad and Flora. Other trams that go to Vinohrady include 4, 10 and 16. Tram 4 also services Vršovice.

SIGHTS

CHURCH OF THE MOST SACRED
HEART OF OUR LORD   CHURCH
Map p344 (Kostel Nejsvětějšího Srdce Páně; ☑222 727 713; www.srdcepane.cz; náměstí Jiřího z Poděbrad 19, Vinohrady; ⊙services 8am & 6pm Mon-Sat, 9am, 11am & 6pm Sun; Ⓜ Jiřího z Poděbrad) This church, from 1932, is one of Prague's most original pieces of 20th-century architecture. It's the work of Jože Plečnik, a Slovenian architect who also worked on Prague Castle. The church is inspired by Egyptian temples and early Christian basilicas. It's usually only open to the public during mass.

RIEGROVY SADY   GARDENS
Map p344 (Rieger Gardens; entrance on Chopinova, across from Na Švíhance, Vinohrady; ⊙24hr; Ⓜ Jiřího z Poděbra) Vinohrady's largest and prettiest park was designed as a classic English garden in the 19th century, and it's still a good place to put down a blanket and chill out. The bluff towards the back of the park affords photo-opworthy shots of Prague Castle. In summer the park's open-air beer garden (p141) is the place to be.

🍴 EATING

Outside the centre, Vinohrady has Prague's largest concentration of good restaurants, and the choice is only getting better as the area continues to move upmarket. Most are clustered around Peace Square and residential street Mánesova, which parallels Vinohradská from the Muzeum to the Jiřího z Poděbrad metro stops.

VINOHRADSKÝ PARLAMENT   CZECH €
Map p344 (☑224 250 403; www.vinohradsky-parlament.cz; Korunní 1, Vinohrady; mains 170-239Kč; ⊙11am-midnight Mon-Wed, 11am-1am Thu-Sat, 11.30am-11.30pm Sun; ⊛🖥; Ⓜ Náměstí Míru) This clean, bright and well-run pub features both a handsome early-modern, art nouveau interior and a daring, inventive cooking staff who are willing to look beyond the standard pork and duck to other traditional Czech staples such as goose, rabbit and boar. Perfect for both lunch or dinner, but phone ahead to book a table as it's often jammed.

DISH   BURGERS €
Map p344 (☑222 511 032; www.dish.cz; Římská 29, Vinohrady; burgers 169-209Kč; ⊙11am-11pm Mon-Sat, noon-10pm Sun; ⊛🖥; Ⓜ Náměstí Miru) The burger wars are heating up, but Dish has emerged the city's favourite. The 'Dish' burger is a classic bacon-cheese, but other varieties feature mushrooms, lamb, red beets, or even highly aromatic cheese from Olomouc. The homemade buns are shiny, brioche-style. The chips (fries) are served with inventive sauces like lime-cilantro mayonnaise. Reservations essential.

CAFE SLADKOVSKÝ   INTERNATIONAL €
Map p344 (☑776 772 478; www.cafesladkovsky.cz; Sevastopolská 17, Vršovice; mains 135-155Kč; ⊙10am-1am Mon-Fri, 5pm-1am Sat, 11am-1am Sun; 🖥🖊; 🚋4, 22 to Krymská) Every Prague neighbourhood could use a Cafe Sladkovský. By day, a quiet spot to meditate over a meal of tapas, burgers, or felafel and hummus; by night, the same great food, but more of a party or pub vibe, filled with students and neighbours. The interior is old-school Viennese cafe, with high ceilings, tiled floors and faded print wallpaper.

THE TAVERN   BURGERS €
(www.eng.thetavern.cz; Chopinova 26, Vinohrady; burgers 139-199Kč; ⊙5-10pm Tue, 11.30am-10pm Wed-Sun; ⊛; 🚋11, Ⓜ Jiřího z Poděbrad) This cosy sit-down burger joint is the dream of a husband-and-wife team of American expats who wanted to create the perfect burger using organic products and free-range, grass-fed beef. Great pulled-pork sandwiches, fries and bourbon-based cocktails too. Reservations are taken only via the website or email and only for dinner on Thursday, Friday and Saturday.

U DĚDKA   INTERNATIONAL €
Map p344 (☑222 522 784; www.udedka.cz; Na Kozačce 12, Vinohrady; mains 130-240Kč; ⊙11am-1am Mon-Fri, 4pm-1am Sat & Sun; 🖥; Ⓜ Náměstí Míru, 🚋4, 22) This pleasantly upmarket pub-restaurant has a quiet, tree-covered terrace out front. The contemporary interior pulls in a mix of Czech professionals, students and the occasional tourist from a nearby pension. The menu is a blend of Czech specialities, plus well-done bar food, such as chicken quesadillas and cheeseburgers.

PLEVEL   VEGETARIAN €
Map p344 (☑273 160 041; www.restauraceplevel.cz; Krymská 2, Vršovice; mains 135-185Kc;

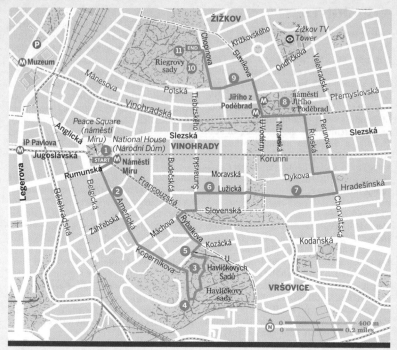

🚶 Walking Tour
Handsome Vinohrady

START PEACE SQUARE
END RIEGROVY SADY
LENGTH 4KM; TWO TO THREE HOURS

Leafy **①Peace Square** (náměstí Míru) is the lively heart of Vinohrady. Leave the square via **②Americká**, a quiet residential street leading south.

At the end of the street, the rocky hillside park **③Havlíčkovy sady** marks the border between Vinohrady and Vršovice and is popular with lovers. There's no prescribed walk for exploring the park – just choose the most inviting path leading downhill. Look for signs to the Viniční Altán wine garden.

Open-air wine gardens are a rarity in Prague and none is as attractive as **④Viniční Altán** (p141), with its wooden gazebo overlooking a terraced hillside lined with grapevines.

Retrace your steps through the park, back to the street **⑤U Havlíčkových Sadů**. Follow this to the right, then make a left onto Rybalkova. At Máchova turn right, crossing Francouzská onto Šumavská, and then make a right at **⑥Lužická**. Cut through the park and onto the street Hradešínská.

This street has some of the most beautiful villas in the city. The most famous is at **⑦Hradešínská 6**, built by early-modern architect Jan Kotěra in 1908. Turn left at Chorvatská and left again onto Dykova, then right onto Řípská, with a view of Žižkov's TV Tower.

Řípská takes you to Vinohradská and the **⑧Church of the Most Sacred Heart of Our Lord** (náměstí Jiřího z Poděbrad; p137). Find the street Slavíkova that runs past the church's front entrance and follow it to Polská.

Walk left onto **⑨Polská** for another row of handsome townhouses. Take a right onto Chopinova and walk slightly uphill to Na Švíhance. The entrance to **⑩Riegrovy sady** (p137) is opposite Na Švíhance. The **⑪Riegrovy sady beer garden** (p141) is 30m from the entrance.

VINOHRADY'S VINEYARDS

Prague is generally known for beer, not wine. And that's probably for good reason. It may come as a surprise, then, that several centuries ago vineyards in Prague produced a substantial amount of wine, and the centre of this activity was Vinohrady (which means 'vineyards'). Vinohrady, so the story goes, got its start in winemaking back in the 14th century, when Emperor Charles IV ordered the first grapes to be planted. The vineyards lasted around 400 years before the area was given over mostly to farms and eventually the luxury townhouses you see today. A small section of the vineyards survives to this day around the area of the Viniční Altán (p141) open-air wine garden.

⊙10am-10pm Mon-Fri, 11am-11pm Sat & Sun; 🌐🛜🖊; 🚋4, 22 to Krymská) Vegan and raw food are becoming more and more popular. This warm, rustic spot with big wooden tables and exposed beams opened in 2013 to cement the Krymská corridor as the centre of Prague hipsterdom. It has arguably the best hummus in the city and many other great choices, like vegan kebabs and grilled peppers. Daily lunch specials.

LAS ADELITAS
MEXICAN €

Map p344 (📞222 542 031; www.lasadelitas. cz; Americká 8, Vinohrady; mains 150-200Kč; 🌐🛜🖊; Ⓜ Náměstí Míru) This small, informal Mexican restaurant run by a group of friends from Mexico offers the closest thing to authentic Tex-Mex you're likely to find in Prague. Delicious tacos, burritos and enchiladas are crafted with love from handmade tortillas. The ambience is a little sterile, but no one is here for a candle-lit dinner – just very good, good-value nosh.

PHO VIETNAM
VIETNAMESE €

Map p344 (http://photuanlan.com; Slavíkova, Vinohrady; mains 80-120Kč; ⊙10am-10pm; 🌐🖊; Ⓜ Jiřího z Poděbrad, 🚋11) This stand-up and takeaway Vietnamese joint gets jammed at lunchtime for arguably the best Vietnamese-style *pho* in town, at very reasonable prices. Snippets from the menu include spicy beef with green beans, and *pho bo* (beef noodle soup). There are plenty of items for vegetarians.

MADAME LYN
VIETNAMESE €

Map p344 (📞606 307 777; www.facebook. com/MadameLynRestaurant; Šafaříkova 18, Vinohrady; mains 130-230Kč; ⊙11am-10pm; 🌐🛜🖊; Ⓜ IP Pavlova) Very good Vietnamese and Thai restaurant. The daily luncheon specials offer good value, as do the hearty *pho bo* (beef noodle) and *pho ga* (chicken noodle) soups, and the fresh and fried spring rolls. The service is friendly and attentive. The clean and bright modern interior is a step up from the usual Vietnamese restaurant in Prague.

LOVING HUT
VEGETARIAN €

Map p344 (📞222 515 006; www.lovinghut.cz; Londýnská 35, Vinohrady; mains under 100Kč; ⊙11am-9pm Mon-Sat; 🌐🛜🖊; Ⓜ Náměstí Míru, IP Pavlova) Part of a citywide chain of non-smoking, no-alcohol vegan/vegetarian restaurants. The menu includes items such as curry soup, vegetarian sushi, and other Asian-inspired vegetarian dishes. There's a great-value self-service buffet on weekdays from 11am to 4pm.

CAFÉ FX
VEGETARIAN €

Map p344 (📞603 193 711; www.radostfx.cz; Bělehradská 120, Vinohrady; mains 120-230Kč; 🌐🛜🖊; Ⓜ IP Pavlova) For more than two decades Café FX has been a vegetarian beacon in the gritty but slowly gentrifying neighbourhood surrounding the IP Pavlova metro stop. The food – mostly salads, Mexican, stir-fries and veggie burgers – is reliably good, though the menu has changed little since opening day.

HA NOI
VIETNAMESE €

Map p344 (📞222 521 430; http:// restauracehanoi.webnode.cz; Slezská 57, Vinohrady; mains 80-150Kč; ⊙10am-10pm Mon-Fri, 2-11pm Sat; Ⓜ Jiřího z Poděbrad, Flora) Ha Noi was one of the first Vietnamese restaurants to open in Prague and is still one of the best. Decent spring rolls, both fresh and fried, and two types of seasoned *pho* are on offer. The unremarkable set-up – just a few wooden tables and oriental kitsch – make it better suited to a hearty lunch than a special night out.

PIZZERIA GROSSETO
ITALIAN €

Map p344 (☏224 252 778; www.grosseto.cz; Francouzská 2, Vinohrady; mains 130-200Kč; ⊙11.30am-11pm; 📶📷; Ⓜ Náměstí Míru) This bustling Vinohrady pizzeria serves very good pizzas, with inventive toppings such as asparagus and ricotta cheese, as well as homemade pastas and original desserts. The garden terrace at the back is a secluded gem and something of a local secret.

PIVO A PÁREK
CZECH €

Map p344 (☏734 201 195; www.pivnipoutnik. cz; Korunní 105, Vinohrady; sausages 40-70Kč; ⊙10am-10pm Mon-Fri, 2pm-10pm Sat & Sun; 📷; 🚊10, 16 to Perunova) The names translates as 'Beer and Hot Dogs' and that's what you'll find at this tiny, mostly stand-up joint on the eastern fringe of Vinohrady. Order your beer and sausage at the counter and find a quiet spot (there are a few tables in the back). It's too informal for a real meal, but a great spot for a quick bite.

OSTERIA DA CLARA
ITALIAN €€

Map p344 (☏271 726 548; www.daclara.com; Mexická 7, Vršovice; mains 200-350Kč; ⊙11am-3pm & 6-11pm Mon-Fri, noon-3.30pm & 6-11pm Sat, noon-4pm Sun; 📷📶📷; 🚊4, 22) This minuscule Tuscan-style trattoria offers some of the most authentic and best-value Italian cooking in the city, though it will take a good map to find the place. The menu varies, but expect a handful of creative pasta dishes and main courses built around duck, beef, pork and seafood. Reserve in advance – there are only a few tables.

KOFEIN
SPANISH €€

Map p344 (☏273 132 145; www.ikofein.cz; Nitranská 9, Vinohrady; 3 tapas plates 270Kč; ⊙11am-midnight Mon-Fri, 5pm-midnight Sat & Sun; 📷📶📷; 🚊11, Ⓜ Jiřího z Poděbrad) One of the hottest restaurants in town is this Spanish-style tapas place not far from the Jiřího z Poděbrad metro station. Descend into a lively space to see a red-faced chef minding the busy grill. Our faves include marinated trout with horseradish and pork belly confit with celeriac. Service is prompt and friendly. Book ahead.

RESTAURACE U BULÍNŮ
CZECH €€

Map p344 (☏224 254 676; www.ubulinu.cz; Budečská 2, cnr Francouzká, Vinohrady; mains 189-300Kč; ⊙11am-11pm; 📷📶🚻; 🚊4, 22, Ⓜ Náměstí Míru) Delicious traditional Czech cooking served in a clean, warm setting. This is the

place to try duck liver pate, rabbit, venison, *strapačky* (small flour-potato dumplings often served with sheep's cheese) and other local specialities, cooked by a kitchen that knows what it's doing. There's a small terrace at the back. Book in advance.

MOZAIKA
INTERNATIONAL €€

Map p344 (☏224 253 011; www.restaurantmozaika.cz; Nitranská 13, Vinohrady; mains 180-450Kč; 📷📷; Ⓜ Jiřího z Poděbrad) One of the most dependably good restaurants in the neighbourhood. The theme is an updated French bistro, with beef tournedos and *boeuf bourguignon* sharing the spotlight with international entrees such as stir-fries, chicken breasts and, our personal favourite (occasionally on the menu): salmon wrapped in seaweed and served with wasabi mashed potatoes. Excellent wine list. Advance booking essential.

ORIGINÁL 1869
CZECH €€

Map p344 (Restaurace Kravín; ☏222 540 524; www.restauracekravin.cz; náměstí Míru 18, Vinohrady; mains 140-395Kč; ⊙11am-midnight Mon-Thu, 11am-2am Fri, noon-2am Sat, noon-midnight Sun; 📷; Ⓜ Náměstí Míru) The Gambrinus brewery purchased and renovated this long-time traditional pub on a corner of (Peace Square) and gave it a fresh coat of paint, a swanky modern interior and a new lease on life. Daily lunch specials of Czech favourites such as grilled chicken livers or pork schnitzels are excellent value. It's slightly fancier (and pricier) at night but still fun.

U BÍLÉ KRÁVY
STEAKHOUSE €€

Map p344 (☏224 239 570; www.bilakrava. cz; Rubešova 10, Vinohrady; mains 170-450Kč; ⊙11.30am-11pm Mon-Fri, 5-11pm Sat; Ⓜ Náměstí

GAY-FRIENDLY VINOHRADY

Over the years Vinohrady has evolved into the unofficial centre of gay Prague, and you'll find many of the city's better gay-friendly cafes and clubs in this area. While the scene changes with the season, and venues come and go, some of the more popular places include the following:

➡ Radost FX (p144)

➡ Termix (p144)

➡ Café Celebrity (p143)

➡ Le Clan (p144)

Míru, Muzeum) This French-run, Lyonnais-styled bistro has some of the best steaks, at the best prices, in town. The name 'White Cow' refers to the Charollais breed of white cows from Burgundy, the source of the restaurant's signature steaks. Added charms include an authentic bistro feel and an excellent wine selection.

RESTAURACE CHUDOBA   CZECH €€
Map p344 (⏏222 250 624; www.restaurace-chudoba.cz; Vinohradská 67, Vinohrady; mains 190-280Kč; ⏰11am-1am Mon-Sat, to midnight Sun; ☎; ☒11) This upmarket Czech tavern-restaurant occupies a choice corner on a leafy section of Vinohradská. The patrons are mostly young professionals and couples out for an after-work beer or a good, reasonably priced Czech meal. The decor plays with the 'Ye Olde Vinohrady' theme, with sepia-toned photos on the wall and polished wooden floors.

ZELENÁ ZAHRADA   CZECH €€
Map p344 (⏏222 518 159; www.zelena-zahrada.eu; Šmilovského 12, Vinohrady; mains 150-390Kč; ⏰11am-11.30pm Sun-Thu, to 1am Fri & Sat; ☎; ⓂNáměstí Míru, ☒4, 22) This secluded, upscale restaurant draws a star-studded crowd, including on at least one occasion – judging by the photos on the wall – crooner Karel Gott. Book in advance to snag one of the coveted garden seats. There are great luncheon specials.

PASTIČKA   CZECH €€
Map p344 (⏏222 253 228; www.pasticka.cz; Blanická 25, Vinohrady; mains 149-429Kč; ⏰11am-1am Mon-Fri, 5-1am Sat & Sun; ☎; ⓂJiřího z Poděbrad, ☒11) A warm, inviting ground-floor pub with a little garden out the back, Pastička is great for a beer or a meal. The interior design is part 1920s Prague and part Irish pub. The mix of international and traditional Czech dishes is very good.

AROMI   ITALIAN €€€
Map p344 (⏏222 713 222; www.aromi.cz; Mánesova 78, Vinohrady; mains 400-600Kč; ⏰noon-11pm Mon-Sat, to 10pm Sun; ☎; ☒11 to Jiřího z Poděbrad, ⓂJiřího z Poděbrad) Red brick, polished wood and country-style furniture create a rustic atmosphere in this gourmet Italian restaurant. Brisk and businesslike at lunchtime, romantic in the evening, Aromi has a reputation for authentic, excellent Italian cuisine. Advance booking essential.

🍷 DRINKING & NIGHTLIFE

Vinohrady is a great area for bar- and cafe-hopping. Check out the streets surrounding náměstí Míru (Peace Square), particularly along Americká, as well as Mánesova and those around Riegrovy sady. Vinohrady is also the centre of Prague's gay life, and you'll find many gay-friendly cafes and clubs.

RIEGROVY SADY BEER GARDEN   BEER GARDEN
Map p344 (Riegrovy sady, Vinohrady; ⏰noon-1am May-Sep; ⓂJiřího z Poděbrad, ☒11) There's a good-natured rivalry between this beer garden and the one across the river at Letná as to which one is the best. We're not sure, but this one is pretty good. Order beers at the bar and carry them to your table. To find it, go to Polská, turn up Chopínova, and enter the park across from Na Švíhance.

VINIČNÍ ALTÁN   WINE BAR
Map p344 (www.vinicni-altan.cz; Havlíčkovy sady 1369, Vršovice; ⏰11am-10pm Apr-Oct, 11am-9pm Mon-Wed, Sat & Sun Nov-Mar; ☒4, 7, 22, 24, ⓂNáměstí Miru) Prague's nicest open-air wine garden claims to be its oldest too – apparently established by Emperor Charles IV himself. Enjoy a glass of locally made white or red on a refurbished wooden gazebo overlooking the vineyards and the Nusle valley. There's no easy way to get here; try cutting through Vinohrady, following Americká and then continuing through Havlíčkovy sady.

KAVÁRNA ŠLÁGR   CAFE
Map p344 (⏏607 277 688; www.kavarnaslagr.cz; Francouzská 72, Vršovice; ⏰10am-10pm; ☎; ☒4, 22 to Krymská) Walking into this evocative, old-fashioned bakery-cafe is like stepping back into the last century and the time of the First Republic, when Czechoslovakia was a young, prosperous democracy. There's a big pastry counter at the front (our favourite has to be the calorie-bomb Czech cream puff called *větrník*) and several cosy, secluded tables at the back.

LE CAVEAU   CAFE
Map p344 (⏏775 294 864; www.broz-d.cz; náměstí Jiřího z Poděbrad 9, Vinohrady; ⏰8am-10.30pm Mon-Fri, 9am-10.30pm Sat, 2-8.30pm Sun; ☎; ⓂJiřího z Poděbrad) This charming French cafe is a perfect spot to relax with coffee or one of its excellent French wines. It

also serves French pastries, sandwiches and cheeses, and takeaway. The 1920s-inspired interior, with stylish lamps and wood flooring, is ideal for an intimate meet-up.

COFFEE SOURCE   CAFE

Map p344 (Coffee House; ☑222 780 115; Francouzská 100, Vršovice; ☺8am-5pm; ☏; ☒4, 22 to Krymská) It calls itself 'Coffee Source' and the sign on the outside says 'Coffee House', but whatever the name this is Vršovice's best coffee, bar none. It uses high-quality beans plus various roasting and filtering techniques to deliver the perfect cup every time. They serve light breakfasts, such as croissants, and there's a pretty garden out back for warm weather.

BAR & BOOKS MÁNESOVA   COCKTAIL BAR

Map p344 (☑222 724 581; www.barandbooks.cz; Mánesova 64, Vinohrady; ☺5pm-3am; ☏; ☒11) This upmarket New York–style cocktail and cigar bar occupies a former rugby pub and couldn't be more different in terms of atmosphere. It's been given a bad rap for its cocktail prices, but the truth is if you stick to the basics, the prices aren't much higher here than elsewhere. Try to book a table in advance.

CAFE V LESE   CAFE

Map p344 (☑724 918 236; www.cafevlese.cz; Krymská 12, Vršovice; ☺noon-3am; ☏; ☒4, 22 to Krymská) The epicentre of the Vršovice hipster revival is this popular student cafe, bar and alternative-music club (downstairs). It's always packed and always fun, though try to arrive early in the evening to get a table. Check the website for musical happenings or events, such as blues nights, trance DJs and other funky stuff. Concerts start at 8pm, and admission is usually 100Kč.

PRAGUE BEER MUSEUM   PUB

Map p344 (☑777 679 767; www.praguebeermuseum.com; Americká 43, Vinohrady; ☺noon-3am; ☏; Ⓜ Náměstí Míru) The Vinohrady branch of a popular pub chain that started in the Old Town. The idea is to highlight smaller, regional beers from around the country, rather than pledge allegiance to a big national brewer. It has 33 labels on tap, including our personal favourite, Primátor.

BLATOUCH   CAFE

Map p344 (☑222 328 643; www.blatouch.cz; Americká 17, Vinohrady; ☺noon-midnight Mon-Thu, noon-1am Fri, 2pm-midnight Sat, 2-10pm Sun; ☏;

Ⓜ Náměstí Míru) This popular cafe is an excellent choice in which to relax, surf the net on free wi-fi, and enjoy a good coffee or glass of wine. The vibe is student friendly and relaxed. There are also some light food items such as salads and sandwiches.

HOSPŮDKA OBYČEJNÝ SVĚT   PUB

Map p344 (☑224 257 161; www.obycejnysvet.com; Korunní 96, entry on Chorvatská, Vinohrady; ☺11.30am-1am Mon-Fri, 1pm-1am Sat, 1pm-midnight Sun; ☏; ☒10, 16 to Perunova, Ⓜ Náměstí Jiřího z Poděbrad) This traditional pub has something of a darkly lit, British gentlemen's club feel about it. There's an excellent range of beers on hand, including harder-to-find varieties, plus traditional Czech food and a friendly, welcoming atmosphere.

AL CAFETERO   CAFE

Map p344 (☑777 061 161; www.alcafetero.cz; Blanická 24, Vinohrady; ☺9am-10pm Mon-Thu, to 6pm Fri; ☏; ☒11, Ⓜ Náměstí Míru, Muzeum; ☺) This quirky little cafe and wine bar, just between Vinohradská and Peace Square, has several things going for it, including arguably the best coffee drinks in Prague. There's also an excellent wine selection and an enforced nonsmoking policy, which makes it comfortable for lingering over the newspaper.

CAFÉ KAABA   CAFE

Map p344 (☑222 254 021; www.kaaba.cz; Mánesova 20, Vinohrady; ☺8am-11pm Mon-Fri, 9am-11pm Sat, 10am-11pm Sun; ☏; ☒11) Café Kaaba is a stylish little cafe-bar with retro furniture and pastel-coloured decor that comes straight out of the 1959 Ideal Homes Exhibition. It serves up excellent coffee (made with freshly ground imported beans). Note that the wi-fi is only free for customers from opening until 6pm. Nonsmoking until 9pm.

SOKOLOVNA   PUB

Map p344 (☑222 524 525; www.restaurantsokolovna.cz; Slezská 22, Vinohrady; ☺11am-midnight; Ⓜ Náměstí Míru) It might be a little unfair to consign Sokolovna to the 'pub' category; after all, it's also a pretty good restaurant, serving excellent traditional Czech food, including a good-value luncheon special. But it's a great beer joint too, with unpasteurised Pilsner Urquell *(tankové pivo)* on tap, served in a dignified 1930s interior.

MAMA COFFEE   CAFE

Map p344 (☑773 263 333; www.mamacoffee.cz; Londýnská 49, Vinohrady; ☺8.30am-8pm Mon-

PEACE SQUARE PUB CRAWL

The district of Vinohrady may be named for vineyards, but these days beer is clearly king. In the recent past, no fewer than three major pubs have opened along the perimeter of central náměstí Miru (Peace Square). If you'll pardon the pun, we're starting to wonder when they're going to rename náměstí Miru as 'náměstí Beeru' ...

The proximity of the pubs makes for a perfect, low-energy pub crawl, and since there's a handy metro station nearby, it's a feasible destination no matter where you're staying. If you're still standing by the end of the night, there are dozens of additional watering holes within easy walking distance at which to carry on.

It's a toss-up where to start, as all three pubs serve decent food too. Vinohradský Parlament (p137), on the square's eastern end, is clean, brightly lit, and serves excellent and inventive Czech food, mixing staples such as pork and duck with more unusual entrées like venison and rabbit. It's a Staropramen pub, but it usually has a couple of experimental brews on hand, and the Staropramen unfiltered and 11° are both very drinkable.

From here, wend your way to the Vinohrady branch of the Prague Beer Museum (p142) on the square's southern side. Though the bar food is above average, this place really excels at serious drinking. It has no fewer than 33 beers on tap here, including excellent Czech regional labels such as Primátor, Svijany, Klášter and Rychtář.

Finish up the evening with a Gambrinus across the street at Originál 1869 (p140), which keeps the doors open until 2am on Friday and Saturday. The 10° Gambrinus lager remains the most popular beer in the country – not so much because it's great, but because it goes down like water. At this stage in the evening, that might be all you're looking for.

Fri, 10.30am-8pm Sat & Sun; 🖰🛝; Ⓜ Náměstí Míru) One of several Mama Coffee branches around town that specialises in home-roasted, fair-trade coffees imported from around the world. Mama Coffees are famously stroller- and kid-friendly.

GALERIE KAVÁRNA RÓZA K CAFE
Map p344 (📞 222 544 696; Belgická 17, Vinohrady; ⊗ 8.30am-1am Mon-Fri, noon-1am Sat & Sun; 🖰; Ⓜ Náměstí Míru) We liked this place so much better when it was called Medúza, but it's still one of the best cafes in Vinohrady. The clientele is mostly students who come for coffee and conversation. Serves light food.

ŽLUTÁ PUMPA PUB
Map p344 (www.zluta-pumpa.info; Belgická 11, Vinohrady; 🖰; Ⓜ Náměstí Míru, IP Pavlova) There aren't many student watering holes left in trendy Vinohrady, but the 'Yellow Pump' has been a neighbourhood fixture for over a decade. There's a tiny bar area and several adjacent small rooms, and normally every seat in the house is filled. There's a complete range of beers, wines and cocktails, plus average but edible Mexican food.

DOBRÁ TRAFIKA CAFE
Map p344 (📞 737 907 635; www.dobratrafika.cz; Korunní 42, Vinohrady; ⊗ 7.30am-11pm Mon-Fri,

8am-11pm Sat, 9am-11pm Sun; 🖰; Ⓜ Náměstí Míru, 🚋 10, 16) From the outside you'd never know there was a cute little coffee shop tucked behind this tobacconist on busy Korunní. The shop is a great place to buy teas, sweets and gifts. At the back there's a small room for drinking coffee and a larger garden for hanging out. Popular with students.

KAVÁRNA ZANZIBAR CAFE
Map p344 (📞 222 520 315; www.kavarnazanzibar. cz; Americká 15, Vinohrady; ⊗ 8am-11pm Mon-Fri, 10am-11pm Sat & Sun; 🖰; Ⓜ Náměstí Míru) Zanzibar started out years ago as a place to buy newspapers and tobacco products. Over the years it's evolved into a homey space that serves as either a cafe, bar or informal restaurant, depending on your mood. The terrace out the front is pleasant in nice weather.

CAFÉ CELEBRITY CAFE
Map p344 (📞 222 511 343; www.celebritycafe. cz; Vinohradská 40, Vinohrady; ⊗ 8am-2am Mon-Fri, 10am-2am Sat, 10am-midnight Sun; 🖰; Ⓜ Náměstí Míru) This cafe is part of the cluster of gay-friendly places that makes up the old Radio Palác building. The Celebrity offers early-morning breakfasts on weekdays and a relaxed brunch on weekends. At other times, it's great for coffee and people-watching.

⭐ ENTERTAINMENT

TERMIX
CLUB

Map p344 (📞222 710 462; www.club-termix.cz; Třebízského 4a, Vinohrady; ⏱9pm-5am Wed-Sun; Ⓜ Jiřího z Poděbrad) **FREE** Termix is one of Prague's most popular gay dance clubs, with an industrial hi-tech vibe (lots of shiny steel, glass, and plush sofas) and a young crowd that contains as many tourists as locals. The smallish dance floor fills up fast and you may have to queue to get in.

RADOST FX
CLUB

Map p344 (📞224 254 776; www.radostfx.cz; Bělehradská 120, Vinohrady; cover 100-250Kč; ⏱10pm-6am; 🛜; Ⓜ IP Pavlova) Though not quite as trendy as it once was, slick and shiny Radost is still capable of pulling in the crowds, with themed dance parties each night of the week. The regular Thursday night hip-hop and R & B party remains the most popular. The place has a chilled-out, bohemian atmosphere, with an excellent lounge and vegetarian restaurant.

TECHTLE MECHTLE
CLUB

Map p344 (📞222 250 143; www.techtle-mechtle. cz; Vinohradská 47, Vinohrady; ⏱6pm-4am Tue-Thu, to 5am Fri & Sat; 🛜; 🚋11 to Vinohradská tržnice, Ⓜ Muzeum, Jiřího z Poděbrad) A popular cellar dance bar on Vinohrady's main drag. In addition to a well-tended cocktail bar, you'll find a decent restaurant and dance floor, and occasional special events. Arrive early to get a good table.

LE CLAN
CLUB

Map p344 (www.leclan.cz; Balbínova 23, Vinohrady; cover 80-200Kč; ⏱2am-10am Tue-Fri, 2am-noon Sat & Sun; Ⓜ Muzeum) DJs on two floors, lots of bars, cosy armchairs and myriad rooms stuffed with people who want to party until dawn. It's got a decadent vibe, and tends to get more crowded as the night wears on.

INFINITY
CLUB

Map p344 (📞731 109 639; www.infinitybar.cz; Chrudimská 2a, Vinohrady; ⏱6pm-3am Mon-Sat, to 1am Sun; Ⓜ Flora) Smart-casual clubbing gear is the order of the day in this midsized cellar with exposed brick walls and sophisticated lighting. Alternating between upbeat happy house and nostalgic '60s to '90s nights, it's much more enjoyable than its reputation as the second-biggest pick-up joint in Prague might suggest. (We're not telling you the first!)

🛍 SHOPPING

OBCHOD S UMĚNÍM
ART, ANTIQUES

Map p344 (📞224 252 779; Korunní 34, Vinohrady; ⏱11am-5pm Mon-Fri; Ⓜ Náměstí Míru, 🚋10, 16) The 'Shop with Art' specialises in original paintings, prints and sculpture from 1900 to 1940, when Czech artists were at the forefront in movements such as constructivism, surrealism and cubism. The artworks fetch astronomical prices these days, but it's still fun to drop by and browse.

VINOHRADSKÝ PAVILON
INTERIOR DESIGN

Map p344 (Vinohradská tržnice; www.pavilon. cz; Vinohradská 50, Vinohrady; ⏱10am-7.30pm Mon-Fri, to 6pm Sat; 🚋11 to Vinohradská tržnice, Ⓜ Muzeum, Jiřího z Poděbrad) Vinohrady's grand old market hall dates from 1902; in 2013 the interior was given a lavish makeover to display high-end home and furniture design. Stroll the upper floors to see the best modern lighting, tables, and furnishings from Italian, German and local designers.

KAREL VÁVRA
MUSIC

Map p344 (📞222 518 114; www.housle-vavra.cz; Lublaňská 65, Vinohrady; ⏱9am-5pm Mon-Fri; Ⓜ IP Pavlova) Handmade fiddles decorate the interior of this old-fashioned violin workshop where Karel and his assistants beaver away making and repairing these instruments in time-honoured fashion. Even if you are not in search of a violin, it's worth a look just for the time-warp atmosphere.

JIŘÍHO Z PODĚBRAD FARMERS MARKET
MARKET

Map p344 (Farmářské tržiště; www.farmarsket-rziste.cz; náměstí Jiřího z Poděbrad, Vinohrady; ⏱8am-6pm Wed & Fri, to 2pm Sat; 🚻; Ⓜ Jiřího z Poděbrad) Every Wednesday, Friday and Saturday food vendors and farmers descend onto the square above the Jiřího z Poděbrad metro station to sell their fresh fruits and vegetables, as well as baked goods, coffees, meats and cheeses.

DŮM PORCELÁNU
GLASS

Map p344 (📞221 505 320; www.dumporcelanu. cz; Jugoslávská 16, Vinohrady; ⏱9am-7pm Mon-Fri, 9am-5pm Sat, 2-5pm Sun; Ⓜ IP Pavlova, Náměstí Miru) The 'House of Porcelain' is a kind of factory outlet for the best Czech porcelain makers, including Haas & Czjzek and Thuna. The flatware, china, blue onion pattern porcelain and other items are priced to draw in local buyers – not tourists.

Žižkov & Karlín

Neighbourhood Top Five

1 Pay a visit to one of Prague's most prominent landmarks, the **National Monument** (p147), where you can learn about 20th-century Czech history, and visit the laboratory where communist president Klement Gottwald was enbalmed.

2 Ascend to the top of Žižkov's other noteworthy landmark, the **TV Tower** (p149), for outstanding city views.

3 Enjoy the ultimate Žižkov experience – a crawl of its classic, crowded pubs, including **U Vystřeleného oka** (p152).

4 Rock up to a live gig at the **Palác Akropolis** (p153), a stalwart of Prague's alternative-music scene.

5 Take a stroll among the art nouveau monuments of **Olšany Cemetery** (p149), Prague's biggest and most atmospheric burial ground.

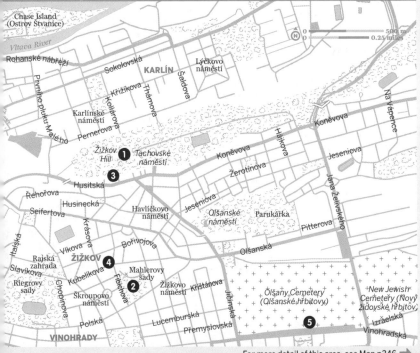

For more detail of this area, see Map p346 ➡

Lonely Planet's Top Tip

The viewing platforms in Žižkov's TV Tower are open until midnight – dodge the daytime crowds and turn up just in time for sunset to enjoy a really special view of the city.

✕ Best Places to Eat

➡ Café Pavlač (p149)
➡ Bisos (p151)
➡ Essence (p151)

For reviews, see p149. ➡

🍷 Best Places to Drink

➡ Bukowski's (p152)
➡ Pivovarský Klub (p152)
➡ U Slovanské Lípy (p152)
➡ U Vystřeleného oka (p152)

For reviews, see p151. ➡

☆ Best Live Music Venues

➡ Palác Akropolis (p153)
➡ Fatal Music Club (p152)
➡ Kuře V Hodinkách (p151)
➡ Hospoda Parukářka (p153)

For reviews, see p153. ➡

Explore: Žižkov & Karlín

Named after the one-eyed Hussite hero Jan Žižka, Žižkov was one of Prague's earliest industrial suburbs. It has long had a reputation as a rough-and-ready neighbourhood, and was full of left-wing revolutionary fervour well before the communist takeover of 1948.

Today it is one of Prague's liveliest districts, with more bars per capita than any other part of Prague. It's pretty rough around the edges, which puts off a lot of visitors, though it's as safe as the rest of the city. There are a couple of major sights which could be covered in an afternoon, but the main attraction here is the bars.

The mostly residential suburb of Karlín lies to the north of Žižkov, squeezed between Žižkov Hill and the Vltava River. It was devastated by the floods of 2002, and since then it has been undergoing massive redevelopment, with office complexes rising along the banks of the river. The older part of the district, along Křižíkova, is another up-and-coming area, with lovely art nouveau buildings, great for some aimless wandering – Lýčkovo náměstí is one of the prettiest squares in the city.

Local Life

➡**Hangouts** Tourists are notable by their absence in Žižkov and Karlín, so most places are 'local'. Café Pavlač (p149) is a popular place for weekend brunch, while Kuře V Hodinkách (p151) pulls in local crowds with live music as well as good food.

➡**Park Life** Sunny days see crowds of locals out for a stroll in the park. The most popular spots are Žižkov Hill (locals often refer to it as Vítkov Hill) and Parukářka – the latter has a great beer garden (p153).

➡**Football** Supporters of FK Viktoria Žižkov are even more passionate than fans of Sparta and Slavia – drop in on a home match for a real Žižkov experience.

Getting There & Away

➡**Bus** Buses 133, 175 and 207 run from outside Florenc metro station along Husitská at the foot of Žižkov Hill, useful for the Army Museum and National Monument.

➡**Metro** There are no metro stations in Žižkov itself; the nearest is Jiřího z Poděbrad on line A, a five-minute walk south from the TV Tower. Line B runs through Karlín.

➡**Tram** Lines 5, 9 and 26 run along Seifertova, in the centre of Žižkov, while lines 3 and 8 run along Sokolovská in Karlín.

TOP SIGHT
NATIONAL MONUMENT

The huge monument atop Žižkov Hill is not, strictly speaking, a legacy of the communist era – construction began in the 1930s. But in the minds of most Praguers over a certain age it is inextricably linked with the Communist Party of Czechoslovakia, and in particular with Klement Gottwald, the country's first 'worker-president'. Although the massive functionalist structure has all the elegance of a nuclear power station, the interior is a spectacular extravaganza of polished art deco marble, gilt and mosaics, and home to a fascinating museum of 20th-century Czechoslovak history.

History

The famous Battle of Vítkov Hill took place in July 1420 on the long, narrow ridge that separates the Žižkov and Karlín districts, when the Hussite forces of Jan Žižka defeated the Holy Roman Emperor Sigismund.

Designed in the 1920s as a memorial to Žižka, and to the soldiers who had fought for Czechoslovak independence in WWI, the National Monument was still under construction in 1939 when the occupation of Czechoslovakia by Nazi Germany made the 'Monument to National Liberation', as it was then called, seem like a sick joke.

After 1948 the Communist Party appropriated the story of Jan Žižka and the Hussites for propaganda purposes, extolling them as shining examples of Czech peasant power. They completed the National Monument with the installation of the **Tomb of the Unknown Soldier** and a gargantuan bronze statue of Žižka. But they didn't stop there.

DON'T MISS

➡ Klement Gottwald's enbalming laboratory
➡ War memorial
➡ View from the rooftop lookout point
➡ Giant statue of Jan Žižka

PRACTICALITIES

➡ Národní Památník na Vítkově
➡ Map p346
➡ ☏222 781 676
➡ www.nm.cz
➡ U Památníku 1900, Žižkov
➡ exhibition only adult/child 60/30Kč, roof terrace 80/40Kč, combined ticket 110/60Kč
➡ ⊙10am-6pm Wed-Sun Apr-Oct, 10am-6pm Thu-Sun Nov-Mar
➡ 🚌133, 175, 207

TAKE A TRAM

Rather than climb steeply up from Husitská immediately below the monument, a much more enjoyable approach is to take tram 1, 9 or 16 to the Ohrada stop on Koněvova at the eastern end of Žižkov Hill, and enjoy an easy walk along the crest of the hill, with great views to either side – south across the rooftops of Žižkov to the TV Tower, and north over Karlín to the Vltava River and the hills above Troja.

In the 1950s a visit to Klement Gottwald's tomb was a compulsory outing for Czechoslovak school groups and busloads of tourists from Warsaw Pact countries. Gottwald's morticians, however, were not as adept as Lenin's – by 1962 the body had decayed so badly that it had to be cremated.

ROOFTOP VIEWS

The lookout point on the museum's roof offers a superb view over the city, and there's an appealing cafe on the 1st floor with an outdoor terrace.

In 1953 the monument's mausoleum – originally intended to hold the remains of Tomáš Garrigue Masaryk, Czechoslovakia's founding father – received the embalmed body of the recently deceased Klement Gottwald, displayed to the public in a refrigerated glass chamber, just like his more illustrious comrade Lenin in Moscow's Red Square.

After 1989, the remains of Gottwald and other communist dignitaries were removed, and the building lay closed for 20 years. However, after a two-year renovation project it reopened to the public in 2009 as a museum of Czechoslovak history from 1918 to 1992.

Museum

The monument's central hall – home to a dozen marble sarcophagi that once bore the remains of communist luminaries – houses a moving **war memorial** with sculptures by Jan Štursa. There are exhibits recording the founding of the Czechoslovak Republic in 1918, WWII, the 1948 coup, the Soviet invasion of 1968 – poignant newsreel footage and a handful of personal possessions record the tragic story of Jan Palach, who set himself alight to protest the Soviet invasion – and the Velvet Revolution of 1989. Upstairs you can visit the **Ceremonial Hall** and the **Presidential Lounge**.

But the most grimly fascinating part of the museum is the Frankenstein-like **laboratory** beneath the Liberation Hall, where scientists once battled to prevent Klement Gottwald's corpse from decomposing. On display in a glass-walled sarcophagus by day, his body was lowered into this white-tiled crypt every night for another frantic round of maintenance and repair. In the corner is the refrigerated chamber where Gottwald spent his nights (now occupied by the shattered remains of his sarcophagus), and in the adjoining room is a phalanx of 1950s control panels, switches and instruments that once monitored the great leader's temperature and humidity.

Žižkov Hill

Next to the monument, dominating the western end of Žižkov Hill (formerly called Vítkov Hill), is a **giant statue of Jan Žižka** on horseback. It was commissioned in 1931 from the Prague sculptor Bohumil Kafka (no relation to Franz), who had a huge studio specially constructed for the project and worked on the statue until his death in 1941, by which time he had succeeded only in creating a full-size plaster version. The statue was eventually cast in bronze – 16.5 tonnes of it – in 1950 and unveiled on 14 July of that year, the anniversary of the Battle of Vítkov Hill.

⊙ SIGHTS

NATIONAL MONUMENT MUSEUM
See p147.

TV TOWER TOWER
Map p346 (Televizní Vysílač; ☑210 320 081; www.
towerpark.cz; Mahlerovy sady 1, Žižkov; adult/
child/family 180/100/420Kč; ◎observation
decks 8am-midnight; ☎; Ⓜ Jiřího z Poděbrad)
Prague's tallest landmark – and, depending on your tastes, either its ugliest or its
most futuristic feature – is the 216m-tall
TV Tower, erected between 1985 and 1992.
But more bizarre than its architecture are
the 10 giant crawling babies that appear to
be exploring the outside of the tower – an
installation called **Miminka** (Mummy; Map
p346), by artist David Černý.

Completely renovated in 2013, the 93m-
high observation decks are fitted out with
comfortable sofas and futuristic hanging
armchairs, with screens showing film clips
of the tower's construction. There's also a
cafe, cocktail bar and restaurant at the 66m
level, and even a luxury one-room 'hotel' (all
clearly aimed at the 'oligarch' market).

OLŠANY CEMETERY CEMETERY
Map p346 (Olšanské Hřbitovy; Vinohradská 153,
Žižkov; ◎8am-7pm May-Sep, to 6pm Mar, Apr &
Oct, to 5pm Nov-Feb; ☐5, 10, 11, 13, 26) Huge
and atmospheric, Prague's main burial
ground was founded in 1680 to handle the
increased deaths during a plague epidemic.
Jan Palach (Map p346), the student who set
himself on fire in January 1969 to protest
the Soviet invasion, is buried here. To find
his grave, enter the main gate (flanked by
flower shops) on Vinohradská and turn
right; it's about 50m along on the left of the
path.

The oldest gravestones can be found in
the northwestern corner of the cemetery,
near the 17th-century **Chapel of St Roch**
(kaple sv Rocha; Map p346). There are several
entrances to the cemetery running along
Vinohradská, east of Flora metro station,
and also beside the chapel on Olšanská.

For our walking tour of the cemetery, see
p150.

ARMY MUSEUM MUSEUM
Map p346 (Armádní muzeum Žižkov; ☑973
204 900; www.vhu.cz; U památníku 2, Žižkov;
◎10am-6pm Tue-Sun; ☐133, 175, 207) FREE
On the way up Žižkov Hill you will find this
grim-looking barracks of a museum, with

a rusting T34 tank parked outside. It's for
military enthusiasts only, with exhibits on
the history of the Czechoslovak Army and
resistance movement from 1918 to 1945, including a small display of personal effects
of one of the paratroopers who took part
in the 1942 assasination of Reichsprotektor
Reinhard Heydrich.

NEW JEWISH CEMETERY CEMETERY
Map p346 (Nový židovské hřbitov; ☑226 235 216;
www.kehilaprag.cz; Izraelská 1, Žižkov; ◎9am-
5pm Sun-Thu, to 2pm Fri Apr-Oct, 9am-4pm Sun-
Thu, to 2pm Fri Nov-Mar, closed on Jewish holidays; Ⓜ Želivského) Franz Kafka is buried in
this cemetery, which opened around 1890
when the older Jewish cemetery – now at
the foot of the TV Tower – was closed. To
find **Kafka's grave** (Map p346), follow the
main avenue east (signposted), turn right
at row 21, then left at the wall; it's at the end
of the 'block'. Fans make a pilgrimage on 3
June, the anniversary of his death.

The entrance is beside Želivského metro
station; men should cover their heads (yarmulkes are available at the gate). Last admission is 30 minutes before closing.

KARLÍN STUDIOS GALLERY
Map p346 (☑608 955 150; www.karlinstudios.cz;
Křižíkova 34, Karlín; ◎noon-6pm Wed-Sun, closed
btwn exhibitions; Ⓜ Křižíkova) FREE Housed in a
converted factory building, this complex of
artists' studios includes a public art gallery
that showcases the best of Czech contemporary art, plus two small commercial galleries. This is the place to come and see what's
happening at the cutting edge of art in the
city. (Access from Křižíkova street, via the
car park behind the Vitra office building.)

✕ EATING

**Žižkov is more famous for its pubs
than its restaurants, but there are new
places springing up every year to add
to the stalwarts that have been around
for ages. As well as the restaurants, it's
worth checking out Pivovarský Klub
(p152), a drinking venue that serves
good traditional pub grub.**

CAFÉ PAVLAČ CAFE €
Map p346 (☑222 721 731; www.cafepavlac.
cz; Víta Nejedlého 23, Žižkov; mains 90-190Kč;
◎10am-11pm Mon-Fri, noon-midnight Sat, noon-
11pm Sun; ☎📶; ☐5, 9, 26) This smart and

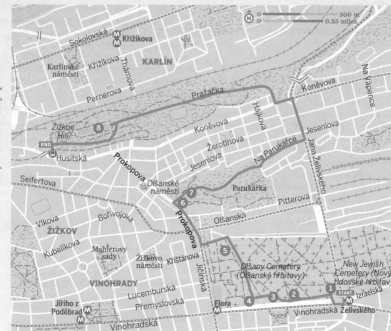

Neighbourhood Walk
Žižkov's Hidden History

START ŽELIVSKÉHO METRO STATION
END NATIONAL MONUMENT
LENGTH 4.5KM; TWO HOURS

From the Želivského metro head west on Vinohradská. At the first kiosk, go right and enter **1 Olšany Cemetery** (Olšanské hřbitovy; p149). Prague's largest burial ground is famous for its ornate family memorials, many in art nouveau style.

Follow the path running west, parallel to the wall; 250m along, just after the start of the main entrance building on the left, is the **2 grave of Jan Palach** (on the right), littered with flowers and votive candles. Just past the main entrance is Olšany's most elaborate monument, the **3 Hrdličkova family tomb**; it shows soldier Hans appearing to his mother in a dream, while she is comforted by Emperor Franz Josef I.

Continue west, keeping close to the south wall; at the far end of Section V is the grey granite slab marking the **4 grave of Klement Gottwald**, the first Communist president of Czechoslovakia; his remains were reinterred here after being removed from the National Monument in 1990.

Now follow the main path northwest towards the far side of the cemetery, passing the open space where the **5 17th-century plague victims** were buried. Turn left to exit onto Jičínska; turn right, cross busy Olšanská and go up the stairs to the right of the footbridge. In a grafitti-strewn hollow on the right are two massive steel doors that lead into a Cold War **6 nuclear bunker** (accessible by guided tour; see p32).

Above is the tiny **7 Parukářka** (p153) pub and beer garden, a focus for the local community. Take the main path east through Parukářka park (note the concrete ventilation towers for the vast bunker below) and continue along Na Parukařce. Go left on Jana Želivského, across Koněvova, then left and first right on Pražačka, which leads for 1.5km along the crest of Žižkov Hill to the **8 National Monument**, with fantastic views in all directions.

stylish cafe-bar is a sign of the new Žižkov, forsaking spit-and-sawdust earthiness for designer metalwork, edgy art and architectural magazines. It serves excellent coffee and hot chocolate, and the food menu runs from breakfast (ham and eggs, croissants or muesli with yoghurt), to lunch specials, to dinner dishes of pasta, salads and steaks.

RESTAURACE AKROPOLIS INTERNATIONAL €

Map p346 (📞296 330 990; www.palacakropolis.com; Kubelíkova 27, Žižkov; mains 90-250Kč; ⏰11am-11pm; 🖳🖊🖼; 🚃5, 9, 26) The cafe in the famous Palác Akropolis club is a Žižkov institution, with its eccentric combination of marble panels, quirky metalwork light fittings and weird fishtank installations designed by local artist František Skála. The menu has a good selection of vegetarian dishes, from nachos to gnocchi, plus great garlic soup, searingly hot buffalo wings and steak tartare. Can be smoky.

★BISOS ITALIAN €€

Map p346 (📞608 550 970; http://bisos.eu; U Rajské zahrady 16, Žižkov; mains 255-355Kč; ⏰7.30am-11.30pm Tue-Sun; 🖳🖂; 🚃5, 9, 26) The lyrics of a love song (in Sardinian dialect) by Sardinian band Tazenda adorn the walls of this cool little restaurant on the fringes of Žižkov. And you may well fall in love with the food (also Sardinian, courtesy the good folk at Ichnusa, p91), ranging from unusual breakfast dishes (buckwheat pancake with goat's cheese, pistachios and maple syrup) to seafood sauté and venison with pumpkin purée.

ESSENCE FRENCH, ITALIAN €€

Map p346 (📞773 106 832; www.essence-restaurant.cz; Štítného 35, Žižkov; mains dinner 270-350Kč, lunch 90-100Kč; ⏰11am-11pm Mon-Sat; 🖳🖂🖊; 🚃5, 9, 26) Locals linger over the excellent-value lunches at this minimalist, Mediterranean-inspired bistro, where the kitchen focuses on good-quality, freshly prepared produce. The lunch menu is limited to a couple of choices, but dinner expands to include galantine of quail, beef carpaccio, roast pork osso buco (shank) and seafood, plus a decent choice of vegetarian dishes.

INDIAN BY NATURE INDIAN €€

Map p346 (📞222 968 622; www.ibn-restaurant.cz; Pernerova 1, Karlín; mains 180-290Kč; ⏰11am-11pm Mon-Thu, 11am-11.30pm Fri, noon-11.30pm Sat, noon-10pm Sun; 🖳🖂🖊; 🚃3, 8) Prague's selection of Indian and Pakistani restaurants just keeps getting better, and this place – hidden away in a corner of Karlín – is one of the best. Classic curry dishes are fragrant with fresh herbs and zinging with ginger, chilli and spices, while the authentic tandoor turns out tender chicken tikka and fluffy naan breads.

HANIL JAPANESE, KOREAN €€

Map p346 (📞222 715 867; www.hanil.cz; Slavíkova 24, Žižkov; sushi per piece 70-50Kč, mains 350-500Kč; ⏰11am-2.30pm & 5.30-11pm Mon-Sat, 5.30-11pm Sun; 🖂; Ⓜ Jiřího z Poděbrad) White walls, lattice screens, paper lanterns and polished-granite tables create a relaxed and informal setting where a mixed crowd of businesspeople, locals and expats enjoys authentic Japanese and Korean cuisine. Tuck into a bowl of *bibimbap* (rice topped with meat and pickled vegetables spiced with hot pepper paste), or order a sashimi platter – the sushi here is among the best in town.

KUŘE V HODINKÁCH CZECH, INTERNATIONAL €€

Map p346 (📞222 734 212; www.kurevhodinkach.eu; Seifertova 26, Žižkov; mains 150-320Kč; ⏰11am-1am Mon-Fri, noon-1am Sat & Sun; 🖂; 🚃5, 9, 26) This music-themed pub is decked out in rock memorabilia, and with a choice of buzzing street-level bar or more intimate brick-vaulted basement, it's more upmarket than most Žižkov pubs and has a classy kitchen to match. The menu includes chicken Caesar salad, barbecued steak with Dijon mustard sauce, and a rich, dark and tasty goulash with bacon dumplings.

The pub is named after a 1972 album by Czech jazz-rock band Flamengo, which was banned by the communist authorities (it means 'Chicken in the Watch' – hey, it was the '70s, psychedelic drugs and all that...).

🍷 DRINKING & ⚓ NIGHTLIFE

Žižkov is famous for having more pubs per head of population than any other city district in Europe, and – depending on your tastes – offers the most authentic or the most terrifying pub-crawling experience in Prague. Be prepared for smoke, sticky floors, wall-to-wall noise and some heroically drunk companions.

ŽIŽKOV & KARLÍN DRINKING & NIGHTLIFE

WORTH A DETOUR

PIVOVAR U BULOVKY

Opened in 2004 during the first wave of new microbreweries, **Pivovar U Bulovky** (Richter Brewery; ☑602 431 077; www.pivovarubulovky.cz; Bulovka 17; ⊙11am-11pm Mon-Thu, to midnight Fri, noon-midnight Sat; ☺3, 10) is a genuine neighbourhood bar, a homely wood-panelled place with quirky metalwork, much of it home-built by the owner/brewer, František Richter. The delicious house *ležák* (lager; 32Kč for 0.5L) is a yeast beer, cloudy in appearance, and crisp, citrusy and refreshing in flavour. The bar is set in a nondescript eastern suburb, but is well worth the tram trip (from Náměstí Republiky or Florenc, take tram 3 to Bulovka). Just don't expect the staff to speak much English!

BUKOWSKI'S
COCKTAIL BAR

Map p346 (☑222 212 676; Bořivojova 86, Žižkov; ⊙7pm-3am; ☺5, 9, 26) Like many of the drinking dens that are popular among expats, Bukowski's is more a cocktail dive than a cocktail bar. Named after hard-drinking American writer Charles Bukowski, it cultivates a dark and slightly debauched atmosphere – the decor is self-consciously 'interesting' (when you can see it through the smoke-befogged candlelight) – but it peddles quality cocktails and cigars, and has friendly bartenders and cool tunes.

PIVOVARSKÝ KLUB
PUB

Map p346 (☑222 315 777; www.pivovarskyklub. com; Křižíkova 17, Karlín; ⊙11.30am-11.30pm; ⓂFlorenc) This bar is to beer what the Bodleian Library is to books – wall-to-wall shelves lined with myriad varieties of bottled beer from all over the world, and six guest beers on tap. Perch on a bar stool or head downstairs to the snug cellar and order some of the pub's excellent grub (such as authentic *guláš* with bacon dumplings) to soak up the beer.

U SLOVANSKÉ LÍPY
PUB

Map p346 (☑734 743 094; www.uslovanskelipy. cz; Tachovské náměstí 6, Žižkov; ⊙11am-midnight; ⓦⓗ; ☺133, 175, 207) A classic Žižkov pub, plain and unassuming outside and in, 'At the Linden Trees' (the linden is a Czech and Slovak national emblem) is something of a place of pilgrimage for beer lovers. The reason is its range of artisan brews, such as those from the Kout na Šumavě brewery, including a superb *světlý ležák* (pale lager).

U VYSTŘELENÉHO OKA
PUB

Map p346 (☑222 540 465; www.uvoka.cz; U Božích Bojovníků 3, Žižkov; ⊙4.30pm-1am Mon-Sat; ☺133, 175, 207) You've got to love a pub that has vinyl pads on the wall above the gents' urinals to rest your forehead on. 'The

Shot-Out Eye' – the name pays homage to the one-eyed Hussite hero atop the hill behind the pub – is a bohemian (with a small 'b') hostelry with a raucous Friday-night atmosphere where the cheap Pilsner Urquell pulls in a typically heterogeneous Žižkov crowd.

MŮJ ŠÁLEK KÁVY
CAFE

Map p346 (☑222 981 874; www.mujsalekkavy. cz; Křižíkova 105, Karlín; ⊙9am-10pm Mon-Sat, 10am-6pm Sun; ⓦⓗ; ⓂKřižíkova) A symbol of Karlín's up-and-coming, neighbourhood-to-watch status, 'My Cup of Coffee' uses Direct Trade beans prepared by expert baristas, and serves what is probably the city's best caffeine hit. Add on a friendly, laid-back atmosphere and tasty food (mains 70Kč to 120Kč), and you can see why it's often full – reservations are recommended for weekend breakfasts.

BAJKAZYL
CAFE

Map p346 (☑739 681 839; www.bajkazyl.cz; Tachovské náměstí 3; ⊙11am-midnight; ⓦ; ☺133, 175, 207) The 'bike asylum' is a combined cafe and workshop where cyclists (and anyone else) can hang out, work on their bike and chat to friends. It's right on one of Prague's most popular cycle trails, and rents out bikes (from 150Kč for two hours) if you fancy working up a thirst for one of its artisan beers or homemade lemonades.

FATAL MUSIC CLUB
BAR

Map p346 (☑222 783 463; www.xt3.cz; Rokycanova 29, Žižkov; cover free-100Kč; ⊙bar 11am-2am Mon-Thu, 11am-5am Fri, 2pm-5am Sat, 2pm-2am Sun, club from 6pm; ☺5, 9, 26) Some of the more hard-core Žižkov clubs can be a bit intimidating for nonlocals, but this relaunch of the much-loved XT3 is scruffy, laid-back, eclectic and great fun. There's a lively cafe-bar at street level, plus a cavern-like club venue downstairs that hosts local

DJs and live music from heavy metal to acoustic singer-songwriters.

HOSPODA PARUKÁŘKA   PUB, BEER GARDEN

Map p346 (http://parukarka.cz; Olšanské náměstí, Žižkov; ☺1pm-1am Apr-Oct, 4pm-midnight Nov-Mar; 🚻; 🚃5, 9, 26) This friendly community pub is little more than a ramshackle wooden hut in a park overlooking Žižkov, where locals, accompanied by kids and/or dogs, gather for a chat at the outdoor tables. There's Gambrinus on tap, a hot-dog stand in summer, occasional live music, and lots of sweet-smelling smoke wafting about in the evenings.

 **ENTERTAINMENT**

PALÁC AKROPOLIS   LIVE MUSIC, CLUB

Map p346 (☏296 330 911; www.palacakropolis.cz; Kubelíkova 27, Žižkov; cover free-200Kč; ☺club 7pm-5am; 🚇; 🚃5, 9, 26 to Lipanska) The Akropolis is a Prague institution, a smoky, labyrinthine, sticky-floored shrine to alternative music and drama. Its various performance spaces host a smorgasbord of musical and cultural events, from DJs to string quartets to Macedonian Roma bands to local rock gods to visiting talent – Marianne Faithfull, the Flaming Lips and the Strokes have all played here.

KINO AERO   CINEMA

Map p346 (☏271 771 349; www.kinoaero.cz; Biskupcova 31, Žižkov; tickets 60-110Kč; 🚇; 🚃9, 10, 11, 16) The Aero is Prague's best-loved art-house cinema, with themed programs, retrospectives and unusual films, often in English or with English subtitles. This is the place to catch reruns of classics from *Smrt v Benátkách* (Death in Venice) to *Život Briana* (The Life of Brian). The same managers run a similar venue in the city centre, Kino Světozor (p133).

Holešovice

Neighbourhood Top Five

❶ Spend a day touring the excellent modern art museum at **Veletržní Palác** (p156). This overlooked branch of the National Gallery has fine examples of early modern Czech surrealist and cubist art. Oh, and you might want to see the stuff from Schiele, Klimt, Picasso and Van Gogh too.

❷ Admire the view over the Old Town and Charles Bridge from the bluff overlooking the Vltava River at **Letná Gardens** (p157).

❸ Take the kids to Prague's best interactive museum, the **National Technical Museum** (p157).

❹ Splurge on some fancy Asian cooking at **Sasazu** (p157), then dance at the energetic club next door.

❺ Get out of town (well, briefly) with a short excursion to the **Prague Zoo** (p158).

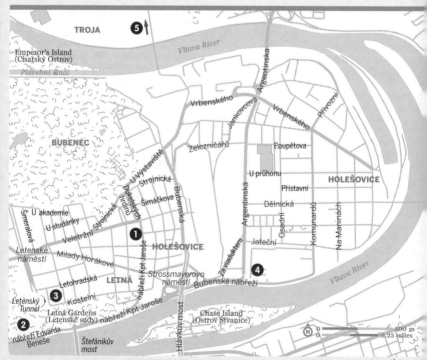

For more detail of this area, see Map p348 ➡

Explore: Holešovice

Holešovice is a mainly industrial district north of the centre defined by the big eastern bulge of the Vltava River and bounded by the river on three sides. It's divided into eastern and western halves by the main north–south rail line and a busy highway. Main transport hubs include Strossmayerovo náměstí in the west and the Holešovice train station (Nádraží Holešovice) in the northeast. The neighbourhood is gritty in spots, but possesses both the city's best art museum at Veletržní Palace and one of its nicest pieces of green at Letná Gardens.

Local Life

→**Hangouts** The Letná Beer Garden (p158) is the place to drink on a warm evening in summer.

→**Shopping** Pražská Tržnice (p161) is no longer the city's main food market, but it's still fun to people-watch.

→**Spectator sports** Ice hockey is a religion here, and home ice for Sparta Praha is Tipsport Aréna (p161).

Getting There & Away

→**Metro** Holešovice is accessible by metro via line C (red). To reach points on the western side of the district, use the Vltavská station. To reach the eastern side, go one stop further to Nádraží Holešovice.

→**Tram** The main tram junction for the western side of Holešovice is Strossmayerovo náměstí, served by lines 1, 8, 12, 17, 24, 25 and 26. Lines 1, 24 and 25 continue on into the district's eastern end. Line 14 also serves eastern Holešovice.

Lonely Planet's Top Tip

The National Gallery's Veletržní Palác (p156) is an art museum that won't disappoint. An amazing array of Western European masters, the best of Czech modern art, and 20 epically proportioned canvases by none other than Alfons Mucha – a must-visit.

HOLEŠOVICE

✗ Best Places to Eat

→ Sasazu (p157)
→ Korbel (p157)
→ Letenský zámeček (p158)
→ Pivovar Marina (p158)
→ Peperoncino (p158)

For reviews, see p157.➡

🍷 Best Places to Drink

→ Letná Beer Garden (p158)
→ Erhartova Cukrárna (p160)
→ Park Cafe & Bar (p160)
→ Kumbal (p160)
→ Klášterní Pivnice (p160)

For reviews, see p158.➡

☆ Best Places to Party

→ Cross Club (p160)
→ Sasazu (p160)
→ Mecca (p161)
→ Hells Bells (p160)
→ Letná Beer Garden (p158)

For reviews, see p160.➡

TOP SIGHT
VELETRŽNÍ PALÁC

The National Gallery's vast Museum of Art of the 19th, 20th and 21st Centuries (Trade Fair Palace) is often overlooked by visitors more bedazzled by Prague's Gothic and baroque heritage. A short tram ride from the centre, the entire building is stuffed with works by Van Gogh, Picasso, Schiele, Munch and Klimt, as well as many Czech masterpieces.

Through 2015, the museum is home to a special exhibition (adult/concession 180/90Kč) of Alfons Mucha's grandiose *Slovanská epopej* (*Slav Epic*), a collection of 20 giant paintings that tell the story of the Slavic peoples.

The permanent holdings are arranged on four floors, in rough chronological order from top to bottom. Take the elevator to the 4th floor and work your way down.

Highlights on the 4th floor (Czech art to 1930) include paintings by Alfons Mucha, Max Švabinský and the early master of abstraction, František Kupka (tracing his shift from representational art to abstraction post-WWI).

On the 3rd floor (the Interwar Period and French Masters), look for Czech cubists Bohumil Kubišta and Josef Čapek. Impressive French holdings include works by Rodin, Cézanne, Gauguin, Van Gogh, Monet and Picasso. Don't miss the functionalist architecture exhibition.

On the 2nd floor (Czech art from 1930 to 1980), our favourite is surrealist Josef Šima and his beautifully spare and subtly sexualized landscapes.

The 1st floor (International Masters) features greatest hits from Klimt, Schiele, Munch and Oskar Kokoschka, whose expressionist paintings of Prague in the 1930s are simply mind-blowing.

DON'T MISS

→ *Green Corn*, Van Gogh
→ *Self Portrait*, Picasso
→ *Dead Town*, Schiele
→ *Charles Bridge*, Kokoschka
→ *Fugue in Two Colours*, Kupka

PRACTICALITIES

→ Museum of Art of the 19th, 20th & 21st Centuries
→ Map p348
→ ☎224 301 122
→ www.ngprague.cz
→ Dukelských hrdinů 47
→ adult/concession 180/90Kč
→ ⏱10am-6pm Tue-Sun
→ 🚊1, 8, 12, 17, 24, 25, 26 to Strossmayerovo náměstí, Ⓜ Vltavská

◉ SIGHTS

Holešovice is divided into distinct western and eastern halves, with most of the important sights in the western part near Veletržní Palác.

VELETRŽNÍ PALÁC   MUSEUM
See p156.

LETNÁ GARDENS   PARK
Map p350 (Letenské sady; ⊘24hr; 🚹; 🚋1, 8, 12, 25, 26 to Letenské náměstí) Lovely Letná Gardens is a large park that occupies a bluff over the Vltava River, north of the Old Town, with postcard-perfect views out over the city, river and bridges. It's ideal for walking, jogging and beer drinking at a popular beer garden (p158) at the eastern end. The entrance is 10 minutes on foot south of Letenské náměstí.

⭐NATIONAL TECHNICAL MUSEUM   MUSEUM
Map p348 (Národní Technické Muzeum; ✆220 399 111; www.ntm.cz; Kostelní 42; adult/concession 190/90Kč; ⊘9am-5.30pm Tue-Fri, 10am-6pm Sat & Sun; 🚇🚹; 🚋1, 8, 12, 25, 26 to Letenské náměstí) Prague's most family-friendly museum got a high-tech renovation in 2012 and is a dazzling presentation of the country's industrial heritage. If that sounds dull, it's anything but. Start in the main hall, filled to the rafters with historic planes, trains and automobiles. There are separate halls devoted to exhibits on astronomy, photography, printing, and architecture.

DOX CENTRE FOR CONTEMPORARY ART   ART GALLERY
Map p348 (✆295 568 123; www.dox.cz; Poupětova 1; adult/concession 180/90Kč; ⊘10am-6pm Mon, 11am-7pm Wed & Fri, 11am-9pm Thu, 10am-6pm Sat & Sun; 🚇; 🚋12, 14, 24 to Ortenovo náměstí) This noncommercial art gallery and exhibition space forms the nucleus of Holešovice's expanding reputation as one of the city's more hip districts. The exhibitions highlight a wide range of media, including video, sculpture, photography and painting. You'll find a cafe and an excellent bookstore (heavy on art and architecture) on the upper level. Closed Tuesday.

CHEMISTRY GALLERY   GALLERY
Map p348 (✆606 649 170; www.thechemistry.cz; Bubenská 1; ⊘11am-7pm Wed-Fri, 10am-6pm Sat; Ⓜ Vltavská) Edgy gallery dedicated to show-ing the works of young Czech and international artists working in contemporary urban art, street art and graffiti. Artists include Pasta Oner, arguably the best-known Czech street artist. The setting is a gritty, 1930s functionalist building that once housed the city's electric works and is now home to a community of small businesses, artists and creative types.

✖ EATING

Holešovice is known around town as a culinary wasteland (and that's not far from the truth). There are some notable exceptions, but for the most part you're likely to eat here only if you happen to be staying somewhere nearby. The busy area around the tram hub at Strossmayerovo náměstí offers the best selection.

KORBEL   CZECH €
Map p348 (✆222 986 095; www.restauracekorbel.cz; Komunardů 30; mains 120-240Kč; ⊘11am-midnight Mon-Thu, 11am-1am Fri & Sat, noon-midnight Sun; 🚇; 🚋1, 12, 14, 25 to Dělnická) This slightly below-ground restaurant is packed at lunchtime, a testament to the very good, great-value Czech cooking. The space is noisy and energetic; service is cool but polite. It serves well-tended Pilsner-Urquell from large tanks to preserve freshness.

BOHEMIA BAGEL   AMERICAN €
Map p348 (✆220 806 541; www.bohemiabagel.cz; Dukelských hrdinů 48; mains 120-220Kč; ⊘10am-midnight; 🚇; 🚋12, 17, 24 to Veletržní palác) This hamburger, bagel and breakfast outfit remains the best all-round place to grab a light meal in this barren stretch (at least from a culinary standpoint) of Holešovice. It runs a popular brunch on weekends and inexpensive daily lunch specials, such as baked cod or grilled peppers, for around 125Kč on weekdays.

⭐SASAZU   ASIAN €€
Map p348 (✆284 097 455; www.sasazu.com; Bubenské nábřeží 306, Hall 25, Pražská tržnice; mains 220-460Kč; ⊘noon-midnight Sun-Thu, to 1am Fri & Sat; 🚇🚇; 🚋1, 14, 25 to Pražská tržnice; Ⓜ Vltavská) This upmarket Asian restaurant (connected to the club of the same name) has by many accounts the best high-end Asian cooking in Prague. While prices for

WORTH A DETOUR

PRAGUE ZOO

Prague's family-friendly **zoo** (Zoo Praha; ☑296 112 230; www.zoopraha.cz; U Trojského zámku 120, Troja; adult/concession/family 200/150/600Kč; ☉9am-7pm Jun-Aug, to 6pm Apr, May, Sep & Oct, to 5pm Mar, to 4pm Nov-Feb; ▦; ☐112, Ⓜ Nádraží Holešovice) is north of Holešovice, reachable by bus 112 from Nádraží Holešovice metro station, or a 15-minute walk from Stromovka park. Visit on a weekday if possible – weekends get ridiculously crowded.

The 60-hectare wooded grounds are on the northern banks of the Vltava. Pride of place, atop the hill, goes to a herd of Przewalski's horses (the zoo played an important role in saving them from extinction) and the komodo dragons. Other attractions include a miniature cable car and kids' play area.

individual entrees are not outrageous for what's on offer, portions are on the small side. Book in advance, especially on weekends.

PEPERONCINO ITALIAN €€

Map p348 (☑233 312 438; www.restaurant-peperoncino.cz; Letohradská 34; mains 180-390Kč; ☉11am-11pm; ⊖✐; ☐1, 8, 12, 25, 26 to Letenské náměstí) Insider's choice for good, reasonably priced Italian cooking in the western end of Holešovice. The grilled octopus and beans starter is a neighbourhood favourite, but we're partial to the beef or tuna carpaccio. The pastas and main courses are all excellent, and the wine list has lots of affordable Czech and Italian choices. Beautiful, bucolic garden in summer. Reservations recommended.

LETENSKÝ ZÁMEČEK CZECH €€

(Brasserie Ullmann; ☑233 378 200; www.letenskyzamecek.cz; Letenské sady 341; mains 175-395Kč; ☉11am-11pm; ⊖✆; ☐1, 8, 12, 25, 26 to Letenské náměstí) This upscale brasserie occupies the ground floor of a 19th-century chateau next to the Letná Beer Garden. It's open year-round but comes into its own from May to September, with the terrace open and the spires of the Old Town stretching out in the distance. The kitchen is strong on Czech specialities such as rabbit confit, and beef in cream sauce with dumplings.

PIVOVAR MARINA CZECH, ITALIAN €€

Map p348 (☑220 571 183; www.pivovarmarina.cz; Jankovcova 12; mains 199-489Kč; ☉11am-midnight; ⊖✆; ☐1, 12, 14, 25 to U Průhonu) An unlikely but welcome combination: an excellent Czech microbrewery and the best Italian cooking in eastern Holešovice. For beers, we especially like the wheat beer and

10° Přístavní lager. The food runs to high-end pastas and mains such as slow-cooked lamb knee served with a puréed celery root. During the warmer months, the outdoor tables afford relaxing views over the river.

MOLO 22 INTERNATIONAL €€

Map p348 (☑220 563 348; www.molo22.cz; U Průhonu 22; mains 150-360Kč; ☉11am-11pm; ✆; ☐1, 12, 14, 25 to U Průhonu) This Staropramen brewery-run restaurant has a clean, modern interior and an upscale international menu of Caesar salads, chicken wraps, pastas and steaks. Draws a lively lunch crowd on work days, and makes for a decent dinner before a night spent cubbing at nearby nightspots.

🍷 DRINKING & 🍸 NIGHTLIFE

Holešovice may be a working-class district at heart, but it has some of the city's best cafes and high-styling clubs. Most of the better cafes are in the western side of the district, while the better clubs are on the eastern side.

★ LETNÁ BEER GARDEN BEER GARDEN

Map p348 (☑233 378 208; www.letenskyzamecek.cz; Letenské sady 341; ☉11am-11pm summer only; ☐1, 8, 12, 25, 26 to Letenské náměstí) No accounting of watering holes in the neighbourhood would be complete without a nod toward the city's best beer garden, situated at the eastern end of the Letná Gardens (p157). Buy a takeaway beer from a small kiosk and grab a picnic table, or sit on a small terrace where you can order beer-by-the-glass and decent pizza.

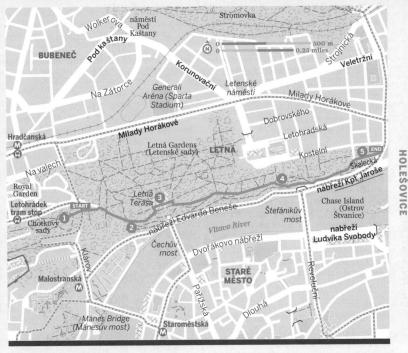

🏃 Neighbourhood Walk
The Heights of Letná

START TRAM 5 OR 18 TO CHOTKOVY SADY STOP
END EXPO '58 RESTAURANT
LENGTH 2KM; ONE HOUR

Catch tram 5 or 18 to Chotkovy sady stop, find a green footbridge and cross it towards the west (in the direction of Prague Castle); here you'll find a ① **stone grotto** dedicated to the novelist Josef Zeyer. There's a park bench nearby, with the first of several photo-op spots, offering superb views out over Malá Strana and up to Prague Castle.

Cross the footbridge again, this time heading east toward Letná Gardens. From here, follow the main path, which bears right from the park entrance, then detour further right to visit the ② **Hanavský pavilón**, where you can enjoy another eye-opening panorama and, perhaps, a little lunch.

The path continues along the top of a bluff above the Vltava, with great views over the river and the eastern and southern parts of the city, before arriving at a monu-

mental stepped terrace topped by a giant, creaking ③ **metronome** that sits on a spot once occupied by a giant statue of Stalin.

Continue east along the path, zigging and zagging but basically hugging the ridge, to arrive at one of the city's most popular summertime watering holes, the ④ **Letná Beer Garden**. Line up at the beer kiosk to buy a Gambrinus in a plastic cup (35Kč) and take a seat at one of the picnic tables. If you're hungry, there's a small terrace here serving pizza, and a fancier, tablecloth place, Letenský zámeček, nearby.

Letná Gardens extend another 300m eastward, before sloping into Holešovice proper. About 100m from the beer garden stands an architectural curiosity, the retro-futuristic ⑤ **Expo '58 Restaurant**. Built for the Brussels World Exposition of 1958, the restaurant was later re-erected here and eventually renovated. It's no longer a restaurant, but instead houses an advertising agency. From here you can head back to the beer garden or walk down the hill to Holešovice.

ERHARTOVA CUKRÁRNA CAFE

Map p348 (✆233 312 148; www.erhartovacukrarna.cz; Milady Horákové 56; ◔10am-7pm; ☎; ◻1, 8, 12, 25, 26 to Kamenická) This stylish 1930s-era cafe and sweetshop in a refurbished functionalist building is adjacent to the local branch of the public library. It draws a mix of students, older folk and mothers with strollers, attracted mainly by the cookies, doughnuts and cinnamon rolls, as well as ice cream in hot weather.

PARK CAFE & BAR CAFE

Map p348 (✆603 193 003; http://parkcafebar.cz; Kamenická 56; ◔5pm-1am Mon-Sat, to 11pm Sun; ☎; ◻1, 8, 12, 25, 26 to Kamenická) This laid-back, alternative cafe is just what the doctor ordered. Two simply adorned rooms, with big wooden tables and wood-plank flooring, provide the perfect setting for a relaxing coffee or glass of wine. There's not much in the way of food, but the toasted panini-style cheese and ham sandwiches, filled with arugula, hit the spot.

KUMBAL CAFE

Map p348 (✆604 959 323; www.kumbal.cz; Heřmanova 12; ◔8am-9.30pm Mon-Fri, 9am-9.30pm Sat & Sun; ☎⊞; ◻1, 8, 12, 17, 24, 25, 26 to Strossmayerovo náměstí) This stylish coffee bar in a 1930s functionalist building manages to be both hip and comfortable at the same time. There are good coffee and tea drinks, though not much on the menu aside from a few simple sandwiches and a daily soup (usually vegetarian). Breakfast is served every day until 11.30am.

KAVÁRNA LIBERÁL CAFE

Map p348 (✆732 222 880; Heřmanova 6; ◔9am-midnight Mon-Sat, 2pm-midnight Sun; ☎; Ⓜ Vltavská, ◻1, 8, 12, 17, 24, 25, 26 to Strossmayerovo náměstí) This Viennese-style coffee house captures something of Prague in the 1920s. By day, it's a quiet spot for coffee and wi-fi surfing; evenings bring out a more publike feel. There are occasional live bands in the recently renovated basement space. It offers coffee, beer and wine, and often – but not always – excellent sweets such as cheesecake and apple strudel.

OUKY DOUKY CAFE

Map p348 (✆266 711 531; www.oukydouky.cz; Janovského 14; ◔8am-midnight; ☎; ◻1, 8, 12, 17, 24, 25, 26 to Strossmayerovo náměstí) This was the original home of the Globe Bookstore & Coffeehouse in the 1990s, and a kind of eclectic, San Francisco funkiness lingers. Today it houses a used bookshop, with a worn-out selection of Czech-language books, and an inviting cafe filled with students, bored housewives and a wandering expat or two (possibly still looking for the Globe).

KLÁŠTERNÍ PIVNICE PUB

Map p348 (✆723 026 104; Ovenecká 15; ◔9.30am-9.30pm; ◻1, 8, 12, 25, 26 to Letenské náměstí) Not for the mild mannered, this old man's pub serves excellent, hard-to-find Klášter beer. The main drinking room gets pretty smoky and crowded with crusty regulars and, indeed, a whole day can go by without a single female visitor, but you can't argue with the beer. A perfectly preserved Prague pub undisturbed by modern life.

HELLS BELLS PUB

Map p348 (✆733 734 918; www.hellsbells.cz; Letohradská 50; ◔11am-12.30am Mon-Thu, 11am-2am Fri & Sat, noon-10pm Sun; ☎; ◻1, 8, 12, 25, 26 to Letenské náměstí) This raucous beer pub with a mostly student-age clientele makes a good place to move on to after the Letná Beer Garden closes down. There's decent Czech food as well, including good-value daily lunch specials.

☆ ENTERTAINMENT

★CROSS CLUB CLUB

Map p348 (✆736 535 010; www.crossclub.cz; Plynární 23; cover free-150Kč; ◔cafe noon-2am, club 6pm-4am; ☎; Ⓜ Nádraží Holešovice) An industrial club in every sense of the word: the setting in an industrial zone; the thumping music (both DJs and live acts); and the interior, an absolute must-see jumble of gadgets, shafts, cranks and pipes, many of which move and pulsate with light to the music. The program includes occasional live music, theatre performances and art happenings.

SASAZU CLUB

Map p348 (✆778 054 054; www.sasazu.com; Bubenské nábřeží 306, Hall 25, Pražská Tržnice; admission 200-1000Kč; ◔9pm-5am; ☎; ◻1, 14, 25 to Pražská Tržnice, Ⓜ Vltavská) One of the most popular dance clubs in the city, Sasazu attracts the fashionable elite and hangers-on in equal measure. If you're into big dance floors and long lines (hint: go early), this is your place. Check the website for occasional big-name acts (such as Bastille or Morcheeba). Book a table in advance by phone (10am to 6pm Monday to Friday, 4pm to 10pm Saturday).

MECCA CLUB

Map p348 (☑734 155 300; www.mecca.cz; U Průhonu 3; cover 100-200Kč; ☺10pm-6am Fri & Sat; ☎; ☐1, 12, 14, 25) This former warehouse in Holešovice had a slick renovation and now boasts fun on three floors (and five bars). It's open weekends only, with Friday usually given over to a weekly R & B party featuring DJs from around the country and occasionally around Europe. The crowd tends to be a bit older – professionals in their 20s, 30s and 40s.

LA FABRIKA THEATRE, PERFORMING ARTS

Map p348 (☑774 417 644 (box office); www.lafabrika.cz; Komunardů 30; admission 100-400Kč; ☺box office 2-7.30pm Mon-Fri; ☐1, 12, 14, 25 to Dělnická) The name refers to a 'factory', but this is actually a former paint warehouse that's been converted into an experimental performance space. Depending on the night, come here to catch live music (jazz or cabaret), theatre, dance or film. Consult the website for the latest program.

BIO OKO CINEMA

Map p348 (Oko Cinema; ☑box office 233 382 606, ticket reservation 608 330 088; www.biooko.net; Františka Křížka 15; tickets from 100Kč; ☎; ☐1, 8, 12, 17, 24, 25, 26 to Strossmayerovo náměstí) This repertory cinema shows a varied program of underground films; selections from film festivals; documentaries; big-budget movies; and classics from around the world. Most films are shown in the original language (not necessarily English), with Czech subtitles. Check the website for the latest film showings. Reserve tickets by phone between 10am and 5pm Monday to Friday.

ALFRED VE DVOŘE THEATRE

Map p348 (☑233 376 985; www.alfredvedvore.cz; Františka Křížka 36; tickets 100-150Kč; ☺box office 5.30-11pm Mon-Fri, 1.30-11pm Sat & Sun; ☐1, 8, 12, 17, 24, 25, 26 to Strossmayerovo náměstí) An artistic treasure in an unlikely spot in Holešovice, the Alfred regularly stages demanding works of drama, dance, cabaret and movement theatre, including occasion-

CATCH A SPARTA PRAHA ICE-HOCKEY MATCH

Czechs have an illustrious history in ice hockey, perennially placing at the top of the world rankings and regularly sending the cream of the crop to the North American National Hockey League. One of the top teams of the Czech Extraliga, Sparta Praha, plays its home games at Holešovice's **Tipsport Aréna** (Sportovní Hala; Map p348; ☑266 727 443; tipsportarena-praha.cz; Za elektrárnou 419; match tickets 180-400Kč; ☺box office 1-5.30pm Mon-Fri; ☐12, 17, 24 to Výstaviště, ⓜNádraží Holešovice). Tickets are usually available for matches during the regular season, which runs from September through April. Buy tickets online at **TicketPortal** (www.ticketportal.cz) or at the stadium box office.

al performances in English. Check what's on and buy tickets through **TicketStream** (www.ticketstream.cz).

🛍 SHOPPING

PIVNÍ GALERIE FOOD, DRINK

Map p348 (☑220 870 613; www.pivnigalerie.cz; U Průhonu 9; ☺11am-7pm Wed-Fri; ☐1, 12, 14, 25 to U Průhonu) If you think Czech beer begins and ends with Pilsner Urquell, a visit to the tasting room at Pivní Galerie (the Beer Gallery) will lift the scales from your eyes. Here you can sample and purchase a huge range of Bohemian and Moravian beers – nearly 150 varieties from 30 different breweries – with expert advice from the owners.

PRAŽSKÁ TRŽNICE MARKET

Map p348 (Prague Market Hall, Holešovická tržnice; ☑220 800 592; www.holesovickatrznice.cz; Bubenské nábřeží 306; ☺7am-6pm Mon-Fri, to 2pm Sat; ☐1, 14, 25 to Pražská Tržnice) Almost a suburb in itself, Prague's sprawling, slightly depressing city market includes a large open-air area selling fresh fruit, vegetables and flowers (Hall 22), and dozens of stalls selling everything from cheap clothes to garden gnomes.

Bubeneč & Dejvice

Neighbourhood Top Five

1 Grab a blanket, pack a picnic lunch and head to **Stromovka** (p164), central Prague's largest city park. You can rent in-line skates or bikes, or ramble the grounds and pair the visit with a trip to the Prague Zoo.

2 Spend a few hours touring the varied sights of the **Výstaviště** (p164) exhibition grounds.

3 Enjoy a carnival-like atmosphere at the **Dejvice Farmers Market** (p168) on a Saturday morning.

4 Hoist a Czech beer or two at one of the neighbourhood's excellent traditional pubs, such as **U Veverky** (p164).

5 Take in a Sparta Praha football (soccer) match at **Generali Aréna** (p169) and see the best football the city can offer.

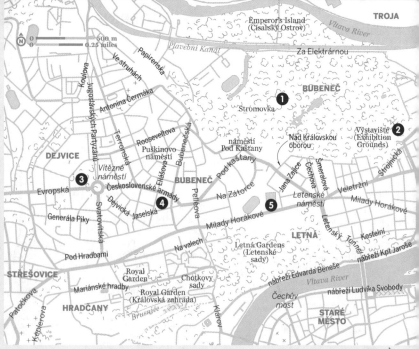

For more detail of this area, see Map p350 ➡

Explore: Bubeneč & Dejvice

Bubeneč and Dejvice are contiguous residential neighbourhoods that run east–west, to the north of the centre. Bubeneč grew up in the 1920s, and the houses and villas here, many of which are embassies, reflect the grand art-nouveau and early-modern styles of the time. Bubeneč encloses the whole of Stromovka park, an oasis of green just a short hop from the centre. Dejvice, further west, is the start of a long string of leafy suburbs that stretch out nearly to Prague's airport. It's short on traditional sights, but long on pubs and restaurants.

Local Life

➡**Hangouts** Enjoy excellent artisanal coffees at a local cafe, such as Kavárna pod Lipami (p168).

➡**Shopping** The Dejvice Farmers Market (p168) is a great place to grab picnic provisions.

➡**Spectator sports** The city's best football (soccer) team plays its home matches at Bubeneč's Generali Aréna (p169).

Getting There & Away

➡**Metro** Dejvice is accessible by metro via line A (green). The main stations are Hradčanská and Dejvická; the latter is useful for accessing attractions around large Victory Square (Vítězné náměstí) and further afield.

➡**Tram** Both Dejvice and Bubeneč are well served by tram. Lines 1, 8, 25 and 26 link Hradčanská to Letenské náměstí. Lines 5, 12, 18 and 20 connect Hradčanská to points in the centre. Victory Square is served by lines 2, 5, 8, 20 and 26. Výstaviště can be reached via lines 12, 17, and 24.

Lonely Planet's Top Tip

Bubeneč is home to Prague's finest piece of green, Stromovka, so once you've tired of the crowds and cobblestones, head here to walk the paths and get some fresh air. It's big, remote and the perfect place to relax with a blanket and a book.

✕ Best Places to Eat

➡ Da Emanuel (p167)
➡ Restaurace U Veverky (p164)
➡ Lokál Nad Stromovkou (p166)
➡ Vozovna Stromovka (p167)
➡ Brown Bag Burger (p166)

For reviews, see p164.➡

🍷 Best Places to Drink

➡ Kavárna pod Lipami (p168)
➡ Na Slamníku (p168)
➡ Alchymista (p168)
➡ La Bodega Flamenca (p168)
➡ Fraktal (p168)

For reviews, see p168.➡

🏃 Best Places for Outdoor Fun

➡ Stromovka (p164)
➡ Šlechtovka (p169)
➡ Generali Aréna (p169)
➡ Dejvice Farmers Market (p168)
➡ Divoká Šárka (p166)

BUBENEČ & DEJVICE

◉ SIGHTS

STROMOVKA
PARK

Map p350 (Královská obora; entry at Výstaviště or Nad Královskou oborou 21, Bubeneč; 🚋1, 8, 12, 25, 26 to Letenské náměstí) Stromovka, just west of Výstaviště, is central Prague's largest park. In the Middle Ages it was a royal hunting preserve, which is why it's sometimes called the Královská obora (Royal Hunting Ground). Rudolph II had rare trees planted here and several lakes created. It's now the preserve of strollers, joggers, cyclists and in-line skaters.

VÝSTAVIŠTĚ
PUBLIC SPACE

Map p350 (Exhibition Grounds; 🕿220 103 111; www.incheba.cz; Areál Výstaviště, Bubeneč; free; ⊘9am-11pm; 🚋12, 17, 24 to Výstaviště) A sprawling area of attractions and buildings of various architectural styles that was first laid out for the 1891 Jubilee Exhibition. These days it holds mainly trade fairs, but also has a branch of the National Museum, a 'singing fountain', the city's biggest aquarium and a slightly scruffy amusement park that's open daily from April to October.

KŘIŽÍK'S FOUNTAIN
FOUNTAIN

Map p350 (Křižíkova fontána; 🕿723 665 694; www.krizikovafontana.cz; U Výstaviště 1, Bubeneč; admission 220Kč; ⊘performances hourly 8-11pm Mar-Oct; 👪; 🚋12, 17, 24 to Výstaviště) Each evening from spring to autumn the musical Křižík's Fountain performs its computer-controlled light-and-water dance. Performances range from classical music such as Dvořák's *New World Symphony* to rousing works performed by Andrea Bocelli, Queen or the Scorpions. Check the website for what's on. The show is best after sunset – from May to July go for later shows.

LAPIDÁRIUM
MUSEUM

Map p350 (🕿233 375 636; www.nm.cz; U Výstaviště 1, Bubeneč; adult/concession 50/30Kč; ⊘noon-6pm Wed-Sun Apr-Oct; 🚋12, 17, 24 to Výstaviště) An outlying branch of the National Museum and an often-overlooked gem, the Lapidárium is a repository for some 400 sculptures from the 11th to the 19th centuries. The exhibits include Bohemia's oldest surviving stone sculpture, parts of the Renaissance Krocín Fountain that once stood on Old Town Square, and several original statues from Charles Bridge.

ZOO MOŘSKÝ SVĚT
AQUARIUM

Map p350 (🕿220 103 275; www.morskysvet. cz; U Výstaviště 1, Bubeneč; adult/concession 280/180Kč; ⊘10am-7pm; 👪; 🚋12, 17, 24 to Výstaviště) The Czech 'Sea World' has the largest water tank in the country, with a capacity of around 100,000L. Some 4500 living species of fish and sea creatures are on display, with a good (and suitably scary) set of sharks. The cramped interior will be disappointing if you're used to larger 'Sea World'–type amusement parks around the world.

PRAGUE PLANETARIUM
PLANETARIUM

Map p350 (Planetárium Praha; 🕿220 999 001; www.planetarium.cz; Královská obora 233, Bubeneč; shows in Czech/English 110/220Kč; ⊘8.30am-noon & 1-8pm Mon-Thu, 9.30am-noon & 1-6pm Sat & Sun; 🚋12, 17, 24 to Výstaviště) The planetarium in Stromovka park, just west of Výstaviště, presents various slide and video presentations in addition to the star shows. Most shows are in Czech only, but one or two of the more popular ones provide a text summary in English (check the website for details). There's also an astronomical exhibition in the main hall.

HOTEL CROWNE PLAZA
HISTORIC BUILDING

Map p350 (Hotel International; 🕿296 537 111; www.crowneplaza.cz; Koulová 15, Dejvice; 🚋5, 8 to Zelená) For architecture buffs, the impressive silhouette of this huge Stalin-era building in Dejvice will be familiar to anyone who has visited Moscow. Originally called the Hotel International, it was built in the 1950s to a design inspired by a tower of Moscow University, right down to the Soviet-style star on top of the spire. The interior is just as impressive.

✖ EATING

★ RESTAURACE U VEVERKY
CZECH €

Map p350 (🕿223 000 223; www.uveverky. com; Eliášova 14, Dejvice; mains 139-240Kč; ⊘10.30am-midnight Mon-Fri, 11am-midnight Sat & Sun; Ⓜ Hradčanská) This highly rated traditional pub has some of the best-tasting, good-value lunches in the city and is worth a detour. The set-up is classic, with a drinking room out the front and two big dining rooms in the back. The restaurant is filled

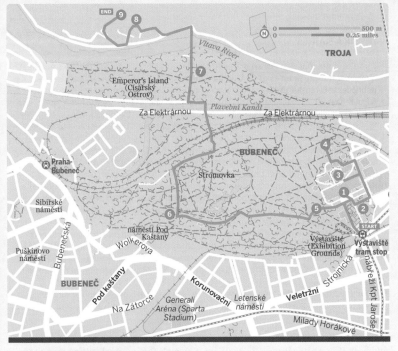

🏃 Walking Tour
Výstaviště & Stromovka

START VÝSTAVIŠTĚ TRAM STOP
END PRAGUE ZOO
LENGTH 3KM; TWO HOURS

Catch tram 12, 17 or 24 to the Výstaviště tram stop at the front of the exhibition grounds, which date from 1891, when Prague hosted a world jubilee. Proceed through the gates (entry free) to find the front of the massive ➊ **Průmyslový Palác** (Industrial Palace), the centrepiece of the exhibition but now closed to the public.

In front of the palace to the right (east), one of the original buildings houses the ➋ **Lapidárium**, a museum of the city's finest sculptures. If you have kids, the same building (enter from the eastern side) holds Prague's biggest aquarium, Mořský svět.

From here, walk along the eastern side of the Industrial Palace to find ➌ **Křižíkova fontána** (Křižík's Fountain), where a 'singing fountain' spritzes to classical and pop music at night during the summer.

Beyond the fountain stadium, an ➍ **amusement park** extends to the grounds' northern boundary. The rides are hit-and-miss (buy tickets individually). We like the big Ferris wheel at the northwestern end.

Retrace your steps back to the entrance of Výstaviště and follow the path to the right of the terminal loop of tram 17, passing the ➎ **Prague Planetarium** as you enter the former royal hunting ground, Stromovka.

From here, wander through Stromovka at your leisure, heading vaguely west and north. In the far distance to the west on a hill, you'll see the Renaissance ➏ **Mistodržitelský Summer Palace**, where royals used to hang out on hunting trips.

Following the signs to 'Troja' and 'Zoo', walk under a railway line. From here climb some steps to enter ➐ **Emperor's Island** (Císařský ostrov); the road eventually leads to a pedestrian bridge over the Vltava.

At this point, it's just a short walk to the ➑ **Troja Chateau** or ➒ **Prague Zoo** (p158).

WORTH A DETOUR

DIVOKÁ ŠÁRKA

If you're in the mood to get away from it all, plan an outing to one of the city's prettiest and most remote nature parks, **Divoká Šárka** (☑603 723 501; www.koupaliste-sarka. webnode.cz; Evropská, Dejvice; adult/concession 80/40Kč; ⊗swimming pool 9am-7pm Jun-Aug; 🖫; 🚊2, 20, 26 to Divoká Šárka). The park is best known for its eerie lunar landscape of barren rocks and hills at its western end, but it actually stretches for miles through forests and valleys along the Šárecký potok (Šárka Creek). The easiest way to access the park is by tram; lines 2, 20 and 26 from Victory Square (Vítězné náměstí) terminate at the edge of the park. You can return by tram the way you came or walk a 7km trail that circles back toward the Vltava, from where you can catch another tram.

The park is named after the mythical warrior Šárka, who is said to have thrown herself off a cliff here after the death of her enemy, the handsome Ctirad – whom she either seduced and murdered (committing suicide afterwards to avoid capture), or fell in love with and failed to protect (killing herself out of grief and guilt), depending on which version of the legend you prefer.

In addition to hiking, the area is perfect for spreading out a picnic blanket. In summer there's an unheated swimming pool (with icy cold water), and a number of pubs.

To hike back towards town, find the red-marked trail that runs all the way to the suburb of Podbaba, where the creek empties into the Vltava. Once you've hit the river, look for the tower of the unmissable Hotel Crowne Plaza (with a gold star on top). Head towards the hotel, from where you can pick up tram 5 or 8, which brings you back to the Dejvická metro station, or stay aboard all the way to Náměstí Republiky.

with the welcoming smell of grilled onions and beer. Reserve in advance.

LOKÁL NAD STROMOVKOU   CZECH €

Map p350 (Nad Královskou Oborou; ☑220 912 319; www.ambi.cz; Nad Královskou oborou 31, Bubeneč; mains 120-220Kč; ⊗11.30am-midnight Mon-Thu, 11.30am-1am Fri, noon-1am Sat, noon-10pm Sun; ⊜🛜; 🚊1, 8, 12, 25, 26 to Letenské náměstí) This lovingly restored, traditional Czech pub is part of the Lokál chain, which has a commitment to high-quality ingredients and, naturally, perfectly tended Pilsner Urquell beer. The menu features simple Czech cooking, such as grilled trout or chicken schnitzels, done well. Pair a visit here with a stroll through nearby Stromovka park. Book in advance.

BROWN BAG BURGER   BURGERS €

Map p350 (☑222 934 773; www.brownbagburger. cz; Československé armády 30, Dejvice; burgers 135-180Kč; ⊗11am-10pm Mon-Sat; ⊜🛜; MDejvická) Delicious gourmet burgers, including a mushroom veggie burger, plus hot dogs, chilli dogs and salads, served in a shiny but tiny diner-type place near the Dejvická metro station. The basic gourmet cheeseburger will suffice for most appetites. There's good Unětice beer on tap,

and even wines brought in from California, though the informal setting doesn't invite a long stay.

YAMYAM   ASIAN €

Map p350 (☑223 004 915; www.yamyam.cz; Mařákova 8, Dejvice; mains 125-180Kč; ⊗11am-11pm; ⊜🛜🞑; MHradčanská) This warm, inviting Thai-influenced Asian spot serves well-prepared curry, rice and noodle dishes, featuring shrimp, duck, chicken and beef as well as a nice range of vegetarian options. We love the mixed appetizer plate, with tiger prawns, chicken satay and fresh spring rolls (almost big enough for a meal in itself). Daily lunch specials offer an appetizer and main for 135Kč.

NA URALE   CZECH €

Map p350 (☑224 326 820; www.dejrest.cz/ na-urale; Uralská 9, Dejvice; mains 120-230Kč; ⊗11am-1am; 🛜; 🚊5, 8 to Lotyšská, MDejvická) A formerly grotty Czech pub, Na Urale has greatly cleaned up its act in recent years, adding beautiful crimson walls and stone-tile floors. The kitchen has also had an upgrade, but the prices for well-done Czech dishes, such as goulash and roast pork, are barely higher than at a typical workers' pub.

U VILÉMA
CZECH €

Map p350 (☑728 916 241; Československé armády 3, Bubeneč; mains 90-150Kč; ⏰11am-midnight Mon-Sat, to 10pm Sun; Ⓜ Hradčanská) This popular neighbourhood pub and beer garden has a welcoming atmosphere and very good 11° Svijany on tap for a bargain 25Kč. The menu includes many simple, home-cooked Czech specialties, such as *pečené hovězí* (roast beef and gravy) and the house goulash served on a potato pancake. Nonsmoking between 11am and 2pm. The garden makes a welcome respite in summer.

VOZOVNA STROMOVKA
INTERNATIONAL €€

Map p350 (☑725 123 705; www.vozovna-stromovka.cz; Královská obora 2, Bubeneč; mains 160-280Kč; ⏰10am-10pm; ⊜🛜🍴; 🚊12, 17, 24 to Výstaviště) This garden restaurant in the middle of Stromovka park is often standing-room only with mums and dads, while kids play in the adjacent playground. The menu borrows heavily from around Europe, with spicy ground beef from the Balkans next to grilled salmon and a very good paella with chorizo sausage. The location is about 200m west of Prague Planetarium.

NAHOŘE A DOLE
INTERNATIONAL €€

Map p350 (Kavárna Nahoře a Restaurace Dole; ☑727 891 986; www.nahoreadole.cz; Na Hutích 9, Dejvice; mains 140-280Kč; ⏰restaurant 11.30am-11pm Mon-Sat, cafe 10am-1am Mon-Fri, 2pm-1am Sat, 4-10pm Sun; ⊜🛜; 🚊5, 8, 20, 26 to Vítězné náměstí, Ⓜ Dejvická) Walk down a flight of stairs to find this handsome, contemporary space serving a welcome mix of Czech and international dishes, such as leg of rabbit pâté served with pistachio. The minimalist space, with concrete walls, wooden floors, and colourful, playful chairs and tables, sets a trendy tone. Repair to the ground-level cafe for an after-meal espresso.

ARGUMENT
INTERNATIONAL €€

Map p350 (☑220 510 427; www.argument-restaurant.cz; Bubenečská 19, Bubeneč; mains 239-389Kč; ⏰11.30am-11.30pm Mon-Sat, noon-10pm Sun; ⊜🛜; Ⓜ Hradčanská) Upscale dining in Prague 6 that perennially gets mentioned alongside the city's best restaurants, but with prices roughly half of what you would pay in the centre. There's no defining culinary theme here, more a hodge-podge of international favourites, steaks, pasta and seafood, and even a terrific burger. Reserve in advance.

KULAT'ÁK
CZECH €€

Map p350 (☑773 973 037; www.kulatak.cz; Vítězné náměstí 12, Dejvice; mains 170-270Kč; ⏰11am-midnight; 🛜; 🚊2, 5, 8, 20, 26 to Vítězné náměstí, Ⓜ Dejvická) The local branch of a Pilsner Urquell–run chain does not disappoint, offering decent Czech cooking in an authentic but spiffed-up atmosphere. This is a good place to try specialities such as *svíčková na smetaně* (braised beef with cranberries and dumplings) or *Moravský vrabec* (Moravian 'sparrow' – a cut of roast pork with a side of bread and bacon dumplings).

SAKURA
JAPANESE €€

Map p350 (☑774 785 077; www.sakuradejvice.cz; náměstí Svobody 1, Dejvice; mains 200-360Kč; ⏰11am-10pm; ⊜🛜🍴; 🚊2, 5, 8, 20, 26 to Vítězné náměstí, Ⓜ Dejvická) This is one of the best sushi places in Prague. It occupies a smart 1930s functionalist building, and the open interior is a blend of contemporary Japanese and Czech modern. The 'volcano' roll features spicy tuna; the 'crunch' roll comes lightly fried, with gently cooked salmon tucked inside. There's a small play area for children.

BUDVARKÁ
CZECH, PUB €€

Map p350 (☑222 960 820; www.budvarkadejvice.cz; Wuchterlova 22, Dejvice; mains 149-320Kč; ⏰11am-midnight; 🛜; 🚊2, 5, 8, 20, 26 to Vítězné náměstí, Ⓜ Dejvická) Handsome Czech pub owned and operated by the Budvar brewery. You'll find the complete 'Budweiser' family of beers here, including the hard-to-find yeast and dark varieties. There's also excellent Czech pub food, heavy on pork and chicken, served in an accurate rendition of a 19th-century tap room. There's a smoking room out front and a large non-smoking area in the back.

DA EMANUEL
ITALIAN €€€

Map p350 (☑224 312 934; www.daemanuel.cz; Charlese de Gaulla 4, Dejvice; mains 400-550Kč; ⏰noon-11pm; ⊜🛜; 🚊5, 8 to Lotyšská, Ⓜ Dejvická) This small, elegant Italian restaurant, on a quiet residential street, is one of Dejvice's true destination restaurants. The main dining room, perched romantically below an arched brick ceiling, holds around a dozen tables, each with a vase of fresh flowers. The menu features homemade pastas as well as grilled meats and fish. Book in advance.

THE DEJVICE FARMERS MARKET

The past few years have a seen a growth in interest in sustainable agriculture and organic foods in the Czech Republic, and thankfully spurred the opening of farmers markets across Prague. The first, and still best, of these is in **Dejvice** (Farmářský trh; Map p350; www.ceskefarmarsketrhy.cz; Vítězné náměstí, Dejvice; ⊙9am-2pm Sat Mar-Nov; Ⓜ︎Dejvická), on the grassy square adjacent to the Dejvická metro station.

Every Saturday morning from March to November, farmers from around the country descend on the square to sell their fruits and vegetables, as well as fresh bread and other baked goods, meats and cheeses.

The markets have evolved into more than just a chance to buy fresh produce. A sunny morning usually brings hundreds of people onto the square and the atmosphere becomes something akin to a carnival. It's a great outing for the whole family.

🍺 DRINKING & NIGHTLIFE

★ KAVÁRNA POD LIPAMI   CAFE

Map p350 (📞777 568 658; www.mamacoffee.cz; Čechova 1, Bubeneč; ⊙8.30am-10pm Mon-Fri, 11am-10pm Sat & Sun; 🛜; 🚋1, 8, 12, 25, 26 to Letenské náměstí) This local branch of the citywide Mama Coffee chain offers fairtrade coffees, as well as teas, other drinks and light meals (such as hummus, soups and salads) in a comfortably dressed-down setting of tiled floors, white walls and light bulbs simply hanging on wires from the ceiling. It's popular with students and there's a terrace out front in summer.

NA SLAMNÍKU   PUB, BEER GARDEN

Map p350 (📞233 322 594; www.koncertynaslamniku.wz.cz; Wolkerova 12, Bubeneč; ⊙noon-midnight; 🚋131 to Sibiřské náměstí, 🚋1, 8, 12, 25, 26 to Letenské náměstí) A great traditional Czech pub and beer garden dating from the 19th century, Na Slamníku is tucked away in a small valley in Bubeneč, just behind the sprawling Russian embassy. There are a couple of drinking rooms inside, and a peaceful shady garden in front in summer. Occasional live music on weekends.

ALCHYMISTA   CAFE

Map p350 (📞732 938 046; www.alchymista.cz; Jana Zajíce 7, Bubeneč; ⊙10.30am-9.30pm; 🛜; 🚋1, 8, 12, 25, 26 to Letenské náměstí) This old-fashioned coffee house with an adjacent art gallery is an oasis in the culturally barren neighbourhood behind Sparta Stadium. Freshly ground coffees, a serious selection of teas (no Lipton in a bag here), and freshly made cakes and strudels draw a mostly local crowd. Beautiful garden out back in summer.

LA BODEGA FLAMENCA   BAR

Map p350 (📞233 374 075; www.labodega.cz; Šmeralová 5, Bubeneč; ⊙4pm-1am Sun-Thu, to 3am Fri & Sat; 🚋1, 8, 12, 25, 26 to Letenské náměstí) La Bodega resides in an atmospheric, red-brick cellar. With the Latin music turned down low, the crowd seems a bit more reflective (at least compared with the rest of the bars in the neighbourhood). Most people come for a beer or sangria, but there's also a nice selection of tapas on hand. Also has live music and dance some nights.

KABINET   CAFE

Map p350 (📞233 326 668; Terronská 25, Dejvice; ⊙noon-10pm Mon-Fri, 3-10pm Sat & Sun; 🛜; 🚋5, 8 to Lotyšská, Ⓜ︎Dejvická) A retro, 1920s-style coffee house, Kabinet is situated in a cool cubist building in a pleasantly residential part of Dejvice. Old cameras, posters and photographs lend a throwback feel. The name of the cafe, for Czechs, recalls early school days – a 'kabinet' being a teacher's office – to add to the nostalgic setting.

FRAKTAL   BAR

Map p350 (📞777 794 094; www.fraktalbar.cz; Šmeralová 1, Bubeneč; mains 120-300Kč; 🛜; 🚋1, 8, 12, 25, 26 to Letenské náměstí) This subterranean space under a corner house near Letenské náměstí is easily the friendliest bar this side of the Vltava. This is especially true for English-speakers, as Fraktal serves as a kind of unofficial expat watering hole. There's also good bar fare such as burgers. The only drawback is the early closing time (last orders at 11.30pm).

POTRVÁ   CAFE

Map p350 (📞222 963 707; www.potrva.cz; Srbská 2, Bubeneč; ⊙3pm-midnight; 🛜; Ⓜ︎Hradčanská) This relaxing cafe just a short walk across the railway tracks from the Hradčanská metro station is a good place for quiet reflection during the day, with occasional live music and open-mic nights in the evening. Mostly coffee and drinks on the menu, but it does serve small bites such as soups and sandwiches.

KAVÁRNA ALIBI
CAFE

Map p350 (www.alibi.cz; Svatovítská 6, Dejvice; ☺9am-midnight Mon-Fri, 2pm-midnight Sat & Sun; ☎; ☒2, 5, 8, 20, 26 to Vítězné náměstí; Ⓜ Dejvická) Lively, smoky coffee house that is usually packed with students. It's a perfect spot to curl up with a coffee or a beer, write some postcards, consult your Lonely Planet guide or have a heart-to-heart chat with your travelling companion.

SIDE DOOR
COCKTAIL BAR

Map p350 (Korunovační 4, Bubeneč; ☺5pm-3am; ☒1, 8, 12, 25, 26 to Letenské náměstí) Side Door is an after-hours cocktail bar with an expat flair. The inviting front room, sporting velvet bar stools and glittery walls, attracts a kind of Edward Hopper *Nighthawks* crowd. The back rooms have a more risqué feel – dark and crowded some nights.

☆ ENTERTAINMENT

SPEJBL & HURVÍNEK THEATRE
THEATRE

Map p350 (Divadlo Spejbla a Hurvínka; ☎224 316 784; www.spejbl-hurvinek.cz; Dejvická 38, Dejvice; tickets 110-220Kč; ☺box office 1-6pm Mon, 9am-2pm & 3-6pm Tue-Fri, 9.30-11.30am & noon-5pm Sat & Sun; ⚑; Ⓜ Dejvická) Created in 1930 by puppeteer Josef Skupa, Spejbl and Hurvínek are the Czech marionette equivalents of Punch and Judy, although they are father and son rather than husband and wife. The shows are in Czech, but most can be followed regardless of which language you speak.

🛍 SHOPPING

STAROŽITNOSTI ROBERT PAVLŮ
ANTIQUES

Map p350 (☎224 318 952; www.antik.pavlu. info; Jaselská 19, Dejvice; ☺10am-5pm Mon-Thu; Ⓜ Hradčanská) Reputable dealer of antiques, including watches, furniture, glass and other decorative items, displayed in several rooms that stretch nearly a block in Dejvice. The holdings are especially rich in early modern, functionalist and art deco styles from the early decades of the 20th century.

WINE FOOD MARKET
FOOD

Map p350 (☎252 540 660; www.winemarket. cz; Národní obrany 29, Dejvice; ☺9am-8pm; ☎; Ⓜ Dejvická) The Dejvice branch of a small citywide chain of high-end Italian food and wine shops is a great place to stock up on meats, cheeses and wines for a day out or back at the hotel. It also has a few tables for a quick coffee or bite in-house.

ANTIKVITA
ANTIQUES

Map p350 (☎233 336 601; www.antikvita.cz; Na Hutích 9, Dejvice; ☺10am-5pm Mon-Fri; Ⓜ Dejvická) This antique shop is a collector's delight, crammed with cases and cabinets overflowing with vintage toys, model trains, dolls, coins, medals, jewellery, clocks, watches, militaria, postcards, porcelain figures, glassware and much more. If you have something to sell, Antikvita holds buying sessions on Wednesday and Thursday.

🏃 SPORTS & ACTIVITIES

GENERALI ARÉNA
SPECTATOR SPORT

Map p350 (Sparta Stadium; ☎296 111 400; www. sparta.cz; Milady Horákové 98, Bubeneč; tickets 100-400Kč; ☺box office 9am-noon & 1-5.30pm Mon, Wed & Fri, 9am-noon & 1-7pm Wed, 9am-noon & 1-4pm Fri; ☒1, 8, 12, 25, 26 to Sparta) Generali Aréna, with a capacity of more than 20,000, is the home ground of Sparta Praha – winner of the top Czech football (soccer) league several times in the past decade. Tickets are available through **Ticketportal** (www.ticketportal.cz) or at the stadium box office during the week or three hours before matches. The season runs from midsummer to the following spring.

ŠLECHTOVKA
EQUIPMENT RENTAL

Map p350 (☎731 354 552; www.slechtovka. com; Královská obora, Stromovka; skate/bike rental per hour 90/100Kč plus deposit; ☺11am-7pm Apr-Oct; ☎⚑; ☒1, 8, 12, 25, 26 to Letenské náměstí) This small shack on the edge of Stromovka park rents in-line skates, bikes and other sports equipment such as longboard skateboards, scooters and even electric bikes. To find it, follow Čechova street to the edge of the park and walk downhill. There's also a playground and a snack bar where you can grab a beer or a grilled sausage and bread.

Smíchov & Vyšehrad

VYŠEHRAD | SMÍCHOV

Neighbourhood Top Five

❶ Spend an afternoon at the **Vyšehrad Citadel** (p173), enjoying views from the rampart walls over the city. Don't miss the evocative cemetery, with its pantheon to Czech arts luminaries. Pack a picnic lunch and, with luck, catch an open-air concert.

❷ While away an evening drinking and discussing at a rowdy Smíchov pub such as **Zlatý klas** (p177).

❸ Enjoy a night of high-quality jazz on the river at **Jazz Dock** (p179).

❹ Check out some off-the-wall art or a crazy club happening at David Černý's **Meet Factory** (p175).

❺ Have a great meal in the open air at **Rio's** (p177) in Vyšehrad.

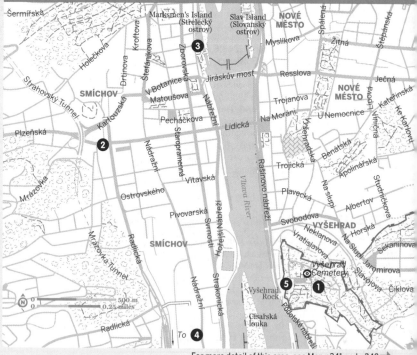

For more detail of this area, see Map p341 and p342 ➡

Explore: Smíchov & Vyšehrad

While the districts of Smíchov and Vyšehrad both lie to the south of the historic centre, they occupy different sides of the Vltava River and couldn't be more different in character. Smíchov, a former industrial area, lacks traditional sights, but has some good old-school pubs and classic restaurants. It's also home to some great hotels, especially around the Anděl metro station, so you might find yourself spending more time in this area than you thought. Bucolic Vyšehrad, by comparison, feels like a sanctuary. In many ways, it's Prague's spiritual home. Come here to tour the Vyšehrad Citadel and pay your respects to the country's cultural giants buried at Vyšehrad Cemetery.

Local Life

➡ **Hangouts** Don't let Smíchov's gleaming office towers fool you, this is a hard-drinkin' 'hood with some great traditional pubs. For starters, try Zlatý Klas (p177), U Bílého lva (p177) or Hlubina (p178). All of these serve decent food, too.

➡ **Strolling** The parkland of the Vyšehrad Citadel is one of the city's most beloved venues for simply walking around and enjoying a fine afternoon.

➡ **Shopping** Going local in Smíchov is all about hitting the mall: Nový Smíchov (p179) to be precise. There are tons of shops, cafes and restaurants, a big supermarket in the basement and a multiplex cinema up top.

Getting There & Away

➡ **Metro** Smíchov lies on line B (yellow). The heart of the district is at Anděl station. A second metro stop, Smíchovské Nádraží, is further south. Vyšehrad lies 15 minutes on foot from Vyšehrad metro station (on line C, red).

➡ **Tram** Smíchov is easily accessible by tram. Lines 4, 7, 10 and 14 rumble across the Vltava from Charles Square (Karlovo náměstí) to Smíchov; from Malá Strana take tram 12 or 20 south. Vyšehrad is better reached by metro, but trams 17 and 21 run along the river bank below the citadel. It's a steep climb up.

Lonely Planet's Top Tip

The hilltop fortress of Vyšehrad is an oasis of calm in a busy city. The grassy bluffs surrounding the cathedral can be a wonderful place to throw down a blanket and have a picnic, while enjoying the gorgeous views out over the river and onto Prague Castle in the distance.

✖ Best Places to Eat

➡ Bejzment (p175)
➡ Rio's (p177)
➡ Na Verandách (p177)
➡ Zlatý klas (p177)
➡ U Bílého lva (p177)

For reviews, see p175. ➡

🍷 Best Places to Drink

➡ Pitomá Kavárna (p178)
➡ Lokal Blok (p178)
➡ Hlubina (p178)
➡ V Cafe (p179)
➡ Cafe Citadela (p179)

For reviews, see p178. ➡

☆ Best Places to Party

➡ Hospoda U Buldoka (p178)
➡ Jazz Dock (p179)
➡ Meet Factory (p175)
➡ Phenomen (p178)
➡ Back Doors (p178)

For reviews, see p179. ➡

TOP SIGHT
VYŠEHRAD CEMETERY

Every national capital has its 'famous' cemetery, where the heroes of the nation are buried. In Prague, the prime piece of permanent real estate is at Vyšehrad. Music lovers will want to see the graves of Czech greats Antonín Dvořák and Bedřich Smetana. But even if you're not familiar with the Czech pantheon, you'll enjoy the intricately designed headstones, lovely gardens and peaceful, reflective atmosphere.

A 'Who's Who' of Czech Luminaries

The cemetery got its start in the 19th century, when the parish graveyard was first made into a memorial for famous figures of Czech culture.

The 600 or so graves in the cemetery read like a 'who's who' of Czech arts and letters. In addition to the graves of composers Bedřich Smetana and Antonín Dvořák, noted writers Karel Čapek, Jan Neruda and Božena Němcová are all buried here. There's a directory of famous names, and where they are located, at the entrance.

Many of the tombs and headstones are themselves works of art – Dvořák's marker, situated on the cemetery's northern wall, is a sculpture by Ladislav Šaloun, the same man who created the Jan Hus monument in Old Town Square. To find it from the entry gate, head north across the cemetery to the opposite wall.

For some of the other 'heroes', an elaborate pantheon called the Slavín (loosely, 'Hall of Fame'), designed by Antonín Wiehl, was added at the eastern end in 1894; its 50-odd occupants include painter Alfons Mucha, sculptor Josef Myslbek and architect Josef Gočár. The haunting motto reads *'Ač Zemřeli Ještě Mluví'* ('Though dead, they still speak').

FAMOUS GRAVES

- ➡ Antonín Dvořák, composer
- ➡ Bedřich Smetana, composer
- ➡ Alfons Mucha, artist
- ➡ Karel Čapek, writer
- ➡ Max Švabinský, painter

PRACTICALITIES

- ➡ Vyšehradský hřbitov
- ➡ Map p341
- ➡ ☎ 274 774 835
- ➡ www.praha-vyseh-rad.cz
- ➡ K Rotundě 10, Vyšehrad
- ➡ ⊙ 8am-7pm May-Sep, shorter hours rest of year
- ➡ Ⓜ Vyšehrad

TOP SIGHT
VYŠEHRAD CITADEL

The complex of buildings and structures that make up the Vyšehrad Citadel has played an important role in Czech history for more than 1000 years. While not many of the ancient buildings have survived to the present day (indeed, most structures date from the 18th century, when the complex was used as a fortress), the citadel is still viewed as Prague's spiritual home. The main sights are spread out over a wide area. Part of the fun is simply to stroll the park grounds and admire the views.

DON'T MISS

➜ Brick Gate & Casements

➜ Northern and southern ramparts

➜ Gothic Cellar

➜ Church of Sts Peter & Paul

➜ Rotunda of St Martin

PRACTICALITIES

➜ Map p341

➜ ☎261 225 304

➜ www.praha-vysehrad.cz

➜ information centre at V pevnosti 159/5b

➜ admission to the grounds free

➜ ⊘grounds 24hr

➜ Ⓜ Vyšehrad

The Birthplace of Prague

Legend has it that this high hill is the very place where Prague was born. According to myth, a wise chieftain named Krok built a castle here in the 7th century, and Libuše, the cleverest of his three daughters, famously prophesied that a great city would rise someday in the valley of the Vltava.

Unfortunately, there's scant evidence for Libuše's prophesy (though it does make for a nice story). According to the legend, Libuše went on to marry a ploughman named Přemysl, who founded both the city of Prague and the Přemysl dynasty. (That last part may be true since there really was a Přemysl dynasty, but records from these days are scarce.)

Archaeological digs at Vyšehrad have turned up proof that the site was permanently settled from as early as the 9th century. Indeed, early Přemysl rulers seemed to like Vyšehrad; Boleslav II (r 972–99) may have lived here for a time. By the mid-11th century there was a fortified settlement, and Vratislav II (r 1061–92) moved his court here from Hradčany, beefing up the walls and adding a castle and religious buildings. His successors stayed until 1140, when Vladislav II returned to Hradčany.

While little physical evidence remains of Vyšehrad from the period, a hint of the area's magnificent past is seen at the 11th-century **Rotunda of St Martin** (Rotunda sv Martina; Map p341; ☎224 911 353; V Pevnosti, Vyšehrad; ⊘mass at 6pm Mon, Wed, Thu, Fri, Sat), Prague's oldest surviving building. The door and frescos date from a renovation made about 1880. The rotunda is normally closed, but the interior can be viewed during Mass (times are posted at the door). In addition, the **Gothic Cellar** (Gotický sklep; Map p341; Vyšehradské sady, Vyšehrad; adult/child 50/30Kč; ⊘9.30am-6pm Apr-Oct, to 5pm Nov-Mar) houses a permanent exhibition called 'The Historic Faces of Vyšehrad', which focuses on both the myths and the facts concerning the origins of Vyšehrad.

Ups & Downs

After Vladislav II moved the court back to Hradčany, Vyšehrad faded into the background for around two centuries. It took the reign of Charles IV, in the 14th century, to recognise the complex's symbolic importance to the Bohemian kingdom. He repaired the walls and joined them to those of his new town, Nové Město. He built a small palace (now gone) and decreed that the coronations of Bohemian kings should begin with a procession from here to Hradčany.

While the Gothic-spired **Church of Sts Peter & Paul** (Kostel sv Petra a Pavla; Map p341; K Rotundé 10, Vyšehrad; adult/child 30/10Kč; ⊘9am-noon & 1-5pm Wed-Mon) certainly looks like

ACCESSING THE CITADEL

The main entrance to Vyšehrad citadel is through a series of gates on the eastern side. The first is the narrow **Tábor Gate** (Táborská brana; Map p341), followed by the grander 17th-century **Leopold Gate** (Leopoldova Brána; Map p341). Between these two main gates, you'll see the only surviving remnants of the 14th-century Gothic **Peak Gate** (Špička brána; Map p341), which now houses the **Špička Information Centre** (Vyšehrad Information Centre; Map p341; V pevnosti 159/5b, Vyšehrad; ⊘9.30am-6pm Apr-Oct, to 5pm Nov-Mar; ☏).

Be sure to check out the **ramparts** on the northern and southern sides of the complex, with wonderful views out over the city in the distance. Beside the southwestern bastion are the foundations of a **royal palace** that was built by Emperor Charles IV in the 14th century but dismantled in 1655. From here, there's no prescribed viewing route, though we've sketched out a handy walking tour (p176).

it may have come from Charles IV's day, in fact the church has been built and rebuilt several times over the centuries. The arresting twin spires are visible from around the city and have become the symbol of Vyšehrad. They date from the end of the 19th century and the brief architectural craze that gripped Prague at that time known as neo-Gothic. Don't miss the church's interior: a swirling acid trip of art nouveau frescoes painted in the 1920s by various Czech artists.

Unfortunately, nearly everything truly ancient was wiped out during the Hussite Wars of the 15th century. The fortress remained a ruin – except for a ramshackle township of artisans and traders – until after the Thirty Years' War, which ended in 1648, when Habsburg Emperor Leopold I once again re-fortified it.

A Baroque Fortress

While most Praguers these days associate Vyšehrad with the early founding of the city around the first millennium, much of what you see today dates from more recent times, when the fortress was used by the Austrian Habsburgs to secure their western and northern borders from Prussian and French advances in the 17th and 18th centuries. Both the French and the Prussians did occupy Vyšehrad for brief periods in the mid-18th century and contributed to the citadel's development as a fort.

This military history is on display at the **Brick Gate & Casements** (Cihelná brána; Map p341; Vratislavova, Vyšehrad; adult/child 50/30Kč; ⊘9.30am-6pm Apr-Oct, to 5pm Nov-Mar), situated on the northern side of the fortress. The Brick Gate houses a fascinating exhibition explaining the military history of Vyšehrad, as well as other fortresses in the city. The casements, in particular, are a real treat. A 20-minute tour takes you through a system of vaulted brick tunnels within the ramparts that were built up in the 18th century. The highlight is the barrel-vaulted **Gorlice Hall**, which was once used as a place for troops to muster in secret. Now it is home to six of the original **baroque statues** from Charles Bridge.

⊙ SIGHTS

⊙ Vyšehrad

VYŠEHRAD CEMETERY   CEMETERY
See p172.

VYŠEHRAD CITADEL   FORTRESS
See p173.

⊙ Smíchov

STAROPRAMEN BREWERY   BREWERY TOUR
Map p342 (☑273 132 589; www.staropramen.com; Pivovarská 9; tours 199Kč; ☉10am-6pm; MAnděl) More of a museum visit than an actual brewery tour, the presentation here focuses on the 100-plus years of history of the brewery, the only big Czech brewer based in Prague. The reward for your time is a glass of Staropramen at the end. Call or check tour times on the door. English tours are normally conducted at 10am, 1pm and 4pm.

FUTURA GALLERY   GALLERY
Map p342 (☑604 738 390; www.futuraprojekt.cz; Holečkova 49; admission by voluntary donation; ☉11am-6pm Wed-Sun; ☐4, 7, 9, 10) The Futura Gallery focuses on all aspects of contemporary art, ranging from painting, photography and sculpture to video, installations and performance art. In the garden, you'll find a rather shocking and amusing permanent installation by David Černý, called **Brownnosers** (Map p342).

MEET FACTORY   GALLERY
(☑251 551 796; http://meetfactory.cz; Ke Sklárně 15; ☉varies according to performance; ☐12, 14, 20 to Lihovar) FREE David Černý's 'Meet Factory' is a remarkable project that unites artists from around the world to live and create in an abandoned factory south of Smíchovské nádraží. The space is used for exhibitions, happenings, film screenings, theatrical performances and concerts. The location is out of the way, so be sure to check the website for the program before heading out.

✗ EATING

Of the two districts, Smíchov and Vyšehrad, the former offers much more variety. The area around Anděl metro station has exploded with restaurants in recent years. Many of these are chains, but there are several good, traditional pubs to choose from too. Offerings are more limited in Vyšehrad.

✗ Smíchov

BEJZMENT   BURGERS €
Map p342 (☑731 406 163; www.bejzment.cz; Zborovská 6, Smíchov; burgers 89-239Kč; ☉11am-11pm; ☺☎; MAnděl) This popular American-themed burger joint gets crowded at meal times, so be sure to reserve in advance. The burgers, grilled in a smoky kitchen at the back, are some of the best in Prague, but it also serves excellent BBQ chicken wings, hot dogs and Caesar salads. The US

DAVID ČERNÝ: ARTIST-PROVOCATEUR

Czech artist David Černý (b 1967) first made international headlines in 1991 when he painted Prague's memorial to the WWII Soviet tank crews bright pink, a shocking display that managed to mock both the former communist government's overenthusiastic celebration of Soviet war prowess and its rewriting of history. Since then, Černý has cultivated a reputation as the enfant terrible of the Prague art scene – his works often turn into major media events, occasionally with the police involved.

Černý achieved international notoriety in 2009 with his massive installation *Entropa*, exhibited in Brussels as part of the Czech Republic's holding of the EU's rotating presidency. The installation, comprised of mini sculptures dedicated to each member of the EU, was meant to poke fun at national stereotypes. Bulgaria, for example, was depicted as a Turkish-style toilet. It's no longer hanging in Prague, but has found a permanent home at the Techmania Science Centre (p222) in Plzeň.

Černý is heavily involved in promoting cross-cultural links with artists abroad through his sprawling Meet Factory artist-in-residency project in southern Smíchov.

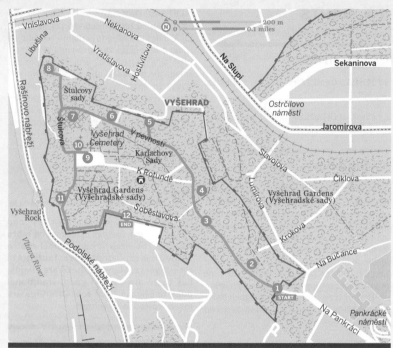

🚶 Walking Tour
Vyšehrad's Treasures

START TÁBOR GATE
END SOUTHERN WALL VYŠEHRAD FORTRESS
LENGTH 2KM; TWO HOURS

The narrow **1 Tábor Gate** (p174) can be found 200m west of the Vyšehrad metro stop. Just beyond it, you'll find the helpful **2 Špička Information Centre** (p174). From here, continue along the road and walk through the larger and more impressive **3 Leopold Gate** (p174).

Once inside the fortress proper, bear right to find the **4 Rotunda of St Martin** (p173), dating from the 11th century.

Continue along the main path to locate the fortress's **5 northern ramparts** for stunning views out over Prague below.

Retrace your steps and bear right to see the **6 Brick Gate & Casements** (p174), with a small exhibition on the fortress's military role and a few original statues that once stood on Charles Bridge.

From the Brick Gate, walk west in the direction of the neo-Gothic **7 New Provosts' Residence**. Bear right to reach the fortress's northwestern corner, which holds the **8 Letní scéna**, a small amphitheatre with dramatic views.

Trace the fortress's western wall to reach the Rio's Vyšehrad restaurant, and then round the bend to see the impressive facade of the **9 Church of Sts Peter & Paul** (p173). Just to the left of the church is the entrance to **10 Vyšehrad Cemetery** (p172), the final resting place of a host of Czech luminaries from the 19th and 20th centuries.

From the cathedral and cemetery, walk south through an archway to enter a large park. From here, a path leads to the right to the **11 Gothic Cellar** (p173), which holds a permanent exhibition on Vyšehrad's history.

You'll find more photo-ops and dramatic views along the **12 southern wall** of the fortress. Trace the southern ramparts to the east, which will eventually loop you back to Leopold Gate.

number plates on the wall add a touch of authenticity.

ZLATÝ KLAS
CZECH €

Map p342 (☑251 562 539; www.zlatyklas.cz; Plzeňská 9; mains 130-200Kč; ☺11am-11pm Sun-Thu, 11.30am-1am Fri & Sat; ⓜAnděl) This very popular pub and restaurant offers well-done Czech grub such as roast pork, goulash and fried chicken breast in a kitsch but comfortable space. Zlatý klas also offers *tankové pivo* (fresh unpasteurised beer) from Plzeň, a local badge of honour. The service is fast and friendly, but you'll have to book in advance in the evening.

FOOD LOVE
FRENCH €

Map p342 (www.foodlove.cz; Štefánikova 37; mains 79-119Kč; ☺8am-9pm Mon-Fri; ⊖⑨⑦; ⑤6, 9, 12, 20 to Arbesovo náměstí) This casual, counter-service place specialises in freshly made quiches, soups and salads and is deservedly beloved by the kids at the French grammar school nearby. There are only a few tables, so try to avoid the most popular meal times, such as noon. It also serves excellent cakes and coffee.

U BÍLÉHO LVA
CZECH €

Map p342 (☑257 316 731; www.ubileholva.eu; Na Bělidle 30; mains 135-240Kč; ☺11am-11pm; ⑦; ⓜAnděl) There's been a pub here since 1883, and everything at the 'White Lion' certainly feels authentic, down to the hardwood bench seating and shiny taps at the bar. The menu is a greatest hits list of traditional dishes, including local 'Smíchovský' goulash, served with fresh onions on top and big bread dumplings on the side.

PIZZERIA CORLEONE
PIZZA €

Map p342 (☑251 511 244; www.corleone.cz; Na Bělidle 42; mains 120-240Kč; ☺11am-11.30pm; ⑦⑨; ⓜAnděl) This lively neighbourhood restaurant is arguably the best pizza option in Smíchov, though not as good as other pizza places around town. The wood-fired pizza oven turns out all the classics, from margherita to moscardina, or you can choose your own toppings.

NA VERANDÁCH
CZECH €€

Map p342 (☑257 191 200; www.phnaverandach.cz; Nádražní 84; mains 150-280Kč; ☺11am-midnight Mon-Wed, 11am-1am Thu-Sat, to 11pm Sun; ⑨; ⑤7, 12, 14, 20 to Na Knížecí; ⓜAnděl) This pub and restaurant, managed by the Potrefená husa chain, is inside the Staropramen brewery, and while lots of people come here to eat, it's perfectly fine to come in just for a superfresh beer (there are seven varieties on tap). The menu here is high-end fast food: ribs, burgers and chicken breasts, as well as standard Czech dishes.

U MÍKULÁŠE DAČÍCKÉHO
CZECH €€

Map p342 (☑257 322 334; www.umikulasedacickeho.com; Victora Huga; mains 150-300Kč; ☺11am-midnight; ⓜAnděl) This is an honest-to-goodness, old-fashioned *vinárna* (wine bar) – complete with traditional atmosphere and excellent Czech cooking. The food here is classic Czech, with well-prepared roast pork and duck main courses, as well as grilled sausages and goulash.

The owners have gone for the 'Ye Olde Middle Ages' look, with dark woods, red tablecloths, and pictures showing the lords enjoying their wine. Reserve in advance.

✖ Vyšehrad

ARROSTO
ITALIAN €

(www.arrostoristorante.cz; Mikuláše z Husi 1709/1; mains 120-190Kč; ⊖⑦; ⓜVyšehrad) This inviting Italian-Balkan restaurant is tucked away behind a football pitch in the distant shadow of the Vyšehrad spires. It's a beacon of good cooking and civility in the bleak urban landscape that unfolds south of the Vyšehrad metro station. You'll find good pizzas and pastas, and Balkan specialities such as *pljeskavica* (spicy meat patties) and *pršut* (air-dried ham).

RIO'S VYŠEHRAD
MEDITERRANEAN €€

Map p341 (☑224 922 156; www.riorestaurant.cz; Štulcova 2; mains 250-600Kč; ☺10am-midnight; ⊖⑦; ⓜVyšehrad) Located opposite the Church of Sts Peter & Paul, this is an attractive modern restaurant set in an ancient building. There's an elegant indoor dining room, but the main drawcard is the garden, a lovely spot for an outdoor meal in summer. The international gourmet menu includes dishes such as salad of grilled octopus, veal saltimbocca and chargrilled Argentinian beef.

SMÍCHOV & VYŠEHRAD EATING

🍷 DRINKING & NIGHTLIFE

Smíchov continues to surprise. Every year brings at least one or two new bar or cafe openings. Most of the action is clustered near Anděl metro station, anchored by Nový Smíchov shopping centre. Vyšehrad is a different story. There's no real nightlife to speak of here, though there are a couple of cafes in which to relax as you take in the sights.

🍸 Smíchov

HOSPODA U BULDOKA   PUB
Map p342 (At the Bulldog; www.ubuldoka.cz; Preslova 1; ⊙bar 11am-midnight Mon-Thu, 11am-1am Fri, noon-midnight Sat, noon-11pm Sun; club 8pm-4am Mon-Sat; 🛜; Ⓜ Anděl) The Bulldog pub has it all: a quiet setting with good beer and decent Czech pub food during the day, while evenings bring out a rowdier vibe (women drink free on Wednesday nights). By night the Bulldog morphs into a college-style dance club, with DJs and theme nights; depending on the crowd it can go well into the wee hours.

PITOMÁ KAVÁRNA   CAFE
Map p342 (📞774 608 971; www.pitoma-kavarna.cz; Preslova 3; ⊙8.30am-11pm Mon-Fri, 11am-11pm Sat & Sun; 🛜; Ⓜ Anděl) This likeable and

---

THE TRUTH ABOUT SMÍCHOV

Smíchov has got to be Prague's most economically varied district. For years it languished as a depressed industrial backwater that was home to Prague's largest Roma community. At the same time, the hills south and west of Anděl metro station, not far from the Barrandov film studios, had some of the city's swankiest villas.

These days, those jarring contrasts are seen in the area around Anděl. It's filled with gleaming office towers, the vast Nový Smíchov shopping centre, the Staropramen brewery, and some of the city's hottest boutique hotels – but just down the road, near Smíchovské Nádraží train station, the poverty and neglect set in again.

---

popular neighbourhood cafe has friendly service and a quiet back room that's perfect for writing postcards home or having a friendly chat over coffee and a piece of cake. In summer it serves delicious homemade iced teas and ice-cream shakes.

LOKAL BLOK   PUB
Map p342 (📞251 511 490; http://lokalblok.cz; náměstí 14, října 10; ⊙noon-1am Mon-Fri, 4pm-1am Sat & Sun; 🛜; Ⓜ Anděl) The perfect Prague combination: a raucous pub and a state-of-the-art climbing wall (though presumably you're supposed to climb before you drink and not vice versa). Most nights there's a lively crowd, fuelled by Pilsner Urquell on tap and some good Mexican eats, such as nachos and quesadillas. Highly recommended.

HLUBINA   PUB
Map p342 (📞257 328 184; www.restaurace-hlubina.cz; Lidická 37; ⊙11am-midnight Mon-Sat, to 11pm Sun; Ⓜ Andel) This traditional neighbourhood pub serves unfiltered Pilsner Urquell from large tanks (tankové pivo) to ensure freshness. The pub is bigger than it looks and there's space for drinking (and eating) on several levels. Most come for the beer, but the cheap, classic pub food is not bad at all.

PHENOMEN   CLUB
Map p342 (📞774 366 636; www.phenomen.cz; Nádražní 84, Smíchov; ⊙7pm-3am Tue-Thu, to 4am Fri & Sat; 🛜; 🚃7, 12, 14, 20 to Na Knížecí, Ⓜ Anděl) This upscale dance club draws a well-heeled crowd in their 20s and 30s who come for the cocktails, champagne, DJ theme nights and occasional live music. They also serve pretty decent bar food such as burgers, wings and salads (kitchen closes at 2am). The Thursday night 'singles party' is particularly popular.

BACK DOORS   BAR
Map p342 (📞257 315 824; www.backdoors.cz; Na Bělidle 30; ⊙11am-3pm, 5pm-1am Mon-Fri; 5pm-2am Sat; 🚃4, 6, 7, 9, 10, 14, 20, Ⓜ Anděl) This upmarket cellar/bar/restaurant/club is inspired by similar spaces in New York and Amsterdam (though the subterranean Gothic-cellar look could only be Prague). It offers decent Czech DJs and a relaxed vibe most nights, though it can get stuffy on a crowded weekend night. If you're hungry, there's a full menu of well-done international dishes.

DOG'S BOLLOCKS
BAR

Map p342 (☑775 736 030; www.dogsbollocks.cz; Nádražní 82; ⏱5pm-3am Tue-Thu, to 5am Fri & Sat; MAnděl) This classy bar, restaurant and nightspot is not far from the Staropramen Brewery and is a great choice if you're staying in the area and don't want to go far for your fun. In spite of the English-friendly name, it draws mostly Czech students and young professionals letting loose.

HELLS BELLS
BAR

Map p342 (☑722 302 559; www.hellsbells.cz; Na Bělidle 27; ⏱3pm-3am Mon-Fri, 5pm-3am Sat, 5pm-midnight Sun; MAnděl) In spite of the glitzy office towers, Smíchov is still a down-and-dirty kind of place, and this Goth-friendly, heavy-metal bar is where the locals let it all hang out. Loud, crowded and fun – the late closing time makes it a perfect ticket for that last drink of the night.

🍷 Vyšehrad

V CAFE
CAFE

Map p341 (☑725 740 717; www.vcafe.cz; K Rotundě 3; ⏱11am-9.30pm; ☎; MVyšehrad) This pretty summer terrace may be the nicest place within the Vyšehrad citadel area to relax over a coffee, beer or a light meal of grilled sausages.

CAFE CITADELA
CAFE

Map p341 (Vyšehrad Citadel; ⏱9.30am-6pm; MVyšehrad) This relaxed beer garden and cafe is the perfect place to cool off under the trees. You'll find it just on the edge of the sculpture garden, south of the cathedral. Most come for coffee or beer, but there's also a small menu of salads, omelettes and sweets.

☆ ENTERTAINMENT

JAZZ DOCK
JAZZ

Map p342 (☑774 058 838; www.jazzdock.cz; Janáčkovo nábřeží 2, Smíchov; cover 150Kč; ⏱4pm-3am; ☐7, 9, 12, 14, MAnděl) Most of Prague's jazz clubs are smoky cellar affairs – this riverside club is a definite step up, with modern decor and a romantic view out over the Vltava. It draws some of the best local talent and occasional international acts. Go early or book to get a good table. Shows normally begin at 7pm and 10pm.

ŠVANDOVO DIVADLO NA SMÍCHOVĚ
THEATRE

Map p342 (Švandovo Theatre in Smíchov; ☑box office 257 318 666; www.svandovodivadlo.cz; Štefánikova 57, Smíchov; tickets 150-300Kč; ⏱box office 2-8pm Mon-Fri, 2hr before performances Sat & Sun; ☐6, 9, 12, 20) This experimental theatre space, performing Czech and international dramatic works, is admired for its commitment to staging 'English-friendly' performances. It also hosts occasional live music and dance, as well as regular 'Stage Talks', unscripted discussions with noted personalities.

🛍 SHOPPING

★ WINE FOOD MARKET
FOOD

Map p342 (☑733 338 650; www.winemarket.cz; Strakonická 1, Smíchov; ⏱9am-9pm; ☎; MSmíchovské Nádraží) This rather unpromising, industrial corner in a forgotten Smíchov neighbourhood holds arguably the city's best Italian market, with all manner of breads, cheeses, meats, and Italian goodies such as marinated mushrooms and peppers. It's the perfect spot to assemble a picnic lunch. There's a dining room in the back where you can treat yourself to the spoils. A real treasure.

NOVÝ SMÍCHOV
SHOPPING CENTRE

Map p342 (☑251 511 151; www.novysmichov.eu; Plzeňská 8, Smíchov; ⏱9am-9pm; ☎; MAnděl) Nový Smíchov is a vast shopping centre that occupies an area the size of several city blocks. It's an airy, well-designed space with plenty of fashion boutiques and niche-market stores. Besides all the big brand names, there's a large computer store, a food court, a virtual-games hall, a 12-screen multiplex cinema and a well-stocked Tesco hypermarket.

TRIBO
HANDICRAFTS

Map p342 (☑736 689 472; www.tattooshop.cz; Lidická 8, Smíchov; ⏱9am-5pm Mon-Fri; ☐4, 7, 10, 14, MAnděl) Though Tribo advertises itself as a tattoo shop, it feels more like an artists' collective, selling an eclectic range of handmade goods, ranging from urban streetwear to funky diaries and journals, composed of artisanal paper and found objects such as old postcards and tram tickets. It also does tattoos and piercings.

SMÍCHOV & VYŠEHRAD ENTERTAINMENT

Day Trips from Prague

Karlštejn Castle p181

Visiting the Czech Republic's most famous castle, perched on a hilltop like a fairy-tale fortress, is the most popular day trip from Prague.

Konopiště Chateau p183

The former country retreat of Archduke Franz Ferdinand (whose assassination sparked WWI) offers a fascinating insight into its aristocratic owner.

Kutná Hora p184

Built on the riches generated by silver mining, Kutná Hora once rivalled Prague in importance, and still boasts a treasure house of historical monuments.

Mělník p186

The Lobkowicz family chateau and its tiny, but historic, vineyard are the focus of Bohemia's modest winegrowing region.

Terezín p188

This grim 18th-century fortress served as a concentration camp during WWII, and is today a moving museum to the horrors of the Holocaust.

RICARDO LIBERATO / GETTY IMAGES ©

TOP SIGHT
KARLŠTEJN CASTLE

Rising above the village of Karlštejn, 30km southwest of Prague, Karlštejn Castle is rightly one of the top attractions in the Czech Republic. This fairy-tale medieval fortress is in such good shape that it wouldn't look out of place on Disney World's Main Street. Unfortunately, the crowds that throng its courtyards come in theme-park proportions too – in summer it's mobbed with visitors, ice-cream vendors and souvenir stalls.

Thankfully, the peaceful surrounding countryside offers views of Karlštejn's stunning exterior that rival anything you'll see on the inside. If at all possible, visit midweek or out of season, and avoid the queues at the castle ticket office by purchasing your tickets in advance via the link on the castle's website.

Karlštejn Information Centre (Informační centrum Karlštejn; ☑ 311 681 370; www.karlstejnsko.cz; Pension Vinice, Karlštejn 334; ☉ 8am-8pm) is across the road from the main car park.

History
Perched high on a crag overlooking the Berounka River, Karlštejn was born of a grand pedigree, starting life in 1348 as a hideaway for the crown jewels and treasury of the Holy Roman Emperor Charles IV. Run by an appointed burgrave, the castle was surrounded by a network of landowning knight-vassals, who came to the castle's aid whenever enemies moved against it.

Karlštejn again sheltered the Bohemian and the Holy Roman Empire crown jewels during the Hussite Wars of the early 15th century, but fell into disrepair as its defences became

DON'T MISS...

➡ Chapel of the Holy Cross
➡ Knight's Hall
➡ Charles IV's Bed-chamber
➡ Audience Hall
➡ Jewel House
➡ Views from the Great Tower

PRACTICALITIES

➡ Hrad Karlštejn
➡ ☑ 311 681 617
➡ www.hradkarlstejn.cz
➡ ☉ 9am-6.30pm Jul & Aug, 9.30am-5.30pm Tue-Sun May, Jun & Sep, to 5pm Apr, to 4.30pm Oct, to 4pm Mar, reduced hours Sat & Sun only Dec-Feb

EATING & DRINKING

Get away from the hordes milling up and down the main route to the castle at **Restaurace Pod Dračí Skálou** (☎311 681 177; www.pod-draciskalou.eu; Karlštejn 130; mains 100-240Kč; ☺11am-11pm Mon-Sat, 11am-8pm Sun; ☜), an appealing country inn with outdoor tables and a barbecue grill, where a half-litre of Pilsner Urquell is only 26Kč. The menu is rustic Czech, with lots of grilled or roast pork, beef and chicken. Take the first road on the left heading up to the castle, or walk down the footpath just outside the castle gate (red markers, signposted 'Beroun').

From the train station, you can travel to the castle in a horse-drawn cart (per person 150Kč).

A RIDE IN THE COUNTRY

Karlštejn is a straightforward 35km bike ride from Prague, mostly on dedicated cycle tracks, and with no hills. Biko (p301) offers a leisurely day trip by bike, stopping to swim in the river or pick cherries on the way, and returning to Prague by train.

outmoded. Considerable restoration work, not least by Josef Mocker – the king of Prague's neo-Gothic architecture – in the late 19th century has returned the castle to its former glory.

Guided Tours

Admission to the castle is by guided tour only; there are three tours available in English. Tour 1 (adult/child 270/180Kč, 50 minutes) passes through the **Knight's Hall**, still daubed with the coats-of-arms and names of the knight-vassals; **Charles IV's Bedchamber**; the **Audience Hall**; and the **Jewel House**; which includes treasures from the Chapel of the Holy Cross and a replica of the St Wenceslas Crown.

Tour 2 (adult/child 300/200Kč, 70 minutes, May to October only) must be booked in advance and takes in the **Marian Tower**, with the Church of the Virgin Mary and the Chapel of St Catherine, then moves on to the Great Tower for the castle's star attraction, the exquisite **Chapel of the Holy Cross**. Designed by Charles IV for the safekeeping of the crown jewels of the Holy Roman Empire, and of sacred relics of the Crucifixion, the chapel's walls and vaulted ceiling are adorned with thousands of polished semiprecious stones set in gilt stucco in the form of crosses, and with religious and heraldic paintings. For Tour 2, book as far in advance as possible.

Tour 3 (adult/child 150/100Kč, 40 minutes, daily June to August, weekends only May and October) visits the upper levels of the **Great Tower**, the highest point of the castle, which provides stunning views over the surrounding countryside.

Tours run to a complicated timetable; however, when you purchase your tickets online, you can select the time of your tour.

Getting There & Away

Trains from Prague's main train station to Beroun (via Praha-Smíchov) stop at Karlštejn (101Kč return, 45 minutes, every 30 minutes). Note that trains are shown as departing from platform 1J, which means the southern (*jih* in Czech) end of platform 1. From the train station or the main car park, it's a 20- or 30-minute uphill walk to the castle. If this doesn't appeal, you can take a shared taxi (per person 100Kč).

Drivers should leave Prague on the D5 motorway towards Plzeň and leave at exit 10 (Loděnice), then follow signs via Bubovice to Karlštejn.

TOP SIGHT
KONOPIŠTĚ CHATEAU

Konopiště Chateau is not only a monument to the obsessions of early 20th-century Habsburg aristocrats, but also an insight into one of the most famous names in European history – the Archduke Franz Ferdinand d'Este, heir to the Austro-Hungarian throne, whose assassination in 1914 sparked WWI.

You'll need a full day to make the most of a visit here: do one of the guided tours of the chateau (Tour 3 is the best), and leave time to explore the beautiful landscaped grounds that surround it.

The Chateau

Konopiště is a testament to the archduke's twin obsessions – hunting and St George. Having renovated the massive Gothic and Renaissance building in the 1890s and installed all the latest technology – including electricity, central heating, flush toilets, showers and a lift – Franz Ferdinand decorated his home with his hunting trophies.

His game books record that he shot about 300,000 creatures. About 100,000 animal trophies adorn the walls. The crowded **Trophy Corridor** (Tours 1 and 3), with a forest of mounted animal heads, and the antler-clad **Chamois Room** (Tour 3), with its 'chandelier' fashioned from a stuffed condor, are truly bizarre sights.

The archduke's collection of art and artefacts relating to St George amounts to 3750 items, many of which are in the **St George Museum** (muzeum sv Jiří; adult/child 30/15Kč; ⊗10am-1pm & 1.30-5pm Sat & Sun Jun-Aug, to 4pm Sep, closed Oct-May).

Guided Tours

There are three guided tours in English. Tour 3 (adult/child 320/220Kč) is the most interesting, visiting the **private apartments** used by the archduke and his family, which have remained unchanged since the state took possession of the chateau in 1921. Tour 2 (adult/child 220/140Kč) takes in the **Great Armoury**, one of the most impressive collections of weapons in Europe, while Tour 1 (adult/child 220/140Kč) visits the grand apartments of the south wing. Tours depart hourly, on the hour.

Getting There & Away

There are buses from Prague's Roztyly metro station to Benešov (112Kč return, 40 minutes, twice hourly); their final destination is usually Pelhřimov or Jihlava. There are also buses from Prague's Florenc bus station (114Kč return, 40 minutes, eight daily).

Trains run from Praha hlavní nádraží (Prague main train station) to Benešov u Prahy (141Kč return, 1¼ hours, hourly). Konopiště is 2km west of Benešov. Local bus 2 (12Kč, six minutes, hourly) runs from a stop on Dukelská, 400m north of the train station (turn left out of the station, take first right on Tyršova and then first left) to the castle car park. If you'd rather walk, turn left out of the train station, go left across the bridge over the railway, and follow the yellow markers west along Konopištská street.

Drivers should take the D1 from Prague towards Brno, exiting at Mirošovice, then follow the signs to Benešov; there's parking near the castle.

DON'T MISS...

➡ Chamois Room
➡ Trophy Corridor
➡ St George Museum

PRACTICALITIES

➡ Zámek Konopiště
➡ ☑317 721 366
➡ www.zamek-konopiste.cz
➡ ⊗10am-noon & 1-5pm Tue-Sun Jun-Aug, to 4pm Apr, May & Sep, 10am-noon & 1-3pm Sat & Sun Oct & Nov, closed Dec-Mar

EATING

After visiting the chateau, head down the hill to **Stará Myslivna** (☑317 700 280; www.staramyslivna.com; Konopiště 2; mains 150-360Kč), a Czech restaurant set in a 19th-century gamekeeper's lodge.

Kutná Hora

Explore

Enriched by the silver ore that veined the surrounding hills, the medieval city of Kutná Hora became the seat of Wenceslas II's royal mint in 1308, producing silver groschen that were then the hard currency of Central Europe. Boom-time Kutná Hora rivalled Prague in importance, but by the 16th century the mines began to run dry, and its demise was hastened by the Thirty Years' War (1618–48) and a devastating fire in 1770. The town became a Unesco World Heritage Site in 1996, luring visitors with a smorgasbord of historic sights. It looks its flower-bedecked best in May and June but is worth a full day's visit at any time of year.

The Best...

➡ **Sight** Sedlec Ossuary
➡ **Place to Eat** Pivnice Dačický
➡ **Place to Drink** Kavárna Mokate

Top Tip

Buy a return train ticket to Kutná Hora Město station, near the centre of the Old Town, so that you don't have to walk or take a bus between the town centre and main train station.

Getting There & Away

➡ **Bus** There are hourly buses on weekdays (three or four on Saturdays) from Háje bus station on the southern edge of Prague to Kutná Hora (136Kc return, 1¾ hours); the train is a better bet.

➡ **Car** Head east from Prague on the D11 towards Hradec Kralové and, at Poděbrady, take exit 39 south on Rte 38 towards Kolín and Kutná Hora.

➡ **Train** There are direct trains from Prague's main train station to Kutná Hora hlavní nádraží every two hours (201Kč return, 55 minutes). It's a 10-minute walk from here to Sedlec Ossuary, and a further 2.5km to the Old Town. However, five minutes after the arrival of the Prague train (and before the departure of return trains) a little railcar shuttles from platform 1 to Kutná Hora Město station (six minutes).

Need to Know

➡ **Location** 65km (1½ hours) east of Prague.

➡ **Kutná Hora Tourist Office** (Informační centrum; ☑327 512 378; www.guide.kh.cz; Palackého náměstí 377; ☺9am-6pm Apr-Sep, 9am-5pm Mon-Fri, 10am-4pm Sat & Sun Oct-Mar) Books accommodation, rents bicycles (per day 220Kč) and offers internet access (per minute 1Kč, minimum 15Kč).

➡ **Sedlec Tourist Office** (Informační centrum Sedlec; ☑326 551 049; www.ossuary. eu; Zámecká 279; ☺9am-5pm Mar-Oct, to 4pm Nov-Mar)

◉ SIGHTS

SEDLEC OSSUARY CHURCH

(Kostnice; ☑327 561 143; www.ossuary.eu; Zámecká 127; adult/concession 90/60Kč; ☺8am-6pm Mon-Sat, 9am-6pm Sun Apr-Sep, 9am-5pm Mar & Oct, 9am-4pm Nov-Feb) When the Schwarzenbergs purchased Sedlec monastery in 1870 they allowed a local woodcarver to get creative with the bones piled in the crypt (the remains of around 40,000 people), resulting in the remarkable 'bone church' of Sedlec Ossuary. Garlands of skulls hang from the vaulted ceiling, around a chandelier containing at least one of each bone in the human body.

Four pyramids of stacked bones squat in each of the corner chapels, and crosses, chalices and monstrances of bone adorn the altar. From April to October a minibus runs on demand (per person 35Kč, minimum three people) between Sedlec, Kutná Hora town centre and the Cathedral of St Barbara.

CZECH SILVER MUSEUM MUSEUM

(České muzeum stříbra; ☑327 512 159; www. cms-kh.cz; Barborská 28; Tour 1 adult/concession 70/40Kč, Tour 2 120/80Kč, combined 140/90Kč; ☺10am-6pm Jul & Aug, 9am-6pm May, Jun & Sep, 9am-5pm Apr & Oct, 10am-4pm Nov, closed Mon year-round) Originally part of the town's fortifications, the **Hrádek** (Little Castle) was rebuilt in the 15th century as the residence of Jan Smíšek, administrator of the royal mines, who grew rich from silver mined illegally right under the building. It now houses the Czech Silver Museum. Visiting is by guided tour, which includes the chance to visit an ancient silver mine.

Kutná Hora

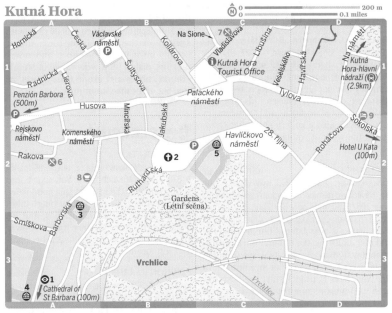

Tour 1 (one hour) leads through the main part of the museum where the exhibits celebrate the mines that made Kutná Hora wealthy, including a huge wooden device once used to lift loads weighing as much as 1000kg from the 200m-deep shafts. **Tour 2** (90 minutes) allows you to don a miner's helmet and explore 500m of medieval mine shafts beneath the town. Kids need to be aged at least seven for this tour.

CATHEDRAL OF ST BARBARA   CHURCH
(Chrám sv Barbora; ☑775 363 938; www.khfarnost.cz; Barborská; adult/concession 60/40Kč; ☺9am-6pm Apr-Oct, 10am-5pm Mon-Fri, 10am-6pm Sat & Sun Nov-Dec, 10am-4pm Jan-Mar) Kutná Hora's greatest monument is the Gothic Cathedral of St Barbara. Rivalling Prague's St Vitus in size and magnificence, its soaring nave culminates in elegant, six-petalled ribbed vaulting, and the ambulatory chapels preserve original 15th-century frescos, some of them showing miners at work. Take a walk around the outside of the church, too; the terrace at the east end enjoys the finest view in town.

Construction was begun in 1380, interrupted during the Hussite Wars and abandoned in 1558 when the silver began to run out. The cathedral was finally completed

Kutná Hora

in neo-Gothic style at the end of the 19th century.

BARBORSKÁ   STREET
Barborská street runs along the front of the 17th-century former Jesuit College, and is decorated with a row of 13 baroque **statues** of saints, an arrangement inspired by the statues on Prague's Charles Bridge. All are related to the Jesuits and/or the town; the second statue – the woman holding a chalice, with a stone tower at her side – is

St Barbara, the patron saint of miners and therefore of Kutná Hora.

GALLERY OF CENTRAL BOHEMIA   GALLERY
(Galerie Středočeského kraje; ☑327 311 135; www.gask.cz; Barborská 53; adult/concession 220/110Kč; ☺noon-5pm) The town's 17th-century former Jesuit College has been restored and now houses this regional gallery devoted to 20th- and 21st-century art. There's also a gallery shop that showcases the work of young Czech artists and designers.

ITALIAN COURT   HISTORIC BUILDING
(Vlašský dvůr; ☑327 512 873; www.vlassky-dvur. cz; Havlíčkovo náměstí 552; adult/concession full tour 105/65Kč, mint only 65/54Kč; ☺9am-6pm Apr-Sep, 10am-5pm Mar & Oct, 10am-4pm Nov-Feb) Just east of St James Church (Kostel sv Jakuba; 1330) lies the Italian Court, the former Royal Mint – it gets its name from the master craftsmen from Florence brought in by Wenceslas II to kick-start the business, and who began stamping silver coins here in 1300. The original treasury rooms hold an exhibit on coins and minting.

The full **guided tour** (in English) visits all the historical rooms open to the public, notably the **Royal Mint** itself, the **Royal Chapel**, and 15th-century **Audience Hall**, with two impressive 19th-century murals depicting the 1471 election of Vladislav Jagiello as king of Bohemia, and the Decree of Kutná Hora being proclaimed by Wenceslas IV and Jan Hus in 1409.

🍴 EATING & DRINKING

PIVNICE DAČICKÝ   BEER HALL €
(☑327 512 248; www.dacicky.com; Rakova 8; mains 140-360Kč; ☺11am-11pm; 🛜🚸) Get some froth on your moustache at this old-fashioned, wood-panelled Bohemian beer hall, where you can dine on dumplings and choose from five draught beers including Pilsner Urquell, Primátor yeast beer and local Kutná Hora lager.

U SŇEKA POHODÁŘE   ITALIAN €
(☑327 515 987; www.usneka.cz; Vladislavova 11; mains 70-250Kč; ☺11am-10pm Mon-Thu, to 11pm Fri & Sat; 🍽🛜) Kutná Hora's best Italian flavours are found at this cosy local favourite that's very popular for takeaway or dine-in pizza and pasta. And no, we don't know why it's called 'The Contented Snail'.

KAVÁRNA MOKATE   CAFE
(Barborská 37; ☺8am-10pm Mon-Fri, 10am-10pm Sat, 10am-8pm Sun) This cosy little cafe, with ancient earthenware floor tiles, timber beams, mismatched furniture and oriental rugs, dishes up a wide range of freshly ground coffees and exotic teas, as well as iced tea and coffee in summer.

🛏 SLEEPING

HOTEL U KATA   HOTEL €
(☑327 515 096; www.ukata.cz; Uhelná 596; s/d/tr 870/1160/1740Kč; 🅿@🛜) You won't lose your head over the rates at this good-value family hotel called the 'Executioner'. Bikes can be rented for 220Kč per day, and it's a short stroll from the bus station. Downstairs there's a welcoming Czech beer hall and restaurant.

PENZIÓN BARBORA   PENSION €
(☑327 316 327; www.penzionbarbora.cz; Kremnická 909; s/d/tr 1400/1800/2500Kč; 🅿😋🛜) A friendly family pension and restaurant, with a lovely (and quiet) location overlooking St Barbara's Cathedral, and secure parking.

HOTEL ZLATÁ STOUPA   HOTEL €€
(☑327 511 540; www.zlatastoupa.cz; Tylova 426; s/d from 1350/2150Kč; 🅿🛜) If you feel like spoiling yourself, the most luxurious place in town is the elegantly furnished 'Golden Mount'. Friendly staff, secure parking, and a location halfway between the town centre and KH Město train station.

Mělník

Explore
Mělník sprawls over a rocky promontory surrounded by the flat Central Bohemian plains. The bus station is 800m east of the town centre, so you begin with a gentle uphill walk along Kapitan Jaroše street. Pass below the prominent clock tower to the main square, then bear left for the chateau.

Plan on taking a chateau tour in the morning, followed by lunch, then a stroll around the other sites – they're all close together. Don't miss the terrace on the far side of the chateau, with superb views across the river to the Central Bohemian plains. The vines below the terrace are supposedly descendants of the first vines introduced to Bohemia, by Charles IV in the 14th century. They're now used to make the chateau's own wines.

The Best...

→ **Sight** Ossuary
→ **Place to Eat** U Císaře
→ **Place to Drink** Galerie/Café Ve Věží

Top Tip

Bring along a packed lunch, grab a bench on the terrace on the far side of the chateau, and enjoy a picnic with a view.

Getting There & Away

→ **Bus** Buses run to Mělník (48Kč, 45 minutes, every 30 minutes weekdays, hourly weekends) from stop 10 in the bus station outside Prague's Praha-Holešovice train station; buy your ticket from the driver (one way only, no return tickets).

→ **Car** From Prague, take D8 north to Nová Ves, then follow Rte 16 east to Mělník.

Need to Know

→ **Location** 30km (one hour) north of Prague.
→ **Mělník Tourist Office** (☑315 627 503; www.melnik.cz; Legionářů 51; ⊙9am-5pm) Sells maps and historical guides and can help with accommodation.

SIGHTS

MĚLNÍK CHATEAU   PALACE
(Zámek Mělník; ☑315 622 121; www.lobkowicz-melnik.cz; Svatováclavská 19; adult/concession 100/80Kč; ⊙10am-6pm May-Sep) This Renaissance chateau was acquired by the Lobkowicz family in 1739; the family opened it to the public in 1990. You can wander through the former living quarters, which are crowded with a rich collection of baroque furniture and 17th- and 18th-century paintings, on a **self-guided tour** with English text.

Additional rooms have changing exhibits of modern works and a fabulous collection of 17th-century maps and engravings detailing Europe's great cities. A separate

tour descends to the 14th-century wine cellars, where you can taste the chateau's wines; a shop in the courtyard sells the chateau's own label. Wine-tasting sessions held in the shop cost from 100Kč to 250Kč.

CHURCH OF STS PETER & PAUL   CHURCH
(Kostel sv Petra a Pavla; ☑315 622 337; Na Vyhlídce; tower adult/child 40/20Kč; ⊙tower 10am-6pm Tue-Sat, 11am-6pm Sun Apr-Oct, 1am-5pm Sat, 11am-5pm Sun Nov-Mar, closed 12.30-1.30pm) Next to the chateau is this 15th-century Gothic church, with baroque furnishings and remnants of its Romanesque predecessor incorporated into the rear of the building. Climb to the top of the **church tower** (Vyhlídková věž) for superlative views.

The church crypt is now an **ossuary** (Kostnice; adult/child 30/20Kč; ⊙9.30am-4pm Tue-Fri, 10am-4pm Sat & Sun, closed 12.30-1.15pm), packed with the bones of around 10,000 people, dug up to make room for 16th-century plague victims. The bones are arranged in the shapes of anchors, hearts and crosses (symbols of faith, love and hope). This crypt is much more visceral and claustrophobic than the Sedlec Ossuary; the floor is of beaten earth, and you literally rub shoulders with the bones.

 EATING & DRINKING

U CÍSAŘE   AMERICAN, CZECH €
(☑608 600 005; www.ucisare.cz; Palackého 135; mains 100-260Kč; ⊙11am-10pm; ☎) Just 150m southeast of the main square, this American-inspired restaurant has a laid-back atmosphere, a summer garden out the back, and a menu that includes steaks, burgers, BBQ pork ribs and finger-lickingly authentic buffalo wings. There's a choice of Pilsner Urquell and Krušovice beers.

GALERIE/CAFÉ VE VĚŽÍ   CAFE
(☑315 621 954; www.mekuc.cz; ulice 5 května; ⊙2-11pm Tue-Sun) Inside the medieval Prague Gate tower, this atmospheric cafe and art gallery spreads across three floors and is served by an ingenious dumbwaiter: write your order on the note pad, ding the bell, and the tray goes down, returning moments later with your order. Choose from a range of freshly ground coffees, exotic teas, local wines, beer and *medovina* (mead).

Terezín

Explore

The former concentration camp of Terezín provides a sobering reminder of the horrors inflicted on Czech Jews during WWII.

It's possible to visit Terezín on a guided day trip from Prague, but in our experience these tours tend to be a bit rushed. Our advice is to allow a full day, bring a picnic lunch, and begin by visiting the Ghetto Museum (where you can pick up information leaflets and maps) and Magdeburg Barracks. It's worth walking past the old railway siding to see the crematorium before crossing the river to take a self-guided tour of the Lesser Fortress.

Top Tip

Rather than eat at one of Terezín's crowded tourist restaurants, take a bus or taxi to attractive Litoměřice, 3km to the north. The town square has several good eateries.

Getting There & Away

➥**Bus** Direct buses from Prague to Litoměřice (166Kč return, one hour, hourly) stop at Terezín. They depart from the bus station outside Praha-Holešovice train station. There are buses between Litoměřice bus station and Terezín (11Kč, eight minutes, at least hourly).

➥**Car** Head north from Prague on the D8 and leave at junction 45 at Lovosice. Go north on Rte 247, then east on 15 to reach Terezín.

Need to Know

➥**Location** 60km (one hour) north of Prague.

➥**Terezín Information Centre** (Městské infocentrum; ☑416 782 616; www.terezin.cz; náměstí Československé armády 179; ☺8am-5pm Mon-Thu, 8am-1.30pm Fri, 9am-3pm Sun, closed Sat)

 SIGHTS

MAIN FORTRESS   HISTORIC SITE

(Hlavní pevnost) The sheer scale of the walls and moats surrounding the Main Fortress is impossible to fathom – mainly because the town is inside the fortifications. Initially, you may think the central square looks no different from other Czech old town centres. Wander past the walls en route to the Lesser Fortress, however, and a different picture emerges.

At the heart of the Main Fortress is the neat grid of streets that makes up the town of Terezín. There's little to see except the 19th-century Church of the Resurrection, the former Commandant's office, the neoclassical administrative buildings and the surrounding grid of houses with their awful secrets. South of the square are the remains of a railway siding, built by prisoners, on which carriageloads of further prisoners arrived – and departed.

GHETTO MUSEUM   MUSEUM

(Muzeum Ghetta; ☑416 782 225; www.pamatnik-terezin.cz; Komenského 151; adult/child 170/140Kč, combined with Lesser Fortress 210/160Kč; ☺9am-6pm Apr-Oct, to 5.30pm Nov-Mar) The Ghetto Museum explores the rise of Nazism and life in the Terezín ghetto. The building once accommodated the camp's 10- to 15-year-old boys; haunting images painted by them still decorate the walls.

The former **Magdeburg Barracks** (Magdeburská kasárna), which served as the seat of the Jewish 'town council', houses an annex to the main museum. Here you can visit a reconstructed dormitory and see exhibits on the rich cultural life that somehow flourished against this backdrop of fear.

There is also a small exhibit in the grim **Crematorium** (Krematorium; ☺10am-6pm Sun-Fri Apr-Oct, to 4pm Sun-Fri Nov-Mar) in the **Jewish Cemetery** just off Bohušovická brána, about 750m south of the main square.

The Ghetto Museum has multilingual pamphlets and tour guides (some of them ghetto survivors) to offer assistance.

LESSER FORTRESS   HISTORIC SITE

(Malá Pevnost; ☑416 782 576; www.pamatnik-terezin.cz; Pražská; adult/child 170/140Kč, combined with Ghetto Museum 210/160Kč; ☺8am-6pm Apr-Oct, to 4.30pm Nov-Mar) The best way to see Terezín's Lesser Fortress is to take a **self-guided tour** through the prison barracks, isolation cells, workshops and morgues, past execution grounds and former mass graves. The Nazis' mocking concentration camp slogan, *Arbeit Macht Frei* (Work Makes You Free), hangs above

TEREZÍN'S HISTORY

A massive bulwark of stone and earth, the fortress of Terezín (Theresienstadt in German) was built in 1780 by Emperor Joseph II with a single purpose: to keep the enemy out. Ironically, it is more notorious for keeping people in – it served as a political prison in the later days of the Habsburg empire. **Gavrilo Princip**, the assassin who killed Archduke Franz Ferdinand in 1914, was incarcerated here during WWI, and when the Germans took control during WWII, the fortress became a grim holding pen for Jews bound for extermination camps. In contrast to the colourful, baroque face of many Czech towns, Terezín is a stark but profoundly evocative monument to a darker aspect of Europe's past.

The bleakest phase of Terezín's history began in 1940 when the Gestapo established a prison in the Lesser Fortress. Evicting the inhabitants from the Main Fortress the following year, the Nazis transformed the town into a transit camp through which some 150,000 people eventually passed en route to the death camps. For most, conditions were appalling. Between April and September 1942 the ghetto's population increased from 12,968 to 58,491, leaving each prisoner with only 1.65 sq metres of space and causing disease and starvation on a terrifying scale. In the same period, there was a 15-fold increase in the number of deaths within the prison walls.

Terezín later became the centrepiece of one of the Nazis' more extraordinary public relations coups. Official visitors to the fortress, including representatives of the Red Cross, saw a town that was billed as a kind of Jewish 'refuge', with a Jewish administration, banks, shops, cafes, schools and a thriving cultural life – it even had a jazz band – in a charade that twice completely fooled international observers. In reality Terezín was home to a relentlessly increasing population of prisoners, regular trains departing for the gas chambers of Auschwitz, and the death by starvation, disease or suicide of some 35,000 people.

the gate to the inner yard. It would be hard to invent a more menacing location, and it is only while wandering through the seemingly endless tunnels beneath the walls that you begin to fully appreciate the vast dimensions of the fortress.

In front of the fortress is a **National Cemetery**, established in 1945 for the victims exhumed from the Nazis' mass graves.

 EATING

MEMORIAL CAFÉ CZECH €
(☎416 783 082; náměstí Československé armády; meals 130-270Kč) There aren't any restaurants in Terezín that are genuinely recommendable. This place in the Hotel Memorial, serving hearty Czech meals and kosher wines on a sunny terrace, is the best of a mediocre bunch.

Sleeping

Prague offers a wide range of accommodation options, from cosy, romantic hotels set in historic town houses to luxurious international chain hotels, and from budget hostels and pensions to sharply styled boutique hotels. Meanwhile, more and more travellers are discovering the pleasures of renting an apartment in Prague.

Room Rates & Seasons

A double room in a midrange hotel in central Prague costs around 4000Kč (€160) in high season; outside the centre, this might fall to about 3000Kč. Top-range hotels cost from 4000Kč up, with the best luxury hotels charging 6000Kč and more. Budget options charge less than 2000Kč for a double room.

Note that some midrange and top-end hotels quote rates in euros. At these hotels you can pay cash in Czech crowns if you like, but the price will depend on the exchange rate on the day you settle the bill.

We provide high-season rates, which generally cover April to June, September and October, and the Christmas/New Year holidays. July and August are midseason, and the rest of the year is low season, when rates can drop by 30% or 40%.

Even high-season rates can be inflated by up to 15% on certain dates, notably at New Year, Easter, during the Prague Spring festival, and at weekends (Thursday to Sunday) in May, June and September.

Apartments

The cost of a short-term stay in a self-catering apartment is comparable with a midrange hotel room, and can mean you have minimal transport costs, access to cheap local food, and the freedom to come and go as you like. Typical rates for a two-person apartment with a combined living room/bedroom, bathroom, TV and kitchenette range from around 2000Kč per night in the outer suburbs, to around 3500Kč or 4500Kč for an apartment near the Old Town Square.

Agencies & Websites

➡ **Alfa Tourist Service** (☑224 230 038; www. alfatourist.cz; Opletalova 38, Nové Město; ☉9am-5pm Mon-Fri; 🚊5, 9, 26) Accommodation in hostels, pensions, hotels and private rooms.

➡ **AVE Travel** (☑251 551 011; www. praguehotellocator.com) A 24-hour call centre and web-based agency with a huge range of hotels and apartments on offer.

➡ **Happy House Rentals** (☑224 946 890; www.happyhouserentals.com; Jungmannova 30, Nové Město; ☉9am-6pm Mon-Fri) Specialises in short- and long-term rental apartments.

➡ **Hostel.cz** (☑415 658 580; www.hostel.cz) Website database of hostels and budget hotels, with a secure online booking system.

➡ **Lonely Planet** (www.lonelyplanet.com/hotels) For more accommodation reviews and recommendations by Lonely Planet authors; you can also book online here.

➡ **Mary's Travel & Tourist Service** (Map p344; ☑222 254 007; www.marys.cz; Italská 31, Vinohrady; ☉9am-6pm Mon-Fri, 10am-1pm Sat & Sun; 🚊11) Friendly, efficient agency offering private rooms, hostels, pensions, apartments and hotels in Prague and surrounding areas.

➡ **Prague Apartments** (☑604 168 756; www. prague-apartment.com) Web-based service with comfortable, IKEA-furnished flats. Availability of apartments shown online.

➡ **Stop City** (☑222 521 233; www.stopcity.com; Belgická 36, Vinohrady; ☉10am-8pm; Ⓜ Náměstí Míru) Specialises in apartments, private rooms and pensions in the city centre, Vinohrady and Žižkov areas.

Lonely Planet's Top Choices

Fusion Hotel (p195) It's a hostel, it's a hotel, it's designer heaven...

Golden Well Hotel (p194) Historic, luxury hotel in the ultimate location – right beneath the castle walls.

Icon Hotel (p196) This cutting-edge designer hotel is a hangout for Prague's beautiful people.

Mosaic House (p196) A stylish blend of four-star hotel and boutique hostel.

Absolutum Hotel (p199) Boutique gorgeousness at reasonable prices; it's out of the centre but right on the main tram route.

Czech Inn (p197) Great value and atmosphere in an up-and-coming neighbourhood.

Best by Budget

€

Fusion Hotel (p195) An 'affordable design hotel' with style in abundance.

ArtHarmony (p196) Quirkily decorated with an easygoing, family-friendly atmosphere.

Holiday Home (p197) Popular family-owned pension in one of the city's best neighbourhoods.

Mosaic House (p196) Designer details with a mix of dorm and private rooms.

Czech Inn (p197) Industrial design with a range of accommodation options from dorm room to private apartment.

€€

Domus Henrici (p193) Peaceful seclusion in a historic building just a short stroll from the castle.

Lokál Inn (p193) Lovely baroque setting with excellent bar and restaurant close to Charles Bridge.

Hunger Wall Residence (p193) Spotlessly clean and modernised short-stay apartments.

Dům u velké boty (p193) Lovely old pension set on a quiet square halfway between Charles Bridge and the castle.

Absolutum Hotel (p199) Eye-catching boutique hotel across from Nádraží Holešovice metro station.

€€€

Golden Well Hotel (p194) Rooms have a superb outlook over the city or the Palace Gardens below.

Savic Hotel (p195) Housed in a former monastery, this hotel is bursting with character.

Icon Hotel (p196) Everything in this gorgeous boutique hotel has a designer stamp on it.

Hotel Aria (p194) Romantic hotel that offers five-star luxury with a musical theme.

Le Palais Hotel (p198) Luxury hotel housed in a gorgeous belle époque building.

NEED TO KNOW

SLEEPING

Price Guide

The following price ranges indicate the cost per night of a standard double room in high season.

€ less than 2000Kč (less than €70)

€€ 2000Kč to 4000Kč (€70 to €145)

€€€ more than 4000Kč (more than €145)

Reservations

Booking your accommodation in advance is strongly recommended (especially if you want to stay in or near the centre), and there are dozens of agencies that will help you find a place to stay. The more reliable agencies should be able to find you a bed even if you turn up in peak periods without a booking.

Smoking

The ban on smoking in public places that came into effect in the Czech Republic in 2010 does not apply to hotels – each establishment comes up with its own rules. In our listings we have used the no-smoking icon for places that are entirely nonsmoking (though they may have an outdoor 'designated smoking area').

Where to Stay

Neighbourhood	For	Against
Prague Castle & Hradčany	Very convenient for the castle, and generally a quiet and peaceful neighbourhood.	Limited choice of restaurants, few bars, and a long walk uphill from the Malá Strana nightlife.
Malá Strana	In the thick of things, close to Charles Bridge; accommodation is often in beautiful historic buildings.	Accommodation is quite expensive, but still gets booked out well in advance.
Staré Město	As central as it gets, in easy walking distance of most attractions; many hotels in historic properties.	Can be noisy and crowded in high season; a bit of a hike to the nearest tram stops.
Nové Město	Central, with good transport connections and a vast choice of eating places; handy for the main train station.	The prime area for visiting stag parties, so can be noisy at nights, and in parts slightly seedy.
Vinohrady & Vršovice	Classy neighbourhood with often spacious and elegant accommodation, excellent restaurants and sophisticated nightlife.	Few attractions in the immediate area, and a bit of a hike from the city centre.
Žižkov & Karlín	Competitively priced accommodation; though it feels out of the centre, it's only three or four tram stops from Wenceslas Square. Excellent local bars.	Some parts look a bit rough and rundown; can be noisy on main streets. Lots of steep hills and long staircases, many places without elevators.
Holešovice	Good-value accommodation away from the centre and decent transport connections (including the metro) into town and back.	Some parts of Holešovice (particularly the eastern half) can look pretty grim. Not many good restaurants in the neighbourhood.
Bubeneč & Dejvice	Good transport options to and from the airport, as well as some very pretty properties in one of the greenest parts of the city.	Not much nightlife to speak of; if you like to party, you'll find yourself on the tram heading in and out of the centre.
Smíchov & Vyšehrad	Lower prices. Both neighbourhoods have metro stations just two stops from the city centre.	Not easily walkable to main sights; some parts have a rough-around-the-edges atmosphere.

Hradčany

DOMUS HENRICI HOTEL €€

Map p330 (☎220 511 369; www.domus-henrici.cz; Loretánská 11; s/d/ste 3150/3600/4400Kč; @📶; 🚊22) This historic building in a quiet corner of Hradčany is intentionally nondescript out front, hinting that peace and privacy are top priorities here. There are eight spacious and stylish rooms, half with private fax, scanner/copier and internet access (via an ethernet port), and all with polished wood floors, large bathrooms, comfy beds and fluffy bathrobes. Wi-fi in lobby only.

ROMANTIK HOTEL U RAKA HOTEL €€

Map p330 (☎220 511 100; www.romantikhotel-uraka.cz; Černínská 10; s/d from 2500/3700Kč; 🚭❄📶; 🚊22) Concealed in a manicured rock garden in a quiet corner of Hradčany, this historic hotel is an atmospheric, late-18th-century timber cottage with just six elegant, low-ceilinged doubles, complete with timber beams, wooden floors and red-brick fireplaces. With its cosy bedrooms, attentive staff, artistic decor and farmhouse-kitchen-style breakfast room, it's ideal for a romantic getaway. Book at least a few months ahead.

HOTEL MONASTERY HOTEL €€

Map p330 (☎233 090 200; www.hotelmonastery.cz; Strahovské nádvoří 13; d/tr from 2900/4000Kč; P🚭@📶; 🚊22) Ancient meets modern at this small hotel, where the only noise that's likely to disturb you is the occasional tolling of a church bell. The 12 quirkily shaped rooms in this 17th-century building have been given a bright, modern makeover and feature polished wood floors, plain white walls hung with photos of Prague, and a splash of colour from the bedspread and sofa.

Malá Strana

LITTLE QUARTER HOSTEL HOSTEL €

Map p328 (☎257 212 029; www.littlequarter.com; Nerudova 21; dm/tw from 400/1300Kč; @📶; 🚊12, 20, 22) This new place is not your average hostel – it's gleamingly clean, reception is staffed 24 hours, the five- or 10-bed dorms have single beds (no bunks!) with secure storage boxes underneath, and there's working wi-fi on every floor. Add in the fact that it's halfway between Charles Bridge and the castle, and you'll see the need to get your booking in early.

LITTLE TOWN BUDGET HOTEL HOSTEL/HOTEL €

Map p328 (☎242 406 965; www.littletownhotel.cz; Malostranské náměstí 11; dm/s/d/tr 550/1750/2000/2400Kč; @📶; 🚊12, 20, 22) A brilliant location in Malá Strana reveals excellent-value rooms arrayed around a quiet, central courtyard. Rooms are simply furnished with whitewashed walls and have a relaxed ambience verging on monastic. The more expensive three- and four-person self-contained rooms/apartments with kitchen and bathroom are excellent value for groups.

★**DŮM U VELKÉ BOTY** PENSION €€

Map p328 (☎257 532 088; www.dumuvelkeboty.cz; Vlašská 30; d/family ste 3150/4000Kč; 🚭📶👪; 🚊12, 20, 22) Location, location, location – those three little words that mean so much. The quaint little 'House at the Big Boot' is set on a quiet square, just five minutes' walk from the castle, and the same from Charles Bridge. The warren of ancient rooms is furnished in an understated and elegant way, with a period atmosphere (no TVs), and the owners are unfailingly helpful.

For families, there is a suite with two neighbouring doubles that share a bathroom.

LOKÁL INN INN €€

Map p328 (☎257 014 800; www.lokalinn.cz; Míšeňská 12; d/ste 3800/4900Kč; 🚭📶; 🚊12, 20, 22) Polished parquet floors and painted wooden ceilings abound in this 18th-century house designed by Prague's premier baroque architect, Kilian Dientzenhofer. The eight rooms and four suites are elegant and uncluttered, and the rustic, stone-vaulted cellars house a deservedly popular pub and restaurant run by the same folk as Lokál (p111), a popular Czech beer hall in Staré Město.

(Best ask for a quiet room if you plan to be in bed before the pub shuts.)

HUNGER WALL RESIDENCE APARTMENTS €€

Map p328 (☎257 404 040; www.hungerwall.eu; Plaská 8; 2-person apt from 3000Kč; 🚭📶; 🚊6, 9, 12, 20) The Hunger Wall offers bright, stylish, modernised apartments at reasonable short-stay rates. From the smiling welcome at reception to the spotlessly clean rooms, the atmosphere here is resolutely 'new Prague', with facilities that include an excellent cafe (p91), conference room and a tiny gym. Located in the quieter southern part of Malá Strana, only two tram stops from Malostranské náměstí.

DESIGN HOTEL SAX
HOTEL €€

Map p328 (📞257 531 268; www.hotelsax.cz; Jánský vršek 3; s/d 2700/3500Kč; 🌐❄️@🛜; 🚊12, 20, 22) Set in a quiet corner of Malá Strana, amid embassies and monastery gardens, the Sax is refreshingly different. The building is 18th century on the outside, but the interior has been remodelled with classic furniture and design from the 1950s, '60s and '70s. There's a dramatic glass-roofed atrium where the courtyard used to be; bold and colourful retro decor; stylish, uncluttered bedrooms, and impeccable service.

★GOLDEN WELL HOTEL
HOTEL €€€

Map p328 (📞257 011 213; www.goldenwell.cz; U Zlaté Studně 4; d/ste from 6850/14,250Kč; 🅿️🌐❄️@🛜; 🚇Malostranská) The Golden Well is one of Malá Strana's hidden secrets, tucked away at the end of a cobbled cul-de-sac – a Renaissance house that once belonged to Emperor Rudolf II, perched on the southern slope of the castle hill. The rooms are quiet and spacious, with polished wood floors, reproduction period furniture, and luxurious bathrooms with underfloor heating and whirlpool baths.

Many rooms have a superb outlook over the city or the Palace Gardens below, as does the hotel's excellent restaurant and terrace.

HOTEL ARIA
BOUTIQUE HOTEL €€€

Map p328 (📞225 334 111; www.ariahotel.net; Tržiště 9; d from 6850Kč; 🅿️❄️@🛜; 🚊12, 20, 22) The Aria offers five-star luxury with a musical theme – each of the four floors is dedicated to a musical genre (jazz, opera, classical and contemporary), and each room celebrates a particular artist or musician and contains a selection of their music that you can enjoy on the in-room hi-fi system.

Service is professional and efficient, and the rooms are furnished with crisp bedlinen, plump continental quilts, Molton Brown toiletries and complimentary chocolates.

🛏️ Staré Město

AHOY! HOSTEL
HOSTEL €

Map p332 (📞773 004 003; www.ahoyhostel.com; Na Perštýně 10; dm/tw 450/1200Kč; @🛜; 🚊6, 9, 18, 22) No big signs or branding here, just an inconspicuous card by the blue door at No 10. But inside is a very pleasant, welcoming and peaceful hostel (definitely not for the party crowd), with eager-to-please staff, some self-consciously 'arty' decoration, clean and comfortable six- or eight-bed dorms, and a couple of private twin rooms. Ideal location too.

OLD PRAGUE HOSTEL
HOSTEL €

Map p332 (📞224 829 058; www.oldprague-hostel.com; Benediktská 2; dm from 380Kč, s/d 1100/1300Kč; 🌐@🛜♿; 🚇Náměstí Republiky) Cheerful and welcoming, with colourful homemade murals brightening the walls, this is one of Prague's most sociable hostels, with a good mix of people from backpackers to families. Facilities are good, with lockers in the dorms, luggage storage and 24-hour reception, though the mattresses on the bunks are a bit on the thin side.

The staff are very helpful and the location could hardly be more central, just five minutes' walk east of the Old Town Square.

RESIDENCE KAROLINA
APARTMENTS €€

Map p332 (📞224 990 990; www.residence-karolina.com; Karoliny Světlé 4; 2-/4-person apt 3000/5200Kč; 🅿️🌐❄️@🛜; 🚊6, 9, 18, 22) We're going to have to invent a new category of accommodation – boutique apartments – to cover this array of 20 beautifully furnished flats. Offering one- or two-bedroom options, all apartments have spacious seating areas with comfy sofas and flat-screen TVs, sleek modern kitchens and dining areas.

The location is good too, set back on a quiet street but close to a major tram stop, and just two blocks from a Tesco supermarket for your self-catering supplies.

U ZELENÉHO VĚNCE
PENSION €€

Map p332 (📞222 220 178; www.uzv.cz; Řetězová 10; s/d/tr 2300/2900/3200Kč; @🛜; 🚊17, 18) Located on a quiet side street, the 'Green Garland' is a surprisingly rustic retreat right in the heart of the city. The bedrooms vary in size – some cramped and some spacious – but all are spotlessly clean, and simply but appealingly decorated, with exposed medieval roof beams in the attic rooms. The English-speaking owner is unfailingly polite and helpful.

Set in a restored 14th-century building, the pension takes its name from the house-sign above the door, and is only a few minutes' stroll from the Old Town Square.

HOTEL JOSEF   BOUTIQUE HOTEL €€

Map p332 (☏221 700 111; www.hoteljosef.com; Rybná 20; s/d from 3500/3800Kč; ✸ @ 🛜; MNáměstí Republiky) Designed by London-based Czech architect Eva Jiřičná, the Josef is one of Prague's most stylish contemporary hotels. The minimalist theme that is evident in the stark, white lobby (with its glass spiral staircase) is continued in the bedrooms, where things are kept clean and simple with plenty of subtle neutral tones. The glass-walled en suites are especially attractive, boasting extralarge rainfall shower heads and glass bowl basins.

PERLA HOTEL   BOUTIQUE HOTEL €€

Map p332 (☏221 667 707; www.perlahotel. cz; Perlová 1; s/d from 2450/3500Kč; ⊜✸🛜; MMůstek) The 'Pearl' is typical of the slinky, appealing designer hotels that have sprung up all over central Prague. Here the designer has picked a – surprise, surprise – pearl motif that extends from the giant pearls that form the reception desk to the silky, lustrous bedspreads and huge screen prints on the bedroom walls.

The rooms are on the small side, but the decor is sleek and modern with muted colours offset by bright-red lacquered chairs and glossy black-tiled bathrooms.

SAVIC HOTEL   HOTEL €€€

Map p332 (☏224 248 555; www.savic.eu; Jilská 7; r from 5200Kč; ✸ @ 🛜; MMůstek) From the complimentary glass of wine when you arrive to the comfy king-size beds, the Savic certainly knows how to make you feel pampered. Housed in the former monastery of St Giles, the hotel is bursting with character and full of delightful period details including old stone fireplaces, beautiful painted timber ceilings and fragments of frescos.

The huge bedrooms are furnished in antique style with parquet floors, dark wooden furniture, wingback armchairs and plush sofas, while the bathrooms are lined with polished marble.

DESIGN HOTEL JEWEL   BOUTIQUE HOTEL €€€

Map p332 (☏224 211 699; http://hoteljewel-prague.com; Rytířská 3; s/d 2500/4400Kč; ✸🛜; MMůstek) Housed in a medieval building that was once home to a royal jeweller (check out the early-20th-century painted ceiling in the cafe-bar, with gemstone motifs), this diamond of a hotel is themed around jewels. Comfort and service are as dazzling as the decor, with rooms named after precious stones, gold and silver detailing, glittering crystals and mirror mosaic tiles (although it doesn't have an elevator).

🛏 Nové Město

★FUSION HOTEL   HOSTEL, BOUTIQUE HOTEL €

Map p336 (☏226 222 800; www.fusionho-tels.com; Panská 9; dm from 400Kč, d/tr from 2100/2700Kč; @🛜; 🚊3, 9, 14, 24) Billing itself as an 'affordable design hotel', Fusion certainly has style in abundance. From the revolving bar and spaceshiplike UV corridor lighting, to the individually decorated bedrooms that resemble miniature modern-art galleries, the place exudes 'cool'. You can choose from the world's most stylish back-packer dorm, private doubles, triples and family rooms, and there's a Skype booth in the lobby.

Special bedrooms are decorated in vintage or romantic style, with works by young Czech artists, and kitted out with hi-tech extras such as Apple TV; one even has a communal bed for up to six people!

MISS SOPHIE'S   HOSTEL €

Map p338 (☏296 303 530; www.miss-sophies. com; Melounova 3; dm from 510Kč, d/apt from 2100/2600Kč; ⊜✸ @ 🛜; MIP Pavlova) This hostel makes a pleasant change from the usual characterless backpacker hive. There's a touch of contemporary style here, with oak-veneer floors and stark, minimalist decor – the main motif is 'distressed' concrete, along with neutral colours and black metal-framed beds – and the place is famous for its 'designer' showers, with autographed glass screens and huge rainfall shower heads.

There is a very cool lounge in the basement, with red-brick vaults and black leather sofas, and reception (open 24 hours) is staffed by a young, multilingual crew who are always eager to help.

ARTHARMONY
PENSION, HOSTEL €

Map p338 (☎222 542 931; www.artharmony.cz; Ječná 12; dm/d from 440/1800Kč; ◉🛜🖩; 🚊4, 10, 16, 22) Quirkily decorated with colourful wall paintings, rustic timber and real silver-birch trees, this pension stands out from the crowd. There's an easygoing, family-friendly, vaguely hippy-ish atmosphere; you can choose to stay in a shared room (from three to six people, doesn't really feel like a dorm), a private room with shared bathroom, or a private room with en suite.

Staff are superhelpful, and there's a residents' lounge and communal kitchen. Note – reception is on the 2nd floor, and there is no elevator.

★MOSAIC HOUSE
HOTEL, HOSTEL €€

Map p338 (☎221 595 350; www.mosaichouse.com; Odborů 4; dm/tw from 370/2400Kč; ◉🖩@🛜; Ⓜ️Karlovo Náměstí) 🏊 A blend of four-star hotel and boutique hostel, Mosaic House is a cornucopia of designer detail, from the original 1930s mosaic in the entrance hall to the silver spray-painted tree branches used as clothes racks. The backpackers dorms are kept separate from the private rooms, but have the same high-quality decor and design, as does the in-house music bar and lounge.

The top-floor private bedrooms cost about 33% more than standard doubles but are worth it for the spacious balconies with city views, and the relative peace and quiet. All have incredibly stylish bathrooms with water-efficient raindance showers; other green technology includes the use of intelligent heating systems, solar panels and greywater recycling.

MOODS HOTEL
BOUTIQUE HOTEL €€

Map p336 (☎222 330 100; www.hotelmoods.com; Klimentská 28; r from 3300Kč; 🖩🛜; 🚊5, 8, 24, 26) Staff are as important as style – if not more so – when it comes to enjoying a hotel stay, and the people here play a huge part in the visitor experience: welcoming, friendly and helpful. One of the best examples of Prague's 'design hotels', Moods is sharply styled and tech savvy, with clever colour schemes, adjustable mood lighting and intriguing quotations gracing the walls.

The location is off the beaten track, but still only 10 minutes' walk from the Old Town Square, with the option of a scenic stroll along the bank of the Vltava.

HOTEL SUITE HOME
APARTMENTS €€

Map p338 (☎222 230 833; www.hotelsuitehome-prague.com; Příčná 2; 2-person ste from 3650Kč; P◉🖩@🛜🖩; Ⓜ️Karlovo Náměstí) Straddling the divide between apartments and hotels, this place offers the space and convenience of a suite with private bathroom and kitchen along with hotel facilities such as 24-hour reception, maid service and breakfast room. It's a good choice for families, with suites for up to six; the rooms are pleasantly old-fashioned, and some on the upper floors have good views towards the castle.

There's a lift, though it's a bit on the small side – important, as the building has five floors. Check the website for special rates.

HOTEL 16 U SV KATEŘINY
HOTEL €€

Map p338 (☎224 920 636; www.hotel16.cz; Kateřinská 16; s/d/tr incl breakfast 2500/3100/3800Kč; ◉🖩@🛜🖩; 🚊4, 10, 16, 22) Hotel 16 is a friendly, family-run little place with just 14 rooms, tucked away in a very quiet corner of town where you're more likely to hear birdsong than traffic. The rooms vary in size and are simply but smartly furnished; the best, at the back, have views onto the peaceful terraced garden. Staff are superb, and can't do enough to help.

Buffet breakfast is included in the price, and the hotel is equipped with a lift. It's near the Botanic Gardens and about five minutes' walk from Štěpánská tram stop or IP Pavlova metro station.

★ICON HOTEL
BOUTIQUE HOTEL €€€

Map p338 (☎221 634 100; www.iconhotel.eu; V jámě 6; r from 3800Kč; 🖩@🛜; 🚊3, 9, 14, 24) Staff clothes by Diesel, computers by Apple, beds by Hästens – pretty much everything in this gorgeous boutique hotel has a designer stamp on it. Appearing on Europe's trendiest hotels lists, the Icon's sleekly minimalist rooms are enlivened with a splash of imperial purple from the silky bedspreads, while the curvy, reproduction art deco armchairs are supplied by Modernista (p117).

Hi-tech touches include iPod docks, Skype phones and fingerprint-activated safes, while the in-house Asian spa offers guests relaxing massages and beauty treatments.

Vinohrady & Vršovice

★CZECH INN
HOSTEL, HOTEL €

Map p344 (☑267 267 600; www.czech-inn.com; Francouzská 76, Vršovice; dm 260-450Kč, s/d 1320/1540Kč, apt from 3100Kč; Ⓟ♋@🛜; 🚋4, 22) The Czech Inn calls itself a hostel, but the boutique label wouldn't be out of place. Everything seems sculpted by an industrial designer, from the iron beds to the brushed-steel flooring and minimalist square sinks. The Czech Inn offers a variety of accommodation, from standard hostel dorm rooms to good-value private doubles (with or without attached bathroom) and apartments.

A bank of internet terminals in the lobby and an excellent buffet breakfast in the adjoining bar-cafe round out the charms. The nearest metro station is 10 minutes on foot or a short tram ride away.

HOLIDAY HOME
PENSION €

Map p344 (☑222 512 710; www.holidayhome.cz; Americká 37, Vinohrady; s/d from 1225/1450Kč; Ⓟ♋@🛜; ⓂNáměstí Míru) This popular family-owned pension offers excellent value in one of the city's choicest residential neighbourhoods. The secret here is no frills: simple, plain rooms and small beds at an unbeatable price. The hotel manager is superfriendly. The location is ideal, just a short walk to several nearby cafes and the Náměstí Míru metro stop.

PENZION MÁNES
PENSION €

Map p344 (☑222 252 180; www.penzionmanes.cz; Mánesova 46, Vinohrady; s/d from 1100/1600Kč; ♋@; ⓂJiřího z Poděbrad, 🚋11) It's bare-bones accommodation here, but a great price given the location on handsome Mánesova, close to some of the area's best bars, restaurants and clubs. There are few facilities, but rooms (some with a courtyard view) are comfortable and quiet, and staff are friendly.

ARKADA
BOUTIQUE HOTEL €€

Map p344 (☑242 429 111; www.arkadahotel.cz; Balbínová 8, Vinohrady; s/d from 1750/2250Kč; Ⓟ♋@🛜; 🚋11, ⓂMuzeum) This 35-room hotel in Vinohrady offers a great combination of style, comfort and location. The rooms are well appointed, with a retro-1930s feel that fits the style of the building. Rooms have flat-screen TVs, free internet access and minibars. Ask to see a couple before choosing, as the decor differs from room to room.

The location is about five minutes by foot to the top of Wenceslas Square and is within easy walking distance of some of the best Vinohrady clubs and restaurants.

LOUREN HOTEL
BOUTIQUE HOTEL €€

Map p344 (☑224 250 025; www.louren.cz; Slezská 55, Vinohrady; s/d/ste 3500/4000/5000Kč; ♋@🛜; 🚋10, 16 to Perunova, ⓂJiřího z Poděbrad) Popular with business travellers, this small luxury hotel with 27 rooms, including several suites, is set in a grand 19th-century apartment building. Stylish decor and attentive service are accompanied by thoughtful touches such as bathrobes and fresh flowers. The rooms are decorated in restful, neutral tones (lots of cream and light wood).

The building dates from 1889 and has been restored to its former grandeur. Service can't be faulted, and staff are courteous and very helpful. Rates are sometimes discounted on its website.

HOTEL ANNA
HOTEL, PENSION €€

Map p344 (☑222 513 111; www.hotelanna.cz; Budečská 17, Vinohrady; s/d/ste from €70/90/100; Ⓟ♋@🛜; ⓂNáměstí Míru) This small, friendly hotel has helpful and knowledgable employees. The late-19th-century building retains many of its original art nouveau features, and the bedrooms are bright and cheerful, with floral bedspreads and arty black-and-white photos of Prague buildings on the walls. There are two small suites on the top floor, one of which has a great view towards the castle.

The hotel is tucked away on a quiet backstreet but is close to the metro and lots of good restaurants and bars; you can walk to the top end of Wenceslas Square in 10 minutes.

HOTEL LUNÍK
HOTEL €€

Map p344 (☑224 253 974; www.hotel-lunik.cz; Londýnská 50, Vinohrady; s/d from 2100/3000Kč; Ⓟ♋@🛜; ⓂNáměstí Míru or IP Pavlova) Clean, attractive and smallish, Hotel Luník is on a quiet residential street a block from Peace Square, between the Náměstí Míru and IP Pavlova metro stations. The lobby and public areas exude a quiet sophistication, while the rooms are homey and slightly old-fashioned, with attractive green-tiled bathrooms. The friendly receptionist may be willing to negotiate room rates on slow nights.

ORION
APARTMENTS €€

Map p344 (☎222 521 706; www.okhotels.
cz; Americká 9, Vinohrady; 2-/4-person apt
2200/2600Kč; P⊜@☎⊞; MNáměstí Míru)
Good-value apartment rentals in an upmarket section of Vinohrady, within easy
walking distance of Peace Square and
Havlíčkovy sady. All 26 apartments are
equipped with a small kitchen, including a
fridge and coffee maker. Several have multiple rooms and can accommodate groups.
Ask to see a couple of rooms as they are
slightly different. Some come with hardwood floors, others carpet.

AMETYST
BOUTIQUE HOTEL €€€

Map p344 (☎222 921 921; www.hotelametyst.cz;
Jana Masaryka 11, Vinohrady; s/d from €160/225;
P⊜❄@☎; MNáměstí Míru) The polished
Ametyst straddles the line between boutique and hotel, with just enough style
points in the lobby (nice retro flagstone)
and the rooms (hardwood floors, arty
lamps) to put it in the boutique camp. All
rooms have air-conditioning and wi-fi access, and there are tubs and hairdryers in
the bathrooms.

There are dozens of places to relax
within easy walking distance in one of the
nicest parts of leafy Vinohrady. Note, rack
rates have risen steeply in the past couple of
years, though the hotel does offer frequent
discounts on its website.

LE PALAIS HOTEL
HOTEL €€€

Map p344 (☎234 634 111; www.vi-hotels.com/
en/le-palais; U Zvonařky 1, Vinohrady; r from
€220, ste from €400; P⊜❄@☎; ⊠11 to Bru-
selská) Le Palais is housed in a gorgeous
belle époque building dating from the end
of the 19th century that was once home to
Czech artist Luděk Marold (1865–98; his
former apartment is now rooms 407 to
412). It has been beautifully restored, complete with original floor mosaics, period
fireplaces, marble staircases, wrought-
iron balustrades, frescos, painted ceilings
and delicate stucco work.

The luxury bedrooms are decorated in
warm shades of yellow and pink, while the
various suites – some located in the corner
tower, some with a south-facing balcony –
make the most of the hotel's superb location, perched on top of a bluff with views
of the Vyšehrad fortress. Within easy walking distance of bars and restaurants in Vinohrady and about 15 minutes by foot from
the top of Wenceslas Square.

🛏 Žižkov & Karlín

HOSTEL LÍPA
HOSTEL €

Map p346 (☎602 211 182; www.hostellipa.com;
Tachovské náměstí 6, Žižkov; dm/d 400/1150Kč;
P@☎⊞; ⊠133, 175, 207) Several good hostels have opened recently in Žižkov, but this
place – upstairs from an excellent pub, U Slovanské Lípy (p152) – is a little gem, run by a
young Czech couple (with good English). It
feels more like a shared apartment, consisting of only four rooms (maximum four beds)
and a modern fitted kitchen. Bike rental
from Bajkazyl (p152) across the square.

HOTEL ALWYN
BOUTIQUE HOTEL €€

Map p346 (☎222 334 200; www.hotelalwyn.
cz; Vítkova 26, Karlín; s/d from 2900/3400Kč;
❄@☎; ⊠3, 8) The Alwyn is the first designer hotel to appear in the up-and-coming
district of Karlín. Set on a quiet side street
only a few tram stops east of Staré Město,
the hotel sports deliciously modern decor in
shades of chocolate brown, beige and burnt
orange, with lots of polished wood and deco-
style sofas in the cocktail bar, and super-
comfortable Hästens beds in the rooms.

It's designed for both business and pleasure, with a conference room, gym, sauna
and massage centre.

PENTAHOTEL PRAGUE
HOTEL €€

(☎222 332 800; www.pentahotels.com; Sokolovská 112, Karlín; r from 2350Kč; P❄☎; MKřižíkova)
This German budget hotel chain is aimed
at business and independent travellers,
with sleek modern styling, quality beds
and bathrooms, a large gym, and a 'pen-
talounge' – a combined reception, bar, cafe
and sitting area where guests can meet and
mingle. The Karlín location has good tram
and metro connections, and there are many
good restaurants and bars in the vicinity.

🛏 Holešovice

SIR TOBY'S HOSTEL
HOSTEL €

Map p348 (☎246 032 610; www.sirtobys.com;
Dělnická 24; dm 370-570Kč; s/d 1190/1400Kč;
P⊜❄☎; ⊠1, 12, 14 to Dělnická) Set in a
refurbished apartment building with a
spacious kitchen and common room, Sir
Toby's is only 10 minutes north of the city
centre by tram. The dorms have between
five and 12 bunks, including a six-bed, all-
female room, and the bigger dorms are

some of the cheapest in Prague. All rooms are light and clean, but don't expect anything fancy.

HOTEL EXTOL INN
HOTEL **€**

Map p348 (☑220 802 549; www.extolinn.cz; Přístavní 2; s/d from 1200/1800Kč; P ⊖ @ 🛜; 🛗12, 14 to U průhonu) The bright, modern Extol Inn provides budget accommodation in an up-and-coming neighbourhood within easy reach of the city centre by tram. The cheapest rooms (on the upper floors) are basic, no-frills affairs with shared bathrooms. More expensive three-star rooms (doubles from 1800Kč) have private bathrooms, TVs, minibars and free use of the hotel spa. There's a public internet terminal in the lobby. Wheelchair-accessible.

PLUS PRAGUE HOSTEL
HOSTEL **€**

Map p348 (☑220 510 046; www.plusprague.com; Přívozní 1; dm 280–440Kč, r 1200Kč; P ⊖ @ 🛜 ≋; 🛗12, 14, 24 to Ortenovo náměstí, MNádraží Holešovice) The cheerful Plus Prague Hostel is one tram stop from Nádraží Holešovice. Cheap rates, clean rooms with en suite bathrooms, friendly staff and an indoor swimming pool make this a special place. It also offers four- to eight-bed, female-only dorm rooms, outfitted with hairdryers and fluffier towels.

HOTEL LEON
HOSTEL, HOTEL **€**

Map p348 (☑220 941 351; www.leonhotel.eu; Ortenovo náměstí 26; s/d from 980/1500Kč; P ⊖ @; 🛗12, 14, 24 to Ortenovo náměstí, MNádraží Holešovice) The Hotel Leon advertises itself as something between a hostel and a small hotel. In truth, it's actually much nicer than a standard hostel and not much more expensive (especially if you share a three- or four-bed room). The rooms are basic, with no TV or much of anything else, but are quiet and clean, with adjoining bathrooms.

If noise is an issue, ask for a quieter room overlooking the back garden. There's a common room for TV and a shared computer for internet access. It's one tram stop (Ortenovo náměstí) from the Nádraží Holešovice train and metro station.

AUTOCAMP TROJSKÁ
CAMPGROUND **€**

(☑283 850 487; www.autocamp-trojska.cz; Trojská 157, Troja; site per person 100Kč, plus per tent/car 150/90Kč; ⊙year-round; P 🛜 📶; MNádraží Holešovice then bus 112 to Kazanka) The most comfortable and secure of half a dozen campgrounds in this quiet northern suburb, Trojská offers a garden bar and restaurant, a laundry and an on-site shop.

★ABSOLUTUM HOTEL
BOUTIQUE HOTEL **€€**

Map p348 (☑222 541 406; www.absolutumho-tel.cz; Jablonského 639/4; s/d 2400/3200Kč; P ⊖ ❄ @ 🛜; 🛗12, 24, ℝPraha-Holešovice, MNádraží Holešovice) A highly recommended, eye-catching boutique hotel, the Absolutum is located across from Nádraží Holešovice metro station. While the industrial neighbourhood wouldn't win a beauty contest, the hotel compensates with a nice list of amenities, including smartly designed rooms with exposed brickwork, well-appointed modern bathrooms (some rooms have a tub), air-conditioning, an excellent restaurant, a wellness centre and free parking.

PLAZA ALTA HOTEL
HOTEL **€€**

Map p348 (☑220 407 082; www.plazahotelalta. com; Ortenovo náměstí 22; s/d from €80/100; P ⊖ @ 🛜; 🛗12, 14, 24 to Ortenovo náměstí, MNádraží Holešovice) ✈ The snazziest hotel in this part of town draws mostly business clientele and travellers looking for a full-service property within easy reach (one tram stop) of the Praha-Holešovice train station and the Nádraží Holešovice metro station. The rooms have a tasteful contemporary look, with comfy mattresses and bold, striped bedspreads. All rooms have air-conditioning and minibar.

🛏 Bubeneč & Dejvice

HOTEL DENISA
PENSION, HOTEL **€**

Map p350 (☑224 318 969; www.hotel-den-isa.cz; Národní Obrany 33, Dejvice; s/d from 1620/1800Kč; P ⊖ @ 🛜; MDejvická) This small, family-run hotel in a turn-of-the-century apartment building on a quiet side street has been thoroughly renovated and represents excellent value for money. Rooms have nice thick mattresses, minibars and high-speed wi-fi connections. The location has always been a plus, just a few minutes' walk to the Dejvická metro stop, as well as being convenient to the airport.

ART HOTEL
BOUTIQUE HOTEL **€€**

Map p350 (☑233 101 331; www.arthotel. cz; Nad Královskou oborou 53, Bubeneč; s/d from €95/110; P ⊖ @ 🛜; 🛗1, 8, 12, 25, 26 to Sparta) There are lots of word-of-mouth recommendations for this small, well-managed hotel hidden away in the normally quiet neighbourhood behind Generali Aréna, where Sparta Praha plays football (soccer). The hotel has sleek, modern styling, with a display of contemporary Czech art in the lobby, and art photography on the walls of the rooms.

HOTEL VILLA SCHWAIGER BOUTIQUE HOTEL €€
Map p350 (220 400 840; www.villaschwaiger.cz; Schwaigerova 59/3, Bubeneč; s/d from €80/120; P@; 131 to Sibirské náměstí) This elegant, colonial-style villa in a quiet valley in Bubeneč feels a world away from the bustle of Old Town Square. Great care has gone into designing the 22 rooms; some have dark hardwood floors and dramatic, eye-catching curtains and fabrics. The public areas are stunning, with white woods, marble floors and comfortable wicker furniture.

Smíchov & Vyšehrad

IBIS PRAHA MALÁ STRANA HOTEL €
Map p342 (221 701 700; www.ibishotel.com; Plzeňská 14, Smíchov; r from €69; P@; Anděl) Offering a little splash of the neighbourhood's more upscale properties, but at half the price. Nevermind that it's nowhere near Malá Strana (but nice try by the marketing department), Smíchov's Ibis hotel is a great addition to the neighbourhood. The rooms are standard issue, but they have air-conditioning and free wi-fi. Breakfast not included.

HOTEL ARBES-MEPRO HOTEL €
Map p342 (257 210 410; www.hotelarbes.cz; Viktora Huga 3, Smíchov; s/d from 1800/2000Kč; P@; Anděl) Clean, quiet and excellent value, the Arbes is a down-to-earth tonic to the many high-rise, flashier hotels in Smíchov. The hotel is family-run and friendly, and the rooms are basic, with modern furnishings and clean bathrooms. Ask for a courtyard room if noise is an issue. There's limited street parking, but there's paid parking near the hotel (per night 375Kč).

ANDĚL'S HOTEL PRAGUE BOUTIQUE HOTEL €€
Map p342 (296 889 688; www.vi-hotels.com; Stroupežnického 21, Smíchov; r from €120; P@; Anděl) This sleek designer hotel, all stark contemporary in white with black and red accents, has floor-to-ceiling windows, DVD and CD players, internet access and modern art in every room. The bathrooms are a wonderland of polished chrome and frosted glass. The website offers packages with significant discounts from the rack rate.

RED & BLUE DESIGN HOTEL HOTEL €€
Map p342 (220 990 100; www.redandblue-hotels.com; Holečkova 13, Smíchov; s/d from €90/110; 6, 9, 12, 20 to Švandovo divadlo) This designer boutique sports 26 rooms done out in tasteful red highlights and 26 in blue. The setting is a smartly renovated 19th-century townhouse. The overall style might be termed contemporary minimalist, though the lobby cafe/bar is a riot of colour. Whichever colour scheme, the rooms are similar, with thick carpets, modern furnishings and baths, and air-conditioning.

HOTEL JULIAN HOTEL €€
Map p342 (257 311 150; www.hoteljulian.com; Elišky Peškové 11, Smíchov; s/d from €105/130; P@; 6, 9, 12, 20 to Švandovo divadlo) This deservedly popular small hotel has helpful staff and a quiet location just south of Malá Strana. The smart, well-kept bedrooms are decorated with relaxing pastels and pine-topped furniture. The public areas include a clubby drawing room with a library and open fire. The property markets itself as a 'romantic' hotel and offers special deals over the internet for couples.

If you're travelling with kids or in a group, there are a couple of family rooms that can hold up to six people, and there's also a wheelchair-accessible room. The in-room air-conditioning can be a life-saver in hot weather.

HOTEL UNION HOTEL €€
(261 214 812; www.hotelunion.cz; Ostrčilovo náměstí 4, Vyšehrad; s/d 1800/3000Kč; P@; 7, 18, 24 to Svatoplukova) A grand old hotel from 1906, the Union was nationalised by the communists in 1958 and returned to the former owner's family in 1991. Comfortably renovated, with a few period touches left intact, the hotel is at the foot of the hill below Vyšehrad fortress. Bedrooms are plain but pleasant.

Best of Bohemia

České Budějovice p202
Bustling regional capital with the country's largest town square and home-brewed Czech 'Budweiser' beer.

Český Krumlov p208
A Renaissance town so pretty even Praguers get a teensy bit envious.

Třeboň p213
A sleepy getaway with a pretty Renaissance castle nestled within a protected landscape.

Tábor p216
This old Hussite bastion has some bewildering underground passageways.

Plzeň p220
The EU's 2015 cultural capital, and, did we mention the brewery tour?

Karlovy Vary p226
Waters and wafers at the Czech Republic's best-known spa town.

Mariánské Lázně p233
Goethe, Chopin and even Mark Twain were drawn to the tranquility of this spa resort.

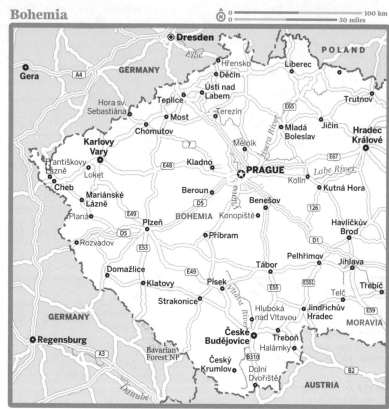

Bohemia

České Budějovice

Explore

České Budějovice (pronounced chesky *bood*-yo-vit-zah or simply 'Budweis') is the provincial capital of southern Bohemia and a natural base for exploring the region. Transport connections to nearby Český Krumlov are good, meaning you could easily take in both places on an overnight excursion from Prague. While České Budějovice lacks top sights, it does have one of Europe's largest main squares and a charming labyrinth of narrow lanes and winding alleyways, some of which hug a sleepy but atmospheric canal. It's also the home of 'Budvar' beer (aka Czech 'Budweiser'), and a brewery tour usually tops the 'must-do' list.

The Best...

➡ **Sight** Budweiser Budvar Brewery (p203)
➡ **Place to Eat** U Tři Sedláku (p205)
➡ **Place to Drink** Modrý Dveře Jazz & Blues (p208)

Top Tip

If you're travelling during the ice-hockey season (September to March) catch the home team **ČEZ Motor České Budějovice** in action at Budvar Arena (p208). Tickets can be bought at the arena on game days.

Getting There & Away

➡ **Bus** From Prague, **Student Agency** (☎386 111 000; www.studentagency.cz; Lannova 27; ⏱9am-6pm Mon-Fri) buses leave from Na Knížecí bus station (150Kč, 2½ hours) at the Anděl metro station (Line B). There are decent bus services from České Budějovice to Český Krumlov (35Kč, 45 minutes), Tábor (70Kč, one hour) and Třeboň (40Kč, 30 minutes). České Budějovice's **bus station** (⚐266 014 111; Nádražní 1759) is east of the centre, near the train station.

➡**Train** From Prague, there's frequent train service (222Kč, 2½ hours, hourly). Regular (slow) trains trundle to Český Krumlov (32Kč, 45 minutes). České Budějovice's **train station** (Vlakové nádraží; ⚐840 112 113; www. cd.cz; Nádražní) is 10 minutes walk east of the centre, following Lannova street.

➡**Car** From Prague, the drive takes 2½ hours following the D1 motorway towards Brno and then heading south on Hwy E55.

Need to Know

➡**Location** 160km south of Prague.

➡**Municipal Information Centre** (Městské Informační Centrum; Map p204; ⚐386 801 413; www.cb-info.cz; náměstí Přemysla Otakara II 2; ☉8.30am-6pm Mon-Fri, to 5pm Sat, 10am-4pm Sun May-Sep, 9am-5pm Mon-Fri, to 1pm Sat Oct-Apr) Books tickets, tours and accommodation, and has free internet.

➡**Oberbank** (www.oberbank.cz; Náměstí Přemysla Otakara II 4) Convenient ATM situated just on the main square.

◉ SIGHTS

BUDWEISER BUDVAR BREWERY   BREWERY
(Budějovický Budvar; ⚐387 705 347; www.visit-budvar.cz; cnr Pražská & K Světlé; adult/child 100/50Kč; ☉9am-5pm daily Mar-Dec, Tue-Sat Jan & Feb; trolley bus 2 to Budvar) One of the highlights of a trip to České Budějovice is a chance to see where original Budweiser beer was born. Brewery tours depart daily at 2pm (less frequently from November to March). The tour highlights modern production methods, with the reward being a glass of Budvar in the brewery's chilly cellars. The brewery is 2km north of the main square.

NÁMĚSTÍ PŘEMYSLA OTAKARA II   SQUARE
(náměstí Přemysla Otakara II) **FREE** This mix of arcaded buildings grouped around **Samson's Fountain** (Samsonova kašna; 1727) is the broadest plaza in the country, spanning 133m. Among the architectural treats is the 1555 Renaissance **Town Hall** (Radnice), which received a baroque facelift in 1731. The figures on the balustrade – Justice, Wisdom, Courage and Prudence – are matched by an exotic quartet of bronze gargoyles.

BLACK TOWER   TOWER
(Černá věž; ⚐386 352 508; U Černé věže 70/2; adult/concession 30/20Kč; ☉10am-6pm daily Jun-Aug, Tue-Sun Apr, May, Sep & Oct) The dominating, 72m Gothic-Renaissance Black Tower was built in 1553. Climb its 225 steps (yes, we counted them) for fine views. The tower's two **bells** – the Marta (1723) and Budvar (1995; a gift from the brewery) – are rung daily at noon.

Beside the tower is the **Cathedral of St Nicholas** (Katedrála sv Mikuláše), built as

BEST OF BOHEMIA ČESKÉ BUDĚJOVICE

EXPLORE BOHEMIA

The Czech Republic's western province boasts surprising variety. Český Krumlov, with its riverside setting and Renaissance castle, is in a class by itself, but lesser-known towns such as Třeboň in the south and Loket in the west exude unexpected charm. Big cities like České Budějovice and Plzeň, the EU Cultural Capital for 2015, offer great museums and restaurants. The spa towns of West Bohemia were world famous in the 19th century and retain old-world lustre.

Bohemia in One Week

Focus your efforts: choose between the historic castle towns of the south or the spa resorts of the west. Český Krumlov deserves two nights, with your remaining time split between Třeboň and České Budějovice. If you opt for the west, spend a night in Plzeň and divide the rest of the week between Karlovy Vary and Mariánské Lázně.

Bohemia in Two Weeks

Two weeks is enough time to fully explore the province. Spend one week in the south, enjoying Český Krumlov and České Budějovice. For the second week, head west: book a long stay at a spa and treat yourself like royalty.

České Budějovice

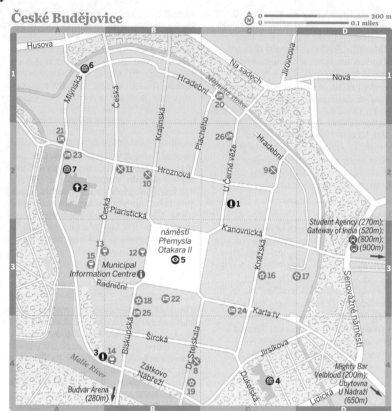

České Budějovice

BEST OF BOHEMIA ČESKÉ BUDĚJOVICE

a church in the 13th century, rebuilt in 1649, then made a cathedral in 1784.

MUSEUM OF SOUTH BOHEMIA MUSEUM

(Jihočeské muzeum; www.muzeumcb.cz; Dukelská 1; adult/child 60/30Kč; ⊙9am-12.30pm, 1-5pm Tue-Fri, to 5.30pm Sat & Sun) The Museum of South Bohemia holds an enormous collection of historic books, coins and weapons. It was closed in 2014 for long-term reconstruction and during research for this book it wasn't clear when it would reopen. Check the website for the latest information.

SOUTH BOHEMIAN MOTORCYCLE MUSEUM MUSEUM

(Jihočeské Motocyklové muzeum; ☑723 247 104; www.motomuseum.malse.eu; Piaristické náměstí; adult/concession 60/30Kč; ⊙10am-6pm Apr-Oct) There are dozens of historic motorcycles on display here at this unlikely, ecclesiastical setting for a motorcycle museum. In addition to motorbikes, there are old-time bicycles and model aeroplanes on display.

✖ EATING & DRINKING

U TŘI SEDLÁKU CZECH €

(☑387 222 303; www.utrisedlaku.cz; Hroznová 488; mains 100-170Kč) Locals celebrate that nothing much has changed at U Tři Sedláku since its opening in 1897. The traditional Czech food here might very well be the best in town and the price represents great value. The meaty dishes go with the Pilsner Urquell that's constantly being shuffled to busy tables.

GATEWAY OF INDIA INDIAN €

(Indická Restaurace; ☑386 359 355; www.indicka restaurace.cz; Chelčického 121/10; mains 120-240Kč; ⊙11am-11pm; ⊜☎) Oddly for a city of its size, České Budějovice has two decent Indian restaurants, but we prefer this smaller, more intimate place close to the train and bus stations. Climb the stairs to the cosy dining room, infused with the smell of curries cooking. The lamb Madras is our favourite, but all the dishes are good and authentic.

HOSPŮDKA U DIVADLA CZECH, FISH €€

(☑607 078 486; www.hospudkaudivadla.cz; Dr Stejskala 13; mains 170-300Kč; ⊙11am-2pm, 5-10pm; ⊜☎) Hospůdka means 'little pub' in Czech, but this refined restaurant that opened in 2013 is much more than that. The highlight here is fish, sourced locally and served fresh, but there are also a few traditional meat dishes. The daily lunch specials, with mains priced around 130Kč, are particularly good value. Try the microbrew Glokner beer.

MASNÉ KRAMÝ CZECH €€

(☑387 201 301; www.masne-kramy.cz; Krajinská 13; mains 170-270Kč; ⊙10.30am-midnight) No visit to České Budějovice would be complete without stopping at this renovated 16th-century meat market for very good Czech food and a cold, locally made Budvar beer. You'll find all the Czech staples, including the house 'brewer's goulash', on the food menu. The drinks menu is equally important: try the superb unfiltered yeast beer. Advance booking is essential.

LIFE IS A DREAM INTERNATIONAL €€

(☑733 609 225; www.lifeisdream.cz; Kněžská 31; mains 190-300Kč; ⊙11am-11pm; ☎⏚) This eclectic restaurant traditionally scores high on user-generated websites, but more for the variety of the menu than the quality of the food. Mains such as chicken wrapped in chocolate, turkey served in red lentils, and a local variety of Peking duck are inventive and quite good. Several dishes incorporate tofu and seitan, making this a good choice for vegetarians.

STARÉ ČASY PUB

(☑728 873 434; Zátkovo nábřeží 13; ⊙1-11pm Mon-Fri, 3-11pm Sat & Sun; ☎) It's hard to pinpoint why exactly, but we love this smoky old-style pub by the canal. Maybe it's the wood-panelled walls, dotted with old photos and maps, the hidden tables that invite long chats, or the friendly service. Even the Platan 11° lager is pretty good. In summer, try to grab a wobbly table by the water.

VINÁRNA SOLNICE WINE BAR

(☑775 579 427; www.vinarnasolnice.cz; Česká 66; ⊙11am-11pm Mon-Thu, to midnight Fri, 6pm-midnight Sat; ☎) This clean and friendly wine bar offers an amazing selection of the best Czech wines, as well as carefully selected bottles from Austria, Germany, Italy and elsewhere. They also have light appetisers, soups and salads to nibble on between sips.

SINGER PUB PUB

(☑386 360 186; www.singerpub.cz; Česká 7/55; ⊙5pm-1am Mon-Fri, 7pm-1am Sat & Sun; ☎)

BEST OF BOHEMIA ČESKÉ BUDĚJOVICE

With Czech and Irish beers, and good cocktails, don't be surprised if you get the urge to rustle up something on the Singer sewing machines scattered around here. If not, challenge the regulars to a game of *foosball* with a soundtrack of noisy rock.

CAFE PLAZA
CAFE

(☎728 272 958; www.cafeplaza.cz; Náměstí Přemysla Otakara II 4; ◷8am-10pm Mon-Fri, 9am-10pm Sat & Sun; ☎) The kind of breezy, busy cafe that every big town needs, right on the main square next to the Municipal Information Centre. Pop in for a coffee, soft drink, beer or wine. They also serve cakes and ice cream. The wi-fi signal is fast and reliable and the service is friendly.

🛏 SLEEPING

PENZIÓN CENTRUM
PENSION €

(☎387 311 801; www.penzioncentrum.cz; Biskupská 130/3; s/d/tr 1000/1400/1800Kč; ☺@☎) Huge rooms with satellite TV, queen-sized beds with crisp, white linen, and thoroughly professional staff all make this a top reader-recommended spot near the main square. Call ahead or try to arrive before 8pm since the reception desk closes early.

UBYTOVNA U NÁDRAŽÍ
HOSTEL €

(☎972 544 648; www.ubytovna.vors.cz; Dvořákova 161/14; s 450-490Kč, d 720-760Kč; ☺@☎) This unattractive but clean tower block, just behind the bus station and about 200m from the train station, offers good-value accommodation with shared bathrooms (usually sharing with just one other room). Shared kitchens are also available. This hostel is popular with longer-stay students.

★RESIDENCE U ČERNÉ VĚŽ
APARTMENTS €€

(☎725 178 584; www.residenceucerneveze.cz; U Černé věž 13; apt from 2300Kč; P☺✳☎) Four centrally located townhouses have been given a thoroughly 21st-century makeover to create 18 furnished, self-contained apartments. The decor is crisply modern with high ceilings, spotless bathrooms and fully equipped kitchens. Rates exclude breakfast.

HOTEL BUDWEIS
HOTEL €€

(☎389 822 111; www.hotelbudweis.cz; Mlýnská 6; s/d 2200-2800Kč; P☺✳@☎) The Hotel Budweis opened its doors in 2010, hived out of an old grain mill with a picturesque canal-side setting. The owners have opted for a smart contemporary look. All the rooms have air-con and are wheelchair accessible. There are two good restaurants in-house, and the central location puts other eating and drinking options just a short walk away.

HOTEL KLIKA
HOTEL €€

(☎387 318 171; www.hotelklika.cz; Hroznová 25; s/d/apt incl breakfast 1100/1600/2500Kč; P☺☎) This is a good-value option, with an attractive riverside location. The modern rooms are light and airy, and anywhere that integrates 14th-century walls into their design is OK by us.

HOTEL BOHEMIA
HOTEL €€

(☎723 468 738; www.bohemiacb.cz; Hradební 20; s/d 1490/1790Kč; ☎) Carved wooden doors open to a restful interior inside these two old burghers' houses in a quiet street. The location near the canal is atmospheric, but the centre is just a few steps away. Take a map or get directions in advance, since the small street, Hradební, can be hard to find the first time.

HOTEL DVOŘAK
HOTEL €€

(☎386 322 349; www.hoteldvorakcb.cz; náměstí Přemysla Otakara II 36; s/d 1400/1800Kč; P@☎) Don't be fooled by the elegant facade: the Dvořak's rooms are modern and clean, but lacking character. The friendly staff and good-value last-minute specials (up to 40% off) still make this a worthwhile standby, and the location is excellent.

HOTEL MALÝ PIVOVAR
HOTEL €€

(☎386 360 471; www.malypivovar.cz; Karla IV 8-10; s/d 2000/2800Kč; P☺@) With a cabinet of sports trophies and sculpted leather sofas, the lobby resembles a gentlemen's club. However the elegant and traditionally furnished rooms will please both men and women, and it's just a short stroll to the cosy Budvarka beer hall downstairs.

☆ ENTERTAINMENT

CHAMBER PHILHARMONIC ORCHESTRA OF SOUTH BOHEMIA
CLASSICAL MUSIC

(Jihočeská komorní filharmonie; ☎box office 386 321 084; www.jcfilharmonie.cz; Kněžská 6; tickets around 180Kč; ◷box office 1-5pm Mon-Fri)

A WHIFF OF WINDSOR AT HLUBOKÁ NAD VLTAVOU

The delightful confection known as **Hluboká Chateau** (☎387 843 911; www.zamek -hluboka.eu; Zámek; adult/concession tour 1 250/160Kč, tour 2 230/160Kč, tour 3 170/80Kč; ☺9am-5pm Tue-Sun May-Jun, to 6pm Jul & Aug, shorter hours Sep-Feb, closed Mar) is one of the most popular day trips from České Budějovice. Buses make the journey to the main square in Hluboká nad Vltavou every 30 to 60 minutes (20 minutes, 20Kč).

A crow pecking the eyes from a Turk's head (the grisly Schwarzenberg family crest) is the recurrent motif of the chateau's decor, but this image is at odds with the building's overt romanticism.

Built by the Přemysl rulers in the latter half of the 13th century, Hluboká was taken from the Protestant Malovec family in 1662 as punishment for supporting an anti-Habsburg rebellion, and then sold to the Bavarian Schwarzenbergs. Two centuries later, they gave the chateau the English Tudor/Gothic face it wears today, modelling its exterior on Britain's Windsor Castle.

Crowned with crenellations and surrounded by a dainty garden, Hluboká is too prissy for some, but this remains the second-most visited chateau in Bohemia after Karlštejn, and for good reason.

There are three English-language tours available: tour 1 (called the 'representation room' on the website) focuses on the castle's public areas; tour 2 goes behind the scenes in the castle apartments; tour 3 explores the kitchens. Tour 1 is all most visitors will need to get the flavour of the place. The last tour commences an hour before closing time. Tours in Czech are 100Kč cheaper. The surrounding park is open throughout the year (admission free).

An annual **music festival** (www.sinfonie.cz) is held in the chateau grounds in late summer. Performances range from Czech folk to jazz and chamber music.

The exquisite **South Bohemian Aleš Gallery** (Alšova jihočeská galérie; ☎387 967 041; www.ajg.cz; Zámek 144; adult/concession 80/40Kč; ☺9am-6pm Apr-Oct) is to the right of the castle gate in a former riding school (*jízdárna*). On display is a fabulous permanent collection of Czech religious art from the 14th to 16th centuries, plus 17th-century Dutch masters and changing exhibits of modern art.

While most visitors treat Hluboká as a day outing, it is possible to stay the night. The **Hotel Bakalář** (☎730 585 463; www.hotel-bakalar.cz; Masarykova 69; s/d 400/750Kč; P ☺), in the middle of town, has functional rooms and a decent pub/restaurant on site, and rents out bikes (per day 200Kč). Alternatively, the **Tourist Information Centre** (☎387 966 164; www.hluboka.cz; Zborovská 80 cnr Masarykova; ☺9am-6pm Apr-Oct, to 5pm Tue-Sun Nov-Mar; ☏), which has internet access and publishes a useful map, can recommend private rooms (also watch for 'Zimmer frei' or 'privát' signs along the main street, Masarykova).

There are a few restaurants scattered about that cater to day-trippers. An easy in-out option is **Pizzerie Ionia** (☎387 966 109; www.pizzerieionia.cz; Masarykova 35; pizza 120-170Kč; ☺11am-10pm Mon-Sat, noon-5pm Sun), just near the information centre.

A highlight of a visit to České Budějovice is to hear a concert at this former church that's been converted into a concert hall. The repertoire ranges from baroque all the way to modern, and there are also regular performances of folk and pop music. Buy tickets at the box office or the Municipal Information Centre.

CONSERVATORY CLASSICAL MUSIC
(Konzervatoř; ☎386 352 089; www.konzervator cb.cz; Kanovnická 22) **FREE** This music academy hosts regular classical-music performances.

SOUTH BOHEMIAN THEATRE THEATRE
(Jihočeské divadlo; ☎box office 386 356 925; www.jihoceskedivadlo.cz; Dr Stejskala 19; ☺10am-7pm Mon-Fri) The main building of the South Bohemian Theatre mostly stages dramatic works and small operas. Do note that the plays are normally performed in Czech.

MODRÝ DVEŘE JAZZ & BLUES JAZZ, BLUES
(☎386 359 958; www.modrydvere.cz; Biskupská 1; admission 50-70Kč; ☎) By day Modrý Dveře is a welcoming bar-cafe with vintage pics of Sinatra. At dusk the lights dim for live music – blues and jazz on Thursdays (from 8pm), and DJs on most Friday nights. Pop in for a drink even if there's nothing on the cards; it's one of the few lively bars near the centre.

MIGHTY BAR VELBLOUD CLUB, LIVE MUSIC
(www.velbloud.info; U Tří lvů 4; ☺from 7pm Tue-Sat) Loud and fun club with an eclectic schedule of live music, covering anything from neopunk to Roma DJs to German rockabilly. Check the website to see what's on offer during your visit.

🏃 SPORTS & ACTIVITIES

BUDVAR ARENA ICE HOCKEY
(ČEZ Motor České Budějovice; ☎tickets 606 877 674; www.hcmotor.cz; F. A. Gerstnera 7/8; tickets 60-100Kč; ☺box office from 1pm match days Sep-Mar) Home ice for the city's professional ice hockey team, **HC ČEZ Motor České Budějovice**, which now plays in the country's first division after being relegated from the top Extraliga in 2013. Purchase tickets on match days at the arena box office, or over the club's website. Check the website to see if there's a match scheduled during your visit.

Český Krumlov

Explore

Outside of Prague, Český Krumlov is arguably the Czech Republic's only other world-class sight and must-see. From a distance, the town looks like any other in the Czech countryside, but once you get closer and see the Renaissance castle towering over the undisturbed 17th-century townscape, you'll feel the appeal; this really is that fairytale town the tourist brochures promised. Český Krumlov is best approached as an overnight destination; it's too far for a comfortable day trip from Prague. Consider staying two nights, and spend one of the days hiking or biking in the surrounding woods and fields.

The Best...

➡**Sight** Český Krumlov Castle (p210)
➡**Place to Eat** Krčma v Šatlavské (p211)
➡**Place to Drink** Zapa Cocktail Bar (p211)

Top Tip

If you're visiting in July or August, try to book tickets to catch the annual **International Music Festival** (Mezinárodní hudební festival; ☎380 711 797; www.festivalkrumlov. cz; ☺concerts mid-Jul–Aug), one of the highlight's of the Czech festival season.

Getting There & Away

➡**Train** From Prague (260Kč, 3½ hours), the train requires a change in České Budějovice. Buses are quicker and cheaper. There's regular train service between České Budějovice and Český Krumlov (40Kč, 45 minutes). Český Krumlov **train station** (Vlakové nádraží; ☎840 112 113; www. cd.cz; Třída Míru 1) is a long 30-minute walk north of the historic centre.

➡**Bus Student Agency** (www.studentagency. cz) coaches (195Kč, three hours) leave regularly from Prague's Na Knížecí bus station at Anděl metro station (Line B). Book in advance for weekends or in July and August. Český Krumlov **bus station** (Autobusové nádraží; www.vlak-bus.cz; Nemocniční 586) is 10 minutes on foot east of the centre.

➡**Car** The drive from Prague is a strenuous three hours along a mostly two-lane highway. Take the D1 motorway in the direction of Brno, and turn south on Hwy E55.

Need to Know

➡**Location** 180km south of Prague.
➡**Infocentrum** (Map p209; ☎380 704 622; www.ckrumlov.info; náměstí Svornosti 2; ☺9am-7pm Jun-Aug, to 6pm Apr, May, Sep & Oct, to 5pm Nov-Mar) Provides transport and accommodation information, as well as maps and audio guides. Sells bus and shuttle tickets as well as the handy and

Český Krumlov

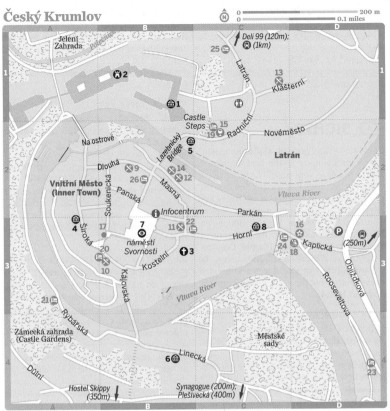

Český Krumlov

◎ Sights
1 Castle Museum & Tower B1
2 Český Krumlov State
   Castle..B1
3 Church of St Vitus.................................B3
4 Egon Schiele Art Centrum....................A3
5 Marionette Museum..............................B2
6 Museum Fotoateliér Seidel B4
7 Náměstí Svornosti................................B3
8 Regional Museum.................................C3

⊗ Eating
9 Cikánská Jizba B2
10 Hospoda Na Louži B3
11 Krčma v Šatlavské................................B3
12 Laibon...B2
13 Nonna Gina...C1
14 U Dwau Maryí B2

⊕ Drinking & Nightlife
Café Schiele......................................(see 4)

15 Zapa Cocktail Bar....................................C2

✪ Entertainment
Divadelní Klub Ántré ....(see 16)
16 Městské Divadlo D3

⊕ Sports & Activities
17 Expedicion...B3
18 Maleček...D3

⊜ Sleeping
19 Castle Apartments................................C2
20 Hospoda Na Louži.................................B3
21 Hostel Postel..A3
22 Hotel Konvice.......................................B3
23 Krumlov House......................................D4
24 Pension Barbakán.................................C3
25 Pension Danny...................................... C1
26 U Malého Vítka......................................B2

good-value **Český Krumlov Card** (www.ckrumlov.cz/card; adult/concession 200/100Kč), which includes entry into four popular attractions.

➡**Internet Access** The Infocentrum has computers on hand for internet access (per five minutes 5Kč).

◉ SIGHTS

There's no neatly prescribed plan for exploring Český Krumlov, so the best strategy is simply to follow your nose. The basic layout will soon become clear: a giant Renaissance castle on top and a web of backstreets and alleyways, bridges and riverbanks below. The centre of the Old Town is defined by **Náměstí Svornosti**, with its 16th-century **Town Hall** and **Marian Plague Column**, dating from 1716. Several buildings on the square feature valuable stucco and painted decorations: note the hotel at **No 13** and the house at **No 14**.

ČESKÝ KRUMLOV STATE CASTLE   CASTLE
(☑380 704 711; www.zamek-ceskykrumlov.eu; Zámek 59; adult/concession tour 1 250/160Kč, tour 2 240/140Kč, theatre tour 300/200Kč; ⊘9am-6pm Tue-Sun Jun-Aug, to 5pm Apr, May, Sep & Oct) Český Krumlov's striking Renaissance castle, occupying a promontory high above the town, began life in the 13th century. The castle acquired its present appearance in the 16th to 18th centuries under the stewardship of the noble Rožmberk and Schwarzenberg families. The interiors are accessible by guided tour only, although you can stroll the grounds on your own.

Three main tours are offered: tour 1 (one hour) takes in the opulent Renaissance rooms; tour 2 (one hour) visits the Schwarzenberg portrait galleries and their 19th-century apartments. The theatre tour (40 minutes, 10am to 4pm Tuesday to Sunday May to October) explores the chateau's remarkable rococo theatre.

CASTLE MUSEUM & TOWER   MUSEUM, TOWER
(☑380 704 711; www.zamek-ceskykrumlov.eu; Zámek 59; adult/concession combined entry 130/60Kč, museum only 100/50Kč, tower only 50/30Kč; ⊘9am-6pm Jun-Aug, to 5pm Apr & May, to 5pm Tue-Sun Sep & Oct, to 4pm Tue-Sun Jan-Mar) Located within the castle complex, this small museum and adjoining tower is an ideal option if you don't have the time or energy for a full castle tour. Through a series of rooms, the museum traces the castle's history from its origins through the present day. Climb the tower for the perfect photo-op shots of the town below.

EGON SCHIELE ART CENTRUM   MUSEUM
(☑380 704 011; www.schieleartcentrum.cz; Široká 71; adult/concession 120/70Kč; ⊘10am-6pm Tue-Sun) This excellent private gallery houses a small retrospective of the controversial Viennese painter Egon Schiele (1890–1918), who lived in Krumlov in 1911, and raised the ire of townsfolk by hiring young girls as nude models. For this and other sins he was eventually driven out. The centre also houses interesting temporary exhibitions.

MUSEUM FOTOATELIÉR SEIDEL   MUSEUM
(☑380 712 354; www.seidel.cz; Linecká 272; adult/concession 100/70Kč; ⊘9am-noon, 1-5pm daily Apr & Oct-Dec, Tue-Sun Jan-Mar; 9am-noon, 1-6pm daily May-Sep) This photography museum presents a moving retrospective of the work of local photographers Josef Seidel and his son František. Especially poignant are the images recording early-20th-century life in nearby villages. In the high season you should be able to join an English-language tour; if not, you can let the pictures tell the story.

SYNAGOGUE   SYNAGOGUE
(☑605 335 353; www.synagoga-krumlov.cz; Za Soudem 282; adult/concession 60/30Kč; ⊘11am-4pm Tue-Sun) Český Krumlov's renovated synagogue was built in neo-Romanesque style in 1909. The building survived the Nazi occupation in World War II and was used as a nondenominational place of worship by American soldiers shortly after the war. It's now used to house photo exhibitions and has a cute cafe around the corner. Buy your entry tickets at the synagogue's cafe.

CHURCH OF ST VITUS   CHURCH
(Kostel sv Víta; ☑380 711 336; www.farnostck.bcb.cz; Horní 156; ⊘9am-6pm) **FREE** This pretty church, with its signature neo-Gothic tower, is worth a peek inside. The church occasionally hosts classical music concerts. Ask at the nearby Infocentrum at náměstí Svornosti.

REGIONAL MUSEUM MUSEUM

(Regionální muzeum v Českém Krumlové; ☎380 711 674; www.museum-krumlov.eu; Horní 152; adult/concession 50/25Kč; ☻9am-noon & 12.30-5pm Tue-Sun) This small museum features folk art from the Šumava region, archaeology, history, fine arts, furnishings and weapons. The highlight is a room-sized model of Český Krumlov c 1800. Just next to the museum is a small grassy area with an amazing view out over the castle.

MARIONETTE MUSEUM MUSEUM

Map p209 (☎380 711 175; www.mozart.cz; Latrán 6; adult/concession 80/50Kč; ☻9am-6pm Apr-Aug, 10am-4pm Sep & Oct) This is the better of two museums in town dedicated to puppetry and marionettes. It's a branch of the National Marionette Theatre in Prague and is housed in the former Church of St Jošt. On display is a full range of Czech marionettes and puppets through the ages, including theatres and stage sets.

✕ EATING & DRINKING

We recommend booking ahead for dinner in July and August.

NONNA GINA ITALIAN €

(☎380 717 187; Klášteriní 52; pizza 100-170Kč; ☻11am-10pm; ☻) Authentic Italian flavours from the Italian Massaro family feature in this pizzeria down a quiet lane. Grab an outdoor table and pretend you're in Naples. In winter, the upstairs dining room is snug and intimate.

LAIBON VEGETARIAN €

(☎728 676 654; www.laibon.cz; Parkán 105; mains 90-180Kč; ☻☎✐) This rustic vegetarian restaurant, with several riverside picnic tables with castle views, is extremely popular on user-generated sites. We like it too, but the cooking admittedly is only above-average. Still, menu items such as guacamole and hummus can start the mouth watering after too many days of pork or chicken. Book in advance in summer and request an outside table.

HOSPODA NA LOUŽI CZECH €

(☎380 711 280; www.nalouzi.cz; Kájovská 66; mains 90-170Kč; ☻) Nothing's changed in this wood-panelled *pivo* (beer) parlour for almost a century. Locals and tourists pack Na Louži for huge plates of Czech staples

such as chicken schnitzels or roast pork and dumplings, as well as dark (and light) beer from the Eggenberg brewery. Get the fruit dumplings for dessert if you see them on the menu.

DELI 99 SANDWICHES €

(☎721 750 786; www.hostel99.cz/deli-99; Latrán 106; snacks & sandwiches 60-80Kč; ☻7am-7pm Mon-Fri, 8am-7pm Sat, 8am-5pm Sun; ☻☎✐) Bagels, sandwiches, organic juices and wi-fi all tick the 'Slightly Homesick Traveller' box.

U DWAU MARYÍ CZECH €

(☎380 717 228; www.2marie.cz; Parkán 104; mains 135-185Kč; ☻☎) The 'Two Marys' medieval tavern re-creates old recipes and presents an opportunity to try dishes made with buckwheat and millet (all tastier than they sound). Wash the food down with a goblet of mead or choose a 21st-century Pilsner. In summer it's a tad touristy, but the stunning riverside castle views easily compensate.

CIKÁNSKÁ JIZBA CZECH €

(☎380 717 585; Dlouhá 31; mains 120-250Kč; ☻3pm-midnight Mon-Sat) At the 'Gypsy Room' there's often live Roma music at the weekends to go with the menu of meaty Czech favourites. Reserve a table in advance during summer, especially over weekends.

★KRČMA V ŠATLAVSKÉ CZECH €€

(☎380 713 344; www.satlava.cz; Horní 157; mains 180-280Kč; ☻11am-midnight) This medieval barbecue cellar is hugely popular with visitors and your tablemates are much more likely to be from Austria or Asia than from the town itself, but the grilled meats served up with gusto in a funky labyrinth illuminated by candles are excellent and perfectly in character with Český Krumlov. Advance booking is essential.

ZAPA COCKTAIL BAR COCKTAIL BAR

(☎380 712 559; www.zapabar.cz; Latrán 15; ☻6pm-1am) Český Krumlov empties out after dinner, but Zapa keeps on going most nights until after midnight. You can expect the town's best cocktails and a relaxed vibe.

CAFÉ SCHIELE CAFE

(☎380 704 011; www.schieleartcentrum.cz; Široká 71; ☻10am-6pm Tue-Sun; ☎) A lovely cafe housed in the art gallery, with ancient oak floorboards, mismatched furniture

BEST OF BOHEMIA ČESKÝ KRUMLOV

and a grand piano with sawn-off legs serving as a coffee table. Excellent fair-trade coffee.

🛏 SLEEPING

★KRUMLOV HOUSE HOSTEL €

(☑380 711 935; www.krumlovhostel.com; Rooseveltova 68; dm/d/tr 300/1000/1350Kč; ❄@🛜) *Perched above the river, Krumlov House is friendly and comfortable, and has plenty of books, DVDs and local information to feed your inner wanderer. Accommodation is in six-bed en suite dorms as well as private double and triple rooms or private, self-catered apartments. The owners are English-speaking and traveller-friendly.

HOSTEL SKIPPY HOSTEL €

(☑380 728 380; www.hostelskippy.webs.com; Plešivecká 123; dm/d 350/880Kč; ❄🛜) Located in the near suburb of Plešivec on the Vltava, about 15 minutes walk south of the historic centre. The owners are a musician and artist and the hostel has a relaxed, indie vibe. Unlike some hostels with racks of bunks, Skippy is more like hanging out at a friend's place. It's small, so you'll need to book ahead.

HOSTEL POSTEL HOSTEL €

(☑776 720 722; www.hostelpostel.cz; Rybářská 35; dm/d 350/700Kč; ⊘closed Jan-Mar; ❄@🛜) Situated near a couple of good local pubs, Hostel Postel has a sunny courtyard with shady umbrellas to help you wake up slowly after a big night on the town. All the accommodation here is in super-clean, two- to four-bed rooms. Do note that the hostel is closed between January and March.

PENSION DANNY PENSION €

(☑380 712 710; www.pensiondanny.cz; Latrán 72; d incl breakfast from 1190Kč; ❄🛜) Exposed beams plus restored brickwork equals simple charm. As with many other places in town, the pension tends to fill up in summer, but is much emptier and cheaper in winter.

HOTEL KONVICE HOTEL €€

(☑380 711 611; www.boehmerwaldhotels.de; Horní 144; s/d 1300/2000Kč; ℗❄🛜) Attractive old-fashioned hotel with romantic rooms and period furnishings. Many rooms, such as No 12, have impressive wood-beamed ceilings, and all have homey architectural quirks that lend atmosphere. The service is somewhat reserved but friendly. The cook at breakfast is more than happy to whip up an egg upon request (which will go nicely with the usual cold cuts and cheeses).

CASTLE APARTMENTS APARTMENTS €€

(☑380 725 110; www.zameckaapartma.cz; Zámek 57; apt 1800-3000Kč; ⊘reception 9am-4pm; ❄🛜) Several apartments, situated in three historic buildings near the castle district, have been transformed into comfortable short-term rental units that offer wooden floors, and modern kitchenettes and bathrooms (no additional charge for the romantic views). The central reception is located just inside the castle entrance off Latrán.

U MALÉHO VÍTKA HOTEL €€

(☑380 711 925; www.vitekhotel.cz; Radniční 27; d 1600Kč; ℗❄🛜) We really like this small hotel, which is located in the heart of the Old Town. The simple room furnishings are of very high-quality, hand-crafted wood, and each room is named after a traditional Czech fairytale character. The hotel's downstairs restaurant and cafe are very good too.

PENSION BARBAKÁN PENSION €€

(☑380 717 017; www.barbakan.cz; Kaplická 26; s/d incl breakfast from 1300/1700Kč; ❄@🛜) Originally the town's gunpowder arsenal, Barbakán now creates fireworks of its own with super-comfy rooms featuring bright and cosy wooden decor. Sit in the grill restaurant (mains 150Kč to 210Kč) and watch the tubing and rafting action on the river below.

HOSPODA NA LOUŽI HOTEL €€

(☑380 711 280; www.nalouzi.cz; Kájovská 66; r 1350-1800Kč; ❄) Eleven cosy rooms situated above a great pub in the absolute centre of town. The interiors couldn't be more pleasant, with big wooden, period-piece beds and wooden floors. The bathrooms have all been nicely redone, and noise from the pub isn't an issue. Accommodation is tight in summer; winter rates may drop by up to 40%.

⭐ ENTERTAINMENT

DIVADELNÍ KLUB ÁNTRÉ   LIVE MUSIC

(☑605 882 342; www.klubantre.cz; Horní 2; 🕿)
The best up-and-coming Czech bands often
include the Ántré on their national schedules. The website is not very helpful, so
ask at the tourist Infocentrum in the town
square to see if anything's on during your
visit.

MĚSTSKÉ DIVADLO   THEATRE

(☑380 727 370; www.divadlo.ckrumlov.cz; Horní
2) The town theatre holds regular performances. Check the website for the current
program.

🏃 SPORTS & ACTIVITIES

EXPEDICION   ADVENTURE TOUR

(☑607 963 868; www.expedicion.cz; Soukenická
33; ⊘9am-7pm) Expedicion rents bikes (per
day 290Kč), arranges horse riding (per hour
250Kč), and operates action-packed day
trips (1680Kč including lunch) incorporat-
ing horse riding, fishing, mountain biking
and rafting in the nearby Newcastle Mountains region.

MALEČEK   CANOEING

(☑380 712 508; http://cz.pujcovna-lodi.malecek.
cz; Rooseveltova 28; 2-person canoe per 60min
450Kč; ⊘9am-5pm) In summer, messing
about on the river is a great way to keep
cool. Rent a canoe and splash around locally, or take a full-day trip down the river
from the town of Rožmberk (850Kč, six to
eight hours).

SEBASTIAN TOURS   GUIDED TOUR

(☑607 100 234; www.sebastianck-tours.com; 5
Května Ul, Plešivec; day trip to Hluboká nad Vltavou
per person 599Kč) Sebastian Tours can get
you discovering South Bohemia on guided
tours including stops at Hluboká nad Vltavou and České Budějovice. Also offers shuttle bus service to destinations in Austria.

SLUPENEC STABLES   HORSE RIDING

(☑723 832 459; www.jk-slupenec.cz; Slupenec
1; horse riding per hour/day 300/2200Kč) Slupenec Stables hires horses for trips and les-
sons. The stables are 2.5km south of town.
Book through the tourist Infocentrum in
the town square.

Třeboň

Explore

Třeboň is traditionally known throughout
the Czech Republic for its many fish ponds,
which produce much of the carp consumed
around the country on Christmas Eve. The
ponds are still there, but these days they're
also prized for aesthetic reasons: they make
a picturesque backdrop while hiking or biking through the Třeboňsko Protected Landscape. Třeboň itself is a nicely preserved
period-piece of Bohemian Renaissance architecture, mixed in with a handful of sights
and some decent hotels. It can be visited as
an easy day trip from České Budějovice.

The Best...

➡ **Sight** Třeboň Chateau (p214)
➡ **Place to Eat** Šupina & Šupinka (p215)
➡ **Place to Drink** Zbrojnice (p215)

Top Tip

Třeboň makes an excellent base for exploring the region's ponds and forests on foot
or by bike. The Tourism Information Centre
(p213) sells hiking maps and can advise on
excursions as well as places to rent bikes.

Getting There & Away

➡ **Train** There are a few trains daily from
Prague (210Kč, three hours), though
connections usually require a change in
Veselí nad Lužnicí.

➡ **Bus** Several daily buses leave from
Florenc bus station in Prague (150Kč,
three hours). Hourly buses run from České
Budějovice (40Kč, 30 minutes). The bus
station is a 10-minute walk from the centre.

➡ **Car** Třeboň is a two-hour drive south
of Prague, going towards Brno on the D1
motorway and then turning at the E55
Hwy. From České Budějovice the drive
takes 30 minutes on Hwy 34.

Need to Know

➡ **Location** 145km south of Prague.

➡ **Tourism Information Centre** (Turistické
informační centrum; ☑384 721 169; www.
itrebon.cz; Masarykovo náměstí 103; ⊘9am-
noon, 12.45-4pm Mon-Fri) Provides maps and
information on bike rental.

➡ **ČSOB** (Ceskoslovenska obchodni banka; www.

BEST OF BOHEMIA TŘEBOŇ

Třeboň

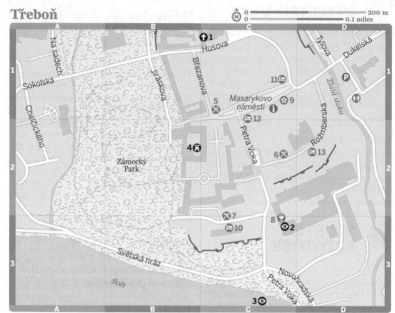

Třeboň

⊙ Sights

1 Decanal Church of the Virgin
Mary & St Giles....................................C1
2 Regent Brewery C3
3 Rybník Svět...C3
4 Třeboň Chateau B2

✖ Eating

5 Fish & Steak...C1
6 Rožmberská Bašta C2
7 Šupina & Šupinka C2

⊙ Drinking & Nightlife

8 Zbrojnice C3

✿ Entertainment

9 Kino Světozor...C1

⊟ Sleeping

10 Apartmány Šupina C3
11 Bílý Koníček...C1
12 Hotel Zlatá Hvězda.................................C1
13 Penzion Modrá Růže.............................. D2

csob.cz; Masarykovo náměstí 104) Handy bank
ATM right on the main square.

⊙ SIGHTS

TŘEBOŇ CHATEAU CASTLE
Map p214 (Zámek; ☑384 721 193; www.zamek
-trebon.eu; Zámek 115; adult 100-150Kč, concession 50-75Kč; ⊙9am-5.15pm Tue-Sun Jun-Aug,
to 4pm Apr-May & Sep-Oct) Třeboň's main attraction is its Renaissance chateau, which
includes a **museum** displaying furniture
and weapons. Today's chateau dates from
1611, the replacement for a Gothic castle
destroyed by fire. Originally built by the

Rožmberk family, it then became one of
the main residences of the Schwarzenberg
family.
Entry is by one of three guided tours:
tour A takes you through the castle's Renaissance interiors; tour B focuses on a
19th-century Schwarzenberg apartment;
and in summer (July and August) a third
tour explores the chateau's cellars.

**SCHWARZENBERG
MAUSOLEUM** MAUSOLEUM
(Švarcenberská Hrobka; ☑384 721 193; www.
zamek-trebon.eu; Park U Hrobky; adult/conces-
sion 60/30Kč, guided tour 100/60Kč; ⊙9am-5pm
Tue-Sun Jun-Aug, to 4pm Apr-May & Sep-Oct)
Many Schwarzenbergs are buried in this

grand neo-Gothic mausoleum, dating from 1877, located in Park U Hrobky on the other side of the pond from Třeboň. The crypt is a 15-minute walk from the centre along well-marked paths. Guided tours in English are possible but must be arranged in advance.

DECANAL CHURCH OF THE
VIRGIN MARY & ST GILES CHURCH
(Kostel Panny Marie Královny a Sv Jiljí; 🖉tours 732 251 103; www.trebon.farnost.cz; Husova; tour 30Kč; ⊙3-4pm, tours 3pm daily) This stately Gothic church and attached Augustine monastery complex date to the 14th century. Peek inside the church to see orginal late-Gothic artwork on the walls and one of the country's most important works of Gothic statuary, a Madonna dating from 1400. Daily tours in Czech are offered at 3pm; ask at the Tourism Information Centre about occasional English tours.

REGENT BREWERY BREWERY
(Pivovar Bohemia Regent; 🖉384 721 319; www.pivolar-regent.cz; Trocnovské náměstí 124) Třeboň's municipal brewery was founded in 1379 and still turns out excellent beers sold under the 'Bohemia Regent' label. Brewery tours need to be pre-booked by telephone or email. Prices depend on the time of day and number of people.

 EATING & DRINKING

FISH & STEAK INTERNATIONAL €
(🖉384 392 595; www.vratislavskydum.cz; cnr Masarykovo náměstí 97 & Březanova; pizza 90-160Kč, mains 140-250Kč; ⊙10.30am-10pm; 🛜🖉) The name is 'Fish & Steak', but giant, thin-crust pizzas are the name of the game here. Have your slice outside in main-square splendour or head inside to enjoy the vaulted ceiling and colourful decor. The fish and meat dishes are also very good. There's a late-night pub below ground where you can continue on after the meal.

⭐ŠUPINA & ŠUPINKA SEAFOOD €€
(🖉384 721 149; www.supina.cz; Valy 155; mains 150-450Kč; ⊙10.30am-11pm; 🖐🛜) Many people come to Třeboň merely to eat here, possibly the best fish restaurant in southern Bohemia. There are two dining areas: Šupina is the fancier option, while Šupinka is cheaper and family-oriented. Both feature regional freshwater fish such as pike, trout, eel and Třeboň carp. The *kapří hranolky,* pieces of carp battered and fried, are a national treasure.

ROŽMBERSKÁ BAŠTA CZECH €€
(🖉731 175 902; www.rozmberska-basta.cz; Rožmberská 59; mains 170-290Kč; ⊙11am-10pm; 🖐) You'll find good fish dishes at this homespun little restaurant, on a quiet side street near the main square. The speciality here is grilled or fried pikeperch. There's an open-air terrace out the back in summer.

ZBROJNICE PUB
(Bohemia Regent Brewery; 🖉722 347 606; www.fajnhospoda.cz/zbrojnice; Trocnovské náměstí 124; ⊙3-10pm) The Bohemia Regent Brewery is home to a few watering holes, including this smoky beer cellar just near the main gate. There's also a cafe/pub on the ground floor and an open-air terrace at the back. A half-litre of beer here is cheaper – and better – than in Prague; our favourite is the Regent 11° light lager.

🛏 SLEEPING

PENZION MODRÁ RŮŽE PENSION €
(🖉603 768 819; www.modra-ruze.cz; Rožmberská 39; s 450-740Kč, d 720-1000Kč; 🖐@🛜) With super-helpful owners providing loads of local information, this pension on a quiet lane is one of Třeboň's best. It's often busy, so it pays to book ahead. The rooms are simple but comfortable.

BÍLÝ KONÍČEK HOTEL €
(🖉724 734 525; www.bilykonicekhotel.cz; Masarykovo náměstí 97; s/d 1000/1200Kč; 🅿) An attractive Renaissance facade hides what's only an ordinary hotel, but the location can't be beaten and the price is fair for what you get. The rooms are unadorned and on the small side. There's free parking at the rear and a decent restaurant downstairs, serving basic Czech food.

APARTMÁNY ŠUPINA APARTMENTS €€
(Supina Apartments; 🖉720 993 825; www.supina.cz; Valy 155; s/d/tr 1400/2400/3400Kč; 🅿🖐🛜) Four well-appointed apartments are available for short-term rental. The units are light and airy, with comfy beds and wooden floors. Some offer small kitchen units for self-catering. One apartment, the 'Svět,' can sleep up to five people.

HOTEL ZLATÁ HVĚZDA   HOTEL €€

(☑384 757 111; www.zlatahvezda.cz; Masarykovo náměstí 107; s/d incl breakfast 1400/2400Kč; P ⊖ @ 🛜) Třeboň's smartest offering has flash rooms, a small bowling alley, and a spa centre, all in a 430-year-old building on the main square. The helpful reception desk serves as a tourist information office and can suggest good hikes and cycling tours. Bikes for hire (per day 300Kč).

☆ ENTERTAINMENT

KINO SVĚTOZOR   CINEMA

(☑384 722 850; www.kinotrebon.cz; Masarykovo náměstí 103) Screens Hollywood movies.

🏃 SPORTS & ACTIVITIES

The area around Třeboň is dotted with literally hundreds of fish ponds, many dating back several centuries. Eating fish is near and dear to the hearts of land-locked Czechs; the most important meal of the year, Christmas Eve, is centred around carp, and much of the nation's carp is raised here.

Much of the area has been designated as a protected landscape and is good for walks. One of the main fish ponds, **Rybník Svět** (Svět Pond), is an easy 10-minute walk south of Třeboň's central square. A 12km leisurely route runs around Rybník Svět on a well-marked trail (around four hours), beginning just south of the Regent Brewery. The trail is flagged with 16 information boards in Czech, German and English, and also takes in the Schwarzenberg Mausoleum. Ask at the Tourist Information Centre for a map; it also has details on other walks in the area and can help with bike-hire info.

Part of the edge of the pond is lined with working fish foundries, where you can see how the fish are stored and harvested for that all-important Christmas meal (the carp are fried and served with potato salad, while inedible bits are boiled to make carp soup).

Another good walk begins at Masarykovo náměstí. Follow the blue-marked trail northeast to **Na Kopečku** (1.5km, 30 minutes). From Na Kopečku, keep on the blue-marked trail to **Hodějov Pond** (7.5km, 2½ hours). A yellow trail then runs west to

Smítka (2km, 45 minutes) where it joins a red trail heading north to **Klec** and a primitive campground (6km, two hours).

From there, for a further 13km (four hours), the red trail runs north, past more fish ponds, forests and small villages to Veselí nad Lužnicí, a major railway junction. Camping is allowed only in official campgrounds throughout the protected landscape region.

Tábor

Explore

The town of Tábor, south of Prague, earned its place in Czech history in the 15th century as home to the most radical wing of the Hussite movement. These days, there aren't many radicals left, but Tábor makes for a convenient lunch-and-a-stroll stopover on the trip south towards České Budějovice and Český Krumlov. The most interesting sights here are Hussite-related: there's an educational museum on Hussite history, and some of the town's centuries-old underground passages have been opened to the public.

The Best...

➡ **Sight** Underground Passages (p218)
➡ **Place to Eat** Goldie (p219)
➡ **Place to Drink** MP7 (p219)

Top Tip

Tábor's Old Town is a beautifully preserved medieval townscape. Be sure to leave time for some aimless wandering through the labyrinth of cobbled lanes. The confusing street plan was originally devised to thwart invaders; these days it serves mainly to charm visitors.

Getting There & Away

➡ **Train** From Prague, regular trains depart from the main station (145Kč, 1½ hours), but they are generally more expensive and less convenient than the bus. Tábor's train station is 1km east of the historic centre, near the bus station.

➡ **Bus** There's regular bus service from Prague's Roztyly station (90Kč, two hours),

Tábor

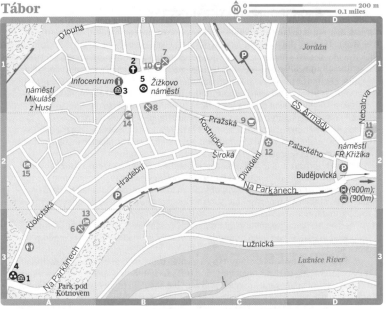

Tábor

⊙ Sights

⊗ Eating

⊙ Drinking & Nightlife

⊗ Entertainment

⊜ Sleeping

a stop along metro line C (red). Tábor's bus station is 1km east of the historic centre.

➡ **Car** By car from Prague, the drive to Tábor takes 90 minutes. Take the D1 motorway in the direction of Brno, bearing south on Hwy E55 and follow the signs to Tábor.

Need to Know
➡ **Location** 90km south of Prague.

➡ **Infocentrum** (☎381 486 230; www.taborcz. eu; Žižkovo náměstí 2; ⊗8.30am-7pm Mon-Fri, 10am-4pm Sat & Sun May-Sep, 9am-4pm Mon-Fri Oct-Apr) Books accommodation and rents audio guides.

➡ **Oberbank** (www.oberbank.cz; Pražská třída 211; ⊗8.30am-5pm Mon-Thu, to 2.30pm Fri) Centrally located ATM.

⊙ SIGHTS

ŽIŽKOVO NÁMĚSTÍ   SQUARE
Tabor's handsome main square is lined with late-Gothic, Renaissance and baroque houses. In the middle is a **fountain** (1567)

A LITTLE BACKGROUND ON THE HUSSITES

Tábor is often regarded as the spiritual home of the radical Hussite movement, but who exactly were the Hussites and what did they stand for?

The movement's history can be traced back to the 15th century and the decision by Catholic authorities to execute Czech religious reformer Jan Hus, who was famously burned at the stake in Constance, Germany, in 1415. The consequences of this act were far greater than the Catholic authorities could have foreseen. Hus's death caused a religious revolt among the Czechs, who had viewed his decision to preach in Czech language as a step towards religious and national self-determination.

Hus himself had not intended such a drastic revolution, focusing on a translation of the Latin rite, and the giving of bread and wine to all the congregation instead of to the clergy alone. But for many, the time was ripe for church reform.

Hus was born around 1372 in Husinec, in southern Bohemia. From a poor background, he managed to become a lecturer at Charles University in Prague and in 1402 was ordained a preacher. He dreamt of a return to the original doctrines of the church – tolerance, humility, simplicity – but such a message had political overtones for a church that treated forgiveness as an opportunity to make money.

Tried on a trumped-up charge of heresy at Constance, Hus's execution was doubly unjust in that he had been granted safe conduct by the Holy Roman Emperor Sigismund.

In Bohemia many nobles offered to guarantee protection to those who practised religion according to Hus's teachings, and Hussite committees became widespread. The movement split over its relationship with the secular authorities, with the moderate Utraquists siding in 1434 with the Catholic Sigismund.

The more radical Taborites, seeing themselves as God's warriors, fought the Catholics in every way. As the military base for the Hussites, Tábor – named after the biblical Mt Tábor – was successfully defended by a mainly peasant army under the brilliant Jan Žižka and Prokop Holý.

The movement also attracted supporters from other Protestant sects in Europe. Many converged on Tábor and the groups joined against the crusading armies of the Holy Roman Empire.

Hussite ideals were never fully extinguished in Bohemia. Although the Utraquists became the dominant force after defeating (with the help of Sigismund's Catholic forces) the Taborites at the Battle of Lipany in 1434, the resulting peace guaranteed religious freedom for the movement. It took almost 200 years before Protestantism was fully suppressed in the Czech lands by the Catholic Habsburg rulers following the Battle of White Mountain, near Prague, in 1620.

and a commanding **statue** of the Hussite leader Jan Žižka, after whom the square is named. The two **stone tables** in front of the Hussite Museum on the square's western end may have been used by the Hussites for religious services.

HUSSITE MUSEUM   MUSEUM
(Husitské muzeum; ☎381 254 286; www.husitskemuzeum.cz; Žižkovo náměstí 1; adult/concession 60/40Kč; ☺9am-5pm daily Apr-Oct, Wed-Sat Nov-Mar) Situated in Tábor's former late-Gothic **Town Hall** (Stará radnice) this museum traces the origins and history of the Hussite movement in the Czech Republic. Here you'll also find the

entrance to underground tunnels below the Old Town.

UNDERGROUND PASSAGES   UNDERGROUND
(Podzemní Chodby; ☎381 254 286; www.husitskemuzeum.cz; Žižkovo náměstí 1; adult/concession 50/30Kč; ☺9am-5pm daily Apr-Oct, Wed-Sat Nov-Mar) At the former Town Hall (which is now the Hussite Museum), you'll find the entrance to a fascinating 650m stretch of underground passageways, which you can visit by guided tour only. The passages, constructed in the 15th century as refuges during fires and times of war, were also used to store food and to mature beer.

DEAN CHURCH OF THE LORD'S TRANSFIGURATION ON MT TÁBOR
CHURCH, TOWER

(Děkanský Kostel Proměnění Páně na hoře Tábor; ☑381 251 226; Žižkovo náměstí; tower adult/concession 50/30Kč; ☺tower 10am-5pm daily Apr-Aug, Sat & Sun Sep-Oct) There has been a church here, on the square's northern side, for several centuries. This church dates from the middle of the 15th century and replaced a wooden structure. The basic style is Gothic, though reconstructions over the years have added Renaissance and baroque elements. The tower soars some 75m (200 steps) and offers sweeping views over Tábor.

KOTNOV CASTLE
RUIN, TOWER

(Hrad Kotnov; ☑381 252 788; www.husitskemuzeum.cz; Klokotská; tower adult/concession 20/10Kč; ☺tower 9am-5pm daily May-Sep, 1-5pm Sat & Sun Apr & Oct) Kotnov castle, marking the oldest site in Tábor, was founded in the 12th century. It was destroyed by fire in 1532 and in the 17th century the ruins were transformed into a brewery. The remnant 15th-century **Kotnov Tower** can be climbed from the adjoining **Bechyně Gate** for a broad view of the city and the Lužnice River.

BECHYNĚ GATE
MUSEUM

(Bechyňská brána; ☑381 252 788; www.husitskemuzeum.cz; Klokotská; adult/concession 40/20Kč; ☺9am-5pm daily May-Sep, 1-5pm Sat & Sun Apr & Oct) The Bechyně Gate, just next to the remains of **Kotnov Castle**, is the last of the town's original Gothic portals to remain standing and still retains the look it had some 500 years ago. It houses a small museum with a permanent exhibition entitled 'Life & Work in Medieval Society', focused mainly on how peasants lived.

EATING & DRINKING

U ZLATÉHO LVA
CZECH, PIZZA €

(The Golden Lion; ☑381 252 397; Žižkovo náměstí 16; mains 120-230Kč; ☺11am-10pm; ☎) From the outside, an ordinary-looking pub serving Budweiser beer from České Budějovice, but locals know it for the excellent, Italian-inspired thin-crust pizza, using fresh ingredients and authentic mozzarella cheese.

★GOLDIE
CZECH €€

(☑380 900 900; www.hotelnautilus.cz; Žižkovo náměstí 20; mains 250-400Kč; ☺☎☑) The house restaurant of the nicest hotel in town also happens to be head and shoulders above everything else around. Head chef Martin Svatek has built a menu around traditional Czech mains such as duck, rabbit and even horse cheeks, but given a lighter touch. It's frequently named on national 'Top 10' lists. Dress up and book in advance in summer.

TANDOOR
INDIAN €€

(Indická Restaurace; ☑381 213 250; www.tabor.indicka.cz; Žižkovo náměstí 8; mains 170-260Kč; ☺11am-10pm Mon-Sat; ☺☎☑) Tábor's highly regarded Indian restaurant offers a spicy alternative to the schnitzels and pizzas on offer at most other places in town, and has a large and delicious section devoted to vegetarian food. Enjoy quality curries and tandoor dishes in a casual, smoke-free environment.

DVOŘÁK
CZECH €€

(☑381 207 211; www.dvoraktabor.cz; Hradební 3037; mains 240-360Kč; ☺☎) One of the better dining choices around town is the restaurant of the Hotel Dvořák (p220), which takes its food seriously indeed. The menu is filled with relatively rare treasures such as venison, duck and rabbit, and each main course is paired with a wine recommendation.

MOCCACAFE
CAFE

(☑725 542 239; www.moccacafe.cz; Pražská 232; ☺9am-7pm Mon-Sat, 10.30am-6.30pm Sun; ☎) You won't find a better cup of coffee anywhere in town, or for miles around for that matter. Moccacafe uses specially roasted beans. It also serves excellent cakes and a wide variety of high-end ice cream. An ideal spot to plant yourself after a day spent hiking around the Old Town.

MP7
BAR

(☑606 856 994; www.facebook.com/cafemp7; Žižkovo náměstí 7; ☺2pm-noon Mon-Thu, to 2am Fri & Sat, to 11pm Sun; ☎) Dance music, jazz, reggae and house all occasionally feature at this art gallery/garden cafe/cocktail bar. It's a good spot to ask about live gigs around town, too.

TÁBOR'S HERO: JAN ŽIŽKA

Hussite Count Jan Žižka, the legendary blind general, was born in Trocnov, just outside České Budějovice, in 1376. He spent his youth at King Wenceslas IV's court and fought as a mercenary in Poland, but returned to the Czech kingdom at the beginning of the Reformation and became the leader of the radical wing of the Hussite movement, the Taborites. His military genius was responsible for all of the Hussite victories, from the 1420 Battle of Žižkov onwards. After losing both eyes in two separate battles, Žižka eventually died of the plague in 1424.

Žižka's army was highly organised and was the first to use a system of wagons with mounted artillery – the earliest tanks in history. These vehicles allowed him to choose where to draw up position, taking the initiative away from the crusaders and making them fight where he wanted. The technique proved almost invincible.

The Hussites successfully held off their enemies for a decade following Žižka's death, but were defeated by a combined army of the rival Hussite faction of the Utraquists and the Holy Roman Empire in 1434. Surprisingly, Žižka's invention was not incorporated into other armies until Sweden's King Gustavus II Adolphus adopted it two centuries later.

🛏 SLEEPING

★ STAROMĚSTSKÝ PENZION — PENSION €

(☎605 538 998; www.staromestsky-penzion.com; Křížová 8; s/d/ste 800/1300/2200Kč; ☺) Nothing fancy here, just a well-run, spotlessly clean pension on a quiet street a few metres away from the main square. There are just four rooms, including a suite that sleeps up to four, so you'll have to book well in advance in summer. Be sure to drop the owners an email ahead of arrival so they can be there to meet you at the door.

HOTEL NAUTILUS — BOUTIQUE HOTEL €€

(☎380 900 900; www.hotelnautilus.cz; Žižkovo náměstí 20; s/d from 2250/2700Kč; ℗☺✳🖳🛜) From the effortlessly cool bar to the elegant rooms decorated with original art, Tábor's first and only real boutique hotel is pure class, and surprisingly affordable for such international ambience right on the main square. Maybe it's time for a bit of a splurge?

HOTEL DVOŘÁK — HOTEL €€

(☎381 207 211; www.dvoraktabor.cz; Hradební 3037; s/d 1850/2350Kč; ℗☺@🛜) The Dvořák occupies a renovated former brewery, just near to the Kotnov Tower and just a short walk from the town centre. The hotel boasts a spa and wellness centre (with special beer massages) as well as clean, fashionable rooms and one of the city's best restaurants. Good value for money.

☆ ENTERTAINMENT

OSKAR NEDBAL THEATRE — THEATRE, LIVE MUSIC

(Divadlo Oskara Nedbala; ☎box office 381 254 070; www.divadlotabor.cz; Divadelní 218; ☺box office 3-6pm Mon-Fri, plus 1 hour before performances) Everything from jazz and classical music to Czech theatre.

KINO SVĚT — CINEMA

(☎381 252 200; www.kinosvettabor.cz; náměstí FR Křižíka 129; ☺cafe 1-10.30pm Mon-Thu, 1pm-1am Fri, 3pm-midnight Sat, 3-10pm Sun) See Hollywood favourites and chat about them after at the laid-back cafe next door.

Plzeň

Explore

Plzeň, the second-biggest city in Bohemia after Prague and the European Union's 'Cultural Capital' selection for 2015, is best known as the birthplace of Pilsner Urquell beer, but as the EU obviously knows, the city's charms run much deeper. In Plzeň's case, literally deeper: exploring the city's extensive underground tunnels is worth the trip here alone. The new Techmania Science Centre joins the zoo and puppet museum to make this a kid-friendly destination as well. The city is close enough to Prague to do in a long day trip, but you'll enjoy the outing much more if you plan to spend the night.

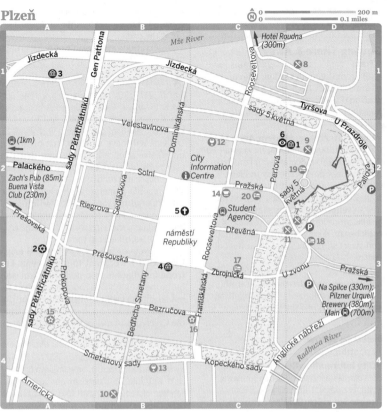

Plzeň

◎ Sights

1 Brewery Museum D2
2 Great Synagogue A3
3 Patton Memorial Pilsen A1
4 Puppet Museum B3
5 St Bartholomew Church B2
6 Underground Plzeň C2

⊗ Eating

7 Aberdeen Angus Steakhouse D3
8 Groll Pivovar D1
9 Na Parkánu D2
10 Slunečnice B4
11 U Mansfelda D3

◉ Drinking & Nightlife

12 Galerie Azyl C2
13 Měšťanská Beseda B4
14 Olala Cafe C2

◉ Entertainment

15 JK Tyla Theatre A4
16 Music Bar Anděl C4

⊜ Sleeping

17 Hotel Rous C3
18 Hotel U Zvonu D3
19 Pension City D2
20 U Salzmannů C2

The Best...

➡ **Sight** Pilsner Urquell Brewery (p222)
➡ **Place to Eat** Na Parkánu (p223)
➡ **Place to Drink** Na Spilce (p223)

Top Tip

Plzeň's designation as EU Cultural Capital in 2015 has brought more visitors to the city and put a strain on hotel rooms. Try to plan and book in advance. The website www.plzen2015.eu provides a good listing for what's on.

Getting There & Away

➜**Train** From Prague, several trains leave daily from the main station, Hlavní nádraží (150Kč, 1½ hours). Plzeň's **train station** (Plzeň hlavní nádraží; www.cd.cz; Nádražní 102) is 1km east of the historic centre.

➜**Bus** From Prague, **Student Agency** (☑841 101 101; www.studentagency.cz; náměstí Republiky 9; ☉9am-6pm Mon-Fri) runs half-hourly buses during the day to Plzeň (100Kč, one hour). Most buses leave Prague from Zličín station, the last stop on metro line B (yellow). Plzeň **bus station** (Centrální autobusové nádraží/CAN; ☑377 237 237; www.csadplzen.cz; Husova 60), marked on maps and street signs as CAN, is 1km west of the centre.

➜**Car** The drive to Plzeň from Prague takes around one hour, depending on traffic, mostly along a four-lane highway. It's a straight shot down the D5 motorway.

Need to Know

➜**Location** 100km southwest of Prague.

➜**City Information Centre** (Informační centrum města Plzně; ☑378 035 330; www.icpilsen.cz; náměstí Republiky 41; ☉9am-7pm Apr-Sep, to 6pm Oct-Mar) Arranges accommodation, organises guides, and sells maps and transport tickets. There's also a **branch** (☑378 035 330; www.icpilsen.cz; Nádražní 102; ☉9am-7pm Apr-Sep, to 6pm Oct-Mar) at the train station.

➜**Internet Cafe Neila** (☑728 852 172; www.neila.cz; Palackého nám 24; per 5 min 5Kč; ☉9am-10pm Mon-Fri, 2pm-9pm Sat & Sun; ☎) has computers to surf the web.

◉ SIGHTS

★**PILSNER URQUELL BREWERY**   BREWERY
(Prazdroj; ☑377 062 888; www.prazdrojvisit.cz; U Prazdroje 7; guided tour adult/child 190/100Kč; ☉8.30am-6pm Apr-Sep, to 5pm Oct-Mar; English tours 12.45pm, 2.15pm & 4.15pm) Plzeň's most popular attraction is the tour of the Pilsner Urquell Brewery, in operation since 1842 and arguably home to the world's best beer. Entry is by guided tour only, with three tours in English available daily. Tour highlights include a trip to the old cellars (dress warmly) and a glass of unpasteurised nectar at the end.

Reservations are possible only for groups of 10 or more. Email the brewery to arrange.

★**TECHMANIA SCIENCE CENTRE**   MUSEUM
(☑737 247 585; www.techmania.cz; cnr Borská & Břeňkova, Areál Škoda; adult/concession incl 3D planetarium 180/110Kč; ☉8.30am-5pm Mon-Fri, 10am-6pm Sat & Sun; ℗☎☢; ☒15, 17) Kids will have a ball at this high-tech, interactive science centre, where they can play with infrared cameras, magnets and many other instructive and fun exhibitions. There's a 3D planetarium (included in the full-price admission) and a few full-sized historic trams and trains manufactured at the Škoda engineering works. Take the trolleybus; it's a hike from the centre.

Art lovers or fans of Czech visual artist David Černý will want to see his epic **Entropa** installation, mounted on a giant wall in the main exhibition room. It's a subtle (or not so subtle) critique of the European Union and originally hung in Brussels during the Czech presidency of the EU in 2009.

UNDERGROUND PLZEŇ   UNDERGROUND
(Plzeňské historické podzemí; ☑377 235 574; www.plzenskepodzemi.cz; Veleslavínova 6; adult/child 100/70Kč; ☉10am-6pm Apr-Dec, to 5pm Feb-Mar, closed Jan; English tour 1pm daily Apr-Oct) This extraordinary tour explores the passageways below the old city. The earliest were probably dug in the 14th century, perhaps for beer production or defence; the latest date from the 19th century. Of an estimated 11km that have been excavated, some 500m of tunnels are open to the public. Bring extra clothing (it's a chilly 10°C underground).

Plzeň's wealthier set used to have wells in their cellars. Overuse led to severe water shortages. When wells dried up they were often filled with rubbish and buried; these have yielded an amazing trove of artefacts. English-language audioguides are available in case you miss the English tour.

BREWERY MUSEUM   MUSEUM
(☑377 224 955; www.prazdrojvisit.cz; Veleslavínova 6; adult/child guided tour 120/90Kč, English text 90/60Kč; ☉10am-6pm Apr-Dec, to 5pm Jan-Mar) The Brewery Museum offers an insight into how beer was made (and drunk) in the days before Prazdroj was founded. Highlights include a mock-up of a 19th-century

pub, a huge wooden beer tankard from Siberia and a collection of beer mats. All have English captions and there's a good English written guide available.

ST BARTHOLOMEW CHURCH   CHURCH

(Kostel Sv Bartoloměje; ☑377 226 098; www.katedralaplzen.org; náměstí Republiky; adult/concession church 20/10Kč, tower 35/25Kč; ☉10am-6pm Wed-Sat Apr-Sep, Wed-Fri Oct-Dec) Gigantic Gothic St Bartholomew Church looms over the surrounding facades from the centre of náměstí Republiky. Ask at the City Information Centre (p222) about guided tours. Look inside at the delicate marble 'Pilsen Madonna' (dating from c 1390) on the main altar, or climb the 301 steps to the top of the tower (weather permitting) for serious views.

PUPPET MUSEUM   MUSEUM

(Muzeum Loutek; ☑378 370 801; www.muzeumloutek.cz; náměstí Republiky 23; adult/concession 60/30Kč; ☉10am-6pm Tue-Sun; ⓗ) Plzeň's museum of marionettes and puppetry is well done and certainly worth a look in, especially if you're travelling with younger children. The exhibits are understandably heavy on Czech puppet tradition, but there's ample signage in English and even some impromptu puppet performances on hand to keep young ones interested.

GREAT SYNAGOGUE   SYNAGOGUE

(Velká Synagoga; ☑377 223 346; www.zoplzen.cz; sady Pětatřicátníků 11; adult/child 60/40Kč; ☉10am-6pm Sun-Fri Apr-Oct) The Great Synagogue, west of the Old Town, is the third-largest in the world – only those in Jerusalem and Budapest are bigger. It was built in the Moorish style in 1892 by the 2000 Jews who lived in Plzeň at the time. The building is now used for concerts and art exhibitions.

PATTON MEMORIAL PILSEN   MUSEUM

(☑378 037 954; www.patton-memorial.cz; Podřežni 10; adult/concession 60/40Kč; ☉9am-1pm & 2-5pm Tue-Sun) The Patton Memorial details the liberation of Plzeň in May 1945 by the American army, under General George S Patton. Especially poignant are the handwritten memories of former American soldiers who have returned to Plzeň over the years, and the museum's response to the communist-era revisionist fabrications that claimed Soviet troops, not Americans, were responsible for the city's liberation.

ZOO PLZEŇ   ZOO

(☑378 038 325; www.zooplzen.cz; Pod Vinicemi 9; adult/concession 140/100Kč; ☉8am-7pm Apr-Oct, 9am-5pm Nov-Mar; ⓗ; ☑1, 4) Plzeň's zoo is one of the best in the country, with a sizeable collection of exotic animals, including rhinos, hippos and giraffes. There are also camel and donkey rides for the kids. You can buy a combined-entry ticket (adult/concession 210/140Kč) for both the Zoo and DinoPark next door.

DINOPARK   THEME PARK

(☑378 774 636; www.dinopark.cz; Nad ZOO 1; adult/concession 90/60Kč; ☉8am-6pm Apr-Oct; ⓗ; ☑1, 4) This dinosaur park has life-sized replicas of some 30 dinosaurs, as well as films and playgrounds. You can buy a combined-entry ticket (adult/concession 210/140Kč) for both the DinoPark and the adjacent Zoo Plzeň.

✖ EATING & DRINKING

Plzeň is a good place to try a big pub meal, complete with excellent Pilsner Urquell beer. It's also a big student town, so there are plenty of good places to kick back afterwards with your beverage of choice.

NA PARKÁNU   CZECH €

(☑377 324 485; www.naparkanu.com; Veleslavínova 4; mains 100-200Kč; ☉11am-11pm Mon-Thu, to 1am Fri & Sat, to 10pm Sun; ☎) Don't overlook this pleasant pub/restaurant, attached to the Brewery Museum. It may look a bit touristy, but the traditional Czech food is top rate, and the beer, naturally, could hardly be better. Try to snag a spot in the summer garden. Don't leave without trying the *nefiltrované pivo* (unfiltered beer). Reservations are an absolute must.

NA SPILCE   CZECH €

(☑377 062 755; www.naspilce.com; U Prazdroje 7; mains 100-249Kč; ☉11am-10pm Sun-Thu, to 11pm Fri & Sat; ☎) The Pilsner Urquell Brewery (p222) tour often ends with a meal (and several more beers, naturally) at this pub, situated within the confines of the brewery itself. The traditional Czech cooking, such as venison stew flavoured with red wine, is reasonably priced and

WORTH A DETOUR

THE 'ELBOW' OF LOKET NAD OHŘE

Surrounded by a wickedly serpentine loop in the Ohře River, the picturesque village of **Loket** may as well be on an island. According to the local tourist office, it was Goethe's favourite town and, after a lazily subdued stroll around the gorgeous main square and castle, it may be yours as well.

Loket's German name is **Elbogen** (meaning 'elbow', after the extreme bend in the river) – a name synonymous with the manufacturing of porcelain since 1815. Shops in town have a fine selection of the local craftsmanship. The neighbouring towns of Horní Slavkov (Schlackenwald) and Chodov (Chodan) also make porcelain.

Most people visit Loket as a day trip from Karlovy Vary, but it's also a sleepy place to ease off the travel accelerator for a few days, especially when the day-trippers have departed. Loket also makes a good base for visiting Karlovy Vary: the bus to/from Karlovy Vary (30Kč) stops across the bridge into the Old Town. Walk across the bridge to reach the castle, accommodation and **Infocentrum** (Loket Information Centre; ☑352 684 123; www.loket.cz; TG Masaryka 12; ☉10.30am-12.30pm & 1-5pm Tue-Sat Jan-Mar, to 5.30pm Apr-Dec), which hands out maps and can advise on transport and sightseeing options.

The main site in town is the beautiful castle, **Hrad Loket** (Loket Castle; ☑352 684 648; www.hradloket.cz; Hrad; adult/concession with English guide 110/90Kč, with English text 95/75Kč; ☉9am-4.30pm Apr-Oct, to 3.30pm Nov-Mar). It was built on the site of an earlier Romanesque fort, of which the only surviving bits are the tall, square tower and fragments of a rotunda and palace.

The castle was regarded as very defensively secure in earlier times, and was known as 'the key to Bohemia'. Its present late-Gothic look dates from the late 14th century. From 1788 to 1947 it was used as the town prison. Highlights of the tour include two rooms filled with the town's lustrous porcelain and views from the castle tower (96 steps). There's also a gleefully gruesome torture chamber, complete with stereophonic sound effects.

Ask at the Infocentrum about hiking possibilities in the surrounding forests, including a semi-ambitious day hike to Karlovy Vary (around four hours) along a 17km blue-marked trail. Karlovy Vary is also the destination for rafting trips.

There are several decent pensions in town. The nicest hotel is the **Hotel Císař Ferdinand** (☑352 327 130; www.hotel-loket.cz; TG Masaryka 136; s/d 1300/1850Kč; ℗ ☉ ☎ ☀), right across from the Infocentrum. This former post office has recently renovated rooms and the best little microbrewery in town.

---

well above average, and the beer is fresh from tanks next door.

U MANSFELDA
CZECH €

(☑377 333 844; www.umansfelda.cz; Dřevěná 9; mains 155-229Kč; ☉11am-11pm Mon-Thu, 11am-midnight Fri & Sat, noon-10pm Sun; ☎) Sure, it's a pub – remember you're in Plzeň now – but it's also more refined and has more interesting food than many other places. Try Czech cuisine such as wild boar *gulaš* (spicy meat and potato soup). Downstairs from the beer-fuelled terrace is a more relaxed *vinárna* (wine bar).

SLUNEČNICE
VEGETARIAN €

(☑377 236 093; www.slunecniceplzen.cz; Jungmannova 4; mains 109-189Kč; ☉11am-11pm Mon-Sat, to 8pm Sun; ☎☎) This casual restaurant specialises in organic and healthy foods, including many vegetarian entrees such as quesadillas with spinach, vegie pastas and burgers made from tempeh.

ABERDEEN ANGUS STEAKHOUSE
STEAKHOUSE €€

(☑725 555 631; www.angussteakhouse.cz; Pražská 23; mains 180-400Kč; ☉11am-11pm; ☎☎) For our money, this may be the best steakhouse in all of the Czech Republic. The meats hail from a nearby farm, where the livestock is raised organically. There are several cuts and sizes on offer; lunch options include a tantalising cheeseburger. The downstairs dining room is cosy; there's also a creekside terrace. Book in advance.

GROLL PIVOVAR   CZECH €€

(☑602 596 161; www.pivovargroll.cz; Truhlářska 10; mains 150-270Kč) If you've come to Plzeň on a beer pilgrimage, then another essential visit is for a beer-garden lunch at this spiffy microbrewery. Meals include well-priced steaks and salads. The highlight is the drinks menu: homemade light and dark beers, including a very good 11° nonfiltered, nonpasteurised light lager.

★ MĚŠŤANSKÁ BESEDA   PUB

(☑378 035 415; http://web.mestanska-beseda.cz; Kopeckého sady 13; ⊘9am-10pm Mon-Fri, 11am-10pm Sat & Sun; ☎) Cool heritage cafe, sunny beer garden, expansive exhibition space and occasional arthouse cinema – Měšťanská Beseda is hands-down Plzeň's most versatile venue. The beautifully restored 19th-century pub is perfect for a leisurely beer or cafe. Check out who's performing at the attached theatre.

OLALA CAFE   CAFE

(☑378 609 699; www.olalacafe.cz; Pražská 2; ⊘8am-10pm Mon-Fri, 9am-10pm Sat, 9am-9pm Sun; ☎) Clean, modern cafe right on the central square that's a lifesaver if you need a strong cup and/or good wi-fi. They also have a nice selection of cakes, sweets and ice cream dishes.

GALERIE AZYL   BAR

(☑377 235 507; www.galerieazyl.cz; Veleslavínova 17; ⊘8am-11pm Mon-Thu, 8am-1am Fri, 4pm-1am Sat, 4-10pm Sun; ☎) Locals kick-off the day with the excellent espresso here. Later in the day, Galerie Azyl morphs into Plzeň's classiest cocktail bar. Quirky artwork surrounds conversation-friendly booths.

 **SLEEPING**

HOTEL ROUDNA   HOTEL €

(☑377 259 926; www.hotelroudna.cz; Na Roudné 13; s/d 1150-1400Kč; P@☎) Might very well be the city's best-value lodging. The exterior is not much to look at; but inside rooms are well-proportioned, with high-end amenities such as flatscreen TVs, minibars and desks. Breakfasts are fresh and ample. The reception is friendly. Note there's no lift. The hotel has an excellent steakhouse two doors down on the same street.

U SALZMANNŮ   PENSION €

(☑377 235 476; www.usalzmannu.com; Pražská 8; s/d 1050/1450Kč, ste 2100Kč; ⊖☎) This pleasant pension, right in the heart of town, sits above a very good historic pub. The standard rooms are comfortable but basic; the more luxurious double 'suites' have antique beds and small sitting rooms, as well as kitchenettes. The pub location is convenient if you overdo it; to reach your bed, just climb the stairs.

PENSION CITY   PENSION €

(☑377 326 069; www.pensioncityplzen.cz; Sady 5. kvetna 52; s/d 1050/1450Kč; ⊖☎) On a quiet street near the river, Pension City has comfortable rooms and friendly, English-speaking staff armed with lots of local information.

HOTEL ROUS   BOUTIQUE HOTEL €€

(☑602 320 294; www.hotelrous.cz; Zbrojnicka 113/7; s/d from 1600/2200Kč; P@☎) This 600-year-old building incorporates the warmth of the original stone walls with modern furnishings. Bathrooms are art deco cool in black and white. Breakfast is taken in a garden cafe concealed amid remnants of Plzeň's defensive walls. Downstairs, the Caffe Emily serves very good coffee.

HOTEL U ZVONU   HOTEL €€

(☑378 011 855; www.hotel-uzvonu.cz; Pražská 27; s/d 1825/2750Kč; P⊖✳@☎) This place is similar to a high-end chain in that it's super clean and modern. It's also conveniently located, close to all the main sights. The rooms are spacious and well-endowed: some are equipped with small kitchenettes, and one room is barrier-free for disabled access. There's ample parking out front.

☆ **ENTERTAINMENT**

ZACH'S PUB   LIVE MUSIC

(☑377 223 176; www.zachspub.cz; Kollárova 6; ⊘1pm-1am Mon-Thu, 1pm-2am Fri, 5pm-2am Sat, 5pm to midnight Sun) Head to Zach's, about a 15-minute walk west of the city centre, for live music and a suitably student atmosphere. There's a big garden for open-air drinking in summer.

BEST OF BOHEMIA PLZEŇ

BUENA VISTA CLUB   LIVE MUSIC

(☑377 921 291; www.buenavistaclub.cz; Kollárova 20; concert tickets 100-200Kč; ⊙11am-3am Mon-Sat; 🎧) This funky multipurpose space, in a studenty area filled with pubs, hosts everything from emerging Czech live acts to an eclectic range of DJs. English-language movies are occasionally screened.

MUSIC BAR ANDĚL   LIVE MUSIC

(☑377 323 226; www.andelcafe.cz; Bezručova 7; tickets for shows 50-200Kč; ⊙7.30am-midnight Mon-Fri, 9am-1am Sat, 11am-10am Sun; 🎧) By day a cool, hip cafe, the Anděl is transformed after dark into a rocking live-music venue featuring the best of touring Czech bands and occasional international acts. It also has a good vegetarian menu.

JK TYLA THEATRE   THEATRE

(☑box office 378 038 190; www.djkt-plzen.cz; Prokopova 14; performances 130-400Kč; ⊙9am-6pm Mon-Fri) Plzeň's main theatre stages regular Czech-language performances, as well as a mix of ballet, opera and classical music. Check the website for what's on during your visit. Buy tickets online, at the theatre box office or at the City Information Centre (p222).

Karlovy Vary

Explore

Karlovy Vary (Carlsbad), or simply 'Vary' to Czechs, has greatly stepped up its game in recent years, thanks largely to a property boom spurred by wealthy Russian investors. Indeed, the first thing you'll notice is the high number of Russian visitors, all following in the footsteps of Tsar Peter the Great, who stayed here for treatments in the early 18th century. Day-trippers come here to admire the grand 19th-century spa architecture and to stroll the impressive colonnades, sipping on allegedly health-restoring sulphuric compounds from ceramic, spouted drinking cups. Despite the exalted spa rep, Karlovy Vary is not entirely welcoming to walk-ins looking for high-end treatments such as exotic massages and peelings; these services are available but make sure to book in advance.

The Best...

➡**Sight** Hot Spring Colonnade (p227)

➡**Place to Eat** Charleston (p227)

➡**Place to Drink** Barracuda (p230)

Top Tip

The **Karlovy Vary International Film Festival** (www.kviff.com; ⊙Jul) is well worth attending. More than 200 films are shown, tickets are relatively easy to get, and there's a funky array of concurrent events (such as buskers, world-music concerts and more).

Getting There & Away

➡**Bus** Buses from Prague (160Kč, two hours) leave hourly during the day from the bus station. The most popular coach operator is **Student Agency** (☑841 101 101; www.studentagency.cz), which maintains a **branch** (☑353 176 333; www.studentagency. cz; T.G. Masaryka 58/34; ⊙9am-6pm Mon-Fri) in Karlovy Vary. Check www.vlak-bus.cz for a timetable.

➡**Train** From Prague, the train takes a circuitous route, which can take as long as seven hours. So unless you have nothing better to do, it's not recommended.

➡**Car** From Prague, Karlovy Vary is an easy two-hour drive due west, heading out of town on Hwy 6 (aka E48).

Need to Know

➡**Location** 127km west of Prague.

➡**Infocentrum Karlovy Vary** maintains two branches, one on **TG Masaryka** (Infocentrum TGM; ☑355 321 171; www. karlovyvary.cz; TG Masaryka 53; ⊙8am-6pm Mon-Fri, 9am-5pm Sat & Sun) in the city area, near the train and bus stations, and another on **Lázeňská** (Infocentrum Lázeňská; ☑355 321 176; www.karlovyvary. cz; Lázeňská 14; ⊙9am-5pm; 🎧) near the Hot Spring Colonnade in the main spa area. They both stocks maps, handle accommodation bookings and provide transport advice.

➡**Česká Spořitelna** (☑956 748 000; www. csas.cz; TG Masaryka 14; ⊙8.30am-4pm Mon-Fri) Centrally located ATM and currency exchange.

○ SIGHTS

HOT SPRING COLONNADE   SPRING
(Vřídelní kolonáda; www.karlovyvary.cz; ⊙6am-
7pm) **FREE** The Hot Spring Colonnade
houses the most impressive of the town's
geysers, **Pramen Vřídlo**. The building itself
is an an incongruous, mid-'70s structure
once dedicated to Soviet cosmonaut Yuri
Gagarin. The geyser belches some 15m into
the air; people lounge about inhaling the
vapours or sampling the waters from a line
of taps in the next room.

CHURCH OF MARY MAGDALENE   CHURCH
(Kostel sv Máří Magdaléná; ☑353 223 668;
www.farnost-kv.cz; náměstí Svobody 2; ⊙9am-
6pm) **FREE** Karlovy Vary's most important
Catholic church and one of its grandest
baroque buildings is this imposing, twin-
steepled structure in the heart of the spa.
The church dates from the 1730s and is the
work of baroque master Kilian Dientzenhofer, the architect of St Nicholas Church in
Prague's Malá Strana.

CHURCH OF STS PETER & PAUL   CHURCH
(Chrám svatých Petra a Pavla; ☑353 223 451;
Krále Jiřího; ⊙9am-6pm) **FREE** This impressive Orthodox Church, with five polished
onion domes and art nouveau exterior
murals, was apparently modelled after a
similar church near Moscow. One of the
church's most prominent decorations is a
relief depicting Tsar Peter the Great.

MOSER GLASS MUSEUM   MUSEUM
(Sklářské muzeum Moser; ☑353 416 132; www.
moser-glass.com; Kpt Jaroše 19; adult/child museum 80/50Kč, glassworks 120/70Kč, combined
ticket 180/100Kč; ⊙9am-5pm, glassworks to
2.30pm; ☑1) The Moser Glass Museum has
more than 2000 items on display. Tours
of the adjacent **glassworks** and combined
tickets are also available. There is a shop
here, too, but the prices are not anything
special, and there's another shop in town.
To get here catch bus 1 from the Tržnice bus
station.

JAN BECHER MUSEUM   MUSEUM
(☑359 578 142; www.becherovka.cz; TG Masaryka 57; adult/concession 120/60Kč; ⊙9am-5pm)
Jan Becher Museum deals with all things
Becherovka, the town's famed herbal liqueur. Entry is by guided tour only, which
must be booked in advance at the museum
cash desk. Most tours are in Czech or Rus-

sian, but there's at least one tour a day in
English.

KARLOVY VARY MUSEUM   MUSEUM
(Krajské muzeum Karlovy Vary; ☑353 226 253;
www.kvmuz.cz; Nová Louka 23; adult/concession
60/30Kč; ⊙9am-noon & 1-5pm Wed-Sun) The
Karlovy Vary Museum has extensive exhibits on the town's history as a spa resort,
Czech glasswork and the area's natural history.

✕ EATING & DRINKING

With a few notable exceptions listed here,
Karlovy Vary's dining scene is bland. Prices
tend to be higher in the spa area than in
other parts of town.

KUS KUS   VEGETARIAN €
(☑777 066 477; www.kus-kus.cz; Bělehradská 8;
mains 60-89Kč; ⊙7.30am-2pm Mon-Fri; ☻☑)
This cosy cafe-bakery serves salads, pasta
and homemade desserts with an organic
and vegetarian tinge. It offers daily vegetarian lunch mains such as soya noodles
or stuffed baked potatoes for 89Kč. Note
the limited menu and opening hours.

CHARLESTON   CZECH €€
(☑353 230 797; www.charleston-kv.cz; Bulharská
1; mains 159-420Kč; ⊙10am-midnight Mon-Sat,
from noon Sun; ☎) Karlovy Vary, alas, is not
a food paradise, but this 1920s-themed
restaurant just outside the spa area is the
best of the lot. In addition to stalwarts such
as roast pork, the menu lists more inventive mains such as venison ragout and a
true Wienerschnitzel (made from veal, not
pork). Book in advance as the seating area
is small.

TANDOOR   INDIAN €€
(☑608 701 341; www.tandoor-kv.cz; IP Pavlova
25; mains 150-270Kč; ⊙noon-10pm Mon-Sat, to
6pm Sun; ☑) Occupying a well-hidden location under a block of flats, Tandoor turns
out a winning combo of authentic Indian
flavours, Gambrinus beer and smooth,
creamy lassis. Vegetarian options abound,
or if you're after a serious chilli hit, order
the chicken *phall*.

HOSPODA U ŠVEJKA   CZECH €€
(☑353 232 276; www.svejk-kv.cz; Stará Louka 10;
mains 160-370Kč; ⊙11am-11pm) A great choice
for lunch or dinner, right in the heart of

Karlovy Vary

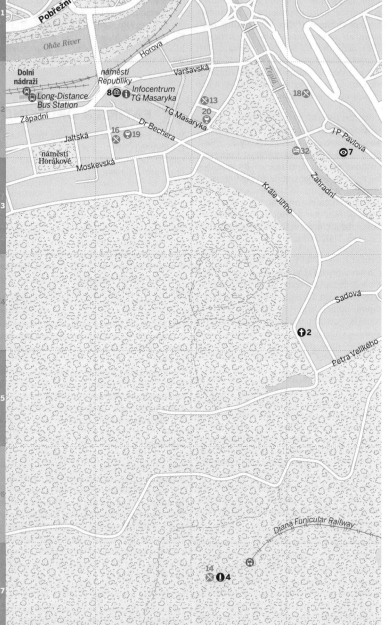

Kino Drahomíra
(500m)

Ohře River

Pobřežní

Horova

náměstí
Republiky

Varšavská

Dolní
nádraží

Long-Distance
Bus Station

8 Infocentrum
TG Masaryka

Západní

TG Masaryka

13

20

18

I P Pavlova

Jaltská

16 19

Dr Bechera

32

7

náměstí
Horákové

Moskevská

Krále Jiřího

Zahradní

Sadová

2

Petra Velikého

5

Diana Funicular Railway

14

4

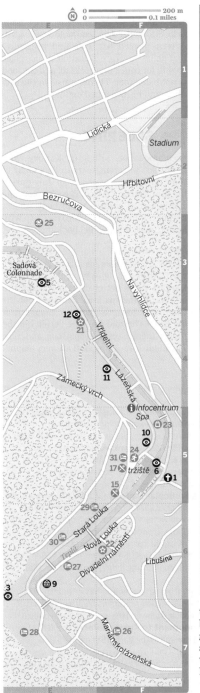

Karlovy Vary

Sights

1	Church of Mary Magdalene	F5
2	Church of Sts Peter & Paul	D4
3	Diana Funicular Railway	E6
4	Diana Lookout Tower	C7
5	Garden Colonnade	E3
6	Hot Spring Colonnade	F5
7	Hotel Thermal	D2
8	Jan Becher Museum	B2
9	Karlovy Vary Museum	E6
10	Market Colonnade	F5
11	Mill Colonnade	F4
12	Spa No 3	E4

Eating

13	Charleston	C2
14	Diana Restaurant	C7
	Embassy Restaurant	(see 27)
15	Hospoda U Švejka	F5
16	Kus Kus	B2
17	Promenáda	F5
18	Tandoor	D2

Drinking & Nightlife

19	Barracuda	B2
20	Retro Cafe Bar	C2

Entertainment

21	Karlovy Vary Symphony Orchestra	E4
22	Town Theatre	F6

Shopping

23	Moser Glasswork Shop	F5

Sports & Activities

24	Castle Spa	F5
25	Swimming Pool	E3

Sleeping

26	Carlsbad Plaza	F7
27	Embassy Hotel	E6
28	Grandhotel Pupp	E7
29	Hotel Boston	E6
30	Hotel Maltézsý Kříž	E6
31	Hotel Romance Puškin	F5
32	Hotel Romania	D2

the spa centre. Though the presentation borders on kitsch, the food is actually very good and the atmosphere not unlike a classic Czech pub. The only ouch factor comes when they bring the bill. A glass of beer here costs a whopping 75Kč.

PROMENÁDA
INTERNATIONAL €€€

(☑353 225 648; www.hotel-promenada.cz; Tržiště 31; mains 250-650Kč; ☺11am-11pm; ☻) The house restaurant of the Hotel Promenáda has appeared in some 'best of' lists for the Czech Republic and is a perennial favourite on online forums. The elegant dining area is conducive to a memorable evening, and the food is very good (though perhaps not always worth the steep prices).

EMBASSY RESTAURANT
CZECH €€€

(☑353 221 161; www.embassy.cz; Nová Louka 21; mains 250-500Kč; ☺11am-11pm) The in-house restaurant of the Embassy Hotel (p231) is a destination in its own right. The dining room is richly atmospheric and the food, mostly Czech standards such as roast pork or duck, is top notch. There's an excellent wine list, and in nice weather they sometimes offer outdoor seating.

BARRACUDA
COCKTAIL BAR

(☑608 100 640; www.barracuda-bar.cz; Jaltská 7; ☺7pm-1am Mon-Thu, to 3am Fri & Sat) This cocktail bar outside the spa area has been going strong for eight years, and is about the only place in town you can be assured of late-night drinking, dancing to cheesy DJs and all that goes with it.

RETRO CAFE BAR
BAR

(☑353 100 710; www.retrocafebar.cz; TG Masaryka 18; ☺10am-midnight Sun-Thu, to 3am Fri & Sat) A retro-themed bar, cafe and restaurant that defies easy categorisation. A nice place to chill for coffee or a cocktail, and the food is not bad either. There's music in the evenings and retro-themed nights.

🛏️ SLEEPING

Accommodation prices in Karlovy Vary have risen in recent years to be similar to those in Prague, especially in July during the film festival. Indeed, if you're planning a July arrival, make sure to book well in advance. Infocentrum (p226) can help with hostel, pension and hotel bookings.

HOTEL ROMANIA
HOTEL €

(☑353 222 822; www.romania.cz; Zahradni 49; s/d 1200/1650Kč; ⓟ☻☻) This is one of Karlovy Vary's better deals if you want to be close to the spa area. The view out the front door towards the ugly monolith of the Hotel Thermal could be better, but the rooms themselves are spacious and tidy. The English-speaking staff are very helpful.

HIKING THE HILLS OF KARLOVY VARY

Once you've wearied of walking around town and taking the waters, a scenic network of trails lies in the hills to the west of the main spa area waiting for exploration.

One of the most popular trails ascends 1.5km from just beside the Grandhotel Pupp (p231) to the hilltop **Diana Lookout Tower** (☑353 222 872; www.karlovy-vary.cz/en/diana-tower; ☺9am-7pm Jun-Sep, to 6pm Apr, May & Oct, to 5pm Feb, Mar, Nov & Dec) FREE . The woods on the way to the lookout are peppered with follies and monuments, a testament to the trail's popularity for several centuries.

If you'd like to skip the hike up, the **Diana Funicular Railway** (☑353 222 638; www.dpkv.cz; Mariánská; one-way/return adult 45/80Kč, child 25/40Kč; ☺9am-7pm Jun-Sep, to 6pm Apr, May & Oct, to 5pm Feb, Mar, Nov & Dec) can whisk you to the top from its base station just at the entrance to the trail, west of the Grandhotel Pupp. The trip takes about five minutes. Just next to the lookout tower, the rustic **Diana Restaurant** (☑777 774 040; www.dianakv.cz; Diana Lookout; mains 180-320Kč; ☺11am-7pm May-Sep, to 6pm Apr & Oct, to 5pm Nov-Mar; funicular), a former hunting lodge, is a great spot for lunch or a cup of coffee.

Stag's Leap (Jelení skok), the promontory from where legend has it that Charles IV, or rather his dogs, first discovered the town's healing waters, is 500m northeast from an intermediate stop on the Diana Funicular Railway. This is a wonderful photo-op spot and even sports an over-the-top **monument to Russia's Peter the Great**, who apparently greatly enjoyed his visits to the spa in the early 18th century.

If you're feeling energetic, it's a 15km hike on a blue-marked trail via the Diana Lookout Tower and along the Ohře River to the romantic castle and village of **Loket**.

HOTEL BOSTON
HOTEL €

(📞353 362 711; www.boston.cz; Luční vrch 9; s/d 1390/1500Kč; P🅿☺☎) Tucked away down a quiet lane, this family-owned hotel offers very good value, with spacious rooms decorated in bright colours and updated bathrooms. Upper-floor rooms have a view out the back towards the forest.

★ HOTEL ROMANCE PUŠKIN
HOTEL €€

(📞353 222 646; www.hotelromance.cz; Tržiště 37; s/d 2450/3450Kč; ☺☎) In a great location just across from the Hot Spring Colonnade, it has renovated rooms with fully updated baths and very comfortable beds. These are just some of the charms at one of the nicest midrange hotels in the spa area. The breakfast is a treat, the usual sausage and eggs is supplemented by inventive salads and smoked fish.

HOTEL MALTÉZSÝ KŘÍŽ
HOTEL €€

(📞353 169 011; www.maltezskykriz.cz; Stará Louka 50; s/d 1650/2800Kč; @☎) This small hotel on the promenade offers very good value, given its upmarket location in the heart of the spa area and the nicely appointed rooms with oriental rugs and wooden floors. The bathrooms are decked out in warm, earthy tones. Request an upper room over the promenade for the best views.

EMBASSY HOTEL
HOTEL €€

(📞353 221 161; www.embassy.cz; Nová Luka 21; s/d from 2260/3130Kč; ☺@☎) Karlovy Vary's not short of top-end hotels, but most lack the personal touch of the family-owned Embassy, with its riverside location and perfectly pitched rooms, some with canopy beds. The hotel's pub and restaurant have seen visits from plenty of film-fest luminaries.

GRANDHOTEL PUPP
HOTEL €€€

(📞353 109 631; www.pupp.cz; Mírové náměstí 2; r 4000-7000Kč; P🅿☀@☎🏊) The sumptuous 18th-century Pupp covers nearly the whole of the spa's southern end and drips Old World glamour. It was featured in the James Bond film *Casino Royale* and inspired Wes Anderson's *Grand Budapest Hotel*. These days, it's a budget-blower, but worth the splurge if you can snag one of the rooms in period style, but you have to ask.

Even if you're not staying here, take a peek inside; the restaurants are very good, and the historic atmosphere is perfect.

CARLSBAD PLAZA
HOTEL €€€

(📞353 225 501; www.carlsbadplaza.cz; Mariánskolázeňská 23; s/d 4000/6000Kč; P🅿☀@☎🏊) Seriously stylish, this relatively new hotel has raised the bar in spa town, with soothingly modern treatment facilities, classy rooms and a vegetarian-friendly Asian restaurant.

 ## ENTERTAINMENT

KARLOVY VARY
SYMPHONY ORCHESTRA
CLASSICAL MUSIC

(Karlovarský symfonický orchestr; 📞353 228 707; www.kso.cz; Mlýnské nábřeží 5, Spa No 3) The town's highly regarded orchestra stages a regular program of concerts; check the website for concerts during your visit. Concerts are held at **Spa No 3** (Lázně III; 📞353 242 500; www.lazneiii.cz; Mlýnské nábřeží 5) in the main spa area. You can buy tickets at the Infocentrum office (p226).

TOWN THEATRE
THEATRE

(Karlovarské městské divadlo; 📞box office 353 225 537; www.karlovarske-divadlo.cz; Divadelní náměstí 21; ☺box office noon-5.30pm) Drama, comedy and musicals all feature here. Tickets are available from the theatre box office or at the Infocentrum tourist offices.

KINO DRAHOMÍRA
CINEMA

(Kino Panasonic; 📞353 222 963; http://kinodrahomira.cz; Vitězná 50; ☺box office from 11am Mon-Fri, from 3pm Sat & Sun; ☎) A compact art-house cinema with a good cafe and free wi-fi access.

Mariánské Lázně

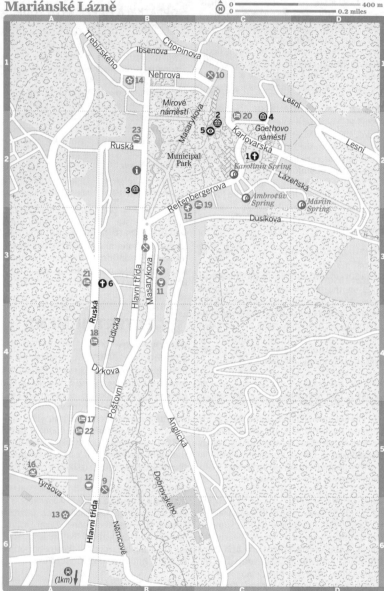

SPORTS & ACTIVITIES

CASTLE SPA SPA

(Zámecké Lázně; ☑353 225 502; www.zamecke
-lazne.com; Zámecký vrch 1; from 2000Kč for 4hr
treatment; ☉7.30am-7.30pm) Most Karlovy

Vary accommodation offers some kind of a
spa treatment for a fee, but if you're just a
casual visitor or day-tripper, consider Castle Spa, a modernised spa centre complete
with a subterranean thermal pool. Consult
the website for a full menu of treatments
and massages.

SWIMMING POOL SWIMMING
(☑359 001 111; www.thermal.cz; IP Pavlova 11;
adult/child 200/140Kč; ⊙10am-8pm Apr-Sep)
The 50m pool of Hotel Thermal is open
to the public from April through to September. The waters of the pool are heated
by thermal springs. To find it, follow the
'Bazén' signs up the hill behind the hotel
to the pool.

Mariánské Lázně

Explore

Mariánské Lázně (mari-*ahn*-skay *lahz*-nyeh; known internationally as Marienbad) is smaller, less urban and arguably prettier than Karlovy Vary, making it feel more like a classic spa destination (but also meaning there's even less to do in the evening). In the resort's heyday, Mariánské Lázně drew such luminaries as Goethe, Thomas Edison, Britain's King Edward VII and even American author Mark Twain. These days, many of its visitors are day-trippers from Germany, hauled in by coach to stroll the gardens and colonnades before repairing to a cafe for the inevitable *apfelstrudel*, then take the ride back home. Besides the colonnades themselves, the town is ringed by deep forests, which make for great walks.

The Best...

➡ **Sight** Colonnade (p234)
➡ **Place to Eat** Medité (p235)
➡ **Place to Drink** Irish Pub (p235)

Top Tip

If you're coming to Mariánské Lázně specifically for a spa treatment, be sure to book in advance: spas are ill-prepared for walk-ins. The website www.marienbad.cz has helpful lists of spas, treatments and prices.

Getting There & Away

➡ **Train** Several fast trains per day run from Prague (240Kč, three hours) via Plzeň. Regular (slow) trains link Mariánské Lázně and Karlovy Vary (63Kč, 1¾ hours). Trolleybuses 5 & 7 (12Kč) run from the station to the spa area, or you can walk (30 minutes).

➡ **Bus** Buses from Prague (180Kč, three hours) and Plzeň (120Kč, 1¼ hours) are less frequent (up to five per day) and take as long as the train.

➡ **Car** From Prague, the drive takes about two hours. Head southwest out of the city

---

Mariánské Lázně

WORTH A DETOUR

THE 'THIRD SPA' OF FRANTIŠKOVY LÁZNĚ

When people talk of western Bohemia's spas, it's usually only the two big ones that are mentioned: Karlovy Vary and Mariánské Lázně. There is, however, a third spa town, Františkovy Lázně (frantish-kovee *lahz*-nyeh), that's worth a day trip from Mariánské Lázně if you're in the area and have the time.

Indeed, with its buttery veneer of yellow paint, well-tended parklands with statues and springs, and spa patients and tourists walking around unbearably s...l...o...w...l...y, Františkovy Lázně may better fulfil your expectations of what a real spa town should look like.

Beethoven and Goethe were Františkovy Lázně's most famous guests, but they were more likely drawn by the lively cafe society than the spa, which was best known for the treatment of female infertility. Czech author Milan Kundera was obviously intrigued by the idea of so many young women concentrated in such a small town that he set his tragic-comic 1970s novel 'The Farewell Waltz' here. These days, that kind of action (or indeed any action at all) is entirely missing. The walks and pavement cafes are soporific, but in a pleasing, relaxing sort of way.

Like its two big-brother spas, Františkovy Lázně is rather short on must-sees. The biggest attraction is simply to stroll the main drag, Národní, admiring the impossibly cute spa architecture and stopping for coffee or cake every couple of hours or so. The key sights are the **Church of the Ascension of the Cross** (Kostel Povýšení sv Kříže) on Ruská, and the town's central spring, the **Františkův pramen**, at the southern end of Národní. To get a better understanding of the spa's history, drop by the **City Museum** (Městské muzeum; ☑354 542 344; www.muzeum-frantiskovylazne.cz; Dlouhá 4, Františkovy Lázně; adult/child 35/25Kč; ☺10am-5pm Tue-Sun). You can also hire a boat at the small pond, the **Rybník Amerika**, about 1km from the city centre.

For a good meal, try **Restaurant Goethe** (☑354 500 180; www.franzensbad-casino. com; Národní 1; mains 150-350Kč; ☺11.30am–11pm, cafe 9am–7pm; ☻☎) for well-prepared international dishes served by waiters decked out in period-piece garb. Hotels line the main drag, though most of these are fancy four-star affairs booked by the week for those seeking spa treatments.

You can get to Františkovy Lázně by bus or train from Plzeň or Mariánské Lázně. From the latter, the trip takes around an hour. Alternatively, the largish city of Cheb is just 30 minutes away by bus: from here you can catch regular trains back to Prague.

---

along the D5 motorway past Plzeň, turning north on Hwy 21 at Bor.

Need to Know

→**Location** Mariánské Lázně is located 173km due west of Prague.

→**Tourist Information Centre** (☑354 622 474; www.marianskelazne.cz; Hlavní třída 47; ☺9am-6pm Mar-Oct, 9am-5pm Mon-Sat, 10am-3pm Sun Nov-Feb) Sells theatre tickets and maps, and can book accommodation for visitors.

→**Československá Obchodní Banka** (☑354 601 611; www.csob.cz; Hlavní třída 81/10; ☺9am-5pm Mon-Fri) Has a handy bank ATM and currency exchange.

⊙ SIGHTS

COLONNADE   HISTORIC BUILDING
(Kolonáda; Lázeňská kolonáda; ☺6am-6pm) **FREE** The restored cast-iron Colonnade, dating from 1889, is the spa's visual centrepiece. Classical and brass-band concerts are presented here two or three times a day in high season. Also here, in its own pavilion, is the **Cross Spring** (Křížový pramen), the spa's first spring. Choose from a galaxy of souvenir porcelain mugs or bring along a plastic bottle.

SINGING FOUNTAIN   FOUNTAIN
(Zpívající fontána; www.marianskelazne.cz/en/marianske-lazne/singing-fountain; Lázeňská kolonáda; ☺7am-10pm May-Oct) **FREE** Just in front of the colonnade, the Singing Foun-

tain sashays to recorded music (everything from Dvořák to Celine Dion) every two hours on the odd hour from May through October, with the last two performances normally at 9pm and 10pm. An information board details the musical schedule.

MUNICIPAL MUSEUM
MUSEUM

(Městské muzeum; ☑354 622 740; www.muzeum-ml.cz; Goethovo náměstí 11; adult/concession 60/30Kč; ☺9.30am-5.30pm Tue-Sun) The tiny Municipal Museum occupies the house where Goethe stayed during his last visit to Mariánské Lázně, though the exhibits here, mostly geological, are not very interesting and signed only in Czech. The most interesting thing to see is a 20-minute video in English on the history of the spa (filmed in 1987 and comically dated in parts).

CHURCH OF THE ASSUMPTION OF THE VIRGIN MARY
CHURCH

(Kostel Nanebevzetí Panny Marie; ☑354 622 434; Goethovo náměstí 31; ☺9am-noon Tue-Fri, 9am-noon, 2-4.30pm Sat, 2-4.30pm Sun) **FREE** This imposing twin-towered white-and-yellow structure is the most important Roman Catholic Church in Mariánské Lázně. It dates from the mid-19th century and is an example of neo-Byzantine style.

FRYDERYK CHOPIN MEMORIAL MUSEUM
MUSEUM

(☑354 622 617; www.chopinfestival.cz; Hlavní třída 47; admission 20Kč; ☺2-5pm Tue, Thu & Sun Apr-Sep) This small museum displays personal effects and information on the life of Polish-French composer Fryderyk Chopin, who visited the spa in 1836. Chopin's music is played in the background.

ST VLADIMÍR CHURCH
CHURCH

(Kostel Sv Vladimíra; Ruská 347-349; admission 20Kč; ☺9.30-11.30am & 2-4pm) The 1901 red-and-yellow brick St Vladimír Church is a plush, Byzantine-style Orthodox church with an amazing porcelain iconostasis.

 **EATING & DRINKING**

CITY CAFE
FISH €

(Rybí Restaurace; ☑734 831 382; Masarykova 626; mains 130-180Kč; ☺10am-10pm; ☻) This casual, light cafe/restaurant in the centre of the spa area stepped up its game in 2014 from serving coffees and cakes. It now has arguably the best fish, including a mouth-watering grilled trout lightly coated in herbs and breadcrumbs, for miles around. The fish soup includes fresh and saltwater varieties. It also does sandwiches and salads.

★MEDITÉ
SPANISH €€

(☑354 422 018; www.medite.cz; Hlavní třída 7/229; tapas 70-130Kč; mains 270-340Kč; ☺11am-11pm; ☻☎☜) Czech owner David Böhm has transformed this unassuming spot into the best tapas restaurant in the Czech Republic. Choose from a small menu of hot and cold tapas dishes, as well as authentic paella and pastas, and pair them with carefully selected Spanish wines. The decor is colourful and minimalist – a welcome response to the languid spa.

ČESKÁ HOSPŮDKA
CZECH €€

(☑720 121 500; www.ceskahospudkaml.cz; Klíčová 179; mains 140-280Kč; ☺11am-10pm; ☻☎) Cozy Czech pub with a wood-burning fire and excellent, inventive local cooking is just the ticket for a perfect evening meal. Opt for something standard like a very good beef goulash or step out a bit with roast leg of venison or marinated pork ribs served in a garlic-honey sauce. The beers on tap include an excellent nonpasteurised Gambrinus.

U ZLATÉ KOULE
CZECH €€€

(☑354 624 455; www.uzlatekoule.com; Nehrova 26; mains 250-580Kč; ☺noon-11pm; ☻) A stunning cocktail of five-star class and cosy informality, this swish eatery features creaking wooden beams, sparkling glassware and antiques. The game-rich menu effortlessly whips up the 'wow' factor. Order a day in advance for roast goose with apple stuffing and bread-and-bacon dumplings.

IRISH PUB
PUB

(☑777 303 838; www.irish-pub.cz; Poštovní 96; ☺5pm-1am; ☎) Old typewriters and vintage green bicycles create a suitably Irish ambience for the best craic in Mariánské Lázně. Lots of Irish whiskeys on hand, as well as light food items and pizza. Follow the signs that say 'Irish Pub'. It's completely nonsmoking.

NEW YORK BARCAFFE
CAFE

(☑776 007 921; www.newyorkml.cz; Hlavní třída 233; mains 60-160Kč; ☺9.30am-11pm Sun-Thu, to 1am Fri & Sat; ☎) Another one of those

BEST OF BOHEMIA MARIÁNSKÉ LÁZNĚ

tough-to-pigeonhole places, this is a popular cafe most of the day, but transforms into a lively bar at night. We like it because they also do light international food items such as salads and pastas – the kind of good (and quick) food that isn't easy to find in Mariánské Lázně.

🛏 SLEEPING

While overnight stays are possible, most of the big hotels and resorts in town are geared for longer-term (one- to two-week) bookings, including full wellness packages. In practice that means reception desks are not always prepared to handle walk-in requests for a one- or two-night stay. You'll get better service (and often better prices) if you reserve a room in advance.

★ VILLA-ART   PENSION €
(☎739 082 358; www.villa-art.cz; Ruská 315; s/d from 1000/1300Kč; P⊖🛜🍴) Owner Miroslav Paral has transformed this 19th-century villa into a cosy but modest pension in the spa's upper end. Rooms are situated on two levels, with some upper-level rooms sporting balconies and shared kitchens. The baths have had a makeover and are gleaming. Rooms have wooden floors and solid-wood beds and desks. Guests take their breakfast at the downstairs cafe.

PENSION EDINBURGH   PENSION €
(☎354 620 804; www.pensionedinburgh.com; Ruská 56; s/d from 800/1100Kč, apt 1500Kč; P⊖@🛜) This friendly, centrally located pension offers five refurbished rooms and one apartment, tucked away above the Scottish Pub. In keeping with the Celtic theme, each room has a well-stocked minibar...and dressing gowns. The owners offer transport around town and further afield.

HOSTEL MILANO   HOSTEL €
(☎774 417 065; www.ubytovani.newyorkml.cz; Ruská 309; per person from 250Kč; P⊖🛜) The cheapest accommodation in town, this hostel features Ikea-furnished dorms and modern art. There's a well-equipped shared kitchen if you're watching your budget. It's run by the same people who own the popular New York Barcaffe.

HOTEL PARIS   HOTEL €€
(☎354 628 897; www.hotelparis.cz; Goethovo náměstí 3; s/d incl breakfast 1450/2400Kč; P⊖🛜🏊) An attractive 19th-century hotel, located just down from the Colonnade in the heart of the spa district. The rooms are on the spare side, though are spotlessly clean and most have balconies. The hotel offers a full range of spa treatments (consult the website for details). Prices here for treatments are lower than for more glamorous resort hotels.

HOTEL RICHARD   HOTEL €€
(☎354 696 111; www.hotelrichard.com; Ruská 487/28; s/d incl breakfast 1850/2890Kč; P⊖❄🛜🏊) This modern hotel is situated just to the west of the main spa area and has a nice view onto the nearby St Vladmir Church. The rooms are done up in a bland,

---

HIKING IN MARIÁNSKÉ LÁZNĚ

Mariánské Lázně is surrounded by dense forest, with dozens of trails winding through the woods and past pavilions and springs. The Tourist Information Centre (p234) hands out a free map – 'Mariánské Lázně a okolí' – that traces four of the most popular and shorter hikes. The longest and most satisfying of these is the 6km-long **Edward Trail** (Edwardova cesta), which is marked in blue and begins from behind the Hotel Nové Lázně (p237). It climbs quickly to the Hotel Panorama and circles around the southen end of the spa all the way out to the Royal Golf Club of Mariánské Lázně (p238).

Another worthwhile path, the 5km-long **Metternich Trail** (Metternichova cesta), marked in green, covers the lesser-explored western side of the spa area and takes in several springs. Find it at the southern end of the spa area, just near the Public Pool (p238). It wends northwards and drops you off at the far northern end of spa, near the top of **Hlavní třída**.

But these are just the tip of the iceberg. Beyond the immediate spa region, trails link Mariánské Lázně to further-flung locales such as **Františkovy Lázně** and the monastery at **Teplá**. The Tourist Information Centre sells hiking maps of the region.

> **WORTH A DETOUR**
>
> ### 'BEER WELLNESS LAND'
>
> In the village of **Chodová Planá**, 20 minutes by bus (26Kč) from Mariánské Lázně, the beer spa at the **Chodovar Brewery** (☑374 617 100; www.chodovar.cz; Pivovarská 107; treatments from 660Kč) is the perfect spot to simultaneously explore both of western Bohemia's claims to fame: world-class spas and beer.
>
> 'Beer spa' treatments at Chodovar's self-proclaimed 'Beer Wellness Land' include a couple of glasses of the village's liquid gold. There are other tantalising menu options, including massages, hot stones and even a 'beer bath for two'. Couples can book in for special Valentine's Day packages.
>
> The beer spa experience goes something like this: after disrobing, you sink yourself into a hoppy bath of warm beer. Confetti-sized fragments of hops and yeast stud the water, and the overriding aroma features the grassy, zesty tones of world-renowned hops from nearby Žatec. The bath is heated to a comfy 34°C (93°F), and you're even allowed to sup on a glass of the Chodovar Brewery's fine golden lager for the duration.
>
> After a relaxing soak of around 30 minutes, an attendant brings you your robe and leads you into some granite tunnels (used for 'lagering' beer as far back as the 12th century) for yet more rest and relaxation. According to the brewery's marketing spiel, the procedures will have 'curative effects on the complexion and hair, relieve muscle tension, warm-up joints and support the immune system of the organism'.
>
> In the attached gift shop there's beer soap, shampoo and cosmetics. After all that hoppy goodness, visitors can even the score with tasty meat-heavy dishes and more brews in the subterranean restaurant and beer hall. Another above-ground restaurant features official beer sommeliers who can instruct in 10 different types of beer.

contemporary style, but are nevertheless clean and well cared for. The main selling point is the comprehensive and good-value menu of spa and treatment options, included hot-stone and honey massages.

HOTEL GRAND SPA MARIENBAD HOTEL €€€
(☑354 929 397; www.falkensteiner.com; Ruská 123; r 3600-5200Kč; P ❋ ❖ @ ❈ ❄) This relatively recent opening towers over the spa resort in more ways than one. The hotel is situated in a sensitively renovated 19th-century spa palace and offers every conceivable amenity. It will help arrange spa treatments too; check the website for special deals and weekend packages.

HOTEL NOVÉ LÁZNĚ HOTEL €€€
(☑354 644 300; www.danubiushotels.cz; Reitenbergerova 53; d 3560-4560Kč; ste from 4700Kč; P ❖ ❋ ❈ ❄) They say 'five star', but we reckon one of Mariánské Lázně's best hotels is a very good 'four star'. Either way you're guaranteed an elegant stay in this 19th-century confection that sits atop the 'new baths'. Exemplary spa services are virtually on tap as you're ushered into the gilded lobby. See the website for spa packages.

☆ ENTERTAINMENT

MĚSTSKÉ DIVADLO THEATRE
(Municipal Theatre; ☑354 622 036; www.marianskelazne.cz; Třebízského 106) Check the website for musical and theatrical performances. Get information and buy tickets from the Tourist Information Centre (p234).

KINO SLAVIA CINEMA
(☑354 622 347; www.kinoslavia.cz; Nerudova 437) This cinema shows mainly Hollywood films.

🏃 SPORTS & ACTIVITIES

As with the other spa resorts, most people come here to stroll the grounds and take a drinking cure by sipping mineral water from one of the various springs from a spouted, porcelain sipping mug. The town website (www.marianskelazne.cz) has information in English on the properties of the various springs. Outside the spa area, there are hundreds of kilometres of marked hiking trails that spread out in all directions. Dozens of hotels and resorts offer various spa treatments for guests and occasionally walk-ins, though often these are more of the medical (and not the pampering) variety.

DANUBIUS HEALTH
SPA RESORT NOVÉ LÁZNĚ   SPA

(☎354 644 111; www.danubiushotels.cz; Reitenbergerova 53; ⊙7am-7pm depending on treatment; ☜) The Danubius chain manages many of the hotels and resorts in town. Consult the website for a full menu of spa treatments, aimed at both longer-term (two weeks) or short-term (overnight) visitors. The chain's main resort is the Hotel Nové Lázně (p237), which includes pools and saunas.

ROYAL GOLF CLUB
OF MARIÁNSKÉ LÁZNĚ   GOLF

(☎354 624 300; www.golfml.cz; Mariánské Lázně 582; greens fees 1500-1700Kč; ⊙7am-9pm May-Sep) Mariánské Lázně is known around the country for its challenging and beautiful 6135-yard, par-72 golf course. The course has a long history, going back more than 100 years. You can hire clubs from the pro club; book in advance.

PUBLIC POOL   SWIMMING

(Městský bazén; ☎354 623 579; www.marianskelazne.cz; Tyršova 6; per 2hr adult/concession 120/60Kč; ⊙11am-9pm Mon-Sat) The public pool is southwest of the city centre.

Best of Moravia

Brno p240
Moravia's brawny capital boasts a spooky hilltop castle, skeletons everywhere, and a masterpiece of early modern architecture.

Telč p248
This small town's colourful Renaissance and baroque main square is so picture-perfect it's a Unesco World Heritage site.

Třebíč p251
This bustling city's former Jewish Quarter is unique in the Czech Republic.

Mikulov p253
A piece of Italy in southern Moravia, with great wine and architecture.

Valtice-Lednice p257
A Unesco-protected heritage landscape amid lush, rolling hills.

Znojmo p259
Pleasant border town with atmospheric alleyways and a magnificent view out over the Thaya (Dyje) River valley.

Olomouc p261
Northern Moravian gem with a main square to rival Prague's, a lively student body and (at least two) great microbreweries.

Kroměříž p267
A Unesco World Heritage site with a magnificent 19th-century chateau.

Brno

Explore

Among Czechs, Moravia's capital has a dull rep: a likeable enough place where not much happens. There was even a hit movie a few years back called *Nuda v Brně (Boredom in Brno)*. The reality is very different. Tens of thousands of students ensure lively cafe and club scenes that easily rival Prague's. The museums are great too. If you add in two excellent microbreweries and at least one of the country's best restaurants, there's plenty to reward a stay of a couple of days. Brno was one of the leading centres of experimental architecture in the early 20th century, and the Unesco-protected Vila Tugendhat is considered a masterwork of functionalist design. The tourist information office has lots of material on the city's rich architectural heritage, including marked-out tours.

The Best...

➡ **Sight** Špilberk Castle (p241)

➡ **Place to Eat** Pavillon (p245)

➡ **Place to Drink** Cafe Podnebi (p245)

Top Tip

Brno is a popular venue for trade fairs, and hotels routinely jack up rates by as much as 50% during large events. Check www.bvv.cz for dates and plan your visit for an off-week.

Getting There & Away

➡ **Train** Express trains to Brno depart Prague's Hlavní nádraží every couple of hours during the day (220Kč, three hours). Brno is a handy junction for onward train travel to Vienna (220Kč, two hours) and Bratislava (210Kč, 1½ hours). Trains arrive at Brno's central **main station** (Brno hlavní nádraží; ☑ 840 112 113; www.cd.cz; Nádražní 1).

➡ **Bus** Buses depart Prague's Florenc bus station hourly for Brno (210Kč, 2½ hours). Brno has two bus stations. Yellow **Student Agency** (☎841 101 101; www.studentagency. cz; náměstí Svobody 17, Dům pánů z Lipé; ⊙9am-6pm Mon-Fri) buses use the bus stop in front of the train station; most other buses use **Zvonařka bus station** (ÚAN Zvonařka; ☎543 217 733; www.vlak-bus.cz; Zvonařka; ⊙information 5am-8pm Mon-Fri, 5.45am-4.15pm Sat & Sun), behind the station.

➡ **Car** Brno is an easy two-hour drive from Prague, a straight shot down the D1 highway. Bratislava is another hour to the east. The drive to Vienna takes two hours.

Need to Know

➡ **Location** 200km southeast of Prague.

➡ **Tourist Information Centre** (TIC Brno; ☎542 211 090; www.ticbrno.cz; Radnická 8, Old Town Hall; ⊙8am-6pm Mon-Fri, 9am-6pm Sat & Sun) Lots of info in English, including free maps. Just next door is a separate **info centre** (Informační centrum - Jižní Morava; ☎542 427 170; www.ticbrno.cz; Radnická 2; ⊙9am-5pm Mon-Fri) dedicated to the sights of South Moravia, outside the city of Brno.

➡ **Internet Access** The Tourist Information Centre has a couple of computers.

⊙ SIGHTS

ŠPILBERK CASTLE   CASTLE
(Hrad Špilberk; ☎542 123 611; www.spilberk.cz; Špilberk 210/1; combined entry adult/concession 400/240Kč, casements only 90/50Kč, tower only 50/30Kč; ⊙9am-5pm Tue-Sun Oct-Apr, 9am-5pm daily May & Jun, 10am-6pm daily Jul-Sep) Brno's spooky hilltop castle is considered the city's most important landmark. Its history stretches back to the 13th century, when it was home to Moravian margraves and later a fortress. Under the Habsburgs in the 18th and 19th centuries it served as a prison. Today, it's home to the **Brno City Museum**, with several temporary and permanent exhibitions.

The menu of visiting options is confusing at first glance. You can choose to visit the exhibitions individually or buy a combined entry ticket to all the sights. The most popular sights are the **casements**, dating from the 18th century, and the **lookout tower**. Interesting permanent exhibitions include **From Castle to Fortress**, about the castle's history, and **Prison of Nations**, on the role Špilberk played as an impenetrable prison.

CATHEDRAL OF STS
PETER & PAUL   CHURCH, TOWER
(Katedrála sv Petra a Pavla; www.katedrala-petrov. cz; Petrov Hill; tower adult/concession 40/30Kč; ⊙11am-6pm Mon-Sat, from 11.45am Sun) This 14th-century cathedral atop Petrov Hill was originally built on the site of a pagan temple to Venus, and has been reconstructed many times since. The highly decorated 11m-high main altar with figures of Sts Peter and Paul was carved by Viennese sculptor Josef Leimer in 1891. You can also climb the **tower** for dramatic views.

The Renaissance **Bishop's palace** (closed to the public) adjoins the cathedral. To the left is the pleasant **Denisovy sady**, a verdant park sweeping around Petrov Hill.

BEST OF MORAVIA BRNO

EXPLORE MORAVIA

The Czech Republic's easternmost province, Moravia is yin to Bohemia's yang. If Bohemians love beer, Moravians love wine. If Bohemia is about towns and cities, Moravia is rolling hills and pretty landscapes. The capital, Brno, has the museums, but the northern city of Olomouc has captivating architecture. The south is dominated by vineyards and, naturally, wine-drinking day-tipplers.

One Week in Moravia
Spend two days in Brno to experience the culture, modern architecture and nightlife. From there, head north to Olomouc for two days, with a day trip to Štramberk, or head south to Mikulov, to enjoy the wine and nature.

Two Weeks in Moravia
In two weeks, you can see everything. Spend four days in Brno and at least a couple in Olomouc, before heading south to Znojmo and Mikulov. Rent a bike, pray for sun and spend the days on the trail and nights at a wine cellar.

Brno

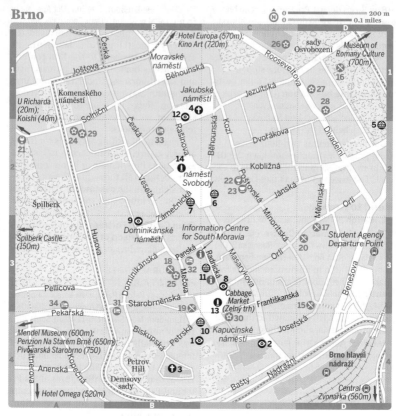

⊙ Cabbage Market & Around

The Cabbage Market (Zelný trh) is the heart of the Old Town. Today it functions as a fruit-and-vegetable market, but at its centre is the curious baroque **Parnassus Fountain** (1695). The images depict Hercules restraining the three-headed Cerberus. The three figures represent the ancient empires of Babylon (crown), Persia (cornucopia) and Greece (quiver of arrows). The woman on top symbolises Europe.

OLD TOWN HALL · HISTORIC BUILDING
(Stará radnice; ☏542 427 150; www.ticbrno.cz; Radnická 8; tower adult/concession 50/30Kč; ⊙9am-5pm) **FREE** Brno's atmospheric Old Town Hall dates from the early 13th century. The tourist office is here, plus oddities including a crocodile hanging from the ceiling (known affectionately as the Brno 'dragon')

and a wooden wagon wheel with a unique story (see p244). You can climb the **tower**.

CAPUCHIN MONASTERY · CEMETERY
(Kapucínský klášter; www.kapucini.cz; Kapucínské náměstí; adult/concession 60/30Kč; ⊙9am-noon & 1pm-4.30pm Mon-Sat, 11am-11.45am & 1pm-4.30pm Sun May-Sep, closed Mon mid-Feb–Apr & Oct–mid-Dec, weekends only mid-Dec–mid-Feb) One of the city's leading attractions is this ghoulish cellar **crypt** that holds the mummified remains of several city noblemen from the 18th century. Apparently the dry, well-ventilated crypt has the natural ability to turn dead bodies into mummies. Up to 150 cadavers were deposited here prior to 1784, the desiccated corpses including monks, abbots and local notables.

LABYRINTH UNDER THE CABBAGE MARKET · UNDERGROUND
(Brněnské podzemí; ☏542 427 150; www.ticbrno.cz; Zelný trh 21; adult/concession 160/80Kč;

Brno

⊘9am-6pm Tue-Sun) In recent years the city has opened several sections of extensive underground tunnels to the general public. This tour takes around 40 minutes to explore several cellars situated 6–8m below the Cabbage Market, which has served as a food market for centuries. The cellars were built for two purposes: to store goods and to hide in during wars.

MINTMASTER'S CELLAR UNDERGROUND
(Mincmistrovský sklep; ☑542 427 150; www.tic-brno.cz; Dominikánské náměstí (enter from Panenská); adult/concession 80/40Kč; ⊘9.30am-6pm Tue-Sun) These medieval cellars were discovered during excavation work carried out in 1999. This is a self-guided tour that takes around 20 minutes. On display is an exhibition of mining and minting, which were once the sources of Moravia's wealth.

MORAVIAN MUSEUM MUSEUM
(Moravské zemské muzeum; ☑533 435 220; www.mzm.cz; Zelný trh 8; adult/concession 50/25Kč; ⊘9am-3pm Tue, 9am-5pm Wed-Fri, 1-6pm Sat & Sun) This natural-history and ethnographic museum holds some 6 million pieces and is the country's second-largest. Exhibits straddle the intellectual gulf between extinct life and the medieval village. In a courtyard next to the museum is the **Bishop's Court**

(Biskupský dvůr; ☑542 321 205; www.mzm.cz; Muzejní 1; adult/concession 60/30Kč; ⊘9am-3pm Tue, 9am-5pm Wed-Fri, 1pm-6pm Sat & Sun), with the largest freshwater aquarium in the country and plenty of info on Moravian wildlife.

⊙ Náměstí Svobody & Around

Spacious náměstí Svobody is the city's bustling central hub. It dates from the early 13th century, when it was called Dolní trh (lower market). The **plague column** here dates from 1680, and the **House of the Lords of Lipá** (Dům Pánů z Lipé; náměstí Svobody 17) FREE at No 17 is a Renaissance palace (1589–96) with a 19th-century sgraffito facade and arcaded courtyard. On the eastern side of the square at No 10 is the **House of the Four Mamlases** (Dům U čtyř mamlasů; náměstí Svobody 10). The facade here is supported by a quartet of well-muscled but clearly moronic 'Atlas' figures, each struggling to hold up the building and their loincloths at the same time.

CHURCH OF ST JAMES CHURCH
(Kostel sv Jakuba; ☑542 212 039; www.svaty jakubbrno.wz.cz; Jakubská 11; ⊘8am-6pm) FREE

BRNO'S QUIRKY OLD TOWN HALL

No visit to Brno would be complete without a peek inside the city's medieval Old Town Hall (p242), parts of which date back to the 13th century. The oddities start right at the entrance on Radnická. Take a look at the Gothic portal made by Anton Pilgram in 1510 and notice the crooked middle turret. According to legend, this was intentional: Pilgram was not paid the agreed amount by the council so, in revenge, he left the turret more than slightly bent.

Take a stroll inside to see the corpse of the legendary Brno 'dragon' that supposedly once terrorised the city's waterways. The animal, in fact (in any event, what we've been told) is an Amazon River crocodile, donated by Archprince Matyáš in 1608. Near the dragon, you'll see a wooden wagon wheel hanging on the wall. It was apparently crafted by an enterprising cartwright from Lednice. In 1636 he bet a mate that he could fell a tree, build a wheel and roll it 50km to Brno – all before dusk. He was successful and the hastily made and quickly rolled wheel has been on display ever since. Unfortunately, someone started the dodgy rumour that the cartwright had received assistance from the devil and he died penniless when his customers went elsewhere.

This austere 15th-century church contains a baroque pulpit with reliefs of Christ dating from 1525. But the biggest drawcard is a small stone figure known as the 'Nehaňba' (The Shameless): above the 1st-floor window of the clock tower at church's west end is the figure of a man baring his buttocks towards the cathedral. Local legend claims this was a disgruntled mason's parting shot to his rivals working on Petrov Hill.

OSSUARY
UNDERGROUND

(Kostnice; ☎542 427 150; www.ticbrno.cz; Jakubské náměstí; adult/concession 140/70Kč; ☉9.30am-6pm Tue-Sun) This ghoulish 20-minute tour through the former burial grounds and crypts below the Church of St James displays the collected bones and remains of some 50,000 people who perished from wars, famines and plagues over the centuries. The remains were discovered in 2001 during the renovation of the square and opened to the public in 2013.

HOUSE OF ARTS
GALLERY

(Dům umění; ☎515 917 553; www.dum-umeni.cz; Malinovského náměstí 2; adult/concession 80/40Kč; ☉10am-6pm Tue-Sun) Holds rotating contemporary art exhibitions, usually focusing on Czech, Moravian and other central European artists. It is open only during shows.

⊙ Outside the Centre

★VILA TUGENDHAT
ARCHITECTURE

(Villa Tugendhat; ☎tour booking 515 511 015; www.tugendhat.eu; Černopolni 45; adult/con-

cession basic tour 300/180Kč, extended tour 350/210Kč; ☉10am-6pm Tue-Sun; ☐3, 5, 11 to Černopolní) Brno had a reputation in the 1920s as a centre for modern architecture in the functionalist and Bauhaus styles. Arguably the finest example is this family villa, designed by modern master Mies van der Rohe in 1930. Entry is by guided tour booked in advance by phone or email. Two tours are available: a 60-minute basic tour and 90-minute extended visit.

Because of the high demand for tickets, it's recommended to book at least a month in advance. If you can't book a tour, the front of the house is still worth a look for how sharply it contrasts with many of the other contemporaneous buildings in the neighbourhood. To find the villa, take tram 3, 5 or 11 from Moravské náměstí up Milady Horákové to Černopolní, then walk 300m north.

MENDEL MUSEUM
MUSEUM

(☎543 424 043; www.mendel-museum.com; Mendlovo náměstí 1a; adult/concession 60/30Kč; ☉10am-6pm Tue-Sun Apr-Oct, to 5pm Nov-Mar) Gregor Mendel (1822–84), the Augustinian monk whose studies of pea plants and bees at Brno's Abbey of St Thomas established modern genetics, is commemorated here in a series of photographs and displays (with plenty of information in English). In the garden are the foundations of Mendel's original greenhouse.

MUSEUM OF ROMANY CULTURE
MUSEUM

(Muzeum romské kultury; ☎545 571 798; www.rommuz.cz; Bratislavská 67; adult/concession

60/30Kč; ⊙10am-6pm Tue-Fri, to 5pm Sun, closed Sat; 🚇2, 4, 11 to Tkalcovská) This excellent museum provides an overdue positive showcase of Romany culture. Highlights include a couple of music-packed videos, period photographs from across Europe, and regular special exhibitions.

 EATING

SPOLEK
CZECH €

(📲774 814 230; www.spolek.net; Orli 22; mains 80-180Kč; ⊙9am-10pm Mon-Fri, 10am-10pm Sat & Sun; 🛜🖊🚼) You'll get friendly, unpretentious service at this coolly 'bohemian' (yes, we're in Moravia) haven with interesting salads and soups, and a concise but diverse wine list. Photojournalism on the walls is complemented by a funky mezzanine bookshop. It has excellent coffee too.

ANNAPURNA
INDIAN €

(📲774 995 122; www.indicka-restaurace-brno. cz; Josefská 14; mains 140-220Kč; ⊙10.30am-10.30pm Mon-Fri, noon-10.30pm Sat & Sun; 🍴🖊) The weekday lunch specials (100Kč for soup, main, rice and salad) are absolutely mobbed at this cramped space not far from the train station. People come for the very good Indian food and prompt service. Outside of lunch, it's less crowded but still worth a trip for curries and lots of varied vegetarian dishes.

ŠPALÍČEK
CZECH €

(📲542 211 526; Zelný trh 12; mains 80-160Kč; ⊙11am-11pm; 🍴) Brno's oldest (and maybe its 'meatiest') restaurant sits on the edge of the Cabbage Market. Ignore the irony and dig into huge Moravian meals, partnered with a local beer or something from the decent list of Moravian wines. The old-school tavern atmosphere is authentic and the daily luncheon specials are a steal.

REBIO
VEGETARIAN €

(📲542 211 110; www.rebio.cz; Orli 26; mains 80-100Kč; ⊙8am-7pm Mon-Fri, 10am-3pm Sat; 🖊) Healthy risottos and veggie pies stand out in this self-service spot that changes its tasty menu every day. There's another all-veggie branch on the 1st floor of the **Velký Spalíček shopping centre** (📲543 214 878; www.rebio.cz; Mečova 2; mains 60-100Kč; ⊙9am-9pm Mon-Fri, 11am-9pm Sat, 11am-8pm Sun; 🍴🛜).

★PAVILLON
INTERNATIONAL €€

(📲541 213 497; www.restaurant-pavillon.cz; Jezuitská 6; mains 250-385Kč; ⊙11am-11pm Mon-Sat, 11am-3pm Sun; 🍴🛜) High-end dining in an elegant, airy space that recalls the city's heritage in functionalist architecture. The menu changes with the season, but usually features one vegetarian entree as well as mains with locally sourced ingredients, such as wild boar or lamb raised in the Vysočina highlands. Daily luncheon specials at 200Kč for soup, main and dessert are a steal.

KOISHI
ASIAN €€€

(📲777 564 744; www.koishi.cz; Údolní 11; mains 395-490Kč; ⊙11am-11pm; sushi served noon-2pm & 5-10pm Tue-Sat; 🍴🛜) Sushi master Noritada Saito and head chef Petr Fučík have combined forces to bring one of the country's top restaurants to Brno. The main drawcard is sushi, served from Tuesday to Saturday, but the menu includes traditional Czech dishes with an Asian twist, such as pike-perch served with barley risotto and apple-vinegar foam. The wine selection is excellent. Book ahead.

🍷 **DRINKING**

★CAFE PODNEBI
CAFE

(📲542 211 372; www.podnebi.cz; Údolní 5; ⊙8am-midnight Mon-Fri, from 9am Sat & Sun; 🛜🚼) This homey, student-oriented cafe is famous citywide for its excellent hot chocolate, but

BEST OF MORAVIA BRNO

AHEAD OF THEIR TIME

The bells of the Cathedral of Sts Peter & Paul (p241) disconcertingly ring noon an hour early, at 11am. Legend has it that when the Swedish laid siege to the city in 1645, their commander, General Torstenson, who had been frustrated by Brno's defences for more than a week, decided to launch a final attack, with one caveat: if his troops could not prevail by noon, he would throw in his hand.

By 11am the Swedes were making headway, but the cathedral's tower-keeper had the inspired idea to ring noon early. The bells struck 12, the Swedes withdrew, and the city was saved.

BRNO FOR KIDS

Brno will be a tough sell for kids. After the charms of the Brno 'dragon' and the wagon wheel in the Old Town Hall (p244) have worn off, you'll have to come up with some more inspired ideas. One possibility is the Brno **Planetarium** (☑541 321 287; www. hvezdarna.cz; Kraví hora 2; adult/concessionn 125/100Kč; ☺7.30am-3pm Mon & Tue, 7.30am-7.30pm Wed-Fri, 9am-7.30pm Sat, 9am-4pm Sun; 🚊4). While most of the shows are in Czech, it may be possible to arrange an English presentation if you contact the staff in advance. Brno's **City Zoological Garden** (Zoologická zahrada; ☑546 432 311; www.zoo brno.cz; Bystrc-Mniší hora; adult/concession 100/70Kč; ☺9am-4pm Nov-Feb, to 5pm Mar & Oct, to 6pm Apr-Sep; 🚊1, 3, 11) on the outskirts of town occupies a lovely setting and has a wide variety of animals. Brno's **Technical Museum** (Technické muzeum vs Brně; ☑541 421 411; www.technicalmuseum.cz; Purkyňova 105; adult/concession 100/50Kč; ☺9am-5pm Tue-Sun; 🚊12) is worth a half-day of anyone's time. Don't miss the panoptikon on the 1st floor: this huge wooden stereoscope allows up to 20 viewers to look at 3D images from antique glass slides that are changed on a regular basis.

it also serves very good espresso drinks. There are plenty of baked goods and sweets to snack on. In summer, the garden terrace is a hidden oasis and there's a small play area for kids.

KAVÁRNA ALFA
CAFE

(☑533 381 199; Poštovská 4; ☺8am-10pm Mon-Fri, 8am-9pm Sat, 2-9pm Sun; 🏠) This tiny, central cafe with retro flair draws students and theatre types who dart in here for a quick shot of very-well-done espresso.

U RICHARDA
PUB

(☑775 027 918; www.uricharda.eu; Údolní 7; ☺11am-11pm Mon-Sat) This microbrewery is highly popular with students, who come for the great house-brewed, unpasteurised yeast beers, including a rare cherry-flavoured lager, and the good traditional Czech cooking (mains 109Kč to 149Kč). Book in advance.

PIVOVARSKÁ STAROBRNO
PUB

(☑543 420 130; www.pivovarskabrno.cz; Mendlovo náměstí 20; ☺11am-midnight; 🚊1, 5, 6, 7 to Mendlovo náměstí) Brno's longest-established brewery is at its best in the beer garden on a warm summer's evening – especially if there is a band playing live music. Catch tram 1 from the train station to Mendlovo náměstí.

PIVNICE PEGAS
PUB

(☑542 210 104; www.hotelpegas.cz; Jakubská 4; ☺11am-midnight) *Pivo* melts that old Moravian reserve as the locals become pleasantly noisy. Don't miss the 12° wheat beer with a slice of lemon. Try to book a table in advance, or grab a spot at one of Brno's longest bars. The food's pretty good too, but the interior can get smoky.

AVIA
CAFE

(☑739 822 215; www.aviacafe.cz; Botanická 1; ☺11am-10pm; 🏠) Popular student cafe/restaurant situated on the ground floor of the Jan Hus Congregational Church, a landmark functionalist building from 1929. The architecture and location, close to the university, lend an intellectual atmosphere. Catch tram 1 or 6 to the Antonínská stop, turn left into Smetanova and then right into Botanická.

MINACH
CAFE

(www.cokoladovna.com; Poštovská 6; per chocolate 13Kč; ☺9am-9pm Mon-Fri, 9am-7pm Sat, 2-7pm Sun) More than 50 kinds of handmade chocolates and bracing coffee make this an essential mid-morning or mid-afternoon detour. You'll find it inside the small shopping passageway.

🛏 SLEEPING

★HOSTEL MITTE
HOSTEL €

(☑734 622 340; www.hostelmitte.com; Panská 22; dm 500Kč, s/d incl breakfast 1000/1300Kč; ⊜◎🏠) Set in the heart of the Old Town, this clean and stylish hostel smells and looks brand new. The rooms are named after famous Moravians (eg Milan Kundera) or famous events (Austerlitz) and decorated accordingly. There are dorms in six-bed rooms and private singles and doubles. Cute cafe on the ground floor.

PENZION NA STARÉM BRNĚ
PENSION €

(☑543 247 872; www.pension-brno.com; Mendlovo náměstí 1a; s/d incl breakfast 1010/1360Kč; 🅿⊜; 🚊1, 5, 6, 11 to Mendlovo náměstí) The atmospheric Augustinian monastery where Gregor Mendel first experimented with pea plants also holds a simple but good-value pension. The five compact rooms are bare bones but clean and comfortable. The Mendlovo náměstí location is convenient to several tram lines.

HOSTEL FLÉDA
HOSTEL €

(☎731 651 005; www.hostelfleda.com; Štefánikova 24; dm/d from 300/1000Kč; ☻☎; 🏠1, 6 to Hrnčirská) A quick tram ride from the centre, one of Brno's best music clubs offers funky and colourful rooms. A nonsmoking cafe and good bar reinforces the social vibe. Catch tram 1 or 6 to the Hrnčirská stop.

HOTEL EUROPA
HOTEL €€

(☎515 143 100; www.hotel-europa-brno.cz; třída kpt Jaroše 27; s/d 1400/1800Kč; P☻☎) Set in a quiet neighbourhood a 10-minute walk from the centre, this self-proclaimed 'art'

hotel (presumably for the wacky futuristic lobby furniture) offers clean and tastefully furnished modern rooms in a historic 19th-century building. The lobby has free wi-fi, while the rooms have cable (ethernet) connections. There is free parking out front and in the courtyard.

HOTEL OMEGA
HOTEL €€

(☎543 215 152; www.hotelomega.eu; Křídlovická 19b; s/d incl breakfast 950-1300/1450-1700Kč; ☻☎🛗; 🏠1 to Václavská) In a quiet neighbourhood 1km from the centre, Omega has spacious rooms with modern pine furniture. A couple of three- and four-bed rooms cater to travelling families, and breakfast comes complete with castle views. Catch tram 1 from the railway station to the Václavská stop.

HOTEL & PIVNICE PEGAS
HOTEL €€

(☎542 210 104; www.hotelpegas.cz; Jakubská 4; s/d 2000/2500Kč; ☻☎) Centrally located,

---

WORTH A DETOUR

CAVING IN MORAVIA

The area to the immediate north of Brno has some of the Czech Republic's best caving in a region known as the **Moravian Karst** (Moravský kras). Carved with canyons and some 400 caves, the landscape is very pretty, with lots of woods and hills.

The karst formations here resulted from the seepage of faintly acidic rainwater through limestone, which over millions of years slowly dissolves it, creating hollows and fissures. In the caves themselves, the slow dripping of this water has produced extraordinary stalagmites and stalactites.

The organisational centre for any caving expedition is the town of **Blansko**, which has a good **tourist information office** (Blanenská Informační Kancelář; ☎516 410 470; www.blansko.cz; Rožmitálova 6, Blansko; ⊙9am-6pm Mon-Fri, to noon Sat) which sells maps and advance tickets to two of the main caves: the Punkva and Kateřinská caves. The office can field transport questions and can help with accommodation. On weekends, particularly in July and August, cave-tour tickets sell out in advance, so try to book ahead with the tourist information office.

The most popular tour is through the **Punkva Cave** (Punkevní jeskyně; ☎516 413 575; www.caves.cz; Skalní Mlýn; adult/child 170/90Kč; ⊙8.40am-2pm Tue-Sun Jan-Mar, 10am-4pm Mon, 8.20am-4pm Tue-Sun Apr-Sep, 8.40am-2pm Tue-Sun Oct-Dec). It involves a 1km walk through limestone caverns to the bottom of the Macocha Abyss, a 140m-deep sinkhole. Small, electric-powered boats then cruise along the underground river back to the entrance.

Another popular tour is to the **Kateřinská Cave** (Kateřinská jeskyně; ☎516 413 161; www.caves.cz; Skalní Mlýn; adult/child 80/60Kč; ⊙8.20am-4pm daily May-Aug, 9am-4pm Tue-Sun Apr & Sep, 9am-2pm Tue-Sun Oct, 10am-2pm Tue-Fri Mar & Nov, closed Dec-Feb). It's usually a little less crowded than the Punkva option. The 30-minute tour here explores two massive chambers.

Though it's easiest to explore the cave region with your own wheels, it is possible with some advance planning to see the caves on a day trip from Brno with public transport. Trains make the 30-minute run to Blansko hourly most days (38Kč). After that, it's about an 8km hike to the caves, though from May to September special tour buses make the run. Before setting out, be sure to arrange transport at the Information Centre for South Moravia (p241) in Brno.

the Pegas has been refurbished to include huge beds, flat-screen TVs and updated bathrooms. Expect a friendly welcome at reception and the lure of the Pegas microbrewery and pub downstairs. The rooms are on the 4th floor, so there is no problem with noise from the bar.

HOTEL POD ŠPILBERKEM   HOTEL €€
(✆543 235 003; www.hotelpodspilberkem. cz; Pekařská 10; s/d/tr incl breakfast 1400/1600/2100Kč; P🅿️🅰️@🛜🐕) This small, family-run and family-friendly pension is located on a busy street just below Špilberk Castle. The rooms are clean and relatively quiet (ask for courtyard-facing). Breakfast is cold cuts and cheeses. The secure car park is a good option for self-drive travellers.

BARCELÓ BRNO PALACE   LUXURY HOTEL €€€
(✆532 156 777; www.barcelo.com; Šilingrovo nám 2; r from €135; P🅿️❄️@🛜) Five-star heritage luxury comes to Brno at the Barceló Brno Palace. The lobby blends glorious 19th-century architecture with thoroughly modern touches, and the spacious rooms are both contemporary and romantic. The location in Brno's old town is excellent.

☆ ENTERTAINMENT

STARÁ PEKÁRNA   CLUB, LIVE MUSIC
(✆541 210 040; www.starapekarna.cz; Štefánikova 8; ⏰5pm-late Mon-Sat; 🚊1, 6, 7) Old and new music with blues, world beats, DJs and rock. Catch the tram to Pionýrská. Gigs usually kick off at 8pm.

FLÉDA   LIVE MUSIC
(✆533 433 559; www.fleda.cz; Štefánikova 24; ⏰to 2am; 🚊1, 6) DJs, Brno's best up-and-coming bands and occasional touring performers all rock the stage at Brno's top music club. Catch tram 1 or 6 to the Hrnčirská stop.

KLUB DESERT   LIVE MUSIC
(✆608 079 226; www.dodesertu.com; Rooseveltova 11; ⏰4pm-3am Mon-Sat, 6pm-1am Sun) Part cool bar/cafe and part intimate performance venue, Klub Desert features Brno's most eclectic live late-night line-up. Gypsy bands, neofolk – anything goes.

BRNO PHILHARMONIC ORCHESTRA   CLASSICAL MUSIC
(Besední dům; ✆539 092 811; www.filharmonie -brno.cz; Komenského náměstí 8) The Brno Philharmonic is the city's leading orchestra for performing classical music. It conducts some 40 concerts a year, plus tours around the Czech Republic and Europe. It's particularly strong on Moravian-born, 20th century composer Leoš Janáček. Most performances are held at Besední dům concert house. Buy tickets at the venue **box office** (✆tickets 539 092 811; www.filharmonie-brno.cz; Besední; ⏰9am-2pm Mon & Wed, 1pm-6pm Tue, Thu & Fri).

JANÁČEK THEATRE   OPERA, BALLET
(Janáčkovo divadlo; ✆542 158 345; www.ndbrno. cz; Rooseveltova 1-7, Sady Osvobození) This modern performance hall is home to the National Theatre's highly acclaimed opera and ballet companies. Performances are held several times weekly in season. Check the National Theatre website for a current schedule. Buy tickets at the **National Theatre Box Office** (Národní Divadlo v Brně Prodej Vstupnek; ✆542 158 120; www.ndbrno.cz; Dvořákova 11, cnr Rooseveltova; ⏰8am-5.30pm Mon-Fri, to noon Sat) or at the theatre 45 minutes before the performance.

REDUTA THEATRE   CLASSICAL MUSIC, OPERA
(Reduta divadlo; www.ndbrno.cz; Zelný trh 4) Opera and classical music with an emphasis on Mozart (he played there in 1767). Buy tickets at the National Theatre Box Office (p248).

KINO ART   CINEMA
(✆541 213 542; www.kinoartbrno.cz; Cihlářská 19; 🚊1, 6 to Antonínská) Screens art-house films, and also has a handy cafe. Check the website for a current schedule of what's on.

CINEMA CITY   CINEMA
(✆255 742 021; www.cinemacity.cz; Mečova 2, Velký Spaliček) On the upper level of the Velký Spaliček shopping centre, showing the latest from Hollywood.

Telč

Explore

The Unesco-protected town of Telč, perched on the border between Bohemia and Moravia, possesses one of the country's prettiest and best-preserved historic town squares. Actually, we can't think of another that comes close! The main attraction is the beauty of the square itself, lined by

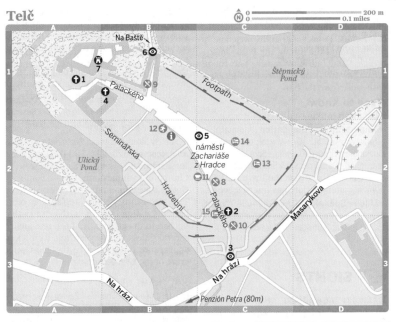

Telč

Renaissance and baroque burgers' houses, with their brightly coloured yellow, pink and green facades. Spend part of your visit simply ambling about, taking in the classic Renaissance chateau on the square's north-western end and the parklands and ponds that surround the square on all sides. Telč empties out pretty quickly after the last tour bus leaves, so plan an overnight stay only if you're looking for some real peace and quiet.

The Best...
➡ **Sight** Telč Chateau (p250)
➡ **Place to Eat** U Marušky (p250)
➡ **Place to Drink** Kavarná Antoniana (p251)

Top Tip
The best time to visit Telč is in late July and early August, when the town explodes into life during the **Prázdniny v Telči** (www. prazdninyvtelci.cz) music festival.

Getting There & Away
➡ **Train** Passenger train services to/from Telč have been greatly scaled back and are not recommended.

➡ **Bus** Around half-a-dozen buses make the

Telč

⊙ **Sights**

⊗ **Eating**

⊜ **Drinking & Nightlife**

⊕ **Sports & Activities**

⊑ **Sleeping**

run daily from Prague's Florenc bus station (175Kč, 2½ hours), with many connections requiring a change in Jihlava. Regional service is decent, with around five daily buses to and from Brno (100Kč, two hours). Check www.bus-vlak.cz for current times and prices.

➡Car From Prague, Telč is an easy two-hour drive, heading toward Brno on the D1 motorway, and turning off at Jihlava.

Need to Know

➡Location 160km southeast of Prague.

➡Tourist Information Office (Informační Středisko; ☑567 112 407; www.telc.eu; náměstí Zachariáše z Hradce 10; ☺8am-5pm Mon-Fri year-round, 10am-5pm Sat & Sun May-Oct, to 4pm Sat & Sun Nov-Apr) Inside the Town Hall. Can book accommodation; has internet access.

➡Miluše Spázalová (☑606 884 598; náměstí Zachariáše z Hradce 8; per day from around 150Kč; ☺8am-5pm Mon-Fri, 9am-noon Sat) Rents bikes.

◉ SIGHTS

NÁMĚSTÍ ZACHARIÁŠE Z HRADCE SQUARE

(Main Square) **FREE** Telč's stunning town square is a tourist attraction in its own right. Most houses here were built in Renaissance style in the 16th century after a fire levelled the town in 1530. Some facades were given baroque facelifts in the 17th and 18th centuries, but the overall effect is harmoniously Renaissance.

Famous houses on the square include **No 15**, which shows the characteristic Renaissance sgraffito. The house at **No 48** was given a baroque facade in the 18th century. **No 61** has a lively Renaissance facade rich in sgraffito. The **Marian column** in the middle of the square dates from 1717, and is a relatively late baroque addition.

TELČ CHATEAU CASTLE

(Zámek; ☑567 243 943; www.zamek-telc.cz; náměstí Zachariáše z Hradce 1; adult/concession route A 110/70Kč, route B 90/60Kč, combined 170/100Kč; ☺10am-4pm Tue-Sun Apr & Oct, to 5pm May, Jun & Sep, to 6pm Jul & Aug) Telč's sumptuous Renaissance chateau guards the northern end of the Telč peninsula. The chateau was rebuilt from the original Gothic structure in the 16th century and remains in fine fettle, with immaculately tended lawns and beautifully kept interiors. In the ornate Chapel of St George (kaple sv Jiří) are the remains of the chateau's builder, nobleman Zachariáš z Hradce.

Entry to the chateau is by guided tour only. Two tours are available. Route A passes through the Renaissance halls and includes the chateau's most impressive interior, the Golden Hall. Route B explores the castle's residence rooms on the 1st floor, last occupied by the Podstatský family of Liechtenstein in the late 19th and early 20th centuries.

CHURCH OF ST JAMES CHURCH

(Kostel sv Jakuba; náměstí Zachariáše z Hradce; adult/concession 20/15Kč; ☺10-11.30am & 1-6pm Tue-Sun Jun-Aug, 1-5pm Sat & Sun May & Sep) The Church of St James's impressive 60m-high Gothic tower dominates the central square. This 15th-century church replaced an older building dating from the 14th century that burned to the ground. It's been remodelled several times over the years and its modern appearance owes much to the neo-Gothic craze of the 19th century.

HOLY NAME OF JESUS CHURCH CHURCH

(Kostel Jména Ježíš; náměstí Zachariáše z Hradce 3; ☺8am-6pm) **FREE** Watching over the square are the twin towers of the baroque Holy Name of Jesus Church, completed in 1667 as part of a Jesuit college.

 EATING & DRINKING

U MARUŠKY CZECH €

(☑602 771 031; Palackého 28; mains 90-170Kč) This simple pub caters more to locals than visitors, but offers decent home-cooked Czech meals with the added bonus of very good Ježek beer on tap. There's also a small beer garden open during summer. The daily lunch menu is a steal at 75Kč.

RESTAURANT ŠVEJK NA ZÁMECKÉ CZECH €

(www.svejk-telc.cz; náměstí Zachariáše z Hradce 1; mains 105-165Kč; 🛜) Classic Czech cooking in a pub-like setting next to the castle. The names of menu items, unsurprisingly, are taken from the classic WWI anti-war book, *The Good Soldier Švejk*. 'Cadet Biegler' chicken, for example, turns out to be a schnitzel that's stuffed with ham and cheese. The outdoor terrace is popular in nice weather.

PIZZERIE ITALIAN €

(☑567 223 246; www.pizzerietelc.cz; náměstí Zachariáše z Hradce 32; pizza 80-130Kč; ☺10am-10pm Mon-Sat, from 11am Sun) Right on the main square and right on the money for better-than-average pizza.

KAVARNÁ ANTONIANA   CAFE

(📞603 519 903; náměstí Zachariáše z Hradce 23; coffee 24-30Kč, cake 35Kč; ⊙8am-2am) The best coffee on the square, plus beer and other alcoholic drinks, and inspirational black-and-white photos of Telč plastered on the wall. There are only limited food options, but the late opening hours mean it's one of the few places in the centre where you can get a drink in the evening.

🛏 SLEEPING

PENSION STEIDLER   PENSION €

(📞721 316 390; www.telc-accommodation.eu; náměstí Zachariáše z Hradce 52; s/d 500/800Kč; ⊜) Rooms reconstructed with skylights and wooden floors combine with a town-square location to deliver one of Telč's best-value places to stay. Some rooms have views of the lake. Breakfast costs 50Kč per person. Note there's a surcharge of 100Kč per room in summer (June to August) for stays of less than two nights.

PENZIN KAMENNÉ SLUNCE   PENSION €

(📞732 193 510; www.kamenne-slunce.cz; Palackého 27; s/d 600/900Kč; 🅿⊜🛜) Lots of brick, exposed beams and warm wooden floors make this a very welcoming spot just off the main square. Hip bathrooms with colourful tiles add weight to claims that this is arguably Telč's coolest place to stay. Breakfast costs 100Kč.

PENZIÓN PETRA   PENSION €

(📞567 213 059; www.penzionpetra.cz; Srázná 572; s 300-500Kč, d 600-1000Kč; 🅿⊜🛜🏊) This modern house just across the bridge from the town square has brightly coloured rooms, spotless bathrooms and a wading pool in the garden. The separate 'Garden House' (300Kč to 500Kč per person) sleeps up to five and has its own kitchen.

HOTEL CELERIN   HOTEL €€

(📞567 243 477; www.hotelcelerin.cz; náměstí Zachariáše z Hradce 43; s/d 980/1530Kč; ⊜❄🛜) Variety is king in the Celerin's 12 comfortable rooms, with decor ranging from cosy wood to white-wedding chintz (take a look first). Rooms 4, 5, 9 and 10 have views out onto the square. The hotel sometimes closes in winter.

Třebíč

Explore

In the past the medium-sized Moravian city of Třebíč rarely made it onto travellers' itineraries. This changed in 2003, when Unesco placed the city's nearly perfectly preserved former Jewish Quarter on its list of protected World Heritage Sites. While the quarter is small, it's unique in the Czech Republic and worth searching out if you're coming this way. In addition, take in the impressive St Procopius' Basilica, another Unesco site. Třebíč is best approached as a day trip from Brno or Telč, though there are a couple of decent overnight options if you want to stay.

The Best...

➡ **Sight** Rear (New) Synagogue (p252)
➡ **Place to Eat** Coqpit (p253)
➡ **Place to Drink** Kavárna Vrátka (p253)

Top Tip

The **Tourist Information Centre** (TIC Zadní synagoga; 📞568 610 023; www.mkstrebic.cz; Subakova 1/44; tours adult 130-150Kč, concession 70-80Kč; ⊙9am-5pm Jan-Jun & Sep-Nov, to 6pm Jul & Aug, to 4pm Dec) in the former Jewish Quarter offers guided tours of the quarter that must be booked at least two days in advance by phone or email.

Getting There & Away

➡ **Train** From Brno, trains leave every hour or so for Třebíč (92Kč, 1¼ hours). Train travel is less convenient from Prague (280Kč, 5¼ hours), with most connections requiring at least two changes.

➡ **Bus** Buses run regularly to/from Brno (70Kč, 1¼ hours) and Telč (35Kč, 40 minutes). From Prague, there are around five direct buses per day (165Kč, 2½ hours).

➡ **Car** Třebíč is a two-hour drive from Prague, down the D1 motorway in the direction of Brno, turning south at Velké Meziříčí. From Brno, the one-hour drive heads northwest on the D1 toward Prague, turning south at Velké Meziříčí.

Need to Know

➡ **Location** 165km southeast of Prague.
➡ **Tourist Information Centre** (informační

a turistické centrum; ☎568 847 070; www.mkstrebic.cz; Karlovo náměstí 47, Národní dům; ⏱9am-6pm Mon-Fri Apr-Oct, 9am-5pm Sat & Sun Jul & Aug, 9am-1pm Sat & Sun Apr-Jun & Sep-Oct) Reduced hours November to March.

➡**Internet Access** The Tourist Information Centre offers 15 minutes of free web-surfing.

◉ SIGHTS

Most visitors come to see the remains of the town's once-thriving Jewish community, which dates back to the 14th century. The former Jewish Quarter, the best-preserved ghetto in the Czech Republic, is situated along the northern bank of the Jihlava River, about a five-minute walk from the centre. Most of Třebíč's Jews perished in WWII, but the buildings here, including two synagogues, survived and are being slowly refurbished.

REAR (NEW) SYNAGOGUE   SYNAGOGUE
(Zadní (Nová) synagóga; ☎568 610 023; www.mkstrebic.cz; Subakova 1/44; adult/concession 80/40Kč; ⏱9am-5pm Jan-Jun & Sep-Nov, to 6pm Jul & Aug, to 4pm Dec) This Renaissance synagogue, dating from 1669, is the highlight of the Jewish Quarter with its beautifully restored frescoes and a wonderful historical model of the ghetto as it appeared in the mid-19th century. Entry is by 30-minute guided tour, with tours scheduled at least once an hour.

JEWISH CEMETERY   CEMETERY
(Židovský hřbitov; ☎737 180 813; www.mkstrebic.cz; Hrádek; ⏱9am-6pm Sun-Fri May-Aug, to 5pm Mar, Apr, Sep & Oct, 10am-3pm Nov-Feb) FREE The 17th-century burial ground on Hrádek, about 600m north of the Jewish Quarter, is the largest in the country, with more than 11,000 graves. The oldest dates back to 1641.

ST PROCOPIUS' BASILICA   CHURCH
(Bazilika sv Prokopa; ☎568 610 022; www.mkstrebic.cz; Zámek 1; adult/concession 60/30Kč; ⏱9am-5pm Mon-Fri, 10am-6pm Sat & Sun Jun-Sep, 9am-5pm Mon-Thu, 9am-3pm Fri, 12.30-5pm Sat & Sun Oct-May) There was a chapel on this site in the early 12th century, when the church was connected to a Benedictine monastery. Although the church has been remodelled many times since then, parts still show signs of the Gothic renovation the structure received in 1260. Today, it's a Unesco World Heritage site.

DISCOVERING MORAVIAN WINE

Compared to the wine regions of France, California, Australia or New Zealand, the Moravian wine tourism experience is much more low-key and homespun. Rather than flash boutique hotels or Michelin-star restaurants, the wine scene here is more likely to involve energetic harvest festivals and leisurely cycle touring between family-owned vineyards.

South from Brno toward the borders with Austria and Slovakia, the Moravian wine region accounts for 96% of the total area under vine in the Czech Republic. Traditionally, robust red wines were part of the Moravian rural diet, but in recent years, late-ripening white wines have taken centre stage. With grape ripening occurring at a slower pace, the emphasis is on full-bodied, aromatic, and often spicy wines.

The Mikulov sub-region is characterised by the proximity of the Pavlovské hills, creating a local terrain rich in limestone and sand. Wines to look for during your visit include the mineral-rich white varietals of Rulandské šedé, Ryzlink vlašský (better known by its German name of Welschriesling) and Veltlínské zelené (Grüner Veltliner). Müller-Thurgau and Chardonnay grapes also do well.

Further west, the Znojmo sub-region is situated in the rain shadow of the Bohemian and Moravian highlands, and the soils are more likely to be studded with gravel and stones. Aromatic white wines including sauvignon, Pálava and Ryzling rýnský (Riesling) are of notable quality, and red wines, especially Frankovka (Blaufränkisch), are also worth trying.

Keep an eye out for Czech Tourism's excellent *Through the Land of Wine* brochure or see www.wineofczechrepublic.cz for details of wine-touring routes and Moravia's growing profile in international wine competitions.

Top spots to try Moravian wines include Mikulov's Vinařské Centrum (p256) and the National Salon of Czech Republic Wines (p258) in Valtice.

EATING & DRINKING

★COQPIT CZECH €€

(☎607 160 027; www.facebook.com/restaurantcoqpit; Havlíčkovo nábř 146/39; mains 160-270Kč; ⏲11am-10pm Mon-Sat, to 4pm Sun; 🚭📶) One of the best restaurants in this part of Moravia stands on the edge of the Jewish Quarter. The bare-bones interior belies a highly skilled kitchen. On our visit, we went for braised pork tenderloin served with caramelised onion in red-wine reduction, with the pumpkin soup as a starter. The homemade cheese cake is perfection.

KAVÁRNA VRÁTKA CAFE

(☎737 565 011; www.kavarna-vratka.unas.cz; L Pokorného 29/42; coffee 30-60Kč; ⏲10am-8pm Tue-Sun Jun-Sep, 10am-5pm Tue-Sun Oct-May; 📶) This non-smoking, family-friendly coffeehouse has excellent coffee concoctions and homemade cakes, and is just steps away from the Rear (New) Synagogue.

SLEEPING

PENZIÓN U SYNAGOGY PENSION €

(☎775 707 506; www.mkstrebic.cz; Subakova 43; s/d incl breakfast 470/720Kč; 🚭📶) Seven simple rooms in an atmospheric location near the Rear (New) Synagogue. Note that the reception desk is only staffed until 5pm and the pension does not take credit cards.

GRAND HOTEL HOTEL €€

(☎568 848 540; www.grand-hotel.cz; Karlovo náměstí 5; s/d/tr incl breakfast 1380/1780/2500Kč; P🚭@📶🏊) The city's nicest hotel is a modern, four-star offering on the main square, an easy five-minute walk from the Jewish Quarter. There's a good restaurant in-house, plus extras such as a music club, pool, fitness centre and even a bowling alley! The rooms are plain but clean and very comfortable. Excellent value.

Mikulov

Explore

The 20th-century Czech poet Jan Skácel (1922–89) bequeathed Mikulov a tourist slogan for the ages when he penned that the town was a 'piece of Italy moved to Moravia by God's hand'. Mikulov is arguably the most attractive of the southern Moravian wine towns, surrounded by white, chalky hills and adorned with an amazing hilltop Renaissance chateau, visible for miles around. Mikulov was also once a thriving cultural centre for Moravia's Jewish community, and the former Jewish Quarter is slowly being rebuilt. Once you've tired of history, explore the surrounding countryside (on foot or bike) or relax with a glass of local wine.

The Best...

- **Sight** Mikulov Chateau (p254)
- **Place to Eat** Restaurace Templ (p256)
- **Place to Drink** Café Dolce Vita (p256)

Top Tip

Experience the countryside on a bike: the tourist office proffers advice, maps and the brochure *Viticulture and Viticulture Discovery Trails* (also available at pensions and hotels). Many pensions rent bikes.

Getting There & Away

Train Mikulov is poorly served by train. Only a frequent short hop to Valtice (20Kč, 15 minutes) is really of any use. The town's tiny **train station** (www.cd.cz; Nádražní) is a 20- to 30-minute walk southwest of the centre. See the online timetable at www.vlak-bus.cz.

Bus The bus is generally the best way to access Mikulov from Brno (70Kč, 1½ hours), with coaches leaving hourly. Regional bus service is good, with frequent buses to Valtice and Lednice (20Kč, 30 minutes). Buses depart from a **small stop** (Nádražní) near the train station or at another stop, closer to the centre, called **U parku** (Piaristů).

Car Mikulov, situated between Prague and Vienna, is a three-hour drive from Prague. From Brno, the drive takes around an hour.

Need to Know

Location 250km southeast of Prague.

Tourist Information Office (Map p254; ☎519 510 855; www.mikulov.cz; Náměstí 1; ⏲9am-6pm daily Jun-Sep, to 5pm Apr, May & Oct, to 4pm Nov-Mar) Organises tours (including

Mikulov

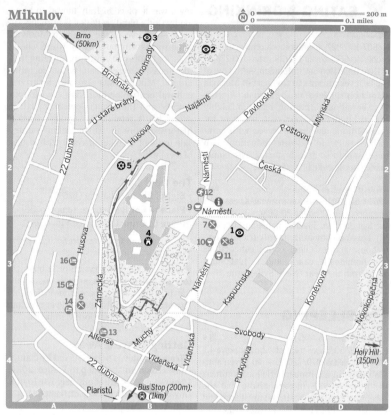

specialist outings for wine buffs) and accommodation.

➡ **Bike Hire RentBike** (Map p254; ☎737 750 105; www.rentbike.cz; Kostelní náměstí 1; rental per hr/day 100/290Kč) rents good-quality mountain bikes.

◉ SIGHTS & ACTIVITIES

Mikulov is filled with beautiful buildings, many still sporting impressive Renaissance and baroque facades. The main square, called simply 'Náměstí' (square), has many houses of interest, including the **Town Hall** at No 1 and the sgraffitoed **Restaurace Alfa** at No 27. The town was also a leading centre of Jewish culture for several centuries until WWII. There's a small former synagogue here as well as a highly evocative

Jewish cemetery, a 10-minute walk north of the Tourist Information Office.

MIKULOV CHATEAU   CASTLE
(Zámek; ☎519 309 019; www.rmm.cz; Zámek 1; adult/concession 150/75Kč; ⊙9am-6pm Tue-Sun Jun-Aug, to 5pm May & Sep, to 4pm Apr & Oct) This chateau was the seat of the Dietrich-stein family from 1575 to 1945, and played an important role in the 19th century, hosting on separate occasions French Emperor Napoleon, Russia's Tsar Alexander and Prussia's King Frederick. Much of the castle was destroyed by German forces in February 1945: the lavish interiors are the result of a painstaking reconstruction.

The castle is accessible by guided tour only. The full history tour takes two hours and visits significant castle rooms as well as exhibitions on viticulture and archaeology. Three specialised shorter tours are also available.

Mikulov

DIETRICHSTEIN BURIAL VAULT   MAUSOLEUM

(Dietrichštejnská hrobka; ☑720 151 793; Náměstí 5; adult/concession 60/30Kč; ⊙10am-5pm Apr, May & Oct; 9am-6pm Jun-Sep) The Dietrichstein family mausoleum occupies the former St Anne's Church. The front of the building features a remarkable baroque facade – the work of Austrian master Johann Bernhard Fischer von Erlach – dating from the early 18th century. Dating from 1617 to 1852, the tombs hold the remains of 45 family members.

SYNAGOGUE   SYNAGOGUE

(Synagóga; ☑519 510 255; www.rmm.cz; Husova 11; adult/concession 50/25Kč; ⊙9am-5pm Tue-Sun May, Jun & Sep, to 6pm Jul & Aug, to 4pm Oct) The main synagogue, the High Synagogue, dates from around 1550 and has an information centre and a small exhibition on the Jews of Mikulov. It reopened in 2014 after a long reconstruction and renovation intended to restore its pre-WWII state.

JEWISH CEMETERY & CEREMONIAL HALL   CEMETERY

(Židovský hřbitov; ☑519 512 368; Hřbitovní náměstí; adult/concession 30/20Kč; ⊙10am-4pm Tue-Fri Apr & Oct, to 5pm May, to 6pm Jun-Sep; ☎) The size of Mikulov's forlorn Jewish cemetery, numbering around 4000 tombstones, is a testament to the importance of the Jewish community to the town over the centuries. The oldest surviving headstone dates back to 1605. Enter the cemetery through the former **Ceremonial Hall**, which holds a small exhibition on the town's Jewish history and Jewish burial traditions.

GOAT HILL   HILL, LOOKOUT

(Kozí hrádek; ☑608 002 976; Kozí hrádek; tower adult/concession 20/10Kč; ⊙tower 9am-6pm May-Sep) Goat Hill is topped with an abandoned 15th-century **lookout tower** offering stunning views over the Old Town. To find it, walk steeply uphill from the entrance to the Jewish Cemetery. Note the tower keeps irregular hours: it's only open when the flag is flying. But even if the tower is closed, the views from the hilltop are spectacular.

HOLY HILL   HILL, CHURCH

(Svatý kopeček; ☑737 382 622; www.farnostimikulovska.cz; Svobody; ⊙church 9am-5pm Sat, to 1pm Sun Jun-Aug) FREE This uphill venture scales the 1km path to a 363m peak, through a nature reserve and past grottoes depicting the Stations of the Cross, to the compact **Church of St Sebastian**. The blue-marked trail begins at the bottom of the main square on Svobody. The whitewashed church and the limestone on the hill give it a Mediterranean ambience.

MIKULOV WINE TRAIL   HIKING, CYCLING

A pleasant way to visit smaller, local vineyards across the rolling countryside is by bicycle on the Mikulov Wine Trail. The tourist office can recommend a one-day ride that also takes in the nearby chateaux at Valtice and Lednice.

EATING

★ SOJKA   INTERNATIONAL €

(☑518 327 862; Náměstí 10; mains 120-160Kč; ⊙9am-9pm; ⊖☑) This light, airy bistro situated above a food shop is a must, both for the quality of the ingredients (fresh, locally grown and organic) and the inventiveness of the menu. On our visit a zesty tomato soup with a slice of tempura-fried courgette (zucchini) was paired with *coq au vin* and homemade apricot cobbler. There are several enticing vegetarian options too.

HOSPŮDKA POD ZÁMKEM　　　CZECH €

(☑519 512 731; www.hospudkapodzamkem.cz; Husova 49; daily special 75Kč; ☎) This combination of old-school pub and coffee bar serves simple but very good Czech meals, usually limited to a few daily specials such as soup plus roast pork or chicken drumsticks. It's also the unlikely home of Mikulov's best coffee and serves very good 11° Gambrinus beer to boot. Find it across the street from the Hotel Templ.

RESTAURACE ALFA　　　CZECH €

(☑519 511 685; Náměstí 27; mains 130-200Kč; ☺10am-10pm) The Alfa's beautifully 'sgraffitoed' Renaissance building, hides what's basically an ordinary Czech pub on the inside. That said, the kitchen turns out well-prepared Czech cooking, and there are even a few game dishes on the menu.

RESTAURACE TEMPL　　　CZECH €€

(☑519 323 095; www.templ.cz; Husova 50; mains 165-280Kč; ☺☎) A leading contender for the best restaurant in town is matched by a fine wine list specialising in local varietals. The menu features an appetising mix of duck, beef and fish dishes. Choose from either the formal restaurant or the relaxed wine garden. There's also a small terrace out the back for dining alfresco on warm evenings.

DRINKING

CAFÉ DOLCE VITA　　　CAFE

(Náměstí 29; cakes 40-70Kč; ☎) Tasty cakes and coffee are dished up in a clean, comfortable setting on the main square, just beside the road leading up to Mikulov Chateau. There's good wi-fi and in summer the front terrace affords a perfect view out over the square.

VINAŘSKÉ CENTRUM　　　WINE BAR

(☑519 510 368; www.vinarskecentrum.com; Náměstí 11; ☺9.15am-noon & 1.15pm-6.15pm Mon-Sat, 10am-12.15pm Sun) This drinking room has an excellent range of local wines

available in small tasting glasses (15Kč to 50Kč), or whole bottles when you've made up your mind.

DOBRÝ ROČNÍK　　　WINE BAR

(www.dobryrocnik.eu; Náměstí 27; ☺10am-9pm Mon-Sat, to 6pm Sun; ☎) A pleasant little wine and coffee bar, serving local wines by the glass or the bottle.

SLEEPING

Mikulov has some beautiful small hotels and pensions, and is a good town for an overnight stay. Most of the better properties are clustered along Husova in the former Jewish Quarter. Many properties offer sightseeing tours and wine tastings, and have bikes to rent; ask when booking.

FAJKÁ PENZION　　　PENSION €

(☑732 833 147; www.fajka-mikulov.cz; Alfonse Muchy 18; s/d 600/1000Kč; P ☺) These bright, newly decorated rooms sit above a cosy wine bar. Out the back is a garden restaurant if you really, really like the local wine.

★HOTEL TEMPL　　　HOTEL €€

(☑519 323 095; www.templ.cz; Husova 50; s/d from 1390/1650Kč; P☺☎) This beautifully reconstructed, family-run hotel comprises a main building and an annex, two doors down. The updated rooms are done out in cheerful tiles and stained glass. The baths are as stylish as the rooms. Some rooms (such as No 11 in the annex) open onto a secluded patio with tables for relaxing in the evening.

PENSION BALTAZAR　　　PENSION €€

(☑720 611 712; www.pensionbaltazar.cz; Husova 44; d 1200-1800Kč; P ☺☎) You'll find this place in the former Jewish quarter, a few doors up from the Hotel Templ. Beautifully renovated rooms effortlessly combine modern furniture with exposed-brick walls and wooden floors.

PENZIÓN HUSA　　　PENSION €€

(☑605 573 788; www.penzionhusa.cz; Husova 30; d 1590Kč; P ☺☎) A beautiful pension on Husova, the 'Goose' boasts furnishings with period flare, such as canopy beds and big oriental rugs on top of hardwood floors. This place is well known, so book well in advance.

Valtice-Lednice

Explore

The Unesco-protected historic landscape of Valtice-Lednice is a popular weekend destination for Czechs, who tour the historic architecture, hike and bike, and sample the region's wines. The two towns are about 10km apart, connected by regular buses. Neither Valtice nor Lednice offer much in terms of nightlife, so they're best visited as a day trip from either Mikulov or Brno. But if you've got more time, either town makes a perfect base for exploring the rolling hills of the southern Moravian wine country: hundreds of miles of walking and cycling trails criss-cross a mostly unspoiled landscape. Tourist information offices in both towns have maps, and you can rent bikes from Cykloráj in Valtice.

The Best ...

➡ **Sight** Lednice Chateau (p258)

➡ **Place to Eat** Grand Moravia (p258)

➡ **Place to Drink** Vinotéka V Zámecké Bráně (p258)

Top Tip

Instead of taking the bus, hike the 10km trail between Valtice and Lednice. The path runs through some pretty hills and takes about two hours at a leisurely pace.

Getting There & Away

➡ **Train** Both Valtice and Lednice are poorly served by train, but Valtice has regular service to/from Mikulov (20Kč, 15 minutes). The Mikulov trains use the tiny **Město Valtice** (Stanice Valtice město; www.cd.cz; Petra Bezruče, Valtice) train station, 2km north of the centre along the main road to Lednice.

➡ **Bus** This is the best way to reach Valtice and Lednice, though connections from Brno are complicated and sometimes require both bus and train. To get to Lednice from Brno, take the train to Podivín (70Kč, 30 minutes) and bus (16Kč, 10 minutes) from there. Bus is the best way to shuttle between Lednice and Valtice (20Kč, 15 minutes). In Lednice, buses leave

from in front of the Tourist Information Centre. In Valtice, buses arrive at and depart from a small stop at the corner of Za Radnicí and Sobotní, west of the Valtice Chateau.

➡ **Car** From Brno, the drive to Valtice takes around an hour. Head south along the E65 highway, turning off at Podivín and following the signs.

Need to Know

➡ **Location** 263km southeast of Prague.

➡ **Tourist Information Offices Valtice** (Turistické Informační Centrum; ☑ 519 352 978; www.valtice.eu; náměstí Svobody 4, Valtice; ◷ 9am-5pm daily Apr-Sep, 7am-3.30pm Mon-Fri Oct-Mar); **Lednice** (Lednice Informační Centrum; ☑ 519 340 986; www.lednice.cz; Zámecké náměstí 68, Lednice; ◷ 9-11am & noon-3pm Mon-Fri, 10am-3pm Sat & Sun Apr-Oct)

➡ **Bike Hire Cykloráj** (☑ 605 983 978; www.cykloraj.com; Malá strana 781, Valtice ; rental per day 250Kč; ◷ 9am-5pm Mon-Fri) rents high-quality mountain and touring bikes, and offers maps and advice on where to ride.

◉ SIGHTS & ACTIVITIES

◉ Valtice

VALTICE CHATEAU   CASTLE

(Zámek; ☑ 519 352 423; www.zamek-valtice.cz; Zámek 1, Valtice; standard tour adult/concession 100/80Kč; ◷ 9am-noon & 1-6pm Tue-Sun May-Aug, to 5pm Sep, to 4pm Apr & Oct) Valtice's 12th-century castle is one of the country's finest baroque structures, the work of JB Fischer von Erlach and Italian architect Domenico Martinelli. Entry is by guided tour only, with two different tours on offer (in Czech, with English text available). The grounds and gardens are free for you to explore during opening times.

The standard 45-minute 'Prince's Tour' (Knížecí okruh) visits 15 castle rooms. The one-hour 'Emperor's Tour' (Císařský okruh; adult/concession 150/100Kč) includes 20 rooms (add wine tasting for 50Kč). Highlights include belongings left behind when the Liechtensteins fled the advancing Soviets in 1945. Notice the walls themselves, plastered with kilos of gold.

ASSUMPTION OF THE VIRGIN MARY
CHURCH

(Kostel Nanebevzetí Panny Marie; náměstí Svobody, Valtice; ⊘8am-5pm) **FREE** Valtice's most significant church is this early baroque work, dating from the middle of the 17th century. Take a look inside to admire the rare baroque organ from the 18th century. Behind the main altar are two significant paintings: the larger is a copy of a Rubens, but the smaller one above it, depicting the Holy Trinity, is a Rubens original.

NATIONAL SALON OF CZECH REPUBLIC WINES
WINE TASTING

(☑519 352 744; www.salonvin.cz; Zámek 1, Valtice; tastings 100-250Kč; ⊘9.30am-5pm Tue-Thu, 10.30am-6pm Fri, 10.30am-5pm Sat & Sun Jun-Sep) This handy wine salon at the Valtice Chateau is the place to try and to buy local wines.

⊙ Lednice

★LEDNICE CHATEAU
CASTLE

(Zámek; ☑519 340 128; www.zamek-lednice.com; Zámek, Lednice; tours adult/child 150/100Kč; ⊘9am-6pm Tue-Sun May-Aug, to 5pm Tue-Sun Sep, to 4pm Sat & Sun only Apr & Oct) Lednice's massive neo-Gothic chateau, owned by the Liechtenstein family from 1582 to 1945, is one of the country's most popular weekend destinations. The crowds come for the splendid interiors and extensive gardens, complete with an exotic-plant greenhouse, lakes with pleasure boats, and a mock Turkish minaret – architectural excess for the 19th-century nobility.

Entry is by guided tour only, with two main tours (45 minutes each) available. Tour 1 visits the chateau's major rooms, including the famous wooden spiral staircase. Tour 2 concentrates on the Liechtenstein apartments: the highlight is the lovely 19th-century Chinese salon.

 EATING & DRINKING

ALBERO
CZECH €

(☑519 352 615; www.alberovaltice.cz; náměstí Svobody 12, Valtice; mains 130-180Kč; ⊘10.30am-10pm Mon-Sat, 10.30am-6pm Sun; ⊜🖉) This lively Czech restaurant and pub, with a raucous terrace in summer, is the place to enjoy grilled meats and local favourites, washed down with wine or beer.

GRAND MORAVIA
CZECH €€

(☑519 340 130; www.grandmoravia.cz; ul 21. dubna 657, Lednice; mains 130-280Kč; ⊜🖥) This restaurant, part of a hotel complex, is arguably Lednice's best (out of an admittedly meagre bunch). You'll find nicely done local specialities, including a couple of fish entrees such as trout and pikeperch. Many of the menu items are given a special twist, for example baked lamb with a hint of rosemary, served with leaf spinach. Call ahead to book a table on weekends.

VINOTÉKA V ZÁMECKÉ BRÁNĚ
WINE BAR

(☑606 712 128; Zámek 1, Valtice; ⊘4-6pm Fri, 10am-6pm Sat & Sun, 10am-3pm Mon) Situated just to the right of the front of the Valtice Chateau, this little wine shop and bar is a friendly place to sip the local varietals.

🛌 SLEEPING

PENSION KLARET
PENSION €

(☑733 348 305; www.pensionklaret.cz; Střelecká 106, Valtice; s/d incl breakfast 1000/1400Kč; 🅿⊜🖥) This pristine modern pension is set amid grassy lawns and has 12 rooms and two larger apartments. The cosy, brick-lined wine cellar is slightly less modern; it dates back to 1890.

★HOTEL MARIO
HOTEL €€

(☑731 607 210; www.hotelmario.cz; ul 21. dubna 55, Lednice; r incl breakfast 1400-1800Kč; 🅿⊜@🖥) The fully renovated Hotel Mario stands head and shoulders above any of the smaller hotels or pensions in the Valtice-Lednice area. The immaculate rooms are furnished in muted contemporary style, with thick cotton sheets on the beds and tastefully updated bathrooms. There's a small wine cellar in the basement and a few garden tables out the back.

HOTEL HUBERTUS
HOTEL €€

(☑519 352 537; www.hotelhubertus.cz; Zámek 1, Valtice; s/d incl breakfast 1300/1600Kč; 🅿@) Valtice's most unusual lodging option is to sleep in the chateau itself. While the facilities are not quite as bedazzling as the website might indicate, and there is a slight whiff of neglect about the place, the setting is amazing and the price affordable. The rooms are plainly furnished, in stark contrast to the opulence of the rest of chateau.

Znojmo

Explore

The border town of Znojmo is one of southern Moravia's most-beloved day trips, particularly for travellers from neighbouring Austria. People come for the wine and to stroll the town's village-like alleys, linking intimate plazas with bustling main squares. Znojmo lies midway between Prague and Vienna and could easily be covered in a few hours as a stopover en route. Alternatively, there are some very nice small hotels and pensions here, and Znojmo is a convenient base for exploring the entire southern Moravian wine region. The tourist information office has a wealth of brochures on hiking, biking and drinking possibilities. Time your visit for September to catch the town in full riot for the annual Znojmo Wine Festival.

The Best...

➡ **Sight** Znojmo Underground (p259)
➡ **Place to Eat** Veselá 13 (p261)
➡ **Place to Drink** Na Věčnosti (p260)

Top Tip

Don't miss the breathtaking view out over the Thaya (Dyje) River valley from behind the Church of St Nicholas (p260).

Getting There & Away

➡ **Train** The bus is better for reaching Znojmo from Brno or Prague, but there is regular train service to Mikulov (69Kč, one hour). The **train station** (Železniční stanice Znojmo; ☎840 112 113; www.cd.cz; 28. října) is located about 1km southeast of the historical centre.

➡ **Bus** Znojmo lies near the major north–south E59 highway and has hourly bus service most days from Brno (88Kč, one hour), plus a couple of direct buses per day from Prague (210Kč, three hours). The **bus station** (Autobusové nádraží; Dr. Milady Horákové) is located next to the train station, about 1km southeast of the centre.

➡ **Car** From Prague, Znojmo is an easy 2½-hour drive: head south on the D1 motorway then exit at route 38 (aka E59 highway) toward Jihlava and follow the signs. From Brno, head an hour south on Hwy E461.

Need to Know

➡ **Location** 210km southeast of Prague.
➡ **Tourist Information Centre** (☎515 222 552; www.znojmocity.cz; Obroková 10; ◷8am-6pm Mon-Fri, 9am-5pm Sat, 10am-5pm Sun May, Jun, Sep & Oct, longer hours Jul & Aug, shorter hours Nov-Apr) is centrally located; there's a **branch** (☎515 222 552; www.znojmocity.cz; Hrad; ◷9am-4pm daily May-Sep, 9am-4pm Tue-Sat Oct-Apr) at Znojmo Castle.
➡ **Internet Access** The tourist office has a computer for visitors to check email.

⊙ SIGHTS

ZNOJMO UNDERGROUND   UNDERGROUND
(Znojemské podzemí; ☎515 221 342; Slepičí trh 2; classic tour adult/concession Jun-Sep 95/55Kč, Oct-May 65/45Kč, adrenaline tour 110-200Kč; ◷9am-5pm daily May-Sep, 10am-5pm Mon-Sat, 1-4pm Sun Oct-Apr) Znojmo's labyrinth of underground corridors below the old town is one of the most extensive in Central Europe, snaking around for some 27km. Two types of guided tours are offered: the classic tour is designed for families and features fairy-tale characters; the 'adrenaline' tour is more hard-core and involves actually climbing walls and crawling through tunnels.

Three types of adrenaline tours (blue, red and black) are available and ranked by difficulty (black is the hardest). Hardhats and proper outer gear are provided. Children under 15 are not permitted on the red and black tours.

ZNOJMO CASTLE   CASTLE
(Znojemský hrad; ☎515 222 311; www.znojmuz.cz; Hrad; adult/concession 40/30Kč; ◷9am-5pm Tue-Sun May-Sep, Sat & Sun only Apr) Znojmo has traditionally occupied a strategic position on the border between Austria and Moravia, and there's been a fortress here since the 11th century. The castle has served as a residence for Moravian nobles, a garrison, and even housed a brewery in the 18th century. In 1335, King John of Luxembourg held a wedding ceremony for his daughter Anne here.

Entry is by guided tour only. Tours leave at the top of the hour, with the day's last tour at 4pm. Tours are normally in Czech, but English and German text is provided on request.

ROTUNDA OF OUR LADY
& ST CATHERINE
CHURCH

(Rotunda Panny Marie a sv Kateřiny; ☑515 222 311; www.znojmuz.cz; Hrad; admission 90Kč; ◷9.15am-5pm Tue-Sun May-Sep, Sat & Sun only Apr) This 11th-century church is one of the republic's oldest Romanesque structures and contains a beautiful series of 12th-century frescoes depicting the life of Christ. Because of the sensitive nature of the frescoes, visitors are limited to groups of 10 or fewer, and are allowed in for 15 minutes at a time once per hour (at a quarter past the hour).

CHURCH OF ST NICHOLAS
CHURCH

(Kostel sv Mikuláše; www.farnostznojmo.cz; náměstí Mikulášské; ◷8am-6pm) **FREE** This beautiful 13th-century church was originally Romanesque and was rebuilt in Gothic style. Toward the front on the right side is the 'Bread Madonna' chapel. According to legend, during the Thirty Years' War a box beneath the image was always found to be full of food. Beside the church is the small **St Wenceslas Chapel** (kaple sv Václava).

TOWN HALL TOWER
TOWER, ARCHITECTURE

(Radniční věž; ☑739 389 094; www.znojmocity.cz; Obroková 12; adult/concession 40/20Kč; ◷9am-5pm May-Sep, 10am-4pm Thu-Sun Oct-Apr) The handsome and scalable 66m tower on Znojmo's town hall is one of Moravia's best examples of late Gothic architecture (c 1448).

EATING & DRINKING

NA VĚČNOSTI
VEGETARIAN €

(☑776 856 650; www.navecnosti.cz; Velká Mikulášská 11; mains 80-140Kč; lunch 79Kč; ◷10.30am-1am Mon-Thu, to 2am Fri & Sat, 11am-1am Sun; ☺🛜♪) We're big fans of this (mainly) vegetarian restaurant (there are a couple of fish dishes on the menu). Mains such as Thai noodles and dal (spiced lentils) are above average for these parts, and the intimate dining room, with wood-plank walls, red brick and plants, is very cosy. They also have a club with occasional touring bands.

LA CASA NAVARRA
MEDITERRANEAN €€

(☑515 266 815; www.lacasanavarra.cz; Kovářská 10; mains 100-220Kč; ◷10am-10pm Mon-Sat, 11am-10pm Sun; ☺🛜) Casa Navarra is well known locally for homemade gnocchi (usually served with cheese), but the pastas and grilled meats and steaks are also very

---

WORTH A DETOUR

ZLÍN'S FUNKY FUNCTIONALISM

In the early 20th century, Moravia was a hotbed of groundbreaking modern architecture. Brno is recognized as the centre of the action, but the smaller industrial town of Zlín (pronounced 'zleen') was also home to some radical and fascinating experimentation in functionalist town planning, following the vision of philanthropist shoe millionaire Tomáš Baťa ('bah-tya').

Adhering to Baťa's plan, the factories, offices, shopping centres and houses all used lookalike red bricks and a functionalist template to provide 'a total environment' to house, feed and entertain the workers at Baťa's massive shoe factory. Wide avenues and planned gardens produce a singular ambience, giving Zlín an expansive and unnervingly modern appearance, in contrast with the sometimes-saccharine historical centres of other towns.

The **Zlín Tourist Information Office** (Městské Informační a Turistické Středisko; ☑577 630 270; www.zlin.eu; Náměstí Míru 12; ◷8am-5pm Mon-Fri, to noon Sat Jun-Sep) has lots of information on the town's architectural heritage, including maps and walking tours (in English) of the most important buildings.

For a taste of the importance of Baťa and his ideas to the town, stop by **Building 14|15** (14|15 Baťův Institut; ☑573 032 111; www.muzeum-zlin.cz; Vavrečkova 7040, Building 14/15, Baťa Institute; adult/concession 129/59Kč; ◷10am-6pm Tue-Sun) of the Baťa Complex to see a permanent exhibition entitled 'The Baťa Principle: Today Fantasy, Tomorrow Reality.' There are tons of interesting and interactive displays on the history of Zlín and the Baťa shoe company, filled with old photos, machinery and maps (and, of course, lots of shoes over the ages).

The best way to reach Zlín is by bus: there are regular links to Brno (110Kč, two hours) and Olomouc (90Kč, one hour).

good. The small dining room is warm and inviting, with lots of red brick centred on a fireplace. There aren't many tables, so it's a good idea to book ahead or visit outside of standard meal times.

VESELÁ 13 — CZECH €€

(☑515 220 323; www.lahofer.cz; Veselá 13; mains 185-400Kč; ◎11am-10pm Mon-Sat, 11am-8pm Sun; ⊖🎵) The in-house restaurant of the Hotel Lahofer is a real treat. The chef is talented at turning out great regional cooking with an international twist, such as grilled trout served with fresh rosemary; menu items are paired with wines from the Lahofer winery. Book a table in advance.

🛏️ SLEEPING

CYKLOPENZION CAFÉ KULÍŠEK — PENSION €

(☑608 811 313; www.pensionkulisek.cz; Velká Michalská 7; s/d/tr 700/1300/1950Kč; ⊖@🎵) This family-run pension built over a cafe has lots of charm. The public areas and corridors have an antique-shop feel, and the rooms retain many old-world touches such as period lamps and elegant crown mouldings. The location, at the edge of the historic area, is not particularly beautiful, but the sights are a few minutes' walk away. Breakfast costs 100Kč.

★HOTEL LAHOFER — HOTEL €€

(☑515 220 323; www.lahofer.cz; Veselá 13; d/ste 1400/2100Kč; P⊖❄@🎵) This small hotel, connected to a winery of the same name, is one of the nicest lodging options in the country. The setting is a renovated 14th-century house, a three-minute walk from the main square. We love the simple, fresh contemporary styling and the attention to detail that extends to the excellent restaurant. Bikes can be hired for 220Kč per day.

REZIDENCE ZVON — PENSION €€

(☑775 611 128; www.rezidence-zvon.cz; Klácelova 61/11; s/d incl breakfast from 1200/1500Kč; @🎵) Concealed in a restored 18th-century residence near the castle are six comfortable rooms featuring wooden floors, flat-screen TVs and modern furniture. The central location couldn't be better or more picturesque. The minor downside is that there are lots of steps. There's no reception desk, so be sure to agree on an arrival time so someone can meet you with the keys.

Olomouc

Explore

Olomouc is a sleeper. Practically unknown outside the Czech Republic and underappreciated at home, the city is surprisingly majestic. The main square is among the country's very nicest, surrounded by historic buildings and blessed with a Unesco-protected trinity column. The evocative central streets are dotted with beautiful churches, testifying to the city's long history as a bastion of the Catholic Church. Explore the foundations of ancient Olomouc Castle at the must-see Archdiocesan Museum, then head for one of the city's many pubs or microbreweries. Don't forget to try the cheese, *Olomoucký sýr.*

The Best...

➡**Sight** Holy Trinity Column (p262)
➡**Place to Eat** Moritz (p265)
➡**Place to Drink** Cafe 87 (p266)

Top Tip

Be sure to take a walk through the beautiful parks and gardens that surround the town, with glimpses of pieces of the old town walls.

Getting There & Away

➡**Train** Olomouc is on a main international rail line, with regular services from both Prague (220Kč, three hours) and Brno (100Kč, 1½ hours). From Prague, you can take normal trains or a private RegioJet service. Buy RegioJet tickets from Student Agency ticket offices at Prague's main station or in **Olomouc** (☑841 101 101; www.studentagency.cz; Riegrova 28; ◎9am-6pm Mon-Fri). The Olomouc **train station** (Olomouc hlavní nádraží; ☑840 112 113; www.cd.cz; Jeremenkova; ☒2, 4, 6) is a 15-minute walk east of the centre.

➡**Bus** There are around 15 buses daily to/from Brno (92Kč, 1¼ hours); see www.vlak-bus.cz. The Olomouc **bus station** (Autobusové nádraží Olomouc; ☑585 313 848; www.studentagency.cz; Sladkovského 142/37; ☒4) is a 15- to 20-minute walk from the centre.

➡**Car** From Prague, Olomouc is an easy three-hour drive along the main D1 motorway through Brno; turn off on highway E462 and follow the signs. From Brno, the drive takes one hour along the same route.

Olomouc

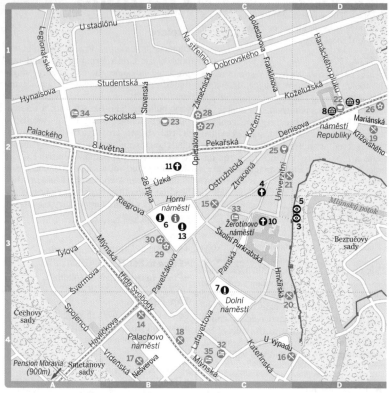

Pension Moravia (900m)

Need to Know

➡️ **Location** 280km southeast of Prague.

➡️ **Olomouc Information Centre** (Olomoucká Informační Služba; ☑585 513 385; www.tourism. olomouc.eu; Horní náměstí; ☺9am-7pm) Sells maps and books accommodation.

➡️ **Slam** (☑774 723 740; www.slam.cz; Slovenská 12; per min 1Kč; ☺9am-9pm; 🛜) Internet access with wi-fi capability.

👁 SIGHTS

👁 Horní Náměstí & Around

Olomouc's main square, Horní ('upper') náměstí, is home to the Town Hall as well as the city's most important sight: a gargantuan trinity column. The square also con-

tains two of the city's six baroque fountains: the **Hercules Fountain** (Herkulova kašna) dates from 1688 and features the muscular Greek hero standing astride a pit of writhing serpents; while the **Caesar Fountain** (Caeserova kašna), east of the town hall, was built in 1724 and is Olomouc's biggest. The tradition of building fountains was continued in 2002 when an **Orion Fountain** featuring turtles and a graceful dolphin was erected on the square.

HOLY TRINITY COLUMN   MONUMENT
(Sloup Nejsvětější Trojice; Horní náměstí) `FREE`
The town's pride and joy is this 35m-high (115ft) baroque sculpture that dominates the square and is a popular meeting spot for local residents. The trinity column was built between 1716 and 1754 and is allegedly the biggest single baroque sculpture in Central Europe. In 2000, the column was awarded an inscription on Unesco's World Heritage list.

Olomouc

⊙ Sights

⊗ Eating

☕ Drinking & Nightlife

✪ Entertainment

🛏 Sleeping

The individual statues depict a bewildering array of Catholic religious motifs, including the Holy Trinity, the twelve apostles, the assumption of Mary, and some of the best-known saints. There's a small **chapel** at the base of the column that's sometimes open during the day for you to poke your nose in.

TOWN HALL TOWER

(Radnice; Horní náměstí; tower 15Kč) `FREE`
Olomouc's Town Hall dates from the 14th century and is home to one of the quirkier sights in town: an astronomical clock from the 1950s, with a face in Socialist-Realist style. The original was damaged in WWII. At noon the figures put on a little performance. The tower is open twice daily by guided tour, at 11pm and 3pm.

ST MORITZ CATHEDRAL CHURCH

(Chrám sv Mořice; www.moric-olomouc.cz; Opletalova 10; ⊗tower 9am-5pm Mon-Sat, noon-5pm Sun) `FREE` This vast Gothic cathedral is Olomouc's original parish church, built between 1412 and 1540. The western tower is a remnant of its 13th-century predecessor. The cathedral's amazing sense of peace is shattered every September with an **International Organ Festival**; the cathedral's organ is Moravia's mightiest. The **tower** (more than 200 steps) has the best view in town.

◉ Dolní Náměstí & Around

Dolní náměstí, or 'lower' square, runs south of Horní náměstí, and is lined by shops and restaurants. It sports its own **Marian Plague Column** (Mariánský morový sloup; Dolní náměstí) and **baroque fountains** dedicated to Neptune and Jupiter.

ST MICHAEL'S CHURCH   CHURCH
(Kostel sv Michala; www.svatymichal.cz; Žerotínovo náměstí 1; ◈8am-6pm) **FREE** This beautiful church on Žerotínovo náměstí is topped by an aging green dome and a robust baroque interior with a rare painting of a pregnant Virgin Mary. Wrapped around the entire block is an active Dominican seminary (Dominikánský klášter).

CHAPEL OF ST JAN SARKANDER   CHURCH
(Kaple sv Jana Sarkandra; Žerotínovo náměstí; ◈10am-noon & 1-5pm) **FREE** This tiny, round chapel is named after a local priest who died under torture in 1620 for refusing to divulge false confessions. It's built on the site of the jail where he died, part of which is preserved in the cellar. Downstairs is an exhibition about his pious life.

◉ Náměstí Republiky & Around

MUSEUM OF MODERN ART   MUSEUM
(Muzeum moderního umění; ☑585 514111; www.olmuart.cz; Denisova 47; adult/child 70/35Kč, Sun & first Wed of month free; ◈10am-6pm Tue-Sun) On two floors, the museum showcases art from the 20th century under the heading 'A Century of Relativity'. One floor focuses on movements from the first half of the century, including expressionism, cubism and surrealism. A second part features postwar movements such as abstractionism and Czech trends from the 1970s and '80s.

You can buy a combined entry **ticket** (adult/concession 100/50Kč) that includes admission to the Archdiocesan Museum (p264).

REGIONAL HISTORY MUSEUM   MUSEUM
(Vlastivědné muzeum; ☑585 515 111; www.vmo.cz; náměstí Republiky 5; adult/child 60/30Kč; ◈9am-6pm Tue-Sun Apr-Sep, 10am-5pm Wed-Sun Oct-Mar) Housed in a former convent, this is part-ethnographic museum and part-natural-history museum. One section focuses on the history of Olomouc from the 6th century to modern times. The second section focuses on the geology of the region, as well as photos of scenic landscapes and information on endangered species. There are films and interactive displays.

ARCHBISHOP'S PALACE   MUSEUM
(Arcibiskupský palác; ☑587 405 421; www.arcibiskupskypalac.ado.cz; Wurmova 9; adult/concession 60/30Kč; ◈10am-5pm Tue-Sun May-Sep, 10am-5pm Sat & Sun Apr & Oct) This expansive former residence of the archbishop was built in 1685. Entry to see the lavish interiors is by guided tour only (free audioguide provided in English). It was here that Franz-Josef I was crowned Emperor of Austria in 1848 at the tender age of 18.

◉ Václavské Náměstí & Around

Václavské náměstí, northeast of the centre, was where Olomouc began. A thousand years ago, it was the site of Olomouc Castle. You can still see the castle foundations in the lower levels of the Archdiocesan Museum. The area still holds Olomouc's most venerable buildings and darkest secrets. Czech King Wenceslas III (Václav III) was murdered here in 1306 under circumstances that are still not clear to this day.

ARCHDIOCESAN MUSEUM   MUSEUM
(Arcidiecézni muzeum; ☑585 514 111; www.olmuart.cz; Václavské náměstí 3; adult/concession 70/35Kč, Sun free; ◈10am-6pm Tue-Sun) The impressive holdings of the Archdiocesan Museum trace the history of Olomouc back 1000 years. The thoughtful layout, with helpful English signage, takes you through the original Romanesque foundations of Olomouc Castle, and highlights the cultural and artistic development of the city during the Gothic and baroque periods.

Don't miss the magnificent Troyer Coach, definitely the stretch limo of the 18th century. Spring for the 30Kč English-language audioguide to get more out of the visit. You can buy a combined entry **ticket** (adult/concession 100/50Kč) that includes admission to the Olomouc Museum of Modern Art (p264).

ST WENCESLAS CATHEDRAL   CHURCH
(Dóm sv Václava; Václavské náměstí; ◈8am-6pm) **FREE** This magnificent cathedral, the seat of the Olomouc Archbishop, was originally

a Romanesque basilica that was first conse-crated way back in 1131. It was rebuilt several times before finally (in the 1880s) having the neo-Gothic makeover you see today.

⊙ Bezručovy Sady

CIVIL DEFENCE SHELTER HISTORIC STRUCTURE
(Kryt Civilní Obrany; Bezručovy sady; admission 20Kč; ⊙tours at 10am, 1pm & 4pm Thu & Sat mid-Jun–mid-Sep) Olomouc is all about centuries-old history, but this more recent relic of the Cold War is also worth exploring on a guided tour. The shelter was built between 1953 and 1956 and was designed to shelter a lucky few from a chemical or nuclear strike. Tours are arranged by and begin at the tour-ist information office.

BEZRUČOVY SADY PARK
(Bezručovy sady) **FREE** A staircase at the rear of St Michael's Church on the southern end of Univerzitní leads through the walls of the old town to Bezručovy sady, a pretty park wrapped around the meandering Mlýnský potok.

✕ EATING

NEPAL NEPALESE €
(☑585 208 428; www.nepalska.cz; Mlýnská 4; mains 110-150Kč; ⊙11am-1am Mon-Thu, 11am-2am Fri & Sat; 🛜🍴) Located in a popular Irish pub, this Nepalese-Indian eatery is the place to go for something a little differ-ent. The 110Kč buffet lunch is an excellent deal (choice of four or five mostly vegetar-ian items), but try to arrive just before noon to get a seat (the buffet is popular).

DRÁPAL CZECH €
(☑585 225 818; www.restauracedrapal.cz; Havlíčkova 1; mains 110-170Kč; ⊙10am-midnight Mon-Fri, 11am-midnight Sat, 11am-11pm Sun; 🛜) It's hard to go wrong with this big historic pub on a busy corner near the centre. The unpasteurised 12° Pilsner Urquell is argu-ably the best beer in Olomouc. The menu is loaded with Czech classics, such as the ever-popular *Španělský ptáček* (literally 'Spanish bird'), a beef roulade stuffed with smoked sausage, parsley and a hard-boiled egg.

GREEN BAR VEGETARIAN €
(☑777 749 274; www.greenbar.cz; Ztracená 3; meals 100Kč; ⊙10am-5pm Mon-Fri, 10am-2pm Sat; ⊝🍴) Around 100Kč will get you a feast of salads, couscous and veggie lasagne at this self-service vegetarian cafe. It's popu-lar with a cosmopolitan mix of overseas students.

MICHALSKÝ VÝPAD STEAKHOUSE €€
(☑585 222 563; www.michalskyvypad.cz; Blažejské náměstí 2; mains 140-300Kč; ⊙11am-10pm Mon-Thu, 11am-11pm Fri & Sat; ⊝🛜) Noth-ing flash about this family-run place, just very good, well-prepared steaks, burgers and grilled meats (including some pork and chicken dishes). The chips (fries) are thin and perfectly cooked, and pair well with the homemade mayonnaise. The 10° Bernard beer on tap makes a nice alternative to the standard Pilsner Urquell and Staropramen.

MORITZ CZECH €€
(☑585 205 560; www.hostinec-moritz.cz; Nešverova 2; mains 120-260Kč; ⊙11am-11pm; ⊝🛜) This microbrewery and restaurant is a local favourite. We reckon it's a combina-tion of the terrific beers, good value food, and a praise-worthy 'no smoking' policy. In summer, the beer garden's the only place to be. Advance booking is a must. The loca-tion is about a 10-minute walk south of the centre, across the busy street třída Svobody.

SVATOVÁCLAVSKÝ PIVOVAR CZECH €€
(☑585 207 517; www.svatovaclavsky-pivovar.cz; Mariánská 4; mains 170-290Kč; ⊙8am-midnight Mon-Fri, 11am-midnight Sat, 11am-9pm Sun; ⊝) This is one of a number of popular micro-breweries in town, with the speciality here being well-crafted, unpasteurised wheat and cherry beers. The menu features most-ly Czech standards done well, plus a few dishes that experiment with Olomouc's sig-nature stinky cheese.

VILA PRIMAVESI INTERNATIONAL €€
(☑585 204 852; www.primavesi.cz; Univerzitní 7; mains 200-380Kč; ⊙11am-11pm Mon-Sat, 11am-4pm Sun; ⊝) In an art nouveau villa that played host to Austrian artist Gustav Klimt in the early 20th century, the Vila Primavesi is one of Olomouc's most exclusive restau-rants. On summer evenings enjoy meals such as tuna steak and risotto on the terrace overlooking the city gardens. Lunch specials are better value than evening meals.

U ANDĚLA CZECH €€
(☑585 228 755; www.uandela.cz; Hrnčířská 10; mains 170-380Kč; ⊙11am-10pm; ⊝) You may

have to wander some to find this atmospheric haunt, down a tiny lane behind Dolní náměstí. While the cooking is only a step or two above average, the warm, country-pub setting is perfect for a relaxing dinner. Try to grab a table towards the back, which overlooks the city gardens below.

🍷 DRINKING

★ CAFE 87   CAFE
(☎585 202 593; www.cafe87.cz; Denisova 47; chocolate pie 45Kč, coffee 40Kč; ⏰7.30am-9pm Mon-Fri, 8am-9pm Sat & Sun; 🛜) Locals come in droves to this funky cafe beside the Olomouc Museum of Modern Art for coffee and their famous chocolate pie. It's a top spot for breakfast and toasted sandwiches too. Seating on two floors and a rooftop terrace.

THE BLACK STUFF   PUB
(☎774 697 909; www.blackstuff.cz; 1. máje 19; ⏰4pm-2am Mon-Fri, 5pm-3am Sat, 5-11pm Sun) Cosy, Irish bar with several beers on tap and a large and growing collection of single-malts and other choice tipples. Attracts a mixed crowd of students, locals and visitors.

TÉ & CAFÉ KRATOCHVÍLE   TEAHOUSE
(☎603 564 120; www.kratochvile-cajovna.cz; Sokolská 36; ⏰11am-11pm Mon-Fri, from 3pm Sat & Sun) A global array of teas and coffees, an interesting array of beers and wines, and a laid-back Zen ambience (fuelled by water pipes) make this a good spot to recharge.

VERTIGO   BAR
(www.klubvertigo.cz; Univerzitní 6; ⏰7pm-2am Mon-Thu, 4pm-2am Fri-Sun) A dark, dank student bar that reeks of spilled beer and stale smoke. In other words, a very popular drinking spot in a college town like Olomouc.

🛏 SLEEPING

POET'S CORNER   HOSTEL €
(☎777 570 730; www.hostelolomouc.com; Sokolská 1, 4th fl; dm/s/d 350/700/900Kč; 🌐🛜; 🚌2, 4, 6) The Australian-Czech couple who mind this exceptionally well-run hostel are a wealth of information. There are dorms in eight-bed rooms, and singles and doubles. Bicycle hire is 100Kč per day. In summer there's sometimes a two-night minimum stay, but Olomouc is worth it, and there's plenty of day-trip information on offer.

UBYTOVNA MARIE   GUESTHOUSE €
(☎585 220 220; www.ubytovnamarie.cz; třída Svobody 41; per person 390Kč; 🌐🛜) Spick and span (if spartan) double and triple rooms with shared bathrooms and kitchens make this spot popular with long-stay overseas students. Discounts kick-in after two nights.

PENSION MORAVIA   PENSION €
(☎603 748 188; www.pension-moravia.com; Dvořákova 37; s/d/tr 700/900/1400Kč; 🅿🌐🛜; 🚌19 to Dvořákova) A 10-minute walk from the town centre, this pension provides good value in a quiet street without the parking hassles of the Old Town. Catch bus 19 from the railway station to the Dvořákova stop.

★ PENZIÓN NA HRADĚ   PENSION €€
(☎585 203 231; www.penzionnahrade.cz; Michalská 4; s/d 1390/1890Kč; 🌐❋🛜) In terms of price/quality ratio, this is Olomouc's best deal. Worth the minor splurge if you can swing it. The location, in the shadow of St Michael's Church, is central. The sleek, cool rooms have a professional design touch and there's a garden terrace for relaxing out back. Reserve in advance in summer.

PENSION ANGELUS   PENSION €€
(☎776 206 936; www.pensionangelus.cz; Wurmova 1; s/d 1450/1850Kč; 🅿🌐🛜; 🚌2, 4, 6) With antique furniture, crisp white duvets and Oriental rugs on wooden floors, the Angelus is a splurge-worthy romantic getaway. To get here catch tram 2 or 6 from the train station, jumping off at the U Domú stop.

PENSION KŘIVÁ   PENSION €€
(☎585 209 204; www.pension-kriva.cz; Křivá 8; s/d 1550/2000Kč; 🌐🛜) This modern pension gets a lot of things right: spacious rooms with cherry-wood furniture, flash bathrooms with even flasher toiletries, and a cosy cafe downstairs.

☆ ENTERTAINMENT

JAZZ TIBET CLUB   LIVE MUSIC
(☎585 230 399; www.jazzclub.olomouc.com; Sokolská 48; admission free-250Kč; ⏰box office 11am-2pm) Blues, jazz and world music, including occasional international acts, feature at this popular spot, which also incorporates a good restaurant and wine bar. Buy tickets in advance at the club box office or at the Olomouc Information Centre.

HOSPODA U MUSEA
CLUB, LIVE MUSIC

(Ponorka; www.ponorka.com; třída 1 maje 8; ⊙10am-midnight Mon-Fri, noon-midnight Sat, 4pm-midnight Sun) This is possibly the loudest, smokiest and most crowded rock club/pub in the Czech Republic. The scene is mostly aging rockers and punks living in the good ol' days; on occasional evenings there are legendary concerts.

KINO METROPOL
CINEMA

(☑722 955 466; www.kinometropol.cz; Sokolská 25; ⊙9am-8pm Mon-Fri, 2-8pm Sat & Sun) For Hollywood hits and art-house surprises. Small cafe and a children's play area.

MORAVSKÉ DIVADLO
OPERA, BALLET

(☑box office 585 500 500; www.moravskedivadlo. cz; Horní náměstí 22; ⊙box office 9am-6pm Mon-Fri) From opera to ballet, all well priced.

MORAVIAN PHILHARMONIC OLOMOUC
CLASSICAL MUSIC

(Moravská Filharmonie Olomouc; ☑585 206 520, tickets 585 513 392; www.mfo.cz; Horní náměstí 23; concerts 70-200Kč) The local orchestra presents regular concerts and hosts Olomouc's International Organ Festival. Buy tickets one week in advance at the Olomouc Information Centre or at the venue one hour before the performance starts.

Kroměříž

Explore

Sleepy Kroměříž merits a detour if you happen to be in this part of the country. The main draw is the sumptuous baroque Archbishop's Chateau, with its commanding tower, rococo interiors and even a certifiable masterpiece: Titian's *The Flaying of Marsyas*. The palace is a Unesco World Heritage site – a great place to while away a few hours. Outside the palace there are some attractive Renaissance and baroque churches and other buildings scattered about, and two lovely gardens: the formal **Flower Garden** and a sprawling park below the chateau itself. Kroměříž is also home to an excellent microbrewery, an essential retreat once you've taken in the sights.

The Best...

➡**Sight** Archbishop's Chateau (p267)

➡**Place to Eat** Černý Orel (p268)

➡**Place to Drink** Černý Orel (p268)

Top Tip

The gardens below the Archbishop's Chateau are beautiful patches of green that merit an hour or two of strolling. There are paths, lakes and a zoo for kids. Entry is free.

Getting There & Away

➡**Train** Train service is poor. Trains to and from Brno (115Kč, 1½ hours) require a change in Kojetín. Trains from Olomouc (70Kč, one hour) require a change in Kojetín or Hulín. See www.vlak-bus.cz for details. The **train station** (Vlakové nádraží; www.cd.cz; Nádražní) is a 10-minute walk northeast of the centre.

➡**Bus** Buses are generally better than trains. There are regular buses, including Student Agency coaches, to/from Brno (88Kč, 1¼ hours). The **bus station** (Stoličkova) is a 10-minute walk northeast of the centre.

➡**Car** From Brno, it's a 45-minute drive northeast along the D1 motorway.

Need to Know

➡**Location** 271km southeast of Prague.

➡**Tourist Information Centre** (Informační Centrum Kroměříž; ☑573 321 408; www. kromeriz.eu; Velké náměstí 115; ⊙9am-6pm Mon-Fri year round, 9am-4pm Sat & Sun May-Sep, 9am-2pm Sat Oct-Apr) Helpful office assists in arranging accommodation; also sells tickets for Student Agency coaches to Brno and Prague.

➡**Internet Access** The Tourist Information Centre has computers.

⊙ SIGHTS

Most visitors come to see the Archbishop's Chateau. After you've done that, meander over to the town's impressive main square, **Velké náměstí**. The 16th-century Renaissance **Town Hall** stands on the corner with Kovářská. At No 30 is the town's oldest **pharmacy**, U Zlatého lva, established in 1675. The cobblestone square also has a decorative **fountain** and **plague column**.

ARCHBISHOP'S CHATEAU
CASTLE

(Arcibiskupský zámek; ☑573 502 011; www. zamek-kromeriz.cz; Zámek; adult/concession 180/160Kč, art gallery 90/80Kč; ⊙9am-6pm

Tue-Sun Jul & Aug, to 5pm Tue-Sun May, Jun & Sep, to 4pm Sat & Sun only Apr & Oct) The Unesco-protected Archbishop's Chateau dates from the late 17th century and is Kroměříž's big-ticket sight, with an 84m-high baroque **tower** visible for miles around. Main attractions include impressive interiors, boasting baroque and rococo murals, as well as the tower, the castle **gardens**, and an impressive **art gallery**.

FLOWER GARDEN GARDENS
(Květná zahrada; ☑cash desk 723 962 891; www.zamek-kromeriz.cz; ulice Gen Svobody; adult/concession 40/30Kč; ☺8am-6pm May-Sep, to 4pm Oct-Apr; ⏧) This 17th-century baroque garden is managed by the Archbishop's Château, but is located on the opposite side of town, about a 15-minute walk west of the chateau. The appeal here is an immaculately kept formal garden. The main sights are a frequently photographed **rotunda** and **colonnade**. Enter from Gen Svobody street.

KROMĚŘÍŽ MUSEUM MUSEUM
(Muzeum Kroměřížska; ☑573 338 388; www.muzeum-km.cz; Velké náměstí 38; adult/concession 60/30Kč; ☺9am-noon & 1-5pm Tue-Sun) The biggest drawcard here is a permanent collection of the works of Czech painter and graphic artist **Max Švabinský**, who was born in Kroměříž in 1873. Several rooms of Švabinský's paintings and sketches are located on the 1st floor. The top floor is dedicated to wildlife. The cellar holds an interesting exhibition of archeological finds (information only in Czech).

 EATING & DRINKING

RADNIČNÍ SKLÍPEK CZECH €
(☑608 117 226; www.radnicnikm.cz; Kovářská 20/2; mains 80-140Kč; ☺8am-10pm Mon-Fri, 9am-midnight Sat, 9am-6pm Sun; ⏧) This cute-and-cosy subterranean space just off Velké náměstí offers good-value Czech dishes such as chicken schnitzel served with potato salad. The homemade soups are brought to the table in big tureens for the whole family.

GREEN BAR VEGETARIAN €
(☑724 176 926; www.greenbar.717.cz; Ztracená 68; mains 50-80Kč; ☺11.30am-4pm Mon-Thu, to 2.30pm Fri; ⏧) Salads and veggie main dishes, a nonsmoking environment and a kids' play area add up to a family-friendly joint. Also offers vegan entrees.

★ČERNÝ OREL CZECH €€
(☑573 332 765; www.pivovar-kromeriz.cz; Velké náměstí 24; mains 159-259Kč; ☺11am-midnight; ⏧) Some of the best food in this part of Moravia is served at this microbrewery on the main square. Choose from a full range of duck, pork and venison mains and pair your meal with one of the house brews.

SLEEPING

PENZIÓN EXCELLENT PENSION €
(☑573 333 023; www.excellent.tunker.com; Riegrovo náměstí 163/7; s/d 1090/1420Kč; ⏧⏧⏧) This pension offers brightly furnished rooms and big buffet breakfast, with a central location on a quiet square about a five-minute walk from the Archbishop's Chateau. While it lacks the polish of a couple of other places in town, it's nevertheless good value and a decent choice for a short stay.

HOTEL LA FRESCA BOUTIQUE HOTEL €€
(☑573 335 404; www.lafresca.cz; Velké náměstí 109/55; s 1100-1300, d 1500-1800Kč; ⏧⏧) The La Fresca occupies a beautifully restored 16th-century burgher's house, with wooden floors, high ceilings and exposed brick in some rooms. The apartments feature furnishings that recall 19th-century styles. The house restaurant is very good. Book well in advance in summer.

HOTEL OCTÁRNA HOTEL €€
(☑573 505 655; www.octarna.cz; Tovačovského 318; s 1150-1400Kč, d 1500-2050Kč; ⏧⏧⏧) We love this small hotel tucked away inside a quiet, shaded courtyard that once belonged to a Franciscan monastery. From the original Max Švabinský paintings on the garden wall to the clean and modern rooms, everything feels classy and well taken care of. A short stroll from the main square.

HOTEL ČERNÝ OREL HOTEL €€
(☑573 332 769; www.cerny-orel.eu; Velké náměstí 24; s 1100-1400Kč, d 1200-1700Kč; ⏧⏧) One of the nicest hotels in town just happens to occupy prime real estate above the town's highly recommended restaurant/microbrewery. The rooms have a clean, modern look and are equipped with fancy baths and high-end amenities such as flat-screen TVs and DVD players. Book in advance on weekends in summer.

Understand Prague & the Czech Republic

Prague & the Czech Republic Today

Prague has emerged as one of Europe's leading tourist destinations. The capital heaves with more than five million foreign tourists a year, and most locals are accustomed to the throng. The crowds can make crossing the Charles Bridge trying on summer's day, but they bring vitality to the city and invigorate an already-booming culinary and cultural scene. The pace slows down markedly in the countryside, where unique aspects of Czech culture still flourish.

Best on Film

Amadeus (1985) Mozart's love affair with Prague gets brilliant treatment.
Kolya (1996) Velvet Revolution–era Prague never looked lovelier.
Loves of a Blonde (1965) Miloš Forman's 'New Wave' classic.
Burning Bush (2013) HBO miniseries on Jan Palach, the student who immolated himself in 1969.
Divided We Fall (2000) Director Jan Hřebejk's hard look at the Nazi occupation and Czechs who collaborated.

Best in Print

The Unbearable Lightness of Being (Milan Kundera; 1984) Prague before the 1968 Warsaw Pact invasion.
I Served the King of England (Bohumil Hrabal; 1990) The Hotel Paříž is the backdrop to this humorous classic.
The Castle (Franz Kafka; 1926) We wonder which castle Kafka was thinking about?
The Good Soldier Švejk (Jaroslav Hašek; 1923) Hašek's absurdist novel is set throughout the Czech Republic.
My Merry Mornings (Ivan Klima; 1986) The sweeter side of life in communist Prague.

Getting that 'Velvet' Mojo Back

It's been some years now since the death in 2011 of Václav Havel, the country's first post-communist president and undisputed moral authority of the 1989 Velvet Revolution. Havel's death at 75 wasn't unexpected, but seemed to catch the country by surprise. The outpouring of grief was uncharacteristically intense for normally stoic Czechs. News of the death brought tens of thousands onto Wenceslas Square to lay candles at the statue of St Wenceslas. Thousands more lined up days later to file past his coffin and pay their final respects.

Havel's passing left a moral vacuum at the heart of the country that in many ways has yet to be filled. The election in 2013 of a frankly embarrassing president, with a fondness for a drink, and a parliamentary vote that same year that's now mired in allegations that the winner was a former communist agent, have done little to convince Czechs the country is on the right path. To be sure, Havel wasn't always an effective president, but at least one knew where his conscience was. To many, especially younger Czechs, this moral component to public life appears to be missing. Indeed, for the time being at least, there appear to be no new Havels on the horizon.

How 'Not' to Govern a Country

In the 25 years since the Velvet Revolution there have been many strange elections and election years in the Czech Republic. Long-term observers still remember 2009, when the Czech government fell in a no-confidence vote, but new elections weren't held for more than a year. That escapade gave rise to the running joke at the time: 'What's the world's biggest nongovernmental organisation? Answer: the Czech Republic.'

But even by Czech standards, 2013 may go down as the weirdest yet. First, outgoing President Václav Klaus was replaced in office by the centre-left Miloš Zeman in the country's first-ever direct popular vote for the presidency. Zeman is a canny, old-school politician with a rumoured taste for drink, who has already embarrassed the country with his off-the-cuff comments and videos showing him falling down stairs or weaving tipsily at the podium.

Later the same year, parliamentary elections brought to power a bizarre left-right coalition, linking the Social Democratic Party and a mysterious new movement, ANO (Yes), led by billionaire businessman Andrej Babiš. In 2014 Babiš fought allegations he spied for the secret police during the communist period. For vote-weary Czechs, this is simply the new normal.

Hopeful Signs for the Economy

After wallowing for years in the wake of the global recession, the Czech Republic has taken aggressive measures to claw its way out of the muck, including devaluing the Czech crown by 5% with respect to the euro. That move and others appear to be having some effect. After suffering a decline in growth as recently as 2013, the Czech economy was poised to grow by 1.1% in 2014 and 2.3% in 2015. Much will depend on continued recovery in Germany, the Czechs' largest export market.

Visitors are not likely to notice any sign of a downturn in Prague, which remains partially buffered from the global economy due to tourist income. Indeed, a near 25-year boom in tourism has helped the Czech capital to become the seventh-richest region in the European Union. The effects are more pronounced in the countryside – particularly West Bohemia and North Moravia – where much of the industry is located.

Oh No, Not Again

When a historic and catastrophic flood inundated Prague in 2002, it was was widely reported as a '100-year' event, meaning presumably it was something that might happen once in a century. At the time, that made sense, since the last big flood before that occurred in 1890.

So it came as something of a shock when the waters started rising again in June 2013. Fortunately, the city learned a lot from the high water of 2002, so the response was quicker and more effective. This time around, the temporary barriers along the river were erected quickly and held, sparing the city near-certain disaster.

religion
(% of population)

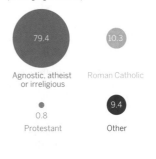

Agnostic, atheist or irreligious — 79.4

Roman Catholic — 10.3

Protestant — 0.8

Other — 9.4

if Prague were 100 people

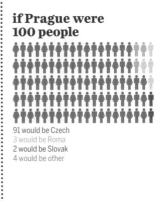

91 would be Czech
3 would be Roma
2 would be Slovak
4 would be other

population per sq km

PRAGUE   CZECH REPUBLIC

= 135 people

History

While modern-day visitors still tend to see the Czech Republic as part of 'Eastern Europe' or a former member of the Soviet bloc, for more than 1000 years the kingdoms of Bohemia and Moravia stood at the very heart of European affairs. Indeed, for much of the 14th century, under Emperor Charles IV, Prague was the seat of the Holy Roman Empire – in effect, the capital of Europe as it existed during those times. Later, in the 16th century under Rudolf II, Prague served as the centre of the sprawling Habsburg Empire, overseeing territories as far-flung as modern-day Italy and Poland.

Early Years with the Celts

There's been human habitation on the territory of the modern-day Czech Republic for some 600,000 years, with permanent communities since around 4000 BC, but it's the Celts, who came to the area around 500 BC, that arouse the most interest. The name 'Bohemia' for the western province of the Czech Republic derives from one of the most successful of these Celtic tribes, the Boii. Traces of Boii culture have been found as far away as southern Germany, leading some archaeologists to posit a relation between Celts here and those in France, and possibly even further afield to tribes in the British Isles.

Some archaeologists believe there was an early Celtic settlement where Prague Castle now stands, but so far there's no physical evidence to support the claim.

In Come the Slavs

It's unclear what prompted the great migration of peoples across Europe in the 6th and 7th centuries, but during this time large populations of Slavs began arriving in central Europe from the east, driving out the Celts and pushing German tribes further to the west. The newcomers established several settlements along the Vltava, including one near the present site of Prague Castle and another upriver at Vyšehrad.

It was a highly unstable time, with the new arrivals under threat from incoming peoples such as the Avars. A Frankish trader named Samo briefly succeeded in uniting the Slavs to repel the Avars, but the Slavs quickly resumed their squabbling.

TIMELINE	500 BC	AD 500	Early 600s
	Celtic tribes arrive in the territory of the modern-day Czech Republic, building settlements whose remains will later be discovered in and around Prague.	Slavic tribes enter Central Europe during the Great Migration, forming settlements along the Vltava River. Excavations indicate the largest of these are near Roztoky, northwest of Prague.	Princess Libuše, the fabled founder of the Přemysl dynasty, looks out over the Vltava valley and predicts that a great city will emerge there someday.

The Myth of Libuše & the Founding of Prague

Fittingly for a city that embraces so much mystery, the origins of Prague are shrouded in a fairy tale. Princess Libuše, the daughter of early ruler Krok, is said to have stood on a hill near the city's Vyšehrad castle one day around the 7th century and predicted a glorious city that would one day become Prague. According to the legend, Libuše needed to find a strong suitor who could yield sturdy heirs to the throne. Passing over a field of eligible bachelors, including some sickly-looking royals, she selected a simple ploughman, Přemysl. She chose well. The Přemysl dynasty would go on to rule for some 400 years.

In the 9th century, the Přemysl prince Bořivoj selected an outcropping in Hradčany to build Prague Castle, the dynasty's seat. Amazingly, the castle – the official seat of the Czech presidency – remains the centre of power to this day.

Christianity became the state religion under the rule of the pious Wenceslas (Václav in Czech), the Duke of Bohemia (r 925–29) and now the chief patron saint of the Czech people (immortalised on horseback at the top of Wenceslas Square). Wenceslas was the 'Good King Wenceslas' of the well-known Christmas carol, written in 1853 by English clergyman John Mason Neale. Wenceslas's conversion to Christianity is said to have angered his mother and his brother, Boleslav, who ended up killing the young duke in a fit of jealousy.

Despite the dysfunctional family relations, the Přemysls proved to be highly effective rulers. During the 13th century, the Přemysl lands stretched from modern-day Silesia (near the Czech–Polish border) to the Mediterranean Sea.

Archaeologists working near the town of Roztoky, northwest of Prague, recently unearthed what may be the largest and oldest of the early Slavic settlements, dating from the early 6th century.

Charles IV & the Holy 'Prague' Empire

It's hard to imagine that Prague and the Kingdom of Bohemia will ever exceed the position of power they held in the 14th century, when Prague for a time became the seat of what was known then as the Holy Roman Empire, under Emperor Charles IV (Karel IV, r 1346–78).

The path to glory began predictably enough with the murder of a Přemysl ruler, Wenceslas III, in 1306, leaving no male successor to the throne. Eventually, John of Luxembourg (Jan Lucemburský to the Czechs) assumed the Czech throne through his marriage to Wenceslas III's daughter Elyška in 1310.

Under the enlightened rule of John's son, Charles IV, Prague grew into one of the continent's largest and most prosperous cities. Charles greatly expanded the limits of the city and commissioned both the bridge that now bears his name and St Vitus Cathedral, among other

HISTORY THE MYTH OF LIBUŠE & THE FOUNDING OF PRAGUE

870s	1278	August 1306	1346
Prince Bořivoj begins construction of Prague Castle in Hradčany to serve as the seat of his Přemysl dynasty – as it will for kings, emperors and presidents for centuries to come.	King Otakar II is thrashed by the Habsburgs at the Battle of Marchfeld (*Moravské Pole* in Czech) at the height of the Přemysl dynasty's influence.	The last Přemysl king, Wenceslas III, is murdered, leaving no male heir. The dynasty passes to John of Luxembourg, who will give Bohemia its greatest ruler, his son Charles IV.	John of Luxembourg dies and Charles IV becomes Bohemian king. Later, he adds 'Holy Roman Emperor' to his list of titles. Prague booms as the seat of the empire.

RELIGIOUS REFORMER JAN HUS

Jan Hus was the Czech lands' foremost (and one of Europe's earliest) Christian reformers, preceding Martin Luther and the Lutheran reformation by more than a century.

Hus was born into a poor family in southern Bohemia in 1372. He studied at the Karolinum (Charles University) and eventually became dean of the philosophical faculty.

Like many of his colleagues at the time, Hus was inspired by the English philosopher and radical reformist theologian John Wycliffe. The corrupt practices of the Roman Catholic clergy proved to be an easy target for Wycliffe's criticisms and fuelled a growing Czech resentment of the wealth and corruption of the clergy.

In 1391 Prague reformers founded the Bethlehem Chapel, where sermons were given in Czech rather than Latin. Hus preached there for about 10 years, while continuing his duties at the university.

Hus's criticisms of the Catholic Church, particularly the practice of selling indulgences, endeared him to his followers but eventually put him in the Pope's black book. In fact, the Pope had him excommunicated in 1410, but Hus continued to preach. In 1415, he was invited to the Council of Constance in modern-day Germany to recant his views with the understanding that he would be granted safe passage. He refused to concede and was burned at the stake on 6 July 1415.

projects. He also established Charles University as the first university in central Europe.

The Hussite Wars & Religious Strife

In contrast to the 14th century, the 15th century brought little but hardship and war to the territory of the Czech Republic. Much of the good of the preceding years was undone in an orgy of religion-inspired violence and intolerance. The period witnessed the rise of an impassioned Church-reform movement led by Jan Hus. Hus's intentions to rid Rome's papal authorities of corruption were admirable, but his movement ended up dividing the country. In 1419, supporters of Hussite preacher Jan Želivský stormed Prague's New Town Hall and tossed several Catholic councillors out the windows – thus introducing the word 'defenestration' (throwing someone from a window in order to do him or her bodily harm) into the political lexicon.

The Hussites (as the followers of Jan Hus were known) assumed control of Prague after the death of Holy Roman Emperor Wenceslas IV in 1419. The move sparked the first anti-Hussite crusade, launched in 1420 by Emperor Sigismund, with the support of many pro-Catholic rulers

1415	1419	15th century	1583
Religious reformer Jan Hus is burned at the stake at Konstanz, Germany, for refusing to recant his criticisms of the Catholic Church. His death inflames decades of religious strife.	Angry Hussite supporters rush into the New Town Hall and toss several Catholic councillors out the window, introducing the word 'defenestration' to the world.	The Hussite Wars – pitting radical reformers against Catholics and Hussite factions against each other – rage throughout Bohemia.	Habsburg Emperor Rudolf II moves the dynasty's seat from Vienna to Prague. This second golden age lasts three decades until Rudolf dies, when Protestant/Catholic tensions boil over.

around Europe. Hussite commander Jan Žižka successfully defended the city in the Battle of Vítkov Hill, but the religious strife spilled into the countryside. The Hussites were split into factions – those wanting to make peace with the emperor and those wanting to fight to the end. The more radical Hussites, the Taborites, were ultimately defeated in battle at Lipany, east of Prague, in 1434.

The Habsburgs Take Over

The weakening of the Bohemian state due to the religious wars left the region open to foreign intervention. Austria's Habsburg empire, ruled from Vienna, was able to take advantage and eventually came to dominate both Bohemia and Moravia. At first, in the mid-16th century, the Habsburgs were invited in by a weary Czech nobility weakened by constant warfare. Decades later, in 1620, the Austrians were able to cement their control over the region with a decisive victory over Czech forces at Bílá Hora, near Prague. The Austrians would continue to rule the Czechs for another 300 years, until the emergence of independent Czechoslovakia at the end of WWI.

Though the Austrians are generally knocked in Czech history books, it must be admitted that their leadership established some much needed stability in the region. Indeed, the latter part of the 16th century under Habsburg Emperor Rudolf II (r 1576–1612) is considered a second 'golden age' in Czech history, comparable to Charles IV's rule in the 14th century. Eccentric Rudolf preferred Prague to his family's ancestral home in Vienna and moved the seat of the Habsburg Empire to the Czech capital for the duration of his reign.

Rudolf is typically viewed by historians as something of a kook. He had a soft spot for esoteric pursuits such as soothsaying and alchemy, and populated his court with wags and conjurers from around Europe. The English mathematician and occultist John Dee and his less-esteemed countryman Edward Kelly were just two of the noted mystics Rudolf kept at the castle in an eternal quest to turn base metals into gold. It's also true, though, that Rudolf's tutelage led to real advances in science, particularly astronomy.

For all his successes, though, Rudolf failed to heal the age-old rift between Protestants and Catholics, and the end of his reign in 1612 saw those tensions again rise to the forefront. The breaking point came in 1618 with the 'Second Defenestration of Prague', when a group of Protestant noblemen stormed into a chamber at Prague Castle and tossed two Catholic councillors and their secretary out the window. The men survived – legend has it they fell onto a dung heap – but the damage was

Following Emperor Sigismund's death, George of Poděbrady (Jiří z Poděbrad) ruled as Bohemia's one and only Hussite king (1452–71), with the backing of moderate Hussites, the Utraquists. By that time, however, the Hussite cause was lost and once-prosperous Bohemia lay in ruin.

HISTORY THE HABSBURGS TAKE OVER

During the 17th and 18th centuries, Prague got a major baroque facelift, including the statues on Charles Bridge and construction of St Nicholas Church in Malá Strana. This was mainly the work of the Austrians and the Jesuits, eager to mark their triumph.

1618	1620	1787	1883
A Protestant mob throws two Catholic councillors and their secretary from a window at Prague Castle. This pushes the Habsburgs to start the Thirty Years' War.	Czech soldiers, united under Protestant leader Frederick V, lose a crucial battle at Bílá Hora, to Austrian Habsburg troops. It begins 300 years of Austrian rule.	Wolfgang Amadeus Mozart, already more popular in Prague than Vienna, conducts the premiere of his opera *Don Giovanni* at the Estates Theatre near Old Town Square.	German-Jewish writer Franz Kafka is born near Old Town Square. He'll lead a double life: mild-mannered insurance clerk by day, harried father of the modern novel by night.

Austrian archduke and heir to the throne, Franz Ferdinand d'Este – whose 1914 assassination in Sarajevo sparked WWI – had a Czech wife and a main residence just south of Prague, Konopiště Chateau. He was not a fan of the Imperial capital, Vienna, and preferred to spend as little time there as possible.

done. The act sparked the Thirty Years' War that ultimately consumed the whole of Europe and left Bohemia again in ruins.

Revival of the Czech Nation

Remarkably, though German was the official language, Czech language and culture managed to endure through the years of Austrian occupation. As the Habsburgs eased their grip in the 19th century, Prague became the centre of the Czech National Revival. The revival found its initial expression not in politics – outright political activity was forbidden – but in Czech-language literature and drama. Important figures included linguists Josef Jungmann and Josef Dobrovský, and František Palacký, author of *Dějiny národu českého* (The History of the Czech Nation).

While many of the countries in post-Napoleonic Europe were swept up by similar nationalist sentiments, social and economic factors gave the Czech revival particular strength. Educational reforms by Empress Maria Theresa (r 1740–80) had given even the poorest Czechs access to schooling, and a vocal middle class was emerging through the Industrial Revolution.

Independence at Last

President Masaryk is a beloved figure in Czech history and regarded as the father of the country. Historians, though, question his legacy, which pushed for the creation of independent, weak states in Central Europe, leaving a power vacuum for the Germans and Russians.

For Czechs, the tragedy of WWI had one silver lining: the defeat of the Central powers, including Austria-Hungary, left the empire too weak to fight for its former holdings, paving the way for the creation of independent Czechoslovakia in 1918. Czech patriots Tomáš Masaryk and Edvard Beneš had spent the war years in the United States, where they lobbied ceaselessly with Czech and Slovak émigré communities to win American backing for a joint state, Czechoslovakia, that would link ethnic Czechs with their linguistic cousins, Slovaks, further to the east.

This plea appealed especially to the idealistic American president, Woodrow Wilson, and his belief in the self-determination of peoples. The most workable solution appeared to be a single federal state of two equal republics, and this was spelled out in agreements signed in Cleveland, Ohio, in 1915 and Pittsburgh, Pennsylvania, in 1918 (both cities having large populations of Czechs and Slovaks).

As WWI drew to a close, the newly created Czechoslovakia declared its independence, with Allied support, on 28 October 1918. Prague became the capital and the popular Masaryk, a writer and political philosopher, the new republic's first president.

1918	1920s	1938	1939
A newly independent Czechoslovakia is proclaimed at Municipal House (Obecní dům) in the final days of WWI. Crowds celebrate in Wenceslas Square.	The heyday of the First Republic, now seen as another golden age. Prague intellectuals are heavily influenced by modern movements in art, architecture, literature and photography.	European powers meet in Munich, agreeing to Hitler's demand to annex the Sudetenland region. British PM Chamberlain declares 'peace in our time'.	German soldiers cross the Czechoslovak frontier and occupy Bohemia and Moravia. Czechoslovak soldiers, ordered in advance not to resist, allow the Germans to enter without firing a shot.

THE JEWS OF PRAGUE

Prague was for centuries a traditional centre of Jewish life and scholarship. Jews first moved into a walled ghetto north of the Old Town Square in about the 13th century, in response to directives from Rome that Jews and Christians should live separately. Subsequent centuries of repression and pogroms culminated in a threat from Habsburg Emperor Ferdinand I (r 1526–64) – that was never carried out – to throw all the Jews out of Bohemia.

Official attitudes changed under Emperor Rudolf II at the end of the 16th century. Rudolf bestowed honour on the Jews and encouraged a flowering of Jewish intellectual life. Mordechai Maisel, the mayor of the ghetto at the time, became Rudolf's finance minister and the city's wealthiest citizen. Another major figure was Judah Loew ben Bezalel (Rabbi Loew), a prominent theologian, chief rabbi, student of the mystical teachings of the Cabbala, and nowadays best known as the creator of the Golem (a kind of proto-robot made from the mud of the Vltava).

When they helped to repel the Swedes on Charles Bridge in 1648, the Jews won the favour of Ferdinand III to the extent he had the ghetto enlarged. But a century later they were driven out of the city, only to be welcomed back later when the residents missed their business.

In the 1780s, Habsburg Emperor Joseph II (r 1780–90) outlawed many forms of discrimination, and in the 19th century the Jews won the right to live wherever they wanted. Many chose to leave the ghetto for nicer areas of the city. At the end of the 19th century, municipal authorities decided to clear the ghetto, which had become a slum.

The ghetto, renamed Josefov in Joseph II's honour, remained the spiritual heart of Prague's Jewish community. That came to a brutal end with the Nazi occupation during WWII. Today the city is home to roughly 5000 Jews, a fraction of the community's former size.

A Taste of Freedom, then Nazi Domination

Czechoslovakia, in the two decades between independence and the 1938 Munich agreement (that paved the way for the Nazi German invasion), was a remarkably successful state. Even now, both Czechs and Slovaks consider the 'First Republic' another golden age of immense cultural and economic achievement.

Czechoslovakia's proximity to Nazi Germany and its sizable German minority in the border area known as the Sudetenland made the country a tempting target for Adolf Hitler. Hitler correctly judged that neither Britain nor France had an appetite for war, and at a conference in Munich in 1938, the Nazi leader demanded that Germany be allowed to annex the Sudetenland. British Prime Minister Neville Chamberlain

1942	May 1945	May 1945	1948
Czechoslovak patriots assassinate German Reichsprotektor Reinhard Heydrich. They hide in a church but are trapped by Nazi soldiers. Some take their own lives; others are killed.	Prague residents begin an armed uprising against the Germans, liberating the city after three days. The Germans are granted free exit in exchange for agreeing not to destroy the city.	The Soviet Army formally liberates the city though most German soldiers are already gone. Later the communists recognise this as the official day of liberation.	Communists stage a bloodless coup. Party leader Gottwald proclaims the news on Old Town Square. The coup leads to four decades of oppressive communist rule.

acquiesced, famously calling Germany's designs on Czechoslovakia a 'quarrel in a faraway country between people of whom we know nothing'. To this day, the words 'Munich' and 'appeasement' are intertwined in the minds of many Czechs.

On 15 March 1939 Germany occupied all of Bohemia and Moravia, declaring the region a 'protectorate', while Slovakia was permitted 'independence' as long as it remained a Nazi puppet state. During the war, Prague was spared significant physical damage, though the Germans destroyed the Czech resistance. Around two-thirds of Bohemia and Moravia's Jewish population of 120,000 perished in the war.

On 5 May 1945, with the war drawing to a close, the citizens of Prague staged an uprising against the Germans. The Red Army was advancing from the east and US troops had made it as far as Plzeň to the west, but were holding back from liberating the city in deference to their Soviet allies. Many people died in the uprising before the Germans pulled out on 8 May, having been granted free passage out in return for an agreement not to destroy more buildings.

In 1945, Czechoslovakia was reconstituted as an independent state. One of its first acts was the expulsion of the remaining Sudeten Germans from the borderlands. By 1947, some 2½ million ethnic Germans had been stripped of their Czechoslovak citizenship and forcibly expelled to Germany and Austria.

Prague could have been liberated by US soldiers under General George S Patton, based in Plzeň, as early as 6 May 1945. Despite Patton's pleas, US commanders called off the American advance to allow the Russians the 'honour' of liberating the capital.

From Hitler's Arms into Stalin's

Czechoslovak euphoria at the end of the war did not last long. The communists seized power just three years later, in 1948. While these days the takeover is usually viewed as a naked power grab by Stalin's henchmen, the reality is more complicated. For many Czechs, WWII had tarnished the image of the Western democracies, and Stalin's Soviet Union commanded deep respect

By the 1950s, however, this initial enthusiasm faded as communist economic policies bankrupted the country and a wave of repression sent thousands to labour camps. In a series of Stalin-style purges staged by the KSČ (Communist Party of Czechoslovakia) in the early 1950s, many people, including top members of the party itself, were executed.

In the 1960s, Czechoslovakia enjoyed something of a renaissance, and under the leadership of reform communist Alexander Dubček, became a beacon for idealists wanting to chart a 'third way' between communism and capitalism. The reform movement was dubbed 'Socialism with a Human Face' and mixed elements of democracy with continued state control over the economy. This easing of hardline communism became known around the world as the 'Prague Spring'.

1952	1968	1969	1977
In a Soviet-style purge, communists accuse party functionaries, including General Secretary Slánský, of treason. The prisoners are executed at Pankrác prison.	Soviet-led Warsaw Pact forces invade Czechoslovakia to end 'Prague Spring' reforms. Hard-liner Gustáv Husák replaces Communist leader Alexander Dubček.	Student Jan Palach immolates himself at Wenceslas Square to protest the Warsaw Pact invasion. Thousands visit the square to mark his memory.	Prague reaches a political and cultural nadir during 'normalisation'. Dissidents sign Charter 77, asking Czechoslovakia to meet its human-rights obligations.

In the end, though, it was the movement's success that eventually undid it. Soviet leaders were alarmed by the prospect of a partially democratic society within the Eastern bloc and any potential spillover it might have on Poland and Hungary. The Prague Spring was eventually crushed by a Soviet-led invasion of Eastern bloc states on the night of 20–21 August 1968. Much of the fighting took place near the top of Wenceslas Square – the front of the National Museum still bears the bullet marks.

In 1969 Dubček was replaced by hardliner Gustáv Husák and exiled to the Slovak forestry department. Thousands of people were expelled from the party and lost their jobs. Many left the country, while others were relegated to being manual labourers and street cleaners. The two decades of stagnation until 1989 are known today as the period of 'normalisation'.

Velvet Revolution & Velvet Divorce

The year 1989 was a momentous one throughout Eastern Europe as communist governments fell like dominoes in Hungary, Poland, East Germany, Bulgaria and Romania. But the revolution that toppled communism in Czechoslovakia was perhaps the greatest of them all. It remains the gold standard around the world for peaceful antigovernment protest.

Ironically, the Velvet Revolution actually had its start in a paroxysm of violence on the night of 17 November, when Czech riot police began attacking a group of peaceful student demonstrators. The protesters had organised an officially sanctioned demonstration in memory of students executed by the Nazis in 1939, but the marchers had always intended to make this demo a protest against the communist regime. What they didn't count on was the fierce resistance of the police, who confronted the crowd of about 50,000 on Prague's Národní třída and beat and arrested hundreds of protesters.

Czechs were electrified by this wanton police violence, and the following days saw nonstop demonstrations by students, artists, and finally most of the population, peaking at a rally on Prague's Letná hill that drew some 750,000 people. Leading dissidents, with Havel at the forefront, formed an anticommunist coalition, which negotiated the government's resignation on 3 December. A 'government of national understanding' was formed with the communists as a minority group. Havel was elected president by the Federal Assembly on 29 December.

Almost immediately after the revolution, problems arose between Czechs and Slovaks. The Slovaks had long harboured grievances against the dominant Czechs, and many Slovaks dreamed of having their own

Prague was the major objective in the 1968 Warsaw Pact invasion. Soviet special forces, with the help of the Czech secret police, secured Prague airport for Soviet transport planes. At the end of the first day of fighting, 58 people had died.

1989	1993	2004	January 2009
Police violently halt student protests at Národní třída, sparking mass demonstrations. The communists relinquish power – the 'Velvet Revolution'.	The Czech and Slovak republics agree peacefully to split into independent countries, formally bringing an end to Czechoslovakia. The split becomes known as the 'Velvet Divorce'.	The Czech Republic achieves its biggest foreign policy objective since the Velvet Revolution and joins the European Union, along with several other former communist countries.	Czech Republic assumes the rotating six-month EU presidency. The period is marked by gaffes and errors, and is hailed as the most chaotic EU presidency ever.

state. On 1 January 1993, amid much hand-wringing on both sides, especially from Havel, the Czechs and Slovaks peacefully divided into independent states.

Best Books by Václav Havel

To the Castle and Back (2008)

Open Letters, Selected Writings (1992)

Disturbing the Peace (1991)

The Czech Republic Rejoins 'Europe'

It would be impossible to summarise in just a few paragraphs the changes that have taken place in the more than 20 years since the Velvet Revolution. The big-picture view is largely positive. The Czech Republic achieved its two major long-term foreign-policy goals: joining NATO in 1999 and the European Union in 2004.

In terms of domestic politics, the country continues to ride a knife-edge. Neither major centrist party – the right-leaning Civic Democratic Party (ODS) or the left-leaning Social Democrats (ČSSD) – has been able to cobble together a truly lasting consensus, so the country seems to lurch from side to side, scandal to scandal with each election cycle.

At the time of research, the country was led by a fragile left-right coalition, linking the Social Democrats with an upstart liberal, pro-business movement called 'ANO' (Yes), headed by a Slovak billionaire with a Czech passport, Andrej Babiš. The country's first-ever direct popular vote for the presidency in 2013 (until now the president was chosen by parliament) swept long-time Social Democratic politician Miloš Zeman into office.

Perhaps the biggest news since 1989 was the death of Havel himself on 18 December 2011. The former president and leader of the Velvet Revolution had served both as a symbol of the Czech Republic's commitment to Western ideals of democracy and human rights, and as a moral compass for a society still badly deformed by corrupt communist rule. At the time of research, that symbolic position had yet to be filled and may not be for years to come.

March 2009	April 2009	2011	2013
Despite the fact the Czechs hold the EU presidency, the government collapses in a no-confidence vote. The unprecedented move throws the EU into disarray.	US President Barack Obama addresses thousands of well-wishers at a speech near Prague Castle during which he promotes a policy of eventual nuclear disarmament.	Former president and leader of the Velvet Revolution, Václav Havel, dies after a long battle with cancer. The nation goes into prolonged mourning.	Miloš Zeman is elected president, replacing Václav Klaus who served 10 years in office, in the country's first-ever direct popular vote for president.

Czech Life

A quarter of a century after the fall of communism, a welcome normality has descended on the Czech Republic. Seen from any measure – from what they value, how they work, what they study or how they relax – Czechs are well within the European mainstream. And that's not a bad thing. After a combined 50 years of war and communism, the overriding social goal after 1989 was to create – or re-create – a prosperous, fully functioning democracy in the heart of Europe. In that, they've – happily – succeeded.

A Nation of Czechs...& Vietnamese?

Compared with western European countries such as Germany, France and the Netherlands, the Czech Republic remains relatively homogenous. According to the most recent census, in 2011, nearly 95% of people living here identified themselves as either Czech or Moravian. (The figures mask the number of Roma in the country, estimated at somewhere between 200,000 and 300,000.) Of the rest, only about 2% are Slovaks, with smaller numbers of Poles, Germans and Hungarians.

It wasn't always this way. Until the start of WWII, the territory of Czechoslovakia was home to around 3 million ethnic Germans. Many of those people were either killed in the war or forcibly expelled in the months after.

What the recent census numbers don't reflect, however, is the increasingly diverse mix of people coming to the Czech Republic to work, either permanently or temporarily. These include relatively large populations of Ukrainians and Russians, and, perhaps most curiously, Vietnamese. Partly because of close ties forged between the former communist government and the government of Vietnam, the Czech Republic has emerged as the destination of choice for Vietnamese people moving to Europe.

It's thought that Vietnamese guest workers may total as many as 85,000. Indeed, the Vietnamese surname Nguyen is reportedly the 9th most common family name in the country, according to a survey conducted by Czech website www.kdejsme.cz. Most of the Vietnamese live in Prague or the West Bohemian city of Cheb. Many make a living by running neighbourhood grocery shops, known in Czech as a *večerka*.

A Modern-Day Lack of Faith

Despite having an active and often violent religious history that stretches back several centuries, Czechs take a much more hands-off approach to the question of religion these days. While hard data are hard to come by, surveys indicate that more than half of all Czechs are either atheists or agnostics. Just 20% or so of the population professes a belief in God.

Among believers, the largest church is the Roman Catholic Church, which claims membership of around a tenth of the population. This compares to neighbouring Poland, where 90% of the population say they are Catholic, and Slovakia, where the figure is around 70%. Protestant and other denominations make up another 10% or so.

Catholicism has always been bound to some degree with the Austrian conquest and overzealous efforts by the Jesuits in the 16th and 17th

Guest Workers by Country

Ukraine (130,000 estimated)

Slovakia (90,000)

Vietnam (85,000)

Russia (40,000)

The increase in guest-worker numbers has pressured the government to limit the inflow through desperate measures. In 2009, responding to the economic crisis, officials offered some guest workers up to €500 and a plane ticket home just to get them to leave.

centuries to convert the local population. In more recent times, the former communist government went out of its way to discourage organised religion, going so far as to lock up priests and close down churches.

There are anecdotal signs of a modest rebirth in faith. More and more couples are choosing to be married in a church, and parents are increasingly opting to baptise their children. Also, interest appears to be growing in more esoteric and spiritual beliefs.

The Czech Republic has earned a reputation for tolerance of homosexuality. Prague's first gay-pride march drew thousands onto the streets when it was held in August 2011 and it's now a staple of the summer calendar.

World Beaters at Ice Hockey

Czechs excel at many international sports, including tennis and speed skating, but they are truly masters of the universe when it comes to ice hockey. Since the debut of the annual World Hockey Championships in 1920, the Czech and Czechoslovak national teams have won gold no less than 12 times and taken home a total of 45 medals. Ice hockey plays such a role in the country's psyche that if you ask a Czech what the most significant year was in modern history, you might not hear 1989 or 1968, but rather 1998. That was the year the Czechs beat the Russians 1-0 for gold at the Nagano Winter Olympics, and the country erupted in joy.

Czech players are a staple on the rosters of many teams in the North American National Hockey League. Past greats – and still household names – include Jaromír Jágr (b 1972), who won the Stanley Cup with Pittsburgh in 1991 and '92, and who still plays for the New Jersey Devils. Dominik Hašek (b 1965), the 'Dominator', was once regarded as the world's best goaltender after winning a Stanley Cup with the Detroit Red Wings in 2001.

The communists discouraged priesthood and church attendance. Priests were hounded by the StB (Státní bezpečnost, the Czech secret service) and people who attended services were persecuted. Priests were ordained in secret and performed religious rites behind closed doors.

A Sceptical View Towards the EU

For a country that so passionately protested during the 1989 Velvet Revolution to rejoin the West and put itself back in the heart of Europe, it may come as a surprise to visitors to learn how unpopular the European Union remains among many Czechs. Surveys routinely find only around a third of Czechs hold favourable views towards the EU.

It's not immediately clear why Czechs would be more critical of the EU than, say, Slovakia or Poland, but perhaps the influence of former President Václav Klaus plays a role. Klaus, in office for 10 years until 2013, fashioned himself a disciple of the late British Prime Minister

WHERE TOLERANCE ENDS: CZECHS & ROMA

Generally speaking, Czechs are a remarkably tolerant people, with relatively open attitudes when it comes to race, religion and sexual preference. That tolerance tends to fly out the window, however, when discussing the subject of the country's Roma minority.

The Roma, descendants of a tribe that migrated to Europe from India in the 10th century, have never been made to feel particularly welcome. Despite making up less than 3% of the population, they are a perpetual object of prejudice, harassment and occasional incidents of violence – such as a wave of Molotov cocktail attacks around the country from 2011 to 2013.

There are no easy answers. Under increased pressure in recent years from international groups, Czech authorities have introduced more enlightened policies to try to educate and mainstream the Roma population. To date, these have had only mixed results.

The Budapest-based European Roma Rights Centre is a watchdog organisation that has kept a close eye on Czech authorities grappling with a rise in anti-Roma violence. The group maintains an informative website at www.errc.org.

TENNIS, ANYONE?

In addition to ice hockey, Czechs have excelled at international tennis. This is a source of national pride and the reason why nearly every park or field of green in the country has a tennis court nearby. Indeed, two of the sport's all-time greatest players, Ivan Lendl (b 1960) and Martina Navrátilová (b 1956), honed their craft here before moving to the big stage. Lendl dominated the men's circuit for much of the 1980s, winning a total of 11 Grand Slam tennis titles and participating in some 19 finals matches (a record only broken in recent years by Roger Federer).

Navrátilová's feats, if anything, are even more impressive. In the late 1970s and throughout the 1980s, she won some 18 Grand Slam singles titles, including a whopping nine victories at Wimbledon, the last coming in 1990. At one point she won six Grand Slam singles titles in a row.

Czechs continue to do well in the international game. The current darling is Petra Kvitová (b 1990), who won Wimbledon in 2011 and was ranked sixth in the world at the time of research. Another young star, Tomáš Berdych (b 1985), is ranked seventh among male players.

Margaret Thatcher, including the 'Iron Lady's' legendary derision for all things EU. In 2009, in a speech before European lawmakers in Brussels, Klaus infamously compared the EU to the Soviet Union, saying: 'we learned the bitter lesson that with no opposition, there is no freedom'.

Klaus was considered a bit of an extremist even in his own country, but some of his scepticism was bound to rub off. And with the EU's recent woes with its common currency, the euro, during the global economic crisis, it's not hard to imagine why Europe's once-untouchable prestige among Czechs has reached a low point. Just one in five Czechs today favours adopting the euro.

In defence of Brussels, much of this EU criticism is overblown. Since the Czechs joined the bloc in 2004, millions of euros have poured across the border to help improve waste management, air and water quality, food testing, and a thousand other parts of life that tend to go unnoticed. As you walk around Prague, amid all the construction, you'll see dozens of signs saying that this bridge or building or tunnel was funded by the EU. It's no stretch to say that without this money, the city would be a far less pleasant place.

> The Czech Republic, along with nine other countries mainly from Central and Eastern Europe, joined the European Union on 1 May 2004. It was the EU's biggest ever expansion.

Man's Best Friend

It's sometimes said that 'Russians love their children and Czechs love their dogs'. That's not to say that Czechs don't love their kids (of course they do), but dogs occupy a special place in the hearts of many people here. Nearly 40% of Czech families own a dog (one of the highest rates in Europe), and the most popular breeds remain those adorable apartment-sized ones, such as dachshunds, terriers and schnauzers. Among larger breeds, the most sought after are German shepherds, Labradors and golden retrievers.

Czechs routinely bring their dogs along when they go out for dinner, and all but the fanciest restaurants normally allow dogs (on a leash) to accompany their owners. Waiters might even bring a bowl of water to the table and, indeed, many restaurants keep doggie water bowls on hand just for those occasions.

About the only time dogs run afoul of Czech society is when it comes to soiling the footpaths. In recent years, efforts to keep roads and pavements free of dog doo-doo have gained pace, and in many neighbourhoods around Prague you'll see stands with paper bags for owners to clean up after their animals.

> **Top English News Websites**
>
> Aktuálně.cz (http://aktualne.centrum.cz/czechnews)
>
> Radio Prague (www.radio.cz/en)
>
> The Prague Post (www.praguepost.cz)
>
> Czech Happenings (www.ceskenoviny.cz/news)
>
> Prague Daily Monitor (www.praguemonitor.com)

The Arts in Prague & the Czech Republic

Czechs have always been active contributors to the arts, and no trip to Prague would be complete without a stroll through the city's major museums and galleries to admire the work of local painters, photographers and sculptors. For evenings, you'll be spoiled for choice among offerings of classical music, jazz and rock. Two Czechs, Antonín Dvořák and Bedřich Smetana, are household names in classical music. Czechs are less well known outside the country for visual arts, but are still impressive in this field.

Music

Classical

Mozart actively embraced Czech audiences. Following the premiere of his opera *Don Giovanni* in Prague's Estates Theatre in 1787, he famously said of his adoring Prague public, 'My Praguers understand me'.

Classical music has a long, rich tradition in the Czech Republic, and Czechs have basked for centuries in the reputation that they know good music when they hear it. It was audiences in Prague, after all, who first 'discovered' the genius of Mozart long before the listening public in Mozart's home country of Austria warmed up to the composer.

Early classical music was heavily influenced by Austrian composers but began to develop distinctly Czech strains in the mid-19th century with the Czech National Revival. As part of this national awakening, Czech composers consciously drew on Czech folk music and historical legends for their compositions. The best-known composer to emerge from this period was Bedřich Smetana (1824–84). While Smetana wrote several operas and symphonies, his signature work remains his *Moldau* (Vltava) symphony.

Antonín Dvořák (1841–1904) is the composer that most non-Czechs will have heard of. He too was heavily influenced by the Czech National Revival, which inspired his two *Slavonic Dances* (1878 and 1881), the operas *Rusalka* and *Čert a Káča* (The Devil and Kate), and his religious masterpiece, *Stabat Mater*. Dvořák spent four years in the USA, where he composed his famous *Symphony No 9, From the New World*.

Czech mastery of classical music continued into the 20th century, with the compositions of Moravian-born Leoš Janáček (1854–1928). Janáček's music is an acquired taste, though once you have an ear for the haunting violin strains, it tends to stay with you. Janáček's better-known compositions include the operas *Cunning Little Vixen* and *Káťa Kabanová,* as well as the *Glagolská mše* (Glagolitic Mass).

Smetana's *Moldau* (Vltava) is arguably the most beloved piece of classical music among Czechs and is traditionally played to start the annual Prague Spring music festival.

Jazz

Jazz imported from the USA first burst onto the local scene in the 1930s, and has remained a fixture of the Prague music scene ever since (though it was frowned upon by the communist authorities in the late 1940s and '50s).

Czech jazz came into its own in the 1960s, and one of the top bands of this period was SH Quartet, which played for three years at Reduta Jazz Club (p133), the city's first professional jazz club. The club is still going strong (though it's no longer quite the centre of the jazz scene). Another leading band from this period was Junior Trio, with Jan Hamr (1948–) and brothers Miroslav and Allan Vitouš, all of whom left for the USA after

1968. Hamr became prominent in American music circles in the 1970s and '80s as Jan Hammer.

Rock & Pop

Rock has played an outsized role in modern Czech history, perhaps to an extent unique among European nations. It was rock that nurtured and sustained the anti-communist movement in the 1970s and '80s. The late former president Václav Havel was a huge fan, and numbered among his closest friends the members of the Rolling Stones, the late Velvet Underground frontman Lou Reed, and even late rocker Frank Zappa.

Rock music blossomed during the political thaw of the mid-1960s and home-grown rock acts began to emerge, showing the heavy influence of bands such as the Beatles, the Beach Boys and the Rolling Stones. The local 1967 hit single 'Želva' (Turtle) by the band Olympic bears the unmistakeable traces of mid-decade Beatles. One of the biggest stars of the time was pop singer Marta Kubišová (1942–). Kubišová was officially banned by the communists after the 1968 Warsaw Pact invasion, though she was rehabilitated after 1989 and still occasionally performs. Her voice and songs, to this day, capture something of that fated optimism of the 1960s, pre-invasion period.

The Warsaw Pact invasion silenced the rock revolution. Many bands were prohibited from openly performing or recording. In their place, the authorities encouraged more anodyne singers such as Helena Vondráčková (1947–) and Karel Gott (1939–). Many popular songs from those days, such as Gott's classic 'Je jaká je' (She is What She is), are simply Czech covers of the most innocuous Western music of the day.

Best Classical-Music Festivals

Prague Spring (www.festival.cz)

Prague Proms (www.prague proms.cz)

Dvořák Festival (www.dvorako vapraha.cz)

Český Krumlov Music Festival (www.ckrumlov. info)

Janáčkovy Hukvaldy (www. janackovy hukvaldy.cz)

ICONIC CZECH POP TUNES

Czechs tend to be patriotic when it comes to their own music. Pop songs from the 1960s and '70s are beloved because they're sappy and inflected with nostalgia for simpler times. Tunes from the 1990s and 2000s tend to sound more authentic, with a harder edge. Together they form the perfect soundtrack when streaming from your music player as you stroll around town. Here is a highly subjective list of our favourites:

➡ **Trezor** (Safe; 1964) by Karel Gott – the Czech crooner extraordinaire is still going strong today, well into his 70s.

➡ **Želva** (Turtle; 1967) by Olympic – the Czech 'Beatles' in their day had the moves, the tunes and the hair.

➡ **Stín Katedrál** (1968) by Václav Neckář and Helena Vondráčková – one of the most beautiful pop songs to emerge from the 1960s.

➡ **Modlitba pro Martu** (Prayer for Marta; 1969) by Marta Kubišová – a sad song that for many Czechs still instantly recalls the 1968 Warsaw Pact invasion.

➡ **Bratříčku, Zavírej Vrátka** (O' Brother, Shut the Door; 1969) by Karel Kryl – 'shut the door' echoes the hopelessness many felt after the Warsaw Pact invasion.

➡ **Sluneční hrob** (Sunny Tomb; 1969) by Blue Effect – this progressive rock-jazz fusion hit is arguably the best song to come out of a very good decade for music.

➡ **Láska je láska** (Love is Love; 1995) by Lucie Bílá – the ballad of mid-'90s Prague from a tough woman with a voice you won't soon forget.

➡ **Proměny** (2006) by Čechomor – beautiful music from a band that almost single-handedly made folk music hip again.

➡ **Falling Slowly** (2007) by Markéta Irglova and Glen Hansard – addictive Czech/Irish tearjerker that won an Oscar for the film *Once*.

➡ **Pocity** (Feelings; 2013) by Tomáš Kluš – likeable teen pop of the type designed to make girls' hearts swoon.

Rock became heavily politicised in the 1980s in the run-up to the Velvet Revolution. Hard-core experimental bands such as the Plastic People of the Universe were forced underground and developed big cult followings. Another banned performer, Karel Kryl (1944–94), became an unofficial bard of the people, singing from his West German exile. His album *Bratříčku, Zavírej Vrátka* (O' Brother, Shut the Door) came to symbolise the hopelessness of the Soviet-led invasion and the decades that followed.

The Velvet Revolution opened the door to a flood of influences from around the world. Early-'90s Czech bands such as rockers Lucie and Žlutý pes soon gave way to a variety of sounds, from the Nina Hagen–like screeching of Lucie Bílá to the avant garde chirping of Iva Bittová, in addition to a flood of mainstream Czech acts. The best of these included Psí Vojáci, Buty, Laura a její tygři, Už jsme doma, and Support Lesbiens.

A look at the list of top music acts for 2014 shows the charts still dominated by old-schoolers such as Gott and Bílá, but a couple of fresher faces have emerged, including teen idol, pop-rocker Tomáš Kluš, pop balladeer Kryštof, indie folk singer Lenka Dusilová, and hip retro-folk acts like Čechomor and Zrní.

Jan Hammer's theme song for the popular 1980s TV show *Miami Vice* remains one of the most popular jazz recordings of all time, selling some 4 million copies in the USA alone.

Visual Arts

Ask about Czech visual arts and many visitors will probably draw a blank. Some may be able to conjure up art nouveau images by Alfons Mucha, but that's about it. However, the country has much more to offer than Mucha's sultry maidens. Prague has both a long tradition of avant garde photography and a rich heritage of public sculpture, ranging from the baroque period to the present day.

Painting

The Czech Republic can look back on at least seven centuries of painting, starting with the luminously realistic 14th-century works of Magister Theodoricus (Master Theodorus). His paintings, which hang in the Chapel of the Holy Cross at Karlštejn Castle and in the Chapel of St Wenceslas in St Vitus Cathedral, influenced art throughout Central Europe. Another gem of Czech Gothic art is a late-14th-century altar panel by an artist known only as the Master of the Třeboň Altar; what remains of it is at the Convent of St Agnes in Prague's Old Town.

Guns N' Roses frontman Axl Rose legendarily opened his May 1992 concert at Prague's Strahov stadium with the words: 'OK you ex-commie bastards, it's time to rock and roll!'

The Czech National Revival in the 19th century witnessed the revival of a Czech style of realism, in particular by Mikuláš Aleš and father and son Antonín and Josef Mánes. The National Revival emphasised the natural beauty of the Czech countryside.

In the early 20th century, Prague became a centre of avant garde art, concentrated in a group called Osma (The Eight). Prague was also a focus for cubist painters, including Josef Čapek (1887–1945) and the aptly named Bohumil Kubišta (1884–1918). The functionalist movement flourished between WWI and WWII in a group called Devětsíl, led by the adaptable Karel Teige (1900–51). Surrealists followed, including Zdeněk Rykr (1900–40) and Josef Šíma (1891–1971). Many of the best works from this period hang in the National Gallery's Modern and Contemporary Art Exhibition at Veletržní Palác.

Visual arts were driven underground during the Nazi occupation, and in the early years of the communist period painters were forced to work in the official Socialist Realist style, usually depicting workers and peasants building the workers' state. Underground painters included Jiří Kolář (1914–2002), an outstanding graphic artist and poet whose name when pronounced sounds something like 'collage' – one of his favourite art forms. Again, the go-to gallery for much of this is Veletržní Palác.

Photography

Czech photographers have always been at the forefront of the medium. The earliest photographers, in the late 19th and early 20th centuries, worked in the pictorialist style, which viewed photography as an extension of painting.

It was after independence in 1918 and during the 1920s and '30s that early-modern styles captured the Czech imagination. Local photographers seized on trends such as cubism, functionalism, Dadaism and surrealism, turning out jarring abstracts that still look fresh today. Two of the best photographers from that time include František Drtikol (1883–1961) and Jaroslav Rössler (1902–90).

During communism, photography was enlisted in the service of promoting the workers' state. Picture books from that time are comically filled with images of tractors, factories and housing projects. Serious photographers turned inward and intentionally chose subjects – such as landscapes and still lifes – that were, at least superficially, devoid of political content. Arguably, the best Czech photographer from this time was Josef Sudek (1896–1976). During a career that spanned five decades, Sudek turned his lens on the city of Prague to absolutely stunning effect.

Current Czech bad-boy photographer Jan Saudek (1935–) continues to delight his fans (or dismay his critics) with his dreamlike, hand-tinted prints that evoke images of utopia or dystopia – usually involving a nude or seminude woman or child.

Communist-era singers Helena Vondráčková and Karel Gott are still going strong today. Vondráčková turned 67 in 2014 and Gott is already well into his 70s.

Sculpture

Public sculpture has always played a prominent role in Prague, from the baroque saints that line the parapets of Charles Bridge to the monumental statue of Stalin that once faced the Old Town from atop Letná Hill. More often than not, that role has been a political one.

In the baroque era, religious sculptures sprouted in public places; they included 'Marian columns' erected in gratitude to the Virgin Mary for protection against the plague or victory over anti-Catholic enemies. One such Marian column stood in the Old Town Square from 1650 until 1918. The placing of the statue of St John of Nepomuk on Charles Bridge in 1683 was a conscious act of propaganda designed to create a new – and Catholic – Czech national hero who would displace the Protestant reformer Jan Hus. As such, it was successful. John of Nepomuk was canonised in 1729 and the Nepomuk legend, invented by the Jesuits, has passed into the collective memory.

The Czech National Revival saw Prague sculpture take a different tack – to raise public awareness of Czech traditions and culture. One of the most prolific sculptors was Josef Václav Myslbek, whose statue of St Wenceslas dominates the upper end of Wenceslas Square.

The art nouveau sculptor Ladislav Šaloun was responsible for one of Prague's most iconic sculptures, the monument to Jan Hus that was unveiled in the Old Town Square in 1915 (to commemorate the 500th anniversary of Hus being burned at the stake).

Probably the most imposing and visible sculpture in Prague – reputedly the biggest equestrian statue in the world – is the huge, mounted figure of Hussite hero Jan Žižka that dominates the skyline above Žižkov (the city district named after him).

Street art has long been a legitimate form of dissent in the Czech Republic. In the 1980s, the Lennon Peace Wall in Malá Strana was a vital anticommunist protest space (long before it became a tourist attraction). The Chemistry Gallery in Holešovice has the best street art today.

Theatre

Theatre remains a popular and vital art form in spite of rising competition from the internet, film and TV. Openings for key performances, such as Tom Stoppard's riveting *Rock 'n' Roll* at the National Theatre

WEIRD ART OF DAVID ČERNÝ

David Černý's sculpture is often controversial, occasionally outrageous and always amusing. Although temporary Černý installations occasionally pop up here and there, the following are permanently on view in Prague:

Quo Vadis (p90; 1991) – in the garden of the German Embassy in Malá Strana. A Trabant (an East German car) on four human legs serves as a monument to the thousands of East Germans who fled the communist regime in 1989 prior to the fall of the Berlin Wall, and who camped out in the embassy garden seeking political asylum.

Viselec (Hanging Out, 1997; Map p332; Husova; 6, 9, 18, 21, 22) – above Husova street in Staré Město. A bearded, bespectacled chap with a passing resemblance to Sigmund Freud, casually dangling by one hand from a pole way above the street.

Kun (Horse, 1999; Map p338; Lucerna Palace, Vodičkova 36) – in the Lucerna Palace shopping arcade, Nové Město. Amusing alternative version of the famous St Wenceslas Statue in Wenceslas Square, only this time the horse is upside down.

Miminka (p149; 2000) – on the TV Tower, Žižkov. Creepy, giant, slot-faced babies crawling all over a TV transmitter tower – something to do with our attachment to media. We think.

Brownnosers (p175; 2003) – in the Futura Gallery, Smíchov. Stick your head up a statue's backside and watch a video of the former Czech president and the director of the National Gallery feeding each other baby food.

Proudy (p88; 2004) – in the courtyard of Hergetova Cíhelná, Malá Strana. Two guys pissing in a puddle (whose irregular outline, you'll notice, is actually the map outline of the Czech Republic) and spelling out famous quotations from Czech literature with their pee. (Yes, the sculpture moves! It's computer controlled.)

(p133) or Václav Havel's acclaimed *Odcházení* (Leaving) at **Archa Theatre** (Divadlo Archa; Map p336; 221 716 111; www.archatheatre.cz; Na poříčí 26; tickets 150-880Kč; box office 10am-6pm Mon-Fri, & 2hr before show; 5, 8, 14), are often sold out months in advance.

Unfortunately for non-Czech speakers, much of the action remains inaccessible. Occasionally, big theatrical events will be subtitled in English, but the bread and butter of Czech drama is performed in Czech. Two theatres, Archa and the Švandovo Divadlo Na Smíchově (p179), are committed to English-friendly performances and occasionally host English drama in the original language.

Theatre has always played a strong role in Czech national consciousness, both as a way of promoting linguistic development and defending the fledgling culture against the dominant Habsburg, German and later communist influences. Historical plays with a nationalist subtext flourished during the 19th century as part of the Czech National Revival.

The decade-long construction of the National Theatre and its opening in 1881 was considered a watershed in Czech history. The theatre tragically burned down shortly after opening but was completely rebuilt, following a public outcry, just two years later.

Drama flourished in the early years of independent Czechoslovakia in the 1920s and '30s, but suffered under the Nazi occupation, when many Czech-language theatres were closed or converted into German theatres. Under communism, classical performances were of a high quality, but the modern scene was largely stifled. Many fine plays during this period, including those by Havel, were not performed locally because of their antigovernment tone, but appeared in the West.

The centrality of theatre to Czech life was confirmed in 1989 during the Velvet Revolution, when Havel and his Civic Forum movement chose to base themselves at the Laterna Magika (p134) for their epic negotiations to push the communists from power.

Marionette plays have been popular since the 16th century, and puppet plays since before that. This form peaked in the 17th and early 18th centuries. A legendary figure was Matěj Kopecký (1775–1847), who performed original pieces.

The Czech Republic on Page & Screen

Reading a book or watching a film can facilitate a deeper understanding of a destination, and add texture and depth. This is especially true for the Czech Republic, which has spawned many masterpieces. In literature, heavyweights such as Milan Kundera and Franz Kafka honed their craft here. The underrated, anti-war novel *The Good Soldier Švejk* is a stroke of comic genius that recalls something of *Catch-22*. In film, the Czech 'New Wave' of the 1960s took the world by storm with its bittersweet take on everyday life in a dysfunctional dictatorship.

Czechs in Print

The communist period produced two Czech writers of world standing, both of whom hail originally from Brno: Milan Kundera (b 1929) and Bohumil Hrabal (1914–97). For many visitors, Kundera remains the undisputed champ. His wryly told stories weave elements of humour and sex along with liberal doses of music theory, poetry and philosophy that appeal to both our low- and high-brow literary selves. His best known book, *The Unbearable Lightness of Being* (also made into a successful film in 1988), is set in Prague in the uncertain days before the 1968 Warsaw Pact invasion. Look out too for Kundera's *The Joke, The Book of Laughter and Forgetting*.

Ask any Czech who their favourite author is and chances are they will say Hrabal, and it's not hard to see why. Hrabal's writing captures what Czechs like best about themselves – a keen wit, a sense of the absurd and a fondness for beer. Hrabal is also a great storyteller, and popular novels such as *I Served the King of England* and *The Little Town Where Time Stood Still* are both entertaining and insightful. Hrabal died in 1997 in classic Czech fashion: falling from a window. In 2014 Archipelago Books published a new translation in English of Hrabal's *Harlequin's Millions*.

Other major talents who came of age during the period from the Warsaw Pact invasion in 1968 to the 1989 Velvet Revolution include Ivan Klíma (b 1931) and Josef Škvorecký (1924–2012). Klíma, who survived the WWII Terezín concentration camp as a child and who still lives in Prague, is probably best known for his collections of bittersweet short stories of life in the 1970s and '80s, such as *My First Loves* and *My Merry Mornings*. Klima's long-awaited memoir *My Crazy Century* was published by Grove Press in 2013 and is getting glowing reviews on its Amazon book page.

There's no shortage of new Czech literary talent. Names such as Jáchym Topol (b 1962), Petra Hůlová (b 1979), Michal Viewegh (b 1962), Michal Ajvaz (b 1949), Emil Hakl (b 1958) and Miloš Urban (b 1967) are taking their places among the country's leading authors, pushing out old-guard figures such as Kundera and Klíma, who are now seen as chroniclers of a very different age.

Until relatively recently, few books from these younger novelists had been translated into English. That's changing slowly, however, as the writers start to find an audience in English. In 2013, Portobello Books

The 2002 best seller *Prague* by American writer Arthur Phillips is not actually set in Prague, but in Budapest in the 1990s. Phillips apparently chose the title to reflect the envy his expat characters felt for their countrymen hanging out and partying at the time in the Czech capital.

published Topol's acclaimed *The Devil's Workshop.* This followed successful debuts in English for Hůlová's *All this Belongs to Me*, and Urban's thriller *The Seven Churches,* among others, a couple of years earlier.

And Then There's Franz Kafka

No discussion of Czech literature would be complete without mentioning Franz Kafka (1883–1924), easily the best-known writer to have ever lived in Prague and the author of modern classics *The Trial* and *The Castle,* among many others. Though Kafka was German-speaking and Jewish, he's as thoroughly connected to the city as any Czech writer could be. Kafka's birthplace is just a stone's throw from the Old Town Square and the author rarely strayed more than a couple of hundred metres in any direction during the course of his short life.

Kafka's Czech contemporary, and polar opposite, was the pub scribe Jaroslav Hašek (1883–1923), author of *The Good Soldier Švejk,* a book that is both loved and reviled in equal doses. For those who get the jokes, it is a comic masterpiece of a bumbling, likeable Czech named Švejk and his (intentional or not) efforts to avoid military service for Austria-Hungary during WWI. Some Czechs, however, tend to bridle at the assertion that an idiot like Švejk could somehow embody any national characteristic.

> Czech contributions to literature are not limited to fiction. Czech poet Jaroslav Seifert (1901–86) won the Nobel Prize for Literature in 1984, though Seifert is not universally considered by Czechs to be their best poet. That distinction often belongs to poet-scientist Miroslav Holub (1923–98).

Czechs on Film

Though films have been made on the territory of the Czech Republic since the dawn of motion pictures in the early 20th century, it wasn't until the 1960s and the Czech New Wave that Czechoslovak film finally caught the attention of international audiences.

The 1960s, though under communism, was a decade of relative artistic freedom, and talented young directors such as Miloš Forman and Jiří Menzel crafted bittersweet films that charmed moviegoers with their grit and wit, while at the same time poking critical fun at their communist overlords. During that decade, Czechoslovak films twice won the Oscar for Best Foreign Language Film: for the *Little Shop on Main Street* in 1965 and *Closely Watched Trains* in 1967. Forman eventually left the country and went on to win Best Picture Oscars for *One Flew Over the Cuckoo's Nest* and *Amadeus.*

Since the Velvet Revolution, Czech directors have struggled to make meaningful films, given the tiny budgets and a constant flood of Hollywood blockbusters. At the same time, they've had to endure non-stop

> Czech film-maker Jan Švankmajer is celebrated for his bizarre, surrealist animation work and stop-motion feature films, including his 1988 version of *Alice in Wonderland* (*Něco z Alenky*) and his 1994 classic, *Faust* (*Lekce Faust*).

BEST POST-'89 CZECH LITERATURE

More and more books by younger Czech writers are finding English-language publishers. Here's a short list of some of our favourites:

➡ **The Seven Churches** (Miloš Urban, 2011) A brilliant modern-day Gothic murder story set among the seven major churches of Prague's Nové Město by one of the rising stars of Czech literature.

➡ **All this Belongs to Me** (Petra Hůlová, 2009) Hůlová's debut novel chronicles the lives of three generations of women living in Mongolia. It was a local sensation on its first Czech printing in 2002.

➡ **Bringing Up Girls in Bohemia** (Michal Viewegh, 1996) Humorously captures the early years of newly capitalist Prague.

➡ **City Sister Silver** (Jáchym Topol, 1994) Translator Alex Zucker modestly describes this rambling, words-on-speed novel as 'the story of a young man trying to find his way in the messy landscape of post-communist Czechoslovakia'.

BEST NEW-WAVE FILMS

Many of the best Czech films from the 1960s are available on DVD or through streaming services such as Netflix. A few all-time classics include:

Closely Watched Trains (1966) Jiří Menzel's adaptation of Bohumil Hrabal's comic WWII classic set in a small railway town won an Oscar for best foreign film in 1967 and put the Czech New Wave on the international radar. Watch for the scene where young Miloš gently broaches the subject of premature ejaculation with an older woman while she lovingly strokes the neck of a goose.

Loves of a Blonde (1965) Miloš Forman's bittersweet love story between a naive girl from a small factory town and her more sophisticated Prague beau. Arguably Forman's finest film, effortlessly capturing both the innocence and the hopelessness of those grey days of the mid-1960s.

Black Peter (1963) This early Forman effort wowed the New York critics on its debut with its cinematic allusions to the French New Wave and its slow but mesmerising teenage-boy-comes-of-age storyline.

critical scrutiny that their output meet the high standards for Czech films set during the New Wave.

Given these high expectations, the newer Czech directors have had some success, settling for smaller, ensemble-driven films that focus on the hardships and moral ambiguities of life in a society rapidly transiting from communism to capitalism. If the Czech New Wave was mostly about making light of a bad situation, it wouldn't be a stretch to say that today's films strive to make bad out of a comparatively light situation.

Films such as David Ondříček's *Loners* (2000), Jan Hřebejk's *Up and Down* (2004), Sasha Gedeon's *Return of the Idiot* (1999), Bohdan Sláma's *Something Like Happiness* (2005) and Petr Zelenka's *Wrong Side Up* (2005) are all different, yet each explores the familiar dark terrain of money, marital problems and shifting moral sands.

In more recent years, historical films have made a comeback, particularly films that explore WWII and the Nazi and communist periods. The best include director Adam Dvořák's *Lidice* (2011), Hřebejk's *Kawasaki Rose* (2009) and Tomáš Lunák's *Alois Nebel* (2010). The latter is an inventive interpretation of a graphic novel concerning a murder committed in the final days of WWII and the subsequent expulsion of Czech Germans. In 2013, HBO released a critically acclaimed miniseries, *Burning Bush,* on Jan Palach, the Czech student who immolated himself in 1969 to protest the Warsaw Pact invasion of the country the previous year.

Running against the grain has been director Jan Svěrák, who continues to make big-budget films that have attracted international attention. In 1996 he took home the country's first Oscar since the 1960s – for the film *Kolja.*

Hollywood Films Shot in Prague

Amadeus (1980)

Mission Impossible (1996)

Hostel (2005)

Casino Royale (2006)

The Chronicles of Narnia: Prince Caspian (2008)

Hollywood Comes to Prague

In addition to Czech films, the Czech Republic has managed to position itself as a lower-cost production centre for Hollywood films. Part of the pitch has been the excellent production facilities at the Barrandov studios, south of Prague centre in Smíchov. The effort has paid off and dozens of big-budget films and television shows, including the first instalment of Tom Cruise's epic *Mission Impossible* (1996), have been filmed here.

A Nation of Beer Lovers

No matter how many times you tell yourself, 'today is an alcohol-free day', Czech beer (pivo) will be your undoing. Light, clear, refreshing and cheaper than water, Czech beer is recognised as one of the world's best – the Czechs claim it's so pure it's impossible to get a hangover from drinking it. (Scientific tests conducted by Lonely Planet authors have found this to be not entirely true.) Brewing traditions go back nearly 1000 years, and the beer has only gotten better since then.

Czechs drink more beer per capita than anywhere else in the world: around 150L per head per year, and the local *hospoda* or *pivnice* (pub or small beer hall) remains the social hub of the neighbourhood.

Types of Czech Beers

Nearly all Czech beers are bottom-fermented lagers, naturally brewed using Moravian malt and hand-picked hops from Žatec in northwestern Bohemia. The brewing and fermentation process normally uses only natural ingredients – water, hops, yeast and barley – though some brewers these days use a chemically modified hops extract that, regrettably, probably wouldn't pass German purity laws.

While both light – *světlé* – and dark – *tmavé* or *černé* – beers are readily available, the overwhelming favourite among Czech drinkers remains the classic golden lager, or pilsner, developed in the city of Plzeň in the mid-19th century. These light lagers are marked by a tart flavour and crisp finish. It's worth pointing out that the word 'light' here refers to colour and is not to be confused with the light, low-calorie beers sold in the USA and other countries.

Dark beers are slowly gaining in popularity but run a distant second to light beers at most pubs, and among old-school beer drinkers dark beers still retain a faint wisp of not being entirely a man's drink. It's perfectly acceptable, even common, in pubs to order half and half, a Czech 'black and tan', known locally as *řezané pivo* (literally 'cut' beer). This is an agreeable compromise that reduces the tartness of the pilsner without adding the heaviness of a dark beer.

The Czech language is filled with proverbs about beer. Our favourite is: *'Kde se pivo vaří, tam se dobře daří',* which translates loosely as 'Life is good wherever beer is brewed'.

Czech beer drinkers are conservative, and more exotic brews such as wheat beer *(pšeničné pivo)* and yeast beer *(kvasnicové pivo)* have only recently begun to gain traction. You'll almost never find these at traditional pubs, but they're often a staple at the growing number of brew pubs and at more modern, multi-tap places that specialise in a wider variety of beers.

Drinking by Degrees

By tradition, Czech beers are usually labelled either *dvanáctka* (12°) or *desítka* (10°) – or occasionally even a *jedenáctka* (11°) – a designation that can lead to understandable confusion among visitors. This measure does not refer directly to the percentage of alcohol; instead, it's an indicator of specific gravity known as the 'Balling' rating (invented by Czech scientist Karl Josef Balling in the 19th century).

In technical speak, 1° Balling represents 1% by weight of malt-derived sugar in the brewing liquid before fermentation. In practice, a typical 12°

BEER & BOOKS

Perhaps nowhere in the world is there a stronger link between beer and literature as in the Czech Republic, and in contrast to many cultures where novels are often concocted in coffee houses or literary salons, as often as not Czech books are written in (and are about) pubs. The great Czech writer Jaroslav Hašek (1883–1923), author of *The Good Soldier Švejk*, wrote many of his best works in a pub. Švejk more or less starts out with the main character swilling beers in the neighbourhood saloon.

Bohumil Hrabal (1914–97), arguably the country's favourite writer, was actually raised in a brewery in Nymburk, and recounts many of his funny brewery memories in his book *Cutting it Short*. He spent many an evening whiling away the hours at Prague's famous U Zlatého Tygra (p115), before falling from a hospital window to his death in 1997.

brew, such as Pilsner Urquell, tends to be richer in flavour (as well as being slightly stronger in alcohol) than a 10° label, such as Gambrinus, which will be slightly sweeter and less bitter.

Czech beers are also rated according to the alcohol-by-volume (ABV) content, and the law recognises a handful of categories: *'výčepní pivo'* (less than 4.5% ABV), *'ležák'* (4.5% to 5.5% ABV) and 'special' (more than 5.5% ABV).

Land of the Giants

Though there are more than 100 breweries around the country, the local market is dominated by a handful of giants. The largest and most important remains the Pilsner Urquell brewery in Plzeň, now a subsidiary of global mega-brewer SABMiller. Pilsner Urquell produces not only its signature 12° brew, but also the 10° Gambrinus (often shortened to 'Gambáč' and inexplicably the country's most popular beer) and Velkopopovický Kozel. Pilsner Urquell pubs around the country, including the brewery's own chain of casual restaurants, often called Pilsner Urquell Original, will normally carry the first two beers, and usually the dark version of Kozel.

The country's number-two brewer is Prague-based Staropramen, owned by the Central European brewing group Starbev, which in turn is owned by American giant Molson Coors. The company's brands include the flagship Staropramen lager and Granát, a semi-dark, as well as international names such as Stella Artois and Hoegaarden, which are produced under license. Staropramen pubs, including the ubiquitous brewery-owned chain Potrefena Husa, usually carry the brewer's light lagers (including an increasingly popular unfiltered variety), as well as Stella, Hoegaarden and occasionally Leffe. While it was once viewed as nothing short of blasphemy to order a Stella in a Czech pub, we've – gasp – even seen Czechs do it.

Beers made by Budvar (Budweiser) of České Budějovice, the country's third-biggest brewer, are a little harder to find in Prague but are common throughout southern Bohemia and much of the rest of the country. The brewery's 12° premium lager is worth seeking out, as well as its highly regarded premium dark. The Budvar Brewery is partly state-owned and, despite a long-running battle with the far-larger US-based Budweiser, owned by the InBev group, and persistent rumours of an imminent privatisation, it remains the only major brewery in the country that's still 100% Czech-owned.

Microbrewers & Multi-Tap Pubs

The takeover of the Czech Republic's breweries by multinational companies has been accompanied by a welcome resurgence of interest in

Argentinean expat Max Bahnson has established himself as a local beer expert, and his blog, *Pivní Filosof* (the Beer Philosopher), is a great place to catch up on local trends and beer lore. Find it at www.pivni-filosof. com.

Best Smaller Breweries

Primátor (www. primator.cz)

Klášter (www. pivovarklaster.cz)

Svijany (www. pivovarsvijany.cz)

Bernard (www. bernard.cz)

THE KING OF BEERS VS THE BEER OF KINGS

In this big wide world, who could have imagined that two major brewers located thousands of miles apart on different continents would each want to sell beer by the name 'Budweiser'? As remarkable as it seems, that's the case, and for more than 100 years now, US-based Anheuser-Busch, owned by the InBev group, and the Czech Budvar Budweiser brewery have been locked in a trademark dispute to determine where each brewer can sell their beer and what they can call it.

The dispute arose innocently enough in the 1870s, after the co-founder of the American brewery, Adolphus Busch, returned home from a tour of Bohemia. Busch wanted to create a light lager based on his experience abroad and dubbed his new concoction 'Budweiser' to lend an air of authenticity. Ironically, the American claim may actually pre-date the Czech one. Though beer has been brewed in the town of České Budějovice for some 800 years, the Czech 'Budweiser' name was apparently only registered in the 1890s.

By the early 20th century, the two brewers, eyeing eventual overseas markets, were already locked in battle. In 1907, they agreed that the American company could use the Budweiser name in North America, while the Czechs could keep it in Europe. That fragile compromise held up remarkably well for decades, though there have been signs for years now that it's fraying around the edges.

InBev sells what many consider its inferior Budweiser brand throughout Europe under the 'Bud' label. In some markets, including in the UK, the courts have ruled that neither company can claim ownership over the name, allowing both companies to use Budweiser. The American Budweiser is not sold in the Czech Republic. In the USA, Czech Budweiser is sold under the somewhat awkward name of 'Czechvar'.

Meantime, rumours abound in the Czech Republic about the eventual privatisation of the state-controlled Czech brewer and its possible sale someday to the far-larger InBev group. Such a move wouldn't shock many people, though true beer lovers would likely shed a few tears into their beer mugs.

traditional beer-making and a growing appreciation for smaller and regional breweries.

The microbrew trend is most prominent in Prague, which boasts around a dozen brew pubs where DIY brewers proffer their own concoctions, usually accompanied by decent-to-very-good traditional Czech cooking. Because of the discerning beer-drinking public, standards are remarkably high. Additionally, these pubs are often free to experiment with more exotic variations, such as wheat- and yeast-based beers or fruit-infusions, that bigger breweries seem loathe to take on.

Alongside this brew-your-own trend, there's been a similar increase in the number of taverns that offer beers produced by the country's smaller, but highly regarded, regional breweries. This represents a change in how pubs normally operate. Traditionally, the big national brewers have forced exclusivity deals on pubs whereby the pubs agree to sell only that brewer's beer in exchange for publicity material, discounts, and mountains of swag such as beer mats and ashtrays. Increasingly, however, more and more pubs are setting aside a 'fourth tap' – *čtvrtá pípa* in Czech – for dispensing independently sourced smaller brews of invariably excellent quality.

The big brewers are not taking the trends lying down. To compete with the microbrews, the larger breweries have come up with no end of innovations, including offering unfiltered *(nefiltrované)* beer (cloudier and arguably more authentic than its filtered cousin) and hauling beer directly to pubs in supersized tanks (called, unsurprisingly, *tankové pivo*). Tank beer is said to be fresher than beer transported in traditional kegs. Who are we to argue with that?

Brewery Tours

Pilsner Urquell Brewery (www. prazdrojvisit.cz).

Budweiser Budvar Brewery (www. visitbudvar.cz).

Velké Popovice Brewery (www. kozel.cz).

Survival Guide

Transport

GETTING THERE & AWAY

Prague sits at the heart of Europe and is well served by air, road and rail.

If arriving by air from outside the EU's common border and customs area, the Schengen zone (this includes arrivals from Ireland and the UK), you must go through passport control. If arriving from a European hub within the Schengen zone, such as Amsterdam or Frankfurt, you will not pass through passport control in Prague.

If arriving overland by train, bus or car, the Czech Republic is surrounded on all sides by EU Schengen countries and there are no passport or customs checks on the border.

Air

Václav Havel Airport Prague (Prague Ruzyně International Airport; ☑220 111 888; www.prg.aero; K letišti 6, Ruzyně; ☎; ▢100, 119), 17km west of the city centre, is the main international gateway to the Czech Republic and the hub for the national carrier **Czech Airlines** (ČSA; ☑239 007 007; www.csa.cz; V Celnici 5), which operates direct flights to Prague from many European cities.

The airport has two terminals: Terminal 1 for flights to/from non–Schengen Zone countries (including the UK, Ireland and countries outside Europe); Terminal 2 for flights to/from Schengen Zone countries (most EU nations plus Switzerland, Iceland and Norway).

In both terminals the arrival and departure halls are next to each other on the same level. The arrival halls have exchange counters, ATMs, accommodation and car-hire agencies, public-transport information desks, taxi services and 24-hour left-luggage counters (per piece per day 120Kč). The departure halls have restaurants and bars, information offices, airline offices, an exchange counter and travel agencies. Once you're through security, there are plenty of shops, restaurants, bars, internet access and wi-fi.

Bus

Several bus companies offer coach service connecting Prague to cities around Europe. Nearly all international buses (and most domestic services) use the renovated and user-friendly **Florenc bus station** (ÚAN Praha Florenc; Map p346; ☑900 144 444; www.florenc.cz; Křižíkova 4, Karlín; ◷4am-midnight, information counter 6am-10pm; Ⓜ Florenc).

International bus operators include the excellent **Student Agency** (☑841 101

CLIMATE CHANGE & TRAVEL

Every form of transport that relies on carbon-based fuel generates CO_2, the main cause of human-induced climate change. Modern travel is dependent on aeroplanes, which might use less fuel per kilometre per person than most cars but travel much greater distances. The altitude at which aircraft emit gases (including CO_2) and particles also contributes to their climate change impact. Many websites offer 'carbon calculators' that allow people to estimate the carbon emissions generated by their journey and, for those who wish to do so, to offset the impact of the greenhouse gases emitted with contributions to portfolios of climate-friendly initiatives throughout the world. Lonely Planet offsets the carbon footprint of all staff and author travel.

GETTING INTO PRAGUE FROM VÁCLAV HAVEL AIRPORT

To get into Prague from the airport, buy a full-price public transport ticket (32Kč) from the **Prague Public Transport Authority** (DPP; ☑296 191 817; www.dpp.cz; ⊙7am-9pm) desk (there's one located in each arrivals hall) and take bus 119 (20 minutes; every 10 minutes from 4am to midnight) to the end of metro line A (Dejvická), then continue by metro into the city centre (another 10 to 15 minutes; no new ticket needed). Note you'll also need a half-fare (16Kč) ticket for your bag or suitcase (per piece) if it's larger than 25cm x 45cm x 70cm.

If you're heading to the southwestern part of the city, take bus 100, which goes to the Zličín metro station (line B). There's also an **Airport Express bus** (AE, 60Kč, 35 minutes, every 30 minutes from 5am to 10pm) which runs to Praha hlavní nádraží (Prague main train station), where you can connect to metro line C (buy ticket from driver, luggage goes free).

Alternatively, take a **Cedaz** (☑220 116 758; www.cedaz.cz; MNáměstí Republiky) mini-bus from outside either arrival terminal to the Czech Airlines office near Náměstí Republiky (150Kč, 20 minutes, every 30 minutes from 7.30am to 7pm); buy a ticket at the Cedaz info centre in the terminal or from the driver.

AAA Radio Taxi (☑14014, 222 333 222; www.aaataxi.cz) operates a 24-hour taxi service, charging around 500Kč to 650Kč to get to the centre of Prague. You'll find taxi stands outside both arrivals terminals. Drivers usually speak some English and accept credit cards.

101; www.studentagency.cz) and **Eurolines** (☑245 005 245; www.elines.cz; ⊙8am-7pm); both have offices at Florenc bus station, or you can buy tickets online.

Car & Motorcycle

Prague lies at the nexus of several European four-lane highways and is a relatively easy drive from many major regional cities, including the following:

Berlin four hours
Budapest five hours
Munich four hours
Nuremberg three hours
Vienna four hours

Train

Prague is well integrated into the European rail networks. **České dráhy** (☑840 112 113; www.cd.cz), which is the Czech state rail operator, sells tickets for international destinations.

Most domestic and international trains arrive at Praha hlvní nádraží. Some trains, particularly from Berlin, Vienna and Budapest, also stop at **Praha-Holešovice** (☑840 112 113; www.cd.cz; Vrbenského, Holešovice), north of the centre. Both stations have stops on metro line C (red).

Negotiating Prague's Main Station

Prague's main station, **Praha hlavní nádraží** (main train station; ☑840 112 113; www.cd.cz; Wilsonova 8, Nové Město), is a cacophonous space in the midst of a multi-year renovation. On arrival, take the underpass from the platforms to the busy main concourse, where you'll find shops, restaurants and ATMs, as well as a **left-luggage office** (Úschovna Zavazadel; Wilsonova 8, Praha hlavní nádraží; per bag per day 60Kč or 100Kč; ⊙6am-11pm; MHlavní nádraží) and luggage lockers (60Kč).

Wenceslas Square is a 10-minute walk south of the station; alternatively take metro line C one stop (direction Háje) to Muzeum. Public-transport tickets are available at ticketing ma-

chines (have coins ready) or at newspaper kiosks in the station.There are taxi ranks at either end of the concourse. To find the nearest tram stop (for trams 5, 9 and 26), exit the main concourse and turn right; the stop is at the far end of the park.

Try not to arrive late at night – the station closes from 12.30am to 3.30am, and the surrounding area is a magnet for pickpockets and drunks.

Leaving by Train

The main ticketing office, **ČD Centrum** (☑840 112 113; www.cd.cz; Wilsonova 8, Praha hlavní nádraží; ⊙3am-midnight; MHlavní Nádraží), is located on the lower (street) level of Prague's main train station (Praha hlavní nádraží). Sales counters are divided into domestic tickets (*vnitrostátní jízdenky*) and international tickets (*mezinárodní jízdenky*), so make sure you're standing in the right line. The windows also sell seat reservations. Credit cards are accepted.

Just to the left of the ticket windows, you'll find

the **ČD Travel** (☏972 241 861; www.cdtravel.cz; Wilsonova 8, Praha hlavní nádraží; ⊙9am-6pm Mon-Fri, 9am-2pm Sat Apr-Sep, 9am-5pm Mon-Fri Oct-Mar; ⓜHlavní Nádraží) agency, which specialises in international connections. You can also buy tickets online through the České dráhy main website (www.cd.cz).

GETTING AROUND

Bus

Within the Czech Republic, buses are often faster, cheaper and more convenient than trains. Many bus routes have reduced frequency (or none) at weekends. Buses occasionally leave early so get to the station at least 15 minutes before the official departure time. Main bus companies:

➡ **Student Agency** (☏841 101 101; www.studentagency. cz) Popular, private bus company with several destinations, including Prague, Brno, České Budějovice, Český Krumlov, Karlovy Vary and Plzeň.

➡ **CSAD** (☏information line 900 144 444) The national bus company links cities and smaller towns.

Florenc bus station (ÚAN Praha Florenc; Map p346; ☏900 144 444; www.florenc. cz; Křižíkova 4, Karlín; ⊙4am-midnight, information counter 6am-10pm; ⓜFlorenc) is the departure and arrival point for most domestic bus services in Prague. In addition to the main station, there are several smaller bus stations that service regional destinations and lie along outlying metro stations. Buses to the northeastern Czech Republic (including Mělník) depart from **Holešovice bus station** (ÚAN Praha Holešovice; Map p348; ☏900 144 444; www.florenc.cz; Vrbenského, Holešovice; ⓜNádraží

Holešovice). Other buses leave from a small stop at the Černý Most station (line B, yellow) or Roztyly station (line C, red). Check the online timetable at www. vlak-bus.cz to make sure you have the right station. On these services, you buy your ticket from the driver.

Car & Motorcycle

Driving Licence
Foreign driving licences are valid for up to 90 days.

Fuel
Unleaded petrol is available as natural (95 octane) or natural plus (98 octane). The Czech for diesel is nafta or just diesel.

Car Hire
Small local companies offer better prices than major international companies, but are less likely to have fluent, English-speaking staff. It's often easier to book by email than by phone. Typical rates for a Škoda Fabia are around 800Kč a day, including unlimited kilometres, collision-damage waiver and value-added tax (VAT). Bring your credit card as a deposit. A motorway tax coupon is included with most rental cars. Major car-hire companies have desks at Václav Havel Airport Prague.

Driving Rules
➡ The minimum driving age is 18.

➡ Traffic moves on the right.

➡ The use of seat belts is compulsory for front- and rear-seat passengers.

➡ Children under 12 or shorter than 1.5m (4ft 9in) are prohibited from sitting in the front seat and must use a child-safety seat.

➡ Headlights must be always on, even in bright daylight.

➡ The legal blood-alcohol

limit is zero; if the police pull you over for any reason, they are required to administer a breathalyser.

➡ For highway driving, motorists are required to display on their windscreen a special prepaid sticker (*dálniční známka*), purchased on the border or at post offices and petrol stations. A sticker valid for 10 days costs 310Kč, for 30 days 440Kč, and for a year 1500Kč.

➡ In Prague, trams have the right of way when making any signalled turn across your path. Drivers may overtake a tram only on the right, and only if it's in motion. You must stop behind any tram taking on or letting off passengers where there's no passenger island.

➡ In case of an accident, contact the police immediately if repairs are likely to exceed 20,000Kč or if there is an injury. Even if damage is slight, it's a good idea to report the accident to obtain a police statement for insurance purposes.

➡ For emergency breakdowns, the **ÚAMK** (ÚAMK; ☏1230) (Central Automobile & Motorcycle Club) provides nationwide assistance 24 hours a day.

Driving in Prague
If you've brought your own car, don't even think of trying to use it for getting around Prague. Car travel in the centre is often restricted, and the warren of one-way streets takes years of driving to get to know well. The only exception might be to desti-

---

CZECH SPEED LIMITS

50km/h (30 mph) in towns and cities

90km/h (56 mph) on the open road

130km/h (78 mph) on expressways

YOU'RE GOING WHERE?

Although most staff at the international ticket counters in Prague's main train station, Praha hlavní nádraží, speak at least some English, those selling domestic tickets may not. In order to speed up the process of buying a ticket, and to avoid misunderstandings, it's often easier to write down what you want on a piece of paper and hand it to the clerk (this works for bus tickets, too).

Write it down in the following way:

➡ **z** departure station, eg PRAHA

➡ **do** destination station, eg KARLŠTEJN

➡ **čas** departure time, using 24-hour clock

➡ **datum** date, eg for 2.30pm on 20 May, write '14.30h. 20.05', or just *dnes* (today)

➡ **osoby** number of passengers

➡ **jednosměrný** (one way) or **zpáteční** (return)

If you're making a reservation on an EC (international) or IC (domestic) train, you may also want to specify *1. třídá* or *2. třídá* (1st or 2nd class), and whether you want an *okno* (window) or *chodba* (aisle) seat.

nations outside the centre or to cross town, but even then you'll have to contend with soul-crushing traffic jams. Instead, find a secure place to leave your vehicle for the duration and use public transport.

PARKING IN PRAGUE
Parking in Prague is tight and in several districts, including the centre, mostly off limits to nonresidents. In areas with restricted parking, a blue marking on the street indicates that only residents may park there. A white line allows for metered, paid parking. Meter fees in the centre are 40Kč per hour. In outlying areas, you're generally allowed to park where you want, but finding an available space is tough.

The **Kotva** (www.od-kotva. cz; Revoluční 1; Ⓜ Náměstí Republiky) department store has a centrally located parking garage, where paid parking is allowed, though at 50Kč per hour rates can add up. Most hotels offer some form of parking for an additional fee (per night 200Kč to 300Kč).

A cheaper alternative is to use the 'Park & Ride' (P&R) spaces near metro stations on the outskirts. The best of these include Skalka (metro

line A); Zličín, Nové Butovice, Palmovka, Rajská Zahrada and Černý Most (line B); and Nádraží Holešovice, Ladví and Opatov (line C).

The fine for illegal parking is normally a clamp on the car wheel or (worse) having the car towed to a police parking compound. Figure on a couple of hours of bureaucracy and fines and fees of about 1500Kč.

Train

The Czech rail network is operated by **České dráhy** (☎840 112 113; www.cd.cz), though a smaller private operator, **RegioJet** (☎841 101 101; www.regiojet.cz; Wilsonova 8, Praha hlavní nádraží; ⊘5.15am-8pm Mon-Wed, 5.15am-8.45pm Thu-Sat, 7.15am-8.45pm Sun; Ⓜ Hlavní Nádraží), operates daily high-speed trains from Prague to the Moravian cities of Olomouc and Ostrava. Timetable information for all trains is available online at www.vlak-bus.cz.

Several different categories of train run on Czech rails, differing mainly in speed and comfort.

➡ **EuroCity (EC)** Fast, comfortable international trains, stopping at main stations only,

with 1st- and 2nd-class coaches; supplementary charge of 60Kč; reservations recommended. Includes 1st-class only SC Pendolino trains that run from Prague to Olomouc, Brno and Ostrava, with links to Vienna and Bratislava.

➡ **InterCity (IC)** Long-distance and international trains with 1st- and 2nd-class coaches; supplement of 40Kč; reservations recommended.

➡ **Express (Ex)** Similar to IC trains, but no extra charge.

➡ **Rychlík (R)** The main domestic network of fast trains with 1st- and 2nd-class coaches and sleeper services; no supplement except for sleepers; express and *rychlík* trains are usually marked in red on timetables.

➡ **Osobní (Os)** Slow trains using older rolling stock that stop in every one-horse town; 2nd class only.

Public Transport in Prague

The centre of Prague is compact and walking is usually the best option. For longer distances, look no further than the city's excellent public-transportation system

DON'T BLAME US...

...when it comes to sorting out Prague's ever-changing tram and bus schedules. While we love Prague's transport system, even we get a little flustered by the constant rerouting and line cancellations brought on by the nearly nonstop construction and maintenance projects. Depending on the day or the week, some trams disappear, others are rerouted and, mercifully, a few stay the same – but figuring out which is which is nearly impossible. The **Prague Public Transport Authority** (DPP; ☑296 191 817; www.dpp.cz; ⊙7am-9pm) lists changes on its website, but you need to know the system well to get much out of it. If you do find yourself on a tram that zigs when it should have zagged, just settle in and enjoy the ride.

of metros, trams and buses. The system is integrated, meaning that tickets bought for one mode of transport are transferable to another. For late-night transit, there is a special line of night trams that operate past midnight.

Prague's excellent public-transport system is operated by the **Prague Public Transport Authority** (DPP; ☑296 191 817; www.dpp.cz; ⊙7am-9pm), which has information desks in both terminals of Prague's Václav Havel airport and in several metro stations, including Muzeum, Můstek, Anděl and Nádraží Holešovice. The metro operates daily from 5am to midnight.

The metro has three lines:
➡ **Line A** (shown on transport maps in green) Runs from the northwestern side of the city at Dejvická to the east at Depo Hostivař.

➡ **Line B** (Yellow) Runs from the southwest at Zličín to the northeast at Černý Most

➡ **Line C** (Red) Runs from the north at Letňany to the southeast at Háje.

Convenient stops for visitors include Staroměstská (closest to Old Town Square), Malostranská (Malá Strana), Můstek (Wenceslas Square), Muzeum (National Museum),

and Hlavní Nádraží (main train station).

After the metro closes, night trams (51 to 58) rumble across the city about every 40 minutes through the night (only full-price 32Kč tickets are valid on these services).

Tickets

You need to buy a ticket before boarding a tram or bus or descending into the metro. Tickets are sold from machines at metro stations and some tram stops (coins only), as well as at DPP information offices and many news stands and kiosks. Tickets are valid on all Prague metros, trams and buses, as well as the **Petřín funicular** (Lanová draha na Petřín; Map p328; ☑800 191 817; www.dpp.cz; Újezd; adult/child 24/12Kč; ⊙9am-11.30pm Apr-Oct, 9am-11.20pm Nov-Mar; 🚋6, 9, 12, 20, 22 to Újezd).

Tickets can be purchased individually or as discounted day passes valid for one or three days. A full-price individual ticket costs 32Kč per adult, and 16Kč per child aged six to 15 years and senior aged 65 to 70 (kids under six ride free) and is valid for 90 minutes of unlimited travel, including transfers. For shorter journeys, buy short-term tickets that are valid for 30 minutes of unlimited travel. These cost 24/12Kč

per adult/child and senior. You'll also need a 16Kč ticket if you're carrying a dog or for each large suitcase or backpack. Bikes (metro only) and prams travel free.

If you're planning on staying more than a few hours, it makes sense to buy either a one- or three-day pass. These not only save money but are more convenient. One-day passes cost 110/55Kč per adult/child and senior; three-day passes cost 310Kč (no discounts available for children or seniors).

Note: you must validate (punch) your ticket before descending into the metro or on entering a tram or bus (day passes must be stamped the first time you use them). For the metro, you'll see stamping machines at the top of the escalators. In trams and buses there will be a stamping machine in the vehicle by the door. While ticket inspections are infrequent, getting caught without a validated ticket can be expensive. The fine if paid on the spot is 800Kč, or 1500Kč if paid later at a police station.

Bicycle

The Czech Republic has a growing network of marked cycling trails that connect cities and pass through scenic areas. Most towns and cities popular with tourists will have rental and repair outfits. The local tourist information office should be able to provide info and trail maps. Many trains will transport bikes (look for a bicycle sign on internet timetables), though be sure to tell the ticket agent you have a bike, since you'll have to pay a small fee for transport.

Several parts of Prague now have marked bike lanes (look for yellow bike-path signs). Still, with its cobblestones, tram tracks and multitudes of pedestrians, Prague has a long way to go to catch up with far bike-friendlier cities such as Vienna or Amsterdam.

➡ Nearly everyone wears a helmet, and this is always a good idea.

➡ The black market for stolen bikes is thriving, so don't leave bikes unattended for longer than a few minutes and always use the sturdiest lock money can buy.

➡ Cycling is prohibited in pedestrian zones such as on Charles Bridge. Technically you could be fined up to 1000Kč, but more often than not, the police will simply tell you to dismount.

➡ Bikes are transported free of charge on the metro, but cyclists are required to obey certain rules. Bikes can only ride near the last door of the rear carriage, and only two bikes are allowed per train. Bikes are not permitted if the carriage is full, or if there's already a pram in the carriage.

For more on cycling in Prague and the Czech Republic, see p34.

Bicycle Hire in Prague

Several companies in Prague rent bikes:

Biko Adventures Prague

(☑733 750 990; www.bikoadventures.com; Vratislavova 3, Nové Město; standard rental per day 450Kč, group tours per person from 1250Kč; ☀9am-6pm Apr-Oct; 🚆7, 17 to Výtoň) Italian owner Fillippo Mari loves to cycle, ski and hike and has created this small outfit dedicated to outdoor pursuits of all kinds. From April to October Biko rents bikes and offers day-long guided cycling trips (both on- and off-road) for riders of all levels. Rental bikes include standard mountain bikes and high-end hardtails, and full-suspension rides from Giant.

City Bike (☑776 180 284;

www.citybike-prague.com; Králodvorská 5, Staré Město; rental per day 500Kč, tours per person 550-800Kč; ☀9am-7pm Apr-Oct; Ⓜ Náměstí Republiky) Rental includes helmet, padlock and map; good-quality Trek mountain bikes are available per day for 600Kč.

Taxis

Taxis in Prague are frequent and relatively expensive. The official rate for licensed cabs is 40Kč flag fall plus 28Kč per kilometre and 6Kč per minute while waiting. On this basis, any trip within the city centre – say, from Wenceslas Square to Malá Strana – should cost no more than 200Kč. A trip to the suburbs, depending on the distance, should run from 200Kč to 300Kč, and to the airport between 500Kč and 700Kč.

While the number of dishonest drivers has fallen in recent years, taxi rip-offs are still an occasional problem, especially among drivers who congregate in popular tourist areas like Old Town Square and Wenceslas Square. The usual tactic is to quote an inflated fare upon arriving at the destination and then refuse to budge when you complain that it seems high. Ask the driver in advance for an approximate fare and if it feels too high, don't get in. Also, avoid unmarked cabs, ie those that aren't obviously part of a reputable firm.

Instead of hailing cabs off the street, call or ask someone to call a radio taxi, as they're better regulated and more responsible. The following companies have honest drivers and offer 24-hour service and English-speaking operators:

➡ **AAA Radio Taxi** (☑14014, 222 333 222; www.aaataxi.cz)

➡ **ProfiTaxi** (☑14015; www.profitaxi.cz)

Directory A–Z

Customs Regulations

Customs formalities have been simplified. On arrival at Prague's Václav Havel airport, if you have nothing to declare, simply walk through the green (customs-free) line. Bags are rarely checked. Formal customs regulations are as follows:

➡ On travel between the Czech Republic and other EU countries, you can import/export 800 cigarettes, 400 cigarillos, 200 cigars, 1kg of smoking tobacco, 10L of spirits, 20L of fortified wine, 90L of wine and 110L of beer, provided the goods are for personal use only (each country sets its own guide levels; these figures are minimums).

➡ Travellers arriving from outside the EU can import or export duty-free a maximum of 200 cigarettes or 100 cigarillos or 50 cigars or 250g of tobacco; 2L of still table wine; 1L of spirits or 2L of fortified wine, sparkling wine or liqueurs; 60mL of perfume; 250mL of eau de toilette; and €175 worth of all other goods (including gifts and souvenirs).

Discount Cards

➡ If you intend to visit several museums during your stay, you might consider purchasing a Prague Card, which offers free or discounted entry to around 50 sights. Included are Prague Castle, the Old Town Hall, the National Gallery museums, the Petřín Lookout Tower and Vyšehrad. Passholders are entitled to a 15% discount on admission to the Prague Jewish Museum.

➡ The pass is available for two to four days, starting at around 850/550Kč per adult/child for two days. Cards can be purchased at **Prague City Tourism** (Prague Welcome; Map p332; ☑221 714 444; www.prague.eu; Old Town Hall, Staroměstské náměstí 5; ☺9am-7pm; MStaroměstská) offices or you can buy the card online at www.praguecitycard.com. When you purchase passes online you have the option to buy unlimited public transport, though prices are about the same as you would pay normally.

Electricity

Electricity in Prague is 230V, 50Hz AC. Outlets have the standard European socket with two small round holes and a protruding earth (ground) pin. If you have a different plug, bring an adapter. North American 110V appliances will also need a transformer if they don't have built-in voltage adjustment.

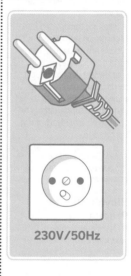

230V/50Hz

Embassies & Consulates

Australian Consulate (☑221 729 260; www.dfat.gov.au/missions/countries/cz.html; 6th fl, Klimentská 10, Nové Město; ☒5, 8, 24, 26 to Dlouhá třída) Honorary consulate for emergency assistance only (eg a stolen passport); the Australian embassy in Warsaw, Poland, is formally responsible for the Czech Republic.

Canadian Embassy (☑272 101 800; www.canadainternational.gc.ca; Ve struhách 2, Bubeneč; 🚌131 to Nemocnice Bubeneč)

French Embassy (🖉251 171 711; www.france.cz; Velkopřevorské náměstí 2, Malá Strana; 🚊12, 20, 22 to Malostranské náměstí)

German Embassy (🖉257 113 111; www.prag.diplo. de; Vlašská 19, Malá Strana; 🚊12, 20, 22 to Malostranské náměstí)

Irish Embassy (🖉257 011 280; www.embassyofireland. cz; Tržiště 13, Malá Strana; 🚊12, 20, 22 to Malostranské náměstí)

Netherlands Embassy (🖉233 015 200; http:// tsjechie.nlambassade.org; Gotthardská 6/27, Bubeneč; 🚌131 to Sibiřské náměstí)

New Zealand Consulate (🖉234 784 777; www.nzembassy.com; Václavské náměstí 11, Nové Město; Ⓜ Můstek) Honorary consulate providing emergency assistance only (eg stolen passport); the nearest NZ embassy is in Berlin.

Russian Embassy (🖉233 374 093; www.czech.mid. ru; Korunovační 34, Bubeneč; 🚌131 to Sibiřské náměstí)

UK Embassy (🖉257 402 111; www.gov.uk/government/world/czech-republic; Thunovská 14, Malá Strana; 🚊12, 20, 22 to Malostranské náměstí)

US Embassy (🖉257 022 000; http://czech.prague. usembassy.gov/; Tržiště 15, Malá Strana; 🚊12, 20, 22 to Malostranské náměstí)

Emergency

Ambulance (🖉155)
Breakdown assistance for motorists (ÚAMK; 🖉1230)
EU-wide emergency hotline (🖉112) English- and German-speaking operators are available.

Fire (🖉150)
Prague municipal police (🖉156)
State police (🖉158)

Gay & Lesbian Travellers

The Czech Republic is a tolerant destination for gay and lesbian travellers. Homosexuality is legal, and since 2006 the country has allowed gay couples to form registered partnerships.

➡ Prague has a lively gay scene and was home to the country's first 'gay pride' march (in 2011). Attitudes are less accepting outside of the capital, but even here homosexual couples are not likely to suffer overt discrimination.

➡ Many gay bars and clubs in Prague are located in Vinohrady.

➡ Useful websites include the **Gay Guide Prague** (http:// prague.gayguide.net) and **Prague Saints** (www.prague saints.cz).

Internet Access

The Czech Republic is well wired. Wi-fi (pronounced 'vee-fee' in Czech) is ubiquitous. Most hotels, including pensions and youth hostels, offer it free of charge to guests; though occasionally more expensive properties charge (or only offer free wi-fi in the lobby). Many bars, cafes and restaurants offer free wi-fi (usually marked on the door with the international wi-fi sign).

➡ Often the most convenient and reliable places to get wi-fi access in a pinch are McDonald's and KFC restaurants, which offer free wi-fi around the country.

➡ Many hotels regrettably are dropping the practice of making a computer terminal available for guests, though some still do, including many hostels. Larger hotels will sometimes have a business centre for guests to use (often for a fee).

➡ For those without a laptop, Prague has dozens of internet cafes.

Globe Bookstore & Café (🖉224 934 203; www. globebookstore.cz; Pštrossova 6, Nové Město; per min 1Kč; ⏰9.30am-midnight Mon-Thu, to 1am Fri-Sun; 🛜; 🚊14 to Myslíkova, Ⓜ Karlovo Náměstí) No minimum usage. Also has ethernet ports so you can connect your own laptop (same price; cables provided, 50Kč deposit), and free wi-fi.

Relax Café-Bar (🖉224 211 521; www.relaxcafebar.cz; Dlážděná 4; per 10min 10Kč; ⏰8am-10pm Mon-Fri, 2-10pm Sat; 🛜; Ⓜ Náměstí Republiky) A conveniently located internet cafe. Wi-fi is free.

We use the 🛜 icon to identify hotels, restaurants, cafes and bars that have wi-fi access for guests and customers. We use the @ icon to indicate hotels that have computers available for guests.

Legal Matters

Foreigners in the Czech Republic, as elsewhere, are subject to the laws of the host country. While your embassy or consulate is the best stop in any emergency, bear in mind that there are some things it can't do for you, like getting local laws or regulations waived, investigating a crime, providing legal advice or representation, getting you out of jail and lending you money.

A consul can, however, issue emergency passports, contact relatives and friends, advise on how to transfer funds, provide lists of reliable local doctors, lawyers and interpreters, and visit you if you've been arrested or jailed.

In the Czech Republic, the legal blood-alcohol level for drivers is 0.0.

Cannabis occupies a legal grey area; it's been decriminalised but is not technically legal. What that means in practice is that police will rarely hassle you for smoking a joint, but one should always exercise discretion and not smoke indoors. Buying and selling drugs of any kind, including cannabis, is illegal.

Medical Services

The quality of medical care in the Czech Republic is high and, rest assured, if you do suffer a medical emergency you will receive proper care. Citizens of EU countries can obtain a European Health Insurance Card (EHIC); this entitles you to free state-provided medical treatment in the Czech Republic (see www.cmu.cz – click on the UK flag – for information on using the card in the Czech Republic).

Non-EU citizens must pay for treatment, and at least some of the fee must usually be paid upfront. Bring cash or credit cards.

If you do need to seek emergency medical treatment, in addition to cash, be sure to bring along your passport and any insurance information you have with you. Save all bills and receipts for later reimbursement with your insurance company.

Clinics in Prague
Canadian Medical Care
(☏235 360 133; www.cm-cpraha.cz; Veleslavínská 1, Veleslavín; ⊗8am-6pm Mon, Wed & Fri, to 8pm Tue & Thu, 9am-2pm Sat; 🚋2, 20, 26 to Veleslavín) A pricey but professional private clinic with

English-speaking doctors; an initial consultation will cost from 1500Kč to 2500Kč.

Polyclinic at Národní (Poliklinika na Národní; ☏222 075 119, 24hr emergencies 777 942 270; www.poliklinika.narodni.cz; Národní třída 9, Nové Město; ⊗8.30am-5pm Mon-Fri; 🚇6, 9, 17, 18, 22 to Národní divadlo) A central clinic with staff who speak English, German, French and Russian. Expect to pay around 800Kč to 1500Kč for an initial consultation.

Emergency Rooms in Prague
Na Homolce Hospital
(☏257 271 111; www.homolka.cz; 5th fl, Foreign Pavilion, Roentgenova 2, Motol; 🚌167, 168 to Nemocnice Na Homolce) The best hospital in Prague, equipped and staffed to Western standards, with staff who speak English, French, German and Spanish.

Pharmacies
You'll see plenty of pharmacies (lékárna or apteka) throughout the Czech Republic. These are identified by a big green cross on the outside.

In addition to dispensing prescription medications, pharmacies are the only places that can sell common over-the-counter drugs like aspirin, cough syrup, cold medications and the like.

Most pharmacies keep normal business hours, but each district has at least one late-hour dispensary for emergencies. To find the pharmacy in your district, go to any nearby pharmacy; information is usually posted on the door.

Lékárna U Sv Ludmily
(☏222 513 396; www.lekarnabelgicka.cz; Belgická 37, Vinohrady, Prague; ⊗7am-7pm Mon-Fri, 8am-noon Sat; 🚇Náměstí Míru) Has a 24-hour pharmacy window.

Money

The Czech crown (Koruna česká, or Kč) is divided into 100 hellers or haléřů. Bank notes come in denominations of 100Kč, 200Kč, 500Kč, 1000Kč, 2000Kč and 5000Kč; coins are in denominations of 1Kč, 2Kč, 5Kč, 10Kč, 20Kč and 50Kč. Hellers do not circulate, but prices are sometimes denominated in fractions of crowns. In these instances, the total will be rounded to the nearest whole crown.

Keep small change handy for use at public toilets and tram-ticket machines, and try to keep some small-denomination notes for shops, cafes and bars – getting change for the 2000Kč notes that ATMs often spit out can be a problem.

ATMs
You'll find ATMs all around Prague and in the central areas of towns and cities around the country. There are ATMs in the concourse of Prague's main train station as well as at both arrivals terminals at Prague's airport. Most ATMs accept any valid credit or debit card, provided you have a four-digit PIN code.

Black Market
Changing money on the black market is illegal and dangerous. Rates are no better than at the banks or ATMs and the chance of getting ripped off is infinitely greater. Firmly decline any offers you may hear to 'change money?'. If you are foolish enough to change money on the street, make sure you receive valid Czech notes in exchange. The black market is flooded with outdated Polish zlotys and other worthless bills.

Changing Money
The main banks – including Komerční banka, Česká spořitelna and UniCredit

PRACTICALITIES

⇒ **Current Events** The English-language weekly online news service the *Prague Post* (www.praguepost.com) is a good source of local news. Foreign newspapers can be found at larger newsagents, bookshops and news stands.

⇒ **Radio** The BBC World Service broadcasts part of the day in English on FM101.1. The state-run **Czech Radio** (www.rozhlas.cz) is the main Czech broadcaster, operating on FM around the country; all programs are in Czech.

⇒ **Smoking** It is prohibited to smoke at most indoor public places, including schools, government offices, hospitals, libraries, railway stations and on public transport. Smoking is permitted in some restaurants and bars, provided the smoking section is physically separated from the nonsmoking section. In practice, most upscale restaurants are nonsmoking, while most pubs and bars allow smoking. Most hotels are nonsmoking.

⇒ **Television** Most hotels offer satellite television with some English-language channels, including usually at a minimum CNN International, Eurosport and BBC World. **Czech Television** (www.ceskatelevize.cz) operates two state-controlled broadcast channels; additionally, there are several private channels. All broadcasts are in Czech.

⇒ **Tipping** In restaurants, tip 10% of the bill to reward good service. Leave the tip on the tray that the bill is delivered in or hand the money directly to the waiter. Taxi drivers won't expect a tip, but it's fine to round the fare up to the nearest 10Kč increment to reward special service.

⇒ **Weights & Measures** The Czech Republic uses the metric system.

Bank – are the best places to exchange cash. They normally charge around a 2% commission with a 50Kč minimum (but do always check, as commissions vary). They will also provide a cash advance on Visa or MasterCard without commission.

The easiest and cheapest way to carry money is in the form of a credit or debit card from your bank, which you can use to withdraw cash either from an ATM or over the counter in a bank. Using an ATM will result in your home bank charging a fee (usually 1.5% to 2.5%), but you'll get a decent exchange rate, and provided you make withdrawals of at least a couple of thousand crowns at a time, you'll pay less than the assorted commissions on travellers cheques etc. Check with your home bank about transaction fees and withdrawal limits.

Avoid private exchange booths (*směnárna*) in the main tourist areas. They lure you in with attractive-looking exchange rates that turn out to be 'sell' (*prodej*) rates; if you want to change foreign currency into Czech crowns, the 'buy' (*nákup*) rate applies. Moreover, the best rates are usually only for very large transactions, above €500. Check the rates carefully, and ask exactly how much you will get before parting with any money. Similarly, hotel reception desks sometimes exchange money for guests, however, they seldom offer an attractive rate.

Credit Cards

Visa and MasterCard are widely accepted for goods and services. The only places you may experience a problem are at small establishments or for small transactions (under 250Kč). American Express cards are typically accepted at larger hotels and restaurants, though they are not as widely recognised as other cards.

Travellers Cheques

Travellers cheques are not much use, as they are not accepted by shops and restaurants and can be exchanged only at banks and currency-exchange counters.

Opening Hours

Most places adhere roughly to the hours listed below. Shopping centres and malls have longer hours and are open daily from at least 10am to 8pm. Museums are usually closed on Mondays, and have shorter hours outside of high season.

⇒ **Banks** 9am to 4pm Monday to Friday, with some banks offering limited hours on Saturday from 9am to 1pm.

⇒ **Bars and clubs** 11am to 1am Tuesday to Saturday, normally shorter hours Sunday and Monday.

⇒ **Museums** 9am to 5pm Tuesday to Sunday; some attractions are closed or have shorter hours October to April.

→ **Offices** 8am to 5pm Monday to Friday, 9am to 1pm Saturday (varies).

→ **Post offices** 7am to 7pm Monday to Friday, 8am to 1pm Saturday (cities).

→ **Restaurants** 11am to 11pm daily; many kitchens close by 10pm.

→ **Shops** 9am to 6pm Monday to Friday, 9am to 1pm Saturday (varies). Shops that cater mainly to tourists in the centre have longer hours and are normally open weekends.

Post

The Czech postal service (Česká Pošta; www.cpost.cz) is efficient, though post offices can be tricky to negotiate since signage is only in Czech. For mailing letters and postcards, be sure to get into the proper line, identified as 'listovní zásilky' (correspondence). Anything you can't afford to lose should go by registered mail (doporučený dopis) or by Express Mail Service (EMS).

A standard postcard or letter up to 20g costs about 20Kč to other European countries and 30Kč for destinations outside Europe. Buy stamps at post offices but be sure to have the letter weighed to ensure proper postage.

Prague's **main post office** (Map p336; ☑221 131 111; www.cpost.cz; Jindřišská 14, Nové Město; ☉2am-midnight; MMůstek) is centrally located not far from Wenceslas Square in Nové Město. It uses an automated queuing system: take a ticket from one of the machines in the entrance corridors, press button No 1 for stamps, letters and parcels; then watch the display boards in the main hall – when your ticket number appears (flashing), go to the desk number shown. It keeps longer hours

than other post offices and can be a lifesaver if you've got something that needs to be sent quickly. In addition, there are copy and fax services here, and you can use the telephone booths to dial international numbers.

Public Holidays

Banks, offices, department stores and some shops are closed on public holidays. Restaurants, museums and tourist attractions tend to stay open, though many may close on the first working day after a holiday.

New Year's Day 1 January

Easter Monday March/April

Labour Day 1 May

Liberation Day 8 May

Sts Cyril & Methodius Day 5 July

Jan Hus Day 6 July

Czech Statehood Day 28 September

Republic Day 28 October

Struggle for Freedom & Democracy Day 17 November

Christmas Eve (Generous Day) 24 December

Christmas Day 25 December

St Stephen's Day 26 December

Taxes & Refunds

Czech prices, including at shops, restaurants and hotels, normally include the value added tax (VAT), so the price you see is the price you pay. Only rarely will this not be the case and it will be clearly marked or stated in advance.

Non-EU residents can qualify for a tax refund on large purchases (over 2000Kč), subject to certain conditions. Look for retailers displaying a 'Tax Free Shopping' sign and then inform the clerk you intend to get a refund. You'll need to save the sales receipt and ensure

the goods are not used. Normally you collect the tax at the airport on departure or by mail once you return home. For details, see the Global Blue website (www.globalblue.com).

Telephone

Most Czech telephone numbers, both landline and mobile (cell), have nine digits. There are no city or area codes, so to call any Czech number, simply dial the nine-digit number.

→ To call abroad from the Czech Republic, dial the international access code (00), then the country code, then the area code (minus any initial zero) and the number.

→ To dial the Czech Republic from abroad, dial your country's international access code, then 420 (the Czech Republic country code) and then the unique nine-digit local number.

Mobile Phones

The Czech Republic uses the GSM 900/1800 system, the same system in use around Europe, as well as in Australia and New Zealand. It's not compatible with most mobile phones in North America or Japan (though many mobiles have multiband GSM 1900/900 phones that will work in the Czech Republic). If you have a GSM phone, check with your service provider about using it in the Czech Republic, and beware of calls being routed internationally (very expensive for a 'local' call).

→ If your mobile phone is unlocked, a cheaper and often better option is to buy a prepaid SIM card, available from any mobile-phone shop for around 450Kč (including 300Kč of calling credit). Prepaid SIMs allow you to make local calls at cheaper local rates. In this case, of course, you can't use your existing mobile number.

➡ The situation is more complicated if you plan on using a 'smartphone' like an iPhone or Android device that may not be easily unlocked to accommodate a local SIM card. With these phones, it's best to contact your home provider to consider short-term international calling and data plans appropriate to what you might need.

➡ Smartphones can still be used as handy wi-fi devices, even without a special plan. Be sure to switch your phone to 'airplane' mode on arrival, which blocks out calls and text messages, but still allows wi-fi. Also turn off your phone's 'data roaming' setting on arrival to avoid unwanted roaming fees.

➡ The three main mobile operators are **Telefonica O2** (www.o2.cz), **T-Mobile** (www.t-mobile.cz) and **Vodafone** (www.vodafone.cz). All have service centres scattered around Prague and offer prepaid SIM cards and temporary calling plans at similar price.

Phonecards

Local prepaid cards for payphones in the Czech Republic include **Smartcall** (www.smartcall.cz) and Karta X Plus – you can buy them from hotels, newspaper kiosks and tourist information offices for 300Kč to 1000Kč. To use one, follow the instructions on the card: dial the access number, then the PIN code beneath the scratch-away panel, then the number you want to call (including any international code). Rates from Prague to the UK, USA and Australia with Smartcall are around 6.6Kč to 10Kč a minute; as a rule, the more expensive the card, the better the rate.

Time

The Czech Republic lies within the same time zone,

GMT/UTC+1, as most of Continental Europe. Czech local time is one hour ahead of London and six hours ahead of New York. The Czech Republic observes Daylight Saving Time (DST), and puts the clock forward one hour at 2am on the last Sunday in March, and back again at 3am on the last Sunday in October. The 24-hour clock is used for official purposes, including all transport schedules. In everyday conversation people commonly use the 12-hour clock.

Toilets

Public toilets are free in state-run museums, galleries and concert halls. Elsewhere, such as in train, bus and metro stations, public toilets are staffed by attendants who charge 5Kč to 10Kč. Men's are marked *muži* or *páni,* and women's *ženy* or *dámy.*

In the main tourist areas of Prague, there are public toilets in Prague Castle; opposite the tram stop on Malostranské náměstí; next to the Goltz-Kinský Palace on Old Town Square; on Templova, just off Celetná close to the Powder Gate; on Uhelný trh in the Old Town; and next to the Laterna Magika on Národní třída.

Tourist Information

The official travel-promotion bureau for the Czech Republic is **Czech Tourism** (www.czechtourism.com), which maintains offices in several major countries. Check the website for contact information.

In Prague

The **Czech Tourism Information Centre** (Map p332; ☑224 861 476; www.czechtourism.cz; Staroměstské náměstí 5; ⊙9am-6pm Mon-Fri, 10am-5pm Sat, 10am-

3pm Sun) offers official travel information throughout the Czech Republic. There's a helpful, centrally located office in Prague.

The official provider of Prague tourist information is Prague City Tourism (formerly called Prague Welcome). Branches are scattered around town, including at Prague's airport. Offices are good sources of maps and general information, as well as an excellent resource for finding what's on during your stay. The main website (www.prague.eu) provides extensive information in English.

Prague City Tourism - Old Town Hall (Map p332; ☑221 714 444; www.prague.eu; Old Town Hall, Staroměstské náměstí 5; ⊙9am-7pm; Ⓜ Staroměstská) The busiest of the Prague City Tourism branches occupies the ground floor of the Old Town Hall (enter to the left of the Astronomical Clock).

Prague City Tourism - Rytírská (Map p332; ☑221 714 444; www.prague.eu; Rytírská 31, Staré Město; ⊙10am-6pm; Ⓜ Můstek) Conveniently situated near the Můstek metro station, this office tends to be less crowded and more helpful than at the other, busier branches. In addition to the usual services, such out handing out maps and advice, this office is a good place to buy tickets for various events around town.

Prague City Tourism - Malá Strana (Map p328; ☑221 714 714; www.prague.eu; Malá Strana Bridge Tower, Mostecká, Malá Strana; ⊙10am-6pm Apr-Oct; 🚋12, 20, 22) Situated inside the north tower on the Malá Strana side of Charles Bridge, this office is often jammed. It's good for maps and basic info, though the harried staff can also offer advice on accommodation, tours and events, and sell transport passes.

Prague City Tourism - Airport (☑221 714 714; www.prague.eu; Terminal 2, Václav Havel Airport Prague; ☉8am-8pm; ☐100, 119) The airport branch of Prague's official tourist-information office is situated in the arrivals hall of Terminal 2 (though there were plans afoot to open a branch in Terminal 1 during the lifetime of this book).

Travellers with Disabilities

The Czech Republic is behind the curve when it comes to catering to the needs of travellers with disabilities. Cobblestones and high curbs present challenging mobility issues, and many older buildings, including hotels and museums, are not wheelchair accessible.

The situation is better with newer buildings. Many McDonald's and KFC restaurants are accommodating to wheelchairs.

In terms of public transport, Prague is slowly making progress on accessibility. Some buses and trams are low riders and, in theory, should accommodate a wheelchair. These services are marked on timetables with a wheelchair symbol. A handful of metro stations, including newer stations, are equipped with lifts. Consult the Prague Public Transport

Authority website (www.dpp.cz) for details.

➡ In the USA, travellers with disabilities may like to contact the **Society for Accessible Travel & Hospitality** (www.sath.org).

➡ In the UK a useful contact is the **Royal Association for Disability & Rehabilitation** (www.radar.org.uk).

Local Organisations

Czech Blind United (Sjednocená Organizace Nevidomých a Slabozrakých v ČR; Map p338; ☑221 462 462; www.braillnet.cz; Krakovská 21, Nové Město; Ⓜ Muzeum) Represents the vision-impaired; provides information but no services.

Prague Wheelchair Users Organisation (Pražská organizace vozíčkářů; Map p332; ☑224 827 210; www.pov.cz; Benediktská 6, Staré Město; ☉9am-4pm Mon-Thu, to 3pm Fri; Ⓜ Náměstí Republiky) This is a watchdog organisation for people with disabilities. While it's mostly geared toward local residents, it can help to organise a guide and transportation at about half the cost of a taxi, and has information on barrier-free Prague in Czech, English and German (though the website is only in Czech).

Visas

Citizens of EU countries do not need a visa to visit the

Czech Republic and can stay indefinitely.

Citizens of the USA, Canada, Australia, New Zealand, Israel, Japan and many other countries can stay in the Czech Republic for up to 90 days without a visa. Other nationalities should check current visa requirements with the Czech embassy in their home country. There's more information on the **Czech Ministry of Foreign Affairs** (www.mzv.cz) website.

The Czech Republic is a member of the EU's common border and customs area, the Schengen Zone, which imposes its own 90-day visa-free travel limit on many visitors from outside the EU. In practice this means your time in the Czech Republic counts against your stay within the entire Schengen Zone – so plan your travel accordingly.

Women Travellers

Solo female travellers are not likely to experience any special difficulties in the Czech Republic. Walking alone on the street is generally as safe – or as dangerous – as in most large European cities.

In Prague, a couple of areas for women to avoid at night would be the park in front of the main train station, which attracts a lot of vagrants, and the upper part of Wenceslas Square, which becomes effectively a red-light district at night.

Language

Czech (*Čeština* chesh·tyi·nuh) belongs to the western branch of the Slavic language family, with Slovak and Polish as its closest relatives. It has approximately 12 million speakers.

Most of the sounds in Czech are also found in English. If you read our coloured pronunciation guides as if they were English, you shouldn't have problems being understood. Note that ai is pronounced as in 'aisle', air as in 'hair' (without the 'r') aw as in 'law', oh as the 'o' in 'note', ow as in 'how' and uh as the 'a' in 'ago'. An accent mark over a vowel in written Czech indicates it's pronounced as a long sound.

For the consonants, note that kh is pronounced like the *ch* in the Scottish *loch* (a throaty sound), zh is pronounced as the 's' in 'pleasure' and r is rolled. The apostrophe (') indicates a slight y sound. The sounds r, s and l can be used as quasi-vowels – this explains why some written Czech words or syllables appear to have no vowels, eg *krk* krk (neck), *osm* o·sm (eight), *vlk* vlk (wolf). If you find these clusters of consonants difficult, just try putting a tiny uh sound between them. Stress is always on the first syllable of a word – this is indicated with italics in our pronunciation guides. Masculine and feminine forms are indicated with (m/f) where needed.

BASICS

Hello.	*Ahoj.*	uh·hoy
Goodbye.	*Na shledanou.*	nuh·skhle·duh·noh
Excuse me.	*Promiňte.*	pro·min'·te
Sorry.	*Promiňte.*	pro·min'·te
Please.	*Prosím.*	pro·seem

WANT MORE?

For in-depth language information and handy phrases, check out Lonely Planet's *Czech Phrasebook*. You'll find it at **shop.lonelyplanet.com**, or you can buy Lonely Planet's iPhone phrasebooks at the Apple App Store.

Thank you.	*Děkuji.*	dye·ku·yi
You're welcome.	*Prosím.*	pro·seem
Yes./No.	*Ano./Ne.*	uh·no/ne

How are you?
Jak se máte? — yuhk se ma·te

Fine. And you?
Dobře. A vy? — dob·rzhe a vi

What's your name?
Jak se jmenujete? — yuhk se yme·nu·ye·te

My name is ...
Jmenuji se ... — yme·nu·yi se ...

Do you speak English?
Mluvíte anglicky? — mlu·vee·te uhn·glits·ki

I don't understand.
Nerozumím. — ne·ro·zu·meem

One moment, please.
Počkejte chvíli. — poch·key·te khvee·li

ACCOMMODATION

Do you have a double room?
Máte pokoj s — ma·te po·koy s
manželskou postelí? — muhn·zhels·koh pos·te·lee

Do you have a single/twin room?
Máte jednolůžkový/ — ma·te yed·no·loozh·ko·vee/
dvoulůžkový pokoj? — dvoh·loozh·ko·vee po·koy

How much is it per ...?	*Kolik to stojí ...?*	ko·lik to sto·yee ...
night	*na noc*	nuh nots
person	*za osobu*	zuh o·so·bu
week	*na týden*	nuh tee·den

campsite	*tábořiště*	ta·bo·rzhish·tye
guesthouse	*penzion*	pen·zi·on
hotel	*hotel*	ho·tel
youth hostel	*mládežnická ubytovna*	mla·dezh·nyits·ka u·bi·tov·nuh

DIRECTIONS

Where's the (market)?
Kde je (trh)? — gde ye (trh)

What's the address?
Jaká je adresa? — yuh·ka ye uh·dre·suh

Can you show me (on the map)?
Můžete mi to — moo·zhe·te mi to
ukázat (na mapě)? — u·ka·zuht (nuh muh·pye)

It's ...	Je to ...	ye to ...
behind ...	za ...	zuh ...
in front of ...	před ...	przhed ...
near	blízko	bleez·ko
next to ...	vedle ...	ved·le ...
on the corner	na rohu	nuh ro·hu
opposite ...	naproti ...	nuh·pro·tyi ...
straight ahead	přímo	przhee·mo

Turn ...	Odbočte ...	od·boch·te ...
at the corner	za roh	zuh rawh
at the traffic lights	u semaforu	u se·muh·fo·ru
left	do leva	do le·vuh
right	do prava	do pruh·vuh

EATING & DRINKING

What would you recommend?
Co byste doporučil/ — tso bis·te do·po·ru·chil/
doporučila? (m/f) — do·po·ru·chi·luh

What's the local speciality?
Co je místní — tso ye meest·nyee
specialita? — spe·tsi·uh·li·tuh

Do you have vegetarian food?
Máte vegetariánská — ma·te ve·ge·tuh·ri·ans·ka
jídla? — yeed·luh

That was delicious!
To bylo lahodné! — to bi·lo luh·hod·nair

I'll have ...	Dám si ...	dam si ...
Cheers!	Na zdraví!	nuh zdruh·vee

I'd like the ..., please.	Chtěl/Chtěla bych ..., prosím. (m/f)	khtyel/khtye·luh bikh ... pro·seem
bill	účet	oo·chet
menu	jídelníček	yee·del·nyee·chek

Key Words

bar	bar	buhr
bottle	láhev	la·hef

To get by in Czech, mix and match these simple patterns with words of your choice:

When's (the next bus)?
V kolik jede — f ko·lik ye·de
(příští autobus)? — (przhee·shtyee ow·to·bus)

Where's (the station)?
Kde je (nádraží)? — gde ye (na·dra·zhee)

Where can I (buy a ticket)?
Kde (koupím — gde (koh·peem
jízdenku)? — yeez·den·ku)

How much is (a room)?
Kolik stojí (pokoj)? — ko·lik sto·yee (po·koy)

Is there (a toilet)?
Je tam (toaleta)? — ye tuhm (to·uh·le·tuh)

Do you have (a map)?
Máte (mapu)? — ma·te (muh·pu)

I'd like (to hire a car).
Chtěl/Chtěla bych — khtyel/khtye·luh bikh
(si půjčit auto). (m/f) — (si pooy·chit ow·to)

I need (a can opener).
Potřebuji (otvírák — po·trzhe·bu·yi (ot·vee·rak
na konzervy). — nuh kon·zer·vi)

Can I (camp here)?
Mohu (zde stanovat)? — mo·hu (zde stuh·no·vuht)

Could you please (help me)?
Můžete prosím — moo·zhe·te pro·seem
(pomoci)? — (po·mo·tsi)

bowl	miska	mis·kuh
breakfast	snídaně	snee·duh·nye
cafe	kavárna	kuh·var·nuh
children's menu	dětský jídelníček	dyets·kee yee·del·nyee·chek
cold	chladný	khluhd·nee
delicatessen	lahůdky	luh·hood·ki
dinner	večeře	ve·che·rzhe
dish	pokrm	po·krm
drink list	nápojový lístek	na·po·yo·vee lees·tek
food	jídlo	yeed·lo
fork	vidlička	vid·lich·kuh
glass	sklenička	skle·nyich·kuh
grocery store	konzum	kon·zum
highchair	dětská stolička	dyet·ska sto·lich·kuh
hot (warm)	teplý	tep·lee
knife	nůž	noozh

lunch	oběd	o·byed
market	trh	trh
plate	talíř	tuh·leerzh
restaurant	restaurace	res·tow·ruh·tse
spoon	lžíce	lzhee·tse
with	s	s
without	bez	bez

Meat & Fish

bacon	slanina	sluh·nyi·nuh
beef	hovězí	ho·vye·zee
chicken	kuře	ku·rzhe
duck	kachna	kuhkh·nuh
fish	ryba	ri·buh
ham	šunka	shun·kuh
herring	sleď	sled'
lamb	jehněčí	yeh·nye·chee
meat	maso	muh·so
mussel	slávka jedlá	slaf·kuh yed·la
pork	vepřové	vep·rzho·vair
pork sausage	vuřt	vurzht
prawn	kreveta	kre·ve·tuh
salami	salám	suh·lam
salmon	losos	lo·sos
steak (beef)	biftek	bif·tek
tuna	tuňák	tu·nyak
turkey	krůta	kroo·tuh
veal	telecí	te·le·tsee
oyster	ústřice	oost·rzhi·tse

Fruit & Vegetables

apple	jablko	yuh·bl·ko
apricot	meruňka	me·run'·kuh
banana	banán	buh·nan
bean	fazole	fuh·zo·le
broccoli	brokolice	bro·ko·li·tse
cabbage	kapusta	kuh·pus·tuh
capsicum	paprika	puh·pri·kuh
carrot	mrkev	mr·kef
cauliflower	květák	kvye·tak
cherry	třešeň	trzhe·shen'
corn	kukuřice	ku·ku·rzhi·tse
cucumber	okurka	o·kur·kuh
date	datle	duht·le
eggplant	lilek	li·lek
garlic	česnek	ches·nek

grapes	hrozny	hroz·ni
legume	luštěnina	lush·tye·nyi·nuh
lemon	citron	tsi·tron
lentil	čočka	choch·ka
lettuce	hlávkový salát	hlaf·ko·vee suh·lat
mushroom	houba	hoh·buh
nut	ořech	o·rzhekh
olive	oliva	o·li·vuh
onion	cibule	tsi·bu·le
orange	pomeranč	po·me·ruhnch
pea	hrách	hrakh
peach	broskev	bros·kef
pear	hruška	hrush·kuh
pepper (bell)	paprika	puh·pri·kuh
pineapple	ananas	uh·nuh·nuhs
plum	švestka	shvest·kuh
potato	brambor	bruhm·bor
pumpkin	dýně	dee·nye
radish	ředkvička	rzhed·kvich·kuh
raisin	hrozinka	hro·zin·kuh
raspberry	malina	muh·li·nuh
spinach	špenát	shpe·nat
strawberry	jahoda	yuh·ho·duh
tomato	rajské jablko	rais·kair yuh·bl·ko
zucchini	cuketa	tsu·ke·tuh

Other

bread	chléb	khlairb
butter	máslo	mas·lo
cheese	sýr	seer
chilli	feferon	pfe·fe·ron
egg	vajíčko	vuh·yeech·ko
honey	med	med
ice cream	zmrzlina	zmrz·li·nuh
jam	džem	dzhem

noodles	nudle	nud·le
pasta	těstovina	tyes·to·vi·nuh
pepper	pepř	pe·przh
rice	rýže	ree·zhe
salad	salát	suh·lat
salt	sůl	sool
sauce	omáčka	o·mach·kuh
soup	polévka	po·lairf·kuh
sugar	cukr	tsu·kr
vinegar	ocet	o·tset

Drinks

beer	pivo	pi·vo
coffee	káva	ka·vuh
lemonade	limonáda	li·mo·na·duh
milk	mléko	mlair·ko
orange juice	pomerančový džus	po·me·ruhn·cho·vee dzhus
red wine	červeného víno	cher·ve·nair·ho vee·no
soft drink	nealkoholický nápoj	ne·uhl·ko·ho·lits·kee na·poy
tea	čaj	chai
(mineral) water	(minerální) voda	(mi·ne·ral·nyee) vo·duh
white wine	bílého víno	bee·lair·ho vee·no

EMERGENCIES

Help!	Pomoc!	po·mots
Go away!	Běžte pryč!	byezh·te prich
Call ...!	Zavolejte ...!	zuh·vo·ley·te ...
a doctor	lékaře	lair·kuh·rzhe
the police	policii	po·li·tsi·yi

I'm lost.
Zabloudil/
Zabloudila jsem. (m/f) — zuh·bloh·dyil/ zuh·bloh·dyi·luh ysem

Question Words		
How?	Jak?	yuhk
What?	Co?	tso
When?	Kdy?	gdi
Where?	Kde?	gde
Who?	Kdo?	gdo
Why?	Proč?	proch

I'm ill.
Jsem nemocný/
nemocná. (m/f) — ysem ne·mots·nee/ ne·mots·na

Where are the toilets?
Kde jsou toalety? — gde ysoh to·uh·le·ti

SHOPPING & SERVICES

I'd like to buy ...
Chtěl/Chtěla bych
koupit ... (m/f) — khtyel/khtye·la bikh koh·pit ...

I'm just looking.
Jenom se dívám. — ye·nom se dyee·vam

Do you have any others?
Máte ještě jiné? — ma·te yesh·tye yi·nair

Can I look at it?
Mohu se na to
podívat? — mo·hu se nuh to po·dyee·vuht

How much is it?
Kolik to stojí? — ko·lik to sto·yee

That's too expensive.
To je moc drahé. — to ye mots druh·hair

Can you lower the price?
Můžete mi snížit
cenu? — moo·zhe·te mi snyee·zhit tse·nu

ATM	bankomat	uhn·ko·muht
internet cafe	internetová kavárna	in·ter·ne·to·va kuh·var·nuh
mobile phone	mobil	mo·bil
post office	pošta	posh·tuh
tourist office	turistická informační kancelář	tu·ris·tits·ka in·for·muhch·nyee kuhn·tse·larzh

TIME & DATES

What time is it?
Kolik je hodin? — ko·lik ye ho·dyin

It's (10) o'clock.
Je (deset) hodin. — ye (de·set) ho·dyin

Half past 10.
Půl jedenácté.
(lit: half eleven) — pool ye·de·nats·tair

am (midnight–8am)
ráno — ra·no

am (8am–noon)
dopoledne — do·po·led·ne

pm (noon–7pm)
odpoledne — ot·po·led·ne

pm (7pm–midnight)
večer — ve·cher

yesterday	včera	fche·ruh
today	dnes	dnes
tomorrow	zítra	zee·truh

Numbers

1	jeden	ye·den
2	dva	dvuh
3	tři	trzhi
4	čtyři	chti·rzhi
5	pět	pyet
6	šest	shest
7	sedm	se·dm
8	osm	o·sm
9	devět	de·vyet
10	deset	de·set
20	dvacet	dvuh·tset
30	třicet	trzhi·tset
40	čtyřicet	chti·rzhi·tset
50	padesát	puh·de·sat
60	šedesát	she·de·sat
70	sedmdesát	se·dm·de·sat
80	osmdesát	o·sm·de·sat
90	devadesát	de·vuh·de·sat
100	sto	sto
1000	tisíc	tyí·seets

Monday	pondělí	pon·dye·lee
Tuesday	úterý	oo·te·ree
Wednesday	středa	strzhe·duh
Thursday	čtvrtek	chtvr·tek
Friday	pátek	pa·tek
Saturday	sobota	so·bo·tuh
Sunday	neděle	ne·dye·le

January	leden	le·den
February	únor	oo·nor
March	březen	brzhe·zen
April	duben	du·ben
May	květen	kvye·ten
June	červen	cher·ven
July	červenec	cher·ve·nets
August	srpen	sr·pen
September	září	za·rzhee
October	říjen	rzhee·yen
November	listopad	li·sto·puht
December	prosinec	pro·si·nets

TRANSPORT

What time does the bus/train leave?
V kolik hodin odjíždí · f ko·lik ho·dyin od·yeezh·dyee
autobus/vlak? · ow·to·bus/vluhk

Please tell me when we get to ...
Prosím vás řekněte · pro·seem vas rzhek·nye·te
mi kdy budeme v ... · mi kdi bu·de·me f ...

Does it stop at ...?
Staví v ...? · sta·vee v ...

What's the next stop?
Která je příští · kte·ra ye przheesh·tyee
zastávka? · zuhs·taf·kuh

Please stop here.
Prosím vás zastavte. · pro·seem vas zuhs·tuhf·te

Please take me to (this address).
Prosím odvezte mě · pro·seem od·ves·te mye
na (tuto adresu). · na (tu·to uh·dre·su)

One ... ticket to (Telč), please.	... jízdenku do (Telče), prosim.	... yeez·den·ku do (tel·che) pro·seem
one-way	Jedno-směrnou	yed·no·smyer·noh
return	Zpáteční	zpa·tech·nye

first	první	prv·nyee
last	poslední	po·sled·nyee
next	příští	przhee·shtyee

bus	autobus	ow·to·bus
plane	letadlo	le·tuhd·lo
train	vlak	vluhk
tram	tramvaj	truhm·vai

I'd like to hire a ...	Chtěl/Chtěla bych si půjčit ... (m/f)	khtyel/khtye·luh bikh si pooy·chit ...
bicycle	kolo	ko·lo
car	auto	ow·to
motorbike	motorku	mo·tor·ku

Is this the road to ...?
Vede tato silnice · ve·de tuh·to sil·ni·tse
do ...? · do ...

Can I park here?
Mohu zde parkovat? · mo·hu zde puhr·ko·vuht

Where's a petrol station?
Kde je benzinová · gde ye ben·zi·no·va
pumpa? · pum·puh

I need a mechanic.
Potřebuji · pot·rzhe·bu·yi
mechanika. · me·khuh·ni·kuh

Do I need a helmet?
Potřebuji helmu? · pot·rzhe·bu·yi hel·mu

The car/motorbike won't start.
Auto/Motorka nechce · ow·to/mo·tor·kuh nekh·tse
nastartovat. · nuhs·tuhr·to·vuht

I have a puncture.
Mám defekt. · mam de·fekt

GLOSSARY

Becherovka – potent herb liqueur

čajovná – teahouse

ČD – Czech Railways

chrám/dóm – cathedral

ČSSD – Social Democratic Party

cukrárna – cake shop

dámy – sign on women's toilet

divadlo – theatre

doklad – receipt or document

dům – house or building

dům umění – house of art, for exhibitions and workshops

galérie – gallery, arcade

hlavní nádraží (hl nád) – main train station

hora – hill, mountain

hospoda or **hostinec** – pub

hrad – castle

hřbitov – cemetery

kaple – chapel

katedralá – cathedral

kavárna – café or coffee shop

Kč – koruna česká; Czech crown

kino – cinema

kostel – church

lékárna – pharmacy

město – town

most – bridge

muzeum – museum

muži – sign on men's toilet

nábřeží – embankment

nádraží – station

náměstí (nám) – square

národní – national

ostrov – island

palác – palace

páni – sign on men's toilet

pasáž – passage, shopping arcade

pekárna – bakery

penzión – guest house

pivnice – small beer hall

pivo – beer

pivovar – brewery

potok – stream

Praha – Prague

radnice – town hall

restaurace – restaurant

Roma – a tribe of people who migrated from India to Europe in the 10th century

rybník – fish pond

sady – garden, park, orchard

sgraffito – mural technique whereby the top layer of plaster is scraped away or incised to reveal the layer beneath

stanice – train stop or station

svatý – saint

tramvaj – tram

třída – avenue

ubytovna – dorm accommodation

ulice (ul) – street

ulička (ul) – lane

Velvet Divorce – separation of Czechoslovakia into fully independent Czech and Slovak republics in 1993

Velvet Revolution – bloodless overthrow of Czechoslovakia's communist regime in 1989

vinárna – wine bar/restaurant

vlak – train

záchod – toilet

zahrada – gardens, park

zámek – chateau

ženy – sign on women's toilet

Zimmer frei – room free (for rent)

Behind the Scenes

SEND US YOUR FEEDBACK

We love to hear from travellers – your comments keep us on our toes and help make our books better. Our well-travelled team reads every word on what you loved or loathed about this book. Although we cannot reply individually to your submissions, we always guarantee that your feedback goes straight to the appropriate authors, in time for the next edition. Each person who sends us information is thanked in the next edition – and the most useful submissions are rewarded with a selection of digital PDF chapters.

Visit **lonelyplanet.com/contact** to submit your updates and suggestions or to ask for help. Our award-winning website also features inspirational travel stories, news and discussions.

Note: We may edit, reproduce and incorporate your comments in Lonely Planet products such as guidebooks, websites and digital products, so let us know if you don't want your comments reproduced or your name acknowledged. For a copy of our privacy policy visit lonelyplanet.com/privacy.

OUR READERS

Many thanks to the travellers who used the last edition and wrote to us with helpful hints, useful advice and interesting anecdotes:
Janet Noonan, Gareth Owen, Petr Vůjtěch

AUTHOR THANKS

Neil Wilson

Many thanks to the usual gang, especially Carol Downie, and also to all the bartenders, bookshop owners, baristas and bellhops who helped out with my endless questions about the best places to eat, drink etc. Plus a big thank you to co-author Mark for making the book so much fun to research, and to Joe and Gemma at LP for behind-the-scenes support.

Mark Baker

I would like to thank the many employees of the Czech tourist information offices whom I relied on for help and guidance during my research, particularly my friend Katerina Pavlitova at Prague City Tourism, and Eliška Koričarová at the Information Centre in Český Krumlov. I also owe a debt of gratitude to my friends in Prague, particularly Czechs, for always showing me new things about this city and country. Lastly, thanks to my co-author Neil Wilson for picking up the dining tab on more than one occasion while researching Prague. Cheers!

ACKNOWLEDGMENTS

Cover photograph: Church of Our Lady Before Týn, Old Town Square, Prague, Francesco Iacobelli/AWL Images.

THIS BOOK

This 11th edition of Lonely Planet's *Prague & the Czech Republic* was researched and written by Neil Wilson and Mark Baker. The previous three editions were also written by Neil and Mark. This guidebook was commissioned in Lonely Planet's London office and produced by the following:

Commissioning Editor Joe Bindloss

Destination Editor Gemma Graham

Coordinating Editor Lauren O'Connell

Product Editor Katie O'Connell

Senior Cartographer Valentina Kremenchutskaya

Book Designer Virginia Moreno

Senior Editor Karyn Noble

Assisting Editors Bruce Evans, Kate Mathews, Charlotte Orr

Cover Researcher Naomi Parker

Thanks to Elin Berglund, Ryan Evans, Larissa Frost, Genesys India, Jouve India, Indra Kilfoyle, Wayne Murphy, Wibowo Rusli, John Taufa, Juan Winata

Index

See also separate subindexes for:

🍴 **EATING P321**

🍷 **DRINKING & NIGHTLIFE P322**

☆ **ENTERTAINMENT P323**

🛍 **SHOPPING P323**

🏃 **SPORTS & ACTIVITIES P323**

🛏 **SLEEPING P323**

EATING

DRINKING & NIGHTLIFE

Prague Maps

Sights

- Beach
- Bird Sanctuary
- Buddhist
- Castle/Palace
- Christian
- Confucian
- Hindu
- Islamic
- Jain
- Jewish
- Monument
- Museum/Gallery/Historic Building
- Ruin
- Sento Hot Baths/Onsen
- Shinto
- Sikh
- Taoist
- Winery/Vineyard
- Zoo/Wildlife Sanctuary
- Other Sight

Activities, Courses & Tours

- Bodysurfing
- Diving
- Canoeing/Kayaking
- Course/Tour
- Skiing
- Snorkelling
- Surfing
- Swimming/Pool
- Walking
- Windsurfing
- Other Activity

Sleeping

- Sleeping
- Camping

Eating

- Eating

Drinking & Nightlife

- Drinking & Nightlife
- Cafe

Entertainment

- Entertainment

Shopping

- Shopping

Information

- Bank
- Embassy/Consulate
- Hospital/Medical
- Internet
- Police
- Post Office
- Telephone
- Toilet
- Tourist Information
- Other Information

Geographic

- Beach
- Hut/Shelter
- Lighthouse
- Lookout
- Mountain/Volcano
- Oasis
- Park
- Pass
- Picnic Area
- Waterfall

Population

- Capital (National)
- Capital (State/Province)
- City/Large Town
- Town/Village

Transport

- Airport
- Border crossing
- Bus
- Cable car/Funicular
- Cycling
- Ferry
- Metro station
- Monorail
- Parking
- Petrol station
- S-Bahn/Subway station
- Taxi
- T-bane/Tunnelbana station
- Train station/Railway
- Tram
- Tube station
- U-Bahn/Underground station
- Other Transport

Note: Not all symbols displayed above appear on the maps in this book

Routes

- Tollway
- Freeway
- Primary
- Secondary
- Tertiary
- Lane
- Unsealed road
- Road under construction
- Plaza/Mall
- Steps
- Tunnel
- Pedestrian overpass
- Walking Tour
- Walking Tour detour
- Path/Walking Trail

Boundaries

- International
- State/Province
- Disputed
- Regional/Suburb
- Marine Park
- Cliff
- Wall

Hydrography

- River, Creek
- Intermittent River
- Canal
- Water
- Dry/Salt/Intermittent Lake
- Reef

Areas

- Airport/Runway
- Beach/Desert
- Cemetery (Christian)
- Cemetery (Other)
- Glacier
- Mudflat
- Park/Forest
- Sight (Building)
- Sportsground
- Swamp/Mangrove

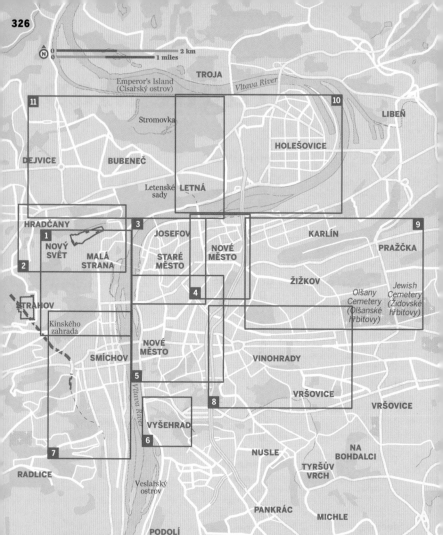

2 km
1 miles

TROJA

Emperor's Island
(Císařský ostrov)

Vltava River

LIBEŇ

Stromovka

HOLEŠOVICE

DEJVICE

BUBENEČ

Letenské
sady

LETNÁ

HRADČANY

JOSEFOV

KARLÍN

PRAŽČKA

NOVÝ
SVĚT

MALÁ
STRANA

STARÉ
MĚSTO

NOVÉ
MĚSTO

ŽIŽKOV

*Olšany
Cemetery
(Olšanské
hřbitovy)*

*Jewish
Cemetery
(Židovské
hřbitovy)*

STRAHOV

Kinského
zahrada

NOVÉ
MĚSTO

VINOHRADY

SMÍCHOV

VRŠOVICE

VRŠOVICE

VYŠEHRAD

NUSLE

NA
BOHDALCI

RADLICE

Veslařský
ostrov

TYRŠŮV
VRCH

PANKRÁC

MICHLE

ZLÍCHOV

PODOLÍ

HLUBOČEPY

SPOŘILOV

MAP INDEX

MALÁ STRANA

MALÁ STRANA Map on p328

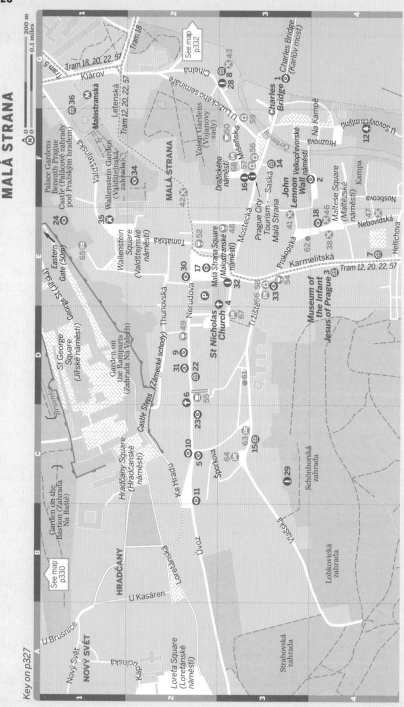

MALÁ STRANA

Key on p327

Key on p332

0   200 m
0   0.1 miles

See map p330

See map p332

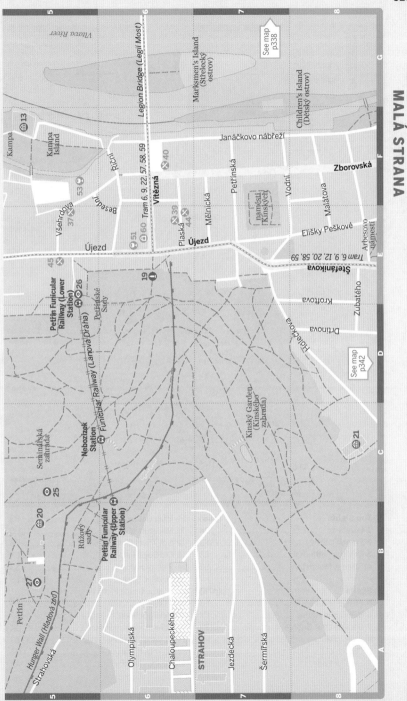

Vltava River

🚇 13 Kampa

Kampa Island

Legion Bridge (Legii Most)

Marksmen's Island (Střelecký ostrov)

Children's Island (Dětský ostrov)

See map p338

Janáčkovo nábřeží

Zborovská

Říčni

❌ 40

Všehrdova

53 ◉

37 ◉

Besední

Tram 6, 9, 22, 57, 58, 59

🚊 60

Vítězná

Petřínská

Mělnická

náměstí Kinských

Vodni

Malátova

Eliška Peškové

Arbesovo náměstí

🚇 51

Plaská

❌ 39

❌ 44

Újezd

Újezd

Tram 6, 9, 12, 20, 58, 59.

Střbřanikova

❌ 45

Petřín Funicular Railway (Lower Station)

🚇 26

Petřínské Sady

19 ℹ

Krotlova

Zubatého

Hlávkova

Drtinova

See map p342

Seminářská zahrada

◉ 25

Nebozízek Station

Funicular Railway (Lanová Dráha)

Kinský Garden (Kinského zahrada)

21 🚇

🚇 20

Kružový sady

Petřín Funicular Railway (Upper Station)

27 ◉

Petřín

Hunger Wall (Hladová zeď)

Strahovská

Olympijská

Chaloupeckého

STRAHOV

Jezdecká

Šermířská

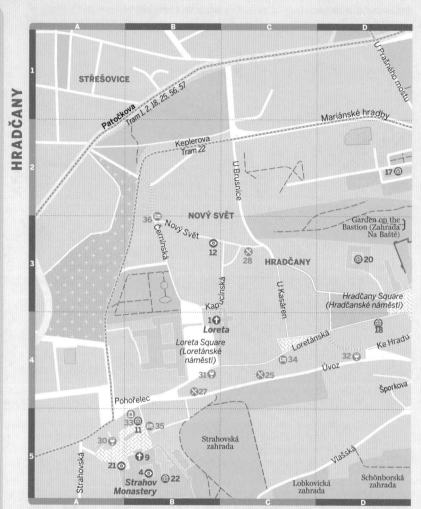

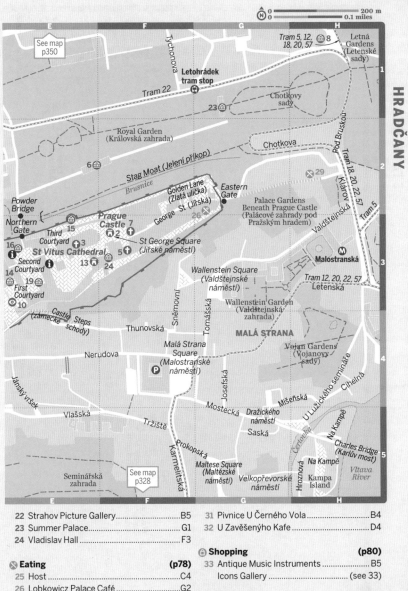

STARÉ MĚSTO

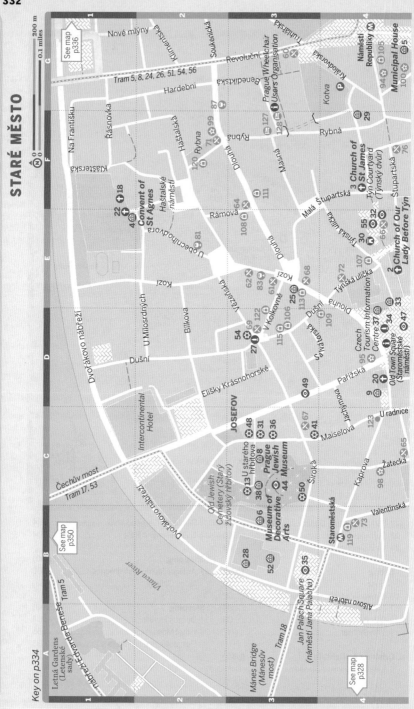

Key on p334

See map p336

Tram 5, 8, 24, 26, 51, 54, 56

Nové mlýny

Revoluční

Hardebni

Na Františku

Řásnovka

Klimentská

Soukenická

Benediktská

Tuhlišská

Prague Wheelchair
Users Organisation

Náměstí
Republiky

Municipal House

Králodvorská

Kotva

Rybná

29

Haštalská

Rybna

Rybná

Masná

Church of
St James

Tyn Courtyard
(Týnský dvůr)

Štupartská

Klášterská

Convent of
St Agnes

Haštalské
náměstí

U Obecního dvora

Rámová

Dlouhá

Malá Štupartská

Týnská

Týnská ulička

Church of Our
Lady Before Týn

Dvořákovo nábřeží

U Milosrdných

Kozí

Bílkova

Veleslávova

Kozí

Dlouhá

Dušní

Týnská ulička

Czech
Tourism Information
Centre

Old Town Square
(Staroměstské
náměstí)

Intercontinental
Hotel

Eliśky Krásnohorské

Pařížská

JOSEFOV

Maiselova

Rachmanova

U radnice

Čechův most
Tram 17, 53

Old Jewish
Cemetery (Starý
židovský hřbitov)

U starého
hřbitova

Prague
Jewish
Museum

Široká

Kaprova

Žatecká

Dvořákovo nábřeží

Museum of
Decorative Arts

Staroměstská

Valentinská

Vltava River

Letná Gardens
(Letenské
sady)

náměstí Edvarda Beneše
Tram 5

Čechův most

Máněs Bridge
(Mánesův
most)

Tram 18

Jan Palach Square
(náměstí Jana Palacha)

Alšovo nábřeží

See map
p350

See map
p328

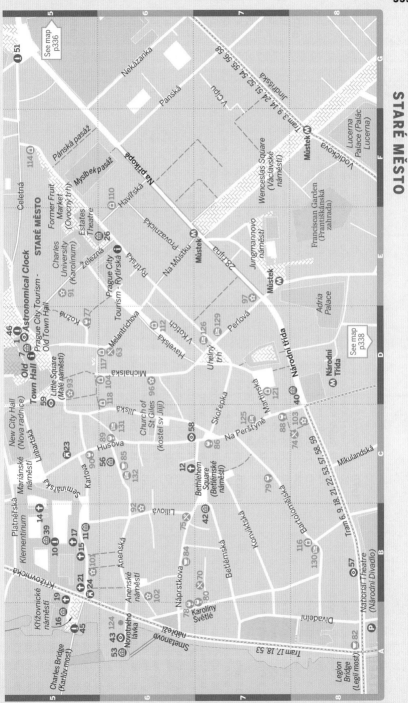

STARÉ MĚSTO

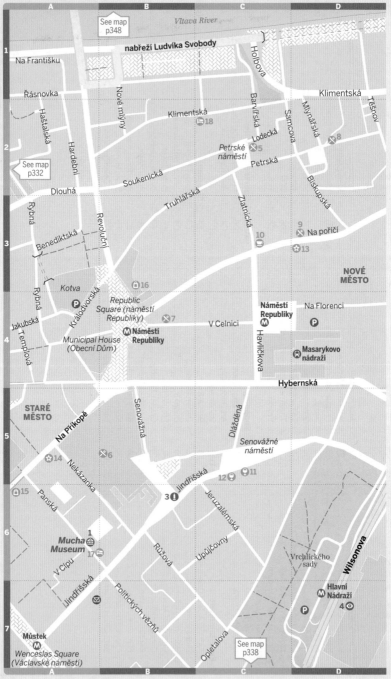

◎ Top Sights (p124)
1 Mucha Museum A6
2 Prague City Museum............E3

◎ Sights (p124)
3 Jindřišská Tower.................B6
4 Prague Main Train Station...D7

✕ Eating (p129)
5 Al Forno.............................C2
6 Kogo..................................B5
7 La Gare/Le Winstub............B4
8 Sansho D2
9 Siam Orchid.......................D3

◉ Drinking & Nightlife (p131)
10 Café Imperial C3

11 Hoffa.......................................C5
12 Vinograf C5

◎ Entertainment (p133)
13 Archa Theatre D3
14 Bohemia Ticket
International......................A5

🔒 Shopping (p134)
15 Moser A6
16 Palladium Praha Shopping
Centre B3

🛏 Sleeping (p195)
17 Fusion Hotel A6
18 Moods Hotel..........................C2

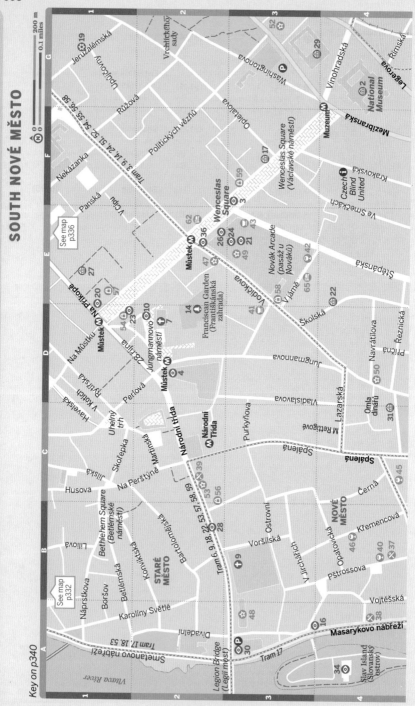

Key on p340

200 m
0.1 miles

Vltava River

Smetanovo nábřeží

Tram 17, 18, 53

Legion Bridge (Legii most)

Tram 17

See map p332

STARÉ MĚSTO

Bethlehem Square (Betlémské náměstí)

Liliová

Husova

Náprstkova

Boršov

Betlémská

Konviktská

Karoliny Světlé

Divadelní

Skořepka

Jilská

Na Perštýně

Bartolomějská

Martinská

Uhelný trh

V kotích

Perlová

Rytířská

Havelská

Na Můstku

Na Příkopě

Nekázanka

Panská

V Cípu

Politických vězňů

Washingtonova

Opletalova

Jeruzalémská

Jindřišská

Růžová

Uhelníkovy

Vrchlického sady

Jungmannovo náměstí

Národní třída

Voršilská

Ostrovní

V Jirchářích

Opatovická

Křemencová

Pštrossova

Vojtěšská

Masarykovo nábřeží

Spálená

Černá

Lazarská

Vladislavova

Purkyňova

Jungmannova

Školská

Štěpánská

Ve Smečkách

Krakovská

Mezibranská

Legerova

Říční

Ječná

Vodičkova

M Rettigové

Omla dinářů

Navrátilova

Příčná

Řeznická

Spálená

NOVÉ MĚSTO

Slav Island (Slovanský ostrov)

Franciscan Garden (Františkánská zahrada)

Wenceslas Square (Václavské náměstí)

Wenceslas Square

National Museum

Novák Arcade (pasáž u Nováků)

Czech Blind United

See map p336

Tram 3, 9, 14, 24, 51, 52, 54, 55, 56, 58

Tram 6, 9, 18, 22, 53, 57, 58, 59

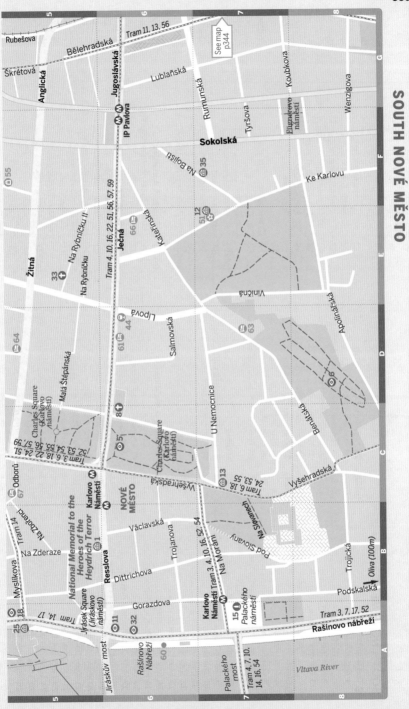

SOUTH NOVÉ MĚSTO Map on p338

⊚ Top Sights (p122)
1 National Memorial to the Heroes of the
   Heydrich Terror.. B5
2 National Museum.. G4
3 Wenceslas Square...................................... F3

⊚ Sights (p124)
4 Adria Palace.. D2
5 Charles Square.. C6
6 Charles University Botanical Garden......... D8
7 Church of Our Lady of the Snows............. D2
8 Church of St Ignatius................................. C6
9 Convent of St Ursula................................. B3
10 Cubist Lamp Post...................................... D2
11 Dancing Building....................................... A6
12 Dvořák Museum... E7
13 Faust House... C7
14 Franciscan Garden.................................... D2
15 František Palacký Memorial....................... A7
16 Goethe Institute.. A4
17 Hotel Jalta Nuclear Bunker....................... F3
18 House of the Hlahol Choir........................ A5
19 Jubilee Synagogue.................................... G1
20 Koruna Palace.. E1
21 Kun (David Černý Sculpture)..................... E3
22 Leica Gallery.. E4
23 Lindt Building.. D1
24 Lucerna Palace.. E3
25 Mánes Gallery... A5
26 Melantrich Building................................... E2
27 Museum of Communism............................ E1
28 Národní Třída.. B2
29 National Museum New Building................. G3
30 National Theatre.. A3
31 New Town Hall... C4
32 Rašínovo nábřeží 78.................................. A6
33 Rotunda of St Longinus............................. E5
34 Slav Island.. A4
35 U Kalicha.. F7
36 Wiehl House... E2

⊗ Eating (p129)
37 Globe Bookstore & Café............................ B4
38 Klub cestovatelů....................................... A4
39 Le Patio... D2
   Room.. (see 65)

⊙ Drinking & Nightlife (p131)
40 Bokovka.. D2
41 Friends Coffee House................................ D3
42 Jáma... E3
43 Kavárna Lucerna............................... (see 24)
44 Kávovarna.. E3
45 Pivovarský Dům... D6
46 U Flekůů.. C4
   Red Room... B4

✪ Entertainment (p133)
47 Kino Světozor.. E2
48 Laterna Magika.. A3
49 Lucerna Music Bar..................................... E3
50 Minor Theatre.. D4
   National Theatre............................. (see 30)
51 Original Music Theatre of Prague............. E7
52 Prague State Opera................................... G3
53 Reduta Jazz Club....................................... C2
   Rock Café... (see 53)

⊞ Shopping (p134)
54 Baťa.. D1
55 Bazar.. F5
56 Belda Jewellery... C2
57 Bontonland... E1
   Globe Bookstore & Café.................. (see 37)
58 Jan Pazdera.. E3
59 Palác Knih Neo Luxor................................ F3

⊛ Sports & Activities (p32)
60 Prague Passenger Shipping...................... A6

⊟ Sleeping (p195)
61 ArtHarmony.. D6
62 Grand Hotel Evropa................................... E2
63 Hotel 16 U Sv Kateřiny.............................. D7
64 Hotel Suite Home...................................... D5
65 Icon Hotel.. E3
66 Miss Sophie's.. E6
67 Mosaic House.. C5

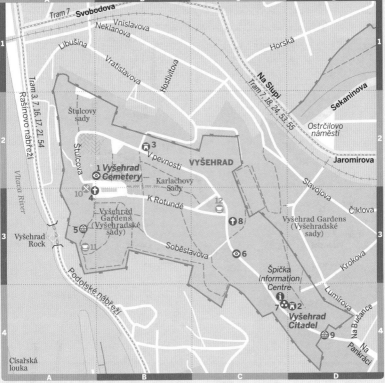

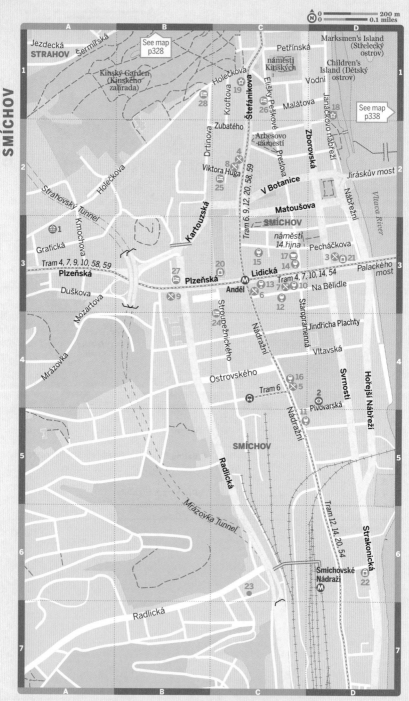

SMÍCHOV

STRAHOV

Jezdecká
Šermířská

See map
p328

Kinský Garden
(Kinského
zahrada)

Holečkova

Holečkova

Štefánikova

Krofftova

19

28

Petřínská

náměstí
Kinských

Eliška Peškové

Malátova

Vodní

Marksmen's Island
(Střelecký
ostrov)

Children's
Island (Dětský
ostrov)

26

18

See map
p338

Zubatého

Drtinova

Arbesovo
náměstí

Preslova

Zborovská

Janáčkovo nábřeží

Jiráskův most

Vltava River

Holečkova

4

8

Viktora Huga

25

V Botanice

Matoušova

Nábřežní

Tram 6, 9, 12, 20, 58, 59

SMÍCHOV

Strahovský Tunnel

Kmochova

1

Grafická

Tram 4, 7, 9, 10, 58, 59

Plzeňská

Duškova

Kartouzská

náměstí
14. října

SMÍCHOV

15

17

14

3

Pecháčkova

21

Palackého
most

Mozartova

27

9

20

Plzeňská

Anděl

Lidická

13

6

7

10

Tram 4, 7, 10, 14, 54

Na Bělidle

12

Mírázovka

Stroupežnického

24

Nádražní

Staropramenná

Jindřicha Plachty

Vltavská

Ostrovského

Tram 6

16

5

2

Pivovarská

11

Svornosti

Hořejší Nábřeží

SMÍCHOV

Radlická

Nádražní

Radlická

Mrázovka Tunnel

23

Tram 12, 14, 20, 54

Strakonická

Smíchovské
Nádraží

22

SMÍCHOV

SMÍCHOV

VINOHRADY & VRŠOVICE

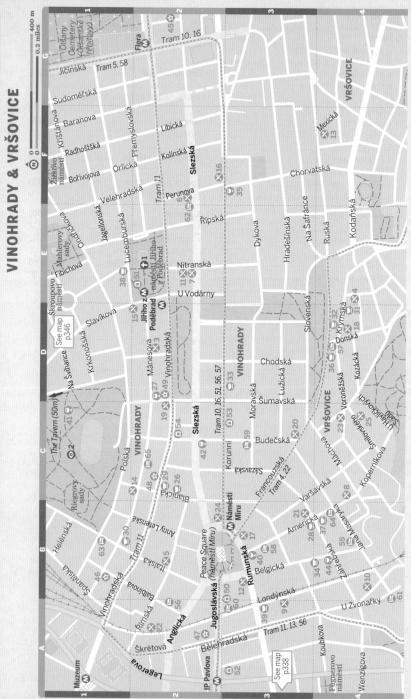

VRŠOVICE

VINOHRADY

Olšany Cemetery
(Olšanské
hřbitovy)

Žižkovo
náměstí

Flora
Tram 10, 16
Tram 5, 58
Jičínská
Sudoměřská
Baranova
Radhošťská
Bořivojova
Orlická
Velehradská
Jagellonská
Lucemburská
Mahlerovy
sady
Fibichova
Škroupovo
náměstí
See map
p346
Slavíkova
Krkonošská
Na Švihance
The Tavern (50m)
Helénská
Španělská
Riegrovy
sady
Polská
Blanická
Anny Letenské
Italská
Tram 11
Balbínova
Vinohradská
Římská
Anglická
Jugoslávská
Škrétova
Bělehradská
IP Pavlova
Legerova
Muzeum
See map
p338

Přemyslovská
Libická
Kolínská
Slezská
Perunova
Říská
Nitranská
U Vodárny
Mánesova
Vinohradská
Jiřího z
Poděbrad
náměstí Jiřího
z Poděbrad
Slezská
Korunní
Sázavská
Francouzská
Tram 4, 22
Náměstí
Miru
Peace Square
(náměstí Míru)
Rumunská
Belgická
Londýnská
Tram 11, 13, 56

Dykova
Chorvatská
Mexická
Na Šafránce
Ruská
Hradešínská
Slovenská
Chodská
Lužická
Šumavská
Moravská
Budečská
Varšavská
Americká
Zahřebská
Jana Masaryka
Kopernikova
Máchova
Voroněžská
Krymská
Donská
Kozácká
Kodaňská
U Havlíčkových
sadů
Havlíčkovy
sady
U Zvonařky
Koubkova
Fügnerovo
náměstí
Wenzigova

Tram 10, 16, 51, 56, 57

VINOHRADY
VRŠOVICE

45
13
16
35
6
62
11
7
4
32
18
31
36
57
20
23
8
10
61
9
39
34
44
55
64
37
21
28
24
17
40
58
12
50
60
52
47
56
22
30
63
46
14
48
29
26
65
2
41
27
49
19
54
42
33
59
53
38
51
1
15
3
5

VINOHRADY & VRŠOVICE

◎ Sights (p137)
1 Church of the Most Sacred Heart of Our Lord	E2
2 Riegrovy sady	C1

◎ Eating (p137)
3 Aromi	D2
Café FX	(see 47)
4 Cafe Sladkovský	E4
5 Dish	B2
6 Ha Noi	F2
7 Kofein	E2
8 Las Adelitas	C4
9 Loving Hut	A3
10 Madame Lyn	B4
11 Mozaika	E2
12 Originál 1869	B3
13 Osteria Da Clara	F4
14 Paštička	C2
15 Pho Vietnam	D2
16 Pivo a Párek	F2
17 Pizzeria Grosseto	B3
18 Plevel	D4
19 Restaurace Chudoba	C2
20 Restaurace U Bulínů	C3
21 Ristorante Sapori	B3
22 U Bílé Krávy	A2
23 U Dědka	C4
24 Vinohradský Parlament	B2
25 Zelená Zahrada	C4
34 Galerie Kavárna Róza K.	B4
35 Hospůdka Obyčejný Svět	F3
36 Kavárna Šlágr	D4
37 Kavárna Zanzibar	B4
38 Le Caveau	E1
39 Mama Coffee	A3
40 Prague Beer Museum	B3
41 Riegrovy Sady Beer Garden	C1
42 Sokolovna	C2
43 Vinični Altán	C5
44 Žlutá Pumpa	B4

◎ Drinking & Nightlife (p141)
26 Al Cafetero	C2
27 Bar & Books Mánesova	D2
28 Blatouch	B3
29 Café Celebrity	C2
30 Café Kaaba	B1
31 Cafe V Lese	D4
32 Coffee Source	D4
33 Dobrá Trafika	D3

◎ Entertainment (p144)
45 Infinity	G2
46 Le Clan	B1
47 Radost FX	A2
48 Techtle Mechtle	C2
49 Termix	D2

◎ Shopping (p144)
50 Dům Porcelánu	B3
51 Jiřího z Poděbrad Farmers Market	E2
52 Karel Vávra	A3
53 Obchod s Uměním	C3
54 Vinohradský Pavilon	C2

◎ Sleeping (p197)
55 Ametyst	B4
56 Arkada	A2
57 Czech Inn	D4
58 Holiday Home	B3
59 Hotel Anna	C3
60 Hotel Luník	A3
61 Le Palais Hotel	B4
62 Louren Hotel	E2
63 Mary's Travel & Tourist Service	B1
64 Orion	B4
65 Penzion Mánes	C2

Tram 11, 13, 56
Bělehradská
Sarajevská
Fričova
Perucká
Havlíčkovy sady
Rybalkova
Tram 4, 22, 57, 59
VRŠOVICE
Tram 7, 22, 24, 55, 57, 59
Vršovická
Tram 7, 24

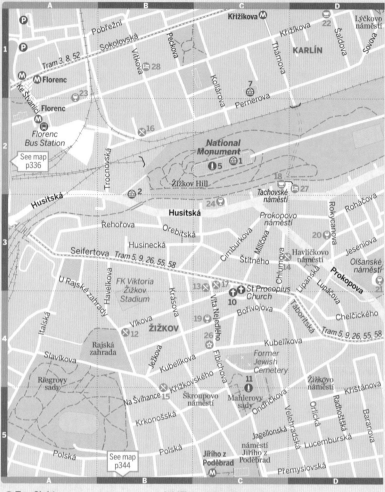

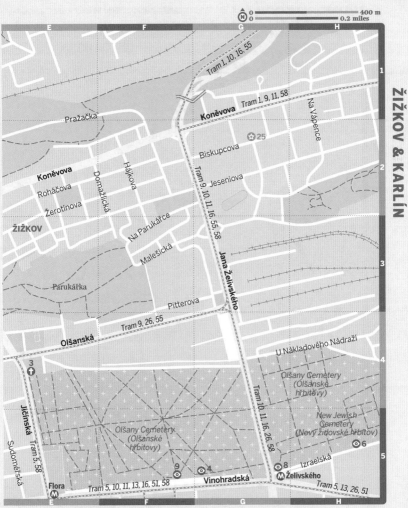

HOLEŠOVICE

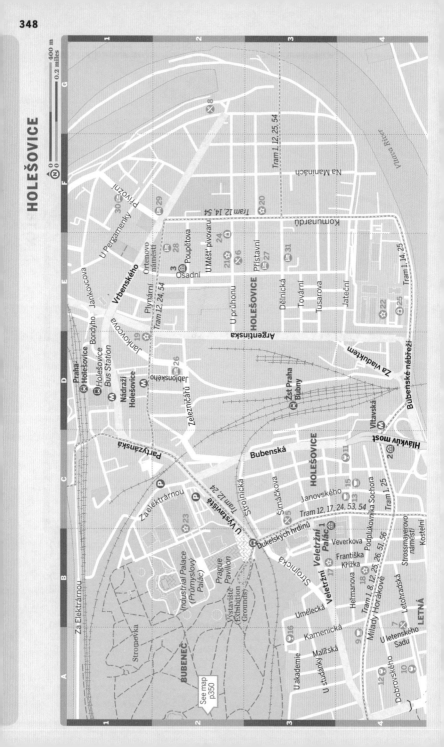

N 0
0 400 m
0 0.2 miles

See map p350

Vltava River

Tram 1, 12, 25, 54

Tram 1, 14, 25

Tram 12, 14, 54

Na Maninách

Komunardů

U Měšť pivovarů

Poupětova

Osadní

Ortenovo
náměstí

U Pergamenky

Přívozní

Vrbenského

Jankovcova

U Pergamenky

Bondyho

Praha-
Holešovice

Holešovice
Bus Station

Nádraží
Holešovice

Jablonského

Železničářů

Argentinská

U průhonu

HOLEŠOVICE

Dělnická

Tovární

Tusarova

Jateční

Za viaduktem

Bubenské nábřeží

Přístavní

Žst Praha
Bubny

Vltavská

Hlávkův most

Za Elektrárnou

Za elektrárnou

Partyzánská

U Výstaviště

Tram 12, 24

Tram 12, 27, 24

Strojnická

Šimáčkova

Bubenská

HOLEŠOVICE

Janovského

Tram 12, 17, 24, 53, 54

Dukelských hrdinů

Veletržní
Palác

Veletržní

Veverkova

Podplukovníka Sochora

Tram 1, 25

Stromovka

Industrial Palace
(Průmyslový
Palác)

Prague
Pavilion

Výstaviště
(Exhibition
Grounds)

BUBENEČ

U akademie

U studánky

Malířská

Kamenická

Umělecká

Heřmanova

Františka
Křížka

Tram 1, 8, 12, 25, 26, 51, 56

Milady Horákové

Strossmayerovo
náměstí

Kostelní

Letohradská

U letenského
Sadu

Dobrovského

LETNÁ

HOLEŠOVICE

◎ Top Sights (p156)
1 Veletržní Palác..................C3

◎ Sights (p157)
2 Chemistry Gallery........................C4
3 Dox Centre for Contemporary Art...............E2
4 National Technical Museum.........A5

◎ Eating (p157)
5 Bohemia Bagel.........................C3
Korbel...............................(see 20)
6 Molo 22...............................E2
7 Peperoncino..........................B4
8 Pivovar Marina........................G2
Sasazu...............................(see 22)

◎ Drinking & Nightlife (p158)
9 Erhartova Cukrárna...................A4
10 Hells Bells...........................A4
11 Kavárna Liberál......................C4
12 Klášterní Pivnice....................C4
13 Kumbal...............................C4
14 Letná Beer Garden....................A5
15 Ouky Douky...........................C4
16 Park Cafe & Bar......................A3

◎ Entertainment (p160)
17 Alfred Ve Dvoře......................B3
18 Bio Oko..............................B4
19 Cross Club...........................G2
20 La Fabrika...........................F3

21 Mecca.................................E2
22 Sasazu...............................E4
23 Tipsport Aréna.......................C2

◎ Shopping (p161)
24 Pivní Galerie........................E2
25 Pražská Tržnice......................E4

◎ Sleeping (p198)
26 Absolutum Hotel......................D2
27 Hotel Extol Inn......................E3
28 Hotel Leon...........................E2
29 Plaza Alta Hotel.....................F2
30 Plus Prague Hostel...................F1
31 Sir Toby's Hostel....................E3

BUBENEČ & DEJVICE

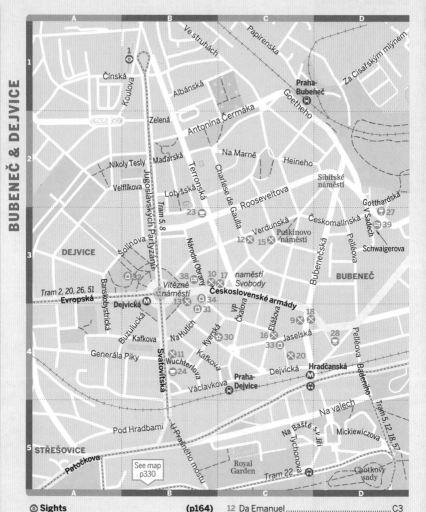

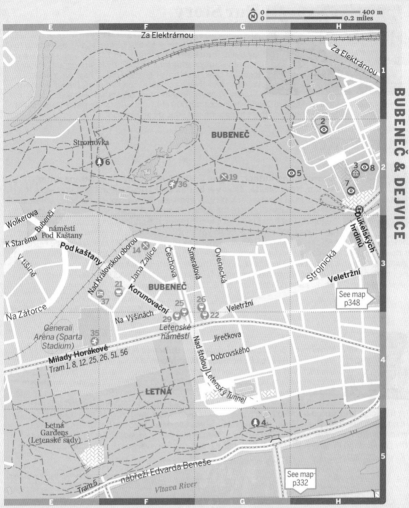

Our Story

A beat-up old car, a few dollars in the pocket and a sense of adventure. In 1972 that's all Tony and Maureen Wheeler needed for the trip of a lifetime – across Europe and Asia overland to Australia. It took several months, and at the end – broke but inspired – they sat at their kitchen table writing and stapling together their first travel guide, *Across Asia on the Cheap*. Within a week they'd sold 1500 copies. Lonely Planet was born.

Today, Lonely Planet has offices in Franklin, London, Melbourne, Oakland, Beijing and Delhi, with more than 600 staff and writers. We share Tony's belief that 'a great guidebook should do three things: inform, educate and amuse'.

Our Writers

Neil Wilson

Coordinating Author, Prague Castle & Hradčany, Malá Strana, Staré Město, Nové Město, Žižkov & Karlín, Day Trips Neil first succumbed to the pleasures of Prague back in 1995, beguiled, like everyone else, by its ethereal beauty, but also drawn to the darker side of its hidden history. He has returned regularly to enjoy the world's finest beers, the city's quirky sense of humour, and the chance to track down yet another obscure monument, having worked now on eight consecutive editions of Lonely Planet's *Prague* guide. A full-time freelance writer since 1988, Neil has travelled in five continents and written more than 60 travel and walking guides for various publishers. He is based in Perthshire, Scotland; for more information see www.neil-wilson.co.uk. Neil also wrote the Plan Your Trip section, the Eating, Drinking, Entertainment and Shopping Overviews and contributed to the Sleeping chapter.

Read more about Neil Wilson at:
lonelyplanet.com/members/neilwilson

Mark Baker

Vinohrady & Vršovice, Holešovice, Bubeneč & Dejvice, Smíchov & Vyšehrad, Best of Bohemia, Best of Moravia Mark first visited Prague in the 1980s as a journalist for the Economist Group. Those were the dark days of communism, yet even then he was hooked by the city's beauty, mysticism and laid-back vibe. He moved to Prague in the early 1990s, and following a stint as a co-founder-owner of the Globe Bookstore & Coffeehouse and a journalist for Radio Free Europe/Radio Liberty, he's found permanent employment as a travel writer. In addition to Lonely Planet *Prague & the Czech Republic*, Mark is co-author of Lonely Planet guides to *Romania & Bulgaria*, *Poland*, and *Slovenia*. Mark also wrote the Architecture chapter, the Understand Prague & the Czech Republic essays, the Survival Guide, and contributed to the Sleeping chapter.

Read more about Mark Baker at:
lonelyplanet.com/members/markbaker

Published by Lonely Planet Publications Pty Ltd
ABN 36 005 607 983
11th edition – November 2014
ISBN 978 1 74220 894 7
© Lonely Planet 2014   Photographs © as indicated 2014
10 9 8 7 6 5 4 3 2 1
Printed in China